Lecture Notes in Artificial Intelligence   11745

Subseries of Lecture Notes in Computer Science

More information about this series at http://www.springer.com/series/1244

Haibin Yu · Jinguo Liu ·
Lianqing Liu · Zhaojie Ju ·
Yuwang Liu · Dalin Zhou (Eds.)

Intelligent Robotics and Applications

12th International Conference, ICIRA 2019
Shenyang, China, August 8–11, 2019
Proceedings, Part VI

Springer

Editors
Haibin Yu
Shenyang Institute of Automation
Shenyang, China

Jinguo Liu
Shenyang Institute of Automation
Shenyang, China

Lianqing Liu
Shenyang Institute of Automation
Shenyang, China

Zhaojie Ju
University of Portsmouth
Portsmouth, UK

Yuwang Liu
Shenyang Institute of Automation
Shenyang, China

Dalin Zhou
University of Portsmouth
Portsmouth, UK

ISSN 0302-9743   ISSN 1611-3349   (electronic)
Lecture Notes in Artificial Intelligence
ISBN 978-3-030-27528-0   ISBN 978-3-030-27529-7   (eBook)
https://doi.org/10.1007/978-3-030-27529-7

LNCS Sublibrary: SL7 – Artificial Intelligence

This Springer imprint is published by the registered company Springer Nature Switzerland AG
The registered company address is: Gewerbestrasse 11, 6330 Cham, Switzerland

Preface

On behalf of the Organizing Committee, we welcome you to the proceedings of the 12th International Conference on Intelligent Robotics and Applications (ICIRA 2019), organized by Shenyang Institute of Automation, Chinese Academy of Sciences, co-organized by Huazhong University of Science and Technology, Shanghai Jiao Tong University, and the University of Portsmouth, technically co-sponsored by the National Natural Science Foundation of China and Springer, and financially sponsored by Shenyang Association for Science and Technology. ICIRA 2019 with the theme of "Robot Era" offered a unique and constructive platform for scientists and engineers throughout the world to present and share their recent research and innovative ideas in the areas of robotics, automation, mechatronics, and applications.

ICIRA 2019 was most successful this year in attracting more than 500 submissions regarding the state-of-the-art development in robotics, automation, and mechatronics. The Program Committee undertook a rigorous review process for selecting the most deserving research for publication. Despite the high quality of most of the submissions, a total of 378 papers were selected for publication in six volumes of Springer's *Lecture Notes in Artificial Intelligence* a subseries of *Lecture Notes in Computer Science*. We sincerely hope that the published papers of ICIRA 2019 will prove to be technically beneficial and constructive to both the academic and industrial community in robotics, automation, and mechatronics. We would like to express our sincere appreciation to all the authors, participants, and the distinguished plenary and keynote speakers.

The success of the conference is also attributed to the Program Committee members and invited peer reviewers for their thorough review of all the submissions, as well as to the Organizing Committee and volunteers for their diligent work. Special thanks are extended to Alfred Hofmann, Anna Kramer, and Volha Shaparava from Springer for their consistent support.

August 2019

Haibin Yu
Jinguo Liu
Lianqing Liu
Zhaojie Ju
Yuwang Liu
Dalin Zhou

Organization

Honorary Chairs

Youlun Xiong   Huazhong University of Science and Technology, China

Nanning Zheng   Xi'an Jiaotong University, China

General Chair

Haibin Yu   Shenyang Institute of Automation, Chinese Academy of Sciences, China

General Co-chairs

Kok-Meng Lee   Georgia Institute of Technology, USA

Zhouping Yin   Huazhong University of Science and Technology, China

Xiangyang Zhu   Shanghai Jiao Tong University, China

Program Chair

Jinguo Liu   Shenyang Institute of Automation, Chinese Academy of Sciences, China

Program Co-chairs

Zhaojie Ju   The University of Portsmouth, UK

Lianqing Liu   Shenyang Institute of Automation, Chinese Academy of Sciences, China

Bram Vanderborght   Vrije Universiteit Brussel, Belgium

Advisory Committee

Jorge Angeles   McGill University, Canada

Tamio Arai   University of Tokyo, Japan

Hegao Cai   Harbin Institute of Technology, China

Tianyou Chai   Northeastern University, China

Jie Chen   Tongji University, China

Jiansheng Dai   King's College London, UK

Zongquan Deng   Harbin Institute of Technology, China

Han Ding   Huazhong University of Science and Technology, China

Xilun Ding	Beihang University, China
Baoyan Duan	Xidian University, China
Xisheng Feng	Shenyang Institute of Automation, Chinese Academy of Sciences, China
Toshio Fukuda	Nagoya University, Japan
Jianda Han	Shenyang Institute of Automation, Chinese Academy of Sciences, China
Qiang Huang	Beijing Institute of Technology, China
Oussama Khatib	Stanford University, USA
Yinan Lai	National Natural Science Foundation of China, China
Jangmyung Lee	Pusan National University, South Korea
Zhongqin Lin	Shanghai Jiao Tong University, China
Hong Liu	Harbin Institute of Technology, China
Honghai Liu	The University of Portsmouth, UK
Shugen Ma	Ritsumeikan University, Japan
Daokui Qu	SIASUN, China
Min Tan	Institute of Automation, Chinese Academy of Sciences, China
Kevin Warwick	Coventry University, UK
Guobiao Wang	National Natural Science Foundation of China, China
Tianmiao Wang	Beihang University, China
Tianran Wang	Shenyang Institute of Automation, Chinese Academy of Sciences, China
Yuechao Wang	Shenyang Institute of Automation, Chinese Academy of Sciences, China
Bogdan M. Wilamowski	Auburn University, USA
Ming Xie	Nanyang Technological University, Singapore
Yangsheng Xu	The Chinese University of Hong Kong, SAR China
Huayong Yang	Zhejiang University, China
Jie Zhao	Harbin Institute of Technology, China
Nanning Zheng	Xi'an Jiaotong University, China
Weijia Zhou	Shenyang Institute of Automation, Chinese Academy of Sciences, China
Xiangyang Zhu	Shanghai Jiao Tong University, China

Publicity Chairs

Shuo Li	Shenyang Institute of Automation, Chinese Academy of Sciences, China
Minghui Wang	Shenyang Institute of Automation, Chinese Academy of Sciences, China
Chuan Zhou	Shenyang Institute of Automation, Chinese Academy of Sciences, China

Publication Chairs

Yuwang Liu   Shenyang Institute of Automation, Chinese Academy
of Sciences, China

Dalin Zhou   The University of Portsmouth, UK

Award Chairs

Kaspar Althoefer   Queen Mary University of London, UK

Naoyuki Kubota   Tokyo Metropolitan University, Japan

Xingang Zhao   Shenyang Institute of Automation, Chinese Academy
of Sciences, China

Special Session Chairs

Guimin Chen   Xi'an Jiaotong University, China

Hak Keung Lam   King's College London, UK

Organized Session Co-chairs

Guangbo Hao   University College Cork, Ireland

Yongan Huang   Huazhong University of Science and Technology,
China

Qiang Li   Bielefeld University, Germany

Yuichiro Toda   Okayama University, Japan

Fei Zhao   Xi'an Jiaotong University, China

International Organizing Committee Chairs

Zhiyong Chen   The University of Newcastle, Australia

Yutaka Hata   University of Hyogo, Japan

Sabina Jesehke   RWTH Aachen University, Germany

Xuesong Mei   Xi'an Jiaotong University, China

Robert Riener   ETH Zurich, Switzerland

Chunyi Su   Concordia University, Canada

Shengquan Xie   The University of Auckland, New Zealand

Chenguang Yang   UWE Bristol, UK

Tom Ziemke   University of Skövde, Sweden

Yahya Zweiri   Kingston University, UK

Local Arrangements Chairs

Hualiang Zhang   Shenyang Institute of Automation, Chinese Academy
of Sciences, China

Xin Zhang   Shenyang Institute of Automation, Chinese Academy
of Sciences, China

Contents – Part VI

Virtual and Augmented Reality

Education in Mechatronics Engineering

Robotic Drilling and Sampling Technology

Automotive Systems

Mechatronics in Energy Systems

Human-Robot Interaction

Robot Motion Analysis and Planning

Research on Optimization of Control Parameters of Coal Sampling Robot Based on Model and Neural Network Algorithm

Xiaodong Liu[1], Haibo Xu[1(✉)], Jun Wang[2], Rui Wang[1], and Li Liu[1]

[1] Xi'an Jiaotong University, Xi'an 710049, Shanxi, China
sclxd95@stu.xjtu.edu.cn, hbxu@mail.xjtu.edu.cn
[2] Xi'an Hongyu Mining Special Mobile Equipment Co.,
Xi'an 710075, Shanxi, China

Abstract. This paper takes the single joint (big arm joint) servo control system of coal sampling robot as the research object, analyzes the structure of servo control system, establishes the model of single joint servo control system to study the method of tuning and optimizing the control parameters of the servo system. The combination of model-based control parameter tuning and improved BP neural network control parameter optimization is adopted to improve the system's ability to adapt to the load and improve the performance of system.

Keywords: Load inertia · BP neural network · Control parameter optimization

1 Introduction

During the operation of mobile coal sampling robot, load variation, change of joint pose and external disturbance will change the equivalent moment of inertia and load inertia torque of each joint motor. If the control parameters do not follow the change at this time, the change of load will affect the performance of the robot servo control system such as motion accuracy, stationarity and service life. This paper takes the single joint (big arm joint) servo control system of coal sampling robot as the research object, analyzes the structure of servo control system, establishes the model of single joint servo control system, and improves the dynamic and static performance and load change of the robot servo control system. The combination of model-based control parameter tuning [1, 2] and improved BP neural network [3] control parameter optimization is adopted to improve the system's ability to adapt to the load and improve the performance of system.

2 Modeling of Robot Single Joint Control System

The arm joint of the sampling robot adopts closed-loop control mode, which can adjust the input control signal of the controller according to the output signals of the end actuator's torque, position, angular velocity and angular acceleration. In the coal sampling robot servo control system, the permanent magnet synchronous AC servo

© Springer Nature Switzerland AG 2019
H. Yu et al. (Eds.): ICIRA 2019, LNAI 11745, pp. 3–15, 2019.
https://doi.org/10.1007/978-3-030-27529-7_1

motor is used to drive. The structure of the arm joint system of the robot model is shown in Fig. 1. Combined with the structural block diagram of the robotic arm joint control system, the control system can be simplified into a closed-loop control system for the servo motor to drive the load. The big arm joint, the arm joint, the wrist joint and the end effector load can be regarded as the total load of the boom joint drive motor in the system, and the load is equivalent to the moment of inertia as J_L on the servo motor rotor, and the external disturbance received by the system is equivalent to torque of the servo motor rotor as T_L. The changes of the load of the end of robot and the joint pose will cause the equivalent load inertia of the drive motor of joint changing.

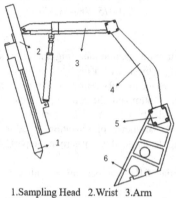

1.Sampling Head 2.Wrist 3.Arm
4.Big Arm 5.Servo Motor 6.Support

Fig. 1. Structure of the sampling robot model.

Based on the vector control strategy with $i_d = 0$, the mathematical model of the robot single joint system is established, and the linear state equation of the robot single joint system is following:

$$\begin{bmatrix} i_q \\ \omega_r \end{bmatrix} = \begin{bmatrix} -R/L & -P_n\psi_f/L \\ 3/2P_n\psi_f/(J_m+J_L) & 0 \end{bmatrix} \begin{bmatrix} i_q \\ \omega_r \end{bmatrix} + \begin{bmatrix} u_q/L \\ -T_L/(J_m+J_L) \end{bmatrix} \quad (1)$$

In Eq. (1): i_d is the d-axis current/A in the d-q coordinate system, i_q is the q-axis current/A in the d-q coordinate system, ψ_f is the coupled flux linkage/Wb, ω_r is the rotational speed of the servo motor/rad/s, J_m is the inertia of the servo motor rotor/ $Kg \cdot m^2$, p_n is the differential operator, J_L is the load inertia of the servo motor/$Kg \cdot m^2$, T_L is the torque of the servo motor load/$N \cdot m$, R is the motor's line resistance/Ω, and L is the motor's line inductance/mH.

According to the principle of permanent magnet synchronous AC servo motor vector control [4] and the mathematical model of servo motor [5], combined with $i_d = 0$ control mode [6], a three-closed loop control system for robot single joint system is established. The current control in the system adopts space voltage vector control mode (SVPWM), and is shown in the Fig. 2.

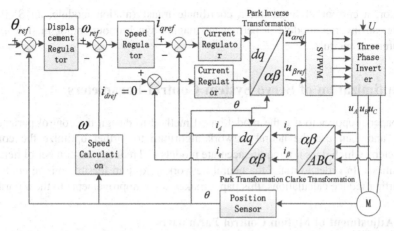

Fig. 2. Three-closed loop control block diagram of single joint system.

As shown in Fig. 2, according to reference speed ω_{ref} and the actual speed ω, the torque current i_{qref} can be calculated by the speed regulator. The $i_d = 0$ mode is used to set i_{dref} as 0. Detecting the phase current of the servo motor to obtain the excitation current i_d and the torque current i_q in the d-q rotating coordinate system through the Clarke and Park transformation, and respectively obtaining the difference of i_{qref} and i_{dref}. The voltage signal u_d and u_q of the system can be obtained by the current regulator. And then the voltage signal in the two-phase stationary coordinate system can be obtained by Park inverse transformation. And the final control pulse can be obtained by SVPWM, which is used to control the three-phase winding resistance current of the stator of the servo motor.

The simulation model of the control system [7, 8] is built in MATLAB/Simulink, as shown in Fig. 3. And it mainly includes a displacement PI regulator, a speed PI

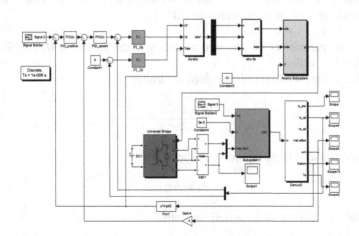

Fig. 3. Simulation model of three-closed loop control system.

regulator, a current PI regulator, a coordinate transformation module, an SVPWM module, an inverter module, a permanent magnet synchronous motor module and a measurement module.

3   Optimization of Servo System Control Parameters

This paper proposes to use the model-based method to design the control parameters firstly, and then use the neural network algorithm to further optimize the control parameters, which does not require accurate models and reduces the number of iteration calculations. In order to make the neural network algorithm feasible on the controller and further reduce calculations, this paper makes some improvements to the algorithm.

3.1   Adjustment of Motion Control Parameters

Adjustment of the Parameters of the Speed Loop. In the motor servo system, the electromagnetic transient process of the system is much faster than the mechanical transient process. In order to simplify the analysis, the current loop is usually equivalent to First-order small inertia system, which is shown in Fig. 4.

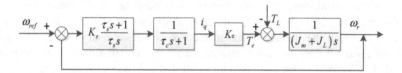

Fig. 4. Simplified servo system speed loop block diagram.

Where: the τ_c is the current loop time constant, K_s and τ_s are the proportional constant and time constant respectively, ω_c is the cutoff frequency, h is the width in the logarithmic coordinates of the band with $-20\ dB/dec$.

In addition, $\omega_1 = 1/\tau_s$, $\omega_2 = 1/\tau_c$.

The system parameters are designed according to the minimum M_r criterion in the oscillation index method.

The proportional constant of the speed controller:

$$K_s = \frac{(h+1)(J_m + J_L)}{2h\tau_c K_e} \tag{2}$$

The time constant of the speed controller:

$$\tau_s = h\tau_c \tag{3}$$

The integral constant of the speed controller:

$$K_i = \frac{K_s}{\tau_s} = \frac{(h+1)(J_m + J_L)}{2h^2 \tau_c^2 K_e} \tag{4}$$

In Eqs. (2)–(4), h, τ_c and K_e are constants, generally taking $h = 5$, τ_c can be obtained from the current loop parameter, K_e is obtained from the servo motor parameters, and K_s and K_i can be calculated in combination with the moment of inertia.

Adjustment of the Parameters of Position Loop. When the servo system position loop is controlled, the speed loop is the inner loop and the bandwidth is much larger than the position loop bandwidth. Therefore, when analyzing the position loop, the speed loop can be simplified into a first-order inertia system [6]. In order to improve the dynamic performance of the servo system and meet the requirements of positional overshoot, the servo system position loop adopts composite control of speed feedforward combined proportional control. The block diagram of the composite control structure is shown as Fig. 5:

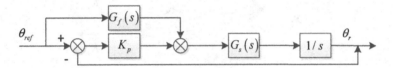

Fig. 5. Compound control structure block diagram of servo system position loop.

In order to obtain the error-free tracking of the position loop, the closed-loop transfer function is following:

$$G_b(s) = \frac{K_P K_v}{\omega_s} \frac{1}{s^2 + \frac{\omega_s}{u} s + \frac{\omega_s}{u} K_P K_v} \tag{5}$$

In Eqs. (5): K_v is the equivalent gain of speed loop; u is the speed loop phase angle margin adjustment coefficient, ω_s is the system's natural frequency, and $u = \omega_s / K_i$, $K_F = \lambda / K_v$ and $\lambda(0 < \lambda < 1)$ is the oscillation coefficients.

Since the system is a typical second-order system model, the position loop requirement can't produce overshoot, so proportional constant of the position loop is:

$$K_P = \frac{4\omega_s}{K_v u} \tag{6}$$

3.2 Optimization of Motion Control Parameters

The motion control parameters obtained by the model design are not the best for the system. This paper proposes the BP neural network algorithm to further optimize the control parameters based on the model tuning and improve the BP neural network algorithm.

The steps of the improved algorithm are as follows: firstly, control the system based on the control parameters obtained as the initial value, and give the system a periodic input (step signal); Then, optimize the target squared error integral ISE as the neural network input layer, control parameters as the output layer, the control parameters and weighting coefficients aren't adjusted in one cycle; Then, after a cycle, the new control parameters and the new weighting coefficients are used for the next cycle. A new ISE will be obtained; Finally, iteratively iterative until the optimal control parameters are obtained. In this paper, F_s is used to represent the $ISE = \int_0^t [r(t) - y(t)]^2 dt$. The F_s^{N-1} of the previous cycle is used as the input layer of the BP neural network. The output layer is the controller parameters K_p and K_i which need to be adjusted, and the output layer and input layer adopt the Sigmoid function.

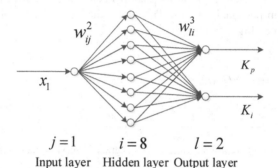

$$j = 1 \qquad i = 8 \qquad l = 2$$

Input layer   Hidden layer   Output layer

Fig. 6. Three-layer BP neural network structure.

In Fig. 6, the input and output of the input layer are:

$$O_j^1 = x = F_s^{N-1} \tag{7}$$

The input and output of the hidden layer are:

$$\begin{cases} I_i^2(k) = w_{ij} O_j^1 \\ O_i^2(k) = f(I_i^2(k)) \end{cases} \tag{8}$$

The input and output of the output layer are:

$$\begin{cases} I_l^3(k) = \sum_{i=1}^{8} w_{li}^3 O_i^2(k) \\ O_l^3(k) = g(I_l^3(k)) \end{cases} \tag{9}$$

In Eqs. (7) to (9), $O_1^3(k) = K_p$, $O_2^3(k) = K_i$, and they are constants over a period. After the performance index function is discretized:

$$E^N = F_s^N = \sum_{k=1}^{n} (r(k) - y(k))^2 = \sum_{k=1}^{n} E(k) \tag{10}$$

The gradient descent method is used to modify the weight coefficients W_{ij}^2 and W_{ij}^3, that is, the negative gradient direction of the weighting coefficient is adjusted according to E^N to obtain the learning algorithm of weighting coefficient of output layer:

$$w_{li}^3(N+1) = w_{li}^3(N)$$
$$- \eta \sum_{k=1}^{n} \left(-2[r(k) - y(k)]\mathrm{sgn}\left[\frac{\partial y(k)}{\partial u(k)}\right] \frac{\partial u(k)}{\partial O_i^3(k)} O_i^3(k)(1 - O_i^3(k))O_i^2(k) \right) \tag{11}$$

Similarly, the learning algorithm for weighting coefficient of hidden layer can be obtained as follows:

$$w_{ij}^3(N+1) = w_{ij}^3(N)$$
$$- \eta \sum_{k=1}^{n} \left(-2[r(k) - y(k)]\mathrm{sgn}\left[\frac{\partial y(k)}{\partial u(k)}\right] \frac{\partial u(k)}{\partial O_i^2(k)} O_i^2(k)(1 - O_i^2(k))f_s^{N-1} \right) \tag{12}$$

In Eqs. (7)–(12): η is the learning rate; N is the number of control parameter optimization cycles.

For each cycle, the input and control parameters and weighting coefficients of the input layer are not adjusted. The parameters of input and output layer of each sampling point are constant. Compared with the conventional PID tuning algorithm of BP neural network, the algorithm can greatly reduce the amount of calculation.

Optimization of Speed Loop Parameters. In order to analyze the influence of adjustment and optimization of the speed loop parameters on the starting performance of the control system, the external disturbance torque T_L is set to 0, the parameters of current controller and the moment of inertia J_m are constant, and the load inertia J_L is from $1J_m$ to $7J_m$. According to the change of load inertia, the control parameters are adjusted through the model-based method, then use the neural network algorithm to further optimize the control parameters.

The given system inputs periodic unit step signals, taking 10,000 sample points per cycle. As the number of iterations increases, the *ISE* changes as shown in Fig. 7. After $N > 28$, ISE basically doesn't reduced constantly, therefore, the control parameters at this time can be the most optimal parameters. The speed is set as *1500r/min*. After adjustment, the system's speed response curves and phase current response curves are shown in Figs. 8 and 9 respectively, the response indicators of system's performance are shown in Table 1.

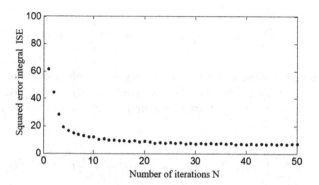

Fig. 7. Trend of ISE.

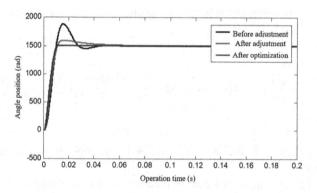

Fig. 8. Speed response curves.

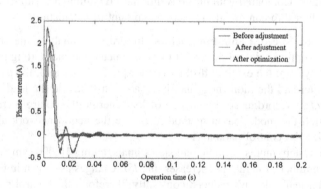

Fig. 9. Phase current response curves.

Table 1. Comparison of system response before and after optimization of control parameters.

System status	Overshoot	Adjusted time	Static error	Maximum current
Before adjustment	26.7%	0.058 s	1.5%	2.10 A
After adjustment	8.20%	0.049 s	0.3%	2.20 A
After optimization	2.90%	0.020 s	0.2%	2.40 A

As shown in Figs. 8, 9 and Table 1 that after the optimization, the system's adjusted time is shortened from 58 ms to 20 ms, the system response speed is obviously improved, and the overshoot is reduced from the original 26.7% to 3%. The system's dynamic performance is significantly improved.

Optimization of Position Loop Parameters. In order to analyze the influence of load inertia change on the system position loop performance, the same method is used to obtain the optimal control parameters of the position loop.

As shown in Figs. 10, 11 and 12 that after optimization of parameters, the system response speed is improved, the position following performance is obviously improved, the adjusted time of speed loop and phase current is shortened, the overshoot is reduced. So the dynamic performance of system is significantly improved.

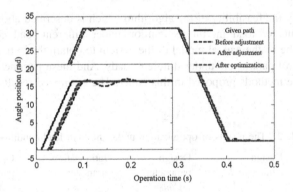

Fig. 10. Position response curves.

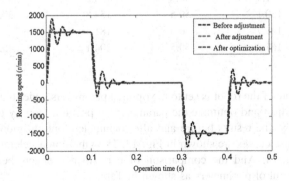

Fig. 11. Speed response curves.

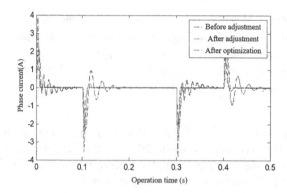

Fig. 12. Phase current response curves.

The result shows that the proposed method in this paper is very effective for improving the performance of the servo system.

4   Experiment of Robot Motion Control

In order to verify the feasibility of the algorithm which is described above. This paper adopts the results of load inertia recognition under different load conditions and combines with the mathematical model of the system to obtain the initial values of the speed loop control parameters under different loads. And these parameters are further optimized by the methods proposed in this paper. The optimized results are shown in Table 2.

Table 2. The results of optimization under different load conditions.

Load situation M/Kg	Design parameter K_{sp}'	Design parameter $\tau si'/ms$	Optimization parameter K_{sp}	Optimization parameter τ_{si}/ms
0.5	92.9	50.5	102.2	26.0
1.0	111.5	50.5	123.2	31.3
1.5	130.1	50.5	154.8	37.8
2.0	148.7	50.5	181.4	40.3
2.5	167.3	50.5	204.1	45.4

The initial state of the robot is set to the optimal parameters under the load situation of 2.0 kg, then adjust and optimize the parameters of position loop by the methods in this paper. Finally, the results before and after parameters optimization are obtained. The speed response curves are shown in Fig. 13. The vibration acceleration curves are as shown in Fig. 14. And the comparison of performance effects before and after optimization of control parameters as shown in Table 3.

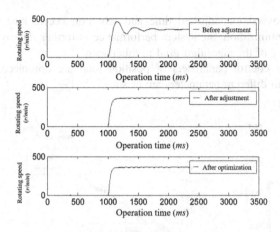

Fig. 13. Speed response curves.

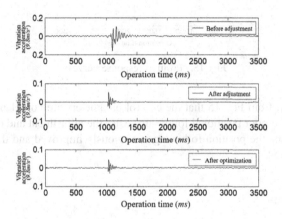

Fig. 14. Vibration acceleration response curves.

Table 3. Comparison of performance effects before and after optimization of control parameters.

Control parameter	Overshoot	Adjusted time	Vibration acceleration
Before adjustment	15.9%	0.750 s	1.67 m/s^2
After adjustment	1.2%	0.140 s	0.49 m/s^2
After optimization	1.0%	0.110 s	0.39 m/s^2

It can be seen from Figs. 13, 14 and Table 3 that when the load inertia changes, if the control parameters can't follow the adjustment, it will affect the performance of the system motion accuracy, stability, and smooth running. After the adjustment of parameters, the overshoot, adjusted time and vibration acceleration of system are reduced. After optimization, the system performance is further improved, which verifies the feasibility of the algorithm used in this paper.

Similarly, the control parameters of position loop are optimized. The position response curves in different parameters are as shown in Fig. 15.

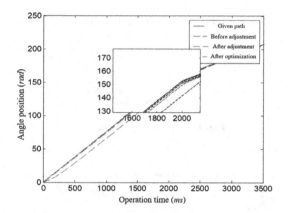

Fig. 15. Position response curves.

It can be seen from Fig. 15 that the control parameters are not adapted to the load inertia, resulting in poor positional follow-up. After the adjustment and optimization of control parameters, the position following is obviously improved and the performance is further improved.

5   Conclusions

In this paper, the structure of single-joint system of coal sampling robot is analyzed, and the three-closed-loop control simulation model of single-joint servo control system of coal sampling robot is established. Then the control parameters are designed by model-based method firstly, and then the parameters are further optimized through the improved BP neural network algorithm, which doesn't require accurate models, and can reduce the possibility of BP algorithm optimization falling into local minimum value and the amount of calculation of iteration. The results of simulation show that the method of adjustment and optimization for control parameters used in this paper can improve the system's ability to adapt to the load and effectively improve the system's performance. And the results of experiments show that the performance of the optimized robot system is significantly improved.

References

1. Mattavelli, P., Tubiana, L., Zigliotto, M.: Simple control autotuning for PMSM drives based on feedback relay. In: European Conference on Power Electronics and Applications, pp. 1–10 (2005)
2. Han, Y., Liu, C., Wu, J.: Backlash identification for PMSM servo system based on relay feedback. Nonlinear Dyn. **84**, 1–13 (2016)
3. Ren, T., Liu, S., Yan, G., et al.: Temperature prediction of the molten salt collector tube using BP neural network. IET Renew. Power Gener. **10**(2), 212–220 (2016)
4. Li, S., Liu, Z.: Adaptive speed control for permanent magnet synchronous motor system with variations of load inertia. IEEE Trans. Ind. Electron. **56**, 3050–3059 (2009)
5. Sharma, R.K., Sanadhya, V., Behera, L., et al.: Vector control of a permanent magnet synchronous motor. In: IEEE India Conference, vol. 1, pp. 81–86 (2009)
6. Xue, T., Wan, Z.J., Xu, W., et al.: The simulation of permanent magnet synchronous motor control system for electric vehicle. In: Control Conference, pp. 7674–7679 (2013)
7. Hongjun, C., Hao, X., Bo, L., et al.: The compensated active disturbance rejection controller based on sliding mode control for PMSM. In: The 5th Annual IEEE International Conference on Cyber Technology, pp. 240–245 (2015)
8. Ichikawa, S.T., Machile, D.S.: Sensorless control of PMSM using online parameter identification based on system identification theory. IEEE Trans. Power Electron. **5**, 363–372 (2011)

A Cooperative Obstacle-Avoidance Approach for Two-Manipulator Based on A* Algorithm

Jinlong Zhao, Yongsheng Chao[(⊠)], and Yiping Yuan

Xinjiang University, Urumqi 830047, Xinjiang, China
cys21st@163.com

Abstract. During the movement process of two 6-dof manipulators, there may be collisions between manipulator and space obstacles or itself. To solve this problem, this paper use A* algorithm to finish the cooperative obstacle-avoidance path planning. Firstly, the model of obstacles is established. A* algorithm is used to plan a feasible path in the static obstacles environment for the main manipulator. Then, the virtual obstacles is set on the feasible path of the main manipulator. A* algorithm is applied to plan a feasible path for the second manipulator. In order to prevent the interference between the manipulators, ensure the smoothness of the manipulators in motion, and the time-energy optimum. By establishing the optimization model of inverse solutions, we realize the two-manipulator smooth motion without interference. Finally, the effectiveness of the algorithm is verified by simulation experiments.

Keywords: Two-manipulator · A* algorithm · Collision · Path smoothness · Optimization model

1 Introduction

In recent years, different types of manipulator are widely used in various areas. However, with the development of complex and intelligent operation, the single manipulator can not effectively complete some complex tasks in the production process, but the coordination of two manipulators can adapt to the increasing complexity of the task and improve the efficiency of the operation as well. However, when the two manipulators operate in the same workspace, there may be interference collision between the manipulators and the space obstacle as well as the manipulators, so the coordinated operation of the two manipulators becomes a hot research topic.

The A* algorithm [1] and RRT algorithm [2] are widely used to plan a collision-free path for manipulator. Park et al. [3] presented a dual arm robot system with a mobile platform for the automatic assembly. Larsen et al. [4] developed a system which allows to generate robot paths on the basis of Computer Aided Design (CAD) data. Zhou [5] proposed a new multi-robot cooperative motion planning method based on the closed kinematic chain constraints between robots. Angerer et al. [6] introduced a novel approach for the automated manufacturing of CFRP materials using cooperating industrial robots. Cheng et al. [7] proposed a simplified model and collision detection method to avoid collision between two robot systems. Zhao et al. [8] presented a path planning algorithm for main-second robot coordinated tracking for the problem of dual

© Springer Nature Switzerland AG 2019
H. Yu et al. (Eds.): ICIRA 2019, LNAI 11745, pp. 16–25, 2019.
https://doi.org/10.1007/978-3-030-27529-7_2

robot coordination welding complex curve. Zhang [9] introduced a collision-free path planning method based on "hypothesis correction" strategy and genetic algorithm to avoid collision between two robots at the same time. Tang et al. [10] combined C space with path planning for the dual robot synchronous welding problem. Wang et al. [11] developed a GC-PSO algorithm to achieve optimal path planning for dual welding robots. Kim et al. [12] proposed an improved fast-expanding random tree algorithm suitable for assembly task system to solve the assembly task operation planning problem of dual-arm robot.

Some methods of collision detection, coordination motion and obstacle avoidance are proposed for the coordination of two manipulators, but they do not take into account that the possibility of interference collision between manipulator and space obstacles or itself when two manipulators is avoiding obstacles at the same time, and not combine motion time and energy with the obstacle avoidance trajectory planning of the manipulator. In this paper, two space 6-dof manipulators are taken as the research object. Firstly, the space manipulator model and obstacle model are reasonably simplified, and the geometric model containing obstacles in three-dimensional coordinates is established. Then, A* algorithm and the method of collision detection is used to plan feasible paths for the main and second manipulators in the obstacles environment. In order to prevent the interference of two manipulators during obstacle avoidance and improve smoothness of motion, and reduce the time and energy cost during obstacle avoidance as well, the optimization model of inverse solutions is established. The inverse solutions is selected by this model to complete the joint trajectory planning.

2 Collision Detection Method

2.1 Model of Two Manipulators

The space 6-dof manipulator studied in this paper satisfies the Pieper criterion, that is, the three consecutive axes of the robot intersect at one point. The combination of two space 6-dof manipulators is shown in Fig. 1. According to its structural characteristics, the model of each link of the manipulator is simplified to a cylindrical model.

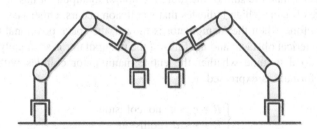

Fig. 1. Model of two manipulators

2.2 Obstacle Model

In the realistic working environment, the geometry of the obstacle is difficult to describe. In order to avoid the collisions between links of manipulator and the obstacles during the movement of the manipulator, this paper uses the common space rule body to approximate the obstacles for model simplification. Although the expansion of the obstacle domain is caused, the simplified model improves the efficiency of the space path planning and ensure the safety of the manipulator in actual operation.

The spherical obstacle can be defined as $A(B_0, r)$, as shown in Fig. 2. Among them, $B_0(x_0, y_0, z_0)$ is the center of the sphere in the base coordinate system, r is the radius of the sphere. The method is simple and intuitive as the obstacle is approximated to a spherical shape, which simplifies the calculation of the distance.

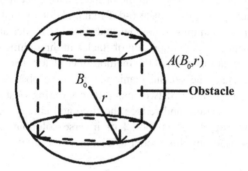

Fig. 2. Obstacle model

2.3 Collision Detection Method

In order to avoid collision between the links of manipulator and obstacles, after enveloping the links of manipulator into a cylinder, it is only need to calculate the space positional relationship between the obstacle and the links of manipulator. When the distance between the axis of the link of manipulator and the center of a spherical obstacle is smaller than the sum of the radii, the link of manipulator has an intersection with the sphere obstacle which indicates that a collision occurs. Otherwise, it means no collision. Therefore, when the manipulator is moved, the space positional relationship between the spherical obstacle and the links of the manipulator is separately calculated. It is possible to determine whether the entire manipulator collides with the space obstacle. The formula is expressed as

$$\begin{cases} R+r>d & \text{no collision} \\ R+r\le d & \text{collision} \end{cases} \tag{1}$$

where R is the radius of the cylinder, r is the radius of the spherical obstacle, d is the distance between the axis of the cylinder and the center of the sphere.

3 Path Planning Method for Two-Manipulator

The A* algorithm is a typical heuristic search method. It is also a more efficient direct search method to optimize the shortest paths in static networks. This method can search for optimal paths in different environments. The core of the A* algorithm is the design of the estimation function $f(n)$. In the process of searching path for obstacle avoidance of manipulator, each step needs to calculate the child node estimation function value of the current position, and select the node with the smallest estimation function value as the node to reach in next step for the manipulator. Until the optimal obstacle avoidance path of the current manipulator obtained, the searching process will be done. It searches for path in a certain direction according to the heuristic function $f(n)$ instead of traversing every node of the space by this method. The A* algorithm can be expressed as follows

$$f(n) = g(n) + h(n) \tag{2}$$

where $f(n)$ is denoted the evaluation function of the current node n, $g(n)$ is denoted the actual cost of the path from the initial nodes to the current node n, $h(n)$ is denoted the evaluation cost of the path from the current node n to the goal node.

4 Optimization Model of Inverse Solutions of Manipulator

4.1 D-H Model of Manipulator

For a given manipulator, the traditional D-H method is used for description. It can establish the coordinate system of joints. $x_0 - z_0$ is a basic coordinate system, $x_6 - z_6$ is a manipulator end coordinate system. The relationship between the $i - 1$ coordinate system and the i coordinate system can be realized by translation and rotation and represented by a matrix A_i, and the relationship can be written as follows

$$A_i = \begin{bmatrix} \cos\theta_i & -\sin\theta_i \cos\alpha_i & \sin\theta_i \sin\alpha_i & a_i \cos\theta_i \\ \sin\theta_i & \cos\theta_i \cos\alpha_i & -\cos\theta_i \sin\alpha_i & a_i \sin\theta_i \\ 0 & \sin\alpha_i & \cos\alpha_i & d_i \\ 0 & 0 & 0 & 1 \end{bmatrix} \tag{3}$$

where θ_i is the angle of joint i, α_i is the link twist of joints i and $i+1$, a_i is the length of joint $i+1$, and d_i is the offset of joint i; $i = 0, 1, 2, 3, \ldots, 6$.

According to the D-H principle, firstly calculate the change matrix A_i of the coordinate system $x_{i-1} - z_{i-1}$ to the coordinate system $x_i - z_i$, and then sequentially multiply the right to obtain the transformation matrix of the end of the manipulator relative to the base coordinate system, the result can be obtained as

$$T = A_1A_2A_3A_4A_5A_6 = \begin{bmatrix} n_x & o_x & a_x & p_x \\ n_y & o_y & a_y & p_y \\ n_z & o_z & a_z & p_z \\ 0 & 0 & 0 & 1 \end{bmatrix} \tag{4}$$

where $n_x, n_y, n_z, o_x, o_y, o_z, a_x, a_y, a_z$ is the posture of the end of the manipulator and p_x, p_y, p_z is the position coordinate of the end of the manipulator.

4.2 Optimization Model of Inverse Solutions

In order to avoid interference between the manipulators during the obstacle avoidance process, ensure the smoothness of motion and reduce the time and energy cost during obstacle avoidance as well, the optimization model of inverse solutions is proposed.

For a certain end position, there may be multiple sets of joint coordinates corresponding to it. It results to the multiplicity of inverse solutions of the manipulator, and the number of inverse solutions depends on the number of non-zero terms of the link length and offset in the structural link parameters of the manipulator.

By the inverse transformation of formula (4), the inverse solutions of manipulator can be obtained as

$$A_3A_4A_5 = A_2^{-1}A_1^{-1}TA_6^{-1} \tag{5}$$

The manipulator satisfying the Pieper criterion has up to 8 sets of inverse solutions. The 12 equations are established according to the equality of the matrix corresponding items and 8 sets of different joint variable values are generated by solving the equations.

According to the multiplicity of inverse solutions, a time-energy optimization model of inverse solutions based on the principle of "closest" and "minimum joint angle variation" is proposed. Formula (6) reflects the principle of "closest" and embodies the weighting idea, so that the selection favors moving smaller joints rather than moving the large joints.

$$Y_1 = \frac{\sum\limits_{i=1}^{E} |\theta_i| l_i}{\sum\limits_{i=1}^{E} l_i} + \frac{1}{F} \sum\limits_{i=1}^{F} |\theta_i| \tag{6}$$

where θ_i is the joint angle of the desired position, l_i is the length of the link i, E is the number of links which are not equal to zero, and F is the number of links which are equal to zero.

Formula (7) reflects the principle of "minimum joint angle variation" and calculates the sum of the joint angle changes, so the optimal model can select the solution with the smallest change in joint angle.

$$Y_2 = \sum_{i=1}^{6} |\Delta\theta_i| \tag{7}$$

where $\Delta\theta_i$ is the amount of change in joint angle.

The model of time-energy optimization can be obtained as

$$Y = \min(Y_1 + Y_2) \tag{8}$$

The specific inverse solutions optimization process is as follows:

(1) Separating the obstacle avoidance path of two manipulators into a number of column nodes in equal amount, the nodes can be written as $x_j, y_j (j = 1, 2, 3 \cdots, i)$.

(2) The eight inverse solutions of these nodes are obtained through the inverse solutions program of the manipulator. The results of inverse solutions can be expressed as $\theta_{m1}, \theta_{m2}, \theta_{m3}, \theta_{m4}, \theta_{m5}, \theta_{m6}$, $m = 1, 2, \cdots, 8$.

(3) According to the range of joint angle of each joint of the manipulator, delete the infeasible solution. The range of joint angle can be described as

$$\min(\theta_n) \leq \theta_{mn} \leq \max(\theta_n)$$

where $m = 1, 2, \cdots, 8, n = 1, 2, \cdots, 6, \min(\theta_n)$ is the minimum joint angle that can be achieved by the n joint, and $\max(\theta_n)$ is the maximum joint angle that the n joint can achieve.

(4) It tests whether the inverse solutions selected by the step (3) interferes in the simulation tool and retain the inverse solutions without interference.

(5) According to the optimization model of inverse solutions (8), from step (4), a set of time-energy optimal inverse solutions are selected for each node of the main-second manipulator.

(6) By interpolating the inverse solutions selected by step (5) on the same joint of the manipulator at different nodes, the joint displacement function will be obtained.

5   Experimental Results and Discussion

In order to complete the obstacle avoidance path planning of the main-second manipulator, an obstacle environment is established in Matlab. The obstacle is a sphere with a radius of 10 cm and the coordinates are (50, 50, 50). The path planning of the main manipulator is completed first. The planning result is shown in Fig. 3(a). Then the virtual obstacles are placed on the feasible path of the main manipulator. The result is shown in Fig. 3(b). Finally, the path for the second manipulator will be planned. The planning result is shown in Fig. 3(c). Through the A* algorithm and setting virtual obstacles, the path planning of the main-second manipulator can be effectively completed and the main-second manipulator can avoid obstacles during the movement.

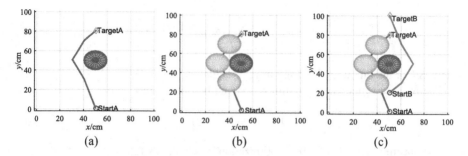

Fig. 3. Main-second manipulator path planning top view. (a) Main manipulator path planning; (b) Place virtual obstacles; (c) Second manipulator path planning.

Meanwhile, the optimization of inverse solutions for each joint of the main-second manipulator is completed by the optimization model of inverse solutions. The optimization results are shown in Fig. 4. It can be seen from the figure that the joint displacement curve changes uniformly through the selection of the optimization model of inverse solutions. The verifications were simulated in Matlab and UG respectively to further identify the effect of the optimization model of inverse solutions in avoiding interference between the manipulators.

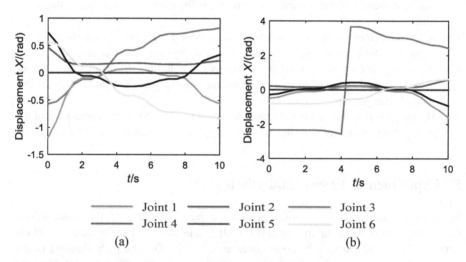

Fig. 4. Joint trajectories obtained by optimization model. (a) Joint trajectories of main manipulator; (b) Joint trajectories of second manipulator.

Matlab and Robotic Toolbox were used to verify the proposed optimization model of inverse solutions through simulation experiments. The model of two manipulators is shown in Fig. 5.

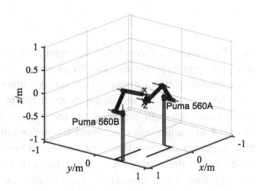

Fig. 5. The model of two manipulator

The simulation process of the two-manipulator in Matlab is shown in Fig. 6. The Main-second manipulator moves from the specified initial position to the specified target position according to the obstacle-avoidance path planned by the A* algorithm. The end effector can effectively avoid the obstacle. At the same time, it can be seen that the inverse solutions which are selected by the optimization model of inverse solutions can avoid interference between the links of manipulator.

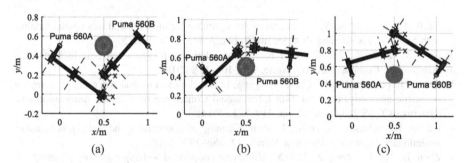

Fig. 6. Simulation results of Matlab top view. (a) Initial state; (b) Intermediate state; (c) End state.

Verification is performed on the UG simulation analysis software to further verify the results of the above Matlab simulation. Figure 7 shows a set of simulation results under the virtual prototype and confirm that the main-second manipulator does not collide with the obstacle, and there is no interference between the manipulators.

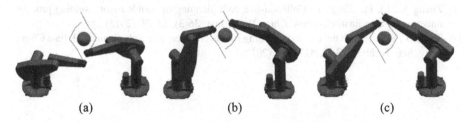

Fig. 7. Simulation results of UG. (a) Initial state; (b) Intermediate state; (c) End state.

6   Conclusion

Aiming at the problem of simultaneous avoidance of obstacles by two six-degree-of-freedom manipulators, this paper proposes and implements a method of two-manipulator obstacle avoidance path planning based on A* algorithm in obstacle environment. Firstly, the A* algorithm is used in the established obstacle environment to complete the obstacle avoidance path planning for the main-second manipulator. Then trajectory planning of the joints are completed by the optimization model of inverse solutions, which improves the smoothness of motion and reduces the time and energy cost in the movement of the manipulator. It can be seen from the simulation results of Matlab and UG that the main-second manipulator can move from the specified initial position to the specified target position along the planned path to avoid obstacles reasonably and eliminate interference between the manipulators, which demonstrates the method is effective.

Acknowledgement. This Research was supported by National Natural Science Foundation of China (No. 51565058).

References

1. Fu, B., Chen, L., Zhou, Y.: An improved A* algorithm for the industrial robot path planning with high success rate and short length. Robot. Auton. Syst. **106**, 26–37 (2018)
2. Cao, X., Zou, X., Jia, C.: RRT-based path planning for an intelligent litchi-picking manipulator. Comput. Electron. Agric. **156**, 105–118 (2019)
3. Park, D.I., Park, C., Do, H., Choi, T., Kyung, J.: Development of dual arm robot platform for automatic assembly. In: 2014 14th International Conference on Control, Automation and Systems (ICCAS 2014), Seoul, pp. 319–321 (2014)
4. Larsen, L., Schuster, A., Kim, J.: Path planning of cooperating industrial robots using evolutionary algorithms. Procedia Manuf. **17**, 286–293 (2018)
5. Zhou, B., Xu, L., Meng, Z., Dai, X.: Kinematic cooperated welding trajectory planning for master-slave multi-robot systems. In: 2016 35th Chinese Control Conference (CCC), Chengdu, pp. 6369–6374 (2016)
6. Angerer, A.: Planning and execution of collision-free multi-robot trajectories in industrial applications. In: Proceedings of ISR 2016: 47st International Symposium on Robotics, Munich, Germany, pp. 1–7 (2016)
7. Cheng, Y., Yan, L., Gu, P.: Detection collision algorithm for two-manipulator system. J. Beijing Univ. Aeronaut. Astronaut. **39**(12), 1644–1648 (2013)
8. Zhao, N., Yue, J., Li, L.: Path planning algorithm for leader-follower of two-robot coordinate welding. Trans. China Weld. Inst. **36**(03), 67–70 (2015)
9. Zhang, L., Li, L., Wang, T.: Collision-free path planning of double robots welding process under loose coordination. Trans. China Weld. Inst. **36**(3), 55–58 (2015)
10. Tang, B., Wang, X., Xue, L.: Dual-welding robots collision-free path planning. J. East China Univ. Sci. Technol. **43**(3), 417–424 (2017)

11. Wang, X., Tang, B., Yan, Y., Gu, X.: Time-optimal path planning for dual-welding robots based on intelligent optimization strategy. In: Chen, S., Zhang, Y., Feng, Z. (eds.) Transactions on Intelligent Welding Manufacturing. TIWM, pp. 47–59. Springer, Singapore (2018). https://doi.org/10.1007/978-981-10-7043-3_3
12. Kim, D.H., Lim, S.J., Lee, D.H.: A RRT-based motion planning of dual-arm robot for (Dis) assembly tasks. In: IEEE ISR 2013, Seoul, pp. 1–6 (2013)

Workspace Simulation and Analysis of a Dual-Arm Nursing Robot

Libo Zhang[1], Su Wang[1,2(✉)], and Xingang Miao[2]

[1] School of Mechanical Engineering and Automation, Beihang University,
Beijing 100191, China
wangsu@bucea.edu.cn
[2] Beijing University of Civil Engineering and Architecture,
Beijing 100044, China

Abstract. Based on the self-innovative dual-arm nursing robot, the kinematics model of the robot is established by D-H method, and the forward kinematics equation of the robot is analyzed and solved. Monte Carlo method was used to analyze the workspace of the nursing robot, and then the MATLAB was used to get the point cloud of the wrist joint at the end of arms. The rationality of the simulation was verified by comparing with the motion boundary graph. By analyzing the relationship between joint variables and workspace boundaries, the influence of joint variables parameters on workspace is further understood, which can provide reference for workspace optimization and control system research, and has important guiding significance for the structural design and practical application of dual-arm robots.

Keywords: Nursing robot · Monte carlo method · MATLAB ·
Joint variables, workspace

1 Introduction

The research of nursing robot with double arm structure has achieved rapid development and great progress along with the development of robotics technology. In complex unstructured environments, dual-arm robots can better meet the needs completely than single-arm robots [1]. Workspace analysis of robots is the basis of kinematics analysis and trajectory planning of robots, and is also an important part of robotics research. Dual-arm can accomplish tasks that single-arm robot cannot accomplish [2], the workspace of a robot is an important index to measure the working capacity of the robot [3]. At present, the common methods to analyse the workspace of robots are geometric method, analytical method and numerical method [4]. Geometric method is not very suitable for multi degree of freedom structure [5]. Analytical method is very complex in solving process, and it is not suitable for practical application [6]. The numerical method has strong computing power, it has obvious advantages [7], and the Monte Carlo method derived from numerical method is a very representative method [8]. In this paper, the workspace of the robot is simulated by Robotics toolbox of MATLAB, Monte Carlo method is used as the basis of workspace research, and the joint variables are taken as the object to further analyse the workspace of the robot.

H. Yu et al. (Eds.): ICIRA 2019, LNAI 11745, pp. 26–34, 2019.
https://doi.org/10.1007/978-3-030-27529-7_3

2 Kinematics Analysis of Dual-Arm Nursing Robot

2.1 Structure Analysis of Robot System

The main structure of the dual-arm nursing robot is composed of two arms and waist, it is a complex multi-body system, as shown in Fig. 1.

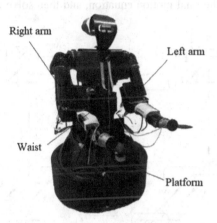

Fig. 1. Structure of nursing robot system

The robot consists of waist with two degrees of freedom and two arms which are identical in structure, and they are symmetrically distributed on the left and right sides of main body structure of the robot. The single arm includes shoulder, upper arm, elbow, lower arm and palm. There are two degrees of freedom at the shoulder joint, front and back swing degrees of freedom and left and right swing degrees of freedom respectively. The front and back swing degrees of freedom are used to realize the front and back swing of the arm relative to the shoulder or the main body. The left and right swing degrees of freedom are used to realize the left and right swing of the arm relative to the shoulder or the main body. The upper arm is close to the elbow and has the degree of freedom of rotation inside and outside, which is used to realize the inner and outer rotation of the lower arm. The elbow joint has the degree of freedom to lift the arm, and the wrist joint has the degree of freedom to swing the hand, which is used to realize the up and down swing of the manipulator. The waist has two degrees of freedom, and the rotating axes of the two joints are arranged vertically with each other, respectively, to realize the lateral tilt freedom of the robot body and the waist pitch of the robot body forward pitch.

2.2 Establishment of Joint Coordinate System

The nursing robot designed in this paper is an open kinematic chain manipulator from waist to wrist. In order to directly compute the kinematic equation of the robot through recursive expression, it is necessary to define the relative position relationship between each link and the adjacent link of the robot. Kinematics is the basis of solving the workspace, the left and right arms of the dual-arm robot are symmetrical. The D-H method is used to establish the link coordinate system for each joint of the dual-arm robot, as shown in Fig. 2. The main contents are structured as follow: firstly, a relative reference coordinate system is established for each member to determine the transformation from one coordinate to the next coordinate; secondly, the transformation is combined from the first member of the base in turn to get the total transformation matrix of the robot, establish the final motion equation, and then solve the pose of the robot.

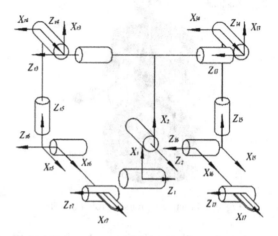

Fig. 2. D-H coordinate system of robot

Considering the initial state of the nursing robot, the kinematics parameters table of the photographic robot is obtained based on the D-H model. As shown in Table 1, I, II and III of serial numbers represent the lumbar joints, left arm joints and right arm joints.

Table 1. Kinematic connecting rod parameter table of robot

No.	Joint	Parameter			
	i	α_{i-1}	a_{i-1}	d_i	θ_i
I	1	0	0	0	0
	2	$-90°$	345.0	65.5	0
II	3	$-90°$	375.0	-313.0	0
	4	$90°$	0	-40.0	$90°$
	5	$90°$	0	-423.0	$90°$
	6	$90°$	0	105.0	0
	7	0	347.5	0	0
III	3	$-90°$	375.0	313.0	0
	4	$90°$	0	-40.0	$90°$
	5	$90°$	0	-423.0	$90°$
	6	$90°$	0	-105.0	$180°$
	7	0	347.5	0	0

For the waist, the range of joint θ_1 ($-\pi/4$–$\pi/3$), the range of joint θ_2 ($-\pi/4$–$\pi/4$). For left and right arms, the range of joint θ_3 (0–$\pi/4$), the range of joint θ_4 ($\pi/2$–π), the range of joint θ_5 (0–π), the range of joint θ_6 ($-pi/0$–0), and the range of joint θ_7 ($-pi/2$–$pi/2$).

2.3 Solution of Forward Kinematics Equation

Forward kinematics analysis is to determine the relative position and attitude between the end of the manipulator and the base coordinate system according to the joint angle of the manipulator and its component parameters. When two coordinate systems corresponding to each other are transformed into each other, there is no relative motion between the two coordinate systems and the corresponding rods. One coordinate system can be matched by rotation, translation and rotation. The corresponding homogeneous coordinate transformation matrix of each rod is established and defined as T matrix.

$$T_i = Rot(z, \theta_i)Trans(0, 0, d_i)Trans(a_i, 0, 0)Rot(x, \alpha_i) \tag{1}$$

Finally, a 4×4 transformation matrix is obtained.

$$
{}^{i-1}_{i}T = \begin{bmatrix}
c\theta_i & -s\theta_i & 0 & a_{t-1} \\
s\theta_i c\alpha_{i-1} & c\theta_i c\alpha_{-1} & -s\alpha_{i-1} & -s\alpha_{i-1}d_i \\
s\theta_i s\alpha_{i-1} & c\theta_i s\alpha_{i-1} & c\alpha_{i-1} & c\alpha_{i-1}d_i \\
0 & 0 & 0 & 1
\end{bmatrix} \tag{2}
$$

Each homogeneous transformation matrix contains only one unknown variable θ_i, and the others are known structural parameters. According to the above formula, each linkage transformation matrix can be obtained. Because the bifurcation structure of the waist and arm can be regarded as the coupling synthesis system of the independent left and right arms at the first two joints by the analysis of the main body structure, the research of the independent manipulator is the foundation and the key to the study of the coupling constraints. The position and attitude of the wrist coordinate system for the independent left arm in the world coordinate system is

$$
{}^{0}_{7}T_L = {}^{0}_{1}T\, {}^{1}_{2}T\, {}^{2}_{3}T_l\, {}^{3}_{4}T_l\, {}^{4}_{5}T_l\, {}^{5}_{6}T_l\, {}^{6}_{7}T_l \tag{3}
$$

The position and attitude of the wrist coordinate system at the end of the independent right arm in the world coordinate system are replaced by the parameters of each link transformation matrix of the independent left arm.

$$
{}^{0}_{7}T_R = {}^{0}_{1}T\, {}^{1}_{2}T\, {}^{2}_{3}T_r\, {}^{3}_{4}T_r\, {}^{4}_{5}T_r\, {}^{5}_{6}T_r\, {}^{6}_{7}T_r \tag{4}
$$

The forward kinematics equation of the robot body structure is

$$^0_7T =^0_1 T^1_2T \begin{cases} ^2_3T_l\,^3_4T_l\,^4_5T_l\,^5_6T_l\,^6_7T_l \\ ^2_3T_r\,^3_4T_r\,^4_5T_r\,^5_6T_r\,^6_7T_r \end{cases} \tag{5}$$

The Eq. (5) is the coupling relationship between the left arm and the left arm of the robot when the first two joints coincide. The origin of the world coordinate system in the formula is the midpoint of the first joint axis. From the coupling relationship, it can be seen intuitively that the position and posture of the end wrist joint of the robot's left and right arms can be determined by 12 joint variables.

3   Robot Workspace Analysis

3.1   Workspace Boundary Analysis

According to the range of the joint angle and the analysis of the structure, the limit position maps of each joint can be drawn. Because the space structure of the robot is complex, we analyze the limit position of the structure from the side structure and frontal structure of the robot.

This Fig. 3 shows that the extreme position of the joint is the main view of the forward-holding action. This view can visually see the boundary position of the connecting rod and the extreme motion trajectory of the red thin line wrist joint.

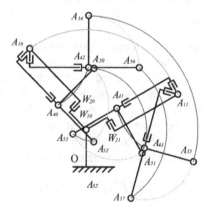

Fig. 3. Boundary map of profile limit position (Color figure online)

The Fig. 4 shows that the two shoulder joints overlap into one joint in the frontal view, and the relationship can be obtained from the side view. When the lower arm is extended horizontally, the front view of the elbow joint and the wrist joint is also combined into one joint, and the spatial position relationship between the joints can also be obtained from the side view. In order to clearly see the boundary relationship in the graph, the emmetropic view only analyses the limit position boundary map of the

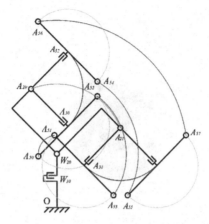

Fig. 4. Boundary map of frontage limit position

independent left arm, and the emmetropic view is the main view of the side release action.

Through the list of the rotation angle of each joint and the boundary map of the limit position of each joint, we can intuitively understand the movement of the whole robot body structure, which is the basis of the robot workspace analysis.

3.2   Workspace Simulation Analysis

According to the motion range of each joint, the motion workspace of the robot is solved and drawn by using the Monte Carlo method of MATLAB based on the analysis of the limit position of the robot joint. Monte Carlo method is a numerical method for solving mathematical problems by means of random sampling. In this paper, Monte Carlo method and D-H model are used to analyze the workspace of the robot, the principle is as follows

$$W = \{\omega(\theta) : \theta \in Q\} \subset R^3 \tag{6}$$

In the Eq. (6), W is the workspace, θ is the generalized joint variable, and $\omega(\theta)$ is the generalized joint variable function, which is the forward kinematics equation. Q is the joint space, R^3 is the three-dimensional space, the motion range of each generalized joint is expressed by a inequality, that is, $\theta_{imin} \leq \theta_i \leq \theta_{imax}$ $(i = 1, 2, \cdots, n)$.

According to the forward kinematics equation and Table 1, each joint variable value is substituted into the forward kinematics equation by using the loop statement of MATLAB. The program runs for 37.23 s and draws 6000 points to get the workspace of the robot's end wrist joint, as shown in Fig. 5.

The workspace map of the robot visually shows the spatial aggregation of the position of the end wrist joint. The blue part is the left wrist joint point cloud, and the orange part is the right wrist joint point cloud. It can be seen from the graph that the structure of the robot workspace is reasonable and the point cloud is symmetrically

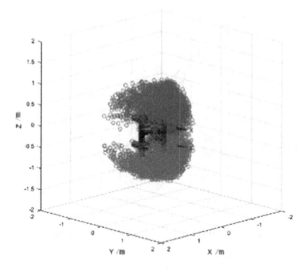

Fig. 5. Robot workspace simulation diagram (Color figure online)

distributed, which proves the correctness of the forward kinematics equation. Through the comparison of Fig. 5, it can be found that the basic profile shape of the robot motion boundary map and the workspace simulation point cloud are consistent, which verifies the correctness of the simulation.

4   The Influence of Joint Variables on Workspace

The workspace is formed by the limit position of the end joints of two arms, and the range of joint variables affects the position of the end joints, thus affecting the workspace of the robot. Because of the symmetry of the main structure of the robot, this paper analyses the influence of joint variables on the workspace based on the independent single arm.

The influence of joint variables on workspace can be expressed mathematically. When a single joint variable takes a certain value, the range of other joint variables takes its value. The maximum distance between the end joint point and the origin of the system coordinates corresponds to the value of a joint variable. The relationship between the joint variable value and the maximum distance is used to analyze the effect of joint variable on the workspace.

Each joint takes 10 values in its variable range, the difference between adjacent values is equal, and the tolerance of each joint variable is different. The joint value is θ_{ij}, and the distance from the end point P (p_x, p_y, p_z) to the origin point (0, 0, 0) is d_{ij}, which is the maximum distance.

$$\theta_{ij} = \theta_{i0} + j \cdot \Delta\theta_i \qquad (7)$$

$$\Delta\theta_i = \frac{\theta_{imax} - \theta_{imin}}{10} \tag{8}$$

$$d_{ij} = \sqrt{p_{ijx}^2 + p_{ijy}^2 + p_{ijz}^2} \tag{9}$$

In the above formula, $i = 1, 2,..., 7$; $j = 1, 2,..., 10$. In order to visually see the relationship between the joint variables and the maximum distance, each joint is drawn in polar coordinate system and Cartesian coordinate system, as shown in Fig. 6. The polar coordinate map is connected with each coordinate point by a broken line, and the Cartesian coordinate map is processed by quadratic fitting.

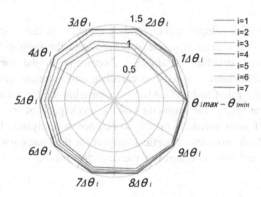

Fig. 6. Polar coordinate diagrams of joint variables and maximal distances

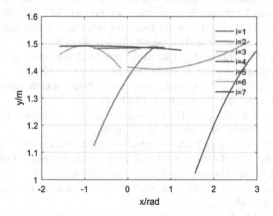

Fig. 7. Fitting curve of joint variables and maximum distance

It can be seen from Fig. 6 that the maximum distance of all joint variables near $9\Delta\theta_i$ is basically the same, and it is the maximum value, and the maximum distance corresponding to the position $\Delta\theta_i$ is the minimum value as a whole. Figure 7 shows that the maximum distance of joint 7 remains almost unchanged within its range of motion. The change of maximum distance corresponding to joint 1 and joint 3 is very small. The change of joint 5 and joint 6 is parabolic, and the change of maximum distance corresponding to joint 2 and joint 4 is the largest.

In Fig. 7, we can know the influence of each joint variable on the maximum distance, so we can see the influence of each joint variable on the workspace boundary. By analyzing the relationship between the joint variable and the boundary, we can analyze the effective solution in the inverse solution process of the robot and guide the trajectory optimization in the trajectory planning process of the robot.

5   Conclusion

In this paper, the self-developed nursing robot is taken as the research object. The kinematics of the robot's main structure is solved, and the motion boundary map is drawn with the main structure parameters. According to the forward kinematics equation, Monte Carlo method is used to calculate and simulate the workspace simulation diagram of the robot in MATLAB. By comparing the boundary graph with the numerical simulation graph, the rationality of the workspace of the robot is verified, and the influence of joint variables on the workspace is analyzed. The workspace is further analyzed, which provides theoretical support for the configuration optimization, trajectory planning and motion control of the dual-arm robot.

References

1. Li, R.F., Ma, G.Q.: Dual-arm kinematic characteristics analysis of humanoid robot based on Matlab. J. Huazhong Univ. Sci. Technol. (Nat. Sci. Ed.) **41**, 343–347 (2013)
2. Zhao, Y.S., Gong, L., Liu, C.L., et al.: Dual-arm robot design and testing for harvesting tomato in greenhouse. IFAC Pap. OnLine **49**(16), 161–165 (2016)
3. Ma, X.M., Shen, H.P., Huang, T., et al.: Kinematics and workspace analysis of redundant anthropomorphic dual-arm robot. J. Mach. Des. **31**(11), 25–28 (2014)
4. Cao, Y., Lu, K., Li, X.J., et al.: Accurate numerical methods for computing 2D and 3D robot workspace. Int. J. Adv. Rob. Syst. **8**(6), 1–13 (2011)
5. Abdel-Malek, K., Yeh, H.J.: Analytical boundary of the workspace for general 3-DOF mechanisms. Int. J. Robot. Res. **16**(2), 198–213 (1997)
6. Botturi, D., Martelli, S., Fiorini, P.: A geometric method for robot workspace computation. In: Proceedings of the 11th International Conference on Autonomous Robots and System, Verona, pp. 17–22. Verona University Publications, Verona (2003)
7. Rastegar, J., Fardanesh, B.: Manipulator workspace analysis using the monte carlo method. Mech. Mach. Theory **25**(2), 233–239 (1990)
8. Yuan, D.D., Deng, S.P., Wang, Z.M.: Analysis of robotic workspace of modular robot based on monte-carlo method. Mach. Tool Hydraulics **45**(11), 9–12 (2017)

A Path Planning Method Under Constant Contact Force for Robotic Belt Grinding

Tao Wang, Huan Zhao$^{(\boxtimes)}$, Qianlong Xie, Xiangfei Li, and Han Ding

State Key Laboratory of Digital Manufacturing Equipment and Technology,
Huazhong University of Science and Technology, Wuhan 430074, Hubei,
People's Republic of China
huanzhao@hust.edu.cn

Abstract. Recently, because of better flexibility and lower cost than CNC machine tools, industrial robots have been widely used in the manufacturing of complex surface parts, especially in blade grinding. However, studies on robotic blade grinding path planning are relatively less and it is still a challenge to realize path planning under constant force constraints. To this end, based on equal arc length method and parameter method, a planning method for robot grinding blades is presented in this paper. Specifically, the equal arc length method is used for plan the step length, the parameter method is used for plan the row spacing, constant force contact is to ensure continuous contact, and the robot speed planning is to guarantee the processing contact time. This method has the advantage of good surface consistency. Some experiments are conducted on an Comau robot NJ-220. The experimental results show that the roughness value can be stabilized at about 0.1 μm, and improves the surface processing quality of the workpiece, which validates the effectiveness of the proposed method.

Keywords: Complex surface parts · Robotic belt grinding ·
Constant force constraints · Path planning · Equal arc length method ·
Parameter method · Roughness

1 Introduction

Aeroengine, as a high-tech equipment in China, is the pearl in the crown of modern industrial technology. Its processing and manufacturing capability is a symbol of the comprehensive strength of a country [1]. Blade parts are one of the key parts in energy conversion, such as steam turbines and aeroengines. Their surface accuracy and surface consistency have great influence on fatigue life and aerodynamic performance in working environment [2].

At present, the accuracy of blade profile is mainly ensured by precision milling, but it is difficult to ensure the true shape of blade profile after milling. Therefore, the blade must be grinded to ensure its shape accuracy and improve surface integrity after precision milling.

Ma et al. [3] used curvature optimization algorithm to determine whether the processing location of all target points needs to be refined by curvature change rate and arc length criterion of adjacent key contact points. This method avoids over-cutting,

© Springer Nature Switzerland AG 2019
H. Yu et al. (Eds.): ICIRA 2019, LNAI 11745, pp. 35–49, 2019.
https://doi.org/10.1007/978-3-030-27529-7_4

large roughness and instability caused by too sparse target points and too single processing direction.

Based on the classical section method, Wang et al. [4] deduced and implemented an arc length optimization algorithm, which improved the grinding efficiency and quality. Wang et al. [5] used Newton iteration method and dynamic tool holder method to complete the generation of abrasive belt trajectory and the optimization of grinding space. Ma et al. [6] pointed out that the best cutting effect could be achieved when the contact axis of the contact wheel coincided with the minimum principal curvature direction at the contact point of the blade profile. The movement mode of the blade grinding process was designed. The tool path was calculated and the NC code was obtained by post-processing. Radzevich et al. [7] put forward the concept of the shortest tool path time, and gave an integral solution of the optimal tool path generation. Ren et al. [8] developed a free-form surface representation method based on discrete Surfel-elements, making full use of the advantages of the new development of point-based rendering technology in computer graphics. Gao et al. [9] proposed a method to optimize the structure size and relative grinding wheel position of the robot using particle swarm optimization, which provided flexible grinding space for the trajectory. Song et al. [10] optimized their control parameters by using the cooperative particle swarm optimization algorithm, improved the smoothness of grinding trajectory and material removal accuracy. Sun et al. [11] proposed a new method of robot abrasive belt grinding, which focused on system calibration and force control to improve grinding performance. Wu et al. [12] proposed a new model for estimating material removal in the process of robot abrasive belt grinding, analyzed the two process parameters of robot speed and contact force between contact wheel and workpiece, and introduced a superposition method to estimate the pressure distribution in the contact area. Jia et al. [13] proposed a curve discretization method based on the principle of equal arc length.

The above methods mainly take curvature of surface, grinding force, material removal rate, feed speed, working efficiency and grinding space as constraints, and generate grinding trajectory through inverse kinematics of robot. However, for constant force grinding, the biggest influence factor is the contact time between abrasive belt and any point on the surface. When the contact time is equal, not only the removal allowance is constant, but also the surface roughness is consistent. Therefore, from the engineering point of view, this paper plans the step size by the equal arc length method and the speed of the robot, so that the contact time of each position on the surface is the same.

The layout of the robotic belt grinding system is described in Sect. 2. Tool path planning and Algorithm process can be found in Sect. 3. In Sect. 4, the effectiveness of the algorithm is verified by the simulation and experiments. The last section presents the conclusion.

2 The Robotic Belt Grinding System

Robot abrasive belt grinding system, as shown in Fig. 1, consists of robot system, constant force grinding unit, off-line programming software and other main subsystems. Comau robot NJ-220, which belongs to the spatial serial kinematic chain, the motion parameters of the robot such as Table 1. Constant force grinding unit is composed of force sensor, lead screw, Yaskawa Electric and Gugao Board, which is used for PID control. Off line programming software is brought out by UG secondary development software which includes inverse kinematics and tool path algorithm of robot. The software interface is shown in Fig. 2.

Fig. 1. The motion parameters of the robot

Table 1. The motion parameters of robots

Joint axis	Range of joint angular velocity
1 Axis Motion Range (Velocity)	±180° (100°/s)
2 Axis Motion Range (Velocity)	+95° ~ −75° (90°/s)
3 Axis Motion Range (Velocity)	−10° ~ −256° (90°/s)
4 Axis Motion Range (Velocity)	±2700° (130°/s)
5 Axis Motion Range (Velocity)	±125° (130°/s)
6 Axis Motion Range (Velocity)	±2700° (195°/s)

Fig. 2. Software interface

3 Tool Path Planning and Algorithm Process

3.1 Problem Description

At present, the main methods of tool path generation are projection method, truncation plane method, parametric curve method and equal residual height method. The main methods of tool path step generation are equal chord height error method, equal chord length method and equal arc length method.

In the section plane method, a set of equidistant planes are used to intercept the surface, and the intersection line is used as the cutting tool path. In order to ensure the same surface removal margin and surface roughness, it is necessary to obtain the maximum curvature of the whole surface and calculate the maximum distance between the planes. Because the generated tool path is too dense, the processing efficiency of this method will be very low. Isoparametric method generates a series of isoparametric curves by surface. This method has the same idea as truncated plane method, which also leads to low processing efficiency. According to the local curvature characteristics of the blade, the equal residual height method generates each machining path dynamically. This method can get the maximum distance of each tool path, which can not only guarantee the machining accuracy, but also improve the processing efficiency. Therefore, the equal residual height method is adopted for row spacing.

The step size is to discretize the tool path into a series of points, and then connect the points into a straight line or arc to fit the tool path curve. This paper mainly studies the step planning under constant force condition. The equal chord height error method obtains the step length by the maximum distance from the constraint curve to the chord. the larger curvature ratio is the longer step length will be. the smaller curvature ratio is the shorter step length will be. This method can easily lead to small machining allowance in places with small curvature but large surface roughness, and excessive machining allowance in places with large curvature but low surface roughness. The equal chord length method discretizes the cutter path by chord length. If chord length is small, it will easily lead to too dense cutter path points and too much calculation. If chord length is large, the surface roughness in the place with large curvature will be too large. The equal arc length method is to discretize the curves into a series of curves with equal arc lengths. This method can make the constant force grinding unit pass through each arc for the same time by controlling the speed of the robot. Therefore, this method can not only ensure the accuracy of the blade profile, but also ensure the surface roughness of the blade. Through the analysis of the above methods, the step size is obtained by using the equal arc length method, which can better solve the surface consistency problem and the problem of removing the margin.

3.2 Blade Machining Trajectory Generation Process

The algorithm flow chart of the blade processing trajectory is shown in the Fig. 3. Firstly, the inlet and exhaust edges and the profile of the machined surface are segmented according to the curvature range. Secondly, the processing area is extracted and the maximum UV parameters of the processing area are obtained. Therefore, the UV parameters of the first path can be obtained and a parametric curve of the surface can be generated. The total length of the parametric curve can be calculated and, generally speaking, for the first time we divide the arc length into ten equal parts. Thirdly, the normal direction vectors of each point are calculated, and the angle between adjacent normal surfaces is calculated. By inverse kinematics, the deflection angles of the joints between two adjacent points are obtained. Then, by calculating the quotient of the deflection angles of the joints and the maximum angular velocity of the corresponding joints, the shortest time T2 required for the robot to complete its motion can be obtained. The speed of arc length planning for each segment is obtained by calculating the distance between two adjacent points and using it to do business with time T2. Finally, the row spacing is calculated by the method of equal residual height, and the next parametric curve is obtained. At this time, it can be judged whether the parametric value of the parametric curve exceeds the UV range. The program can determine whether the parameters of the parametric curve are beyond the UV range. If not, it will return to the step of generating the parametric curve and continue the algorithm process. If it is beyond the UV range, the tool path planning will be completed.

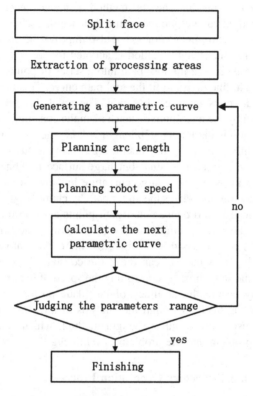

Fig. 3. The follow chart

3.3   Processing Step Calculation

In fact, the process of obtaining cutter contact points on the path curve generated in the processing area is the process of discretization of the processing path, which approximates the spatial curve with a series of low-order piecewise linear interpolation. The distance between adjacent cutter contacts is called step size. In the process of constant force grinding, step size has a great influence on the consistency of surface roughness. When the step size is large, the machined surface roughness is large. When the step size is small, the generated cutter contacts are too dense, the post-processing calculation is large, and the processing efficiency of the robot is reduced.

Processing Step Calculation

Ak-order NURBS curve is defined as follows:

$$C(u) = \frac{\sum_{i=0}^{n} N_{i,p}(u)\omega_i P_i}{\sum_{i=0}^{n} N_{i,p}(u)\omega_i} \quad (a \leq u \leq b) \tag{1}$$

where $P_i = \{P_0, P_1 \cdots, P_n\}$ is the control vertex; $\omega_i = \{\omega_0, \omega_1, \cdots, \omega_n\}$ is the weight factor; $N_{i,p}(\mathbf{u})$ is the k-order B-spline basis function defined on the aperiodic node vector; $\mathbf{U} = \{0, \cdots, 0, u_{k+1}, \cdots, u_n, 1, \cdots, 1\}$ is the node vector.

In order to achieve the purpose of discretization, the curve is divided into N segments according to the specified arc length L_a, and the node vector $\mathbf{u}$ corresponding to the discrete points is obtained. Before discretization, the total length of the curve is obtained.

$$L = \sum_{j=0}^{n-1} l_j = \sum_{j=0}^{n-1} \int_{u_j}^{u_{j+1}} \sqrt{\left[c_x'(u)\right]^2 + \left[c_y'(u)\right]^2 + \left[c_z'(u)\right]^2} \, du$$

$$= \int_0^1 \sqrt{\left[c_x'(u)\right]^2 + \left[c_x'(u)\right]^2 + \left[c_x'(u)\right]^2} \, du \tag{2}$$

The arc length of NURBS curve segment corresponds to l_j belong to

$$L_a = Fix(N_1) = Fix\left(\frac{L}{L_a(s)}\right) = Fix\left(\frac{\sum_{j=0}^{n-1} l_j}{a \cdot s^2 + b \cdot s + c}\right) \tag{3}$$

In this paper, we define a quadratic function related to arc $\mathbf{u} \in [u_j, u_{j+1})$ step size, namely step function $L_a(s)$:

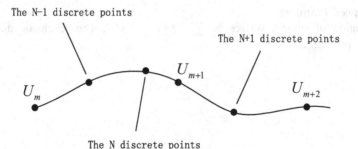

The N-1 discrete points

The N+1 discrete points

U_m U_{m+1} U_{m+2}

The N discrete points

Fig. 4. Schematic diagram for solving discrete node vector **u**.

Among them, a, b and c are coefficients and s is step function parameter. In practical application, different precision curves can be discretized according to the adjustment of coefficients a, b and c and the control of parameters s. Thus the NURBS curve can be discretized into N segments:

The curve segment N_1 obtained at this time is not necessarily an integer, so it is necessary to adjust the calculated value. The number of discrete segments N_1 is determined by the method of adjusting, and the corresponding arc length step is adjusted to achieve a reasonable curve distribution.

Finding the Node Vector of Discrete Points

In order to obtain discrete node vectors, we first need to determine the node interval where u is located. As shown in Fig. 4. The node interval of the first discrete point n is known to be $u \in [u_m, u_{m+1})$, and the corresponding node vector $\mathbf{u}$ of the third discrete point $n+1$ is obtained. The arc length from n + 1 discrete point to the starting point is $L_n = n \times L_a$, and the total length corresponding to $[0, u_m)$ on NURBS curve is $\sum_{j=0}^{m} l_j$. If $L_n > \sum_{j=0}^{m} l_j$, it is known that the discrete point is not in the interval $[u_m, u_{m+1})$, so the arc length $\sum_{j=0}^{m+1} l_j$ of NURBS curve corresponding to $[0, u_{m+2})$ is required. If $L_n < \sum_{j=0}^{m+1} l_j$, the discrete point can be determined in the interval $[u_{m+1}, u_{m+2})$. At this time, the node vector $\mathbf{u}$ corresponding to the discrete point can be obtained by the following formula:

$$\int_{u_{m+1}}^{u} \sqrt{\left[c_x'(u)\right]^2 + \left[c_y'(u)\right]^2 + \left[c_z'(u)\right]^2}\, du = L_n - \sum_{j=0}^{m} l_j \qquad (4)$$

If $L_n > \sum_{j=0}^{m+1} l_j$, the formula continues to iterate. Knowing $L_n < \sum_{j=0}^{m+q} l_j$, we can determine that the discrete points are in $[u_{m+q}, u_{m+q+1})$ interval. Then, $\bm{u}$ can be obtained from the upper formula, and that each discrete point can be obtained by bringing the value of $\mathbf{u}$ into the formula.

Robot Speed Planning

The equation of smooth surface is: $\sum: F(x, y, z) = 0$. The schematic diagram is shown in the Fig. 5.

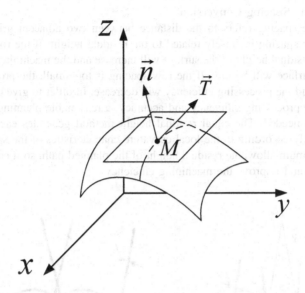

Fig. 5. Curved normal and tangent directions

The normal vector equation at any point $M(x_0, y_0, z_0)$ on the surface can be expressed as:

$$\frac{x - x_0}{F_x(x_0, y_0, z_0)} = \frac{y - y_0}{F_y(x_0, y_0, z_0)} = \frac{z - z_0}{F_z(x_0, y_0, z_0)} \tag{5}$$

The discrete points are brought into the equation and the direction vectors are united. The coordinate system is established by taking the normal direction of each point surface as Z axis and the tangent vector of each point on the parametric curve as X axis. The angle of each joint is solved by inverse kinematics of the robot and the change value of the joint angle between two adjacent points is calculated. The angle of each joint is solved by inverse kinematics of the robot and the change value of the joint angle between two adjacent points is calculated. Then the maximum time t_{max} of the robot motion passing through two adjacent points is obtained by the corresponding maximum angular velocity of each joint.

Through the planned robot speed, the robot passes through two adjacent points in equal time. The formula can be expressed as:

$$T_0 = T_1 = \cdots = T_n$$
$$= \frac{\sqrt{(x_n - x_{|n-1})^2 + (y_n - y_{n-1})^2 + (z_n - z_{n-1})^2}}{v_n} \tag{6}$$

It can be obtained that the efficiency is the highest when the surface roughness is the same.

Processing Line Spacing Conversion

Processing line spacing refers to the distance between two adjacent grinding paths. Processing row spacing is closely related to the residual height. If the row spacing is too large, the residual height of the surface will increase and the machining accuracy of the complex surface will be low. If the row spacing is too small, the processing path will increase and the processing efficiency will decrease. In order to give consideration to both surface processing efficiency and accuracy, a reasonable planning of grinding line spacing is needed. The equal residual height method generates each machining path dynamically according to the local curvature characteristics of the surface. It can make the maximum allowable residual height of the planned path, so it can reduce the grinding times and improve the machining efficiency.

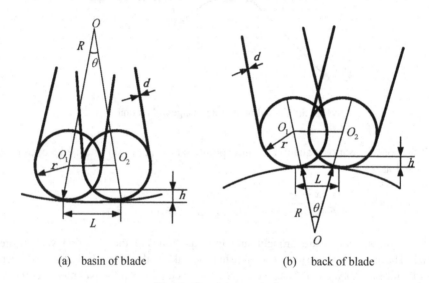

(a) basin of blade   (b) back of blade

Fig. 6. Parameter method

Because the blade basin is concave, the relationship between the blade and the contact wheel is internal tangent. The following formula can be obtained from Fig. 6:

$$R_a = r + d \tag{7}$$

$$\left[(R - h) - (R - R_a) \cdot \cos \frac{\theta}{2}\right]^2 + \left[(R - R_a) \cdot \sin \frac{\theta}{2}\right]^2 = r^2 \tag{8}$$

In formula, $\sin \theta/2 = L/2R$ $\sin \theta/2 = L/2R$. Among them, L represents the distance between adjacent grinding rows, h represents the residual height, and R represents the radius of curvature at the cutter contact.

Because the residual height is usually much smaller than the radius of curvature, formula (8) can be simplified as follows:

$$L \approx 2\sqrt{2R_a h}\sqrt{\frac{R}{R - R_a}} \qquad (9)$$

According to the same principle, when the abrasive belt contact wheel grinds the blade back, the following relationship can be obtained according to Fig. 6:

$$L \approx 2\sqrt{2R_a h}\sqrt{\frac{R}{R + R_a}} \qquad (10)$$

Calculating Processing Line Spacing
Because the distance direction of the path curve in Cartesian space is not the same as that of the parametric space on the surface of the processing area, the distance value of Cartesian space is not equal to the distance value of the parametric space on the surface of the processing area. The following methods can be used to realize the conversion between the processing distance in Cartesian space and the processing distance in the parametric space.

$$L_p = \frac{L}{\sin \theta} \qquad (11)$$

Among them, L represents the processing row spacing calculated in Cartesian space when the abrasive belt contact wheel grinds and polishes the blade profile; L_p represents the processing row spacing in parameter space when the abrasive belt contact wheel grinds and polishes the blade profile, and θ represents the angle between the planned path curve in Cartesian space and the parameter line in parameter space.

$$\theta = \cos^{-1}\left(\frac{\frac{\partial C}{\partial u} \cdot (T)}{\left|\frac{\partial C}{\partial u}\right| \cdot |T|}\right) \qquad (12)$$

The path interval value L_p of parameter space parametric lines needs to be further transformed into the row interval value Δu between parametric lines. Given the parameter curve $C(u)$, Taylor expansion is made at as follows:

$$C(u_{i+1}) = C(u_i) + C'(u_i)\Delta u + \frac{1}{2!}C''(u_i)\Delta u^2 + \frac{1}{3!}C'''(u_i)\Delta u^3 + \cdots \qquad (13)$$

$$L_p = |C(u_{i+1}) - C(u_i)| = |C'(u_i)\Delta u| \qquad (14)$$

Parametric curve $C(u)$ can be expressed as:

$$C(\mathbf{u}) = x(\mathbf{u})i + y(\mathbf{u})j + z(\mathbf{u})k \qquad (15)$$

The following formulas can be obtained:

$$L_p^2 = A\Delta u^2 \tag{16}$$

$$A = \left[\left(\frac{dx}{du}\right)^2 + \left(\frac{dy}{du}\right)^2 + \left(\frac{dz}{du}\right)^2 \right]_{u=u_i} \tag{17}$$

Therefore, the formula for calculating the parameter row spacing Δu corresponding to the spatial processing path in the parameter domain is as follows:

$$\Delta u = \frac{L_p}{\sqrt{\left[\left(\frac{dx}{du}\right)^2 + \left(\frac{dy}{du}\right)^2 + \left(\frac{dz}{du}\right)^2 \right]_{u=u_i}}} \tag{18}$$

4 Simulation and Experiment

4.1 Simulation by Off-Line Programming System

The ultimate goal of the tool path generation of robotic abrasive belt grinding is to assist programmers to quickly generate the processing path program of parts. In order to verify the scientificity and rationality of the equal arc length algorithm in the trajectory planning of robotic abrasive belt grinding, superalloy blades were selected as the research object. The UG software is redeveloped by mixing C and C++ in Visual Studio. The Excel table generated by the UG software is used as simulation, and the PDL language is used as the tool path program of the robot. The framework of the secondary development software is shown in Fig. 7.

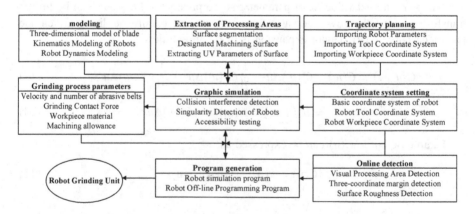

Fig. 7. Software framework of robot off-line programming platform

The cutter path generated by the equal arc length method and the equal residual height method is shown in Fig. 8.

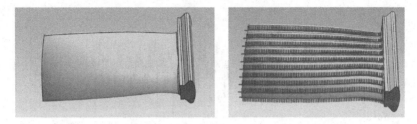

Fig. 8. Simulated tool path trajectory

4.2 Grinding Test

According to the actual processing material and processing allowance, the method of combining rough grinding with fine grinding and the alumina abrasive belt based on abrasive belt cloth are selected. The grinding process parameters are shown in Table 2.

Table 2. Parameter list

Grinding parameters	Rough grinding	Fine grinding
Abrasive belt mesh	80	400
Motor speed	3000 r/min	3000 r/s
Drive wheel size	30 mm	30 mm
Grinding force	5 N	5 N
Arc length	2 mm	2 mm
Maximum velocity	0.05 m/s	0.05 m/s

Processing experiments are carried out according to the generated tool paths and the set process parameters. The processing effect is shown in Fig. 9. By comparing before and after processing, the experimental processing effect is obvious.

(a) before grinding   (b)   after grinding

Fig. 9. Contrast before and after grinding

In order to test the effect of the experiment, Force Talysurf PGI830 surface profile comprehensive measuring instrument is used to measure the surface roughness of three different positions. The results of measurement are shown in Figs. 10, 11 and 12.

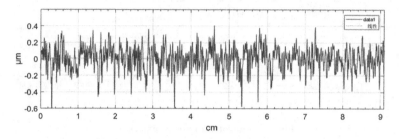

Fig. 10. Measurement results of blade leading edge: $R_a\psi = 0.0987$ μm

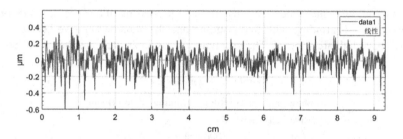

Fig. 11. Measurement results of middle blade: $R_a\psi = 0.1089$ μm

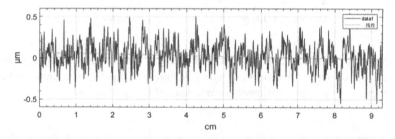

Fig. 12. Measurement results of blade trailing edge: $R_a\psi = 0.1028$ μm

Based on the analysis of the above results, under the condition of reasonable planning of the speed of the robot, the blade surface roughness is about $0.1\mu m$ by using the method of equal arc length to plan the step and the method of equal residual height to plan the row spacing. It can not only ensure the surface accuracy and surface consistency of parts, but also avoid over-cutting. The speed planning of the robot makes the grinding efficiency the highest when the arc length is 2 mm, which guarantees the grinding quality as well as the grinding efficiency.

5 Conclusions

In this paper, a planning method for robotic belt grinding is proposed, and the effectiveness of this method is verified by experiments. The parametric method is to plan the distance of the next tool path through the curvature characteristic of the former tool path, which is more efficient than the equal section method. Under the condition of constant force contact, the blade surface processed by arc length planning robot has good consistency, and the surface roughness can be stabilized at about 0.1 μm. The optimization of this method combined with material removal rate will be further studied and validated in the following work.

Acknowledgements. This work was supported by the National Key Research and Development Program of China under Grant No. 2017YFB1303401, the National Natural Science Foundation of China under Grant Nos. 91748114 and 51535004.

References

1. Hung, Y., Xiao, G.J., Zou, L.: Current situation and development trend of polishing technology for blisk. Acta Aeronaut. Astronaut. Sinica **37**(7), 2045–2064 (2016). (in Chinese)
2. Guo, D.M., Sun, Y.W., Jia, Z.Y.: Methods and research progress of high performance manufacturing. J. Mech. Eng. **50**(11), 119–134 (2014). (in Chinese)
3. Ma, K., Han, L., Sun, X., Liu, P., Zhang, K.: Trajectory planning for robotic belt grinding based on curvature optimization. ROBOT **40**(3), 360–367 (2018)
4. Wang, W., Yun, C., Zhang, L.: Optimization algorithm for robotic belt surface grinding process. Chin. J. Mech. Eng. **47**(7), 8–15 (2011)
5. Wang, W., Zhang, L., et al.: Designing and optimization of an off-line programming system for robotic belt grinding process. Chin. J. Mech. Eng. **24**(4), 647–655 (2011)
6. Ma, Y., Tang, X., Chen, J., et al.: The project and technical study on the track of vertical axis linkage abrasive belt grinding of turbine blade. China Nuclear Power **3**(1), 34–38 (2010)
7. Radzevich, S.P.: A closed-form solution to the problem of optimal tool-path generation for sculptured surface machining on multi-axis NC machine. Math. Comput. Model. **43**(3–4), 222–243 (2006)
8. Ren, X., Kuhlenkotter, B.: Real-time simulation and visualization of robotic belt grinding processes. Int. J. Adv. Manuf. Technol. **35**, 1090–1099 (2008)
9. Gao, Z.H., Lan, X.D., Bian, Y.S.: Structural dimension optimization of robotic belt grinding system for grinding workpieces with complex shaped surfaces based on dexterity grinding space. Chin. J. Aeronaut. **24**(3), 346–354 (2011)
10. Song, Y.X., Liang, W., Yang, Y.: A method for grinding removal control of a robot belt grinding system. J. Intell. Manuf. **23**(5), 1903–1913 (2012)
11. Sun, Y., Giblin, J., Kazerounian, K.: Accurate robotic belt grinding of workpieces with complex geometries using relative calibration techniques. Robot. Comput.-Intergrated Manuf. **25**(1), 204–210 (2009)
12. Whitney, D., Brown, M.: Material removal model and process planning for robot grinding. In: Proceedings of 17th International Symposium on Industrial Robots, pp. 19–29 (1987)
13. Jia, C., Yang, Y., Chen, F.: NURBS curve discrete algorithm based on equal arc-length principle. CEA **50**(3), 165–167 (2014)

Large Contact Area Trajectory Planning Algorithm for Fuel Tank with Irregular Surfaces

Xing Fan, Haibo Xu$^{(\boxtimes)}$, Wenyu Huang, and Yufeng Lin

Xi'an Jiaotong University, Xi'an 710049, Shanxi, China
M18829235412@163.com, hbxu@mail.xjtu.edu.cn

Abstract. When the robot uses the flat scrub head to clean the outer surface of the fuel tank, the recessed structure near the ends of the fuel tank cannot be in good contact. In this paper, the outer contour of the fuel tank is detected by laser ranging sensor and described by NURBS curve. The interference between the scrub head and the fuel tank is divided into 16 cases. It is further divided into 4 types, and different adjustment algorithms are studied for different types. The article also studies the motion characteristics of the end trajectory. The results show that the proposed algorithm can greatly improve the contact area between the scrubbing head and the fuel tank surface, and ensure that the motion characteristic curve is smooth and will not impact the robot.

Keywords: Outline description · NURBS · Trajectory planning · Irregular surface

1 Introduction

Before performing the thermal insulation layer structure on the outer surface of the fuel tank, it is necessary to clean the oil and other pollution on the outer surface of the fuel tank. If the pollution cannot be effectively removed, the pollution will lead to insufficient bonding strength of the thermal insulation structure, and the problem may even cause the rocket to fail to launch.

In the industry, the cleaning of large tanks such as rocket tanks is a research focus. Dry ice cleaning uses dry ice particles to impact the surface of the fuel tank at high speed, and uses the tension of the dry ice to vaporize the top, but it is expensive [1]. Ultrasonic cleaning is widely used, the cleaning cleanliness is consistent, and the operation is safe and reliable [2–4]. High pressure water jet cleaning is the most widely used. If the pressure is too low, the surface of the fuel tank cannot be effectively cleaned, so the cleaning effect is not good [5].

In the existing fuel tank cleaning process, the fuel tank is placed on the roller frame to rotate at a constant speed, and the surface of the fuel tank is scrubbed by a robot-held scrub head with alcohol-filled. However, there is a recessed structure at the position near the ends of the fuel tank, and the scrubbing head cannot obtain a large contact area. The scrub head trajectory planned by this algorithm can maintain a large contact area between the scrub head and the fuel tank surface.

© Springer Nature Switzerland AG 2019
H. Yu et al. (Eds.): ICIRA 2019, LNAI 11745, pp. 50–62, 2019.
https://doi.org/10.1007/978-3-030-27529-7_5

2 Collection and Description of Fuel Tank Surface Signals

2.1 Data Collection

The principle of fuel tank cleaning is shown in Fig. 1. The fuel tank is placed on the roller frame to rotate counterclockwise. A laser ranging sensor is installed above the fuel tank to extract the outer contour of the fuel tank, and a robot carrying a scrubbing head on the left side scrubs the surface of the fuel tank. Fuel tank rotation speed $n = 1\,\text{rpm}$, Fuel tank radius $r = 1750\,\text{mm}$, Scrubbing head width $b = 100\,\text{mm}$ [6, 7].

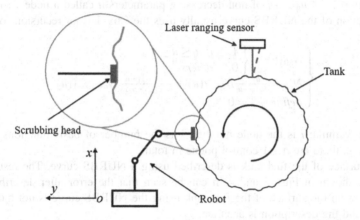

Fig. 1. The principle of collecting and cleaning the outer surface of the fuel tank.

The acquired outer contour information is shown in Fig. 2. In the figure, the positive direction of x is the direction in which the scrub head advances along the surface of the fuel tank, and the positive direction of y is radially outward along the fuel tank.

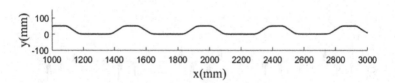

Fig. 2. Fuel tank surface raw data.

2.2 NURBS Curve Description

The NURBS curve has the powerful function of representing and designing free-form curves and surfaces, and is one of the mainstream methods for shape mathematical description. The B-spline method (NURBS) is the basis for the current international

standard for geometric definition of industrial products [8, 9]. The NURBS curve
equation can be written as:

$$p(u) = \sum_{i=0}^{n} d_i N_{i,k}(u) \qquad (1)$$

In the formula: $d_i (i = 0, 1 \ldots n)$ is the control vertex (coordinate), $N_{i,k} (i = 0, 1 \ldots n)$
is the K-norm NURBS curve basis function, and the highest number is k.

The basis function is a K-order piecewise polynomial determined by a sequence
$U : u_0 \le u_1 \le \ldots \le u_{n+k+1}$ of non-decreasing parameters u called a node vector. The
basis function of the NURBS curve usually uses the Cox-deBoor recursion formula:

$$\begin{cases} N_{i,0}(u) = \begin{cases} 1, & if\ u_i \le u \le u_{i+1} \\ 0, & others \end{cases} \\ N_{i,k} = \frac{u-u_i}{u_{i+k}-u_i} N_{i,k-1}(u) + \frac{u_{i+k+1}-u}{u_{i+k+1}-u_{i+1}} N_{i+1,k-1}(u) \\ define\quad \frac{0}{0} = 0 \end{cases} \qquad (2)$$

In the formula: i is the node number, k is the number of basis functions, in this
paper $k = 2$, there are $n + 1$ control points in total.

The surface of the fuel tank is described using a NURBS curve. The results and
errors are shown in Figs. 3 and 4. It can be seen that the error after describing the
information on the surface of the fuel tank using the NURBS curve is not more than
0.8 mm, and the description is accurate.

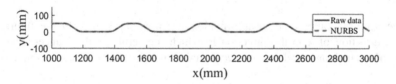

Fig. 3. NURBS description and raw data comparison.

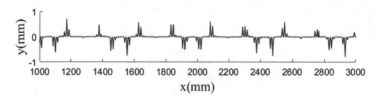

Fig. 4. NURBS described error.

3   Interference Between the Scrub Head and the Fuel Tank

3.1   Scrub Head Initial Position Description

As shown in Fig. 5, the scrub head is at any point i on the trajectory l of the fuel tank, the midpoint P_i of the scrub head coincides with the point i and the scrub head is tangent to the surface of the fuel tank.

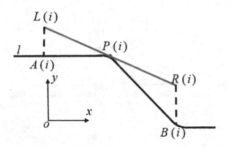

Fig. 5. The initial position of the scrub head.

The initial position of the scrub head is mathematically described as: The position of the scrub head has the same slope as the tangent at i on curve l, and the center of the scrub head coincides with point i on curve l.

$$\begin{cases} k_l(i) = k_p(i) \\ l(i) = P(i) \end{cases} \tag{3}$$

In the formula: $k_l(i)$ is the slope of the tangent of the outer surface curve l of the fuel tank at i, $k_p(i)$ is the slope of the scrub head at curve l at i.

The position of the initial scrub head can be determined by solving Eq. (3).

3.2   Scrub Head Interference Type

Points $A(i)$ and $B(i)$ are the projections on the curve l at the left and right ends of the scrub head, which can be described as:

$$\begin{cases} A(i) \in l \\ x_A(i) = x_L(i) \end{cases}$$

$$\begin{cases} B(i) \in l \\ x_B(i) = x_R(i) \end{cases}$$

The vertical distance between the L_i and R_i points to the curve l is expressed as:

$$h_A(i) = y_L(i) - y_A(i)$$

$$h_B(i) = y_R(i) - y_B(i)$$

According to the state of $h_A(i)$ and $h_B(i)$ in $(-\infty, -C]$, $(-C, C)$, $[C, +\infty)$, and in combination with the actual cleaning process, the interference mode of the initial scrub head and the fuel tank trajectory can be roughly divided into 16 cases. C is the judgment threshold, in this paper $C = 1\,\text{mm}$ (Fig. 6).

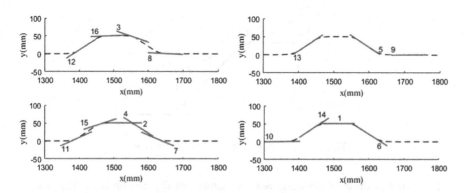

Fig. 6. Interference between the initial scrub head and the fuel tank.

Table 1. The interference of the scrub head is divided into 16 types.

No.	1	2	3	4	5	6	7	8	9	10	11	12	13	14	15	16
$h_A(i)$	+	0	+	+	+	0	−	−	0	0	−	−	−	0	+	+
$h_B(i)$	+	+	+	0	−	−	−	0	0	−	−	0	+	+	+	0

In the Table 1: + means $h_A(i)$ or $h_B(i)$ is in $[C, +\infty)$, 0 means it is in $(-C, C)$, − means it is in $(-\infty, -C]$.

Further, the contact type can be classified into 4 types depending on whether the contact interferes and the number of interference points (Table 2).

Table 2. Scrubbing head interference classification.

Type	Contact situation	Description
A	1, 2, 3, 4, 9, 14, 15, 16	No interference
B	5, 13	Interference at one end, no contact at one end
C	6, 8, 10, 12	Interference at one end, contact at one end
D	7, 11	Both ends interfere

4 Scrubbing Head Adjustment Algorithm

Since no interference occurs in type A, no adjustment is necessary. It is only necessary to adjust the other three types of interference.

4.1 Type B Adjustment Algorithm

In the Type B, one end of the scrub head is in contact with the fuel tank and the other end interferes with the fuel tank. No. 5 and No. 13 are mutually symmetrical, so the adjustment example is only made for No. 5, and the adjustment algorithm of No. 13 is similar to No. 5. Adjustment is mainly divided into 2 steps.

Step 1. The scrub head $\overrightarrow{L_iR_i}$ is rotated about the last contact point T_i on its left side until the right end point R_i of the scrub head is in contact with the fuel tank surface. The initial adjusted scrub head is $\overrightarrow{L'_iR'_i}$, as shown in Fig. 7(a).

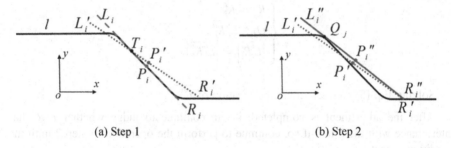

(a) Step 1   (b) Step 2

Fig. 7. Type B adjustment principle.

The last contact point of the scrub head $\overrightarrow{L_iR_i}$ on the left side of the outer surface of the fuel tank is T_i. Assduming $T_{i,j}$ is the j data point on the fuel tank surface light curve l, the definition of T_i has the following equation:

$$T_i = \{T_{i,j} \in l, T_{i,j} \in l_P, T_{i,j-1} \in l, T_{i,j-1} \notin l_P\}$$

In the formula: l_P is the line segment that assumes the scrub head.

The mathematical description of the adjusted scrub head $\overrightarrow{L'_iR'_i}$ is:

$$\begin{cases} \left|\overrightarrow{T_iR_i}\right| = \left|\overrightarrow{T_iR'_i}\right| \\ R'_i \in l \\ T_i \in \overrightarrow{L'_iR'_i} \\ \left|\overrightarrow{L_iR_i}\right| = \left|\overrightarrow{L'_iR'_i}\right| \end{cases} \tag{4}$$

Solving Eq. (4) can determine the location of $\overrightarrow{L_i'R_i'}$.

Step 2. The $\overrightarrow{L_i'R_i'}$ rotates clockwise around R_i' until the left side is tangent to the fuel tank surface. Using the same point on the curve l where the tangent is the same as the slope of the $\overrightarrow{L_i'R_i'}$, the scrub head is rotated to coincide with the point, as shown in Fig. 7(b).

Assume that the slope of the tangent at Q_j is the closest to the slope of the $\overrightarrow{L_i'R_i'}$ in the range of the scrub head, as described below:

$$Q_j = \min(|k_j - k_P'|), x_{Q_j} \in [x_{L_i'}, x_{R_i'}], Q_j \in l$$

In the formula: k_j is the slope of the tangent of the outer surface curve l at j, k_P' is the slope of $\overrightarrow{L_i'R_i'}$.

The mathematical description of the adjusted scrub head $\overrightarrow{L_i''R_i''}$ is:

$$\begin{cases} R_i'' = R_i' \\ Q_j \in \overrightarrow{L_i''R_i''} \\ \left|\overrightarrow{L_i'R_i'}\right| = \left|\overrightarrow{L_i''R_i''}\right| \end{cases} \tag{5}$$

Solving Eq. (5) can determine the location of $\overrightarrow{L_i''R_i''}$.

After the adjustment is completed, it can continue to judge whether $\overrightarrow{L_i''R_i''}$ has interference with the l, and if so, continue to perform the operation of step 2 until the condition is met.

4.2   Type C Adjustment Algorithm

In type C, one end of the scrubbing head is in contact with the outer surface of the fuel tank, and the other end interferes. No. 6 and No. 10 are cases where the left end of the scrub head is in contact with the fuel tank, and the right end interferes. No. 8 and No. 12 are exactly the opposite. The adjustment is relatively simple, and only the end of the scrubbing head that is in contact with the fuel tank is rotated until the other end is in contact with the fuel tank. Take No. 10 as an example, as shown in Fig. 8.

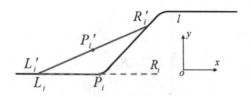

Fig. 8. Type C adjustment principle.

The mathematical description of the scouring head $\overrightarrow{L_i'R_i'}$ at the end of the adjustment is:

$$\begin{cases} R_i' \in l \\ \left|\overrightarrow{L_iR_i}\right| = \left|\overrightarrow{L_i''R_i''}\right| \\ L_i = L_i' \\ \alpha < 90° \end{cases} \tag{6}$$

In the formula: α is the angle of the adjusted scrub head $\overrightarrow{L_i'R_i'}$ relative to the initial scrub head $\overrightarrow{L_iR_i}$, which is positive counterclockwise.

Solving Eq. (6) can determine the location of $\overrightarrow{L_i'R_i'}$.

4.3   Type D Adjustment Algorithm

In type D, both ends of the scrub head interfere with the surface of the fuel tank, and this type corresponds to the case of No. 7 and No. 11. The scrub head is first translated in the normal direction of the fuel tank until one end is in contact with the surface of the fuel tank. Then, according to the type C adjustment algorithm, the scrub head is rotated to bring the two ends into contact.

Taking No. 7 as an example, the scrub head L_iR is translated in a direction perpendicular to its own direction $\overrightarrow{P_iP_i'}$ until L_i or R_i is located on the curve l. At this time, the scrub head is expressed by $\overrightarrow{L_i'R_i'}$, and then adjusted to $\overrightarrow{L_i''R_i''}$ according to the type C adjustment method, as shown in Fig. 9.

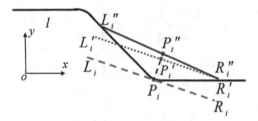

Fig. 9. Type C adjustment principle.

The mathematical description of the scrub head $\overrightarrow{L_i'R_i'}$ is:

$$\begin{cases} \overrightarrow{L_iR_i} \parallel \overrightarrow{L_i'R_i'} \\ \left|\overrightarrow{L_iR_i}\right| = \left|L_i'R_i'\right| \\ \overrightarrow{L_iL_i'} \perp \overrightarrow{L_iR_i} \\ R_i' \in l \vee L_i' \in l \end{cases} \tag{7}$$

Solving Eq. (7) can determine the location of $\overrightarrow{L'_i R'_i}$. Further adjustments can be made according to the type C adjustment method to obtain the position of the $\overrightarrow{L''_i R''_i}$.

5   Result Analysis

5.1   Adjustment Effect

The effects of the adjusted No. 5, No. 6, No. 7, No. 8 are shown in the Fig. 10, and the remaining No. 10, No. 11, No. 12, No. 13 are symmetrical with the display. It can be seen that all of the scrubbing heads have been effectively contacted with the fuel tank surface while avoiding interference by adjusting the adjustment algorithm.

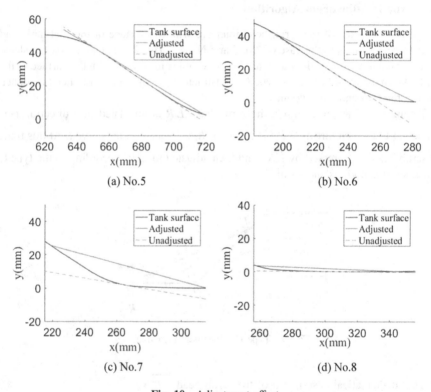

Fig. 10. Adjustment effect.

The contact effect of the scrubbing head and the fuel tank surface adjustment is shown in Fig. 11. It can be seen that the scrubbing head before adjustment only relies on the movement in the y direction to achieve contact with the fuel tank surface, and in many cases maintains the line contact effect with the fuel tank surface. After the adjustment, the position where only one line contact can be made on the inclined surface and the convex surface is changed to the surface contact. The concave surface is changed from one line contact to two line contacts.

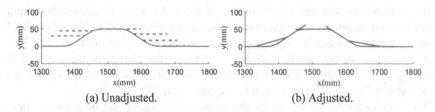

(a) Unadjusted.   (b) Adjusted.

Fig. 11. Comparison of contact effects before and after adjustment.

5.2 Contact Effect Analysis

In order to judge the contact effect between the scrub head and the fuel tank surface, the area between the scrub head and the track directly below was selected for evaluation. When the surface of the scrubbing head and the fuel tank are in sufficient contact, the area is small, and if the contact is insufficient, the area is large [10]. The area is calculated as Eq. (8).

$$S_i = \sum_{j=n}^{m} [(y_P(j) - y_l(j)) \frac{x_P(j+1) - x_P(j-1)}{2}] \tag{8}$$

In the formula: S_i indicates the area formed between the scrubbing head at the i and the track directly below it, $y_P(j)$ indicates the y value of the j point on the scrub head, $y_l(j)$ indicates the y value of the j point on the surface trajectory curve l, $x_P(j)$ indicates the x value of the j point on the scrub head, $m > n$, $x_P(n) = x_L(i)$, $x_P(m) = x_R(i)$.

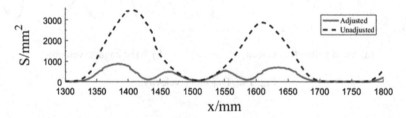

Fig. 12. Area contrast.

As can be seen from Fig. 12, the gap area of the scrub head and the fuel tank surface is significantly reduced after the adjustment algorithm is used. In particular, the drop in the interval between the 1400 mm and 1600 mm attachments is most pronounced, and the two intervals correspond to the slope position of the fuel tank outline.

5.3   Motion Characteristics Analysis

In the robot trajectory where no adjustment is made, the scrub head is always parallel to the fuel tank trajectory without the need to adjust the robot wrist joint. The movement in the *x* direction is achieved by the rotation of the fuel tank itself, so the robot mainly moves in the direction of the *y*. After using the adjustment algorithm, the robot mainly achieves effective contact by adjusting the angle of the scrubbing head, and also has a small amount of motion in the *x* direction to match the change in the angle of the scrubbing head. The angle of the scrub head is defined as the positive direction of *y*, clockwise positive and counterclockwise negative [11, 12].

The re-adjusted trajectory solves the problem of contact and interference, but it must be ensured that the trajectory is continuous in motion to avoid the impact during the robot tracking process. The motion characteristic curve of the end trajectory is shown in Figs. 13, 14 and 15.

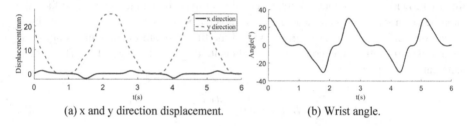

(a) x and y direction displacement.   (b) Wrist angle.

Fig. 13. Trajectory displacement.

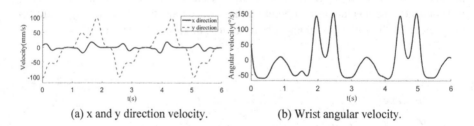

(a) x and y direction velocity.   (b) Wrist angular velocity.

Fig. 14. Trajectory velocity.

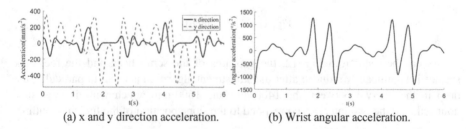

(a) x and y direction acceleration.   (b) Wrist angular acceleration.

Fig. 15. Trajectory acceleration.

6 Conclusion

In this paper, the problem of poor contact effect of the scrubbing head when scrubbing the fuel tank is studied. The information of the rocket fuel tank surface was collected by laser ranging sensor. The contour information was described by NURBS curve. The maximum error described was less than 0.8 mm. Further, the tangential position of the fuel tank surface is taken as the initial position of the scrubbing head. According to the initial position and the interference of the fuel tank, it is divided into 16 cases, 4 types, and different adjustment algorithms are proposed for different types. The gap area between the scrubbing head and the fuel tank surface was used as an evaluation index, and it was found that the adjusted track sticking effect was greatly improved. Finally, the motion characteristics of the new end trajectory are also studied, which proves that the motion is smooth and does not impact the robot.

Acknowledgements. This thesis is supported by the major sub-item of "High-Grade CNC Machine Tools and Basic Manufacturing Equipment" of the major science and technology project "Aerospace Lightweight Structures Complete Manufacturing Equipment Demonstration Line (2017ZX04005001)."

References

1. Jones, R.D., Gurley, D., Bruer, K., et al.: Dry ice cleaning of metal surfaces to improve welding chatacteristics. Google Pantents (2012)
2. Jeong, K.-S., Lee, K.-W., Lim, H.-K.: Risk assessment on hazards for decommissioning safety of a nuclear facility. Ann. Nuclear Energy **37**(12), 1751–1762 (2010)
3. Wani, I.A., Ganguly, A., Ahmed, J.: Silver nanoparticles: ultrasonic wave assisted synthesis, optical characterization and surface area studies. Mater. Lett. **65**(3), 520–522 (2011)
4. Cowan, M., Page, J., Sheng, P.: Ultrasonic wave transport in a system of disordered resonant scatterers: propagating resonant modes and hybridization gaps. Phys. Rev. B **84**(9), 297–305 (2011)
5. Guoqiang, C., Rui, Z.: Review on high pressure water jet. J. Shenyang Aerosp. Univ. **6**, 1–16 (2017)
6. Yang, J., et al.: A double threshold correction method for walk error in pulsed laser ranging system. Infrared Phys. Technol. **100**, 28–36 (2019)
7. Space Research; New Data from Wroclaw University of Environmental and Life Sciences Illuminate Findings in Space Research (Characteristics of Goce Orbits Based On Satellite Laser Ranging). Science Letter (2019)
8. Nguyen, T.N., Thai, C.H., Luu, A.-T., Nguyen-Xuan, H., Lee, J.: NURBS-based postbuckling analysis of functionally graded carbon nanotube-reinforced composite shells. Comput. Methods Appl. Mech. Eng. **347**, 983–1003 (2019)
9. Faroughi, S., Shafei, E., Eriksson, A.: NURBS-based modeling of laminated composite beams with isogeometric displacement-only theory. Compos. Part B **162**, 89–102 (2019)
10. Kljuno, E., Catovic, A.: Estimation of projected surface area of irregularly shaped fragments. Defence Technol. **15**(2), 198–209 (2019)

11. Jia, S., Dong, Z., Li, X., et al.: Distributed intelligent assistance robotic system with sensor networks based on robot technology middleware. Int. J. Distrib. Sensor Netw. **10**(6), 908260 (2014)
12. Choi, J., Cho, Y., Choi, J., et al.: A layered middleware architecture for automated robot services. Int. J. Distrib. Sensor Netw. **10**(5), 201063 (2014)

A General Kinematics Model for Trajectory Planning of Upper Limb Exoskeleton Robots

Qiaoling Meng[1,2,3], Qiaolian Xie[1,2,3], Zhimeng Deng[1,2,3], and Hongliu Yu[1,2,3(✉)]

[1] Institute of Rehabilitation Engineering and Technology,
University of Shanghai for Science and Technology, Shanghai,
People's Republic of China
yhl98@hotmail.com
[2] Shanghai Engineering Research Center of Assistive Devices, Shanghai,
People's Republic of China
[3] Key Laboratory of Neural-Functional Information and Rehabilitation
Engineering of the Ministry of Civil Affairs, Shanghai,
People's Republic of China

Abstract. Trajectory planning is a paramount requirement for upper limb rehabilitation robots because that can help stroke patients to receive rehabilitation training, especially in the implementation of activities of daily life. The patient-customized trajectory planning of the robot system is much more fit with human movement. This paper proposes an equivalent kinematics model of the upper limb, which covers all degrees of freedom of the upper limb. The trajectory planning based on this kinematics model is appropriate for upper limb exoskeleton rehabilitation or assistive robots. In addition, the proposed model has been experimentally validated on the prototype of an upper limb exoskeleton robot. The model of the exoskeleton is obtained by simplifying extra degrees of freedom of the kinematics model. And taking movement trajectory of the exoskeleton by cubic polynomial coincides with that by quintic polynomials, which proves that the approach can optimize the approach of trajectory planning. Furthermore, a significant reduction of trajectory generated operation can be achieved, with a consequent remarkable computational time-saving. Finally, results from taking things experiments with the exoskeleton are presented, which verify the usability of trajectory planning.

Keywords: Trajectory planning · Kinematics model · Exoskeleton · Rehabilitation

1 Introduction

In recent years, the application of robots in the assistive fields and rehabilitation has increased significantly for many reasons, due to high repeatability and intensity of treatment, increasing patients independence and social participation. Robotic motion planning is an important requirement for upper limb rehabilitation robots, which can

© Springer Nature Switzerland AG 2019
H. Yu et al. (Eds.): ICIRA 2019, LNAI 11745, pp. 63–75, 2019.
https://doi.org/10.1007/978-3-030-27529-7_6

help the stroke patients to carry out rehabilitation training [1], especially in activities of daily life (ADL) that the basis for reintegration into society and occupation. The patient-customized trajectory planning is compatible with the human motion control strategy and can replicate the user's personal motion style. This is much more fit with human movement and improves the effects of rehabilitation training [2, 3]. Trajectory generation of upper limb rehabilitation robots, one method is to record the motion of the affected limb following the movement of the therapist. In this method, the therapist moves the patient's affected limb trained with a rehabilitation robot, and the rehabilitation robot records the movement while performing a specific exercise [4]. Another method, mirror movement, is that the healthy limb drives the affected to move. These methods need the help of therapists or require bilateral manipulators of rehabilitation robots or motion capture. These factors may limit the application of rehabilitation robots and take more time and labor.

Most of the path generation of the upper limb rehabilitation robots is based on the rehabilitation robot rather than the human body [5–8], and the D-H convention [2, 6–10], a forward and inverse kinematics analysis [2, 5–9, 11–13], the Jacobian equation [2, 5, 7, 13], geodesic curves [3], the minimum jerk algorithm [14–17], and other methods are used to obtain the trajectory. The goal of trajectory planning for upper limb rehabilitation robots is to obtain smooth and reliable rehabilitation exercise and improve safety and human-robot interaction [18].

The establishment of upper limb model is necessary for upper limb trajectory planning and is combined from the upper limbs of the human body. The most common model of the upper extremity is now composed of the shoulder, elbow, and wrist joints, as shown in Fig. 1 [4, 9, 11, 12]. In addition to the importance of the forearm and upper arm, the movement of the clavicle and the scapula cannot be negligible during the motion of the upper limbs. Scapula and sternoclavicular joint play an important role in ADL. If their role is ignored, the rehabilitation training will not be effective. Each clavicle and scapula has three degrees of freedom of rotation [19]. In [20], the shoulder girdle is modeled as rigid elements which simulate the movement of the scapula and clavicle. The model of the shoulder girdle [21] and arm skeleton [22] focuses on the movement of the shoulder girdle but does not give a general upper limb kinematics mechanism. Kinematic chain of the proposed multibody model (Maria et al. 2012) lists all the joints of upper limbs except the hand, but the counterpart mechanic model did not obtain [23]. In [24], it shows the configuration of the human upper arm and the anthropomorphic arm that consider the scapula girdle, elbow and wrist. The simplified human upper limb kinematic chain reduced freedom of the scapula girdle, so this model is incomplete. Simplified human arm model is composed of the shoulder, elbow and wrist joints [25] that not consider the scapula and clavicle. In Eduardo et al. [26], the shoulder equivalent kinematic model is provided that is an important reference for the equivalent kinematics model of the upper limb. To sum up, there is no general kinematics model of the upper limb with full degrees of freedom.

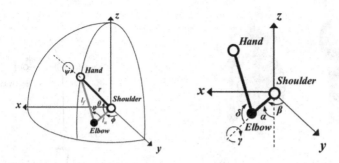

Fig. 1. Kinematic model of the human arm from [Hyosang Moon].

This paper proposes a general kinematics model of the human upper limb with full degrees of freedom. The trajectory planning based on this model for upper limb rehabilitation or assistive robots with multi-DOF manipulators, which is appropriate for upper limb exoskeleton rehabilitation robots. The motion path of the main upper limb consists of shoulder, elbow, and wrist joints as well as the clavicle and scapula. Trajectory planning of ADL in upper limb rehabilitation or assistive robots can improve the motor function of stroke patients and help them return to society and occupation.

The remainder of this paper is organized as follows. Section 2 presents the counterpart mechanic model of the human upper limb. Section 3 gives a general kinematics model of the upper limb with full degrees of freedom and its kinematics equation. The approach to trajectory planning of upper limb exoskeleton is conducted in Sect. 4. Finally, we summarize and conclude this paper in Sect. 5.

2 The Counterpart Mechanic Model of Human Upper Limb

As shown in Fig. 2, the bones and joints of the upper limb are marked, which contain the clavicle, scapula, shoulder, elbow, and wrist. In the analysis of the human upper limb movement, the upper limb should be simplified into an appropriate calculation model [11]. Figure 3 shows the counterpart mechanic model of human upper limb transformed from Fig. 2. The bones of the upper limbs are reduced to links, and point P is the end position of the scapula. The sternoclavicular joint, the acromioclavicular joint, the scapulothoracic joint, and the glenohumeral joint are simplified to the spherical hinge with restricted range of motion. The elbow joint is converted into a revolute joint. In addition, the proximal end of the ulna and radius are immovable with the internal and external rotation of the forearm, so the counterpart mechanic model of the forearm is a four-link structure and the fixed end is located at the proximal end.

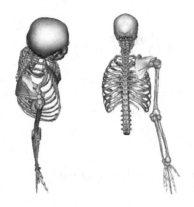

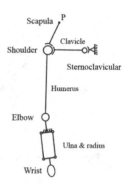

Fig. 2. The human upper limb model.

Fig. 3. The counterpart mechanic model of human upper limb.

3 The Counterpart Mechanic Model of Human Upper Limb

The motion of a rigid body is composed of rotation and translation. In order to represent translation and rotation with a matrix, it is necessary to introduce homogeneous coordinates and homogeneous transformation. The homogeneous coordinate is a description of the spatial position, and the homogeneous transformation is used to describe the transformation of the rigid body's position and postures [27].

Figure 4 shows coordinate systems for the kinematics model of the human upper limb. The coordinate systems are established at the joints, fixed ends, and terminal positions of the model. The coordinate system (X_0, Y_0, Z_0) is the base coordinate frame in the sternum, the coordinate system (X_1, Y_1, Z_1) represents the sternoclavicular joint, the coordinate system (X_2, Y_2, Z_2) describes the shoulder joint, the coordinate system (X_3, Y_3, Z_3) represents the elbow joint, the coordinate system (X_4, Y_4, Z_4) describes the center of rotation of the forearm, the coordinate system (X_5, Y_5, Z_5) represents the wrist joint, the coordinate system (X_6, Y_6, Z_6) describes the scapula. The model has 13 degrees of freedom (DoF) including 3 DoF for the sternoclavicular joint, 3 DoF for the scapulothoracic joint, 3 DoF for the glenohumeral joint, 2 DoF for the elbow joint and 2 DoF for the wrist joint. And the degrees of freedom of acromioclavicular joint is negligible because the range of motion of the acromioclavicular joint is very small ($\leq 10°$) in ADL [28].

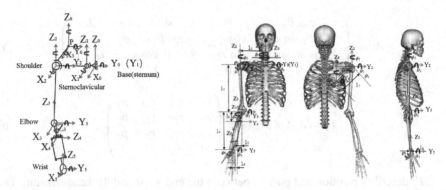

Fig. 4. Build coordinate systems for the mechanical model of human upper limb.

Fig. 5. Set the parameters of the model.

According to the model built in Fig. 4, the model is applied to the human body and parameters are set for the model as shown in Fig. 5. The parameters of the model are different for everyone. And φ is the angle that describes adduction and abduction of the joint, θ is the angle to describe the flexion and extension of the joint. φ is the angle of internal rotation and external rotation of the joint.

In Fig. 5, according to the homogeneous transformation, the following transformation relations can be written:

$$A_1 = \begin{pmatrix} \cos\phi_1\cos\theta_1 - \sin\varphi_1\sin\phi_1\sin\theta_1 & -\sin\phi_1\cos\varphi_1 & \cos\phi_1\sin\theta_1 + \sin\varphi_1\sin\phi_1\cos\theta_1 & 0 \\ \sin\phi_1\cos\theta_1 + \sin\varphi_1\cos\phi_1\sin\theta_1 & \cos\phi_1\cos\varphi_1 & \sin\phi_1\sin\theta_1 - \sin\varphi_1\cos\phi_1\cos\theta_1 & -l_0 \\ -\cos\varphi_1\sin\theta_1 & \sin\varphi_1 & \cos\varphi_1\cos\theta_1 & 0 \\ 0 & 0 & 0 & 1 \end{pmatrix}$$

(1)

$$A_2 = \begin{pmatrix} \cos\phi_2\cos\theta_2 - \sin\varphi_2\sin\phi_2\sin\theta_2 & -\sin\phi_2\cos\varphi_2 & \cos\phi_2\sin\theta_2 + \sin\varphi_2\sin\phi_2\cos\theta_2 & 0 \\ \sin\phi_2\cos\theta_2 + \sin\varphi_2\cos\phi_2\sin\theta_2 & \cos\phi_2\cos\varphi_2 & \sin\phi_2\sin\theta_2 - \sin\varphi_2\cos\phi_2\cos\theta_2 & -l1 \\ -\cos\varphi_2\sin\theta_2 & \sin\varphi_2 & \cos\varphi_2\cos\theta_2 & 0 \\ 0 & 0 & 0 & 1 \end{pmatrix}$$

(2)

$$A_3 = \begin{pmatrix} \cos\theta_3 & 0 & \sin\theta_3 & 0 \\ 0 & 1 & 0 & 0 \\ -\sin\theta_3 & 0 & \cos\theta_3 & -l_2 \\ 0 & 0 & 0 & 1 \end{pmatrix}$$

(3)

$$A_4 = \begin{pmatrix} \cos\phi_4 & -\sin\phi_4 & 0 & 0 \\ \sin\phi_4 & \cos\phi_4 & 0 & -l_5 \\ 0 & 0 & 0 & -l_3 \\ 0 & 0 & 0 & 1 \end{pmatrix}$$

(4)

$$A_5 = \begin{pmatrix} \cos \theta_5 & 0 & \sin \theta_5 & l_8 \\ \sin \theta_5 \sin \varphi_5 & \cos \varphi_5 & -\cos \theta_5 \sin \varphi_5 & -l_5 \\ -\cos \varphi_5 \sin \theta_5 & \sin \varphi_5 & \cos \theta_5 \cos \varphi_5 & l_4 - l_3 \\ 0 & 0 & 0 & 1 \end{pmatrix} \tag{5}$$

$$T_5^0 = A_1 A_2 A_3 A_4 A_5 = \begin{pmatrix} r_{11} & r_{12} & r_{13} & p_x \\ r_{21} & r_{22} & r_{23} & p_y \\ r_{31} & r_{32} & r_{33} & p_z \\ 0 & 0 & 0 & 1 \end{pmatrix} \tag{6}$$

T_5^0 describes position and posture between the end-wrist and the base-sternum. The corresponding elements of the matrix at both ends are equal, and the variable expression of the matrix can be obtained.

$$T_6^2 = \begin{pmatrix} \cos \phi_6 \cos \theta_6 - \sin \varphi_6 \sin \phi_6 \sin \theta_6 & -\sin \phi_6 \cos \varphi_6 & \cos \phi_6 \sin \theta_6 + \sin \varphi_6 \sin \phi_6 \cos \theta_6 & 0 \\ \sin \phi_6 \cos \theta_6 + \sin \varphi_6 \cos \phi_6 \sin \theta_6 & \cos \phi_6 \cos \varphi_6 & \sin \phi_6 \sin \theta_6 - \sin \varphi_6 \cos \phi_6 \cos \theta_6 & -l_7 \cos \beta \\ -\cos \varphi_6 \sin \theta_6 & \sin \varphi_6 & \cos \varphi_6 \cos \theta_6 & -l_7 \sin \beta \\ 0 & 0 & 0 & 1 \end{pmatrix} \tag{7}$$

$$T_6^0 = A_1 A_2 T_6^2 = \begin{pmatrix} r_{11} & r_{12} & r_{13} & p_x \\ r_{21} & r_{22} & r_{23} & p_y \\ r_{31} & r_{32} & r_{33} & p_z \\ 0 & 0 & 0 & 1 \end{pmatrix} \tag{8}$$

T_6^0 describes the position and posture between the end-scapula and the base-sternum. Similarly, the variable expression of the matrix can be obtained by T_6^0.

4   Trajectory Planning of Taking Based on an Exoskeleton Upper Limb Robot

4.1   Method of Trajectory Planning

Section 3 presents a general upper limb kinematics model and the kinematics equation of the wrist and scapula. The model has 13 degrees of freedom (DoF) that covers all joints of the upper limbs, including 3 DoF for the sternoclavicular joint, 3 DoF for the scapulothoracic joint, 3 DoF for the glenohumeral joint, 2 DoF for the elbow joint, and 2 DoF for the wrist joint.

In order to obtain a path generation of upper limb rehabilitation robot, the kinematics equation of the robot will be solved by modeling. The object of upper limb rehabilitation robot is human, and its human-computer interaction is the most important. So the trajectory planning of upper limb rehabilitation robots also needs to be considered from the human. With this general kinematics model, the model of the upper limb rehabilitation robot can be obtained by simplifying extra degrees of freedom. The parameters of the robot can be substituted into the kinematics equation of the model to solve the kinematics equation of the rehabilitation robot, which reduces the process of kinematics calculation.

The concrete implementations are given in Sect. 4, using this model and kinematics equation to model the exoskeleton of the upper limb and solve the kinematics equation.

4.2   The Prototype of an Exoskeleton Upper Limb Robot Based on Wheelchair

The prototype of an exoskeleton upper limb robot based on a wheelchair has 4 DOF for rotation and the length of the exoskeleton can be adjusted. The robot employs a modularization method, which consists of the wrist, elbow, shoulder training module, the lifting module, and the control module. The trajectory planning helps to better control the movement of the joints of the exoskeleton, and improve ADL of stroke patients and help them return to society and occupation.

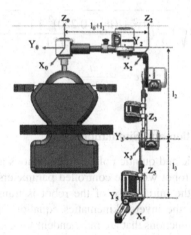

Fig. 6. Modeling on the exoskeleton.

4.3   Kinematics Equation

As shown in Fig. 6, the prototype did not contain the movement of collarbone and scapula. According to Eqs. (1)–(8), $A_1 = 0$, $T_6^2 = 0$. The prototype has flexion and extension of the shoulder, flexion of the elbow, and flexion of the wrist, so $\varphi2 = 0$, $\varphi4 = 0$, $\varphi5 = 0$. The following results can be obtained by substituting the above angles into Eq. (1)–(8). The forward kinematics equation of the exoskeleton robot is as follows ($l_0 + l_1 = 0.220$ m, $l_2 = 0.338$ m, $l_4 = 0.258$ m):

$$p_x = -0.338cos\phi_2 sin\theta_2 - 0.258cos\theta_2 cos\phi_2 sin\theta_3 - 0.258sin\theta_2 cos\phi_2 cos\theta_3 \quad (9)$$

$$p_y = -0.338sin\phi_2 sin\theta_2 - 0.258cos\theta_2 sin\phi_2 sin\theta_3 - 0.258sin\theta_2 sin\phi_2 cos\theta_3 - 0.220$$

$$(10)$$

$$p_z = 0.258sin\theta_2 sin\theta_3 - 0.258cos\theta_2 cos\theta_3 - 0.338cos\theta_2 \tag{11}$$

The inverse kinematics equation of the exoskeleton robot is as follows:

$$\phi_2 = \text{Atan}\,\frac{dy + 0.220}{dx} \tag{12}$$

$$\theta_3 = \text{A}\cos\frac{dx^2 + (dy + 0.220)^2 + dz^2 - 0.181}{0.174} \tag{13}$$

$$\theta_2 = \text{A}\sin c - \text{A}\sin\frac{dz \times c}{a} \tag{14}$$

$$a = -0.258(\frac{dx^2 + (dy + 0.220)^2 + dz^2 - 0.181}{0.174}) - 0.338 \tag{15}$$

$$b = 0.258\sqrt{1 - (\frac{dx^2 + (dy + 0.220)^2 + dz^2 - 0.181}{0.174})^2} \tag{16}$$

$$c = \frac{a}{\sqrt{a^2 + b^2}} \tag{17}$$

4.4   Trajectory Generation and Simulation

In the joint space, the cubic and quintic polynomial methods are used to complete the trajectory planning of the robot with the controlled parameters. In order to obtain the trajectory in joint space, the initial pose of the robot is transformed into the corresponding joints angles by the inverse kinematics equation. The joints variables are mapped into smooth time functions that are independent for each joint whose motion is planned separately.

To reach a target position coordinate (p_x, p_y, p_z), the joints angles can be obtained by inverse kinematics equation. Given the initial and terminal angular velocities of the joints angles, and the trajectory can be obtained by substituting the cubic equation into the positive kinematics equation. The trajectory equation is as follows:

$$p_x = (-0.338\sin\theta_2(t) - 0.258\sin(\theta_2(t) + \theta_3(t)))\cos\phi_2(t) \tag{18}$$

$$p_y = (-0.338\sin\theta_2(t) - 0.258\sin(\theta_2(t) + \theta_3(t)))\sin\phi_2(t) - 0.220 \tag{19}$$

$$p_z = -0.258\cos(\theta_2(t) + \theta_3(t)) - 0.338\cos\theta_2(t) \tag{20}$$

Taking can be divided into two motions, one is taking things, the other is putting things to another place. The coordinate of the original position is $(0.3, -0.22, -0.25)$, coordinate of the final position is $(0.35, 0.1, -0.25)$, the initial and terminal angular velocities of each joint are all 0, and time for each motion is 3 s.

The first trajectory of taking things is obtained by

$$p_{x1}(t) = (-0.338\sin(-2.11t^2 + 0.35t^3) - 0.258\sin(-24.18t^2 + 4.03t^3)\cos(0) \quad (21)$$

$$p_{y1}(t) = (-0.338\sin(-2.11t^2 + 0.35t^3) - 0.258\sin(-24.18t^2 + 4.03t^3))\sin(0) - 0.220 \quad (22)$$

$$p_{z1}(t) = -0.258\cos(-24.18t^2 + 4.03t^3) - 0.338\cos(-2.11t^2 + 0.35t^3) \quad (23)$$

The second trajectory for putting things to another place is obtained by

$$p_{x2}(t) = (-0.338\sin(-9.51 - 6.73t^2 + 1.12t^3) - 0.258\sin(-108.85 + 3.72t^2 \\ - 0.62t^3)\cos(9.43t^2 - 1.57t^3) \quad (24)$$

$$p_{y2}(t) = (-0.338\sin(-9.51 - 6.73t^2 + 1.12t^3) - 0.258\sin(-108.85 + 3.72t^2 \\ - 0.62t^3))\sin(9.43t^2 - 1.57t^3) - 0.220 \quad (25)$$

$$p_{z2}(t) = -0.258\cos(-108.85 + 3.72t^2 - 0.62t^3) - 0.338\cos(-9.51 - 6.73t^2 - 1.12t^3) \quad (26)$$

There are 6 unknowns in the quintic polynomial, and the acceleration values of the starting and ending points are increased on the basis of the cubic polynomial. Jtraj function in MATLAB robotic toolbox is used to plan trajectory by a quintic polynomial. Taking trajectories by cubic polynomial coincides with that by a quintic polynomial, as shown in Fig. 7. It is proved that the formula can reduce the order of quintic polynomial to cubic polynomial, optimize the trajectory and improve the responsiveness of the control system. In addition, the time of trajectory planning by a cubic polynomial (0.086 s) is much shorter than that by jtraj function (0.952 s).

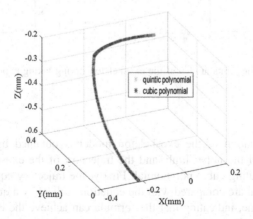

Fig. 7. Compare the taking trajectories by cubic and quintic polynomials.

The kinematics and trajectory equations are programmed into the control program of the exoskeleton robot. The robotic arm can complete this action by giving only one end position coordinate and completing the action time.

One experiment was done to complete the taking movement of the exoskeleton. Given the cup coordinate P_1 (0.3, −0.22, −0.25) and the final position coordinate P_2 (0.35, 0.1, −0.25), the exoskeleton drives the tester's upper limb to complete the taking movement, the experiments are shown in Fig. 8. Figure 8(a) is the exoskeleton in the initial position, Fig. 8(b) is taking the cup, and Fig. 8(c) is putting the cup to another place. The joints angles of the exoskeleton during taking experiment are shown in Fig. 9.

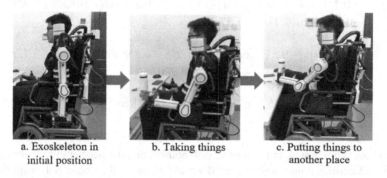

a. Exoskeleton in   b. Taking things   c. Putting things to
initial position   another place

Fig. 8. The experiment of taking movement by the exoskeleton.

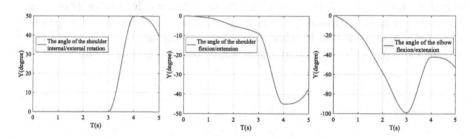

Fig. 9. The joints angles of the exoskeleton during taking experiment.

5 Discussion

The kinematics equation of the exoskeleton model is obtained by simplifying the kinematics model of the upper limb, and the trajectory of the exoskeleton motion is achieved by substituting cubic polynomial. Firstly, the trajectory equations solved by the cubic polynomial are compared with the equations solved by a quintic polynomial. The two are the same, indicating that the formula can achieve the effect of trajectory reduction. Secondly, the trajectory formula is programmed into the control system and the exoskeleton achieves taking motion planning. These results show that the kinematics equation and trajectory planning of the exoskeleton are reasonable, thus verifying that the upper limb kinematics model is correct.

6 Conclusion

This paper presents a general kinematics model for trajectory planning of upper limb exoskeleton robots, which considers the movement of the human upper limb and is closer to the movement law of humanity.

Firstly, a general kinematics model of the upper limb with 13 DoF is proposed, which is appropriate for all upper limb rehabilitation or assistive robots. Secondly, analyze the kinematics of the equivalent mechanism of the upper limb. The kinematics equations are divided into two parts, one is the position and postures the relationship between the end-wrist and the base-sternum, the other is the position and posture relationship between the end-scapula and the base-sternum. Thirdly, the prototype of an exoskeleton upper limb robot was used to verify the feasibility of the model and its kinematics equation. The model of the exoskeleton is obtained by simplifying the extra DoF of the kinematics model and substituting the parameters into the kinematics equation of the model to obtain the kinematics equation of the exoskeleton. Fourthly, the trajectory of the exoskeleton is got by substituting cubic polynomial into the kinematics equation. Finally, the trajectory of the exoskeleton is proved to be feasible and the model is correct by MATLAB simulation and experiments.

References

1. Lauretti, C., Cordella, F., Guglielmelli, E., Zollo, L.: Learning by demonstration for planning activities of daily living in rehabilitation and assistive robotics. IEEE Robot. Autom. Lett. 2(3), 1375–1382 (2017). https://doi.org/10.1109/LRA.2017.2669369
2. Harischandra, P.A.D., Abeykoon, A.M.H.S.: Development of an upper limb master-slave robot for bimanual rehabilitation. In: 2017 Moratuwa Engineering Research Conference (MERCon), Moratuwa, pp. 52–57 (2017). https://doi.org/10.1109/mercon.2017.7980455
3. Soltani-Zarrin, R., Zeiaee, A., Langari, R., Robson, N.: Reference path generation for upper-arm exoskeletons considering scapulohumeral rhythms. In: 2017 ICORR, London, pp. 753–758 (2017). https://doi.org/10.1109/icorr.2017.8009338
4. Xu, H., Ding, X.: Human-like motion planning for a 4-DOF anthropomorphic arm based on arm's inherent characteristics. Int. J. Humanoid Robot. 14(4) (2017). https://doi.org/10.1142/s0219843617500050
5. Fekrache, D., Guiatni, M.: Kinematics and design of a 5 DoF exoskeleton for the rehabilitation of the upper limb. In: 2015 4th ICEE, Boumerdes, pp. 1–5 (2015). https://doi.org/10.1109/intee.2015.7416752
6. Rahman, M.H., et al.: Development of a whole arm wearable robotic exoskeleton for rehabilitation and to assist upper limb movements. Robotica 33(1), 19–39 (2015). https://doi.org/10.1017/s0263574714000034

7. Guo, X., Wang, W., Yan, H.: The trajectory planning and simulation of exoskeleton upper limb rehabilitation robot. China: J. Qingdao Univ. (Nat. Sci. Edn.) **28**(3), 65–69 (2015). https://doi.org/10.3969/j.issn.1006-1037.2015.08.14

8. Tsai, B.C., Wang, W.W., Hsu, L.C., et al.: An articulated rehabilitation robot for upper limb physiotherapy and training. In: 2010 IEEE/RSJ, Taipei, pp. 1470–1475 (2010). https://doi.org/10.1109/iros.2010.5649567

9. Miao, Q., Mcdaid, A., Zhang, M.: A three-stage trajectory generation method for robot-assisted bilateral upper limb training with subject-specific adaptation. Robot. Auton. Syst. **105**, 38–46 (2018). https://doi.org/10.1016/j.robot.2018.03.010

10. Schiele, A., van der Helm, F.C.T.: Kinematic design to improve ergonomics in human machine interaction. IEEE Trans. Neural Syst. Rehabil. Eng. **14**(4), 456–469 (2006). https://doi.org/10.1109/TNSRE.2006.881565

11. Aili, Z.: Analysis and Simulation of Human Upper Limb Motion Based on MATLAB. Tianjin University of Science and Technology, Tianjin (2003)

12. Robson, P., Langari, R., Buchanan, J.J.: Experimental observations on the human arm motion planning under an elbow joint constraint. In: 2012 Annual International Conference of the IEEE Engineering in Medicine and Biology Society, San Diego, CA, pp. 3870–3873 (2012)

13. Zhang, J., Cheah, C.C.: Passivity and stability of human–robot interaction control for upper-limb rehabilitation robots. IEEE Tran. Robot. **31**(2), 233–245 (2015). https://doi.org/10.1109/tro.2015.2392451

14. Guidali, M., Büchel, M., Klamroth, V., et al.: Trajectory planning in ADL tasks for an exoskeletal arm rehabilitation robot. In: Technically Assisted Rehabilitation, TAR 2009; 2nd European Conference, 18–19 March 2009, Deutsche Gesellschaft für Biomedizinische Technik, Berlin (2009)

15. Piazzi, A., Visioli, A.: Global minimum-jerk trajectory planning of robot manipulators. IEEE Tran. Ind. Electron. **47**(1), 140–149 (2000). https://doi.org/10.1109/41.824136

16. Loureiro, R., Amirabdollahian, F., Topping, M.: Upper limb robot mediated stroke therapy —GENTLE/s approach. Auton. Robots **15**(1), 35–51 (2003). https://doi.org/10.1023/a:1024436732030

17. Loconsole, C., Banno, F., Frisoli, A., et al.: A new kinect-based guidance mode for upper limb robot-aided neurorehabilitation. In: IEEE/RSJ, Vilamoura, Algarve, Portugal, October 2012

18. Rahman, M.H., Kittel-Ouimet, T., Saad, M., et al.: Dynamic modeling and evaluation of a robotic exoskeleton for upper-limb rehabilitation. Int. J. Inf. Acquisition **8**(1), 83–102 https://doi.org/10.1142/s0219878911002367

19. Pronk, G.M.: The shoulder girdle, analysed and modelled kinematically (1991)

20. Helm, F.C.T.V.D.: A finite element musculoskeletal model of the shoulder mechanism. J. Biomech. **27**(5), 551–569 (1994). https://doi.org/10.1016/0021-9290(94)90065-5

21. Maurel, W., et al.: A biomechanical musculoskeletal model of human upper limb for dynamic simulation. In: 5th IEEE EMBS International Summer School on Biomedical Imaging, Berder Island, pp. 121–136 (2002)

22. Klopcar, N., Lenarc, J.: Bilateral and unilateral shoulder girdle kinematics during humeral elevation. Clin. Biomech. **21**(Suppl. 1), S20–S26 (2006). https://doi.org/10.1016/j.clinbiomech.2005.09.009

23. Laitenberger, M., Raison, M., Périé, D., et al.: Refinement of the upper limb joint kinematics and dynamics using a subject-specific closed-loop forearm model. Multibody Syst. Dyn. **33**(4), 413–438 (2015). https://doi.org/10.1007/s11044-014-9421-z

24. Wenbin, C.: Human Upper Limb Kinematics Analysis and Humanoid Limb Design and Motion Planning. Huazhong University of Science and Technology, China (2012)

25. Bertomeu-Motos, A., et al.: Human arm joints reconstruction algorithm in rehabilitation therapies assisted by end-effector robotic devices. J. NeuroEngineering Rehabil. **15**(10) (2018). https://doi.org/10.1186/s12984-018-0348-0
26. Piña-Martínez, E., Ricardo, R., Salvador, L.M., et al.: Vision system-based design and assessment of a novel shoulder joint mechanism for an enhanced workspace upper limb exoskeleton. Appl. Bionics Biomech. **2018**, 1–14 (2018). ID. 6019381. https://doi.org/10.1155/2018/6019381
27. Spong, M.W., Hutchinson, S., Vidyasagar, M.: Forward and inverse kinematics. In: Robot Modeling and Control, 2nd edn, pp. 65–103. Wiley, Hoboken (2005)
28. Lin, B., Zhang, H., Guo, Z., et al.: The movement characteristics of acromioclavicular joints in normal Chinese people. China: J. Clin. Orthopaedics **12**(14), 451–454 (2009). https://doi.org/10.3969/j.issn.1008-0287.2009.04.038

A Modified Cartesian Space DMPs Model for Robot Motion Generation

Nailong Liu[1,2,3]($\boxtimes$), Zhaoming Liu[1,2,3], and Long Cui[1,2]

[1] State Key Laboratory of Robotics, Shenyang Institute of Automation (SIA),
Chinese Academy of Sciences (CAS), Shenyang 110016, China
`liunailong@sia.cn`
[2] Institutes for Robotics and Intelligent Manufacturing,
Chinese Academy of Sciences (CAS), Shenyang 110016, China
[3] University of Chinese Academy of Sciences (CAS), Beijing 100049, China

Abstract. DMPs (dynamic movement primitives) are a method to generate trajectory planning or control signal for complex robot movements. Each DMP is a nonlinear dynamical system which can be used as a primitive action for complex movements. The origin DMPs are used to model the robot joint space motion, however in many cases, robot motions are defined in Cartesian space, the model of Cartesian space is necessary. A Cartesian space DMPs variant is proposed which adds a dynamical quaternions goal subsystem to make the generated cartesian space twist more smooth and steady in the initial stage in this paper. This DMPs variant can be useful in some robot tasks which often require low speed operations, such as contact operation.

Keywords: Dynamic movement primitives · DMPs · Robot learning · Learning from demonstration

1 Introduction

In some robotic tasks, the given conditions of the motion trajectory are non-strict, but the trajectories can describe a similar behavior, even under different initial or target conditions, such as robot playing ball [1], helicopter aerobatics [2], etc. In these robotic tasks, there seems to be a loose constraint on trajectory, but in fact they require the trajectory generator to have an understanding of the characteristics of the behavior, and to make the resulting trajectory have a lot of similarity and flexibility, for example, it expects to encode the robot's trajectory, and using this encoding to produce a similar task trajectory when the target position changes. Sometimes it is necessary to scale the time and space profiles of the trajectory execution while maintaining certain trajectory and behavioral characteristics, even the interaction with the environment. For example, in an robotic assembly task, when the workpiece is placed at a position, the robot can be programmed by means of kinesthetic teaching [3], but when the posture of the workpiece changes, we still expect the robot to intuitively produce

© Springer Nature Switzerland AG 2019
H. Yu et al. (Eds.): ICIRA 2019, LNAI 11745, pp. 76–85, 2019.
https://doi.org/10.1007/978-3-030-27529-7_7

a trajectory similar to the previous demonstrated trajectory. The trajectory in the actual robot task may be complex, rather than a simple straight line or arc, and it is not easy to get a similar trajectory to such a complex task trajectory. The learning from demonstration (or programmed by demonstration) framework [3–7] is often used in robotic programming for complex and non-strict motion trajectories, which first acquiring behavioral data, then encode these behavioral data through a learning model, and use appropriate control models to reproduce similar behaviors. DMP is a method commonly used in LfD framework to encode trajectory [8,9]. It uses a nonlinear dynamic system model to encode complex trajectory (p, v, a, t), the basic assumption of the method is that any complex motion can be composed of simple motion primitive.

The DMPs model can not only describe the trajectory about kinematics, but also construct the closed-loop control by adding feedback information [5]. This can be used in learning the interaction behaviors. LfD framework is very efficient method to program some complex robotic tasks, but using LfD directly to learn the trajectory of some contact tasks will be not feasible [10]. In these tasks, the contact feedback information should be considered, and the force controllers are also needed for compliance control. The DMPs model is compatible with the control framework, and this will expand the scope of use of the model [5] (Fig. 1).

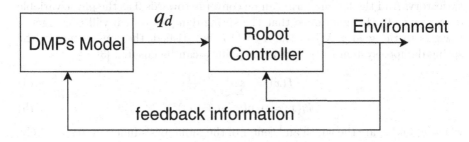

Fig. 1. DMPs control diagram

The origin DMPs are defined in the robot configuration space, and every DMP is designed to learn the trajectory of the robot joint. Since the origin spring-damper system has many issues, such as the convergence with the forcing term, the autonomy of the forcing term, and the scaling about the goal, there are many improvement about the origin spring-damper system. But most of the robotic tasks are defined in cartesian space, the model should learn the trajectory of the cartesian space [3]. But there are some differences between the cartesian pose and the position of the joint space, especially the rotation is in the $SO(3)$ which has many different characters from the Euclid space. It results in the improvements for the joint space DMPs cannot be directly applied in cartesian space DMPs. In this paper, a modified cartesian space DMPs model is proposed which based on the improved method of the joint space DMPs:

- add a dynamic goal subsystem for quaternions DMPs
- add a standalone gating term using the sigmoid systems
- using a constant velocity system to replace the exponential system term.

In the following sections, we will find that these changes, which works well in joint space, also bring some better behaviors in cartesian space.

2   Related Work

A general DMP model is defined as a nonlinear dynamical system, which includes a spring-damper system and a phase system [5].

$$\tau \dot{z} = \alpha_z(\beta_z(g - y) - z) + (g - y_0)x f(x), \tag{1}$$

$$\tau \dot{y} = z, \tag{2}$$

$$\tau \dot{x} = -\alpha_x x \tag{3}$$

where y is the position part of the trajectory, and z is a variable about the velocity part of the trajectory, x is the phase variable, τ is time constant, and $\alpha_x > 0$. The Eq. (1) describes a spring-damper system, and the y_0 is the initial value of y, g is the goal of the y. $f(x)$ is a linear combination of some nonlinear radial basis functions. The $(g - y_0)x f(x)$ is a forcing term in the spring-damper system, and the nonlinearity of the $f(x)$ enable the DMP model to encode any smooth trajectory. And the forcing term can be converge towards 0 as the phase variable decreases to 0, this guarantee that the spring-damper system will convergence towards to the goal g. When the $\alpha_z = 4\beta_z$ is satisfied, the convergence of the spring-damper system to the attractor point g can be ensured [3].

$$f(x) = \frac{\sum_{i=1}^{N} \omega_i \Psi_i(x)}{\sum_{i=1}^{N} \Psi_i(x)} \tag{4}$$

$$\Psi_i(x) = \exp(-h_i(x - c_i)^2) \tag{5}$$

where h_i and c_i are the width and center of the radial basis function, respectively. ω_i is the trainable parameter which should be estimated from the trajectory data.

In this DMP model, the exponential system is used as the gating term in the forcing term, and this will lead that the gating decreases very quickly at the beginning, then the $f(x)$ should be very high at the end of the movement to have any effect at this stage. This leads to scaling issues when training the function approximator. Sigmoid system was proposed as a gating system to solve this issue [11]. Since the samples are not at intervals of time, using the exponential phase system may complicate the learning of the function approximator. A constant velocity phase system was proposed to allow for a more natural integration [12]. The origin spring-damper system can lead to high initial accelerations, and this is not suitable for some robotic tasks. A delayed goal system was proposed [11] can generate a movement trajectory that with zero velocity and acceleration at the start and end of the trajectory. Inspired by these ideas, we applied these to cartesian space DMP in this paper, especially the DMPs which used to encode the quaternions trajectory, and some different properties between the joint space and cartesian space were mentioned.

3   Modified Cartesian Space DMPs

The cartesian space trajectory can be divided into two parts, position trajectory and orientation trajectory. The position trajectory can be easily encoded by the previous DMPs model [13]. Here we focus on the orientation trajectory expressed by the quaternions. And the quaternions DMPs share the same phase system with the position DMPs. The unit quaternions representation for orientation is non-singular, but not minimal. The unit quaternions is in S^3. It has many different properties from the Euclid space. The elements in S^3 have no direct addition operation like Euclid space and every calculation should ensure that the element is unit quaternions.

The general DMPs for quaternions trajectory of the cartesian space [3] is

$$\tau \dot{\eta} = \alpha_z(\beta_z 2 \log(g * \bar{q}) - \eta) + f(x) \tag{6}$$

$$\tau \dot{q} = \tfrac{1}{2}\eta * q \tag{7}$$

$$\tau \dot{x} = -\alpha_x x \tag{8}$$

where the $g \in S^3$ is the goal of the orientation trajectory. $\bar{q}$ is the conjugation of the quaternions q, and $\eta \in R^3$ is a quaternions with zero scalar part, here it is treated as a 3D vector when it is estimated. The forcing term

$$f(x) = D \frac{\sum_{i=1}^{N} \omega_i \Psi_i(x)}{\sum_{i=1}^{N} \Psi_i(x)} x \tag{9}$$

where the trainable parameters are $\omega_i \in R^3$, $D = diag(\log(g * \bar{q}_0)) \in R^{3 \times 3}$ is a diagonal matrix, q_0 is the initial value of the q.

The logarithmic operation from S^3 to R^3 is defined as

$$\log(q) = \log(v + u) = \begin{cases} \arccos(v)\frac{u}{\|u\|}, & \text{if } u \neq 0 \\ [0, 0, 0]^T, & \text{otherwise} \end{cases} \tag{10}$$

where we use the vector representation for quaternions, $q = v + u$, v is the scalar part, and u is the vector part.

The distance metric on the S^3

$$d(q_1, q_2) = 2 \begin{cases} \|\log(q_1 * \bar{q}_2)\|, & \text{if } q_1 * \bar{q}_2 \neq -1 + [0, 0, 0]^T \\ \pi, & \text{otherwise} \end{cases} \tag{11}$$

The distance metric is helpful when integrating the DMPs, and it can be used with the exponential map from R^3 to S^3,

$$\exp(r) = \begin{cases} \cos(\|r\|) + \sin(\|r\|)\frac{r}{\|r\|}, & \text{if } \|r\| \neq 0 \\ 1 + [0, 0, 0]^T, & \text{otherwise} \end{cases} \tag{12}$$

where $\|r\| < \pi$.

Then we can get the orientation difference within time period Δt

$$\chi(\omega\Delta t) = \exp(\frac{\omega\Delta t}{2}) \tag{13}$$

where ω is the angular velocity.

The following integration step can be used for integrating Eq. 6

$$q(t + \Delta t) = \chi(\omega\Delta t)q(t) \tag{14}$$

Since the q and ω at time t have the relationship $\dot{q} = \frac{1}{2}\omega * q$, $\eta = \tau\omega$. Then we can get

$$q(t + \Delta t) = \chi(\frac{\eta(t)}{\tau}\Delta t)q(t) \tag{15}$$

Based on the improvements on the joint space DMPs, we will give the modified cartesian space DMPs, and then the details of the modified model will be introduced.

Modified DMPs for quaternions trajectory is

$$\tau\dot{\eta} = \alpha_z(\beta_z 2\log(g^{gd} * \bar{q}) - \eta) + f(x) \tag{16}$$

$$\tau\dot{q} = \frac{1}{2}\eta * q \tag{17}$$

$$\tau\dot{q}^{gd} = \alpha_g \log(q^g * \bar{q}^{gd}) * q^{gd} \tag{18}$$

$$\tau\dot{x} = 1 \tag{19}$$

$$\tau\dot{v} = \alpha_v v(1 - \frac{v}{v_{max}}) \tag{20}$$

where $f(x)$ has the following formulation,

$$f(x) = D\frac{\sum_{i=1}^{N} \omega_i \Psi_i(x)}{\sum_{i=1}^{N} \Psi_i(x)}v \tag{21}$$

v is the variable of the gating system Eq. 20. In this equation, we replace the phase variable by the gating variable. This gating system change its state from 1 to 0, which will guarantee that the forcing term decreases towards 0, but not as fast as the exponential system in the beginning. And this will guarantee that the function approximator in the forcing term doesn't need to be very high at the end of the movement. The Eq. 19 is the phase system, which using a constant velocity system to replace the exponential system, and this system no longer changes from 1 to 0, but from 0 to 1. This phase system is linear with time which will make the function approximator more natural. Actually the gating system and the phase system can be designed and work like the joint space DMPs, but the delayed goal system Eq. 18 is not same as the situation in joint space. The q^g is the goal orientation of the quaternions trajectory, and the q^{gd} is a dynamic sub-goal. The dynamic sub-goal changes at every integration step which is derived by the difference between the global goal and the current sub-goal. Here it needs to be highlighted that if we formulate the delayed goal system as the formulation in joint space DMPs like

$$\tau\dot{q}^{gd} = \alpha_g \log(q^g * \bar{q}^{gd}) \tag{22}$$

the quaternions trajectory derived from the Eq. 16 can't converge to the final goal quaternions. From joint space DMPs, the Eq. 22 is acceptable, since the logarithmic map about quaternions is similar to the difference of the joint space value. In fact, the Eq. 22 is a quaternions differential equation (QDE), the solution space is mathematically right free module, and the joint space differential equation of the solution space is actually linear vector space [14]. The algebraic structure of the solutions to the QDEs is completely different from ODEs, since the non-commutativity of the quaternion algebra. This should be the reason why there is such a difference between the two situations. Using the delayed goal system Eq. 18, the movement generated from the modified DMPs has low initial angular velocity and acceleration, which has similarity with the human-like point-to-point movements. We use the similar phase system and gating system, and use the similar delayed goal system with the joint space DMPs for the position trajectory. Thus we can encode the whole cartesian space trajectory with the position DMPs and the quaternions DMPs shared the same phase system and gating system. And we use the method of Euler integration to train the modified DMPs.

4   Experiment and Evaluation

In order to demonstrate the effectiveness of the modified cartesian DMPs model, we first sample some cartesian space trajectories by the kinesthetic guiding from KUKA iiwa robot in gravity compensation mode. By the kinesthetic guiding, human operator can intuitively guide the robot to do some tasks, such as the peg-in-hole task. The cartesian space trajectories are recorded during the demonstration by human operator.

We acquired the cartesian space trajectories including cartesian space pose and twist of the TCP (tool center point), and the timestamp of the trajectory point.

$$\text{Data} = \{p_t, q_t, \dot{p}, \omega_t, t\} \tag{23}$$

For training the DMPs, we also need the accelerations $\ddot{p}_t$, $\dot{\omega}_t$, but the accelerations can't get directly from the robot API. We calculated the accelerations using the twist data and the timestamp.

$$\ddot{q}_t = \frac{q_t - q_{t-1}}{\Delta t} \tag{24}$$

$$\dot{\omega}_t = \frac{\omega_t - \omega_{t-1}}{\Delta t} \tag{25}$$

Then the data including cartesian pose, twist and acceleration will feed to the cartesian DMP to train the parameters (Fig. 2).

$$\text{Data} = \{p_t, q_t, \dot{p}, \omega_t, \ddot{q}_t, \dot{\omega}_t\} \tag{26}$$

From the Fig. 3, we can see that our modified position DMPs can reproduce the demonstrated position trajectory completely. From the Fig. 4, we can see that our modified quaternions DMPs can reproduce the demonstrated orientation trajectory completely.

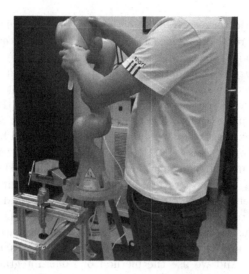

Fig. 2. Demonstration by gravity compensation mode

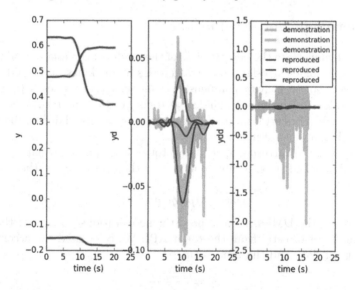

Fig. 3. Modified Cartesian DMPs encode the position of trajectory

From the Fig. 5, it can be seen that the movement generated from the modified position DMPs has lower linear velocity and linear acceleration than the previous position DMPs at the start and end of the movement. And the velocity profile is more natural like the human-like movements. From the Fig. 6, it can be seen that the orientation generated from the modified quaternions DMPs also has lower angular velocity and angular acceleration than the previous quaternions DMPs at the start and end of the movement. This is more appropriate in this contact task which need slow speed to change its orientation.

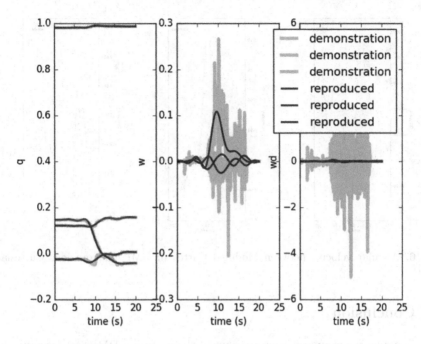

Fig. 4. Modified Cartesian DMPs encode the orientation of trajectory

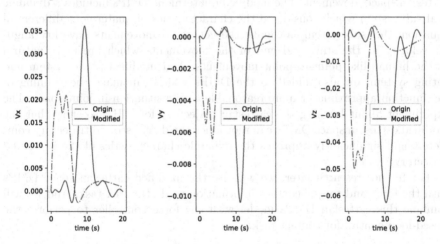

Fig. 5. Linear velocity between Modified Cartesian DMP and previous Cartesian DMP

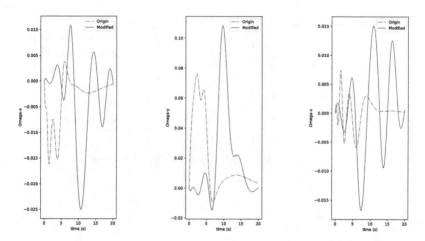

Fig. 6. Angular velocity between Modified Cartesian DMP and previous Cartesian DMP

5   Conclusion

In this paper, we proposed a new variant of the cartesian DMPs for learning the cartesian space movement. The modified quaternions DMPs includes a dynamic goal sub-system which considered the characteristics of quaternions differential equation, this sub-system can make the generated movements have low angular velocity at the start and end of the movements which are more natural as the human-like point-to-point movements. And modified phase system and gating system are also added to the DMPs which can make the training of the function approximator more reasonable as the situation in joint space. The experiment about learning the cartesian trajectory for PiH also show that the modified cartesian space DMPs can reproduce the demonstrated trajectory completely and significantly improves the dynamic characteristics of the generated trajectory.

For further research later, we will use the modified cartesian space DMPs with the force and torque contact information to do the PiH task. And we will combine this cartesian DMPs model with the force controller to perform the closed-loop control for contact task.

References

1. Mülling, K., Kober, J., Kroemer, O., Peters, J.: Learning to select and generalize striking movements in robot table tennis. Int. J. Robot. Res. **32**(3), 263–279 (2013)
2. Abbeel, P., Coates, A., Ng, A.Y.: Autonomous helicopter aerobatics through apprenticeship learning. Int. J. Robot. Res. **29**(13), 1608–1639 (2010)
3. Abu-Dakka, F.J., Nemec, B., Jorgensen, J.A., Savarimuthu, T.R., Kruger, N., Ude, A.: Adaptation of manipulation skills in physical contact with the environment to reference force profiles. Auton. Robots **39**(2), 199–217 (2015)

4. Rozo, L., Jiménez, P., Torras, C.: A robot learning from demonstration framework to perform force-based manipulation tasks. Intell. Serv. Robot. **6**(1), 33–51 (2013)
5. Schaal, S.: Dynamic movement primitives - a framework for motor control in humans and humanoid robots. In: Kimura, H., Tsuchiya, K., Ishiguro, A., Witte, H. (eds.) Adaptive Motion of Animals and Machines, pp. 261–280. Springer, Tokyo (2006). https://doi.org/10.1007/4-431-31381-8_23
6. Savarimuthu, T.R., Liljekrans, D., Ellekilde, L.-P., Ude, A., Nemec, B., Kruger, N.: Analysis of human peg-in-hole executions in a robotic embodiment using uncertain grasps, pp. 233–239. IEEE (2013)
7. Siciliano, B., Khatib, O. (eds.): Springer Handbook of Robotics, 2nd edn. Springer, Cham (2016). https://doi.org/10.1007/978-3-319-32552-1
8. Ijspeert, A., Nakanishi, J., Schaal, S.: Movement imitation with nonlinear dynamical systems in humanoid robots. In: Proceedings 2002 IEEE International Conference on Robotics and Automation (Cat. No. 02CH37292), vol. 2, pp. 1398–1403. IEEE (2002)
9. Xu, J., Hou, Z., Liu, Z., Qiao, H.: Compare contact model-based control and contact model-free learning: a survey of robotic peg-in-hole assembly strategies (2019)
10. Kober, J., Gienger, M., Steil, J.J.: Learning movement primitives for force interaction tasks. In: 2015 IEEE International Conference on Robotics and Automation (ICRA), pp. 3192–3199 (2015)
11. Kulvicius, T., Ning, K., Tamosiunaite, M., Worgötter, F.: Joining movement sequences: modified dynamic movement primitives for robotics applications exemplified on handwriting. IEEE Trans. Robot. **28**(1), 145–157 (2011)
12. Stulp, F.: DmpBbo - a C++ library for black-box optimization of dynamical movement primitives (2014)
13. Pastor, P., Righetti, L., Kalakrishnan, M., Schaal, S.: Online movement adaptation based on previous sensor experiences, pp. 365–371. IEEE (2011)
14. Kou, K.I., Xia, Y.-H.: Linear quaternion differential equations: basic theory and fundamental results. Stud. Appl. Math. **141**, 3–45 (2018)

Robot Brush-Writing System of Chinese Calligraphy Characters

Jie Li, Huasong Min[✉], Haotian Zhou, and Hongcheng Xu

Institute of Robotics and Intelligent Systems,
Wuhan University of Science and Technology, Wuhan, China
mhuasong@wust.edu.cn

Abstract. In this paper, robot calligraphy systems is developed to write Chinese brush characters dynamically. The BBOD algorithm of stroke extraction is optimized by adding a rule for merging stroke. the results show that the accuracy of stroke extraction is 95% for the Simple-style font, 92% for Kai-style font and 90% for Yan-style font. A model of calligraphy features is established, which includes not only the spatial structure features of Chinese characters, but also the dynamic writing features of Chinese characters. In the period of trajectory planning, a rule of Chinese brush characters applies to optimize the trajectory of stroke, and there are two steps of motion planning, cubic B-spline algorithm is used to plan the Cartesian path, then S curve algorithm is used to plan the joint space trajectory, in order to control manipulator smoothly and stably. To verify the proposed method, three types of experiments are conducted and the developed systems achieved good results in Chinese brush calligraphy reproducing.

Keywords: Robot calligraphy system · Stroke extraction ·
Calligraphy feature model · Calligraphy writing rule

1 Introduction

The preservation and reproduction of Chinese calligraphy works is a significant work to inherit and carry forward excellent Chinese traditional culture. Learning calligraphy requires years of training, and it is very difficult to reproduce excellent calligraphy works. With the development of artificial intelligence and robotics, many researchers adopt manipulator to construct calligraphy robot. In general, the pipeline of calligraphy system is: (1) stroke feature of Chinese characters is extracted according to the calligraphy feature extraction algorithm; (2) the calligraphy feature model is established according to the collected features; (3) the trajectory parameters of the manipulator are generated by trajectory planning algorithm (Fig. 1).

Fig. 1. The pipeline of traditional robot calligraphy system

© Springer Nature Switzerland AG 2019
H. Yu et al. (Eds.): ICIRA 2019, LNAI 11745, pp. 86–96, 2019.
https://doi.org/10.1007/978-3-030-27529-7_8

However, there are three problems in present robot calligraphy system: firstly, the stroke extraction of character is not precise [1]. A kind of method proposed in [2] classify strokes by extracting feature points after obtaining the information of stroke skeleton. But he information of stroke width is lost. The method in [3] extracts stroke according to the tangent direction of Chinese character pixels, it keeps the width of strokes, but the stroke may be over-separated. In the second place, the perform of feature model is not well. Calligraphy model in [4, 5] has created lack of the dynamic feature of calligraphy. Lo et al. use digital camera to capture the movement trajectory of brush, [6], but the imitation work is not good since the collected data is not accurate. Li et al. propose a method of dynamic writing information acquisition via touch screen, which can obtain information such as position, stroke width, motion velocity, acceleration [7], but writing brush character with touch screen limits the writing effect. The third point is that the previous calligraphy robot does not study the writing rule of Chinese characters during trajectory planning [6, 7], which leading to the missing of stroke details.

Based on the analysis above, there are three main works in this paper:

- The stroke extraction algorithm in [3] is improved by adding the rule of stroke merging, the over-separated strokes are combined and the accuracy of stroke extraction is increased.
- A model of calligraphy features is presented, which includes not only the spatial structure features of Chinese characters, but also the dynamic writing features of Chinese characters.
- A set of calligraphy writing rules are presented by studying the rule of calligraphy writing. Combining with the model of calligraphy features, the manipulator is controlled to make the trajectory planning, and the dynamic writing process of Chinese characters is reproduced.

The remaining parts of the paper are organized as follows. The calligraphy system is introduced in Sect. 2. The optimized stroke extraction algorithm is described in Sect. 3. The calligraphy feature model is introduced in Sect. 4. The rules of writing control and the algorithm of trajectory planning is presented in Sect. 5. Some experiment results are given in Sect. 6. Section 7 summarizes our work, and looks forward to the next step of improvement.

2 Intelligent Calligraphy System

The pipeline of our intelligent calligraphy system is shown in Fig. 2. At first, the structural features of calligraphy are extracted according to stroke extraction algorithm and the proposed stroke merging rule is used to optimize the stroke extraction effect. Next the calligraphy feature model is established on stroke feature extraction algorithm. Our calligraphy feature model is divided into two parts: structural feature model and writing feature model. The structural feature model includes the size of Chinese characters, the length-width ratio of Chinese characters and stroke features. The writing feature model includes the order, trajectory and width of stroke. In the third step, combining calligraphy feature model and calligraphy writing rule, the key points of calligraphy trajectory are generated. The fourth step, the Cartesian space path of manipulator is fitted by cubic B-spline algorithm. In the end, the algorithm of S-shaped curve is used to plan the joint space trajectory of the manipulator to ensure the best effect of the reproduced Chinese characters.

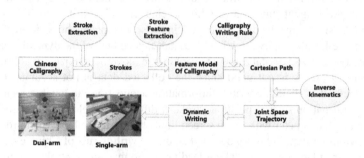

Fig. 2. The pipeline of robot calligraphy system

3 Stroke Extraction

Strokes are extracted according to the tangent direction of pixels. Depending on the tangent direction, pixels can be divided into three areas: regular area, boundary area and singular area. The pixels located in the regular area and the boundary area have only one tangent direction, and the pixels in the singular area have at least 2 tangent directions. At first, the pixels are mapped to a three-dimensional space according to the tangent direction [3].

$$\rho_i = (x_i \ \ y_i \ \ \theta_i) \tag{1}$$

x_i, y_i is the coordinate of pixels, θ_i is the tangent direction of pixels. Generally, the pixel points in the boundary area and the regular area appear only in one plane of the ρ space, and the pixels in the singular area at least appear on 2 planes. Now we need to compute the tangent direction of pixels.

The tangent direction of pixels can be determined by the local maximum of the boundary to boundary orientation distance (BBOD) of pixels. The BBOD is the orientation distance of pixel between two boundary points along the kth quantized orientation, where k = 1, 2, ..., m [3]. We calculate BBOD of pixels in m directions (0–180°) the number of local maximum values is recorded as N. The criteria for determining the region of the pixel are as follows:

– If N = 1, the pixel belongs to the regular region or the boundary region;
– If N > 1, the pixel belongs to the singular region.

The main strokes of Chinese character are separated by the singular region, and then the overlapped strokes are separated according to the tangent directions, but strokes may be over separated. The mathematical model of the strokes is as follows:

$$S_i = [B_i \ \ E_i \ \ \theta_i \ \ P_i \ \ l_i] \tag{2}$$

B_i and E_i are the start point and end point of stroke, θ_i is the tangent direction of stroke, P_i is the number of stroke pixels, l_i is the number of pixels in the stroke skeleton. The parallel thinning algorithm in [8] is used to calculate the stroke skeleton of Chinese characters.

On the basis of the original algorithm [3], we propose a set of stroke merging rules, which combine the over-separated strokes to generate correct strokes. If there are two strokes S_i, S_j, they intersect in region h, the singular area of Chinese character is called β.

1. if $P_i < \overline{P} \times \omega$, delete S_i. ω is threshold, the default value is 0.3. $\overline{P}$ is average value of stroke pixels, it can be calculated by the following equation:

$$\overline{P} = \frac{1}{n} \times \sum\nolimits_{i=1}^{n} P_i \qquad (3)$$

2. If tangent direction of the two strokes is same and they share pixels, merging the strokes.
3. If tangent direction of the two strokes is similar, and they share pixels which don't belong to singular region, merging the strokes.
4. If tangent direction of the two strokes is similar, the distance between start points (B_i, B_j) and end points (E_i, E_j) of two stroke (S_i, S_j) less than $\varepsilon \times \overline{sw}$, merging the strokes. ε is threshold, the default value is 0.5. $\overline{sw}$ is average stroke width, it can be calculated by following equation:

$$\overline{sw} = \frac{1}{n} \times \sum\nolimits_{i=1}^{n} \frac{P_i}{l_i} \qquad (4)$$

The over separated strokes are merged and the correct strokes are obtained after using the algorithm above.

4   Character Feature Model

Establishing calligraphy feature model is necessary before trajectory planning, our model consists of two parts: structural feature model and dynamic writing feature model of Chinese character.

4.1   Structural Feature Model

The structure model of character is following:

$$SF = [Size, LwRatio, Stroke] \qquad (5)$$

Size is the size of Chinese character, *LwRatio* is the length-width ratio of Chinese character, *Stroke* are obtained by our stroke extraction algorithm, It contains the structural features of strokes, which are extracted in Sect. 3.

The size and length-width ratio are computed according to the boundary points of character. The boundary points are saved as an array.

$$BP = [x_{min} \ x_{max} \ y_{min} \ y_{max}] \tag{6}$$

The equations to compute size and length-width ratio of Chinese character are:

$$size = (x_{max} - x_{min}) \times (y_{max} - y_{min}) \tag{7}$$

$$lwRatio = \frac{y_{max} - y_{min}}{x_{max} - x_{min}} \tag{8}$$

Every calligrapher writes brush characters with distinctive structural characteristics. Our structural feature model not only can judge the calligraphy style of calligraphy characters, but also create new calligraphy fonts in the future.

4.2 Dynamic Writing Model

The dynamic writing model of character is following:

$$WF = [StrOrder \ StrTraj \ StrWidth] \tag{9}$$

StrOrder is the writing order of strokes, *StrTraj* is the trajectory of strokes, *StrWidth* is the width of strokes.

The stroke order is obtained according to the habit of Chinese character writing, the stroke order is usually from left to right, from top to bottom, the rules are as follows:

There are two strokes S_i, S_j:

a. if $B_i.x < B_j.x$, the order priority of S_i is higher than S_j;
    if $B_i.x = B_j.x$ and $B_i.y < B_j.y$, the order priority of S_i is higher than S_j;

We can obtain the stroke order of character according to the rule.

The acquisition of stroke trajectory *StrTraj* is divided into two steps: Firstly, we use thinning algorithm to obtain stroke skeleton information [8]. Then we use critical point detection algorithm described in [9] to extract the critical points *KP* of stroke trajectory.

$$StrTraj = [KP_1 \ KP_2 \ldots\ldots KP_n] \tag{10}$$

The width of stroke is the normal line of critical points. The direction of the normal line is perpendicular to the tangential direction. The length is equal to the orientation distance between critical point and boundary of brush character. we save them in an array:

$$StrWidth = [NL_1 \ NL_2 \ldots\ldots NL_n] \tag{11}$$

Our calligraphy feature model describes the structural feature and dynamic writing feature of Chinese character clearly.

5 Chinese Character Trajectory Planning

In the aspect of trajectory planning, previous calligraphy robot systems have two problems: (1) They have not studied the writing rules of Chinese calligraphy, so that the imitated Chinese characters lack of the aesthetics of calligraphy. (2) The previous robot systems only plan the Cartesian space trajectory, but don't consider the joint space trajectory planning. In view of the above two problems, a set of calligraphy writing rules are presented based on the study of the rules of Chinese character writing. Next, B-spline is used for planning path of Cartesian space, which can accurately imitate Chinese character. and S-curve algorithm is used as the basic algorithm for planning trajectory of joint space, in order to ensure the smoothness of the joint motion of the manipulator.

5.1 Calligraphy Writing Rule

Calligraphy is different from simple Chinese characters. If you don't follow the rules of calligraphy, only use the key points SP to plan the trajectory, the imitated Chinese characters will distort in details. The writing process of brush strokes is divided into three parts: head, middle and tail [10]. The writing rule of head and tail has two situations: "CangFeng" and "LuFeng". "CangFeng" means hide the tip of brush when writing calligraphy. "LuFeng" means show the tip of brush when writing calligraphy. The direction of brush is basically same with the direction of stroke in "LuFeng" style. On the contrary, the direction of brush is opposite with the direction of stroke in "CangFeng" style.

There are five basic strokes and writing trajectory of Chinese brush character. In this paper, the rules of five basic strokes (point, horizontal, vertical, left-falling, right-falling) are summarized and calligraphy writing rules are proposed below:

When entering a stroke's trajectory, the writing method of head is determined by the type of stroke.

If it is "LuFeng" style, don't increase the trajectory point;

If it is "CangFeng" style, we should add a trajectory point at the beginning.

The rules apply to the tail of stroke too, the point can be calculated by the equations:

$$\overline{KP_0 \ KP_1} = k * l \tag{12}$$

$$\overrightarrow{KP_0 \ KP_1} = -\overrightarrow{KP_1 \ KP_n} \pm \sigma \tag{13}$$

KP_0 is the new trajectory point, KP_1, KP_n are the start point and end point of *StrTraj*, l is the length of stroke, k is the scale factor, whose size depends on stroke type. For example, the tail of horizontal is about 1/8 of the total length of stroke, so that k is 1/8.

$\overline{KP_0\ KP_1}$ is the distance between KP_0, KP_1, $\overrightarrow{KP_0\ KP_1}$ is the orientation vector of two points, which is in the opposite direction of stroke trajectory $\overrightarrow{KP_1\ KP_n}$. σ is the error compensation, we compensate the angle according to the real brush characters.

For instance, the key points of the extracted trajectory of stroke "Heng" according to our character model are shown in Fig. 3(a), which lack of the process of head and tail. As shown in Fig. 3(b), the start point and end point are added according to calligraphy writing rules.

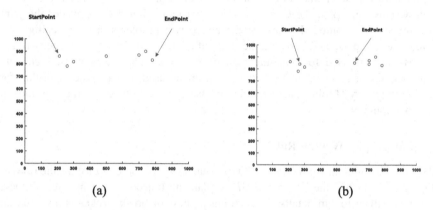

(a)   (b)

Fig. 3. (a) Trajectory without writing rule (b) Trajectory with writing rule

We can obtain the path point of the manipulator motion according to the calligraphy feature model, it is recorded as SP.

$$SP = [SP_1\ SP_2 \dots \dots SP_n] \tag{14}$$

$$SP_i = [x_i\ y_i\ z_i] \tag{15}$$

5.2   Trajectory Planning

Cubic B-spline algorithm is used to plan the path of Cartesian space [11], which has the following advantages:

- B-spline curve only needs low order to describe the complex curve. The curve with lower order has better performance in fitting motion path.
- The B-spline curve is a piecewise continuous curve with local support and can adjust the local shape of the curve without affecting the total curve.

According to the trajectory points of the manipulator and the B-spline algorithm in [11], we obtain the motion path of the manipulator in cartesian space.

In order to smooth the motion of six joints, we use S curve algorithm to plan the trajectory of joint space. The S-curve algorithm is an algorithm whose velocity curve likes S shape in the process of acceleration and deceleration [12].

According to the Cartesian path SP of the manipulator, the rotation angles of six joints are calculated by the inverse kinematics, and the desired maximum velocity V_{max}, maximum acceleration A_{max} and maximum jerk J_{max} are set. According to the given parameters, the total time t_{total} is divided into seven periods: plus-acceleration T_a, uniform acceleration T_b, reduce-acceleration T_c, uniform speed T_d, reduce-deceleration T_e, uniform deceleration T_f and plus-deceleration T_g. The trajectory of joint space are computed according to the formula in [12].

6 Experiments

6.1 Stroke Extraction Experiment

In this experiment, three kinds of fonts, such as Simple-style character, Kai-style character and Yan-style character, are selected as experimental datasets. One hundred Chinese characters in three fonts are randomly selected for the stroke extraction experiment. Compared with the Cao.R's method, the accuracy of Chinese character extraction is increased from 88% to 95%, and the accuracy of stroke extraction is increased from 93% to 98.6%. The experimental results show that our algorithm significantly improves the accuracy of stroke extraction. It's comparison of the Cao.R's method with our method (Fig. 4).

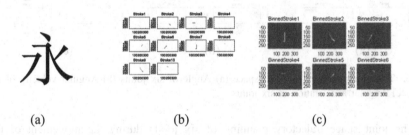

(a)   (b)   (c)

Fig. 4. (a) Chinese character 'Yong' (b) Cao.R's method (c) Our method

Then we continue to test the improved algorithm with Kai-style and Yan-style fonts. The extraction accuracy of the three kinds of fonts is more than 90%, among which the extraction effect of simple characters is the best (95%), and the extraction effect of Yan-style is worst (90%), the accuracy of Kai-style is 92%. Later, the stroke extraction effect of Chinese characters can be improved by adjusting the threshold value. Experimental results show that our stroke extraction algorithm can apply to stroke extraction of commonly-used brush characters.

6.2   Trajectory Planning of Chinese Character

Firstly, a cubic B-spline algorithm is used to plan the Cartesian spatial path, which fits the end path of the manipulator, and the results are shown in Fig. 5. The blue points represent the path point obtained according to the calligraphy characteristic model and the calligraphy writing rule, the red points represent the control point of the spline curve, and the green curve is the fitting Chinese character trajectory.

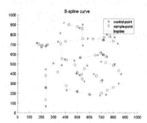

Fig. 5. The path of character 'wang' (Color figure online)

Then S-curve algorithm is used to plan joint space trajectory.

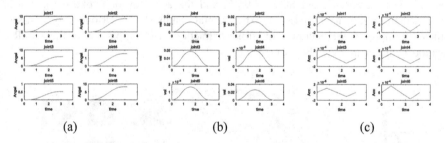

(a)   (b)   (c)

Fig. 6. Trajectory planning of joint space (a) Angle of six joints (b) Angular velocity of six joints (c) Angular acceleration of six joints

The joint space trajectory planning of six joints during the movement of the manipulator (see Fig. 6). The S-curve algorithm not only ensures the smoothness of the movement speed of each joint, but also ensures the continuity of acceleration, which basically satisfies the requirements of writing calligraphy with the manipulator.

We first use cubic B-spline curve to plan Cartesian space path, and then use S-curve algorithm to plan joint space trajectory. The method of trajectory planning not only ensures the manipulator can accurately reproduce the trajectory of Chinese characters, but also ensures the movement smoothness of each joint.

6.3   Writing Effect

Figure 7(a) is the writing effect without calligraphy writing rule, the strokes of character lack of head and tail, so they distort in details the character isn't real brush character. Figure 7(b) is the writing effect with calligraphy writing rule. It accurately imitates the Yan-style Chinese characters, and it adds the head and tail in writing process, accurately reproduces the dynamic writing process of Chinese characters. Obviously, there are still some differences between the real calligraphy work and the imitating calligraphy work. The reason is that the tip of brush will distort when writing brush and our robot system is unable to correct the deviation automatically. It requires further improve by active perception in the future.

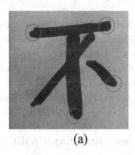   

(a)   (b)

Fig. 7. (a) Writing effect without calligraphy writing rules (b) The writing effect with calligraphy writing rules

7 Conclusion and Future Work

The robot calligraphy system developed by us can imitate Chinese calligraphy works. It can not only accurately describe the structural features of Chinese characters, but also reproduce the dynamic writing process of Chinese characters. The main contributions of this paper include the following: improved algorithm of stroke extraction, mathematical model to describe the features of calligraphy and calligraphy writing rule.

In the future, our robot calligraphy system will extend the calligraphy writing rules to forty basic strokes of Chinese characters. In addition, a visual evaluation mechanism will be researched using camera to collect the Chinese character images written by manipulator, to obtain the writing deviation and compare the robot calligraphy works with the original calligraphy works. The parameters of the calligraphy feature model can be modified dynamically according to the deviation.

Acknowledgements. This work is supported by National Key R&D Program of China (Project No. 2017YFB1300400), National Natural Science Foundation of China (Project No. 61673304) and Wuhan Science and Technology Planning Project (Project No.: 2018010401011275).

References

1. Mueller, S., Huebel, N., Waibel, M., et al.: Robotic calligraphy—learning how to write single strokes of Chinese and Japanese characters. In: 2013 International Conference on Intelligent Robots and Systems (IROS), pp. 1734–1739. Institute of Electrical and Electronics Engineers Inc., Tokyo, Japan (2013)

2. Liu, K., Huang, Y.S., Suen, C.Y.: Robust stroke segmentation method for handwritten Chinese character recognition. In: Proceedings of the Fourth International Conference on Document Analysis and Recognition, pp. 211–215. IEEE, Los Alamitos, CA, United States, Ulm, Ger (1997)
3. Cao, R., Tan, C.L.: A model of stroke extraction from Chinese character images. In: Proceedings 15th International Conference on Pattern Recognition, IEEE, pp. 4: 368–371. Institute of Electrical and Electronics Engineers Inc., Barcelona, Spain (2000)
4. Xu, S., Lau, F.C.M., Cheung, W.K., et al.: Automatic generation of artistic Chinese calligraphy. IEEE Intell. Syst. 20(3), 32–39 (2005)
5. Lyu, P., Bai, X., Yao, C., et al.: Auto-encoder guided GAN for Chinese calligraphy synthesis. In: 14th IAPR International Conference on Document Analysis and Recognition (ICDAR), pp. 1095–1100. IEEE Computer Society, Kyoto, Japan (2017)
6. Lo, K.W., Kwok, K.W., Wong, S.M., et al.: Brush footprint acquisition and preliminary analysis for Chinese calligraphy using a robot drawing platform. In: 2006 IEEE/RSJ International Conference on Intelligent Robots and Systems, pp. 5183–5188. Institute of Electrical and Electronics Engineers Inc., United States, Beijing, China (2006)
7. Li, J., Sun, W., Zhou, M.C., et al.: Teaching a calligraphy robot via a touch screen. In: 2014 IEEE International Conference on Automation Science and Engineering (CASE), pp. 221–226. IEEE Computer Society, Taipei, Taiwan (2014)
8. Zhang, T.Y., Suen, C.Y.: A fast parallel algorithm for thinning digital patterns. Commun. ACM 27(3), 236–239 (1984)
9. Zhu, P., Chirlian, P.M.: On critical point detection of digital shapes. IEEE Trans. Pattern Anal. Mach. Intell. 17(8), 737–748 (1995)
10. Yang, L., Li, X.: Animating the brush-writing process of Chinese calligraphy characters. In: Eighth IEEE/ACIS International Conference on Computer & Information Science. IEEE, pp. 683–688. IEEE Computer Society, Shanghai, China (2009)
11. Shi, F.Z.: Computer-Aided Geometric Design and Non-uniform Rational B-Spline. Higher Education Press, Beijing (2001)
12. Perumaal, S., et al.: Synchronized trigonometric S-curve trajectory for jerk-bounded time-optimal pick and place operation. Int. J. Robot. Autom. 27(4), 385 (2012)

Robot Workspace Optimization
and Deformation Compensation in Grinding

Xiaoteng Zhang, Bing Chen$^{(\boxtimes)}$, Junde Qi, and Zhiyang Niu

School of Mechanical Engineering, Northwestern Polytechnical University,
Xi'an 710072, China
bingchen72@nwpu.edu.cn

Abstract. Industrial robots are becoming a key component of modern manu-facturing due to their flexibility and low-cost. However, the motion singularity and weak stiffness caused by the open series structure of the robot have a strong influence on its positioning accuracy and machining quality. In this paper, considering the dexterity and stiffness illustrated above, the method of work-space optimization and grinding deformation error compensation are utilized to improve the precision of the robot grinding. First of all, the robot dexterity analysis is carried out to obtain its dexterous workspace. And then, the work-space stiffness distribution is analyzed with the compliance ellipsoid model, which results in the acquisition of stiffer workspace. Finally, the characterization method of grinding normal deformation is proposed by setting the material removal rate as an index, and the way to compensate this deformation is brought out accordingly. A robot grinding experimental platform in this paper is set up based on KUKA KR210-2 to validate the method aforementioned. The accuracy is improved from 0.148 mm to 0.189 mm, which verifies the effectiveness of the proposed method.

Keywords: Robot grinding · Dexterity · Stiffness · Workspace optimization · Deformation compensation

1 Introduction

Industrial robots are widely used in modern manufacturing for their flexibility, oper-ability, low-cost and high efficiency. When robots are applied to high-precision machining (e.g. grinding, milling), the singularity and relatively low stiffness turn to be the main obstacle. The transmission relationship between the motion-input and the motion-output is distorted near the singular point. Compared to a machine tool with a stiffness greater than $50\,\mathrm{N}/\mu\mathrm{m}$, a 6 Degrees of Freedom (DOF) industrial robot usually has a stiffness of less than $1\,\mathrm{N}/\mu\mathrm{m}$, presenting a typical weak stiffness. These problems bring out inevitable impact on the positional accuracy and machining accuracy of the robot.

In order to solve these problems, domestic and foreign scholars have put forward a variety of methods to improve the machining performance and accuracy of robots. Yoshikawa [1] introduced the concept of operability to check if the robot is at a singular point. Angeles [2] utilized the condition number of the Jacobian matrix to

H. Yu et al. (Eds.): ICIRA 2019, LNAI 11745, pp. 97–109, 2019.
https://doi.org/10.1007/978-3-030-27529-7_9

measure the distance to the singular point. Zargarbashi [3] improved the joint velocity distribution with the metric condition of the reversibility for the Jacobian matrix to ensure a smoother joint space trajectory of stabilizing the attitude change during robot machining. Guo [4] proposed the performance index of the robot stiffness in the drilling system, namely the compliance ellipsoid, using a redundant degree of freedom in the machining of the 6-DOF robot to find the robot joint configuration with the best stiffness performance. Bu [5] defined the quantitative evaluation index of the end executive stiffness in the robot actuator towards the drilling direction. By optimizing the end attitude to guarantee the maximum performance, the hole depth and the hole axial accuracy could be ensured. Chen [6] defined a surface normal stiffness performance index (NSPI) to evaluate the robot Stiffness performance, and a robot attitude optimization model for adjusting the tool feed direction is established in view of the performance index. Slavkovic [7] proposed an off-line compensation method for the static displacement of the machining tool tip to refine the static displacement deviation of the tool tip caused by the cutting force. Wang [8] presented a practical method to compensate the robot deformation caused by the machining force. A feed forward compensation scheme is implemented in the robot controller.

As far as the author's knowledge of the literatures is concerned, the existed literatures mainly focus on Milling and drilling, while few researches have been made on the application of robot grinding. Moreover, most of the literatures only consider one of the factors to improve the machining accuracy, so there are few researches considering both the dexterity and stiffness of the robot simultaneously.

For the above-mentioned analyses, taking the robot dexterity and stiffness as the research objects, this paper centers on the method of how to optimize the workspace and how to compensate the deformation error of grinding force. Here is the main structure as below: Sect. 2 takes the Jacobian matrix condition number as the index to analyze the robot dexterity, and obtains the dexterous workspace of the robot, so on this basis, the compliance ellipsoid model is used to analyze the stiffness characteristics of the robot, and its stiffer workspace is brought out; Sect. 3 establishes the grinding material removal model with the index as material removal rate, and proposes the characterization method of grinding normal deformation whose error compensation method is constructed simultaneously; in Sect. 4, experiments are carried out to identify the joint stiffness of the robot and to verify the effectiveness of workspace optimization and deformation compensation for improving the grinding accuracy.

2   Robot Workspace Optimization

Given the singularity and low stiffness of the robot, this section intends to find the workspace with the best performance by considering both dexterity and stiffness. In the robot reachable workspace, the dexterity index is used to avoid the singularity and solve the dexterous workspace of the robot. On this basis, the stiffness characteristics of the robot are analyzed, and region with better stiffness in the dexterous workspace is obtained. This region is mapped from the joint space to the Cartesian space, resulting in an optimized robot workspace, i.e., the task space.

2.1 Robot Dexterity Analysis and Dexterous Workspace Solution

Serial industrial robot is a series of kinematic chains composed of links connected by joints. In this paper, Robot kinematics is established by the standard Denavit–Hartenberg (DH) model [9]. The DH model of KUKA KR210-2 is shown in Fig. 1, and the DH parameters are shown in Table 1. In order to ensure that the joint angle θ_i in the DH model is consistent with the actual joint angle θ_i' in the robot controller, θ_i needs to be corrected during the operation of the robot, as shown in Table 1, too.

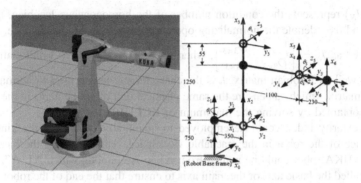

Fig. 1. DH model of the KUKA KR210-2 robot.

Table 1. DH parameters and joint angle correction of KUKA KR210-2.

θ_i	α_i (°)	a_i (mm)	d_i (mm)	θ_i range (°)	θ_i'
θ_1	−90	350	750	−185–+185	$\theta_1' = -\theta_1$
θ_2	0	1250	0	−146–+0	$\theta_2' = \theta_2$
θ_3	−90	−55	0	−209–+65	$\theta_3' = \theta_3 + 90°$
θ_4	90	0	1100	−350–+350	$\theta_4' = -\theta_4$
θ_5	−90	0	0	−125–+125	$\theta_5' = \theta_5$
θ_6	0	0	230	−530–+170	$\theta_6' = -\theta_6 - 180°$

The velocity transfer ratio of the joint space motion to the Cartesian space is represented by Jacobian matrix J, which depends heavily on the robot configuration. When $|J(q)| = 0$, the robot's end effector (EE) would lose one or more DOF, which is called the singular point of the robot. However, in the area near the singular point, the required joint speed will become so large that the transmission relationship between the motion input and the motion output is distorted, which will affect the accurate position control of the robot. In order to ensure the dexterity of the robot, it is essential to escape from not only the singularity but also to its area around. Therefore, the conditional number of Jacobian matrix is put into use to evaluate the robot dexterity, and its reciprocal can quantify the distance to singularities. The dexterity index, which is called the kinetostatic conditioning index (KCI) [10], is defined as:

$$\text{KCI} = \frac{1}{k(J_N)} \times 100\%, J_N \in R^{m \times n}, m \leq n$$

$$k(J_N) = \frac{1}{m} \sqrt{tr(J_N J_N^T) tr\left((J_N J_N^T)^{-1}\right)} \tag{1}$$

where $k(J_N)$ represents the condition number of the homogeneous Jacobian, the subscript N and $tr(\cdot)$ denote the normalizing operation as well as the matrix trace. And J_N is expressed as $J_N = \begin{bmatrix} \frac{1}{L} I_{3 \times 3} & O_{3 \times 3} \\ O_{3 \times 3} & I_{3 \times 3} \end{bmatrix}$, where $O_{3 \times 3}, I_{3 \times 3}, J$ are 3×3 null matrix, unit matrix as well as Jacobian matrix. L is the characteristic length used to normalize the Jacobian matrix, which can ensure the same physical unit of all the items in the matrix. L can be obtained by solving the maximum of KCI [10].

The dexterity index could be employed to quantitatively analyze the kinematics performance of the robot in the reachable workspace. And start with the base, the 6 joints of KUKA robot could be named from A1 to A6, among which A1, A2, A3 are the axes called the basic axis or the main axis to ensure that the end of the robot reaches any position in the working space, and A4, A5, A6 are called the wrist axis or the secondary axis to realize the space attitude of the robot end. In fact, the most important factor that affects its dexterity is the end position.

For the wrist of the robot (the latter three axes), the singular point appears when the 4th axis is parallel with the 6th one, which means A5 equals to zero. A quantitative analysis below is carried out on A5's angle to solve its un-singularity range. Set the joint angles of A1, A2, A3, A6 as 0°, −90°, 0°, 0° (all angles mentioned below are DH model angles), discrete θ_4, θ_5 in the joint workspace, treat KCI as the index, and draw the contour map as shown in Fig. 2(a). It is obvious to see from this figure that the dark blue, which indicate the extraordinary poor dexterity at this time, is displayed at 0 and its neighborhood, thereby verifying the analysis of the wrist singularity aforementioned. The robot is considered to have good dexterity when KCI is above 0.4. So, as can be seen from Fig. 2(a), the boundary value of θ_5 is 0.7156 rad, and the angle range of A5 is [−125°, −41°] and [41°, 125°].

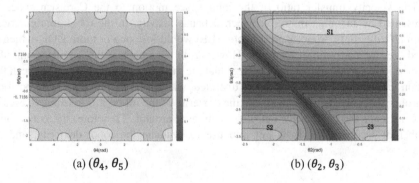

(a) (θ_4, θ_5) (b) (θ_2, θ_3)

Fig. 2. Dexterity contour map. (Color figure online)

As for the basic axis A1, A2 and A3, the rotation of A1 does not affect the dexterity. Set the joint angles of A1, A4, A5, A6 as 0°, −45°, 60°, 0°, discrete θ_2, θ_3 in the joint space, and the contour map could be plotted analogically, as shown in Fig. 2 (b), which indicates that the relatively high dexterity of the joint space is concentrated in regions S1, S2 and S3 whose range of joint angle is listed in Table 2.

Table 2. Joint angle range of S1, S2, S3.

Joint angle	Region		
	S1	S2	S3
θ_2	−118.03°–0°	−90°−−146.11°	−37.52°–0°
θ_3	−25.66°–65°	−209°−−147.25°	−209°−−138.08°

(a)   (b)   (c)

Fig. 3. Typical posture of three regions (a) P1 (b) P2 (c) P3.

As shown in Fig. 3, the typical posture of the robots in each region are selected as P1 $(\theta_2 = −65°, \theta_3 = 10°)$, P2 $(\theta_2 = −120°, \theta_3 = −190°)$ and P3 $(\theta_2 = −35°, \theta_3 = −190°)$. The posture of P2 and P3 have a negative angle rotation of A3, which is necessary in some machining scenes in practical applications. P1's posture matches more with the machining scene in this paper, so S1 is chosen as the dexterity area, which could be mapped from the joint space to the Cartesian space by kinematics, as the red area of Fig. 4(b), and this is the dexterous workspace of the robot-end.

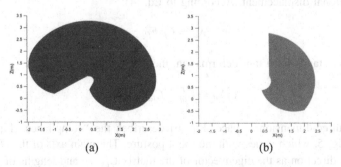

(a)   (b)

Fig. 4. Robot workspace (a) Reachable workspace (b) Dexterous workspace. (Color figure online)

2.2 Robot Stiffness Characteristics Analysis and Stiffer Workspace Solution

To simplify the establishment of the boundary conditions, the following assumptions are proposed: (a) the stiffness of the actuators and transmission components is the main source of the robot stiffness and can be represented by the linear torsion spring for each joint; (b) the active stiffness in actuators due to the robot position control system is time-invariant; (c) the links are infinitely stiff [11].

Salisbbury [12] established the traditional stiffness model of robot using Virtual joint method (VJM):

$$K = J^{-T} K_\theta J^{-1} \tag{2}$$

where K is the robot Cartesian stiffness matrix, J is the robot Jacobian matrix, K_θ is the robot joint stiffness matrix containing six joint stiffness values.

From Eq. (2), the relationship between the six-dimensional force vector F acting at the end of the robot and the end deformation vector dX could be presented as:

$$dX = CF = K^{-1}F = JK_\theta^{-1}J^T F \tag{3}$$

The compliance matrix C here is to avoid the inverse operation of the Jacobian matrix. Since the elements of C are not necessarily dimensionally homogeneous, the force, the moment, the translational displacement, and the rotational displacement are considered separately so that C should be divided into four parts as Eq. (4):

$$\begin{bmatrix} X_d \\ X_\delta \end{bmatrix} = \begin{bmatrix} C_{fd} & C_{md} \\ C_{f\delta} & C_{m\delta} \end{bmatrix} \begin{bmatrix} F_f \\ F_m \end{bmatrix} \tag{4}$$

where F_f, F_m are the end force and moment, respectively. X_d, X_δ are the end translational and rotational displacement, respectively, and C_{fd}, $C_{f\delta}$, C_{md} and $C_{m\delta}$ are 3×3 force-translational, force-rotational, moment-translational and moment-rotational compliance matrices. Considering that the rotational displacement of the tool is negligible compared to the translational one during machining, and the torque acting at the tool end can be ignored [13], here we mainly focus on the relationship between force and translational displacement. According to Eq. (4):

$$X_d = C_{fd} F_f \tag{5}$$

When X_d stands for a unit deformation, then

$$X_d^T X_d = C_{fd}^T F_f^T C_{fd} F_f = 1 \tag{6}$$

In the three-dimensional space, Eq. (6) describes the "compliance ellipsoid" as shown in Fig. 5, which varies with the robot posture. The main axis of the ellipsoid is in the same direction as the eigenvector of the matrix $C_{fd}^T C_{fd}$, and lengths of the semi-axes are equal to its eigenvalues λ_1, λ_2 and λ_3, individually. The compliance ellipsoid

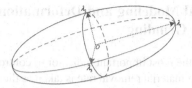

Fig. 5. Compliance ellipsoid.

reflects the overall compliance of the robot in a certain posture, and its overall compliance is proportional to the volume of the ellipsoid. Based on this property, Guo [4] defined the performance index of the robot stiffness (K_s) as:

$$K_s = \frac{1}{\sqrt[3]{det(C_{fd})}} = \frac{1}{\sqrt[3]{det(J_{11}K_{11}^{-1}J_{11}^T + J_{12}K_{22}^{-1}J_{12}^T)}} \tag{7}$$

where $J = \begin{bmatrix} J_{11} & J_{12} \\ J_{21} & J_{22} \end{bmatrix}$, $K_\theta = \begin{bmatrix} K_{11} & K_{12} \\ K_{21} & K_{22} \end{bmatrix}$. The larger K_s is, the stiffer the robot is. Since the robot stiffness is mainly affected by the end position, and the latter three axes need to ensure the tool axis vector during machining, so only the angle ranges of A2 and A3 are optimized here to obtain the position with better stiffness. With the joint stiffness values identified in Sect. 4.1, θ_2 and θ_3 could be discrete in the joint space within the scope of S1 in Sect. 2.1 to achieve the stiffness contour map depicted in Fig. 6(a).

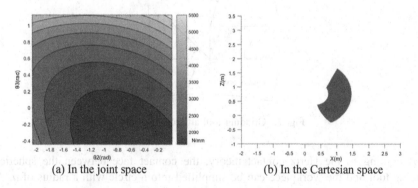

(a) In the joint space   (b) In the Cartesian space

Fig. 6. Stiffness contour map (Color figure online)

For the sake of ensuring the robot's large workspace, the region that Ks above 3000 N/mm is defined as stiffer region. The joint angle range $\theta_2(-118°-0°)$ and $\theta_3(22.52°-65°)$ is mapped to Cartesian space as the red region in Fig. 6(b), namely the stiffer workspace of the robot, in other words, the task space at the end of the robot where the robot holds a relatively better dexterity and stiffness during manufacturing.

3 Material Removal Modeling and Deformation Compensation in Grinding

Material removal depth is the most important indicator to control the grinding accuracy. In this section, the grinding material removal rate is taken as the control object, and error compensation is carried out in the optimized workspace further. Material removal model is established at the first step to reveal that the removal depth is related to the normal grinding force. At the same time, the characterization method of grinding normal deformation is proposed, and so that the deformation of the robot is compensated.

3.1 Grinding Material Removal Depth Model

In the modeling field of grinding material removal rate modeling, the Preston equation is the most prevalent model. On the basis of this model, the material removal depth per unit length w_p could be defined as Eq. (8):

$$w_P = \frac{dh}{dl} = k_p p_c \frac{v_s}{v_a} \tag{8}$$

where p_c represents the normal pressure of the contact area, v_s is the relative speed of the contact area between the grinding tool and the workpiece, v_a is the feed rate, k_p is the coefficient of the Preston equation which is related to the working environment.

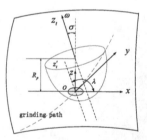

Fig. 7. Grinding tool attitude diagram.

According to the Hertz contact theory, the contact face between the spherical grinding tool and the workpiece can be simplified into a circle with a radius of a. As shown in Fig. 7, set the normal direction of the grinding path as the x-axis, the tangential one as the y-axis, and the contact point as the origin of coordinate, then the coordinate system O-xyz is established. And the pressure distribution in the area could be calculated as Eq. (9):

$$p(x,y) = -\frac{p_0}{a}\sqrt{a^2 - x^2 - y^2} \tag{9}$$

where p_0 is the pressure at the center of the polishing area and $p_0 = \frac{3F_n}{2\pi a^2}$. It is convenient to find out that the grinding removal depth is only related to the normal grinding force F_n. When the spherical grinding tool with radius R is grinded in the posture shown in Fig. 7, the angle formed between the tool axis Z_t and the workpiece surface could be expressed as a function containing forward angle σ and a side angle λ. Then the speed of any point in the contact area could be determined as:

$$v_s = \omega_p \sqrt{\left(-R_p \sin \lambda \, \sin \sigma - \cos \sigma y\right)^2 + \left(x \cos \sigma + R_p \cos \lambda \, \sin \sigma\right)^2} \quad (10)$$

where R_p is the distance from the tool axis and $R_p = \sqrt{R^2 - a^2}$. ω_p is the tool rotation angular velocity. For the integration of w_p over the length of 2a, the removal depth at the contact point could be brought out as Eq. (11):

$$h = \int_{-a}^{a} w_p dy \quad (11)$$

Substituting Eqs. (8), (9) and (10) in Eq. (11), there results,

$$h = -\frac{3k_p F_n \omega_p}{\pi v_a a^3} \int_0^a \sqrt{(a^2 - y^2) \cdot \left[\left(-R_p \sin \lambda \, \sin \sigma - \cos \sigma y\right)^2 + \left(x \cos \sigma + R_p \cos \lambda \, \sin \sigma\right)^2\right]} \, dy$$

$$(12)$$

In accordance with Ref. [14], the tangential grinding force F_t and the radial grinding force F_r are proportional to F_n, where $F_t = 0.26F_n$ and $F_r = 0.74F_n$. And Eq. (12) shows that the normal grinding force has a linear correlation with h. Since the grinding force causes the deformation and affects the removal depth, the normal deformation compensation research will be performed in Sect. 3.2.

3.2 Normal Deformation Compensation

In the robot task space, the dexterity and stiffness during grinding are greatly improved, but under the action of the grinding force, the joint will still be deformed and positional deviation will occur at the EE. To obtain a more precise removal depth, the normal deformation produced at the robot end is compensated towards in the removal depth direction.

For robot programming and calculation convenience, the robot tool center point (TCP) is established at the grinding path point whose feed direction is the x-axis, and vertical one is the y-axis. The conversion matrix between TCP and the six-axis end coordinate system Tool0 is:

$$^{Tool0}_{tcp}T = \begin{bmatrix} ^{Tool0}_{tcp}R & ^{Tool0}P_{tcp} \\ 0 & 1 \end{bmatrix} \quad (13)$$

The relationship between the grinding force and deformation at EE and the force and deformation at the robot end could be presented as Eqs. (14) and (15):

$$F_{grinding} = {}^{Tool0}_{tcp}T_f F \tag{14}$$

$$dX_{tcp} = {}^{Tool0}_{tcp}T_d dX \tag{15}$$

where ${}^{Tool0}_{tcp}T_f$, ${}^{Tool0}_{tcp}T_d$ are the force and deformation transformation matrices,

$$
{}^{Tool0}_{tcp}T_f = \begin{bmatrix} {}^{Tool0}_{tcp}R & 0 \\ S\left({}^{Tool0}P_{tcp}\right){}^{Tool0}_{tcp}R & {}^{Tool0}_{tcp}R \end{bmatrix}
$$

$$
{}^{Tool0}_{tcp}T_d = \begin{bmatrix} {}^{Tool0}_{tcp}R & S\left({}^{Tool0}P_{tcp}\right){}^{Tool0}_{tcp}R \\ 0 & {}^{Tool0}_{tcp}R \end{bmatrix} \tag{16}
$$

$S\left({}^{Tool0}P_{tcp}\right)$ is the antisymmetric matrix of ${}^{Tool0}P_{tcp} = [p_x, p_y, p_z]^T$. Combining Eqs. (3), (14) and (15), the deformation at EE could be expressed as:

$$dX_{tcp} = {}^{Tool0}_{tcp}T_d J K_\theta^{-1} J^T {}^{Tool0}_{tcp}T_f^{-1} F_{grinding} \tag{17}$$

The normal deformation at the end effector (Δh) is also the main factor affecting the removal depth, as shown in Eq. (18):

$$\Delta h = \vec{n} dX_{tcp} \tag{18}$$

where $\vec{n}$ is the normal vector of the workpiece surface. The normal deformation is compensated to the end position of the robot to obtain a new end position, and then the compensated grinding path would be obtained eventually.

4 Experiments and Discussion

4.1 Robot Joint Stiffness Identification

Figure 8(a) shows the KUKA KR210-2 robot joint stiffness identification experimental setup. ATI Omega 160 six-dimensional force sensor (range ±1000 N, ±120 Nm, accuracy 0.0 1N, 0.0 1Nm) is installed at the end of the robot to measure the loading force. The amount of deformation is measured by API T3 laser tracker (accuracy 15 μm). 36 kinds of measurement postures are selected in the dexterous workspace of the robot.

The experimental procedure could be divided into two steps: (1) Move the robot end to the specified position and record the coordinate values of the target ball at this time; (2) After the workpiece is placed, the end should be moved to the same position to contact the workpiece, and the robot is deformed by the reaction force, then collect the force signal at this time and record the coordinate values again, and the deviation

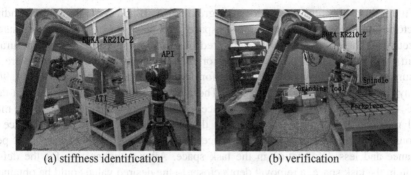

(a) stiffness identification   (b) verification

Fig. 8. Robot experimental setup.

between the values measured twice is the deformation at the target ball. The measured force and deformation are converted from the coordinate of ATI and the target ball to the six-axis end coordinate system, respectively. With the Eq. (5), the stiffness of the six joints K_θ is identified as $diag([3.84 \times 10^9, 2.08 \times 10^{10}, 1.32 \times 10^9, 5.43 \times 10^8, 4.91 \times 10^8, 3.22 \times 10^8])$Nmm/rad.

4.2 Workspace Optimization and Deformation Compensation Verification

Grinding experiments were performed on the KUKA KR210-2 robotic grinding platform with a NSK E400 electric spindle. The experimental setup is shown in Fig. 8(b). The workpiece material is Ti-6Al-4 V. Grinding tool is a 10 mm diameter Besdia diamond spherical grinding head. The process parameters could be selected as $\omega_p = 8000$ rpm, $v_a = 1$ mm/s, $\lambda = 0°$, $\sigma = 30°$ and the desired grinding depth be selected as $h = 0.2$ mm. The experiment is divided into three groups: (1) grind in the non-task space; (2) grind in the task space; (3) grind in the task space with the normal deformation compensated. Each group is implemented for five times.

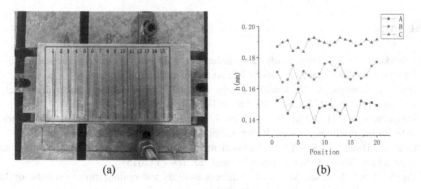

(a)   (b)

Fig. 9. (a) Grinded workpiece (b) Removal depth of three different grinding groups

Figure 9(a) shows the workpiece after grinding, A, B and C are the set of grinding trajectories in the non-task space, task space and task space being compensated, respectively. The removal depth is measured by Alicona Infinite Focus G4 (accuracy 10 nm), with four control points discrete for each grinding trajectory, so there are 20 measurements for each set of experiments for depth removal the. Meanwhile, Fig. 9(b) displays the removal depth in Fig. 9(a). The average removal depth in the non-task space (A), task space (B) and task space being compensated (C) is 0.148 mm, 0.171 mm and 0.189 mm, which means that the removal depth in task space is obviously better than that of non-task space, that is to say, the robot has better performance and less deformation in the task space. After compensating for the deformation in the task space, a removal depth closer to the desired value could be obtained, which could prove that the deformation compensation can obtain a more accurate removal depth.

5 Conclusions

1. Considering the singularity and low stiffness of the robot, this paper works out the workspace with the best performance by considering both dexterity and stiffness. The optimized dexterous workspace and the stiffer workspace are obtained.
2. To control the grinding accuracy, material removal depth model is established. At the same time, the characterization method of grinding normal deformation is proposed, and the normal deformation is compensated accordingly.
3. The joint stiffness of the KUKA KR210-2 robot is obtained with joint stiffness identification experiments. And a further experiment is carried out to verify the effectiveness of grinding in the optimized workspace and with the deformation compensation for improving its precision.

Acknowledgements. This work was supported by China Scholarship Council (No. 201706295033) and the National Science and Technology Major Project of the Ministry of Science and Technology of China (Grant No. 2017ZX04011011).

References

1. Yoshikawa, T.: Manipulability and redundancy control of robotic mechanisms. In: International Conference on Robotics & Automation. IEEE (2003)
2. Angeles, J., Rojas, A.: Manipulator inverse kinematics via condition-number minimization and continuation. Int. J. Robot. Autom. **2**(2), 61–69 (1987)
3. Zargarbashi, S.H.H., Khan, W., Angeles, J.: The Jacobian condition number as a dexterity index in 6R machining robots. Robot. Comput. Integr. Manuf. **28**(6), 694–699 (2012)
4. Guo, Y., Dong, H., Ke, Y.: Stiffness-oriented posture optimization in robotic machining applications. Robot. Comput. Integr. Manuf. **35**, 69–76 (2015)
5. Bu, Y., Liao, W., Tian, W., et al.: Stiffness analysis and optimization in robotic drilling application. Precis. Eng. **49**, 388–400 (2017)

6. Chen, C., Peng, F., Yan, R., et al.: Stiffness performance index based posture and feed orientation optimization in robotic milling process. Robot. Comput. Integr. Manuf. **55**, 29–40 (2019)
7. Slavkovic, N.R., Milutinovic, D.S., Glavonjic, M.M.: A method for off-line compensation of cutting force-induced errors in robotic machining by tool path modification. Int. J. Adv. Manuf. Technol. **70**(9–12), 2083–2096 (2014)
8. Wang, J., Zhang, H., Fuhlbrigge, T.: Improving machining accuracy with robot deformation compensation. In: IEEE/RSJ International Conference on Intelligent Robots & Systems. IEEE Press (2009)
9. Hartenberg, R., Denavit, J.: Kinematic Synthesis of Linkages. McGraw-Hill Book Company, New York (1964)
10. Lin, Y., Zhao, H., Ding, H.: Posture optimization methodology of 6R industrial robots for machining using performance evaluation indexes. Robot. Comput. Integr. Manuf. **48**, 59–72 (2017)
11. Alici, G., Shirinzadeh, B.: Enhanced stiffness modeling, identification and characterization for robot manipulators. IEEE Trans. Robot. **21**(4), 554–564 (2005)
12. Salisbury, J.K.: Active stiffness control of a manipulator in cartesian coordinates. In: IEEE Conference on Decision & Control (1980)
13. Zargarbashi, S.H.H., Khan, W., Angeles, J.: Posture optimization in robot-assisted machining operations. Mech. Mach. Theory **51**, 74–86 (2012)
14. Ren, J., Hua, D.: Grinding Principle. Publishing House of Electronics Industry, Beijing (2011)

A Methodology for Multi-goal Trajectory Planning in Welding

Nianfeng Wang, Yaoqiang He$^{(\boxtimes)}$, and Xianmin Zhang

Guangdong Provincial Key Laboratory of Precision Equipment
and Manufacturing Technology, School of Mechanical and Automotive Engineering,
South China University of Technology, Guangzhou 510640, China
menfwang@scut.edu.cn, xiaoqiangscut@163.com

Abstract. In this paper, a methodology is proposed for multi-goal trajectory planning in welding, which is divided into effective movements
and supporting movements. For effective movements, four objective functions are defined to describe the task requirements. A non-dominated
sorting genetic algorithm (NSGA-II) is used to get the optimum solution. For supporting movements, the classical algorithm RRT-Connect is
adopted to find a minimum-time trajectory and a smoothing algorithm
is proposed to remove the redundant vertices. A simulation is presented
to show that the proposed algorithms are effective and an experiment
is conducted to illustrate that the trajectories meet the welding requirements.

Keywords: Trajectory planning · Multi-goal · Welding ·
Smoothing algorithm

1 Introduction

Industrial robots play an important role in industrial assembly lines and manufacturing systems. It is difficult for robot teaching while considering the task
requirements, so trajectory planning makes a great difference. Voluminous studies have been conducted to address the trajectory planning for the optimization
on minimum time [1,2], minimum energy [3], minimum jerk [4,5], or combining
two of them [6–8].

As for welding, the multi-goal trajectory planning is mainly divided into
two parts according to the robotic movements. One includes movements that
are required for welding, which are called effective movements. And the movements between every two effective movements are called supporting movements.
Supporting movements are not directly needed for welding. However, they are
necessary to sequence one effective movement after the other, which means that
they would move the robot from one welding seam to another [9]. The movements are shown in Fig. 1. Movements ② and ④ are effective movements, while
①, ③ and ⑤ are supporting movements.

© Springer Nature Switzerland AG 2019
H. Yu et al. (Eds.): ICIRA 2019, LNAI 11745, pp. 110–123, 2019.
https://doi.org/10.1007/978-3-030-27529-7_10

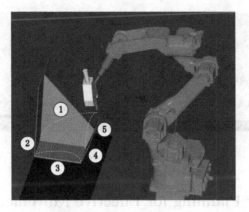

Fig. 1. Robotic movements

For effective movements, a geometric path is given from the workpiece, providing the position as constraints, which makes the trajectory planning in operating space. The speed of the welding torch is predefined so the executing time is constant. The force on the welding torch can be ignored. The optimization objective is not merely the time, jerk or energy. Therefore, some welding requirements should also be considered.

For supporting movements, two geometric points are given. One is at the end of the current weld seam and the other is at the beginning of the next weld seam. The planning is mainly to find a minimum-time trajectory from one point to another without collision. The previous studies about point-to-point trajectory planning are mainly classified into categoriesgrid-based trajectory planning and sample-based trajectory planning. Dijkstra algorithm [10], A* algorithm and some of their improvement [11–13] are widely used for grid-based trajectory planning. It would be hard to build a grid map according to the environment and avoid kinematic singularities and manipulator redundancy in the operating space of 6R robot, so sample-based trajectory planning is preferred in joint space. Rapidly-exploring random trees(RRT) [14] is a classical sample-based trajectory planning and some of its modifications are proposed [15,16]. After getting a trajectory, some post-process smoothing algorithms are used to get a smooth path [17,18]. The executing time of the smoothing algorithms above is long because there are many collision detections between the robot and the obstacle. In order to reduce the executing time, a new post-process smoothing algorithm will be proposed in this paper. The trajectory may not be the minimum-time one but it is qualified.

The rest of this paper is organized as follows. Section 2 describes the trajectory planning for effective movements, where the objective functions of welding are given and NSGA-II is used. Section 3 describes the trajectory planning for supporting movements, from which a new post-process smoothing algorithm is proposed. The simulation, experiment, and conclusion are presented in Sects. 4 and 5.

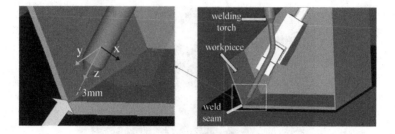

Fig. 2. Effective movements

2   Trajectory Planning for Effective Movements

2.1   Problem Formulation

In this paper, it is assumed that the geometric path is generated by discretizing the weld seam, which provides the initial positions of the welding torch. During effective movements, the distance between the welding torch and the weld seam should be less than 3 mm and the z-axis of the tool coordinate must point to the weld seam, which is shown in Fig. 2. Therefore, the position of the welding torch can be calculated once the orientation is given. And the trajectory can be obtained if the orientations of two geometric points are given in linear interpolation or three geometric points in circular interpolation.

After the analysis above, the trajectory planning for effective movements is to find the suitable orientations of two geometric points in linear interpolation or three geometric points in circular interpolation, from which a sequence of geometric points are generated and the welding robot should meet the constraints while moving along the points successively. Considering the task requirements and collision avoidance, four objective functions are proposed.

Hence, the optimal trajectory planning problem can be formulated as

$$
\begin{cases}
find: \\
\max \ \mathbf{F}\left(\mathbf{X}\right) = \left[\mathbf{f_1}\left(\mathbf{X}\right), \mathbf{f_2}\left(\mathbf{X}\right), \mathbf{f_3}\left(\mathbf{X}\right), \mathbf{f_4}\left(\mathbf{X}\right)\right]^{\mathbf{T}} \\
subject\ to: \\
\mathbf{X}_{\min} \leq \mathbf{X} \leq \mathbf{X}_{\max}
\end{cases}
\tag{1}
$$

where $\mathbf{F}\left(\mathbf{X}\right)$ is a vector of four objective functions, $\mathbf{X}$ is a vector of the optimization variables, which $\mathbf{X} = \left[\alpha_1, \beta_1, \gamma_1, \alpha_2, \beta_2, \gamma_2\right]^{\mathbf{T}}$ in linear interpolation while $\mathbf{X} = \left[\alpha_1, \beta_1, \gamma_1, \alpha_2, \beta_2, \gamma_2, \alpha_3, \beta_3, \gamma_3\right]^{\mathbf{T}}$ in circular interpolation, and α, β, γ represent the RPY angles.

2.2   Getting the Initial Trajectory

Without considering the obstacle, the fittest trajectory for welding is called the initial trajectory in this paper. Relative to a point of the geometric path, the z-axis of the tool coordinate should be in the angular bisector of two planes

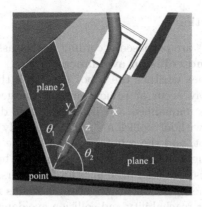

Fig. 3. The pose of the welding torch

adjacent to the weld seam. And the y-axis of the tool coordinate should be parallel to the tangent line at the point. The x-axis is the cross product of the z-axis and the y-axis. As shown in Fig. 3, θ_1 is equal to θ_2. The z-axis of the welding torch points to the specified point and the y-axis is parallel to the tangent line at the point. The distance between the end of the welding torch and the point is 3 mm. Therefore, for each point of the geometric path, the corresponding positions and orientations of the welding torch can be obtained, which builds up the initial trajectory. Usually, the first point and the last point are needed for linear interpolation, the rest can be calculated by interpolation algorithm and a middle point should be added for circular interpolation.

2.3   The Range of the Optimization Variable

It is assumed that the final trajectory should be as similar to the initial trajectory as possible. The smaller the variation of the orientation is, the better the final trajectory will be. Therefore, for linear interpolation, the optimization variable can be defined as

$$\mathbf{X}' = [\alpha_1', \beta_1', \gamma_1', \alpha_2', \beta_2', \gamma_2']^T \tag{2}$$

where $\alpha_1', \beta_1', \gamma_1', \alpha_2', \beta_2', \gamma_2'$ are the variations of the RPY angle of the welding torch at the first point and the last point. Considering the welding requirement, the range of the optimization variable is set to

$$\begin{cases} -30 \le \alpha_1' \le 30 \\ -20 \le \beta_1' \le 40 \\ -180 \le \gamma_1' \le 180 \\ -30 \le \alpha_2' \le 30 \\ -20 \le \beta_2' \le 40 \\ -180 \le \gamma_2' \le 180 \end{cases} \tag{3}$$

2.4   Objective Function

Four objective functions are proposed according to the task requirements.

1. Reachability and collision avoidance

Reachability describes whether the robot can track the weld seam during welding. Singularity may occur at some points of the geometric path, which means the trajectory is unqualified. Collision avoidance describes if the robot tracks the weld seam without collision. Collision usually occurs between the workpiece and the robot, and the robot links may collide with each other. For security, collision is thought to happen if the least distance between the workpiece and the welding torch is less than 0.1 mm. And for others, such as robot links and the workpiece or the robot links themselves, 20 mm is necessary. Therefore, the optimizing index for reachability and collision avoidance is given as

$$f_r = \frac{n_r + n_c}{2N} \tag{4}$$

where n_r and n_c represent the number of the geometric points which the robot can reach and track without collision, N represents the number of the geometric points.

2. Manipulability measure

Manipulability measure indicates the ability of the robot to move and suffer the forces from arbitrary directions. Yoshikawa proposed a measure of manipulability based on the Jacobian of the robot, which is used in this paper [19].

$$f_m = \frac{\sum\limits_{i=1}^{n} w_i}{N} \tag{5}$$

$$w_i = \sqrt{\det J_i\left(\theta\right) J_i^T\left(\theta\right)} \tag{6}$$

where w_i is defined as Eq. (6), representing the manipulability measure of the robot at the ith point, N represents the number of the geometric points.

3. Smoothness

Smoothness describes the variation of the joint. It is assumed that the smaller the variation is, the smoother the motion will be. For the first 3 joints, the motion of them will make a great difference to the end effector, so the weight of each joint should be taken into account.

$$f_s = \sum_{j=1}^{d} r_j \left(1 - \sum_{i=2}^{N} \frac{|q_{i,j} - q_{i-1,j}|}{|q_{j\,\max} - q_{j\,\min}|}\right) \tag{7}$$

where $q_{i,j}$ represents the jth joint of the robot at the ith point, $q_{j\,\min}$ and $q_{j\,\max}$ represent the lower boundary and the upper boundary of the jth joint, r_j represents the weight of the jth joint, d represents the degree of freedom (DOF) of the robot, N represents the number of the geometric points.

4. Welding quality

Welding quality mainly depends on the position and the orientation of the welding torch at a specific speed. The pitch angle and the yaw angle have a great effort on welding quality while the roll angle does not, so the weights of α' and β' should be bigger than that of the γ'. During welding, a better weld seam will be formed if the pitch angle and the yaw angle keep the same, so the difference between α'_1 and α'_2 or β'_1 and β'_2 should be as small as possible. And the orientation of the trajectory mainly depends on α'_1 and β'_1. The objective function for welding quality can be given as

$$
\begin{aligned}
f_w =0.7 \times &\left(\left(1 - \frac{\alpha'_1}{\alpha'_{\max} - \alpha'_{\min}} \right) \times 0.4 + \left(1 - \frac{\beta'_1}{\beta'_{\max} - \beta'_{\min}} \right) \times 0.4 + \right. \\
&\left. \left(1 - \frac{\gamma'_1}{\gamma'_{\max} - \gamma'_{\min}} \right) \times 0.2 \right) + \\
0.3 \times &\left(\left(1 - \frac{|\alpha'_2 - \alpha'_1|}{\alpha'_{\max} - \alpha'_{\min}} \right) \times 0.4 + \left(1 - \frac{|\beta'_2 - \beta'_1|}{\beta'_{\max} - \beta'_{\min}} \right) \times 0.4 + \right. \\
&\left. \left(1 - \frac{|\gamma'_2 - \gamma'_1|}{\gamma'_{\max} - \gamma'_{\min}} \right) \times 0.2 \right)
\end{aligned}
\tag{8}
$$

where $\alpha'_{\max}$, $\alpha'_{\min}$, $\beta'_{\max}$, $\beta'_{\min}$, $\gamma'_{\max}$, $\gamma'_{\max}$ are the boundaries of α', β', γ'.

2.5   Optimization Algorithm

NSGA-II (Deb et al. 2002) is widely used for solving multi-objective problems. It builds a population of competing individuals, ranks and sorts each individual according to nondomination level. The crowding distance in selection operator is used to keep a diverse front by making sure each member stays a crowding distance apart, which keeps the population diverse and helps the algorithm to explore the fitness landscape.

A solution will be chosen from the Pareto optimal set according to the evaluation, which is shown in Eq. (9). For each objective function, the value range is $[0, 1]$. If the value of the objective function for reachability and collision avoidance is less than 1, which means that the robot cannot reach some geometric points or somewhere the collision occurs, the trajectory is thought to be unqualified. In this situation, other objective functions are meaningless, which are set to 0.

$$
f_{eva} = \begin{cases} f_r & , \ if \ f_r < 1 \\ 1 + w_1 f_m + w_2 f_s + w_3 f_w & , \ if \ f_r = 1 \end{cases}
\tag{9}
$$

where w_1, w_2, w_3 are the weights of the objective functions.

3   Trajectory Planning for Supporting Movements

Supporting movements aims to find a minimum-time trajectory. Two geometric points are given from the welding seam and the relevant position and orientation of the welding torch are obtained according to Sect. 2. It is the collision avoidance that needs taking into account. Since there are no constraints of the positions or orientations, planning the trajectory in the joint space rather than in the operating space has a major advantage, which would allow avoiding the problems arising with kinematic singularities and manipulator redundancy. The widely known algorithm Rapidly-exploring Random Trees (RRT) is an efficient randomized algorithm for solving single-query path planning problems in high-dimensional configuration spaces. In order to speed up the search, the RRT-Connect is adopted in this paper, which works by incrementally building two RRTs rooted at the start and the goal configurations.

3.1   RRT-Connect

A brief description of RRT-Connect will be addressed. T_a and T_b represent two Rapidly-exploring Random Trees growing from initial and goal state respectively. The state space can be represented by the set C and the state $q \in C$ represents a configuration of the robot. $C_{obs} \subset C$ represents the obstacle configuration space where the collision occurs. $C_{free} = C/C_{obs}$ represents the traversable states of the robot. E_a and V_a represent the edges and vertices of the tree $T_a \subset C_{free}$, and similarly for the tree $T_b \subset C_{free}$. A solution of the problem means that T_a and T_b must be connected, shown as

$$T_a \cap T_b \neq \emptyset \tag{10}$$

3.2   Smoothing

There may be some redundant vertices in the path connecting T_a to T_b. Therefore, smoothing plays an important role in reducing the length of the path by removing the redundant vertices. If the robot moves from one vertex to another by joint interpolation without collision, the vertices between them are thought to be redundant. As shown in Fig. 4, the collision will not occur if the robot moves from q_{init} to q_9 by joint interpolation, so $q_1, q_2, \ldots, q_8$ are regarded as redundant vertices. The smoothing algorithm is proposed in Algorithm 1. The shortest distance between the robot at a specific state and the obstacle is used as the evaluation criterion. An adaptive threshold based on the shortest distance is proposed to decide whether a vertex is qualified. The algorithm searches from q_{goal}, finding a vertex q_{cur} when the robot moves from q_{init} to it without collision. Then, a threshold is obtained according to the evaluation of the vertices between q_{init} and q_{cur}. A qualified vertex q_{qua} will be chosen and the redundant vertices between q_{init} and q_{qua} are removed. The algorithm repeats until q_{goal} is chosen. The process of smoothing is shown in Fig. 5.

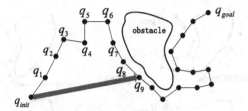

Fig. 4. Redundant vertices

Algorithm 1. Smoothness

---

1 $N_{init} = 1$;
2 $N_{end} = $ PATH.SIZE;
3 **while** $(N_{init} < N_{end})$ **do**
4   **for** $i = N_{end}$ to N_{init} **do**
5   **if** $COLLISION\_FREE(N_{init}, i)$ **then**
6   break;
7   **if** $(i = N_{end})$ **then**
8   NEWPATH.ADD(N_{end});
9   **return** NEWPATH;
10     $S_{min} \leftarrow$ GET_MIN(N_{init}, i);
11     $S_{avg} \leftarrow$ GET_AVERAGE(N_{init}, i);
12     $S_{thr} = S_{min} + (S_{avg} - S_{min}) * S_{weight}$ $(0 \leq S_{weight} \leq 1)$;
13   **for** $k = i$ to N_{init} **do**
14   **if** $EVALUATE(k) \leq S_{thr}$ **then**
15   NEWPATH.ADD(k);
16   break;
17   **if** $(k = N_{init})$ **then**
18   NEWPATH.ADD($k + 1$);
19         $N_{init} = k$;
20   **else**
21         $N_{init} = k + 1$;

---

4 Simulation and Experiment

The trajectories of effective movements and supporting movements will be shown
in this section according to the algorithm proposed above. A 6R industrial robot,
Motoman MH12 and a workpiece with 4 weld seams are used for the experiment.
The robot and the workpiece are placed as Fig. 6(a). A simulation environment
is established as shown in Fig. 6(b).

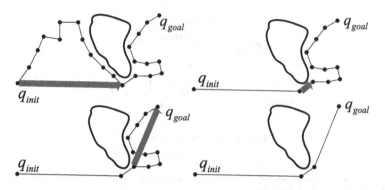

Fig. 5. The process of smoothing

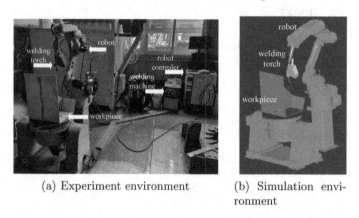

(a) Experiment environment

(b) Simulation environment

Fig. 6. Experiment environment and simulation environment

4.1 Effective Movements

Take a weld seam for an example, as shown in Fig. 7. NSGA-II proposed above is used to get the Pareto front, which is shown in Fig. 8. The size of the population is set to 50; the crossover rate is set to 0.8 and the mutation rate is set to 0.05. After 100 generations, a solution is shown in Fig. 9. The orientations of the welding torch at the first point and the last point of the weld seam are obtained and the positions are calculated subjected to the constraints. The poses at the rest points of the weld seam are obtained by linear interpolation according to these two points. The robot can reach each point of the weld seam without collision while meeting the task requirements. Figure 10 shows the angle variation of six joints and each joint moves smoothly without sudden changes, which means no singularities occur. Figure 11 shows the variation of the pitch angle, the yaw angle and the roll angle of the welding torch. These three angles change in a small range which remains the orientation of the welding torch almost the same and benefits the weld quality.

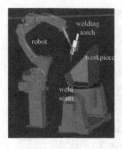

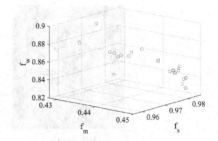

Fig. 7. Example for effective movement

Fig. 8. Pareto front

(a) Pose at the 1st point   (b) Pose at the 10th point   (c) Pose at the last point

Fig. 9. Process of effective movements

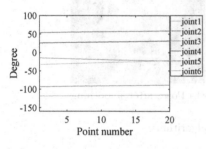
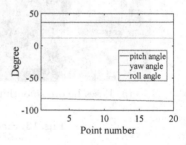

Fig. 10. Angle variation of 6 joints   **Fig. 11.** Variation of RPY angles

4.2 Supporting Movements

Figure 12(a)(d) shows the poses at the end of a weld seam and the beginning of the next weld seam, which provide inputs for supporting movements. RRT-Connect algorithm is used and the poses of the trajectory before smoothing is shown in Fig. 13(a), which consists of lots of states resulting in multiple robot commands. After smoothing, the redundant states are removed and only 5 states

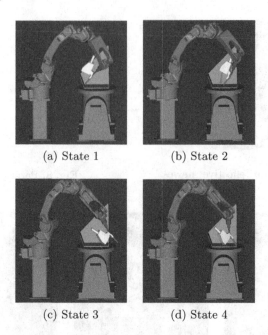

(a) State 1   (b) State 2

(c) State 3   (d) State 4

Fig. 12. Process of supporting movements

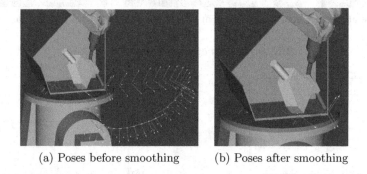

(a) Poses before smoothing   (b) Poses after smoothing

Fig. 13. Smoothing algorithm

are required, as shown in Fig. 13(b). The process of supporting movements is shown in Fig. 12.

4.3 Experiment

A corner pieces of a dyeing machine is shown in Fig. 14, of which 4 weld seams need welding. The trajectories are planned in the simulation environment and the robot commands are generated. During welding, the robot moves smoothly without collision or singularities. Figure 16 shows the trajectories of the robot.

Fig. 14. A workpiece with 4 weld seams to be welded

Fig. 15. Four weld seams formed after welding

Fig. 16. Trajectories of the welding robot

After welding, four weld seams formed in good shapes as shown in Fig. 15, which met the welding requirements.

5 Conclusion

In this paper, a methodology is proposed for trajectory planning in welding, which is divided into effective movements and supporting movements. For effective movements, four objective functions are defined–reachability and collision avoidance, manipulability measure, smoothness, and welding quality, which describe the task requirements. Then NSGA-II is used in order to get an optimum solution from the Pareto optimal set. For supporting movements, the classical algorithm RRT-Connect is adopted to find a minimum-time trajectory according to two geometric points. To make the trajectory smooth and reduce the robot commands, a smoothing algorithm is proposed which simplifies the trajectory while considering its shape. The simulation shows that the algorithms proposed are effective and the experiment illustrates that the trajectories meet the welding requirements.

Acknowledgments. The authors would like to gratefully acknowledge the reviewers comments. This work is supported by National Natural Science Foundation of China (Grant Nos. U1713207), Science and Technology Planning Project of Guangdong Province (2017A010102005), Key Program of Guangzhou Technology Plan (Grant No. 201904020020).

References

1. Verschueren, R., van Duijkeren, N., Swevers, J., Diehl, M.: Time-optimal motion planning for n-DOF robot manipulators using a path-parametric system reformulation. In: 2016 American Control Conference (ACC), pp. 2092–2097. IEEE (2016)
2. Bourbonnais, F., Bigras, P., Bonev, I.A.: Minimum-time trajectory planning and control of a pick-and-place five-bar parallel robot. IEEE/ASME Trans. Mechatron. **20**(2), 740–749 (2015)
3. Zhao, Y., Wang, Y., Bortoff, S.A., Nikovski, D.: Energy-efficient collision-free trajectory planning using alternating quadratic programming. In: 2014 American Control Conference, pp. 1249–1254. IEEE (2014)
4. Piazzi, A., Visioli, A.: Global minimum-jerk trajectory planning of robot manipulators. IEEE Trans. Ind. Electron. **47**(1), 140–149 (2000)
5. Huang, P., Xu, Y., Liang, B.: Global minimum-jerk trajectory planning of space manipulator. Int. J. Control Autom. Syst. **4**(4), 405–413 (2006)
6. Gasparetto, A., Zanotto, V.: A new method for smooth trajectory planning of robot manipulators. Mech. Mach. Theory **42**(4), 455–471 (2007)
7. Gasparetto, A., Zanotto, V.: Optimal trajectory planning for industrial robots. Adv. Eng. Softw. **41**(4), 548–556 (2010)
8. Huang, J., Hu, P., Wu, K., Zeng, M.: Optimal time-jerk trajectory planning for industrial robots. Mech. Mach. Theory **121**, 530–544 (2018)
9. Alatartsev, S., Ortmeier, F.: Thesis abstract: path-planning for industrial robots among multiple under-specified tasks (2013)

10. Dijkstra, E.W.: A note on two problems in connexion with graphs. Numerische mathematik **1**(1), 269–271 (1959)
11. Ammar, A., Bennaceur, H., Châari, I., Koubâa, A., Alajlan, M.: Relaxed dijkstra and a* with linear complexity for robot path planning problems in large-scale grid environments. Soft Comput. **20**(10), 4149–4171 (2016)
12. Duchoň, F., et al.: Path planning with modified a star algorithm for a mobile robot. Procedia Eng. **96**, 59–69 (2014)
13. Kang, H.I., Lee, B., Kim, K.: Path planning algorithm using the particle swarm optimization and the improved Dijkstra algorithm. In: 2008 IEEE Pacific-Asia Workshop on Computational Intelligence and Industrial Application, vol. 2, pp. 1002–1004. IEEE (2008)
14. LaValle, S.M.: Rapidly-exploring random trees: a new tool for path planning (1998)
15. Klemm, S., et al.: RRT?-connect: faster, asymptotically optimal motion planning. In: 2015 IEEE International Conference on Robotics and Biomimetics (ROBIO), pp. 1670–1677. IEEE (2015)
16. Kuffner Jr., J.J., LaValle, S.M.: RRT-connect: an efficient approach to single-query path planning (2002)
17. Hauser, K., Ng-Thow-Hing, V.: Fast smoothing of manipulator trajectories using optimal bounded-acceleration shortcuts. In: 2010 IEEE International Conference on Robotics and Automation, pp. 2493–2498. IEEE (2010)
18. Pan, J., Zhang, L., Manocha, D.: Collision-free and smooth trajectory computation in cluttered environments. Int. J. Robot. Res. **31**(10), 1155–1175 (2012)
19. Yoshikawa, T.: Manipulability of robotic mechanisms. Int. J. Robot. Res. **4**(2), 3–9 (1985)

Kinematics Solution and Workspace Analysis of a Seven (DOF) Redundant Manipulator

Cunfeng Kang⬤, Juan Wu[(⊠)]⬤, Shizheng Zhang⬤, Ting Miao⬤, and Guanchen Zong⬤

Beijing University of Technology, Chaoyang District, Beijing, China
1026502186@qq.com

Abstract. The standard D-H parameter method was used to analyze the kinematic modeling of the redundant manipulator with seven degrees of freedom. By establishing the link coordinate system, the transformation matrix of the end tool coordinate system relative to the fixed coordinate system is obtained, and the positive motion of the manipulator is solved. According to the working condition requirements and the structural constraints of the mechanical arm, the joint angle of the mechanical arm is constrained, and the inverse kinematics solution of the mechanical arm is solved by the matrix inverse multiplication analysis method, and the positive kinematics solution is mutually verified to ensure the correctness of the solution; Matlab Robotics Toolbox 10.3 simulates the working space of the manipulator model, and judges the rationality of the manipulator structure through the simulation space results.

Keywords: Tandem manipulator · Seven DOF · Kinematics · Workspace

1 Preface

With the rapid development of social life and technology, the demand for health medical robots and flexible assembly robots is increasing. The redundant cooperative robot arm has more spare degrees of freedom than the traditional six degree of freedom robot arm, which can complete more complex motion movements such as fault tolerance and singular avoidance. It combines intelligent, secure and flexible features to enhance the collaboration between robots and people to create a harmonious and intelligent environment. In this paper, the kinematics operation of a single seven degree of freedom redundant manipulator is analyzed by analytical method, and the manipulator motion control and path planning are realized.

2 Kinematic Modeling of the Manipulator

2.1 Kinematic Model of D-H Parameters

The UR5 robot is a flexible, lightweight six-joint industrial robot developed by Universal Robots. It is safe and easy to use, and has a compact design. It can perform lightweight cooperative movements such as grabbing and placing, and can be

© Springer Nature Switzerland AG 2019
H. Yu et al. (Eds.): ICIRA 2019, LNAI 11745, pp. 124–133, 2019.
https://doi.org/10.1007/978-3-030-27529-7_11

completed work with people without a protective fence. Its three-axis parallel structure broadens the design of the mechanical arm, as shown in Fig. 1.

The mechanical arm structure studied in this paper is based on the UR5 type mechanical arm, and a rotating joint is added at the end to evolve into a seven-degree-of-freedom redundant mechanical arm (As shown in Fig. 2). Different arm configurations determine the working space of the arm and the flexibility of the arm.

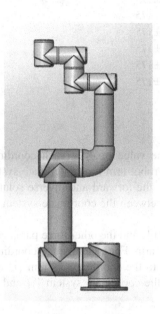

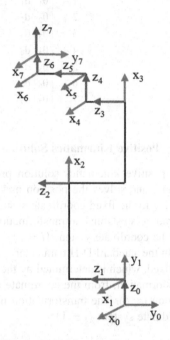

Fig. 1. Mechanical arm three-dimensional model

Fig. 2. D-H joint coordinate model

In this paper, the standard D-H parameter principle is used to indicate the positional relationship and rotation angle between the joints. The relationship between the tool coordinate system and the fixed coordinate system is established to complete the calculation of the forward and backward kinematics of the robot arm.

The standard D-H parameters include four kinematic parameters: link length a_i, link offset d_i, link torsion angle α_i, and joint torsion angle θ_i. The link length a_i represents the distance from z_{i-1} to z_i around the x_i axis; the link offset d_i represents the distance from x_{i-1} to x_i around the z_{i-1} axis; the link torsion angle α_i represents the x_i axis, from The angle of z_{i-1} to z_i; the joint torsion angle θ_i represents the angle from x_{i-1} to x_i around the z_{i-1} axis. The origin of the coordinate system $\{i\}$ is the intersection of the joint axes i and $i - 1$. When the joint axes between the two coordinate systems are parallel to each other, the origin of the coordinate system $\{i\}$ is the intersection of the common perpendicular line between the joint axes i and $i - 1$ and the joint axis i. The direction of the z axis is the same as the orientation of the joint axis $\{i\}$. The direction of the x axis is determined by the z axis of the current coordinate system $\{i\}$ and the axis of the coordinate system $\{i - 1\}$; The right hand rule determines the y axis direction [1]. The D-H parameter table is shown in the Table 1 below.

Table 1. D-H parameters table

Link	θ_i	di/mm	ai/mm	αi	θmin ~ θmax
1	θ_1	d_1	0	0	$\pm175°$
2	θ_2	d_2	a_2	90°	$\pm175°$
3	θ_3	d_3	a_3	0	$\pm175°$
4	θ_4	d_4	0	$-90°$	$\pm175°$
5	θ_5	d_5	0	0	$\pm175°$
6	θ_6	d_6	0	0	$\pm175°$
7	θ_7	d_7	0	0	$\pm175°$

2.2 Positive Kinematics Solution

The positive kinematics solution process knows the value of θ_i in each coordinate system, and solves the position and attitude of the robot arm tool coordinate system relative to the fixed coordinate system. The basis of the forward and inverse solution operation is establish a transformation relationship between the coordinate system $\{i\}$ and the coordinate system $\{i - 1\}$.

In the standard D-H parameter, $_i$ is the joint variable and the other three parameters are fixed, which is determined by the structure of the arm. For a momentary coordinate transformation, from the coordinate system $\{i - 1\}$ to the coordinate system $\{i\}$ axis rotation (α_{i-1}). The transformation matrix between the coordinate system $\{i\}$ and the coordinate system $\{i - 1\}$:

$$^{i-1}_i T = Rz(\theta_i)Dz(d_i)Dx(a_{i-1})Rx(\alpha_{i-1})$$

$$= \begin{bmatrix} \cos\theta_i & -\sin\theta_i\cos\alpha_{i-1} & \sin\theta_i\sin\alpha_{i-1} & a_{i-1}\cos\theta_i \\ \sin\theta_i & \cos\theta_i\cos\alpha_{i-1} & -\cos\theta_i\sin\alpha_{i-1} & a_{i-1}\sin\theta_i \\ 0 & \sin\alpha_{i-1} & \cos\alpha_{i-1} & d_i \\ 0 & 0 & 0 & 1 \end{bmatrix} \quad (1)$$

From Eq. (1), the transformation matrix of the tool coordinate system x$\{7\}$ relative to the fixed coordinate system $\{0\}$:

$$^0_1T\,^1_2T\,^2_3T\,^3_4T\,^4_5T\,^5_6T\,^6_7T = {}^0_7T = \begin{bmatrix} n_x & o_x & a_x & p_x \\ n_y & o_y & a_y & p_y \\ n_z & o_z & a_z & p_z \\ 0 & 0 & 0 & 1 \end{bmatrix} \quad (2)$$

The above formula $R = \begin{bmatrix} n_x & o_x & a_x \\ n_y & o_y & a_y \\ n_z & o_z & a_z \end{bmatrix}$ is the attitude rotation matrix of the tool coordinate system relative to the fixed coordinate system, $[n_x \, n_y \, n_z]^T$, $[o_x \, o_y \, o_z]^T$ and $[a_x \, a_y \, a_z]^T$ are 3 unit vectors, they are perpendicular to each other. Posture rotation matrix R is a standard orthogonal matrix.

$$n_x = -s_7(c_5s_1 + c_{234}c_1s_5) - c_7(c_6s_1s_5 + s_{234}c_1s_6 - c_{234}c_1c_5c_6)$$

$$n_y = -c_7(c_1c_6s_5 + s_{234}s_1s_6 + c_{234}c_5c_6s_1) + s_7(c_1c_5 - c_{234}s_1s_5)$$

$$n_z = c_7(s_{234}c_5c_6 + c_{234}s_6) - s_{234}s_5s_7)$$

$$o_x = s_7(c_6s_1s_5 + s_{234}c_1s_6 - c_{234}c_1c_5c_6) - c_7(c_5s_1 + c_{234}c_1s_5)$$

$$o_y = c_7(c_1c_5 - c_{234}s_1s_5) - s_7(c_1c_6s_5 + s_{234}s_1s_6 + c_{234}c_5c_6s_1$$

$$o_z = -s_7(c_{234}s_6 + s_{234}c_5c_6) - s_{234}c_7s_5$$

$$a_x = s_6(s_1s_5 - c_{234}c_1c_5) - s_{234}c_1c_6$$

$$a_y = -s_6(c_1s_5 + c_{234}s_1c_5) - s_{234}s_1c_6)$$

$$a_z = c_{234}c_6 - s_{234}c_5s_6$$

$$p_x = (d_2 + d_3 + d_4)s_1 + a_2c_1c_2 + d_6c_5s_1 - d_5s_{234}c_1 + a_3c_1c_{23} + d_6c_{234}c_1s_5$$
$$+ d_7s_1s_5s_6 - d_7s_{234}c_1c_6 - d_7c_{234}c_1c_5s_6$$

$$p_y = -(d_2 + d_3 + d_4)c_1 + a_2s_1c_2 - d_6c_5c_1 - d_5s_{234}s_1 + a_3s_1c_{23} + d_6c_{234}s_1s_5$$
$$- d_7c_1s_5s_6 - d_7s_{234}s_1c_6 - d_7c_{234}c_5s_1s_6$$

$$p_z = d_1 + a_3s_{23} + a_2s_2 + d_5c_{234} + d_6s_{234}s_5 - d_7s_{234}s_6c_5 + d_7c_{234}c_6$$

$$s_{234} = \sin(\theta_2 + \theta_3 + \theta_4), c_{234} = \cos(\theta_2 + \theta_3 + \theta_4), c_i = \cos(\theta_i), s_i = \sin(\theta_i).$$

2.3 Inverse Kinematics Solution

The inverse kinematics solution process is find the position and attitude of the robot arm tool coordinate system relative to the fixed coordinate system, and to solve the θ_i in the relative configuration.

The most distinguishing feature of redundant degrees of freedom robots from non-redundant degrees of freedom robots is the self-motion characteristics [2]. Due to the existence of redundant joints, there is zero space in the robot arm. In the case of the specified end position, there is no array solution in the joint space corresponding to the specified end pose. The set of all possible joint angles is the redundant robot movement manifold. In other words, any joint angle combination within the self-motion manifold can be achieved, and there are multiple solutions in the same pose.

At present, there are numerical methods, geometric methods and analytical methods for the inverse kinematics of redundant mechanical arms at home and abroad. The numerical method adopts the principle of numerical iteration, and iterates to the target θi value multiple times until the accuracy requirement is met. The advantage of the numerical method is that it does not limit the number of structures and degrees of freedom of the manipulator. The solution is relatively simple and due to the iterative solution process of the numerical method. The solution speed is slower than the analytical method, and the flexibility of the manipulator motion control cannot be guaranteed. In fact, it uses "time" for "precision".

The analytical method is based on the solution of the analytical form. In general, all inverse solutions in a certain configuration can be obtained. For the six-degree-of-freedom manipulator, Pieper [3] demonstrated that there are closed solutions for the manipulators with three joint axes intersect at one point. Duffy [4] have a closed solution for the manipulators parallel to three adjacent joint axes. It is difficult to solve the seven-degree-of-freedom manipulator analytical method, but it has the advantages of fast calculation speed and other requirements to meet the needs of subsequent PLC motion control. Aiming at the existing manipulator structure, considering the special structure of the parallel axes of the 2, 3 and 4 axes of the manipulator, the inverse kinematics model is analyzed, and an analytical method for the inverse kinematics is derived.

Slove $\theta_1\theta_5$

From Eq. (2), the matrix is inversely multiplied:

$$_1^0T^{-1} {}_7^{10}T_7^6T^{-1} = {}_2^1T_3^2T_4^3T_5^4T_6^5T \tag{3}$$

According to the corresponding elements of the matrix (3, 4):

$$_1^0T^{-1} {}_7^{10}T_7^6T^{-1} = \begin{bmatrix} c_1 & s_1 & 0 & 0 \\ 0 & 0 & 1 & -d_1 \\ s_1 & -c_1 & 0 & 0 \\ 0 & 0 & 0 & 1 \end{bmatrix} \begin{bmatrix} n_x & o_x & a_x & p_x \\ n_y & o_y & a_y & p_y \\ n_z & o_z & a_z & p_z \\ 0 & 0 & 0 & 1 \end{bmatrix} \begin{bmatrix} c_7 & s_7 & 0 & 0 \\ -s_7 & c_7 & 0 & 0 \\ 0 & 0 & 1 & -d_7 \\ 0 & 0 & 0 & 1 \end{bmatrix}$$

$$\tag{4}$$

According to the corresponding elements of the matrix (3, 4):

$$(p_x - a_xd_7)s_1 + (a_yd_7 - p_y)c_1 = d_2 + d_3 + d_4 + d_6c_5 \tag{5}$$

among $A = (a_yd_7 - p_y)c_1$, $B = (p_x - a_xd_7)s_1$, $C = d_2 + d_3 + d_4 + d_6c_5$

From Eq. (5), if θ_1 or θ_5 is known, a corresponding other solution can be obtained. Given θ_5 here:

$$\theta_1 = A\tan 2(B, A) \pm A\tan 2(\sqrt{B^2 + A^2 - C^2}, C) \tag{6}$$

Slove θ_6

From Eq. (7):

$$_1^0T^{-1} {}_7^{10}T = {}_2^1T_3^2T_4^3T_5^4T_6^5T_7^6T \tag{7}$$

According to the corresponding elements of the matrix (3, 3):

$$a_x s_1 - a_y c_1 = s_5 s_6 \tag{8}$$

$$\theta_6 = \arcsin((a_x s_1 - a_y c_1 / s_5) \tag{9}$$

Slove θ_7

From Eq. (7):

According to the corresponding elements of the matrix $(3,2)$:

$$c_6 s_5 s_7 - c_5 c_7 = o_x s_1 - o_y c_1 \tag{10}$$

$$\theta_7 = A \tan 2(c_6 s_5, -c5) \pm A \tan 2(\sqrt{(c_6 s_5)^2 + (-c_5)^2 - (o_x s_1 - o_y c_1)^2}, o_x s_1 - o_y c_1) \tag{11}$$

Slove $\theta_2 \theta_3 \theta_4$

From Eq. (7):

$$^0_1 T^{-1} {}^0_7 T {}^6_7 T^{-1} {}^5_6 T^{-1} {}^4_5 T^{-1} = {}^1_2 T {}^2_3 T {}^3_4 T \tag{12}$$

According to the corresponding elements of the matrix $(1, 4),(2, 4)$:

$$\begin{aligned} t_{14} &= a_3 c_{23} + a_2 c_2 \\ t_{24} &= a_3 s_{23} + a_2 s_2 \end{aligned} \tag{13}$$

Add t_{14} and t_{24} squared :

$$t_{14}^2 + t_{24}^2 = a_3^2 + a_2^2 + 2a_3 a_2 c_3 \tag{14}$$

$$\theta_3 = arc \sin((t_{14}^2 + t_{24}^2 - a_3^2 - a_2^2)/2a_3 a_2 c_2) \tag{15}$$

Substitute the obtained θ_3 into the Eq. (13)

$$t_{14}^2 + t_{24}^2 = a_3^2 + a_2^2 + 2a_3 a_2 c_3 \tag{16}$$

$$\theta_2 = a \tan2((a_3 \cos(\theta_3) + a_2)t_{24} - (a_3 \sin(\theta_3))t_{14}, (a_3 \cos(\theta_3) + a_2)t_{14} + (a_3 \sin(\theta_3))t_{24}) \tag{17}$$

According to the corresponding elements of the matrix $(1, 1)$:

$$\theta_4 = \arcsin(t_{21}) - \theta_2 - \theta_4 \tag{18}$$

3   Algorithm Verification

According to the above D-H parameter, using the rotation matrix, the joint angles θ_1 to θ_7 are known, and the end position and position of the arm are obtained. The initial position of the manipulator is verified by Matlab Robotics Toolbox, and the initial position simulation diagram of the manipulator is obtained (As shown in Fig. 3).

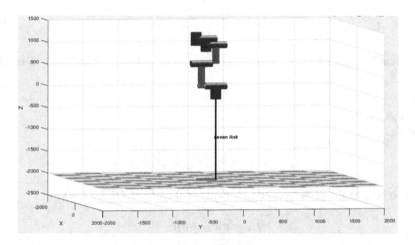

Fig. 3. Initial pose simulation

For the atypical situation during the operation of the manipulator, the inverse kinematics method is used to verify the algorithm, inputing the attitude and position data of the atypical position, and obtain the inverse kinematic joint rotation angle θ1–θ7. On the premise of inverse kinematics solution, the positive motion solution is substituted to verify the correctness of the inverse motion calculation.

Bring θ1 = 25°θ2 = 46°θ3 = 82°θ4 = −146°θ5 = 73°θ6 = −24°θ7 = 27° into the formula (2):

$$
{}_{7}^{0}T = \begin{bmatrix}
-0.065565 & -0.072972 & 0.019397 & 334.284461 \\
0.069959 & -0.049046 & 0.051962 & -8.564704 \\
-0.028405 & 0.047639 & 0.083209 & 1018.89353 \\
0 & 0 & 0 & 1
\end{bmatrix}
\tag{19}
$$

Bring formula (19) into the formula (6), (9), (11), (15), (17), (18) and give $\theta_5 = 50°$.

Get the value of $\theta_1 = 36.37°$ $\theta_2 = 44.90°$ $\theta_3 = 85.63°$ $\theta_4 = -144.20°$ $\theta_5 = 50.00°$ $\theta_6 = -23.33°$ $\theta_7 = 40.15°$.

$$
{}^{0}_{7}T = \begin{bmatrix} -0.065569 & -0.072968 & 0.019400 & 334.33264 \\ 0.069958 & -0.049048 & 0.051964 & -8.553674 \\ -0.028401 & 0.047644 & 0.083207 & 1018.86800 \\ 0 & 0 & 0 & 1 \end{bmatrix} \tag{20}
$$

After several sets of different data verification results, the results of the forward and inverse kinematics are solved, the data is reasonable, and the correctness of the algorithm is verified.

4 Workspace Analysis

The working space of the robot arm refers to the maximum range of the origin of the end tool coordinate system in the normal operation of the robot arm, or the volume occupied by the origin point. This space is also called the reachable space or the total workspace [5]. Monte Carlo method is a method of solving mathematical problems by using the development of stochastic theory. It is used to solve the multi-joint manipulator workspace and construct a robotic arm workspace cloud map by generating random points. The image is displayed on the computer to get the workspace outline [6, 7]. In this paper, the robot arm model is simulated based on Matlab Robotics Toolbox, and the Monte Carlo method is used to analyze the point cloud image of the robot arm up to the working space. First, a robotic arm simulation model is established to calculate the positive kinematics of the manipulator to obtain the pose and position of the end of the manipulator. Then, the value of the random number and the variable range of each joint axis ($\theta_{min} \sim \theta_{max}$). The random number N is 20000. The point cloud diagram of the working space of the robot arm can be obtained by programming in Matlab software. The three-dimensional map and the various directions of the working space (As shown in Figs. 4, 5, 6 and 7)

Through the observation of the point cloud image of the simulation space, it can be known that the working space of the robot arm is an elliptical sphere, and the electric cloud is dense in the working space, indicating that the end of the mechanical arm can reach any point in the working space, which verifies the reasonable design of the mechanical structure. The random number is the key factor that determines the degree of fitting between the simulation workspace and the real workspace. The value of the random number i can be appropriately increased to ensure that the simulation workspace is infinitely close to the real workspace.

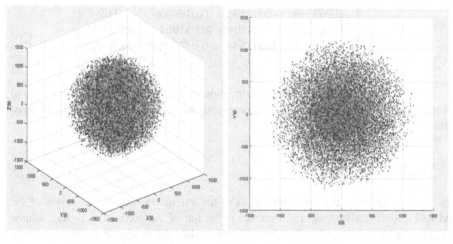

Fig. 4. xyz work space　　　　　　　　　　**Fig. 5.** xy work space

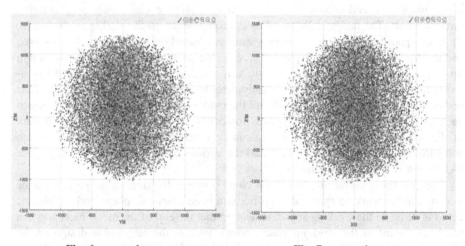

Fig. 6. yz work space　　　　　　　　　　**Fig. 7.** xz work space

5　Conclusions

Based on the seven-degree-of-freedom redundant manipulator, an analytical method for joint angle parameterization is proposed. The joint coordinate system established under the D-H parameter principle obtains the relative relationship between each coordinate system. According to the range of joint angle. The solution of the forward and backward kinematics of the manipulator is combined with Matlab to verify the solution results, which ensures the rationality and correctness of the solution results. Using Matlab Robotics Toolbox, Monte Carlo method is used to simulate the working space of the manipulator model. It is not limited to the number and structure of the freedom of the manipulator, and it is infinitely close to the real working space, which verifies the rationality of the mechanical structure design.

References

1. Craig, J.J.: Introduction to Robotics, 4nd edn. China Machine Press, Beijing (2018)
2. da Graça Marcos, M., Duarte, F.B., Machado, J.T.: Fractional dynamics in the trajectory control of redundant manipulators. Commun. Nonlinear Sci. Numer. Simul. **13**(9), 1836–1844 (2008)
3. Pieper, D.L.: The Kinematics of Manipulators Under Computer Control. Stanford University, Stanford (1968)
4. Daffy, J.: Analysis of mechanisms and robot manipulators. Edward Arnold, London (1980)
5. Zhu, X.: Design of Mechanical Arm Applied to Wall Moving Operation and Its Characteristics Study, pp. 23–24. Shanghai Jiaotong University, Shanghai (2014)
6. Li, B., Sun, H., Jia, Q., et al.: Space robots based on Monte Carlo method space computing field. Spacecraft Eng. **20**(4), 79–85 (2011)
7. Zhao, Y., Zhang, Y., Jiang, J., et al.: Robot workspace based on matlab solution method. Mech. Sci. Technol. 28 (12), 1657 (2009)

A Posture Planning Method in Clustered Synergy Subspace for HIT/DLR Hand II

Li Jiang, Bingchen Liu, Shaowei Fan[✉], and Hong Liu

State Key Laboratory of Robotics and System,
Harbin Institute of Technology, Harbin 150080, China
fansw@hit.edu.cn

Abstract. In this paper, a dexterous hand posture planning method in clustered synergy subspace is proposed, and the HIT/DLR Hand II is used as verification platform. Firstly, posture dataset of the hand is obtained by recording the hand's motion while human teleoperating it. Secondly, the synergy subspace of the hand is created by applying Gaussian process latent variable model on posture data. Thirdly, the data in synergy subspace is further clustered by K-means, because similarities between different postures can be predicted from their inter-distance in synergy subspace. Finally, posture of the dexterous hand is generated from the synergy-level data in specific cluster instead of the whole subspace. To evaluate the method proposed in this paper, comparison of posture reconstruction error between this method and directly posture planning in synergy space is shown. The results show that method proposed in this paper is more accurate and anthropomorphic, and the control paraments of the hand have been considerable reduced.

Keywords: Dexterous hands · Posture planning · Dimensional reduction

1 Introduction

In recent years, many elaborate multi-finger dexterous hands have been developed, like the Shadow Robot Hand [1], the iCub Hand [2] and the HIT/DLR Hand II [3]. With the help of dexterous hands, industrial robots and service robots can perform more complex operational tasks. However, grasp planning of dexterous hand is a tough problem due to its high number of Degrees of Freedom (DoFs). Therefore, the application fields of dexterous hands have been greatly restricted.

A normal way to solve grasp planning problem is to calculate fingertip points which contact with the object in cartesian space. Then, the dexterous hand posture is given via the computation of inverse-kinematics [4]. However, solving the inverse-kinematics problem need large amount of calculation. Besides, this method is lack of generality, because every time encounter a different object the contact points need to replan.

The human-inspired control strategies provide a new approach to solve the tough grasp planning of the dexterous hand. In 1998, Santello et al. proposed a postural synergies model from observing human hand virtually grasping 57 kinds of daily-life objects. Using Principal Component Analysis (PCA), the high-dimensional human hand posture data can be reconstructed from small number of low-dimension principle

H. Yu et al. (Eds.): ICIRA 2019, LNAI 11745, pp. 134–145, 2019.
https://doi.org/10.1007/978-3-030-27529-7_12

components. Using the first two principle components, more than 80% variance of the posture data can be explained. The principle components can be called postural synergy variables, and the low-dimensional space can be called synergy subspace [5]. Based on this idea, researchers attempted to use two synergy variables to control dexterous hands fulfilling serval grasp tasks [6, 7]. Furthermore, in order to reduce the posture reconstruction error, more synergy variables were preserved [8, 9].

However, as a data-driven approach, the outcome of posture planning in synergy subspace heavily depend on the choice of input data [10]. Palli et al. proved that the posture planning error could be quite large when we give an in-hand manipulation posture planning for dexterous hand from the synergy subspace which is the created by power grasp data [11]. Therefore, the input data for the synergy subspace is of great importance for posture planning in synergy level. The aim of this paper is to propose a synergy level posture planning method, while utilizing the most similar posture in the synergy subspace.

This paper is organized as follows: Sect. 2 describes the posture planning method for dexterous hand in a clustered synergy subspace. Section 3 describes the experimental platform and preparations for verification of this method. Section 4 shows the evaluation of this method. Section 5 provides the conclusion.

2   Posture Planning in Clustered Synergy Subspace

In this section, the posture planning method in clustered synergy subspace is described in detail. We will first introduce the creation of the clustered-synergy-subspace. Then, the posture of dexterous hand is predicted from posture data in specialized cluster. The process of dexterous hand's posture generation is given in Fig. 1.

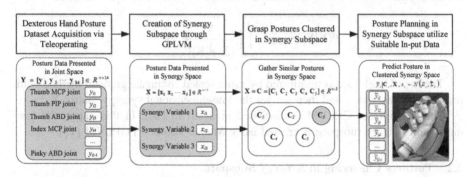

Fig. 1. The synergy level posture planning method for dexterous hand, while extracting the most similar posture as input data in synergy subspace.

2.1   Creation of the Synergy Subspace

Gaussian process latent variable models (GPLVM) is a globally non-linear dimensionality reduction method, and it has been proved to be an effective method to deal with high-dimensional hand posture data. Romero et al. compared GPLVM with PCA and serval common nonlinear methods like Isomap and LLE. The result showed that GPLVM clearly outperform in all these methods [12]. Besides, Xu used the GPLVM to extract nonlinear postural synergy variables, and these synergy variables were applied into controlling of a 13-DoFs dexterous hand [13]. So, in this paper, we also use GPLVM model to create the synergy subspace of dexterous hand instead of PCA.

In this paper, the high-dimensional posture matrix can be defined as $\mathbf{Y} = [\mathbf{y_1 y_2} \cdots \mathbf{y_{14}}] \in R^{n \times 14}$, n is the number of grasp postures recorded in the dexterous hand posture database, and 14 is the recorded DoFs of the dexterous hand. The low-dimensional synergy matrix can be defined as $\mathbf{X} = [\mathbf{x_1 x_2 x_3}] \in R^{n \times 3}$. We set the synergy subspace dimension at 3 because the grasp postures can be already reconstrued effectively proved by the previous studies [7]. Besides, three-dimensional data has a good visualization effect. The mapping of ith row vector in synergy matrix y_i to high-dimensional vector y_i can be presented as

$$y_i = f(x_i) + \varepsilon \tag{1}$$

where $f(x_i)$ is a nonlinear function with GP prior $f \sim GP(\mu, \mathbf{K})$, μ presents the mean of the value and $\mathbf{K}$ presents the kernel matrix. Normally, radial-basis function is chosen as the kernel matrix, and the element in the ith row and jth column of the kernel matrix is given by

$$k(x_i, x_j) = \sigma_r e^{-\frac{\gamma}{2}(x_i - x_j)^T (x_i - x_j)} \tag{2}$$

where x_i and x_j are postures in the synergy subspace, σ_r and γ are paraments need to be optimized.

Due to the assumption that observed data in high dimensions are independent, the marginal likelihood of the model can be obtained by using Bayesian theorem

$$P(\mathbf{Y}|\mathbf{X}, \sigma_r, \gamma) = \prod_{j=1}^{14} \frac{1}{(2\pi)^{\frac{n}{2}}|\mathbf{K}|^{\frac{1}{2}}} e^{-\frac{1}{2}y_j^T \mathbf{K}^{-1} y_j} \tag{3}$$

The log of likelihood is minimized by using scaled conjugate gradient method with respect to $\mathbf{X}$, σ_r and γ, and then we get the low-dimensional synergy matrix $\mathbf{X}$.

The principle of GPLVM is discussed in detail in [14]. In this paper, the low dimension synergy subspace is created using Matlab Toolbox FGPLVM [15].

2.2 Postures Clustering in Synergy Subspace

The GPLVM method can guarantee that points close in synergy subspace remain close in the observed space. So, the inter-distance between different points in synergy subspace reveals the similarity between different postures in high dimension. Then, the postures in synergy subspace are clustered according to the distance measures through a typical cluster analysis method K-means (based on Matlab Statistical Toolbox). We set the number of clusters at 5, because in a previous analysis of grasping behavior, 5 kinds of postures can overfit most of the daily-life works [16].

With this approach, posture data in synergy subspace $X = [x_1 x_2 x_3] \in R^{n \times 3}$ are clustered into 5 groups $\mathbf{X} = \mathbf{C} = [\mathbf{C}_1\ \mathbf{C}_2\ \mathbf{C}_3\ \mathbf{C}_4\ \mathbf{C}_5] \in R^{n \times 3}$ by a least-squares estimator

$$E = \sum_{i=1}^{k} \sum_{x \in C_i} \|x - \bar{x}_i\|_2^2 \tag{4}$$

where $\bar{x}_i = \frac{1}{|C_i|} \sum_{x \in C_i} x$ is the mean vector of $\mathbf{C}_i$. Through multiple iterations, we get the minimized error E, while similarity of samples in the same cluster are highest. Then, posture data in appropriate cluster are used as input data for posture planning in synergy subspace.

2.3 Posture Planning in Synergy Subspace

For any point x_i in synergy subspace, the high-dimensional posture $\tilde{y}_i$ could be inferred with Gauss Process. We first calculate the sums of independent Gaussian random variables as Eq. (5)

$$\begin{bmatrix} \mathbf{C}_i \\ \tilde{y}_i \end{bmatrix} | \mathbf{X}, x_i = \begin{bmatrix} f \\ \tilde{f}_i \end{bmatrix} + \begin{bmatrix} \varepsilon \\ \tilde{\varepsilon}_i \end{bmatrix} \sim N \left(\vec{0}, \begin{bmatrix} K(\mathbf{X}, \mathbf{X}) + \sigma_r^2 I & K(\mathbf{X}, x_i) \\ K(x_i, \mathbf{X}) & K(x_i, x_i) + \sigma_r^2 I \end{bmatrix} \right) \tag{5}$$

Then, the posture $\tilde{y}_i$ can be predicted using the rules for conditioning Gaussians follows Eq. (6)

$$\tilde{y}_i | \mathbf{C}_i, \mathbf{X}, x_i \sim N(\tilde{\mu}_i, \widetilde{\Sigma}_i) \tag{6}$$

where

$$\tilde{\mu}_i = K(x_i, \mathbf{X})(K(\mathbf{X}, \mathbf{X}) + \sigma_r^2 I)^{-1} \mathbf{C}_i \tag{7}$$

$$\widetilde{\Sigma}_i = K(x_i, x_i) + \sigma_r^2 I - K(x_i, \mathbf{X})(K(\mathbf{X}, \mathbf{X}) + \sigma_r^2 I)^{-1} K(\mathbf{X}, x_i) \tag{8}$$

3 Posture Dataset Acquisition for Method Verification

We use the HIT/DLR Hand II as the verification platform. This hand matches the size and shape of an adult hand. It has five identical fingers. The structure of the hand can be seen in Fig. 2. In each finger, it has three DoFs, in which two for flexion/extension of the metacarpophalangeal and proximal interphalangeal joint and another for finger's adduction/abduction. The distal interphalangeal joint moves coupled with proximal interphalangeal joint transmitted by a steel-wire system. As its highly integrated and anthropomorphic, this hand is suitable for complex grasping tasks and teleoperation jobs [3].

In order to quickly obtain large amount of the dexterous hand's posture data, we use the CyberTouch to teleoperate it, while recording the posture data after stably grasping. In this way, we can directly acquire the joint data of the dexterous hand, at the same time exploit the experience of human hand.

Fig. 2. The teleoperation system architecture for acquisition of dexterous hand posture dataset.

The teleoperation system architecture for data acquisition can be seen in Fig. 2, and the sensors' configuration of CyberTouch are also marked in the figure. We neglect the middle finger's abduction, because its range of motion during different grasping tasks is quite small. Then, the sensor variables of CyberTouch can be mapped to corresponding joints of the dexterous hand. Before teleoperation, we need to find out the linear working area of each sensor, then calculate the mapping from the human hand joint angles to the glove joint angles by a least-squares-regression method. Besides, due to the different kinematics between the human hand and the dexterous hand, we also need to map from the human fingertip workspaces to that of the dexterous hand. The mapping method has been described in detail in [17].

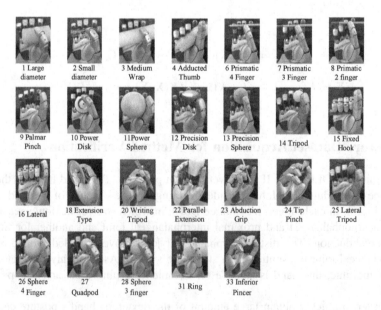

Fig. 3. 26 Grasp Postures the HIT/DLR Hand II could complete. The serial numbers map to the same posture in grasping taxonomy.

During the experiment, the subjects was asked to teleoperate the dexterous hand performing different grasp postures following the human hand grasp taxonomy proposed in [18], since these postures can basically cover the various grasping tasks in daily life. For each posture, ten groups of joint angle data were recorded when dexterous hand had grasped stably (with the CyberTouch fore feedback). Due to the different kinematics between the human hand and the dexterous hand, especially the limitation of thumb's motion range, the dexterous hand completed 26 of the 33 grasp postures (Fig. 3). The obtained posture dataset can basically reveal motion ability of the dexterous hand, and it will be furtherly used in extracting nonlinear synergy variables.

4 Results and Discussion

4.1 Synergy Subspace of the Dexterous Hand

The synergy subspace of the dexterous hand created by the GPLVM is shown in the Fig. 4, and the grasp posture points close in this synergy subspace are gathered together. Unlike the linear method, it is hard to express the relationship between the synergy variables and observed joint angles in exact equations. So, in order to show the meaning of the synergy variables, the Pearman's Correlation Coefficient between the synergy variables and the joint angles are presented in Fig. 5. The similarities between postures in same cluster and the role of synergy variable in posture generation is discussed in this part.

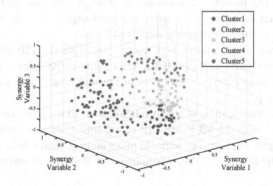

Fig. 4. The distribution of dexterous hand's grasp postures in synergy subspace.

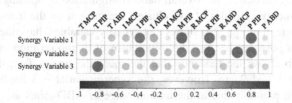

Fig. 5. The Pearman's Correlation Coefficient between synergy variables and joint angles.

Clustering of the Grasp Postures in Synergy Subspace

Cluster one contains posture 8, 20, 23, 24 and 33. These postures take high similarity and close in synergy subspace. They are all precision grasps with the fingertip of thumb, index and middle finger contact the object. The MCP and PIP joints of the fingers flexed in a similar position, and the thumb bends to the inside of the palm in a medium position.

Cluster two contains posture 2, 3, 15 and 18, which are mostly power grasps with both the fingers and the palm contacting the object. The joints of the fingers are in a very flexed position and their positions are quite similar. The function of the thumb in this cluster is to cooperate with the fingers and keep the object stable, so the motion range of thumb is large.

Cluster three contains posture 1, 6, 7, 10 and 31, which are quite similar to the postures in Cluster two, but the flexion of the fingers are smaller. Besides, the main characteristic of postures in this cluster is the adduction of thumb is near the limitation position.

Only lateral grasp belongs to Cluster four. Lateral grasp is quite different from other postures because the thumb position is in opposite direction from other postures. In lateral grasp, the thumb bend to the outside of the palm and other fingers flex a lot.

Cluster five is the biggest group and it contains all the other 11 grasp postures. Most of the postures in this group are precision grasps, with the fingertips contact with the object. Grasps in this cluster are separate in synergy subspace, and the positions of the fingers are mostly mid-flexed.

The Role of Synergy Variables

Considering both the postures distribution in synergy subspace and the correlation coefficients between the synergy variables and joint angles, the role of three synergy variables in grasp posture creation are described here.

The synergy variable 1 shows high correlation with the PIP joints of the four fingers. It is also correlated with the MCP&ABD joints of the index and the ABD joint of the thumb. It mainly controls the flexion of the four fingers and shows a tendency like cylindrical grasp.

The synergy variable 2 shows high correlation with all the joints of thumb. Besides, it is also correlated with the MCP and PIP of the four fingers, especially the middle, ring and pinky finger. This synergy variable plays an important role in grasp task when four fingers and the thumb moving simultaneously. It shows an enveloping tendency like ball grasp.

The synergy variable 3 shows high correlation with the PIP joint of the thumb, and it is also correlated with the ABD joint of all four fingers and the MCP joint of index and middle finger. It controls the overall hand configuration in opening and closing.

The mean synergy variables of five clusters are present by the transparent yellow triangle in radar graph in Fig. 7. It shows that synergy variable 2 have the largest range between different postures, because the importance of thumb position in posture configuration. It also shows the tendency that the more the fingers flex, the higher the synergy variable 1 and 2 are. However, the synergy variable 3 hardly changes in different postures, probably due to the motion range of ABD joints are small.

4.2   The Evaluation of the Posture Planning Method

In order to evaluation the posture planning method proposed in this paper, we compare it with two other synergy level posture planning method, that are directly use PCA and GPLVM for posture planning. We divide the hand posture data into 80% training set $\mathbf{Y}$ and 20% test set $\mathbf{Y}^*$, comparing posture reconstruction error in the test set $\mathbf{Y}^*$.

For PCA method, the posture planning in synergy space is achieved by linear combination of eigenvector. By using the SVD method to the high-dimensional posture matrix $\mathbf{Y}$, and picking the three biggest singular values, a hand posture can be approximated as presented in Eq. (9)

$$\mathbf{Y} = \bar{\mathbf{Y}} + [\mathbf{x_1 x_2 x_3}] \begin{bmatrix} q_{11} & q_{12} & \cdots & q_{1\,14} \\ q_{21} & q_{22} & \cdots & q_{214} \\ q_{31} & q_{32} & \cdots & q_{314} \end{bmatrix} \tag{9}$$

where $\bar{\mathbf{Y}}$ is the average posture matrix and the j row of $\bar{\mathbf{Y}}$ is $\bar{y}_{*j} = \frac{1}{n} \sum_{i=1}^{n} y_{ij}$, $\mathbf{X} = [\mathbf{x_1 x_2 x_3}]$ presents the synergy variables in synergy subspace created by PCA.

For any point $x_i = [x_{i1} x_{i2} x_{i3}]$ in synergy subspace, the posture planning result $\tilde{y}_i$ through PCA can be presented in Eq. (10)

$$\tilde{y}_i = \bar{y} + q_{1i} x_{i1} + q_{2i} x_{i2} + q_{3i} x_{i3}, i = 1, 2, \cdots, 14 \tag{10}$$

Posture Planning in synergy subspace by GPLVM has been described in Sect. 2.3. Besides, when directly use GPLVM for posture planning, input data of synergy subspace is the whole posture dataset $\mathbf{C}_i$ instead of $\mathbf{X}$.

The reconstruction error is used for the evaluation indicator between different methods, and it can be written as

$$y_i^{err} = |y_i - \tilde{y}_i| \tag{11}$$

where y_i is the original posture point in the test set.

Figure 6 shows the result of reconstruction error of the method proposed in this paper compared to the traditional PCA and GPLVM methods. In order to ensure the rationality of comparison, the synergy variables of these three methods are all set at three. Because both PCA and GPLVM are globally dimensional reduction method, the reconstruction error distribution in finger joints space are similar, which can be seen from Fig. 6(A)–(C). GPLVM method shows smaller reconstruction error in most finger joints than PCA, which has been proved before.

During the comparation, the error reduction in PIP joint of thumb and index are obvious. It will be helpful in approaching the objects with a smaller position error, because thumb and index finger both play a vital role in most of the grasp postures. Besides, the reconstruction error of the ring and little finger's joints have also been greatly reduced, which will make the posture of the dexterous hand more anthropomorphic.

Using the PCA method, the average reconstruction error in all postures is 3.86°. When using GPLVM method, the error has been decreased to 3.01°, the average reconstruction error has been reduced by 22.02%. Moreover, we replace the input data $\mathbf{X}$ by $\mathbf{C}_i$, the average reconstruction error in all postures has been further reduced to 1.55°. The reconstruction error is reduced by 48.50% compared with directly using GPLVM method. Besides, the variance of reconstruction error also has been dropped considerably when optimizing the input data. It means the posture reconstruction error is steady between different postures using the method proposed in this paper.

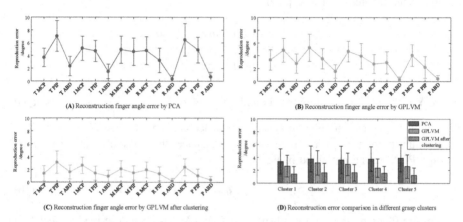

(A) Reconstruction finger angle error by PCA

(B) Reconstruction finger angle error by GPLVM

(C) Reconstruction finger angle error by GPLVM after clustering

(D) Reconstruction error comparison in different grasp clusters

Fig. 6. Comparation of the reconstruction error between the method of PCA, GPLVM, and GPLVM after clustering.

4.3   Experiments of Actual Grasp Posture Planning for HIT/DLR Hand II

The effect of posture planning in synergy subspace has been further validated in actual grasping tasks by HIT/DLR Hand II. We randomly selected one posture from each cluster. Posture planning for dexterous hand real grasp is divided into three parts. Firstly, the synergy variables of the posture to be completed is inferred from the similarity between it and recorded grasps in synergy subspace. Then, the stable grasp posture is obtained by mapping from the synergy subspace to joint angle subspace using the method of Gauss process. Finally, the joint trajectory is established by interpolating between the current posture and stable grasp posture. The posture planning results are shown in Fig. 7. Four images for each of these postures are shown. The process of dexterous hand from pre-grasping to stable grasping can be seen from Fig. 7 from left to right. In radar map, the transparent yellow triangle presents the mean synergy variables in five grasp clusters, and the triangle printed in red solid line presents the synergy variables of the posture to be completed. It shows much similarities between postures in the same grasp cluster.

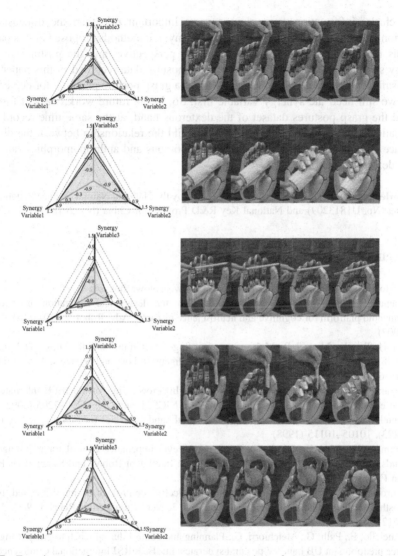

Fig. 7. Experiments of actual grasp postures reconstruction of the dexterous hand and the synergy variable in posture reconstruction. (Color figure online)

5 Conclusion and Future Work

This paper proposes a synergy level posture planning method, while utilizing the most similar postures in the synergy subspace. The synergy subspace is created by GPLVM. Utilizing the revealed similarity between postures in synergy subspace, we further cluster the grasp postures into five groups. During posture planning, only the posture data from a specialized cluster instead of the whole posture dataset is used. Results given by the posture reconstruction error comparation with other methods show that grasp cluster information even plays a more important role than the dimensional reduction method. Besides, unlike grasp taxonomy, the methods proposed in this paper analysis the hand postures from a data-driven perspective, and the postures in the synergy subspace is successive. However, the posture data recorded in this paper are still insufficient. Besides, when we need to give a grasp posture planning for dexterous hand, we still need the synergy variable first. So, in the future work, we will further expand the grasp postures dataset of the dexterous hand, at the same time record the information of object to be grasped. Finally, build the relationship between the object subspace and synergy subspace, realizing autonomous and anthropomorphic planning of the dexterous hand.

Acknowledgements. This work is supported in part by the National Natural Science Foundation of China (No. U1813209) and National Key R&D Program of China (No. 2018YFB1307201).

References

1. Shadow Robot Dexterous Hand Homepage. www.shadowrobot.com
2. Tsagarakis, N.G., Metta, G., Sandini, G.: iCub: the design and realization of an open humanoid platform for cognitive and neuroscience research. Adv. Robot. **21**(10), 1151–1175 (2007)
3. Liu, H., Wu, K., Meusel, P.: Multisensory five-finger dexterous hand: the DLR/HIT Hand II. In: IEEE/RSJ International Conference on Intelligent Robots and Systems, Nice, France, pp. 3692 + (2008)
4. Ferrari, C., Canny, J.: Planning optimal grasps. In: Proceedings of the IEEE International Conference on Robotics & Automation (ICRA), NICE, France, pp. 2290–2295 (1992)
5. Santello, M., Flanders, M., Soechting, J.: Postural hand synergies for tool use. J. Neurosci. **18**(23), 10105–10115 (1998)
6. Thomas, W., Jahn, B., Hirzinger, G.: Synergy level impedance control for multifingered hands. In: IEEE/RSJ International Conference on Intelligent Robots and Systems. (ICRA), San Francisco, CA, USA, pp. 973–979 (2011)
7. Matrone, G.C., Cipriani, C.: Real-time myoelectric control of a multi-fingered hand prosthesis using principal components analysis. J. Neuroengineering Rehabil. **9**(1), 1–13 (2012)
8. Ficuciello, F., Palli, G., Melchiorri, C.: Planning and control during reach to grasp using the three predominant UB hand IV postural synergies. In: IEEE/RSJ International Conference on Intelligent Robots and Systems. (ICRA), Saint Paul, Minnesota, USA, pp. 2255–2260 (2012)
9. Bernardino, A., Henriques, M.: Precision grasp synergies for dexterous robotic hands. In: IEEE International Conference on Robotics and Biomimetics. (ROBIO), Shenzhen, pp. 62–67 (2013)
10. Thomas, W., Reinecke, J., Chalon, M.: Derivation and verification of synergy coordinates for the DLR hand arm system. In: IEEE International Conference on Automation Science & Engineering. Seoul, Korea (2012)
11. Palli, G., Ficuciello, F., Scarcia, U.: Experimental evaluation of synergy-based in-hand manipulation. IFAC Proc. Vol. **47**(3), 299–304 (2014)
12. Romero, J., Feix, T.: Extracting postural synergies for robotic grasping. IEEE Trans. Robot. **29**(6), 1342–1352 (2013)

13. Xu, K., Liu, H., Du, Y.: A comparative study for postural synergy synthesis using linear and nonlinear methods. Int. J. Humanoid Robot. **13**(03), 24 (2016)
14. Li, P., Chen, S.: A review on Gaussian process latent variable models. CAAI Trans. Intell. Technol. **1**(4), 366–376 (2016)
15. Lawrence, N.: Probabilistic non-linear principal component analysis with Gaussian process latent variable models. J. Mach. Learn. Res. **6**, 1783–1816 (2005)
16. Feix, T., Bullock, I.M., Dollar, A.M.: Analysis of human grasping behavior: object characteristics and grasp type. IEEE Trans. Haptics **7**(3), 311–323 (2014)
17. Hu, H.Y., Gao, X.H., Li, J.W.: Calibrating human hand for teleoperating the HIT/DLR hand. In: IEEE International Conference on Robotics and Automation (ICRA), New Orleans, Louisiana, USA, pp. 4571–4576 (2004)
18. Feix, T., Romero, J., Schmiedmayer, H.B.: The GRASP taxonomy of human grasp types. IEEE Trans. Hum.-Mach. Syst. **46**(1), 66–77 (2016)

Continuous Path Planning for Free-Floating Space Manipulator Based on Genetic Algorithm

Long Zhang[(✉)]

Technology and Engineering Center for Space Utilization,
Chinese Academy of Sciences, Beijing, China
buptzlong@163.com

Abstract. In this paper, a path planning method based on Genetic algorithm for free-floating space manipulator is proposed. Considering the non-holonomic characteristics of free-floating space manipulator, the kinematics model and dynamics coupling model are established first. In order to ensure the smoothness and continuity of the joint trajectory, the joint angle is parameterized by sinusoidal function with its arguments in fifth-order polynomial form. And then objective function is designed considering the end-effector position, the obstacle avoidance, and the trajectory cost. Finally, the Genetic algorithm is employed to search for the suitable values of the polynomial coefficients to optimize the objective function. The simulation verifies the effectiveness of the proposed method.

Keywords: Space manipulator · Continuous path planning ·
Genetic Algorithm

1 Introduction

Path planning has always been a research hotspot, especially for mobile robots. Many methods are proposed, such as sampling-based algorithms, heuristic-based algorithms, intelligent optimization algorithms, artificial potential field based algorithms [1, 2], and the enhanced learning algorithms [3] proposed recent years. However, different from mobile robots, the manipulator system which consists of multiple links cannot be treated as a point, and thus the algorithms above cannot be used directly. For this problem, some researchers proposed that the path planning can be implemented in manipulator configuration space [4], where the manipulator multibody system could be seen as a point. On this basis, path planning problem of manipulator is then transformed into that of finding a collision-free path for a point robot among the Cspace obstacles. This idea is effective for ground manipulator because most path planning methods take joint angle as a variable. However, for the space manipulator, as its base not fixed, the end-effector position cannot be determined even for the same configuration. What's more, when the base of space manipulator is in free-floating mode, it has strong coupling relationship between the base and the manipulator, which means the motion of manipulator will have an influence on the base. This is called non-holonomic

© Springer Nature Switzerland AG 2019
H. Yu et al. (Eds.): ICIRA 2019, LNAI 11745, pp. 146–153, 2019.
https://doi.org/10.1007/978-3-030-27529-7_13

characteristics. And when the inertia of the base is comparable to the total inertia of the manipulator links, this influence will be more obvious [5]. Some researchers utilized the non-holonomic characteristics for path planning and both the base attitude and manipulator configuration could reach the target status [6, 7], but the obstacle avoidance problem is not considered. And other researchers utilized the null-space of redundant space manipulator to avoid obstacles while keeping the end-effector tracking desired trajectory [8, 9]. Due to strict restrictions from the end-effector, the optional obstacle avoidance trajectory is greatly reduced.

In this paper, a path planning method based on Genetic Algorithm (GA) for free-floating space manipulator is proposed. The problems of non-holonomic characteristics, obstacle avoidance, joint limit, trajectory cost and final end-effector position accuracy are all considered. In Sect. 2, the model of free-floating space manipulator is established first. Section 3 introduces how the path planning method based on GA is implemented. Section 4 is the simulation of a 3-dof free-floating space manipulator. Section 5 gives the conclusions.

2 Modeling for Free-Floating Space Manipulator

2.1 Kinematics Model

The general model of space manipulator is shown in Fig. 1. The position vector at the centroid of each link of the space manipulator is (if not specified, all vectors are represented in the inertial system):

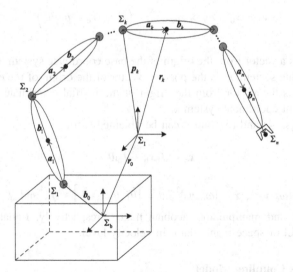

Fig. 1. The general model of space manipulator

$$r_k = r_0 + b_0 + \sum_{i=1}^{k} a_i + \sum_{i=2}^{k} b_{i-1} \tag{1}$$

Where, r_0 is the position vector of the origin of the base coordinate system, a_i is the direction vector of the origin of the joint coordinate system i to the centroid of link i, b_0 is the direction vector of the origin of the base coordinate system to the origin of the joint coordinate system 1, and b_i is the direction vector of the centroid of link i to joint coordinate system $i + 1$.

The angular velocity and linear velocity recursion formula of the kth link is:

$$\omega_k = \omega_{k-1} + z_k \dot{\theta}_k \tag{2}$$

$$v_k = v_{k-1} + \omega_{k-1} \times b_{k-1} + \omega_k \times a_k \tag{3}$$

Where, z_k is the axial direction vector at joint k, and $\dot{\theta}_k$ is the angular velocity of joint k. And the angular acceleration and linear acceleration expressions can also be obtained.

On this basis, for the end-effector, its angular velocity and linear velocity can be solved.

$$\omega_e = \omega_0 + \sum_{k=1}^{n} \left(z_k \dot{\theta}_k \right) \tag{4}$$

$$v_e = v_0 + \omega_0 \times r_{0e} + \sum_{k=1}^{n} \left(z_k \times (r_e - p_k) \dot{\theta}_k \right) \tag{5}$$

Where, r_{0e} is a vector from the origin of the base coordinate system to the origin of the end coordinate system, r_e is the position vector of the origin of the end coordinate system, and p_k is the vector from the origin of the inertial coordinate system to the origin of the joint coordinate system k.

Combine Eqs. (4) and (5), and it can be obtained that

$$\dot{x}_e = J_b \dot{x}_b + J_m \dot{\theta} \tag{6}$$

Where, $\dot{x}_e = [\omega_e, v_e]^T$, $\dot{x}_b = [\omega_0, v_0]^T$, $\dot{\theta} = \left[\dot{\theta}_1, \dot{\theta}_2 \cdots \dot{\theta}_k \right]^T$. J_b and J_m are the base Jacobain matrix and manipulator Jacobian matrix, respectively. Equation (6) is the kinematics model of space manipulator in velocity-level.

2.2 Dynamics Coupling Model

For the free-floating space manipulator system, the angular momentum and the linear momentum are conserved. Assuming that the initial system's linear momentum and angular momentum are both zero, the following equation can be obtained.

$$P = \sum_{k=0}^{n} (m_k v_k) = 0 \tag{7}$$

$$L = \sum_{k=0}^{n} (I_k \omega_k + m_k r_k \times \dot{r}_k) = 0 \tag{8}$$

Where, m_k and I_k are the mass and inertia matrix of each part, respectively. Combine Eqs. (7) and (8), and it can be obtained that

$$H_b \dot{x}_b + H_{bm} \dot{\theta} = 0 \tag{9}$$

Where, H_b and H_{bm} are the inertia matrix of the base and the coupling inertia matrix, respectively. And the final relationship of the base and the manipulator can be obtained after transformation.

$$\dot{x}_b = -H_b^{-1} H_{bm} \dot{\theta} = J_{bm} \dot{\theta} \tag{10}$$

3 Path Planning Based on Genetic Algorithm

The GA is a method of searching for optimal solutions by simulating natural evolutionary processes. It can solve complex nonlinear problems. Before the optimization, the control parameters and objective function needs to be determined.

The success of path planning for space manipulator should meet the following conditions:

- The end-effector of the space manipulator reaches the target point within a given time.
- The joint runs smoothly and meets the joint limit constraint during the movement.
- The obstacles can be detected and a collision-free trajectory should be found.
- For a good performance, the cost of the trajectory (such as the total distance) should also be considered.

3.1 Joint Parameterization

In this paper, the following conditions are set for the space manipulator.

$$\theta(t_0) = \theta_{\text{ini}}, \dot{\theta}(t_0) = 0, \theta(t_f) = \theta_{\text{des}}, \dot{\theta}(t_f) = 0 \tag{11}$$

Where, $\theta_{\text{ini}}, \theta_{\text{des}}$ are the initial configuration and the desired configuration, and t_0, t_f are the start and end time. Also, each joint angle should meet the joint limit constraints:

$$\theta_{i\min} \le \theta_i(t) \le \theta_{i\max} \tag{12}$$

Where, $\theta_{i\min}, \theta_{i\max}$ are the lower and upper limits, respectively.

In order to ensure the smoothness and continuity of the trajectory, the joint trajectory is parameterized by a sinusoidal function, whose argument is a fifth-order polynomial,

$$\theta_i(t) = \Delta_{i1} \sin(a_{i5}t^5 + a_{i4}t^4 + a_{i3}t^3 + a_{i2}t^2 + a_{i1}t + a_{i0}) + \Delta_{i2} \tag{13}$$

Where, $a_{i5}, a_{i4}, \ldots, a_{i0}$ are the coefficients of the polynomial, $i = 1, 2 \ldots, n$ denotes the ith joint, $\Delta_{i1} = \frac{\theta_{i\max} - \theta_{i\min}}{2}$, $\Delta_{i2} = \frac{\theta_{i\max} + \theta_{i\min}}{2}$.

Considering the constraints, the following results can be obtained by Eqs. (11) and (13).

$$
\begin{aligned}
a_{i0} &= \arcsin\left(\frac{\theta_{\text{ini}\_i} - \Delta_{i2}}{\Delta_{i1}}\right) \\
a_{i1} &= 0 \\
a_{i2} &= -\frac{3a_{i3}t_f + 4a_{i4}t_f^2 + 5a_{i5}t_f^3}{2} \\
a_{i3} &= -\frac{2\left(\arcsin\left(\frac{\theta_{\text{des}\_i} - \Delta_{i2}}{\Delta_{i1}}\right) - a_{i0}\right) + 2a_{i4}t_f^4 + 3a_{i5}t_f^5}{t_f^3}
\end{aligned}
\tag{14}
$$

We can see that after parameterization, only two parameters (a_{i4}, a_{i5}) are unknown in each joint function and they can be the control parameters. In the following, we will employ the Genetic Algorithm (GA) to search the values of a_{i4}, a_{i5}.

3.2 Objective Function

The objective function needs to be designed considering many factors such as the obstacle avoidance, trajectory cost and the final end-effector position. Based on this, it is designed as:

$$
f = \begin{cases} \xi_1 \|\boldsymbol{p}_{\text{fin}} - \boldsymbol{p}_{\text{des}}\| + \xi_2 C_{\text{tot}} & \text{if flag} = 0 \\ \chi & \text{else} \end{cases}
\tag{15}
$$

Where, ξ_1, ξ_2 are the weight coefficients, $\boldsymbol{p}_{\text{fin}}, \boldsymbol{p}_{\text{des}}$ are the final position and desired position of the end-effector. flag is the sign of whether a collision has occurred, and if the collision occurs, namely flag $\ne 0$, the objective function will be given a penalty value χ. C_{tot} is the trajectory cost expressed as follows:

$$C_{\text{tot}} = C_{\text{his}} + C_{\text{heu}} \tag{16}$$

Where, $C_{his} = \sum_{i=1}^{n} \|\theta_{i+1} - \theta_i\|, C_{heu} = \|\theta_i - \theta_{des}\|$ are the experience and inspiration for the trajectory searching.

4 Simulation

We take a 3-dof free-floating space manipulator as an example, as shown in Fig. 2, where $a_0 = 0.3\,\text{m}, a_1 = a_2 = a_3 = 0.5\,\text{m}$. The mass of the base is 50 kg, and the mass of each link is 4 kg. The inertia matrix of the base is $I_b = \text{diag}(50, 50, 50)$ and the inertia matrix of each link is $I_1 = I_2 = I_3 = \text{diag}(0.045, 0.083, 0.083)$. The initial configuration is $\theta_{ini} = [0, 90, -90]^\circ$ and the desired configuration is $\theta_{des} = [-5, 0, 20]^\circ$. The joint limits are $\theta_{max} = [90, 180, 180]^\circ$ and $\theta_{min} = [-90, -180, -180]^\circ$.

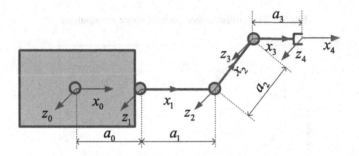

Fig. 2. A 3-dof free-floating space manipulator

Assume that there are two obstacles located at [1.4, 0.2, 0; 0.8, 0.8, 0] m, and the desire target point is [1.78, 0.04, 0] m. Set $\xi_1 = 10000, \xi_2 = 100, \chi = 100000$. The number of population in GA is 20, and the iterative number is 50. By GA, we can get the optimized solution $[0.96, -0.98, 0.90, -0.43, 0.18, -0.28] \times 10^{-5}$. The path of free-floating space manipulator is shown in Fig. 3. It can be seen that a collision-free path is found and due to coupling relationship, the base moves with the manipulator. At the same, the introduction of trajectory cost factor reduces the redundant trajectory effectively. The final position error is about 0.04 m and the whole joint angle curves are shown in Fig. 4, where we can see that the joint runs smoothly within the limits. Another test is carried out with obstacle located at [1.4, 0.2, 0; 0.8, -0.4, 0] m, and it is also working as shown in Fig. 5.

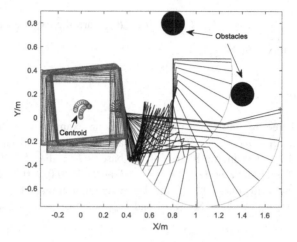

Fig. 3. The collision-free path of space manipulator

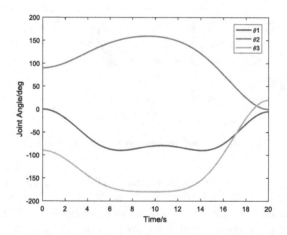

Fig. 4. The joint angle curves

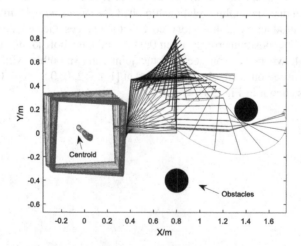

Fig. 5. The collision-free path of space manipulator with different obstacles

5 Conclusions

For the path planning problem of free-floating space manipulator, a GA-based method is proposed in this paper. Different from the ground manipulators, the motion of the base is strongly affected by the motion of manipulator. And thus the dynamics coupling model between the base and the manipulator is established firstly, which could give an intuitive mapping relationship. On this basis, in order to ensure the smoothness and continuity of the joint trajectory, the joint angle is parameterized by sinusoidal function with its arguments in fifth-order polynomial form. In this way, the joint limit avoidance can also be realized by the designed joint function. And then considering the end-effector position accuracy, the obstacle avoidance, and the trajectory cost, the objective function is designed. Finally, the optimized solution is obtained by GA to generate a continuous and smooth joint trajectory. The simulation results verify the effectiveness of the proposed path planning method.

References

1. Zhang, H.Y., Lin, W.M., Chen, A.X.: Path planning for the mobile robot: a review. Symmetry **10**, 1–17 (2018)
2. Thoa, M.T., Copot, C., Trung, T.D., et al.: Heuristic approaches in robot path planning: a survey. Robot. Auton. Syst. **86**, 13–28 (2016)
3. Prases, K.M., Arun, K.S., Vikas, K., et al.: Application of deep Q-learning for wheel mobile robot navigation. In: 3rd International Conference on Computational Intelligence and Networks, pp. 88–93. IEEE, Odisha (2017)
4. Yang, H., Li, L., Gao, Z.: Obstacle avoidance path planning of hybrid harvesting manipulator based on joint configuration space. Trans. Chin. Soc. Agric. Eng. **33**(4), 55–62 (2017)
5. Zhang, L., Jia, Q.X., Chen, G., et al.: Pre-impact trajectory planning for minimizing base attitude disturbance in space manipulator systems for a capture task. Chin. J. Aeronautics **9**(4), 1199–1208 (2015)
6. Xu, W.F., Liu, Y., Liang, B., et al.: Non-holonomic path planning of a free-floating space robotic system using genetic algorithms. Adv. Robot. **22**(4), 451–476 (2008)
7. Shi, Y., Liang, B., Wang, X.Q., et al.: Cartesian non-holonomic path planning of space robot based on quantum-behaved particle swarm optimization algorithm. J. Mech. Eng. **47**(23), 65–73 (2011)
8. Gao, H., Zhang, M.L., Zhang, X.J.: A review of the space trajectory planning of redundant manipulator. Mech. Transm. **40**(10), 176–180 (2016)
9. Chen, G., Ye, P.C., Jia, Q.X., et al.: Obstacle avoidance path planning of manipulator based on speed correction term. Control Decis. **30**(1), 156–160 (2015)

Simulation Analysis of Trajectory Planning for Robot-Assisted Stereotactically Biological Printing

Wanru Fei[1,2], Baosen Tan[1], Shaolong Kuang[3], Yubo Fan[1,2],
and Wenyong Liu[1,2(✉)]

[1] School of Biological Science and Medical Engineering, Beihang University,
Beijing 100083, China
wyliu@buaa.edu.cn
[2] Beijing Advanced Innovation Center for Biomedical Engineering,
Beihang University, Beijing 100083, China
[3] Robotics and Micro-Systems Center, Soochow University,
Suzhou 215021, China

Abstract. Application of 3D printing in the individualized fabrication of biological organ receives more and more attentions. The adopted movement trajectories of nozzle in 3D printing are all based on depositing materials vertically layer by layer. We noticed that the biological organ has always anisotropic property and its natural growing procedure implies a so-called *stereotactic* fabrication method which can be implemented utilizing robotic techniques. In this research, we proposed and simulated a robot-assisted stereotactic printing method. Kinematics analysis of the robotic manipulator was analyzed. Trajectory planning method for stereotactic operation was designed. Motion simulation analysis of the planned trajectory utilizing manipulator was conducted which validated effectiveness of the proposed printing system from aspects of motion accuracy, flexibility, and potential collisions. The results indicated flexibility of the proposed robot-assisted stereotactic printing technology.

Keywords: 3D printing · Robotics · Trajectory planning · Stereotactic · Simulation

1 Introduction

3D printing receives more and more attentions in the field of biomedicine especially the individualized fabrication of biological organs. Movement performance of printing nozzle directly influences the fabrication quality. Currently mainstream types of nozzle's movement trajectory are all based on depositing materials vertically layer by layer. It was noticed that the start and stop of nozzle in these printing techniques will cause *stair-step* effect on the curved surface of the printing model [1], which affects the modeling accuracy and subsequent analysis. Furthermore, we noticed that the biological organ has always anisotropic property and its natural growing procedure implies a so-called *stereotactic* fabrication method which can be implemented utilizing robotic techniques.

© Springer Nature Switzerland AG 2019
H. Yu et al. (Eds.): ICIRA 2019, LNAI 11745, pp. 154–162, 2019.
https://doi.org/10.1007/978-3-030-27529-7_14

In the robot-assisted printing procedure, position and pose of robot's end-effector can be changed stereotactically within a certain range of motion, which enables printing nozzle on the end-effector to deposit materials in any desired directions. Chakraborty et al. proposed an idea of depositing materials on curved surfaces in 2007 [2] which was implemented by Allen et al. in 2015 [3]. Wu et al. presented a RoboFDM robotic system for 3D printing without support-structures [4], which consists of a 6-DOF UR3 robot and an extruder fixed on the cantilever beam. Wang et al. [5] proposed a trajectory planning method for stereotactic printing of 3D bio-scaffold's surface assisted by a 6-DOF ABB IRB 120 robot, in which firstly the designed model is triangulated and mapped to the 2D plane utilizing the least square conformal mapping (LSCM), then the model contour which is obtained with the *marching square* algorithm is used for generating the filling trajectory of nozzle, finally each point of the equidistant line is re-mapped onto the surface of the designed model (3D) to form a final trajectory. In order to satisfy the anisotropic printing requirements of biological organ, a 3D directional printing method is designed in our group which is based on 3D curved layering of model and spiral scanning along the normal inward [6].

It was noticed that the accuracy and efficiency of trajectory planning directly influence the quality of stereotactic printing [7]. In this research, a double-parallelogram manipulator for stereotactic printing and the corresponding trajectory planning strategy is proposed and simulated to verify accuracy, flexibility, and potential collisions during movement procedure of the manipulator.

2 Trajectory Planning

3D printing procedure is generally divided into five steps [8]: modeling the printing entity, discretizing model, slicing the model, intra-layer filling of trajectory, and post-processing of the 3D printing model. Typical slicing methods included the equidistant slicing and the adaptive slicing. Equidistant slicing divides the model into the same thickness, while the adaptive slicing can adjust the slice thickness continuously according to the geometric features of model.

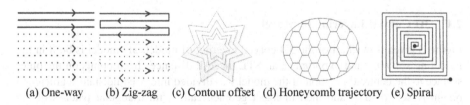

(a) One-way   (b) Zig-zag   (c) Contour offset   (d) Honeycomb trajectory   (e) Spiral

Fig. 1. Trajectory filling method.

Intra-layer trajectory filling is conducted after model slicing. Trajectory filling traditionally adopts one-way scanning method (Fig. 1a) in which the nozzle scans along the horizontal or vertical direction during spraying and directly moved to the start point of next (neighboring) line once it reaches the end point of the current line. Unlike one-way scanning, zig-zag scanning method (Fig. 1b) can keep continuous printing from one line to the neighboring line. These two scanning methods always produce non-ignorable errors when nozzle started or stopped. Contour offset scanning method [9] (Fig. 1c) scans the contour in a selected direction (inward or outward) layer by layer. Honeycomb trajectory scanning method (Fig. 1d) generate contour based on the mechanical properties of model, which can save printing materials [10]. Spiral scanning [11] (Fig. 1e) can improve printing accuracy by emitting rays from the contour center of model and generating next contour ray in a progressive manner. All these trajectory-filling methods are based on planar layering which are increasingly prominent in terms of accuracy.

We proposed a trajectory planning method which transforms layering from planar to 3D surface. Adaptive layering strategy is adopted which can effectively eliminate *stair-step* effect and increase the printing accuracy. From the aspect of intra-layer trajectory planning, the proposed method first cuts horizontally the model into N closed curve layer by layer and then spirals all curves into one curve to obtain the intra-layer printing trajectory of printing nozzle. Flow chart of the stereotactic printing is shown in Fig. 2.

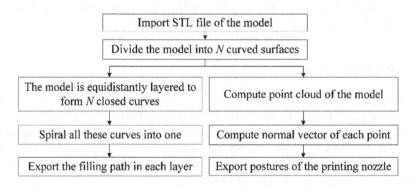

Fig. 2. Flow chart of stereotactic printing.

2.1   3D Curved Layering of Model

Figure 3 gives flow chart of the 3D curved layering of model. 3D model is built in the modeling software and exported as an STL file. All distances from points on the outer surface to the centroid position of the model was divided into N equidistant segments to obtain N sets of data and then intersect geometrically with triangular patches of the STL file to form N closed surfaces, as shown in Fig. 4 (a constructed model of kidney). In this 3D curved layering scheme, the surface of each layer printed by the nozzle is closed after the model is layered, thus there is no *stair-step* effect. Errors caused by 2D planar layering on the printing model can be effectively eliminated.

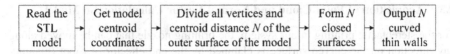

Fig. 3. Flow chart of 3D curved layer of model.

For trajectory planning of the nozzle scan on each curved thin layer (a wall with very small thickness) in the model, posture of the nozzle is designed to inward along the normal vector during printing process, which can eliminate potential interference of nozzle with printed part. Intra-layer trajectory planning algorithm is composed of two stages: spiral line calculation, and normal vector calculation of each thin layer.

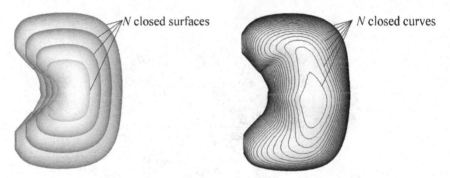

Fig. 4. Curved layering of kidney models.   **Fig. 5.** Equidistant slicing result.

2.2 Acquisition of Spirals

During spiral scan, equiangular rays are emitted from the geometric center of each contour, the spiral line will be generated in an asymptotic manner from one ray to the other. Here we create $N = 30$ equidistant slice from model between maximum and minimum values in the vertical direction to obtain N equidistant horizontal planes. Each horizontal plane intersects with the outer surface of model and form N closed plane. Figure 5 shows the result after equidistant slicing. Since the surface of each layer is formed by merging the triangular faces, the resulting intersection is formed by connecting the segments end to end. We sorted these endpoints of segments in a counter-clockwise (from top to bottom) and the sorted endpoints are used for inter-section spiraling. Thus the surface printing can be implemented according to the trajectories formed by these ordered points. To connect the disjoint curves, we refer to the method of traditional manual kiln shaping curved surface by spiral trajectories, and spiral the N closed curves into one curve.

2.3   Acquisition of Point Cloud and Normal Vector Calculation on Model

For the stereotactic printing in our system, the printing nozzle that can be moved along any direction on the curved surface is clamped by the end-effector of robot (manipulator) for material filling. If the nozzle always maintains a vertically downward pose, it may interact with the surface of printed model during the movement. In our system, the nozzle should be always keep in an inward direction along normal vector of the print model (the normal vector of a surface at a point P is a vector perpendicular to the tangent plane of the point). A local surface fitting-based method [12] is adopted here to estimate normal vector, i.e., by calculating k-neighborhood of each point (here $k = 5$) in the point cloud to obtain a local fitting plane. Normal vector of a point in the point cloud is consistent with the outward normal vector of the local fitting plane around that point. Figure 6 illustrates normal vector distribution of a 3D model.

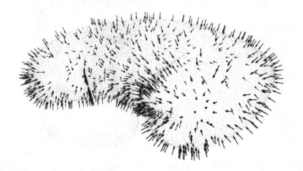

Fig. 6. Normal vector of the kidney model.

3   Simulation Analysis

3.1   Kinematics Analysis of Manipulator

In our system, a double-parallelogram mechanism (Fig. 7) is designed to perform stereotactic printing around any fixed-point in the workspace. During object printing, the pose of manipulator's end-effector consistently keeps a fixed direction. Reachable working space of the end-effector can be analytically calculated from kinematics analysis. Coordinates of the end-effector point denoted as M in Fig. 7 can be expressed as

$$M = (L_1 \cos \theta_1 - L_2 \sin \theta_2 + 30, L_1 \sin \theta_1 + L_2 \cos \theta_2 + 42.42) \qquad (1)$$

where, $\theta_1 \in (-12°, 110°)$, $\theta_2 \in (-70°, 130°)$, $L_1 = 260\text{mm}$, $L_2 = 200\text{mm}$. Figure 8 gives the simulation of point M.

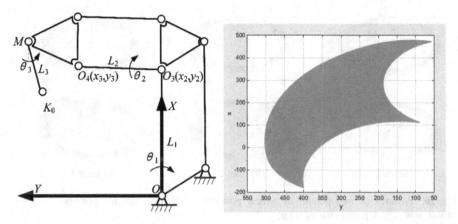

Fig. 7. Diagram of the mechanism.   **Fig. 8.** Kinematics of point M.

3.2 Simulation Analysis

Simulation Analysis of Nozzle Workspace. In order to analysis the workspace of nozzle, a rotation joint denoted as MK_0 in Fig. 7 is added to establish an additional coordinate system. Coordinates of point K_0 can be expressed as

$$X_{K_0} = L_1 \cos \theta_1 - L_2 \sin \theta_2 + 30 - L_3 \cos \theta_3$$
$$Y_{K_0} = (L_1 \sin \theta_1 + L_2 \cos \theta_2 + 42.42 - L_3 \sin \theta_3 - 456.68) * \cos \theta_4 \qquad (2)$$
$$Z_{K_0} = (L_1 \sin \theta_1 + L_2 \cos \theta_2 + 42.42 - L_3 \sin \theta_3 - 456.68) * \sin \theta_4$$

where, $\theta_1 \in (-12°, 110°)$, $\theta_2 \in (-70°, 130°)$, $\theta_3 \in [-195°, 240°]$, $\theta_4 \in [0°, 360°]$ is the rotating angle of manipulator relative to circular track in Fig. 10, $L_1 = 260$mm, $L_2 = 200$mm, $L_3 = 60$mm. Figure 9 gives the kinematic simulation of point K_0.

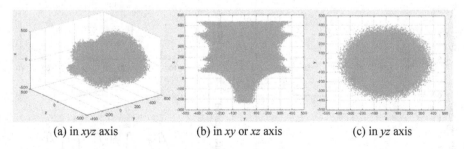

(a) in xyz axis   (b) in xy or xz axis   (c) in yz axis

Fig. 9. Kinematics of K_0 on the nozzle.

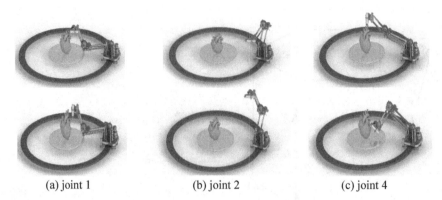

| (a) joint 1 | (b) joint 2 | (c) joint 4 |

Fig. 10. Postures of manipulator at typical positions. Top row: extreme positions of joint; bottom row: acceleration gust of joint.

Simulation of Manipulator Motions in Typical Positions. During motion of the manipulator, there are some typical positions (usually extreme positions) such as acceleration gusts, extreme positions, and collision positions shown in Fig. 10. When first rod is perpendicular to second one, joint 1 reaches extreme position at $\theta_3 = -90°$ and reaches acceleration gust position at $\theta_3 = 0°$ respectively. Joint 2 reaches extreme position at $\theta_2 = -70°$ and reaches acceleration gust position at $\theta_2 = 90°$ respectively. Joint 4 reaches extreme position once first rod and second one is collinear and reaches acceleration gust position once first rod is perpendicular to second one.

Simulation of Joint Angle. In the trajectory simulation, we used a sphere with radius of 100 mm for experimental testing. It is shown in Fig. 11 that the angle of first joint is increasing first and then decreasing, the angle of second joint is always decreasing, the angle of third joint is always zero, and the angle of fourth joint is a broken line (the

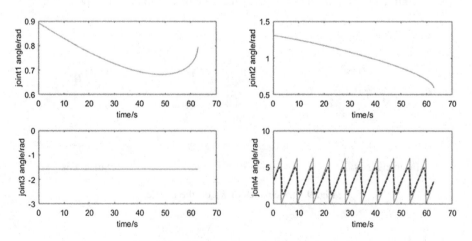

Fig. 11. Joint trajectory planning curve.

solid line). It should be noticed that there are periodical acceleration gust positions in the fourth joint's motion.

To eliminate this phenomenon of acceleration gust position we use non uniform rational B-spline (NURBS) to smooth the trajectory curve, and obtain an optimized curve (the dotted line). From results in Fig. 11, the smoothness of each planned joint trajectory (curve) have illustrated the effectiveness and flexibility of working space of designed manipulator for stereotactic printing.

4 Conclusions

3D printing received more and more attention in biomedicine with the growing demand for individualized fabrication. This research proposed and simulated a robot-assisted stereotactic printing method for biomedical printing. Kinematics of the proposed mechanism can be directly calculated without establishing a D-H coordinate system. Another advantage of the mechanism is that pose of the manipulator' end-effector always keeps fixed in a designed direction during movement of two parallelograms.

For further optimization, the followings should be considered. First, trajectory planning of the printing nozzle should be optimized. Spiral fill trajectory shows good performance when surface of print model is smooth. However, when the contour curve on the layered surface of model is complicated, it is difficult to completely represent contour features, which requires us to explore a new trajectory filling method. Second, spines such as NURBS can be used for smoothing trajectory curves in acceleration gust positions during the manipulator's movement. Third, the deployment of degree-of-freedoms (DOFs) of the system should be rearranged. It is better to increase DOFs by introducing a rotary moving platform, so that the printing nozzle can be kept fixed, and material of deposition module is carried out with rotating DOF of supporting platform. In some sense this requires a better motion planning for support platform.

Acknowledgments. The work is supported by the Beijing Natural Science Foundation (Grant no. Z170001), and the National Key R&D Program of China (Grant no. 2018YFB1307603).

References

1. Hiegemann, L., Agarwal, C., Weddeling, C., et al: Reducing the stair step effect of layer manufactured surfaces by ball burnishing. In: AIP Conference Proceedings on ESAFORM Conference, Nantes, France, pp. 372–378. AIP Publishing (2016)
2. Chakraborty, D., Reddy, B.A., Choudhury, A.R.: Extruder path generation for curved layer fused deposition modeling. Comput. Aided Des. **40**(2), 235–243 (2008)
3. Allen, R.J.A., Trask, R.S.: An experimental demonstration of effective curved layer fused filament fabrication utilising a parallel deposition robot. Addit. Manuf. **8**(1), 78–87 (2015)
4. Wu, C., Dai, C., Fang, G., et al: RoboFDM: a robotic system for support-free fabrication using FDM. In: Proceedings of the 2017 IEEE International Conference on Robotics and Automation (ICRA), Singapore, pp. 1175–1180, IEEE (2017)

5. Wang, Z., Min, J. K., Xiong, G.: Robotics-driven printing of curved 3D structures for manufacturing cardiac therapeutic devices. In: Proceedings of the International Conference on Robotics and Biomimetics (ROBIO), Zhuhai, China, pp. 2318–2323. IEEE (2015)
6. Liu, W.Y., Hou, X.L., Tan, B.S., et al.: Path planning and simulation of curved surface layering-based directional 3D printing. J. Mach. Des. **35**(S1), 10–14 (2018)
7. Kraljić, D., Kamnik, R.: Trajectory planning for additive manufacturing with a 6-DOF industrial robot. In: Aspragathos, N.A., Koustoumpardis, P.N., Moulianitis, V.C. (eds.) RAAD 2018. MMS, vol. 67, pp. 456–465. Springer, Cham (2019). https://doi.org/10.1007/978-3-030-00232-9_48
8. Li, Z., Yang, J., Wang, Q., et al.: Processing and 3D printing of gradient heterogeneous biomodel based on computer tomography images. IEEE Access **4**, 8814–8822 (2016)
9. Yang, Y., Loh, H.T., Fuh, J.Y.H., et al.: Equidistant path generation for improving scanning efficiency in layered manufacturing. Rapid Prototyp. J. **8**(1), 30–37 (2002)
10. Kim, D.S.: Polygon offsetting using a Voronoi diagram and two stacks. Comput. Aided Des. **30**(14), 1069–1076 (1998)
11. Zhao, H.S., Gu, F.L., Huang, Q.X., et al.: Connected Fermat spirals for layered fabrication. ACM Trans. Graph. **35**(4), 1–10 (2016)
12. Wang, X., Cai, J., Wu, Z., et al.: Normal estimation and normal orientation for point cloud model based on improved local surface fitting. J. Comput.-Aided Des. Comput. Graph. **4**, 614–620 (2015)

Adaptive Hybrid Impedance Control Algorithm Based on Subsystem Dynamics Model for Robot Polishing

Zihao Luo[✉], Jianfei Li, Jie Bai, Yaobing Wang, and Li Liu

Beijing Key Laboratory of Intelligent Space Robotic Systems Technology
and Applications, Beijing Institute of Spacecraft System Engineering,
Beijing, China
438940765@qq.com

Abstract. With the continuous application of robots, the accuracy requirements of robot control have been continuously improved. In the past, robot position control systems that can perform good palletizing, clamping, sorting, etc., have been unable to meet people's needs. Therefore, based on theory, simulation and experimental verification, this paper proposes an adaptive hybrid impedance control algorithm based on subsystem dynamics model design, which reduces the computational complexity of the algorithm and solves the problem of inaccurate modeling. Related research and discussion in combination with grinding experiments for different surfaces.

Keywords: Subsystem kinetic model · Adaptive control ·
Hybrid impedance control · Robot polishing system

1 Introduction

Most of the existing robotic robotic arm systems have certain advantages in handling non-refining operations such as gripping and palletizing, and are incapable of handling fine-grained operations such as high-precision assembly. For robots, it is very difficult to perform finer operations (such as high-precision grinding) more strictly than positioning accuracy. Therefore, the robot needs force control to accomplish this task.

On the one hand, the position control strategy of most robots is still not considering the PID control of the dynamic model, but for complex nonlinear strongly coupled robot systems, the PID control strategy has problems of poor stability, poor precision and low bandwidth. Robot Astronaut System in order to achieve some highly demanding tasks, the control strategy needs to consider the dynamics model of the robot. Further, when the robot operation completes the variable load task, the robot has dynamic model parameters and uncertainty of the working environment. The solution is a dynamic algorithm based control algorithm that combines an adaptive strategy or a non-model based control algorithm.

On the other hand, robots often have contact coordination operations in performing tasks, so it is necessary to use force control strategies to provide contact (operation function) and equipment and personnel protection (smooth function) during contact.

H. Yu et al. (Eds.): ICIRA 2019, LNAI 11745, pp. 163–176, 2019.
https://doi.org/10.1007/978-3-030-27529-7_15

Existing force control methods each have different situations and have limitations, so it is important to study the force control methods applicable to robots.

2   Robot Dynamics Model

In this section, we first derive the subsystem-based dynamics model and then derive the dynamic model based on the global system.

2.1   Subsystem Dynamics Model

Derivation of the Newton-Euler equation reference [2]. First, the subsystem label, as shown in Fig. 1 left, defines two coordinate systems at each end of each subsystem, called the inner body coordinate system and the outer body coordinate system.

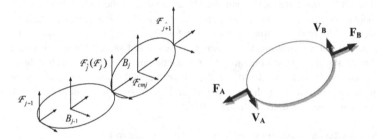

Fig. 1. Definition of subsystem coordinate system (left) & Relationship between velocity and force in different coordinate systems (right)

It is specified that the inner body coordinate system on the rigid body j and the outer body coordinate system on the rigid body $j - 1B$ coincide in the initial state, and the joint jC translates or rotates along the zD axis. In addition, a body coordinate system is established in the rigid body centroid, and the coordinate system direction is consistent with the inner body coordinate system. Define the following symbology (Table 1):

Table 1. Symbols and their meanings in the dynamics formula

Symbol	Meaning
B_j	rigid body j
F_j, $F_{\tilde{j}}$, F_{cmj}	External coordinate system, internal coordinate system, ontology coordinate system
m_j, I_j	The mass of the rigid body j, the inertia in the external body coordinate system
$p^{A,B}$, $C^{A,B}$	The position vector of the coordinate system B relative to the coordinate system A, the rotation matrix (represented in the coordinate system A)
$V_A = \begin{bmatrix} v_A \\ \omega_A \end{bmatrix}$	The speed of the coordinate system A (linear velocity, angular velocity) (representation in coordinate system A)
$F_A = \begin{bmatrix} f_A \\ m_A \end{bmatrix}$	Force (force, moment) at coordinate system A (representation in coordinate system A)

The Newton-Euler formula gives a chain recursion of velocity and force. Before deriving the dynamic equation, the transformation relationship between velocity and force in different coordinate systems is given.

Firstly, the subsystem dynamics equations are constructed, and then the dynamic equations of the complete robot system can be obtained according to the chain relationship between the subsystems. The relationship between the speed and acceleration (kinematic chain) in the positive sequence recursive and the force relationship (kinetic chain) in the reverse order are formed between the subsystems of the robot arm.

2.2   Global Model Dynamics

For a robot system with n-degree-of-freedom end force, the dynamic equations of the joint space and the end task space based on the Lagrange method are respectively the following second-order nonlinear differential equations:

$$\bar{M}(q)\ddot{q} + \bar{C}(q,\dot{q})\dot{q} + \bar{G}(q) = \tau + \tau_{\varepsilon} \tag{1}$$

$$M(X)\ddot{X} + C(X,\dot{X})\dot{X} + G(X) = F_u + F_{\varepsilon} \tag{2}$$

Where $q, \dot{q}, \ddot{q} \in R^n$ represents the joint position, velocity and acceleration vector respectively; $X, \dot{X}, \ddot{X} \in R^n$ represents the pose, velocity and acceleration vector of the task space respectively. If the Jacobian matrix is $J \in R^{6Xn}$, then $\dot{X} = J\dot{q}$ $\bar{M}(q) \in R^{nXn}, \bar{G}(q) \in R^n$ represents the joint space inertia matrix, Coriolis force and Centrifugal force matrix and gravity term vector; $M(X) \in R^{6X6}, C(X,\dot{X}) \in R^{6X6}, G(X) \in R^6$ represents task space inertia matrix, Coriolis force and centrifugal force matrix and gravity term vector, respectively, and $M = J^{-T}\bar{M}J^{-1}, C = J^{-T}\bar{C}J^{-1} + J^{-T}\bar{M}J^{-1}, G = J^{-T}\bar{G}; \tau \in R^n, F_u \in R^6$ represents the driving force vector of the joint and the expression in the task space, respectively, and $\tau = J^T F_u; \tau_e \in R^n, F_e \in R^6$ respectively represent. The expression of the contact force vector acting on the environment by the end effector in the joint space and the task space, and $\tau_e = J^T F_e$.

There are several properties of the robot system that are commons:

Property 1: Both $\bar{M}$ and M are symmetric positive definite matrices.

Property 2: Both $\dot{\bar{M}} - 2\bar{C}$ and $\dot{M} - 2C$ are antisymmetric matrices.

Property 3: The dynamic equations shown in Eqs. (1, 2) can be rewritten as a linear representation of a set of inertial parameters, namely:

$$\tau - \tau_e = \bar{M}(q)\ddot{q} + \bar{C}(q,\dot{q})\dot{q} + \bar{G}(q) = \bar{Y}(q,\dot{q},\ddot{q})\theta \tag{3}$$

$$F_u - F_e = M(X)\ddot{X} + C(X,\dot{X})\dot{X} + G(X) = Y(X,\dot{X},\ddot{X})\theta \tag{4}$$

Where $\theta \in R^k$ is the inertia parameter vector, k is the number of inertia parameters; $Y(X,\dot{X},\ddot{X})\theta \in R^{6k}, \bar{Y}(q,\dot{q},\ddot{q})\theta \in R^{nk}$ is the regression matrix of the task space and the joint space inertia parameter, respectively, and $Y(X,\dot{X},\ddot{X}) = J^{-T}\bar{Y}(q,\dot{q},\ddot{q})$ (Table 2).

Table 2. Dynamic modeling

Algorithm	Global system modeling (Lagrange method)	Subsystem modeling (Newton-Euler method [2])
Characteristics	Simple form, easy to analyze, computationally complex	Flexible form, recursive form, small computational complexity
Formula	**Joint space:** $\bar{M}(q)\ddot{q} + \bar{C}(q,\dot{q}) + \bar{G}(q) = \tau + \tau_e$ **Task space:** $M(X)\ddot{X} + C(X,\dot{X})\dot{X} + G(F) = F_u + F_e$	**Kinematic chain:** $V_i = T^{i,\hat{j}}V_{\hat{j}} + (\sigma_i z_3 + \bar{\sigma}_i z_6)\dot{q}_i$ $V_{\widehat{i+1}} = \dot{T}^{i,\hat{j}}V_i$ **Dynamic chain:** $M_i \cdot \dot{V}_i + C_i \cdot V_i + G_i = F_i^*$ $F_i = F_i^* + \left(T^{\widehat{i+1},i}\right)^T F_{\widehat{i+1}}$ $F_{\hat{j}} = \left(T^{i,\hat{j}}\right)^T F_i$

3 Adaptive Control Scheme

3.1 Inner/Outer Loop Control Strategy

Anderson and Spong [1] proposed an inner/outer loop control strategy, which can be developed into multiple control strategies under this control framework (Fig. 2).

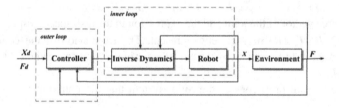

Fig. 2. The structure of the whole system.

Inner loop: PID control, feedback linearization, inverse kinematics (based on kinetic model);
Outer loop: additional controls to achieve more control objectives, trajectory tracking, force control, etc.

3.2 Inner Control Loop Design

As described in Sect. 2, the inner loop uses inverse dynamics and adds adaptive control to solve the problem of inaccurate modeling. The resulting control algorithm is Virtual Decomposition Control (VDC). The virtual decomposition control proposed in [3] is an adaptive control algorithm based on subsystem dynamics model. This article focuses on the proof of stability, please refer to the literature [3]. This article focuses on how our control system is built, as well as its simulation and experimental results.

Kinematic Chain (Control)

$$V_{ri} = T^{i\hat{l}}V_{r\hat{l}} + (\sigma_i z_3 + \bar{\sigma}_i z_6)\dot{q}_{ri}$$
$$V_{\widehat{ri+1}} = T^{l+1,i}V_{ri}$$
$$\dot{V}_{ri} = T^{i,\hat{l}}V_{r\hat{l}} + (\sigma_i z_3 + \bar{\sigma}_i z_6)\ddot{q}_{ri} \tag{5}$$
$$\dot{V}_{\widehat{rl+1}} = T^{l+1,i}\dot{V}_{ri}$$

Where $i \in \{1, 2, \ldots, n\}$, σ_i and $\bar{\sigma}_i$ represent the type of joint i, if it is a moving joint, then $\sigma_i = 0, \bar{\sigma}_i = 1$, if it is a rotating joint, then $z_3 = [0, 0, 1, 0, 0, 0]^T, z_6 = [0, 0, 0, 0, 0, 1]^T$. The initial speed and acceleration of the pedestal are zero and $V_{\widehat{rn+1}} = V_{ee}\dot{X}_r$.

Dynamic Chain (Control)

$$F_{ri}^* = \hat{M}_i \cdot \dot{V}_{ri} + \hat{C}_i \cdot V_{ri} + \hat{G}_i + K_{Di}(V_{ri} - V_i)$$
$$= Y_i(V_{ri}, \dot{V}_{ri})\hat{\theta}_i + K_{Di}(V_{ri} - V_i)$$
$$= Y_i(V_{ri}, \dot{V}_{ri})\theta_i + K_{Di}(V_{ri} - V_i) + Y_i(V_{ri}, \dot{V}_{ri})\tilde{\theta}_i \tag{6}$$
$$F_{ri} = F_{ri}^* + \left(T^{i,\hat{l}}\right)^T F_{ri}$$

Among them, $i \in \{n, n-1, \ldots, 1\}$. The initial condition is given by the external force of the end effector, $F_{\widehat{n+1}} = F_{ee}$. In addition, $\hat{\theta}_i \in R^r (R \leq 13)$ is an estimated value of θ_i, $\tilde{\theta}_i = \hat{\theta}_i - \theta_i$; $K_{Di} \in R^{6 \times 6}$ is a positive diagonal matrix. Note that in the calculation of the control link, the actual accelerations $\ddot{q}_i$ and $\dot{V}_i$ are not required, and the algorithm does not need to measure the amount of acceleration.

Design Adaptive Law:

$$\dot{\hat{\theta}}_i = \Gamma_i^{-1} Y_i^T (V_{ri}, \dot{V}_{ri})(V_{ri} - V_i) \tag{7}$$

There, Γ_i is a positive diagonal matrix.

Finally, the formula for the joint output torque is (Table 3):

$$\tau_i = (\sigma_i z_3 + \bar{\sigma}_i z_6)^T F_{ri} \tag{8}$$

Table 3. Adaptive control strategy

Adaptive algorithm	The computed torque method	Input and Output Theory
Characteristics	*need to calculate $\hat{M}^{-1}$*	*No need to calculate $\hat{M}^{-1}$*
Outer loop design variables	*Acceleration*	*Reference velocity*

Advantages of virtual decomposition control:

1. Advantages of subsystem modeling;
2. Advantages of input and output theory;
3. Reference velocity error $r = \dot{X}_r - \dot{X} \in L_6^2 \cap L_6^\infty$.

3.3 Outer Control Loop Design

The outer loop uses mixed impedance control to provide the following advantage:

1. Advantages of combined force/bit mixing control and impedance control;
2. Continue to follow the control objectives of impedance control;
3. Design impedance for position control subspace and force control subspace respectively;
4. Combine matrix selection for task space reference acceleration and reference speed.

Some characteristics of environmental impedance and expected impedance modeling of the manipulator in order to meet different objectives are given in [4], which is summarized as the dual theorem. This section only gives the goal of achieving position trajectory tracking in the position control subspace and achieving constant force control in the force control subspace. In the following, the control algorithm is derived by two decoupling controls of the bit control subspace and the force control subspace.

Position Control Subspace
The environment is modeled as resistive, that is $K_e = 0, Z_e(S) = M_e s + B_e$, then the contact force with the environment can be obtained:

$$F_e = M_e(\ddot{X} - \ddot{X}_e) + B_e(\dot{X} - \dot{X}_e) \tag{9}$$

In order to simplify the calculation, it is assumed that the contact surface is flat and the origin is at the contact surface, then $X_e = \dot{X}_e = 0$. In fact, in order to simplify the model, $M_e = 0$, there is only a damping term. According to the principle of duality, when the robot arm realizes position control, it is expected that the impedance must be set to capacitive, that is $Z_m(s) = M_d s + B_d + K_d/s$. At this point, we can write the dynamic equation that the mixed impedance control satisfies in the position control subspace:

$$M_d(\ddot{X} - \ddot{X}_d) + B_d(\dot{X} - \dot{X}_d) + K_d(X - X_d) = -F_e \tag{10}$$

If the positional auxiliary deviation is defined as (similar to the sliding surface, the same below):

$$\xi_p = M_d(\ddot{X} - \ddot{X}_d) + B_d(\dot{X} - \dot{X}_d) + K_d(X - X_d) + F_e \tag{11}$$

Then when $\xi_p = 0$, position control is achieved.

For the convenience of derivation, this section uses the global system dynamics model to derive. According to formula (11), the reference acceleration of the position control subspace can be designed as:

$$\ddot{X}_r = \ddot{X}_d - M_d^{-1}\left(B_d(\dot{X} - \dot{X}_d) + K_d(X - X_d) + F_e\right) \tag{12}$$

And define:

$$\dot{r} = \ddot{X}_r - \ddot{X} = \ddot{X}_d - \ddot{X} - \left(B_d(\dot{X} - \dot{X}_d) + K_d(X - X_d) + F_e\right) = -M_d^{-1}\xi_p \tag{13}$$

If $t \to \infty$, $\dot{r} \to 0$, then $\xi_p \to 0$, this satisfies the dynamic equation shown in Eq. (9), that is, position control is achieved.

In order to use the previously derived control law and adaptive law, the Eq. (12) is integrated over time to obtain:

$$\dot{X}_r = \dot{X}_d - M_d^{-1}\left(B_d(X - X_d) + \int_{t_0}^{t} K_d(X - X_d) + F_e)dt\right) \tag{14}$$

$$r = \dot{X}_d - \dot{X} - M_d^{-1}\left(B_d(X - X_d) + \int_{t_0}^{t} K_d(X - X_d) + F_e)dt\right) \tag{15}$$

Where $t \ge t_0 \ge 0$. This is the reference speed of the bit control subspace.

Force Control Subspace

For a fixed environment, the environment is modeled as capacitive, that is $M_e = 0, Z_e(s) = B_e + K_e/s$. At this point, the contact force of the environment can be obtained:

$$F_e = B_e(\dot{X} - \dot{X}_e) + K_e(X - X_e) \tag{16}$$

To simplify the calculation, assume that the contact surface is flat and the origin is at the contact surface, that is $X_e = \dot{X}_e = 0$. According to the principle of duality, when the mechanical arm realizes force control, it is expected that the impedance must be set to resistivity, that is $Z_m(s) = M_d s + B_d$. At this point, we can write the dynamic equation that the mixed impedance control satisfies in the force control subspace:

$$M_d\ddot{X} + B_d\dot{X} = F_d - F_e \tag{17}$$

Similarly, if the force assisted deviation is defined as:

$$\xi_f = M_d\ddot{X} + B_d\dot{X} - (F_d - F_e) \tag{18}$$

Then when $\xi_f = 0$, the force control is realized.

According to formula (16), the reference acceleration of the force control subspace can be designed as:

$$\ddot{X}_r = -M_d^{-1}\left(B_d\dot{X} - (F_d - F_e)\right) \tag{19}$$

If we define:

$$\dot{r} = \ddot{X}_r - \ddot{X} = -\ddot{X} - M_d^{-1}\left(B_d\dot{X} - (F_d - F_e)\right) = -M_d^{-1}\xi_f \tag{20}$$

If $t \to 0$, $\dot{r} \to 0$, then $\xi_f \to 0$, this satisfies the dynamic equation shown in Eq. (17), that is, force control is achieved.

In order to use the previously derived control law and adaptive law, the Eq. (19) is integrated over time to obtain:

$$\dot{x}_r = -M_d^{-1}\left(B_d X - \int_{t_0}^{t} (F_d - F_e)dt\right) \tag{21}$$

$$r = -\dot{x} - M_d^{-1}\left(B_d X - \int_{t_0}^{t} (F_d - F_e)dt\right) \tag{22}$$

Where $t \geq t_0 \geq 0$. This is the reference speed of the force control subspace.

Control Law and Adaptive Law
In order to use the previous conclusions, the control law and the adaptive law in this section are respectively the formulas (6) and (7). For the convenience of formula derivation, it is transformed into global system dynamics, as shown in Eqs. (23) and (24), respectively (Tables 4 and 5).

$$\begin{aligned}\tau &= J^T\left(\hat{M}\ddot{X}_r + \hat{C}\dot{X}_r + \hat{G} + K_D\left(\dot{X}_r - \dot{X}\right) + F_e\right)\\ &= J^T\left(Y\left(X, \dot{X}, \dot{X}_r, \ddot{X}_r\right)\hat{\theta} + K_D\left(\dot{X}_r - \dot{X}\right) + F_e\right)\end{aligned} \tag{23}$$

$$\dot{\hat{\theta}} = \Gamma^{-1}Y^T\left(X, \dot{X}, \dot{X}_r, \ddot{X}_r\right)\left(\dot{X}_r - \dot{X}\right) \tag{24}$$

Table 4. Position/Force control subspace

	Position control subspace	Force control subspace
Control target	$M_d\left(\ddot{X} - \ddot{X}_d\right) + B_d\left(\dot{X} - \dot{X}_d\right) + K_d(X - X_d) = -F_e$	$M_d\ddot{X} + B_d\dot{X} = F_d - F_e$
Reference acceleration	$\ddot{X}_r = \ddot{X}_d - M_d^{-1}\left(B_d\left(\dot{X} - \dot{X}_d\right) + K_d(X - X_d) + F_e\right)$	$\ddot{X}_r = -M_d^{-1}\left(B_d\dot{X} - (F_d - F_e)\right)$

Table 5. Task/joint control subspace

	Position control subspace	Force control subspace
Reference acceleration	$\ddot{X}_r = S\ddot{X}_d - M_d^{-1}\left(B_d\left(\dot{X} - S\dot{X}_d\right) + K_d S(X - X_d) + SF_e - (1 - S)(F_d - F_e)\right)$	$\ddot{X}_r = \int_{t_0}^t \ddot{X}_r dt$
Reference velocity	$\ddot{q}_r = J^{-1}\left(\dot{X}_r - JJ^{-1}\dot{X}_r\right)$	$\dot{q}_r = J^{-1}\dot{X}_r$

4   Simulation Results and Experiment

4.1   Simulation of 2-dof Manipulator

This section verifies and analyzes the control algorithm proposed in Sect. 2 through a series of simulation experiments and physical platform experiments. Note that this section only gives the validity of the algorithm. As for the calculation of the global model and subsystem model algorithms in terms of computational complexity, adaptive ability and control accuracy, reference can be made to [5].

This simulation task requires a two-degree-of-freedom manipulator to control the constant force in the vertical direction (direction) and position control in the horizontal direction (direction) to track the uniform motion.

Figure 3 shows the process of two-degree-of-freedom manipulators performing constant force control on planes and small curved surfaces.

The setup environment is modeled as follows: $M_e = 0, B_e = diag\{0, 1e3\}$, $K_d = diag\{0, 1e6\}$. Set the x direction biasing force to $F_e = 0$, therefore, B_e is also set to 0 in the x direction dimension. Select matrix as $S = diag\{1, 0\}$, Expected speed is $\dot{X}_d = [0.02, 0]^T$, Expected power is $F_d = [0, -5]^T$. The expected inertia matrix is $M_d = diag\{10, 10\}$. The expected damping matrix is $B_d = diag\{1000, 1000\}$. When setting the desired impedance matrix, the expected stiffness value in the z direction is zero, and the expected stiffness matrix is $K_d = diag\{50, 0\}$.

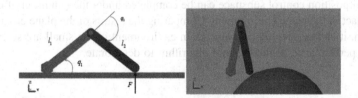

Fig. 3. Two-degree-of-freedom mechanical arm constant force control diagram

The simulation results are shown in the figure below. Figure 4 shows the speed tracking curve in the x direction and the force tracking curve in the z direction in the plane environment. Figure 5 left shows the position tracking error curve in the x direction. The results show that both the velocity and the contact force converge quickly to the desired value, while the oscillation is small. The position tracking error curve indicates that the position tracking task of the orthogonal position control subspace can be completed under the condition of constant force contact in the plane environment.

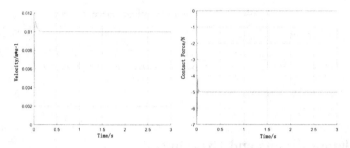

Fig. 4. Plane environment speed tracking and force tracking curve

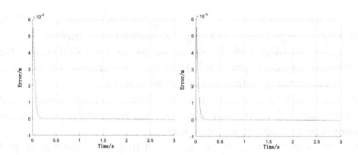

Fig. 5. Position tracking error map for planar environment (left) & Position tracking error map of small curved surface environment (right)

Figure 6 shows the speed tracking curve in the x direction and the force tracking curve in the z direction in a small curved surface environment. Figure 5 right shows the position tracking error curve in the x direction. The results show that both the velocity and the contact force converge quickly to the desired value, while the oscillation is small. The position tracking error curve indicates that the position tracking task of the orthogonal position control subspace can be completed under the condition of constant force contact in the plane environment. Comparing the results of the plane environment simulation, it can be seen that the uncertain environment of the small arc surface will cause the performance of the original algorithm to deteriorate.

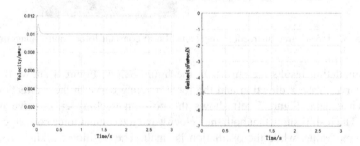

Fig. 6. Small arc surface environmental velocity tracking and force tracking curve

4.2 Experiments on a Manipulator Platform with Multiple Degree of Freedom

In this section, the constant force control experiment is carried out on the physical platform of multiple degree of freedom manipulator. The two engineering applications of hard pen writing and polishing are taken as examples to demonstrate whether the above-mentioned adaptive impedance control algorithm based on subsystem dynamics model is effective

Control algorithm In the robot real-time operating system TwinCAT 3 [6], Twin-CAT 3 supports the code generation technology of Simulink model, which can quickly realize MATLAB simulation code. The control algorithm is fully implemented on the TwinCAT 3 platform, using only the current loop of the servo drive, and the control signals are passed through the EtherCAT fast bus.

Figure 7 show the process of writing a seven-degree-of-freedom manipulator in a flat hard pen and a six-degree-of-freedom manipulator in a small curved surface.

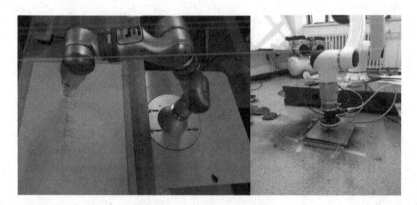

Fig. 7. Mechanical arm hard pen writing "Beijing welcomes you" (left) & Mechanical arm grinding experiment in small curved surface (right)

The following is a detailed analysis of the small arc surface grinding by the mechanical arm of the Han's robot Elfin series 10 kg load. The contact force is measured by a 6-dimensional force sensor with a resolution of 0.01 N. Let the vertical direction (z direction) be constant force control, the horizontal direction (x direction) be uniform speed tracking control, and the other directions keep the position and attitude angle unchanged, that is, the selection matrix is $S = diag\{1, 1, 1, 1, 0, 1\}$. The reference speed is set as shown in Eqs. (10) and (17), and the biasing force of the position control subspace is $F_e = 0$.

The expected speed is $\dot{X}_d = [0.02, 0, 0, 0, 0, 0]^T$ and the expected force is $F_d = [0, 0, -5, 0, 0, 0]^T$. The expected inertia matrix is $M_d = diag\{10, 10, 10, 10, 10, 10\}$, the expected damping matrix is $B_d = diag\{1500, 1500, 1500, 500, 500, 500\}$, and when the desired impedance matrix is set, the expected stiffness value in the z direction is zero, and the expected stiffness matrix is $K_d = diag\{100, 100, 0, 300, 300, 300\}$.

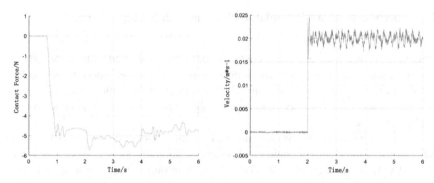

Fig. 8. Contact force curve in the z direction & Speed tracking curve in the x direction

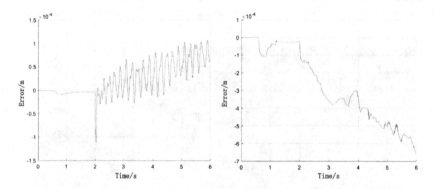

Fig. 9. Position tracking error: x direction (left) and y direction (right)

Figure 8 left shows the contact force in the z direction. From the measurement results, the impact at the time of contact is small, and the contact force quickly converges to the desired value, but there is also oscillation. Figure 8 right shows the speed tracking curve in the x direction. According to the measurement results, the overshoot of the speed is small, and it can quickly converge to the required speed. Figure 9 shows the position tracking error in the x direction and the y direction, respectively. The x direction is the constant speed command, and the y direction is the position where the speed is zero. From the measurement results, the x direction position tracking error is small, and the y direction is small. A position with a zero speed maintains a large error.

5   Conclusion

The control algorithm of this paper is based on the double loop control system. For the inner loop control, the robot dynamics model of the end force system is first established. The subsystem based dynamic model is introduced in detail, and the dynamic model based on the global system is introduced. In contrast, the subsystem-based dynamic model has a small amount of computation; for the terminal force system, an adaptive control algorithm based on subsystem dynamics, namely VDC algorithm, is proposed to replace the traditional global system dynamics. Inner loop control of the model or feedback linearization algorithm design.

A key issue in force control is the lack of accuracy of the robot dynamics model. Adaptive and robust methods are used for hybrid control [7]. The outer loop is designed to satisfy the hybrid impedance control algorithm, and divides the task space into a bit control subspace and a force control subspace according to the desired impedance relationship. Based on the dual model of hybrid impedance control algorithm, the expected impedance and environmental impedance of the manipulator are modeled in two subspaces, and the reference velocity of the corresponding subspace is designed. Then based on the conclusion of the VDC algorithm, the reference velocity of the two subspaces can be known. It can satisfy the relationship of the desired impedance, further explain that the position trajectory tracking of the position control subspace and the constant force contact algorithm of the force control subspace are stable, and can greatly reduce the calculation amount. In order to exploit the computational advantages of the subsystem dynamics model, the expected speed of the task space is transformed into adaptive hybrid impedance control based on the subsystem dynamics model.

In order to verify the effectiveness of the algorithm, a series of simulation experiments and physical platform experiments were designed. In the simulation experiment, the two-degree-of-freedom manipulator is used to perform the constant force control in the vertical direction and the position tracking task in the horizontal direction in the unknown environment model (plane and small arc surface). In the physical platform experiment, the seven-degree-of-freedom mechanical arm was used to perform the hard pen writing experiment on the horizontal surface and the six-degree-of-freedom mechanical arm on the small curved surface. The experimental results show that the algorithm can control the accuracy in the horizontal contact, and the control accuracy in the uncertain environment (surface) is relatively insufficient.

6   Summary

In this work, we propose a hybrid impedance control algorithm based on subsystem dynamics model to reduce the computational complexity of the algorithm and adaptive control to solve the problem of inaccurate modeling. The algorithm can guarantee high control precision in the planar environment (including Position accuracy and force accuracy), while ensuring a certain degree of control accuracy in a curved environment that is not too complicated.

References

1. Anderson, R.J., Spong, M.W.: Hybrid impedance control of robotic manipulators. IEEE J. Robot. Autom. 4(5), 549–556 (1988)
2. Luh, J.Y.S., Walker, M.W., Paul, R.P.C.: On-line computational scheme for mechanical manipulators. J. Dyn. Syst. Measur. Control 102(2), 69–76 (1980)

3. Zhu, W.H.: Virtual Decomposition Control: Toward Hyper Degrees of Freedom Robots. Springer, Heidelberg (2010). https://doi.org/10.1007/978-3-642-10724-5
4. Hosseinzadeh, M., Aghabalaie, P., Talebi, H.A., et al.: Adaptive hybrid impedance control of robotic manipulators. In: IECON 2010-36th Annual Conference on IEEE Industrial Electronics Society, pp. 1442–1446. IEEE (2010)
5. Li, J., Liu, L., Wang, Y., et al.: Adaptive hybrid impedance control of robot manipulators with robustness against environment's uncertainties. In: 2015 IEEE International Conference on Mechatronics and Automation (ICMA), pp. 1846–1851. IEEE (2015)
6. Wannagat, A., Vogel-Heuser, B.: Increasing flexibility and availability of manufacturing systems-dynamic reconfiguration of automation software at runtime on sensor faults. IFAC Proc. Vol. **41**(3), 278–283 (2008)
7. Chen, Y.H., Pandey, S.: Robust hybrid control of robot manipulators. In: Proceedings of IEEE International Conference on Robotics and Automation, vol. 1, pp. 236–241, 14–19 May 1989

Robot Design, Development and Control

Design of Wall Climbing Robot
with Non-magnetic Surface

Liang Zhao[1,2(✉)], Chunlong Liu[1], Shaoyun Zhou[3], Deyong Zhu[1,2],
and Chuang Liu[1,2]

[1] Changchun Institute of Optics, Fine Mechanics and Physics,
Chinese Academy of Sciences, Changchun 130033, China
LiangzhaoSEU@outlook.com
[2] University of Chinese Academy of Science, Beijing 100049, China
[3] Tohoku University, Sendai 980-8579, Japan

Abstract. With the rapid development of economy, the energy consumption in the world is accelerating, and the number of large pressure vessels which are convenient for storing fuels is increasing. Large pressure vessels generally use a welding process to close the wall surface, and the weld seam needs to be inspected regularly to ensure the safe operation of the pressure vessels. At present, the main detection of welds is manual, and it is expected that magnetic pressure vessel can be detected by magnetic adsorption robots. In order to detect large non-magnetic pressure vessels, we conducted a study on a pneumatic adsorption wall climbing robot. We first develop a basic research plan for the mechanical design of wall climbing robot and then build a mathematical model based on the actual situation of the wall climbing robot which is working on the surface of pressure vessels. By CFD simulation technology, the simulation and experiment results of the aerodynamics of the impeller rotation from inside of wall climbing robot can be envisioned and verified.

Keywords: Non-magnetic surface · Wall climbing robot ·
Vacuum adsorption · Aerodynamics

1 Introduction

With the rapid development of the economy, energy consumption is accelerating, the number of large pressure vessels which are convenient for storing fuels and chemical products is increasing [1]. Large pressure vessels are generally connected by a welding process, we need to regularly inspect the weld to ensure the safety of the pressure vessel [2–4]. At present, the main detection of welds is mainly manual, expect that magnetic pressure vessel can be detected by magnetic adsorption robots [5, 6]. The current inspecting work has a lot of problems such as low detection efficiency, poor adaptability and high cost [7–12].

In order to detect large non-magnetic pressure vessels, we conducted a study on a pneumatic adsorption wall climbing robot [12–16]. We use a centrifugal impeller to spin the air at a high speed to generate negative pressure in the shell of robot. This method is highly adaptable and safe [16–20]. In addition to the application of the detection to non-

© Springer Nature Switzerland AG 2019
H. Yu et al. (Eds.): ICIRA 2019, LNAI 11745, pp. 179–189, 2019.
https://doi.org/10.1007/978-3-030-27529-7_16

magnetic pressure vessels [21, 22], we can also apply our robot to high-altitude glass cleaning, wall spraying, ship descaling and military application [22–25].

2   Overall Design and Mechanical Structure

Wheeled motion structure is common in our life, its main advantage is that the structure is simple, light, easy to control and flexible to move [26]. The crawler type mechanism has strong adaptability and stable movement, but its movement structure is cumbersome and poor flexible. Foot-type motion mechanism can cross larger obstacles and complex work surfaces [27], but its speed is very slow. According to the actual working condition of the non-magnetic wall surface, we select the wheeled motion mechanism as it is shown in Fig. 1.

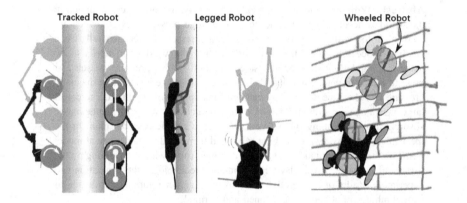

Fig. 1. Three kinds of motion structures of the robot.

We choose eight ordinary DC motors for robot movement, and two high-speed DC brushless motor drives the centrifugal fan to generate negative pressure [28]. We chose the Arduino Uno R3 development board as the control center. The ordinary DC motor is driven by the L298N driver chip. High-speed Maxon motors work with Swiss Maxon drives, the rated power of the motor is 80 W, the rated speed is up to 11888 r/min, and the 100:1 reducer is used to meet the driving torque requirements. We add the infrared receiving module to the circuit, set up the wireless controller, and define each button by writing code, so that the signal can be transmitted through the development board to realize remote control according to the signal transmitted by the button. In terms of power supply, we add an adjustable buck module to meet the power requirements of different components. The moving mechanism is the active mode of the two rear wheels and the two front wheels. According to the overall scheme, we use Solidworks software to complete 3D modeling. The overall mechanical structure model is shown in Fig. 2.

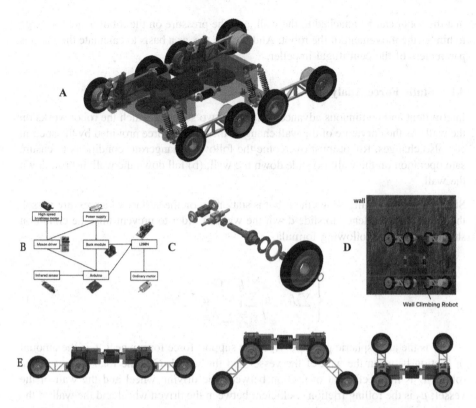

Fig. 2. Overall design and mechanical structure of wall climbing robot. (A) 3D model of the wall climbing robot. (B) Control framework of the wall climbing robot, which is composed of high speed brushless motor, power supply, maxon driver, buck module, L298N driver, infrared sensor, arduino and ordinary motor. (C) Detailed illustration of the wheel of the wall climbing robot. (D) The state of the wall climbing robot is under air adsorption conditions. (E) Three motion states of the wall climbing robot.

3   Robot Safety Adsorption Conditions Analysis

For the wall climbing robot, it cannot fall off the wall during the operation [29–31]. We should prevent the damage of the robot causing a major safe accident. In order to meet the need of the work, the robot also needs to move flexibly on the wall. If the resistance is too large, it is difficult to move. Under normal conditions, the centrifugal impeller rotates at high speed to continuously suck the air inside the casing, so that the internal pressure of the casing is lower than atmospheric pressure [32]. During the operation, as the curvature of the pressure vessels changes, the suction force generated by the suction cup also changes. The force and motion state of the robot during the operation on the wall will be complicated and varied due to change in external conditions, adsorption mechanism needs to have sufficient adsorption and good surface adaptability. For the three main critical conditions, we analyse the force and list the equilibrium equations to find the range of forces required for the robot to be adsorbed on the wall. We guarantee that the robot can be attached to the wall, and the pressure on the robot is not too large to hinder the movement of the robot. And we use this as a basis to calculate the various parameters of the centrifugal impeller.

3.1 Static Force Analysis

Intermittent and continuous advancement is the two states in which the robot works on the wall. As the curvature of the wall changes, the suction force provided by the suction cup also changes. Robot must overcome the following dangerous conditions to ensure safe operation on the wall: (a) slide down the wall; (b) fall down the wall; (c) roll down the wall.

Slide Down the Wall. When the robot is stationary on the surface of a pressure vessel, there may be a tendency to slide down the wall. In order to prevent this, the condition should satisfy the following formula:

$$\begin{cases} \sum f_i \geq G \\ \sum f_i = \mu_1 \sum_1^2 N_i + \mu_2 \sum_3^4 N_i \\ F_X = \sum N_i \end{cases} \tag{1}$$

F_X is the atmospheric pressure; N_i is the support force form wheel; f_i is the amount of friction between the wall of the vessel and the wheel; G is the total weight of the robot; μ_1 is the coefficient of friction between the driving wheel and the wall of the vessel; μ_2 is the rolling friction coefficient between the driven wheel and the wall of the vessel; i is the number of robot wheels $i = 1$–4.

We idealize the wall during the analysis and calculation process. So μ_2 is small and it can be ignored. According to the above formula, we can get the following inequalities:

$$F_X \geq G/\mu_1 \tag{2}$$

Fall Down the Wall. In the case of uneven distribution inside the robot, the center of gravity of the robot may not be at its center, so the body may fall down. We can list the torque balance equation as follows:

$$\frac{W}{2} F_X - W(N_3 + N_4) - GH = 0 \tag{3}$$

W is the distance between the driving wheel and the driven wheel; H is the distance between the center of the robot and the center of gravity of the robot.

In order to prevent the robot from falling down the wall, the wheel of the robot must be in contact with the surface of the pressure vessels. The main driven wheel receives positive support:

$$N_1 > 0, N_2 > 0, N_3 > 0, N_4 > 0 \tag{4}$$

In the end we can get the conditions for the robot not to fall down the wall:

$$F_X \geq \frac{2H}{W} G \tag{5}$$

Roll Down the Wall. If the robot rolls down from the surface of the pressure vessels, the motor is self-locking. The motor uses a 100:1 reducer with high resistance to prevent the robot from rolling down. The static safety adsorption force $[F_X]$ provided by the robot adsorption structure needs to meet the following conditions:

$$[F_X] \geq \max\left(\frac{G}{\mu_1}, \frac{2H}{W} G\right) \tag{6}$$

3.2   Dynamic Force Analysis

On the surface of the pressure vessels, the robot can be at any angle. According to D'Alembert's principle:

$$\begin{cases} \sum f_i - G - ma = 0 \\ W(N_3 + N_4) + GH + maH - \frac{W}{2} F_X = 0 \end{cases} \tag{7}$$

m is the total mass of the robot; a is the motion acceleration of the robot.

Combined with the conclusions obtained from the above static analysis, we can conclude that the conditions required for adsorption are as follows:

$$[F_X] \geq \max\left(\frac{G + ma}{\mu_1}, \frac{2H(G + ma)}{W}\right) \tag{8}$$

Assumed robot parameters is $H = 50\,\text{mm}$. Distance between front and rear wheels is $W = 200\,\text{mm}$. The maximum acceleration is 0.1 g, and constant $\mu_1 < 1$. We get the safe adsorption of the robot in any state:

$$F_X \geq \frac{1.1G}{\mu_1} \tag{9}$$

Because the life of pressure vessels is generally long, there will be rust, oil, and unevenness on the wall of the pressure vessels. Part of the contact between the wheel and the wall is in the boundary friction, we look up the literature and get the range of friction coefficient is 0.5–0.8. When the friction coefficient μ_1 is equal to 0.5, the maximum F_X is 80 N. When the safety factor is 2, We can get F_X minimum is 160 N.

4 Calculation of Geometric Parameters of Centrifugal Fan

According to the work requirements of the wall climbing robot, we can convert the safety adsorption force into the flow, hydraulic head and speed parameters of the centrifugal fan [33]. As is shown in Fig. 3, we design the geometric parameters of the impeller according to the following process:

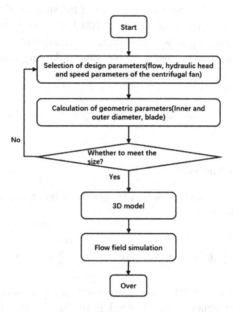

Fig. 3. Blade design flow.

Firstly, we calculate the specific speed according to the hydraulic head and flow of the fan:

$$n_s = 5.54 n q_m^{1/2} / (1.2 H / \rho)^{3/4} \tag{10}$$

According to n_s we can roughly determine the type of centrifugal fan and the form of the blade to calculate the blade geometry.

According to the empirical relationship between the pressure coefficient π_k^* and the exit angle, we can find out the value of the blade exit angle β_{2A}. We can calculate the circumferential speed of the impeller according to the following formula:

$$\mu_2 = \sqrt{H / (\rho \pi_k^*)} \tag{11}$$

From this we can calculate the following parameters:

$$\text{Impeller outer diameter}: \quad D_2 = 60\mu_2/(\pi n) \tag{12}$$

$$\text{Inlet diameter}: \quad D_0 \geq 1.194 D_2 \sqrt[3]{Q} \tag{13}$$

$$\text{Number of blades}: \quad Z \approx 8.5 \sin\beta_{2A}/(1 - D_0/D_2) \tag{14}$$

$$\text{Blade outlet width}: \quad b_2 = \pi_k^* D_2 \mu_2/(4\tau_2 C_{2r}) \tag{15}$$

$$\text{Blade inlet width}: \quad b_1 \approx b_2 D_2/D_0 \tag{16}$$

We have detailed geometric parameters as shown in Table 1:

Table 1. Detailed parameter table of centrifugal fan.

Parameter	Unit	Data
Speed	rpm	6500
Flow	Kg/s	0.03
Hydraulic head	m	310
D0	mm	58
D2	mm	208
B1	mm	15.5
B2	mm	6
Number		11

Based on the above parameters, we use the turbomachine blade design tool Bladegen to model the blade. The blade profile flow follows the B-spline curve to ensure that the impeller has a good aerodynamic performance. The three-dimensional model of the centrifugal fan is shown in Fig. 4.

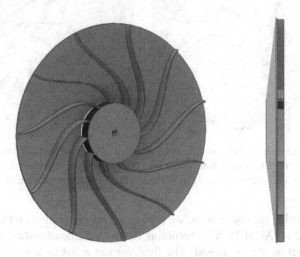

Fig. 4. 3D model of the centrifugal fan.

5   CFD Simulation of Centrifugal Fan

Because the 3D model is complex, we need to simplify the model reasonably during the simulation [34]. Firstly, we import the 3D model into the ANSYS DM module for fluid domain extraction. We use the By Gaps method in Fill to first close the opening position of the 3D model to the surface. After all the closures are completed, we can extract the fluid calculation domain directly. After the fluid domain extraction is completed, we directly delete the simplified 3D model, as shown in Fig. 5(a). After completing the extraction of the fluid domain, we mesh the fan runners, as shown in Fig. 5(b). In order to facilitate the setting of boundary conditions, we rename several boundary surfaces, the entrance boundary is named Inlet, and the exit boundary is named Outlet.

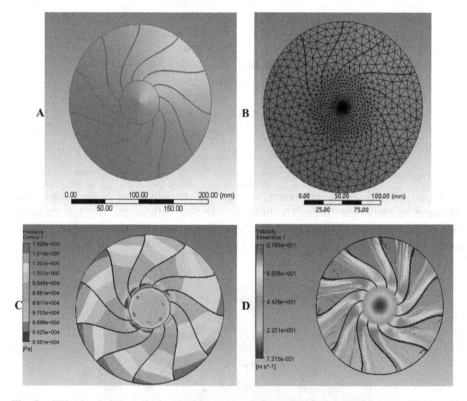

Fig. 5. CFD simulation analysis of the centrifugal fan. (A) Fluid domain model diagram of centrifugal impeller. (B) Finite element meshing of centrifugal impeller. (C) Pressure field distribution diagram of centrifugal fan. (D) Velocity field distribution diagram of centrifugal fan.

After completing the above steps, we next set up pre-processing on the fluid model. The type of fluid is "Air at 25 °C". According to the fluid characteristics, we choose the turbulence model as the k-e model. The fluid domain is set to a wall except for the entrance and exit. The blade rotating wall rotates at 6500 rpm. After the boundary conditions are set, we calculate the fluid domain. The pressure field and velocity field distribution of the centrifugal fan are shown in Fig. 5.

From the pressure field distribution diagram of the centrifugal fan, the air sucked in after the fan rotates at a high speed will rapidly decompress to form a stable pressure gradient. According to the data in the figure, the internal and external pressure difference is approximately 3 kPa. The negative pressure area is calculated according to $300 \times 300\,mm^2$ to produce a pressure of 270 N, we have got minimum force is 160 N from mathematical calculation in Sect. 3, which fully satisfies the safe adsorption condition. The velocity field distribution shows that the circumferential velocity distribution of the airflow from the inlet to the outlet is relatively uniform. Centrifugal fan energy conversion efficiency is high. At the same time, the oil slag and rust in the pressure vessel can be carried away from the wall with a high-speed air stream.

6 Conclusion

In this paper, large non-magnetic pressure vessels are studied. We design a welding seam detecting wall climbing robot that can adapt to different material walls of pressure vessels. We calculate the range of forces that the robot adsorbed on the wall to ensure that it could be attached to the wall while the pressure was not too high to hinder the movement. We design a centrifugal fan that meets the requirements of the work, test the aerodynamic performance of the centrifugal fan through CFD simulation, demonstrate the efficiency of the centrifugal fan, and achieve the expected adsorption effect.

References

1. Omori, H., Nakamura, T., Yada, T.: An underground explorer robot based on peristaltic crawling of earthworms. Ind. Robot Int. J. **36**(4), 358–364 (2009)
2. Zhang, Y., Nishi, A.: Low-pressure air motor for wall-climbing robot actuation. Mechatronics **13**(4), 377–392 (2003)
3. Jiang, Y., Wang, H., Fang, L.: Motion control of micro wall-climbing robot on unsmoothed wall. In: World Congress on Intelligent Control and Automation, pp. 3252–3257 (2008)
4. Guo, L., Rogers, K., Kirkham: A climbing robot for wall exploration. In: Proceedings of IEEE/ASME International Conference on Robotics and Automation, pp. 2495–2500 (1994)
5. Karla, L.P., Gu, J., Meng, M.: A wall climbing robot for oil tank inspection. In: Proceedings of the IEEE International Conference on Robotics and Biomimetics, pp. 1523–1528 (2006)
6. Xu, Z.L., Ma, P.S.: A wall-climbing robot for labelling scale of oil tank's volume. Robotica **20**(2), 209–212 (2002)
7. Hagen, S.: Neptune: above-ground storage tank inspection robot system. IEEE Robot. Autom. Mag. **2**(2), 9–15 (1995)
8. Blander, J., Zealand, M.A.F.B.N.: Review of Options for In-water Cleaning of Ships. MAF Biosecurity New Zealand, Wellington (2009)
9. Ross, B., Bares, J.: A semi-autonomous robot for stripping paint from large vessels. Int. J. Robot. Res. **22**, 617–626 (2003)

10. Xu, Z., Zhang, K.: Design and optimization of a magnetic wheel for a grit-blasting robot for use on ship hulls. Robotic **35**, 712–728 (2017)
11. Shi, Y., Cao, Z.X., et al.: Study on air flow dynamic characteristic of mechanical ventilation of a lung simulator. Sci. China Technol. Sci. **60**, 243–250 (2017)
12. Bogue, R.: Robots in the nuclear industry: a review of technologies and applications. Ind. Robot. **38**, 113–118 (2011)
13. Balaguer, C., Gimenez, A., Abdulrahim, C.M.: ROMA robots for inspection of steel-based infrastructures. Ind. Robot. **29**, 246–251 (2002)
14. Bagherzadeh, M.R., Vosburgh, G.R.: Design and prototyping of a hybrid pole climbing and manipulating robot with minimum DOFs for construction and service applications. In: Manuel, A., Pablo, G.S. (eds.) Climbing and Walking Robots, pp. 1071–1080. Springer, Berlin (2005). https://doi.org/10.1007/3-540-29461-9_105
15. Tawakoni, M., Vosburgh, G.R.: A hybrid pole climbing and manipulating robot with minimum DOFs for construction and service applications. Ind. Robot. **32**, 171–178 (2005)
16. Ortiz, F., Alonso, D.: A reference control architecture for service robots implemented on a climbing vehicle. In: Vardanega, T., Wellings, A. (eds.) Reliable Software Technologies. LNCS, vol. 3555, pp. 13–24. Springer, Berlin (2005). https://doi.org/10.1007/11499909_2
17. Shi, Y., Wang, Y., Cai, M.: Study on the aviation oxygen supply system based on a mechanical ventilation model. Chin. J. Aeronaut. **31**, 197–204 (2018)
18. Xiao, J., Li, B., Song, Q.: Rise-Rover: a wall-climbing robot with high reliability and load-carrying capacity. In: Proceedings of IEEE International Conference on Robotics Biomimetics (ROBIO), pp. 2072–2077, December 2015
19. Pope, M.T.: A multimodal robot for perching and climbing on vertical outdoor surfaces. IEEE Trans. Robot. **33**(1), 38–48 (2017)
20. Jung, Y., Jung, S.W., Jung, Y.H., Myung, H.: Development of a drone-type wall-sticking and climbing robot. In: 12th International Conference Ubiquitous Robots Ambient Intelligence (URAI), pp. 386–389, October 2015
21. Guan, Y., et al.: A modular biped wall-climbing robot with high mobility and manipulating function. IEEE/ASME Trans. Mechatronics **18**(6), 1787–1798 (2013)
22. Qian, Z.Y., Zhao, Y.Z., Fu, Z.: Development of wall-climbing robots with sliding suction cups. In: IEEE/RSJ International Conference Intelligent Robots and Systems, pp. 3417–3422, October 2006
23. Taches, F., Fischer, W.: Magnebike: a magnetic wheeled robot with high mobility for inspecting complex-shaped structures. Field Robot. **26**(5), 453–476 (2009)
24. Lee, G., Woo, J., Kim, J.: High-payload climbing and transitioning by compliant locomotion with magnet adhesion. Robot. Autonomy. Syst. **60**(10), 1308–1316 (2012)
25. Zhu, H., Guan, Y., Wu, W., Zhang, L., Zhou, X., Zhang, H.: Autonomous pose detection and alignment of suction modules of a biped wall-climbing robot. IEEE-ASME Trans. Metatron. **20**(2), 653–662 (2015)
26. Lee, G., Kim, H., So, K.: Series of multilinked caterpillar track-type climbing robots. J. Field Robot. **3**(6), 737–750 (2016)
27. Barometer, P., Gillies, A.G., Fearing, R.S.: Dynamic climbing of near-vertical smooth surfaces. In: International Conference on Intelligent Robots and Systems (IROS), Algarve, pp. 286–292 (2012)
28. Koh, K., Sreekumar, M., Puntambekar, S.: Hybrid electrostatic and elastomer adhesion mechanism for wall climbing robot. Mechatronics **35**, 122–135 (2016)
29. Menon, C., Siti, M.: Biologically inspired adhesion-based surface climbing robot. In: IEEE International Conference on Robotics and Automation, Barcelona, Spain, pp. 2715–2720 (2005)

30. Murphy, M.P., Siti, M.: An agile small-scale wall-climbing robot utilizing dry elastomer adhesives. IEEE/ASME Trans. Metatron. **12**(3), 330–338 (2007)
31. Unver, O., Siti, M.: A palm-size, tank-like climbing robot using soft elastomer adhesive treads. Int. J. Robot. Res. **29**(14), 1761–1777 (2010)
32. Seo, T., Siti, M.: Tank-like module-based climbing robot using passive compliant joints. IEEE/ASME Trans. Metatron. **18**(1), 397–408 (2013)
33. Greeter, M., Shah, G.: Toward micro wall-climbing robots using biomimetic fibrillary adhesives. In: International Symposium on Autonomous Robot for Research and Education (AMIRE), pp. 39–46 (2005)
34. Kahn, J., Liu, Y., Sadeghi, A., Menon, C.: A tailless timing belt climbing platform utilizing dry adhesives with mushroom caps. Smart Mater. Struct. **20**(11), 1–11 (2011)

Kinematic Analysis and Speed Control of 3SPS-1S Parallel Mechanism for End Actuator of Segment Erector

Wang Lintao[⊠], Li Ji, and Zhao Lei

School of Mechanical Engineering, Dalian University of Technology,
Dalian 116024, Liaoning, China
wlt@dlut.edu.cn, {DerekLi,leill05}@mail.dlut.edu.cn

Abstract. In this paper, the 3SPS-1S parallel mechanism is applied under the consideration of the large load and high positioning accuracy of the end actuator of the segment erector. And a complete set of speed control solutions for the end actuators of the segment erector is proposed. The scheme proposes the iterative positive solution of the mechanism by using Newton iteration method, and controls the speed by designing the fuzzy PID controller. By solving the inverse solution of the mechanism, expressions of the rotation angles and the lengths of the legs are obtained. And then the iterative equation is constructed for the positive solution. The convergence of the solution is demonstrate with three set of examples, and all of the relative errors are less than 0.1%. A fuzzy PID controller is designed for the controlled object with parameter uncertainties. The effectiveness is verified by simulation.

Keywords: Speed control · Parallel mechanism · Segment erector

1 Introduction

The segment erector, one of the key components of the shield machine, is a device for the handling and precisely positioning of the segment in the shield machine. The segment is a component of the inner wall of a tunnel. Generally, a complete circular tunnel is formed by splicing 6 pieces of segment with different sizes. Therefore, the weight of the segments is generally large and there are certain difference. Inevitably there is a large load and significant difference as well as a large inertia for the end effector of the segment assembly machine. Under this condition, the end actuator needs to maintain a high positioning accuracy.

Most of the existing end actuators of the segment erectors adopt a series structures (Fig. 1b), which control one degree of freedom by one or two hydraulic cylinders respectively, and realize three rotational degrees of freedom for adjusting the attitude of the segment finally. The structure is complicated and not tight enough. By comparison, 3SPS-1S is a three-degree-of-freedom rigid parallel mechanism with high rigidity, high precision, etc. [1, 2]. It fully meets the requirements of fine-tuning precise positioning and heavy-loading of the segment for the attitude adjustment mechanism of the end of the segment Erector [2]. However, when the mechanism is applied to the end of the

H. Yu et al. (Eds.): ICIRA 2019, LNAI 11745, pp. 190–201, 2019.
https://doi.org/10.1007/978-3-030-27529-7_17

segment erector to realize the attitude adjustment and precise positioning of the segment, there still exist some technical problems that need to be solved. The first issue is the real-time speed control of the mechanism. The real-time speed control mainly includes two parts: 1. kinematic analysis, 2. controller design.

Many scholars have studied on the kinematic analysis of this mechanism. Cui and Wang did a lot of researches on the dynamic analysis, kinematic solution and flexibility analysis about space rotation three-degree-of-freedom parallel mechanism. And they successfully obtained a positive solution and a velocity solution by nonlinear equation method. After this Gan [5] applied Dixon's resultant to the positive solution algorithm, and gave a numerical solution to the parallel mechanism. This exact solution can be obtained with algorithm. The existing kinematics analysis of the mechanism has been relatively complete. However, there is still a complicated computational process and large calculated amount in the positive solution and the solution is not unique, so that it cannot be applied to real-time control and the like.

In terms of the design of the controller, Hu et al. [1] applied 3SPS-1S to the humanoid manipulator system, and proposed a hybrid PID control algorithm. The effectiveness of the algorithm for position control was verified by experiments. Liu, Hu et al. [6] applied the mechanism to the vector thrusters of AUVs, did the dynamic and kinematic analysis and design the control scheme of vector thruster. Li, Cheng et al. [7] gave the singularity analysis of 3SPS-1PS mechanism and gave the corresponding singular evasive strategy. In addition, many scholars have done a lot of researches on the stiffness and deformation of parallel mechanisms [8, 9], but they do not involve the speed control.

In this paper, a complete speed control solution is proposed for the 3SPS-1S parallel mechanism applied to the attitude adjustment of the end of the segment erector. It includes an iterative positive solution and a controller for the end actuator of the segment erector based on a fuzzy PID design considering the uncertainty of system parameters. Through this solution, the real-time speed control of the mechanism is achieved. Finally, the effectiveness of this method is verified through simulation.

2 Kinematic Analysis of Parallel Mechanism

2.1 3SPS-1S Mechanism Modeling

The mechanism which lies at the end of the segment erector only needs three degrees of rotational freedom to adjusting the attitude of the segment. Figure 1a shows a segment erector for existing engineering applications and the end actuator shows in the red frame. The model illustration is shown in Fig. 1b. In order to save the internal space of the shield machine and improve the stiffness and load/weight ratio of the attitude adjustment mechanism [10], it can be replaced with the 3SPS-1S parallel mechanism. As shown in Fig. 2a, the mechanism consists of three parallel SPS(spherical bearing pair, prismatic pair, spherical bearing pair) type legs and one S(spherical bearing pair) shaped fixed rod. Three rotational degrees of freedom can be achieved. The length of the three prismatic pairs can be measured directly by the sensor as d_i ($i = 1, 2, 3$). To facilitate the kinematic analysis, tow coordinate systems as shown in Fig. 2b are

defined. The upper platform is movable. The moving coordinate system O_b is established at the geometric center of the moving platform. The x-axis passes through the
center B_3 of the spherical bearing pair. The z-axis is vertically upward, perpendicular to
the plane $B_1B_2B_3$, and the y-axis direction can be determined by the right-handed spiral
rule. The lower platform is static. Correspondingly, the static coordinate system O_a is
established at the geometric center of the static platform. The x-axis passes through the
center of the spherical bearing pair A_1. The z-axis is vertically upward, perpendicular to
the plane $A_1A_2A_3$, and the y-axis direction can be determined by the right-handed spiral
rule.

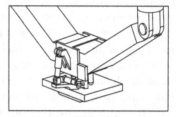

Fig. 1. (a) Existing segment erector. (b) Model of the attitude adjustment mechanism of the
existing segment erector

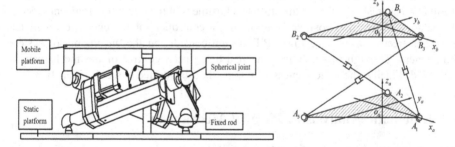

Fig. 2. 3SPS-1S attitude adjustment mechanism (a) Model of the 3SPS-1S mechanism
(b) Coordinate system definition

2.2   Kinematic Analysis of 3SPS-1S Mechanism

In order to realize the real-time speed control of the mechanism to achieve the purpose
of adjusting the attitude of the segment, it is indispensable to solve rotational speeds w_x,
w_y, w_z around x, y, z axes respectively of each actuator. The positive solution is the key
of the solution process. The Newton iteration method is applied herein to give an
approximate solution of the positive solution of the mechanism.

The static and moving platforms are respectively regular triangles with circumradiuses of r_a, r_b respectively. According to the geometric relationship, coordinate values of the points on the dynamic and static platforms can be expressed as

$$A_i^a = r_a \left[\cos\left(\tfrac{2(i-1)\pi}{3}\right) \quad \sin\left(\tfrac{2(i-1)\pi}{3}\right) \quad 0 \right]^T (i = 1,2,3) \tag{1}$$

$$B_i^b = r_b \left[\cos\left(\tfrac{2i\pi}{3}\right) \quad \sin\left(\tfrac{2i\pi}{3}\right) \quad 0 \right]^T (i = 1,2,3) \tag{2}$$

where A_i^a represents the coordinate value of the point A_i in the coordinate system O_a, and B_i^a represents the coordinate value of the B_i point in the coordinate system O_b.

According to the coordinate transformation relationship,

$$B_i^a = R \cdot B_i^b + p \ (i = 1,2,3) \tag{3}$$

where R is the rotation matrix of the coordinate system O_a to O_b written as

$$R = \begin{bmatrix} c\beta c\gamma & s\alpha s\beta c\gamma - c\alpha s\gamma & c\alpha s\beta c\gamma + s\alpha s\gamma \\ c\beta s\gamma & s\alpha s\beta s\gamma + c\alpha c\gamma & c\alpha s\beta s\gamma - s\alpha c\gamma \\ -s\beta & s\alpha c\beta & c\alpha s\beta \end{bmatrix}$$

In the above formula, s represents sin and c represents cos; α, β, γ are the rotation angles of the moving coordinate system with respect to the x, y and z axes of the static coordinate system respectively.

P is the translation matrix of the coordinate system O_b to the coordinate system O_a and $P = [0, 0, d_c]^T$;

According to the formula of the distance between two points in three-dimensional space

$$d_i = \sqrt{\left|x_{A_i^a} - x_{B_i^a}\right|^2 + \left|y_{A_i^a} - y_{B_i^a}\right|^2 + \left|z_{A_i^a} - z_{B_i^a}\right|^2} \ (i = 1,2,3) \tag{4}$$

written as a matrix form

$$d_i = \sqrt{2B_i^{aT} R^T p - 2A_i^{aT} p - 2A_i^{aT} R B_i^a + A_i^{aT} A_i^a + B_i^{aT} B_i^a + p^T p} \ (i = 1,2,3) \tag{5}$$

According to Eq. (5)

$$E_i(\alpha, \beta, \gamma) = 2B_i^{aT} R^T p - 2A_i^{aT} p - 2A_i^{aT} R B_i^a + A_i^{aT} A_i^a + B_i^{aT} B_i^a + p^T p - d_i^2 \ (i = 1,2,3) \tag{6}$$

The parallel mechanism is applied to the attitude adjustment of the segment erector with the range of -0.0524 rad $\leq \alpha \leq 00524$ rad, -0.0524 rad $\leq \beta \leq 0.0524$ rad, -0.0873 rad $\leq \gamma \leq 0.0873$ rad. Therefore, trigonometric functions can be expanded into power series to simplify the equation as $\sin(\bullet) \approx (\bullet)$, $\cos(\bullet) \approx 1 - (\bullet)^2/2$.

Here an iterative equation is constructed as

$$x = x - H^{-1}E \tag{7}$$

where $x = [\alpha, \beta, \gamma]^{\mathrm{T}}$, $E = [E_1, E_2, E_3]^{\mathrm{T}}$; H is the Hesse matrix and

$$H = \begin{bmatrix} \frac{\partial E_1}{\partial \alpha} & \frac{\partial E_1}{\partial \beta} & \frac{\partial E_1}{\partial \gamma} \\ \frac{\partial E_2}{\partial \alpha} & \frac{\partial E_2}{\partial \beta} & \frac{\partial E_2}{\partial \gamma} \\ \frac{\partial E_3}{\partial \alpha} & \frac{\partial E_3}{\partial \beta} & \frac{\partial E_3}{\partial \gamma} \end{bmatrix};$$

As a result, an approximate solution can be obtained as to the positive solution of the institution.

Suppose that the rotation speed around the x, y, and z axes are w_x, w_y and w_z respectively. According to the geometric relationship, the speed of B_i^b can be expressed in the moving coordinate system O_b as

$$\begin{cases} v_1^b = \begin{bmatrix} -y_{B_1^b}\omega_z & x_{B_1^b}\omega_z & y_{B_1^b}\omega_x - x_{B_1^b}\omega_y \end{bmatrix}^{\mathrm{T}} \\ v_2^b = \begin{bmatrix} -y_{B_2^b}\omega_z & x_{B_2^b}\omega_z & y_{B_2^b}\omega_x - x_{B_2^b}\omega_y \end{bmatrix}^{\mathrm{T}} \\ v_3^b = \begin{bmatrix} -y_{B_3^b}\omega_z & x_{B_3^b}\omega_z & y_{B_3^b}\omega_x - x_{B_3^b}\omega_y \end{bmatrix}^{\mathrm{T}} \end{cases} \tag{8}$$

According to the coordinate transformation relationship, the velocity vector of the point is converted to the static coordinate system O_a, which is calculated as

$$v_i^a = R \cdot v_i^b \tag{9}$$

where v_i^a is the velocity value of B_i^b in the coordinate system O_a. Then the speed of each actuator is the projection length of the velocity of the point in the static coordinate system along the push rod.

$$v_{Li} = \frac{v_i^{a\mathrm{T}} \vec{e}_i^a}{|\vec{e}_i^a|} \tag{10}$$

Where v_{Li} ($i = 1, 2, 3$) is the speed of the three push rod; $\vec{e}_i^a = B_i^a - A_i^a$ is the direction vector of the push rod.

2.3 Positive Solution Example

In terms of the above positive solution algorithm, a set of positive solution examples is given. The true angles of α, β and γ are as shown in Table 1. The initial values are all set to 0. The results shown in Fig. 3 can be obtained by applying the above algorithm. It can be seen that after three iterations, the results are almost no longer changed, and the results tend to be stable. By comparison with true values, the maximum relative error is 0.0804%, and the error is within the acceptable range.

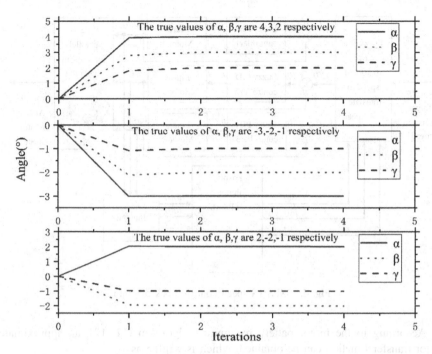

Fig. 3. Positive solution iteration results

Table 1. Iterative data values

	α	β	γ
3rd Iteration Data(°)	3.996785/−2.99862/ 1.999589	2.998564/−1.99967/ −1.99964	1.999513/−0.99997/ −0.99995
True Angle(°)	4/−3/2	3/−2/−2	2/−1/−1
Maximum relative error	0.0804%	0.0479%	0.0244%

3   Controller Design

The segment erector load may vary because of different sizes of segments in assembly process. Moreover, when the segment erector is used in a full circle tunnel, different angles will also cause load changes on the end actuator. These changes directly lead to mathematical models uncertainties of the actuators directly. Therefore, to solve this problem, this paper proposes a fuzzy PID controller which can adapt to parametric uncertainties of the controlled object within a certain range. The block diagram of the speed control is shown in Fig. 4.

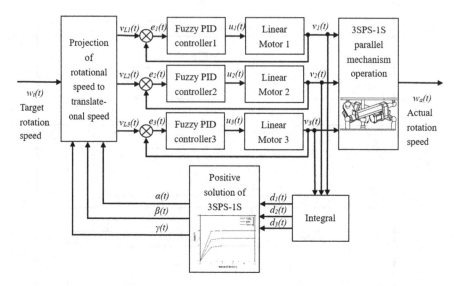

Fig. 4. 3SPS-1S speed control block diagram

According to the motor pattern recognition algorithm [11, 12], an approximate motor transfer function can be obtained, which is written as

$$G(s) = \frac{a}{b_1 s^2 + b_2 s + 1} \tag{11}$$

Through multiple data acquisition and identification, the values of the parameters a, b_1, and b_2 are within a certain range. Considering the different values, a fuzzy PID controller is designed. The block diagram of the fuzzy PID control system is shown in Fig. 5. The controller contains two inputs, namely the deviation e and its derivative ec, and outputs the adjustment parameters K_P, K_I, and K_D of the PID regulator through fuzzy inference and defuzzification. The fuzzy controller can adjust the parameters of the PID regulator in real time.

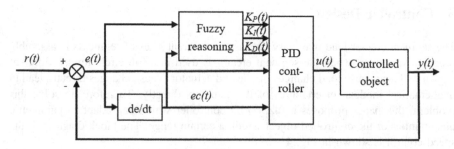

Fig. 5. Schematic diagram of fuzzy PID control system

The fuzzy inference adjusts the PID parameters based on empirical knowledge and fuzzy set theory [13] to establish the relationship between input and outputs. In this paper, the range of inputs is set to $[-6, 6]$, and the range of outputs is set to $[-3, 3]$. The corresponding fuzzy set is [NB, NM, NS, ZO, PS, PM, PB], where NB stands for negative big, NM negative medium, NS negative small, ZO zero, PS positive small, PM positive medium, PB positive big. Select "Mamdani" as the fuzzy inference system and "trimf" as the membership function. Figure 6 shows the membership functions. The adjustment rule table for PID parameters K_P, K_I and K_D are shown in Table 2.

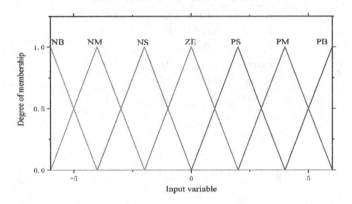

Fig. 6. Membership function

Table 2. K_P, K_I and K_D fuzzy inference rule table

ec	NB	NM	NS	ZO	PS	PM	PB
e	$K_P/K_I/K_D$						
NB	PB/NB/PS	PB/NB/NS	PM/NM/NB	PM/NM/NB	PS/NS/NB	ZO/ZO/NM	ZO/ZO/PS
NM	PB/NB/PS	PB/NB/NS	PM/NM/NB	PS/NS/NM	PS/NS/NM	ZO/ZO/NS	NS/ZO/ZO
NS	PM/NB/ZO	PM/NS/NS	PM/NS/NM	PS/NS/NM	ZO/ZO/NS	NS/PS/NS	NS/PS/ZO
ZO	PM/NM/ZO	PM/NM/NS	PS/NS/NS	ZO/ZO/NS	NS/PS/NS	NM/PM/NS	NM/PS/ZO
PS	PS/NM/ZO	PS/NS/ZO	ZO/ZO/ZO	NS/PS/ZO	NS/PS/ZO	NM/PM/ZO	NM/PB/ZO
PM	PS/ZO/PB	ZO/ZO/PM	NS/PS/PS	NM/PS/PS	NM/PM/PS	NM/PB/PS	NB/PB/PB
PB	ZO/ZO/PB	ZO/ZO/PM	NM/PS/PM	NM/PM/PM	NM/PM/PS	NB/PB/PS	NB/PB/PB

4 Simulation

The progress will be divided into two parts. The first part verifies the effectiveness of the speed control system; the second part adjusts the model of the controlled object within the range of parameter identification, and compares the effect of the fuzzy PID controller with that of the PID controller.

According to the parameter identification, it is found that $a \in [0.6385, 0.6511]$, $b_1 \in [0.00113, 0.0031]$ and $b_2 \in [0.0362, 0.05879]$. Table 3 shows the values of each parameter. The simulation model is built by simulink, as shown in Fig. 7. The left "vel_cal" module is the speed calculation method, and the right "ang_cal" is the positive solution algorithm.

Table 3. Parameter values

Parameter	Value	Parameter	Value
a	0.6385	K_P	10
b_1	0.00113	K_I	120
b_2	0.05879	K_D	0.1
r_a(mm)	140	ΔK_P	1
r_b(mm)	140	ΔK_I	1
d_c(mm)	70	ΔK_D	0.1

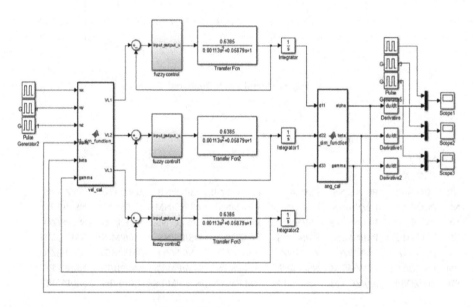

Fig. 7. Simulation system model

The desired rotational speeds of w_x, w_y and w_z are set to 3°/s, 2°/s, and 2°/s, respectively. The simulation results are shown in Fig. 8. It can be seen that the algorithm is very effective for speed control of the 3SPS-1S mechanism.

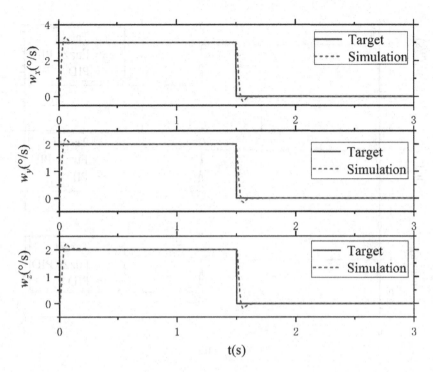

Fig. 8. Simulation results

The second part of the simulation adjusts the controlled object, taking the parameters $a = 0.6511$, $b_1 = 0.002$ and $b_2 = 0.04$ respectively, and the remaining ones are shown in Table 3, to verify the adaptability of the fuzzy PID to the parameter changes. The desired rotational speeds of w_x, w_y and w_z are set to 3°/s, 2°/s, and 2°/s, respectively. The simulation results are shown in Fig. 9. Table 4 shows the comparison of the main performance indicators. It can be seen that compared with the PID controller, the maximum overshoot of the fuzzy one is reduced by no less than 8.8%, the number of oscillations is reduced by 0.5, and the rise time is slightly increases. It is proved that the fuzzy PID controller is more adaptable to parameter changes.

Table 4. Comparison of performance indexes

	Rise time			Overshoot			Number of oscillation		
	w_x	w_y	w_z	w_x	w_y	w_z	w_x	w_y	w_z
Fuzzy PID	0.036 s	0.036 s	0.037 s	30.5%	29.3%	30.5%	2	2	2
PID	0.025 s	0.025 s	0.025 s	39.4%	39.6%	40.0%	2.5	2.5	2.5
Difference	0.011 s	0.011 s	0.012 s	−8.8%	−10%	−9.5%	−0.5	−0.5	−0.5

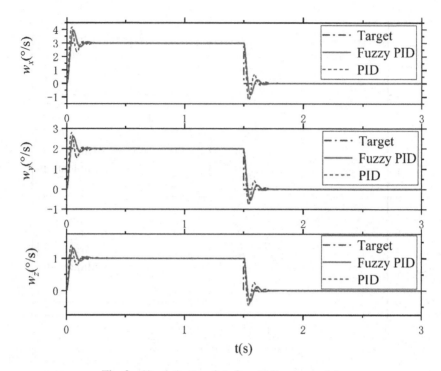

Fig. 9. Simulation results of controller comparison

5 Conclusion

This paper presented a complete solution of the 3SPS-1S parallel mechanism applied to the attitude adjustment mechanism lying at the end of the segment erector. Through the kinematic analysis and the mechanism controller design, the real-time speed control of the mechanism attitude adjustment was realized, which mainly included the following two aspects.

By obtaining the inverse solution of the mechanism, the expressions between the rotation angle and the length of the leg were obtained, and then the iterative equation was constructed to solve the positive solution. The convergence of the solution was demonstrate with three set of examples, and all of the relative errors were less than 0.1%.

The fuzzy PID controller was designed for the controlled object with parameter uncertainties, and its effectiveness was verified by simulation. The results showed the effectiveness on the speed control. The performance indexes of the fuzzy PID controller and the PID controller were compared when the parameters of the controlled object changed. The results showed that the overshoot of the fuzzy PID controller was reduced by no less than 8.8% compared to that of the PID controller, and the number of oscillations was reduced by 0.5.

References

1. Lei, H.: 3SPS-1S parallel mechanism based humanoid manipulator system. J. Harbin Eng. Univ. **36**(11), 1515–1521 (2015)
2. Cuohua, C.: Mechanism design and kinematic analysis on a three rotation degree-of-freedom spatial parallel manipulator. Trans. Chin. Soc. Agric. Mach. **09**, 144–148 (2008)
3. Cuohua, C.: Configuration design and analysis of a new 3-SPS/S spatial rotation parallel manipulator. J. Jilin Univ. (Eng. Technol. Edn.) **39**(S1), 200–205 (2009)
4. Yanwei, Z.: Singular loci analysis of 3-SPS-1-S spatial rotation parallel manipulator. Trans. Chin. Soc. Agric. Mach. **41**(04), 199–203 (2010)
5. Gan, D.: Design and analytical kinematics of a robot wrist based on a parallel mechanism. In: 2012 World Automation Congress, pp. 1168–1184. Institute of Electrical and Electronics Engineers, Puerto Vallarta, Mexico (2012)
6. Tao, L.: Investigation of the vectored thruster AUVs based on 3SPS-S parallel manipulator. Appl. Ocean Res. **85**, 151–161 (2019)
7. Yang, L.: Forward position solution and singularity analysis of a 3SPS + 1PS bionic parallel manipulator. J. Mech. Transm. **39**(05), 76–79 (2015)
8. Nan, W.: Parallel institutions 3-SPS/S static and dynamic stiffness performance study. Mach. Des. Manuf. **08**, 213–215 (2013)
9. Xiuli, Z.: Stiffness and elastic deformation of 3SPS + UP parallel manipulators based on constraint wrench. J. Liaoning Tech. Univ. (Nat. Sci.) **32**(04), 513–516 (2013)
10. Wu, C.: Dimension optimization of an orientation fine-tuning manipulator for segment assembly robots in shield tunneling machines. Autom. Constr. **20**(4), 353–359 (2011)
11. Jianming, Z.: Application of self-tuning fuzzy PID controller for a SRM direct drive volume control hydraulic press. Control Eng. Practice **17**(12), 1398–1404 (2009)
12. Bo, Y., Zhiyong, T.: Fuzzy PID control of Stewart platform. In: Proceedings of 2011 International Conference on Fluid Power and Mechatronics, pp. 763–768. Institute of Electrical and Electronics Engineers, Beijing, China (2011)
13. Ruxun, Z.: Direct identification of DC electromotor model parameter. Comput. Simul. **06**, 113–115 (2006)

The Design of 3-D Space Electromagnetic Control System for High-Precision and Fast-Response Control of Capsule Robot with 5-DOF

Li Song[1], Xiuping Yang[1], Hang Hu[3], Guanya Peng[1], Wenxuan Wei[1], Yuguo Dai[1], and Lin Feng[1,2(✉)]

[1] Beihang University, Beijing 100191, China
linfeng@buaa.edu.cn
[2] Beijing Advanced Innovation Center for Biomedical Engineering, Beihang University, Beijing 100083, China
[3] Beijing University of Technology, Beijing 100124, China

Abstract. In view of the shortcomings of traditional gastroscopy and capsule robot in human stomach detection, a new 6-square coil electromagnetic control device for capsule robot attitude control was proposed in this paper. The device can not only generate uniform magnetic field in arbitrary direction and wide range of three-dimensional space to control the capsule to revolve, but also generate magnetic field with a certain gradient to provide propulsion for the capsule. Compared with the traditional electromagnetic device consisting of Helmholtz coil and Maxwell wire, it is easier to assemble, has higher coil utilization rate and more diverse driving signals. At the same time, it has a pair of movable coils, which can adjust the coil spacing according to the demand and produce different magnetic field configuration. Firstly, the appropriate device parameters were chosen by modeling and simulation, and illustrate the advantages of the system in generating magnetic field. After that, the feasibility of the device to control the capsule robot was proved by experiments such as fixed-point three-dimensional rotation scanning and two-dimensional planar loco-motion. The moving distance in plane point motion of the capsule robot can be adjusted by adjusting the signal type, amplitude and frequency of the driving coil, so as to improve the control accuracy reasonably. It can achieve a maximum accuracy of 1 mm in plane point motion, and the angle control accuracy in three-dimensional scanning motion can reach up to 10°.

Keywords: Electromagnetic control system · Capsule robot · Attitude control

1 Introduction

Gastric diseases are the most common digestive system diseases. Recent studies have shown that the total prevalence of peptic ulcer disease in European population is 4.1%, while the total prevalence of peptic ulcer disease in China is 17.2% [1]. And most gastric diseases are asymptomatic and have a certain probability of developing to gastric cancer. Wireless capsule endoscopy (WCE), as a new method of gastrointestinal

© Springer Nature Switzerland AG 2019
H. Yu et al. (Eds.): ICIRA 2019, LNAI 11745, pp. 202–212, 2019.
https://doi.org/10.1007/978-3-030-27529-7_18

disease examination, has higher patient compliance than traditional gastrointestinal endoscopy. However, the current WCE still has many shortcomings, such as the power supply problem, the movement mode is mostly passive, relying entirely on gastrointestinal peristalsis and gravity to move, which can not replace the traditional gastrointestinal endoscopy. The external magnetic field control of capsules is the most scientific method which has been continuously verified by clinical experiments [2].

In recent years, many improvements and optimizations have been made to the magnetic control device of capsule robot. Lucarini et al. [3] designed a magnetic control platform for active capsule attitude control by synchronizing a single external electromagnet with a capsule robot equipped with permanent magnet. Another kind of magnetic control device based on multiple fixed electromagnets can achieve high-precision multiple-degree-of-freedom motion of micro-robot [4, 5]. But the workspace provided by this device is too small for controlling capsule robot. In addition, large permanent magnet magnetic field control devices are also used for capsule robot control, but most of these devices are expensive and the magnetic field can not be turned off, which may interfere with the experimental equipment [6]. Feng et al. [7–10] has done a lot of experiments on permanent magnet control or other non-contact operation of micro-robots before, which are inspiring to control capsule robots.

The magnetic control system based on the combination of circular three-dimensional Helmholtz coils can provide a large workspace for the control of some specially modified capsules which can realize the spiral forward motion [11]. The electromagnetic control system based on the combination of Maxwell coil and Helmholtz coil group can control independently the coil used to adjust the direction of the capsule and the coil used to provide the capsule propulsion force [12, 13], thus simplifying the capsule attitude control. However, this kind of device usually has redundancy in design, and the heat dissipation of coil is also a problem. Pawaher et al. [14] show us a new possibility: to build the system without following the traditional Helmholtz coil spacing layout requirements. But this may result in smaller effective area of uniform magnetic field or insufficient magnetic field gradient in some directions.

In this paper, a 6-square coil electromagnetic control device which can generate uniform magnetic field in any direction in three-dimensional space and magnetic field with a certain gradient was proposed to move and steer the capsule robot prototype. The device is mainly composed of four movable coils with fixed spacing and two movable coils with variable spacing. Finally, several experiments, such as fixed-point three-dimensional point rotation scanning and two-dimensional plane motion, were carried out to prove the feasibility of the device for the operation of capsule robot.

2 System Design

2.1 Electromagnetic Coils and Capsule Robot Model Design

To insure the independence and simplicity of capsule robot's attitude control, electromagnetic coils are arranged perpendicularly based on X, Y, Z three coordinate axis of Cartesian coordinate system. On each axis there is a pair of coils with the same shape, size and number of turns. In order to satisfy both the simplicity of assembly and the ability to provide magnetic field, the device is assembled with square coils. The device frame model is shown in Fig. 1. Four fixed coils are arranged at equal center distance to generate a magnetic field space that can accommodate the moving coils. The actual effective working space is determined by the size of the moving coils. The suspension wheel and sliding rail are installed above the two smaller coils, so that the spacing between them can be adjusted independently and flexibly according to the control requirements. Copper enameled wire with diameter of 0.85 mm is selected for winding in the coil. To ensure a certain size of workspace, the side length of large coil frame is set to 130 mm, the side length of small coil frame is 110 mm, and the thickness of coil is 60 mm.

2.2 Magnetic Field Simulation and Parametric Analysis

In order to accommodate the moving coils in the effective space of the magnetic field, it is necessary to arrange the distance between the fixed coils reasonably. The actual effective range of the magnetic field consists of at least one cube with a side length of 110 mm. In this paper, COMSOL simulation software is used to simulate the magnetic field produced by the coil. As shown in Fig. 2, when the coil spacing is 240 mm, a larger uniform magnetic field range and a relatively larger flux density are displayed. From the simulation results shown in Fig. 3, it can be seen that the device with fixed coil spacing of 240 mm can meet the initial requirements of uniform magnetic field range and size.

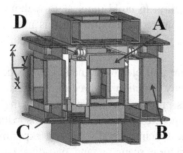

Fig. 1. Frame model of electromagnetic coil. Where (A) is a movable coil sliding in the X-axis direction (B) is a pair of coils with fixed spacing fixed on the Y-axis and Z-axis respectively, (C) is a connecting piece and (D) is hanging wheel.

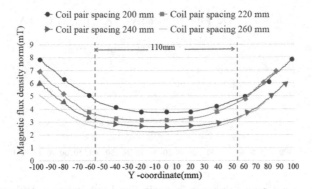

Fig. 2. The line chart of the distribution of magnetic flux density norm along the y-axis. Considering the assembly and distribution of coils, the spacing of fixed coils should be at least 200 mm, coils pass through 1.5 A DC.

After fixed large coil spacing of 240 mm, the influence of the current signal on the magnetic field is shown in Fig. 4. It can be seen that changing the current has little effect on general distribution trend of magnetic field. However, when the current is less than 1 A, the range of uniform magnetic field is larger. Figure 5 shows the distribution of magnetic field in XOZ and XOY cross section when the current in coils is 0.5 A DC.

Figure 6 shows the gradient information of the magnetic field generated by a movable coil (DC 2 A) in the forward direction of the x-axis. The distance between the movable coils is 130 mm at this time.

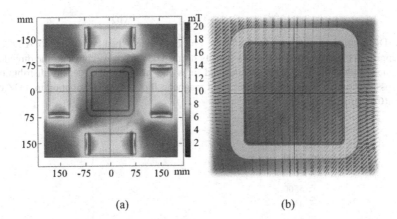

(a)   (b)

Fig. 3. The simulation of YOZ cross-section magnetic field distribution When the distance between fixed coil pairs is 240 mm (DC 1.5 A). The inner box is a projection of a movable coil, and the color legend represents the magnetic flux density norm. The red arrow represents the direction of the magnetic induction line. (a) Magnetic flux density distribution. (b) Distribution of magnetic induction lines within the projection range of movable coils. (Color figure online)

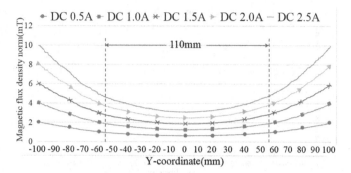

Fig. 4. Magnetic flux density distribution in y axis. Fixed coil spacing is 240 mm. Change the current of the fixed coil placed on the y-axis, and the other coils are not electrified.

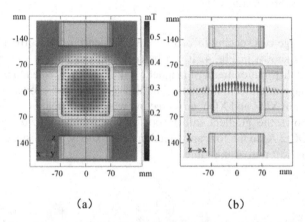

(a)   (b)

Fig. 5. Distribution of magnetic field of large coil on Y axis when current is 0.5 A DC. The color represents the magnitude of the flux density norm. The red arrow represents the direction of the magnetic induction line. (a) Magnetic field lines and magnetic flux density distribution in XOZ cross section (b) Magnetic field lines and magnetic flux density distribution in YOZ cross section. (Color figure online)

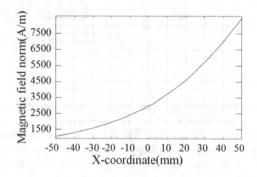

Fig. 6. The gradient of the magnetic field provided by a single coil is uneven.

2.3   Composition of Magnetic Control System

The magnetic control device and the capsule model are shown in Fig. 7. The coil is controlled by a computer based on visual studio 2010, combined with a data acquisition card (USB-6211, National Instruments) to transmit the signal to the coil driver (DZRALTE-040L080, digital driver, maximum output is 80 V, continuous operating current is 20 A). In this way, real-time programmatic control of the current in the coil can be achieved. The magnetic induction intensity is measured by using a Gauss meter (TM-701, KANETEC).

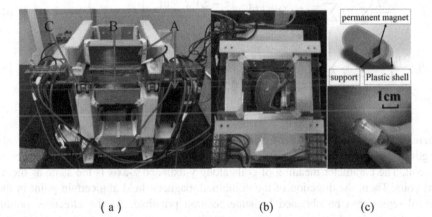

(a)   (b)   (c)

Fig. 7. Magnetic control device and capsule robot model. (a) The whole physical picture of the device (b) Overhead view of the device (c) The capsule is made of plastic injection molding. Its inside is loaded with a cuboid NdFeB permanent magnet (10 mm in length and 4 mm in side length).

3   Magnetic Field and Magnetic Force

Firstly, Biot-Savart law can be used to calculate the magnetic field produced by a single coil with constant current. The formula is as follows:

$$\vec{B}(x,y,z)=\frac{\mu_0 NI}{4\pi}\oint \frac{\vec{dl}\times\vec{e}_r}{r^2} \tag{1}$$

where $\vec{B}(x,y,z)$ refers to the magnetic field intensity generated by a single coil at the point where the capsule robot is located, μ_0 is vacuum permeability ($4\pi\times10^{-7}$Tm/A), N is the number of the coil turns, I is the current in the coil, $\vec{dl}$ refers to the tiny line element of the current, $\vec{e}_r$ is the unit vector of the current element pointing to the field to be obtained, r is the distance from the line element to the target point.

Next, convert the contour integral into the integration of four sides to analyze the square coil system [15]. For the coils along x-axis, we can calculate the magnetic field intensity component on the x, y and z axes as follows:

$$r = \sqrt{(x-c)^2 + (y-y_i)^2 + (z-z_i)^2} \tag{2}$$

$$B_x = \frac{\mu_0 NI}{4\pi} \sum_{i=1}^{2} \sum_{j=1}^{2} (-1)^{i+j} \times \frac{(z-z_i)(y-y_i)}{r} \times \left[\frac{1}{(x-c)^2 + (y-y_i)^2} + \frac{1}{(x-c)^2 + (z-z_i)^2} \right] \tag{3}$$

$$B_y = \frac{\mu_0 NI}{4\pi} \sum_{i=1}^{2} \sum_{j=1}^{2} (-1)^{i+j+1} \times \frac{(z-z_i)(x-c)}{r} \times \left[\frac{1}{(x-c)^2 + (y-y_i)^2} \right] \tag{4}$$

$$B_z = \frac{\mu_0 NI}{4\pi} \sum_{i=1}^{2} \sum_{j=1}^{2} (-1)^{i+j+1} \times \frac{(y-y_i)(x-c)}{r} \times \left[\frac{1}{(x-c)^2 + (z-z_i)^2} \right] \tag{5}$$

$$z \in [a, -a], \; y \in [a, -a]$$

where B_i is the intensity of the magnetic field in the i direction, a is half of the side length of the square coil, and c is the position coordinate on the x-axis of the center of the coil. The parameter meaning of coils along y-axis and z-axis is the same as the x-axis coils. Then, the direction of the combined magnetic field at a certain point in the control region can be obtained by superposition principle. As the effective motion space of capsule robot is mainly concentrated in a small area far from the coils, the above deduction formula can be used.

Magnetic substances in a magnetic field are subject to magnetic force and moment, which can be expressed by the following formula:

$$\vec{T}_m = V_m \vec{M} \times \vec{B}(x,y,z) \tag{6}$$

$$\vec{F}_m = V_m \left(\vec{M} \cdot \nabla \right) \vec{B}(x,y,z) \tag{7}$$

where $\vec{T}_m$ and $\vec{F}_m$ separately is the moment and force that the object receives, V_m is the volume of the magnetized object, $\vec{M}$ is the magnetization intensity of the object [16]. So the combination of uniform and gradient fields on three orthogonal axes can make the capsule robot move in five degrees of freedom.

4 Experiments

4.1 Fixed-Point Three-Dimensional Rotational Scanning Motion of Capsule Robot

Since most stomach examinations are conducted when people are lying down and the internal structure of stomach is complex, a simple and effective method is fixed-point scanning. First, the capsule robot can be fixed to a point on the stomach wall by gravity or magnetic field, and the capsule head equipped with a micro-camera can rotate 360° for scanning inspection. As shown in Fig. 8, the liquid environment in the experiment is water [2]. After examining one area, the capsule moves to another point until finishing the examination of whole stomach.

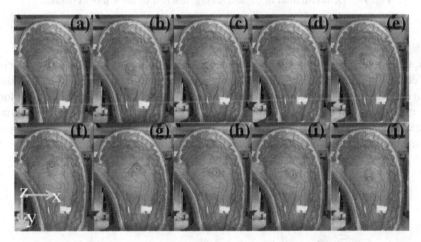

Fig. 8. Fixed-point three-dimensional scanning in the stomach model. (a)–(j) is arranged in clockwise scanning order. During the scanning process, the driving current of the coil varies by 0.1 A each time. Here, only a picture of the capsule rotating around the Z axis at a multiple of 45° is shown.

In the experiment, this method can be used to improve the control accuracy of the capsule rotation angle. If the current of the coil pair on the x-axis increases or decreases by 0.1 A in turn while the axis of the capsule revolves around the z-axis, the rotation angle of the capsule can be changed at a minimum of about 10° (also applicable to the coils on the y-axis) as shown in Fig. 9.

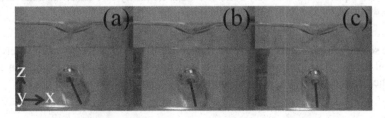

Fig. 9. Three-dimensional rotational scanning motion after improving angle control accuracy.

Figure 10 shows a schematic view of a fixed-point swing attached to the top. The experiment shows that the scan movement attached to the top is unstable and consumes a lot of power, and the capsule can only achieve a small angle swing within 30° (the uniformity of the magnetic field at the top is not enough).

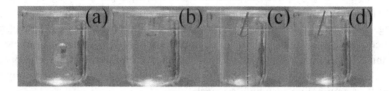

Fig. 10. Demonstration of capsule swing attached to the top of container.

4.2 Two-Dimensional Planar Locomotion of Capsule

A square wave signal with a certain frequency and amplitude is used to drive the coil and control the plane motion of the capsule. The magnetic field generated by this kind of signal can drive the capsule to move, and the moving distance of the capsule is close to 1 mm. As shown in Fig. 11, with the increase of square wave amplitude, the moving distance of capsule increases. Considering the inductance of the coil, the frequency of the square wave signal used is less than 5 Hz.

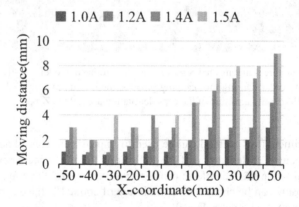

Fig. 11. The square wave with duty cycle of 0.1 and frequency of 1 Hz drives a movable coil (the coordinate of the coil facing the capsule side is x = 65).

The square wave signals are given to the coils on X-axis and Y-axis separately, and each coil drives the capsule to move independently. Therefore, the capsule can move along the desired trajectory in a two-dimensional plane, as shown in Fig. 12.

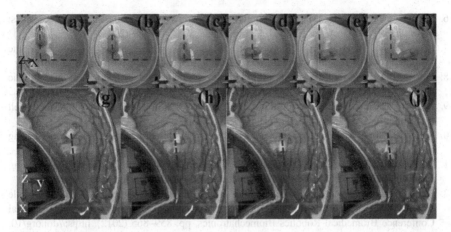

Fig. 12. The locomotion of capsules in two-dimensional plane and in model stomach. Red dotted line represents the assumed trajectory. (Color figure online)

5 Conclusion

This paper introduces a new 6-square coil electromagnetic control device that can be used for wireless control of capsule robots. The device consists of four fixed spacing non-movable coils and two movable coils, which are arranged in Cartesian coordinate system. It can generate uniform magnetic fields with a wide range in any direction and a certain gradient in a specific direction. Through fixed-point 3D rotational scanning motion and 2D planar locomotion, the feasibility of the capsule control was verified. The control accuracy of capsule robot can be improved quickly by changing the power supply sequence, signal type and amplitude of driving signal of coils. Control accuracy of 2D planar linear motion can reach 1 mm, and the angle control accuracy of 3D space can reach 10°.

References

1. Li, Z., et al.: Epidemiology of peptic ulcer disease: endoscopic results of the systematic investigation of gastrointestinal disease in China. Am. J. Gastroenterol. **105**, 2570–2577 (2010)
2. Liao, Z., et al.: Accuracy of magnetically controlled capsule endoscopy, compared with conventional gastroscopy, in detection of gastric diseases. Clin. Gastroenterol. Hepatol. **14**, 1266–1273.e1 (2016)
3. Lucarini, G., Ciuti, G., Mura, M., Rizzo, R., Menciassi, A.: A new concept for magnetic capsule colonoscopy based on an electromagnetic system regular paper. Int. J. Adv. Robot. Syst. **12**, 25 (2015)
4. Borer, R., et al.: OctoMag: an electromagnetic system for 5-DOF wireless micromanipulation. IEEE Trans. Robot. **26**, 1006–1017 (2010)
5. Diller, E., Giltinan, J., Zhan Lum, G., Ye, Z., Sitti, M.: Six-Degrees-of-Freedom Remote Actuation of Magnetic Microrobots (2015). https://doi.org/10.15607/rss.2014.x.013

6. Carpi, F., Pappone, C.: Magnetic robotic manoeuvring of gastrointestinal video capsules: preliminary phantom tests. Biomed. Pharmacother. **62**, 546–549 (2008)

7. Feng, L., Di, P., Arai, F.: High-precision motion of magnetic microrobot with ultrasonic levitation for 3-D rotation of single oocyte. Int. J. Rob. Res. **35**, 1445–1458 (2016)

8. Feng, L., et al.: Cell injection millirobot development and evaluation in microfluidic chip. Micromachines **9**, 590 (2018)

9. Feng, L., et al.: On-chip microfluid induced by oscillation of microrobot for noncontact cell transportation. Appl. Phys. Lett. **111**, 203703 (2017)

10. Feng, L., Song, B., Zhang, D., Jiang, Y., Arai, F.: On-chip tunable cell rotation using acoustically oscillating asymmetrical microstructures. Micromachines **9**, 596 (2018)

11. Fu, Q., Guo, S., Yamauchi, Y., Hirata, H., Ishihara, H.: A novel hybrid microbot using rotational magnetic field for medical applications. Biomed. Microdevices **17**, 31 (2015)

12. Keller, H., et al.: Method for navigation and control of a magnetically guided capsule endoscope in the human stomach. In: Proceedings of IEEE RAS EMBS International Conference Biomedical Robotics Biomechatronics, pp. 859–865 (2012). https://doi.org/10.1109/biorob.2012.6290795

13. Lee, C., et al.: Active locomotive intestinal capsule endoscope (ALICE) system: a prospective feasibility study. IEEE/ASME Trans. Mechatron. **20**, 2067–2074 (2015)

14. Pawashe, C., Floyd, S., Sitti, M.: Modeling and experimental characterization of an untethered magnetic micro-robot. Int. J. Rob. Res. **28**, 1077–1094 (2009)

15. Frix, W.M., Karady, G.G., Venetz, B.A.: Comparison of calibration systems for magnetic field measurement equipment. IEEE Trans. Power Delivery **9**, 4–6 (1994)

16. Yesin, K.B., Vollmers, K., Nelson, B.J.: Modeling and control of untethered biomicrorobots in a fluidic environment using electromagnetic fields. Int. J. Rob. Res. **25**, 527–536 (2006)

Design of Finger Exoskeleton Rehabilitation Robot Using the Flexible Joint and the MYO Armband

Jianxi Zhang, Jianbang Dai, Sheng Chen$^{(\boxtimes)}$, Guozheng Xu,
and Xiang Gao

Nanjing University of Posts and Telecommunications, Nanjing, China
jianxi_zhang@foxmail.com, 1426818@qq.com

Abstract. High-risk diseases such as stroke can do great harm to human hands. Hand rehabilitation for stroke patients is a complex and necessary task. To achieve this goal, this paper introduces a hand exoskeleton equipment with flexible joints and EMG-base motion prediction. Experiment of the equipment includes kinematics analysis, EMG signal detection by MYO armband and motion prediction base on BP neural network. The result shows that the device can not only assists patient bending or extending fingers, but also perform six kinds of rehabilitation exercises with 92% accuracy for target motion recognition.

Keywords: Flexible joints · Wire-driven · Rehabilitation robot

1 Introduction

Stroke is the main cause of dyskinesias [1]. According to statistical results in past two decades, stroke's survival rate is 60%–70% in China. However, in survival patients, about 80% of them suffer from hemiplegia, and likely to appear hand function obstacle. Previous researchers have proposed constraint-induced therapy based on the rehabilitation experience of many clinical patients. Physical therapy has been proved that can help repair some of the damage, and the earlier the treatment begins the result will be better [2]. At present, the clinical rehabilitation method of the hand depends highly on the one-by-one physical therapy by doctor. Compared with the current unstable rehabilitation treatment, machine-assisted treatment can enhance the effect of traditional treatment and greatly improving the rehabilitation result.

Researchers have created some typical hand rehabilitation robots, including mechanical hand, soft material hand and pneumatic hand. It is a good solution to use the mechanical connected rod to drive hand exoskeleton for rehabilitation exercises [3–11]. Although the movement of this device is very precise, but is limited by materials. Because most of the equipment structure uses metal parts, causes it is not only very complicated, but also bulky and heavy, which creates a burden for the patient. Pneumatic actuators are usually as the drive scheme of finger recovery equipment, the actuators integrated into the equipment can make the device very compact [12, 13], but pneumatic actuators usually need backup stable gas source, and actuators control precise is poor, and any structure parts failure will lead to leakage, or part splash, this

© Springer Nature Switzerland AG 2019
H. Yu et al. (Eds.): ICIRA 2019, LNAI 11745, pp. 213–225, 2019.
https://doi.org/10.1007/978-3-030-27529-7_19

has a hidden danger to patients. However wire-driven provides an ideally solution. It does not need the backup air source like pneumatic components or the connecting rod structure, which cause additional burden on patients, and can be properly applied to various rehabilitation hands with in limited installation. However, the tendon can only transmit force in one direction, so actuator should be added to satisfy two-way force transmission [14–19].

According to the background mentioned above, a hand exoskeleton rehabilitation equipment with flexible joints and EMG-base motion prediction is designed. In this device, the knuckle exoskeleton was filled with flexible material, while the finger exoskeleton and hand exoskeleton hand were connected by spring. In this way, the deformation of the spring and the flexible material can be transmitted or converted to the joint. This structure fits well with the distal interphalangeal (DIP), the proximal interphalangeal joint (PIP), and the metacarpophalangeal joint (MCP). The wearable part weighs only 310 grams, which cause no addition burden to the patient. In this design, lubrication is not required, and maintenance steps are reduced. In control strategy, 8 channels of surface myoelectrogram signals (sEMG) were collected by using the Myo armband, the acquired data was identified by BP-neural network. This recognition can be used e used to predict patients' motion and assist perform.

2 Structural Design

2.1 Integral Structure

As an exoskeleton device, it should conform wearer's shape firstly. The principle priority is allow patient performing finger bending and extending movement, and finally assist the patient can perform both the palm relaxation and fist movement. Normal human finger part contains at least 14 degrees of freedom. If these movements are separately given to separate motor controls, it will be very complicated for the whole equipment. If the rod drive is used, although the finger movement is very precise, it is usually necessary to use metal parts to ensure structural stability, which will increase the weight of the system and cause unnecessary burden on the patient. Therefore, it is very appropriate to use an under-driven method to drive the fingers for rehabilitation.

The overall structural design of the system is shown in Fig. 1(a) and (b). It consists of hand-worn part and base part. The base part can place the patient's arm, and has a 220 V AC–24 V DC power supply. Each two servo motor controllers and CAN cable are mounted on a bottom plate, the two bottom plates are fixed by three studs, and the bottom plate is fixed on the base through the chute, the motors' connecting cable is connected to the control board through the square slot on the right side of the base. The hand wearing part is divided into a hand back part and a five-finger wearing part, and the back part of the hand can be worn separately or can be fixed by a stud after being inserted into the base; the back part of the hand provides four mounting holes of the servo motor, the driving wheel and the connection interface of the five fingers. The back part of the hand is divided into two layers, magic sticks is mounted on the back of the bottom layer. When user wears the glove, the wearable structure is bonded with the magic sticks on the back of the glove, the top can fix motor and connect finger wearable structure. Consider various factors, the wire-driven is used as the driving method, the flexible material is used to connect the PIP and DIP joints, and the MCP joint is connected through the double-link structure to ensure the system can have minimize size complexity and weight. Except for the weight of the base part, the system weights only 310 g.

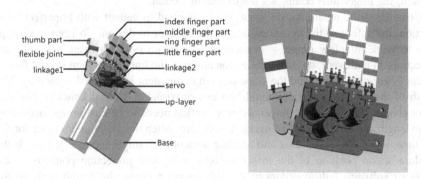

Fig. 1. A design diagram of structure (left-a is the overall design, right-b is the palm part design)

In order to match the movement state of PIP and DIP joint, joint is filled with a flexible material. Compared with the traditional mechanical structure, the flexible joint has the inherent deformation ability and shape memory ability, so it has high safety and adaptability while greatly reducing the complexity of the system. The material of the flexible joint use polyurethane as the filler (the polyurethane material is composed of the elastic material A and the viscous material B. The ratio of the materials is 3:1. And a small amount of agitation is needed during the mixing process to prevent the air from being mixed in the materials. The density and elasticity of the flexible material will be lowered if air bubbles are mixed in).

In driving system, 14 joints have to be controlled in the finger part (2 for the thumb, 3 for the index finger, 3 for the middle finger, 3 for the ring finger, and 3 for the little finger). In order to minimize the number of drives, therefore, the control of the joints in the system is realized by the wire-driven and the three-degree-of-freedom (or two-degree-of-freedom) flexion and extension movement of a single finger is controlled by an actuator, since ring finger and the little finger are fewest used, they are controlled by the same servo. In order to realize the wire-driven, a new driving wheel is designed, which mounted on the rotating shaft of the planetary reducer. The driving wheel can be connected with two reins and separated from each other without entanglement. One of the two reins end is fixed on the driving wheel, and the other end is sequentially passed through the upper side of the hand-back, finger-wearing structure, the ends of the last two reins are fixed to each other. When the action finger bending needs to be performed, the EPOS controller controls the motor to perform a forward rotation, which force the two reins on the revolver gradually tight. During the process, the finger's wearable part moves, and the distance between each joint gradually becomes smaller, so that the fingers perform the adduction action; When the action finger extending needs to be performed, the motor starts to reverse, and the retracted reins are gradually relaxed. During the relaxation of the reins, the flexible material at the joints of the finger's wearing part will gradually recover to the original shape. The joint between the finger part and the hand part will gradually return to the original position by the force of tension spring. When the tension spring and the flexible material returns to the original position, the finger also completes the extending action.

Considered the rehabilitation robot will be applied to patient with imperfect hand function, the safety of the system is one of the focuses in design. To keep the equipment to work in safety range, it is necessary to design both hardware and software protection. In hardware, based on the action angle of the finger, the joint should follow human finger movement, and the slope of each component is designed separately. The length of the flexible material should between proximal and distal knuckles (for different people, the size of the finger-wearing portion needs to be customized according to the length and width of each finger). In software, when the system is running for the first time, it performs extending and bending tests of each finger separately, records the absolute action position of the motor encoder as system protection point, once the circuit or software failure occurs in the subsequent process, the action limit on the system structure also ensures that the rehabilitation robot does not cause any damage to the human hand.

2.2   Motion Analysis

The kinematics relationship between exoskeleton and finger joint is shown in Fig. 2. The point of the wire-driven line is marked with P1–P6 points (for example, the index finger). When the user wears the exoskeleton, the exoskeleton of the adjacent joint is made by human. The finger joint acts as a center of rotation.

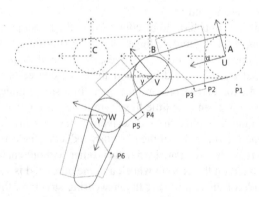

Fig. 2. Finger joint motion

Table 1 shows the symbols of the correlation calculation and their annotations, and the coordinates of the points are represented by a 4 * 1 matrix and the coordinate system transformations are represented by a matrix of 4 * 4.

Table 1. Related symbols of motion analysis and significances.

Symbol	Significance
α	MCP joint rotation angle (0–90°)
β-α	PIP joint rotation angle (0–110°)
γ-β	DIP joint rotation angle (0–70°)
L1	U coordinate system and V coordinate system origin length value
L2	V coordinate system and W coordinate system origin length value
^V_WT	W coordinate system relative V coordinate system transformation matrix
^U_VT	V coordinate system relative U coordinate system transformation matrix
^A_UT	U coordinate system relative A coordinate system transformation matrix
$^WP_6$	The coordinates of point P6 relative to the W coordinate system
$^VP_5$	The coordinates of point P5 relative to the V coordinate system
$^VP_4$	The coordinates of point P4 relative to the V coordinate system
$^UP_3$	The coordinates of the P3 point relative to the U coordinate system
$^UP_2$	The coordinates of the P2 point relative to the U coordinate system
$^AP_1$	The coordinates of point P1 relative to the A coordinate system
D_1	Euclidean distance between P5 and P6
D_2	Euclidean distance between P4 and P3
D_3	Euclidean distance between P4 and P3
DD	Reel total length change value
N1	Encoder change value
r	Drive wheel radius value
i	Planetary reducer reduction ratio

When controlling the forward rotation of the motor, the length of the rope of the MCP joint, PIP joint and DIP joint gradually decreases with the increase of the rotation angle, so that the three joint angles are rotated, and the three joint reins' change of lengths of are calculated as:

DIP joint length: $D1 = |P_5P_6| = \|{}^VP_6 - {}^VP_5\|$ among them ${}^VP_6 = {}^V_WTg{}^WP_6$;

PIP joint length: $D_2 = |P_4P_5| = \|{}^UP_4 - {}^UP_3\|$ among them ${}^UP_4 = {}^U_VTg{}^VP_4$;

MCP joint length: $D_3 = |P_1P_2| = \|{}^AP_2 - {}^AP_1\|$ among them ${}^AP_2 = {}^A_UTg{}^UP_2$;

Total length of reins change: $DD = \sum_{k=1}^{3} D_k(\alpha = 0, \beta = 0, \gamma = 0) - \sum_{k=1}^{3} D_k$ $(\alpha \neq 0, \beta \neq 0, \gamma \neq 0)$;

The relationship between the change of the length of the reins and the rotation angle of the driving wheel is $DD = \theta r = \frac{N1}{64 \times i} \times 2\pi r$, Among them, is the arc value of the driving wheel rotation angle; the encoder receive 64 pulses per revolution of the motor itself.

3 System Features

3.1 System Framework and Control Strategy

The control block diagram of the system is shown in Fig. 3(a). The patient wears the Myo armband on the right arm. Myo connects to the host computer via Bluetooth and transmits data in real time. At the same time, the host computer establishes CAN-bus through the USB-CAN transceiver. The CAN-bus is connected to four EPOS motor controllers, and the motor controller control the motor by five wires. Myo-armband collects 500 times/second of 8-channel sEMG data in real time, and these data are transmitted to the host-computer through Bluetooth. After the host-computer software get the signal, the BP-neural network recognition algorithm is processed to obtain the motion recognition result of the patient, and then according to the setting data and control strategy of active and passive rehabilitation, each motor controller sends a control command, and the encoder is fed back to the motor position for closed-loop control.

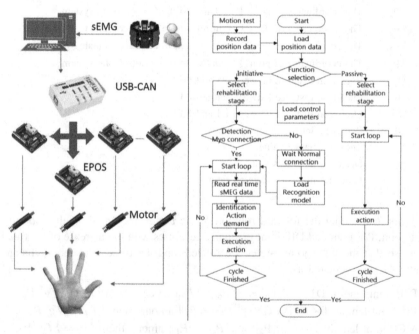

Fig. 3. Structure of the system (left-a) and control flow chart (right-b).

The control flow chart of the system is shown in Fig. 3(b). The system's functions are divided into passive and active rehabilitation effects. Under the passive function, the system performs the cycle-phase control and related motion data settings according to the patient's rehabilitation phase. In each cycle, the patient is subjected to a corresponding angle of rehabilitation exercise, and the angle of completion of the joint motion is measured according to the rotational position of the motor recorded by the encoder until the completion angle and the number of times of the movement reach the preset value, when the current rehabilitation exercise is ended, relaxation posture is returned.

Under the active rehabilitation function, the system maintains a relaxed posture firstly, and detects the patient's sEMG information at a predetermined cycle, and detects the patient's first motion intention in each cycle, such as relaxation state, bending state, extending state, single finger. After the detection is completed, the preset position control is started, and the completion angle of the action is judged by the encoder, and the number of times that action is completed is detected throughout the exercise phase. After the number of cycles is completed, the system returns to the relaxed posture, and the patient can take off Rehabilitation gloves and rest.

3.2 sEMG Signal Data Processing and Analysis

The acquisition and processing of the sEMG signal directly affects the entire control process of the system. Therefore, for the acquisition of sEMG signals, it is especially important to select the appropriate sensor. The Myo-armband is not only easy to wear, but also adaptable to different people's arms, it can be worn on the left and right arm. The human arm's sEMG signal is detected by Myo-armband in real time through eight equally spaced channels.

For the collected 8-channel sEMG signals, feature extraction is needed to distinguish different gestures of the patient. The time domain feature can obtain better classification characteristics, and has the advantages of less computation and quick acquisition, that meets the real-time requirements of the system. For the sEMG signal, six time-domain statistical features were used as the classification criteria, which are mean absolute value (MAV), variance (VAR), zero-crossing point (ZC), slope change (SSC), and waveform length (WL) and mean absolute slope (MAVS).

The average absolute value MAV is as shown in formula (1);

$$MAV = \frac{1}{N}\sum_{i=1}^{N}|x(i)| \tag{1}$$

i is a single sampling point, x(i) is the sEMG data for each sample, and i is the sEMG data acquisition channel of Myo (i = 1,2...8).

The formula for calculating the variance VAR is as shown in Eq. (2), where N is the number of sampling points and $\bar{x}$ is the mean of the sampling points.

$$MAV = \frac{1}{N}\sum_{i=1}^{N}|x(i)| \tag{2}$$

ZC's calculation mark: $\mathrm{sgn}(x) = \begin{cases} 1, x > 0 \\ 0, \ else \end{cases}$, ε is given a value greater than 0 (set 0.012). If the formula (3) satisfies the condition, the ZC value is incremented by one.

$$\text{sgn}(-x_k \bullet x_{k+1}) \&\& (|x_k - x_{k+1}| \geq \varepsilon) \tag{3}$$

Slope change number SSC calculation: for 3 consecutive sampling points x_{k-1}, x_k, x_{k+1}, given a threshold φ greater than 0 (take 0.02). When the condition of the formula (4) is satisfied, the SSC value is increased by one.

$$(x_k - x_{k-1}) \bullet (x_k - x_{k+1}) \geq \varphi \tag{4}$$

The waveform length WL is the cumulative length of the waveform within N data lengths and the waveform amplitude, frequency, and WL can estimate duration simultaneously. The calculation formula is as shown in Eq. (5).

$$WL = \sum_{k=1}^{N} |x_{k+1} - x_k| \tag{5}$$

The average absolute value slope MAVS is the difference between the MAVs in two adjacent analysis windows, and the calculation formula is as shown in Eq. (6).

$$M_{AVS} = M_k - M_{k-1} \tag{6}$$

The motion recognition system uses the BP neural network shown in Fig. 4 as a classifier for offline training and online recognition; it is composed of input layer, hidden layer, and output layer. The input layer is n (n = 6 * 8) neurons, corresponding to 6 characteristic of 8 channels, and the output layer is m (m = 6) neurons, corresponding to six different gestures of the patient. By performing a large number of data training parameters in advance, a related motion data model is generated, and the feasibility of the data model is determined by the accuracy of the trained data model; based on the trained data model, during online operation, online gesture recognition and prediction are realized by analyzing the motion data collected in real-time operation.

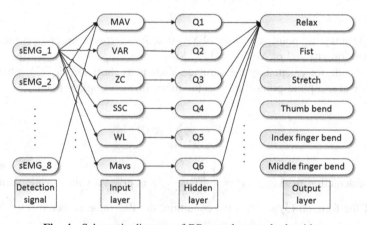

Fig. 4. Schematic diagram of BP neural network algorithm

4   Experiments and Results

In these experiments, we performed two kinds of rehabilitation exercise on volunteers, including test action 1000 times in each group. The results show that the hand equipment in this paper can perform both single-finger and five-fingers combination movement without taking off equipment, and predict motion through the BP neural network, which can help rehabilitation of the patients with better effect.

4.1   Integral Structure

In order to evaluate the effectiveness of the designed rehabilitation robot, it is important to try to reconstruct the system motion when the patient use the robot, which is achieved by analyzing the motion of the device. The analysis of these motion states is based on the wire-driven motion and joint motion association.

In experiment, the attitude sensors GY-25 (measurement accuracy is $0.1°$) are fixed on the back of index finger's wearable structure (As shown in Fig. 5). Those sensors monitor the angle of each joint in real time. In addition, the encoder monitors the rotation angle of the motor in real time. Since encoder receive 1088 pulses per revolution, the length change of rope is 0.018 mm/pulse.

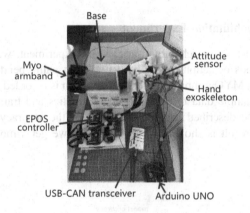

Fig. 5. An experiment environment

The experimental test was conducted according to the purpose of passive rehabilitation experiment. In the preparation stage, maximum speed, acceleration, deceleration and other related parameters of the servo motor should be adjust, and volunteers should fully spread their hand. In experiment, set the position target of each step as 100 pulse points (driving-wheels' radius is 4 mm), the initial value of altitude sensor is relative zero point, and in each step the angle data provided by 3 sensors is recorded until both three sensors' value stop change. The relative value read from altitude sensor and motor encoder are recorded as shown in Fig. 6(a). The error of index finger between the value calculated by altitude sensor and real value (rope length) calculated by motor encoder is shown in Fig. 6(b).

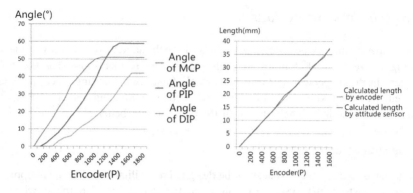

Fig. 6. Experimental results of index finger joint movement (left a, right b)

The experimental data recorded in the Fig. 6(a) shows that the index finger joints' range of motion are: MCP joint: 0–51°, PIP joint: 0–59°, DIP joint: 0–42°. Figure 6(b) shows that error between the value calculated by altitude sensor and the value calculated by motor encoder is less than 1 mm, The closed-loop position control of the servo motor by fuzzification the position of the encoder can make the device control more accurate.

4.2   Initiative Rehabilitation Experiment

Before performing the active rehabilitation exercise experiment, we collected sEMG signal of several kinds of action (relax, hold fist, open palm, bend and extension of singe finger) through MYO armband, each kind of action is recorded with 250 samples. Then we used the sample data to analyzed characteristics and trained the BP neural network with method described in Sect. 3.2, and test the accuracy value during the whole training, the result is shown in Fig. 7. Finally we get a model which predict accuracy reach 92%.

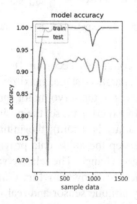

Fig. 7. Data model of BP-neural network training

By performing 100 sets of gestures of active rehabilitation, we got the predict accuracy of BP neural network and convolution neural network respectively and summarize in Fig. 8. The action "hold fist" and "hand extend" both activate the whole hand and have very conspicuous sEMG signal in all six motion, as a result, the predict accuracy is remarkable high. However, in the single-finger movement, the feature of index fingers and middle finger's motion signals have some similarities because there are a lot muscle associated between the index finger and the middle finger. This also leads to a relatively low recognition rate for the movement of the two fingers. The Average accuracy of BP neural network is 92.17% and convolution neural network algorithm is 89.5%. The results show its more effectiveness and reliability to use BP neural network for sEMG signal recognition.

Recognition rate by BP-neural network						
Gesture	Relax	Fist	open palm	thumb bend	index finger	middle finger bend
Accuracy	99%	98%	100%	87%	83%	86%

Recognition rate by convolution neural network						
Gesture	Relax	Fist	open palm	thumb bend	index finger bend	middle finger bend
Accuracy	95%	93%	99%	90%	81%	79%

Fig. 8. Recognition rate of BP-neural network and convolution neural network

Once network training completes, initiative rehabilitation training can be started. The System is designed to reach the aim of rehabilitation by several steps as follows:

First, the control period and control parameters are set according to the user's rehabilitation stage. Then, after MYO is connected, each control cycle is performed within a preset time. In each period, user's action intention is predict by the real time 8-channel EMG signal and BP neural network, after motion predict, the value of motor encoder is read to preform auxiliary action control and execute verification. System calculate the number of required periods according to the patient's rehabilitation status, and finally stop when target period number reached.

5 Conclusion

This paper proposes a new design of five-finger rehabilitation robot device based on the combination of wire-driven and flexible material, and also develops it into a functional prototype. In order to test the device, we use altitude sensors combined with motor encoder for position detection to assess the system's movable angle, stability and rehabilitation effects. Experiment shows that the design allows patients to safely perform single-finger or five-fingers bending and extending exercises. Based on the safety of this design, it can be use to passively rehabilitated when the patient's fingers are weak or help patient regain consciousness of the movement. The device can be used to performs initiative rehabilitation exercises on patient or helps them sense hand actions when they have weak limb perception and unable to control the hand freely. Compared with the predecessor's design, this design can not only complete the finger bend and extend movements, but also achieve the five-finger independent or overall rehabilitation exercise, while ensuring safety and not generating extra weight. It also combined with passive and initiative rehabilitation exercises thus it can be applied to different stages of rehabilitation.

Acknowledgement. This paper is supported by the Primary Research & Development Program of Jiangsu Province (Grant No. BE2015701), the Natural Science Foundation of Jiangsu Province, China (Grant No. BK20170898), the Natural Science Foundation of Higher Education Institutions of Jiangsu Province, China (Grant No. 16KJB460017), and the NUPTSF (Grant No. NY215050, No. NY218027 and No. 2018XZZ06).

References

1. Ates, S., Haarman, C.J.W., Stienen, A.H.A.: SCRIPT passive orthosis: design of interactive hand and wrist exoskeleton for rehabilitation at home after stroke. Auton. Robots **41**(3), 711–723 (2017)
2. Wolf, S.L., Blanton, S., Baer, H., et al.: Repetitive task practice: a critical review of constraint-induced movement therapy in stroke. Neurologist **8**(6), 325–338 (2002)
3. Diez, J.A., Catalan, J.M., Lledo, L.D., et al.: Multimodal robotic system for upper-limb rehabilitation in physical environment. Adv. Mech. Eng. **8**(9), 8/9/1687814016670282 (2016)
4. Sarac, M., Solazzi, M., Sotgiu, E., et al.: Design and kinematic optimization of a novel underactuated robotic hand exoskeleton. Meccanica **52**, 749–761 (2017)
5. Hansen, C., Gosselin, F., Ben Mansour, K., et al.: Design-validation of a hand exoskeleton using musculoskeletal modeling. Appl. Ergon. **68**, 283–288 (2018)
6. Kim, S.J., Kim, Y., Lee, H., Ghasemlou, P., Kim, J.: Development of an MR-compatible hand exoskeleton that is capable of providing interactive robotic rehabilitation during fMRI imaging. Med. Biol. Eng. Comput. **56**, 261–272 (2018)
7. Dicicco, M., Lucas, L., Matsuoka, Y.: Comparison of control strategies for an EMG controlled orthotic exoskeleton for the hand. In: Proceedings of IEEE International Conference on Robotics and Automation, New Orleans, LA, USA, pp. 1622–1627. IEEE (2004)
8. Bouzit, M., Burdea, G., Popescu, G., Boian, R.: The Rutgers Master II new design force feedback glove. IEEE/ASME Trans. Mechatron **7**, 256–263 (2002)
9. Yisheng, T.M.: Robotic Glove for Hand Rehabilitation [OL] (2019). http://www.siyizn.com. Accessed 27 Mar 2019
10. Adamovich, S., Merians, A., Boian, R., Tremaine, M., et al.: A virtual reality-based exercise system for hand rehabilitation post stroke. Teleoperators Virtual Environ. **14**(2), 161–174 (2005)
11. Wang, J., Li, J., Zhang, Y., Wang, S.: Design of an exoskeleton for index finger rehabilitation. In: Annual International Conference of the IEEE Engineering in Medicine and Biology Society, EMBC 2009, pp. 5957–5960. IEEE (2009)
12. Conti, R., et al.: Kinematic synthesis and testing of a new portable hand exoskeleton. Meccanica **52**, 2873–2897 (2017)
13. Randazzo, L., Iturrate, I., Perdikis, S., et al.: mano: A wearable hand exoskeleton for activities of daily living and neurorehabilitation. IEEE Robot. Autom. Lett. **3**(1), 500–507 (2018)

14. Bataller, A., Cabrera, J.A., Clavijo, M., Castillo, J.J.: Evolutionary synthesis of mechanisms applied to the design of an exoskeleton for finger rehabilitation. Mech. Mach. Theory 105, 31–43 (2016)
15. Park, Y., Jo, I., Lee, J., et al.: A dual-cable hand exoskeleton system for virtual reality. Mechatronics 49, 177–186 (2018)
16. Tadano, K., Akai, M., Kadota, K., Kawashima, K.: Development of grip amplified glove using bi-articular mechanism with pneumatic artificial rubber muscle. In: Proceedings of the IEEE International Conference on Robotics and Automation, pp. 2363–2368 (2010)
17. Biggar, S., Yao, W.: Design and evaluation of a soft and wearable robotic glove for hand rehabilitation. IEEE Trans. Neural Syst. Rehabil. Eng. 24(10), 1 (2016)
18. Hu, X., Tong, K., Wei, X., Rong, W., Susanto, E., Ho, S.: The effects of post-stroke upper-limb training with an electromyography (EMG)-driven hand robot. J. Electromyogr. Kinesiol. 23(5), 1065–1074 (2013)
19. Jones, C.L., Wang, F., Morrison, R., et al.: Design and development of the cable actuated finger exoskeleton for hand rehabilitation following stroke. IEEE/ASME Trans. Mechatron. 19(1), 131–140 (2014)

Design and Implementation of Hovering Flapping Wing Micro Air Vehicle

Jiaxiang Li[1], Chao Wang[1,2], Jin Liu[1], Peng Xie[1],
and Chaoying Zhou[1(✉)]

[1] Harbin Institute of Technology, Shenzhen 518055, China
cyzhou@hit.edu.cn
[2] Dongguan University of Technology, Dongguan 523000, China

Abstract. In this paper, a prototype of a hovering flapping wing micro air vehicle is developed. The aerodynamic force of the prototype at different flapping frequencies and pitch angles is measured, and a hovering flight control scheme for the vehicle is designed based on the measured results. Finally, a flight test of the prototype is carried out. The tail deflection of the prototype is controlled by a micro linear rudder, and the pitch attitude of the prototype is adjusted during flight. The hovering flight within a certain range is realized. The feasibility of the hovering flight control scheme of flapping wing micro air vehicle is verified.

Keywords: Flapping Wing Micro Air Vehicle · Hovering · Attitude control

1 Introduction

The Flapping Wing Micro Air Vehicle (FW-MAV) is a new type of bionic aircraft based on the flight principle of birds and insects. Compared with the traditional fixed-wing aircraft and rotating aircraft, the most prominent advantages of the FW-MAVs are their high flight efficiency and excellent hovering abilities [1]. In the case of a large forward speed, the maneuverability of the aircraft will be affected, resulting in a large turning radius. When flying indoors, the obstacle avoidance strategy will be complicated, thereby increasing the design difficulty of the aircraft control system. The FW-MAV with hovering ability is more suitable for flying in a narrow space [2]. Therefore, some progress has been made in the study of hovering flapping wing. The Aero-Vironment of the United States developed a hummingbird-like FW-MAV: Nano Hummingbird, which adopted a combination structure of four links, pulleys and ropes, and used twisted wings to realize the hovering flight of the aircraft. Its structure is complicated and the control method is quite difficult [3]. Konkuk University developed a tailless controllable flapping aircraft: KUBeetle, which could achieve vertical takeoff and hovering through PD control method [4]. The University of Maryland developed a FW-MAV with a weight of 62 g, a flapping frequency of 22 Hz. It successfully achieved a 6 s hover flight [5]. The Delft University developed a fruit-flying tailless flapping wing aircraft with a weight of 28.2 g and a wingspan of 33 cm, which could achieve agile forward and hovering flight. At the flapping frequency of 17 Hz, the hovering flight time could be up to 5 min, in the forward flight state, the flight distance could reach 1 km [6]. Most of the

© Springer Nature Switzerland AG 2019
H. Yu et al. (Eds.): ICIRA 2019, LNAI 11745, pp. 226–233, 2019.
https://doi.org/10.1007/978-3-030-27529-7_20

domestic researches on hovering flapping wing aircraft are in theoretical research, and no prototypes have been developed for actual hovering flight.

The vehicles structure mentioned above are complicated. Basically, there are more than two mechanisms are combined to realize the flapping motion. In terms of attitude adjustment, additional mechanisms are used to realize this function. In this paper, a simple hovering FW-MAV was developed which only used a simple single crank double rocker mechanism. The aerodynamic characteristics of the aircraft were measured and analyzed under different conditions. Based on the analysis results, a simple hovering flight control mechanism was proposed and verified by the flight test. The hovering flight is only realized by changing the flapping frequency of the vehicle, thereby the flying height of the vehicle is adjusted. By controlling the deflection of the tail, the pitch angle of the vehicle is changed, and then the components of the aerodynamic force in the horizontal direction and the vertical direction are changed, thereby realizing the hovering flight of the vehicle.

2 Design of Flapping Mechanism

The FW-MAV provides periodic lift by the flapping mechanism to drive the wings. When the wings are symmetrically flapping and the flapping plane is horizontal, the hovering flight can be achieved. In this paper, the double crank and double rocker mechanism with symmetric swinging is selected, as shown in Fig. 1.

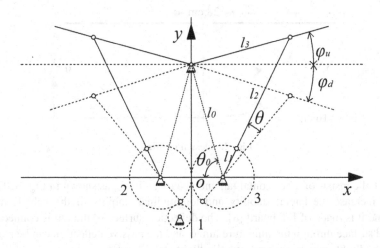

Fig. 1. Schematic diagram of flutter mechanism

The length of each pole satisfies the following mathematical relationship:

$$\phi = \phi_u + \phi_d = ar\cos(\frac{l_3^2 + l_0^2 - (l_2 + l_1)^2}{2l_3l_0}) - ar\cos(\frac{l_3^2 + l_0^2 - (l_2 - l_1)^2}{2l_3l_0}) \quad ((1))$$

where, l_0, l_1, l_2 and l_3 form the four-bar mechanism, l_1 is the crank and l_3 is the rocker.

ϕ_u is the upper flapping amplitude, ϕ_d is the lower flapping amplitude.

$$\phi_u = ar \cos\left(\frac{l_3^2 + l_0^2 - (l_2 + l_1)^2}{2l_3 l_0}\right) \tag{2}$$

$$\phi_d = \theta_0 - ar \cos\left(\frac{l_3^2 + l_0^2 - (l_2 - l_1)^2}{2l_3 l_0}\right) \tag{3}$$

$$\left(2l_3 \sin\frac{\phi}{2}\right)^2 = (l_1 + l_2)^2 + (l_2 - l_1)^2 - 2(l_1 + l_2)(l_2 - l_1)\cos\theta \tag{4}$$

3 Design of Wing and Tail

The Marcos Vanella team carried out a computational investigation to understand the influence of flexibility on the aerodynamic performance of a hovering wing [7]. It can be seen that the flexible wing can obtain higher aerodynamic efficiency and stronger anti-interference ability, so flexible wing is adopted in this vehicle. The wing has a four-wing X-shaped layout with a semi-elliptical shape and a wingspan of 28 cm. The material used in the wing is polyester film, which is shown in Fig. 2.

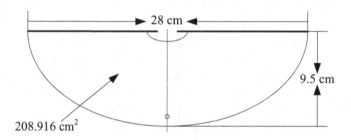

Fig. 2. Design of wing

The tail consists of a horizontal tail and a vertical T-tail, as shown in Fig. 3. The T-tail can increase the lateral stability and longitudinal stability of the vehicle during flight, and it is made of KT board [8]. The deflection surface of the tail is connected to the fixed surface through the miniature hinge, and the passive deflection can be realized during the flight, which can improve the flight stability of the vehicle.

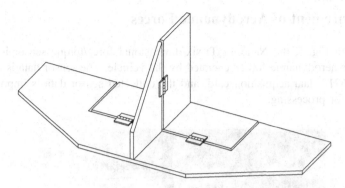

Fig. 3. Tail design

4 Fabrication of the Vehicle

The 3D model of the prototype is designed using 3D modeling software, as shown in Fig. 4(a). Two pairs of wings and flapping mechanism are located at the top of the vehicle, and the control device, battery and tail are in turn. This layout makes the center of gravity of the whole machine below the flapping plane, which improves the stability of the vehicle during flight. The lift generated by the two pairs of wings is vertically upward, which can ensure that the vehicle maintains an upright flight state during flight.

The components of the prototype were fabricated and assembled. The final mass of the vehicle is 18.19 g and the wingspan is 28 cm, as shown in Fig. 4(b).

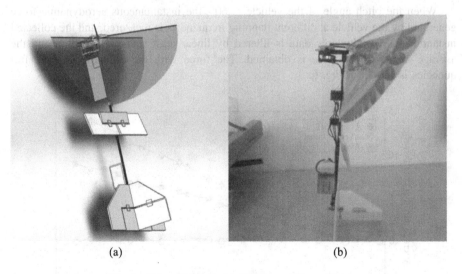

(a)   (b)

Fig. 4. 3D model and physical map of the vehicle

5   Measurement of Aerodynamic Forces

As shown in Fig. 5, the Nano 17 Ti six-dimensional force/torque sensor is used to measure the aerodynamic force generated by the vehicle. The sensor data is collected by the NI-6210 data acquisition card, and the collected sensor data is imported into MATLAB for processing.

Fig. 5. Prototype mounted on the measuring platform

When the pitch angle of the vehicle is 60°, the instantaneous aerodynamic force generated by the vehicle at different flapping frequencies is measured, and the collected instantaneous aerodynamic data is filtered by linear least squares algorithm and the average aerodynamic force is obtained. The force with the different flapping frequencies is shown in Fig. 6.

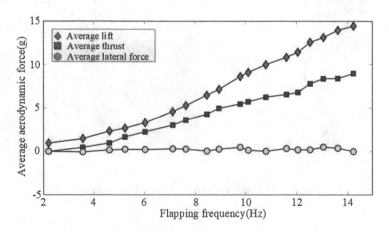

Fig. 6. Average aerodynamic force as a function of flapping frequency

It can be seen from the figure that the average aerodynamic force generated by the wing during a flapping period will increase as the flapping frequency increases, the flying height can be changed by adjusting the flapping frequency of the FW-MAV. When the flapping frequency is 8 Hz, by adjusting the pitch angle, the instantaneous aerodynamic force generated by the vehicle is measured, and the variation law of it can be obtained, which is shown in Fig. 7. It can be seen that as the pitch angle of the prototype increases, the average lift and the average thrust show opposite trends, that is, the average lift will increase, and the average thrust will decrease, so it can be changed by changing pitch angle to reduce the thrust in the horizontal direction to reach a hovering state.

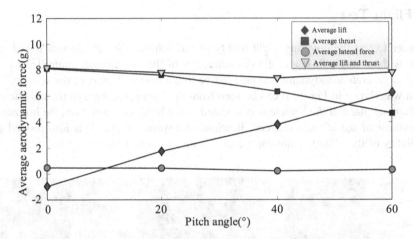

Fig. 7. Average aerodynamic force as a function of pitch angle

6 Design of Control Mechanism

Based on the above aerodynamic analysis results, this paper proposes the following control mechanisms: By changing the flapping frequency of the vehicle, thereby adjusting the flying height of the vehicle; By controlling the deflection of the tail, the pitch angle of the vehicle is changed, and then the components of the aerodynamic force in the horizontal direction and the vertical direction are changed, thereby realizing the hovering flight of the vehicle. The adjustment of pitch attitude of the vehicle is achieved by deflection of the tail, which is controlled by a micro linear servo. The driving mode of tail and deflection range are shown in Fig. 8.

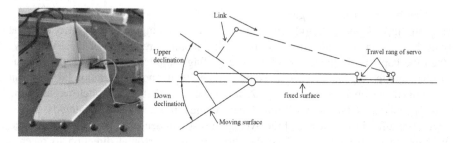

Fig. 8. Driving mode and deflection range of horizontal tail wing

7   Flight Test

In order to test the hovering flight ability of the vehicle, the vehicle was tested in a room without any influx, and the tail deflection of the vehicle was controlled by the servo to generate aerodynamic torque relative to the center of mass of the vehicle. The result was shown in Fig. 9. It can be seen from the figure that through the tail control, the flapping plane of the vehicle was adjusted to the horizontal direction, the horizontal component of the lift was reduced, it achieved hovering flight. This also proved the feasibility of the attitude adjustment mechanism mentioned above.

Fig. 9. Prototype in flight

8   Conclusion

In this paper, a FW-MAV was developed. By measuring the aerodynamic force generated by the Vehicle at different flapping frequencies and different pitch angles, the control mechanism for the hovering flight of the FW-MAV was proposed. By changing the flapping frequency, the height of the vehicle changed, but since the average thrust was also affected by the flapping frequency, the position of the vehicle in the horizontal plane changed, so it was necessary to control the pitch angle of the vehicle to reduce the thrust on the horizontal direction to ensure that the position of the vehicle in the horizontal plane did not change greatly, and the hovering flight of the vehicle was realized. Finally, the test flight results showed that the vehicle had a certain hovering flight capability and could achieve hover flight within a certain range under manual control.

Acknowledgement. The work described in this paper was supported by the National Natural Science Foundation of China (No. U1613227), the Natural Science Foundation of Guangdong Province of China (No. 2018A030310045), the Basic Research Program of Science and Technology Project of Shenzhen (No. JCYJ20170307151117299), the China Postdoctoral Science Foundation(No. 2018M641828), the DGUT innovation center of robotics and intelligent equipment of China (No. KCYCXPT2017006) and the KEY Laboratory of Robotics and Intelligent Equipment of Guangdong Regular Institutions of Higher Education (No. 2017KSYS009).

References

1. Cheng, X., Sun, M.: Wing-kinematics measurement and aerodynamics in a small insect in hovering flight. Sci. Rep. **6**, 1–12 (2016)
2. Deng, X., Schenato, L., Sastry, S.: Hovering flight control of a micromechanical flying insect. In: Proceedings of the 40th IEEE Conference on Decision and Control, Orlando, Florida, USA, pp. 235–240. IEEE (2001)
3. Keennon, M., Klingebiel, K., Won, H.: Development of the nano hummingbird: a tailless flapping wing micro air vehicle. In: AIAA Aerospace Sciences Meeting Including the New Horizons Forum and Aerospace Exposition, pp. 129–134 (2013)
4. Phan, H.V., Kang, T., Park, H.C.: Design and stable flight of a 21 g insect-like tailless flapping wing micro air vehicle with angular rates feedback control. Bioinspiration Biomim. **12**(3), 36–60 (2017)
5. Coleman, D., Benedict, M., Hirishikeshaven, V.: Development of a robotic hummingbird capable of controlled hover. J. Am. Helicopter Soc. **62**, 1–9 (2017)
6. Karásek, M., Muijres, F.T., De Wagter, C.: A tailless aerial robotic flapper reveals that flies use torque coupling in rapid banked turns. Science **361**(6407), 1089–1094 (2018)
7. Vanella, M., Fitzgerald, T., Preidikman, S.: Influence of flexibility on the aerodynamic performance of a hovering wing. J Exp Biol **212**(1), 95–105 (2009)
8. Wang, L.G., Song, B.F., Fu, P., An, W.G.: Engineering design of driving system for flapping-wing micro air vehicles. Mach. Des. Manuf. **08**, 34–37 (2013). (In Chinese)

Design of Embedded Structure Variable Stiffness Pneumatic Actuator

Yiqing Li[1], Wen Zhou[2,3], Yan Cao[1(✉)], and Feng Jia[1]

[1] School of Mechatronic Engineering, Xi'an Technological University,
Xi'an 710021, China
jantonyz@163.com
[2] School of Mechanical Engineering, Xi'an Jiaotong University,
Xi'an 710049, China
[3] State Key Laboratory for Manufacturing and Systems Engineering,
Xi'an 710049, China

Abstract. Soft pneumatic actuator, which is actuated by pneumatic pressure, is the most widely used actuator in the field of soft robotics. During the application of the pneumatic actuator, the chambers inside the actuator expand like balloons. It causes nonlinear problems and gives difficulties in modeling of actuator. A design method of variable stiffness pneumatic actuator is proposed in this paper. The embedded structure is adopted by the actuator. The finite element method (FEM) is used for analyzing the effect of the proposed soft pneumatic actuator. The results show that the proposed design of the pneumatic actuator works well on restraining the balloon problems when the actuator bends.

Keywords: Soft pneumatic actuator · Variable stiffness ·
Embedded structure

1 Introduction

Human-centered technology requires unconventional application of sensors, actuators, and systems close to the body. Composed of soft structures, soft robotics possesses the characteristics of compliance and adaptability, which makes it more adaptive for soft interactions. Therefore, in recent years, soft robotic research attracts more and more attention and gets rapid progress.

The soft pneumatic actuator, which is actuated by pneumatic pressure, is the most widely used actuator in the field of soft robotics. The actuator is made of soft material such as silicone rubber has advantages such as compliance, lightweight, safe human-robot interaction. It is characterized by their inflatable, lowweight, and environmental compliance, are playing a major role in this field [1]. In the actuator, there are several chambers, the gas is filled into it to make the actuator stretch or bend. Many applications of soft pneumatic actuators have already been used in various fields, including biomimetic systems [2,3], soft fingers [4], surgical tools [5] and muscle rehabilitation [6].

© Springer Nature Switzerland AG 2019
H. Yu et al. (Eds.): ICIRA 2019, LNAI 11745, pp. 234–239, 2019.
https://doi.org/10.1007/978-3-030-27529-7_21

Although most pneumatic actuators have similar characteristics, for example, they are made of soft material and have chambers inside, but they may also have differences in structure to suit different task types. Marchese designed a highly compliant continuum manipulator. It composed of multiple bi-directional bending actuator segments [7]. The segment comprises of two chambers which are cured by soft rubber. There is a central tube in it, which is made of stiff rubber. The two chambers are posited symmetrically on both sides of the tube, among which are the airway tubes for all the segments. The segment has a slender shape and can be cascaded together, which make it extremely ideal for manipulator component. Katzschmann developed a uni-directional bending actuator with pleated channel configuration [8]. The actuator has many chambers that are cascaded by a channel. There is a gap between every two adjacent chambers which make the actuator be capable of a large bending angle.

Modeling of soft fluidic robots has been proved to be extremely challenging due to their large deformability and infinite degree of freedom. There are also some works try to analyze the deform behavior of a single actuator segment. Elsayed analyzed and optimized three soft actuator modules with different pneumatic chamber configurations [9]. Moseley describes the modeling, design method of the soft pneumatic actuators and analyzed the performance of the actuators with finite element method [10]. During these applications of soft pneumatic actuators, there is a common problem due to the soft material. When the pressure of the chambers increases, the chambers of the actuator expand like balloons. This causes nonlinear problems and gives a huge obstacle to kinematics modeling of the actuator. On the other hand, when the chambers expand, only one direction of the expand is useful for the actuator. The energy is wasted.

Aiming this problem, this work proposes a design method of variable stiffness pneumatic actuator. The design of this pneumatic actuator is illustrated. General procedures of the fabrication are described. Finite element method is used for modeling the pneumatic actuator. According to the comparison of the variable stiffness pneumatic actuator and pneumatic actuator without variable stiffness part, the effect of the design proposed in this work is validated.

2 Design of Variable Stiffness Actuator

2.1 Structure of the Actuator

In order to bend bidirectionally, the actuator designed in this study has a symmetrical structure. As shown in Fig. 1, the soft pneumatic actuator is comprised of two silicone rubber blocks with multi-chambers inside. The chambers are divided by ribs. There is an ABS plank between the two rubbers as a neutral layer. The actuator prototype is built with the method which can be seen in reference [11]. The fully mixed liquid silicone rubber (Ecoflex 0030 from Smooth-on Co., Ltd) is poured into a casting mold made by 3D printing, and released from the mold after cooling to get the rubber block. Then two rubber blocks are laterally glued to the ABS plank.

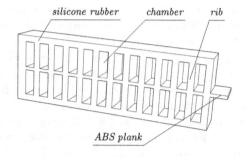

Fig. 1. Structure of the actuator

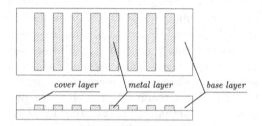

Fig. 2. Structure of the variable stiffness part

2.2   Structure of the Variable Stiffness Part

As mentioned above, the actuator has many chambers inside. When the pressure of the chambers increases, the chambers of the actuator expand like balloons. The reason is that the stiffness of the material on the upper wall of each chamber is too low. If the stiffness of this part increases, the balloon effect of the whole actuator can be improved. In this work, a multi-layer structure is proposed. This structure can only increase the stiffness of the material on the upper wall of each chamber. It has little effect on other parts when the actuator deforms.

The variable stiffness part is composed of three layers, which is shown in Fig. 2. The base layer is made of silicone rubber, which is the same as the actuator. The metal layer is made of copper wires. The copper wires are clustered on the base layer. They are arranged by equal spacing. When the variable stiffness part is applied to the actuator, the space of copper wires is the same as the chambers in the actuator. It is guaranteed that on the upper wall of each chamber, there is a cluster of copper wires. The cover layer is made by the same material as the actuator. And it is covered on the metal layer.

2.3   Embedded Structure of the Variable Stiffness Actuator

The stretch of the variable stiffness actuator is shown in Fig. 3. The multi-layer structure is glued to the actuator. The variable stiffness structure is placed on both sides of the actuator. According to the result of the FEM, the balloon effect is most noticeable in front of the actuator. Therefore, the variable stiffness structure is also placed. Then a compact structure of the actuator is obtained.

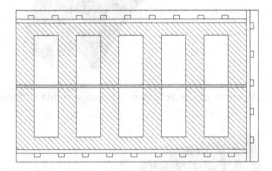

Fig. 3. Embedded structure of the variable stiffness actuator

3   Validation of Simulation

The FEM is used for validating the proposed variable stiffness actuator. The deformation process of the actuator is performed. To compare the effect of the variable stiffness structure, the actuator without variable stiffness structure is also analyzed by the FEM. The different result is shown in Figs. 4 and 5. Figure 4 shows that the air is pumped to the actuator, the actuator is bent at an angle. Each chamber expands like a balloon, the expansion of each chamber is inconsistent. Especially at the last chamber, a large balloon type deformation appears. It brings difficulties to kinematics and dynamic modeling. Figure 5 shows the variable stiffness actuator proposed in this work under the same conditions. It is obvious that the balloon effect is well suppressed due to the design of the metal layer in the variable stiffness structure. All the chambers expand more evenly. This explains that the balloon problem of the pneumatic actuator is improved due to the proposed variable stiffness structure.

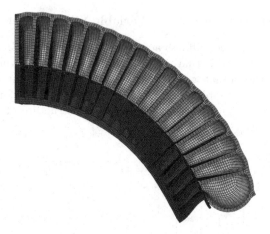

Fig. 4. FEM result of the actuator without variable stiffness part

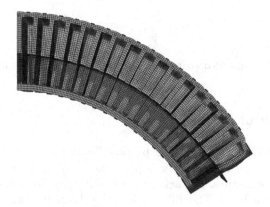

Fig. 5. FEM result of the variable stiffness actuator

4   Conclusions

The soft pneumatic actuator usually fabricated with one or more chambers. When the pressure of the chambers increases, the chambers of the actuator expand like balloons. It brings difficulties to kinematics modeling of the actuator. In order to solve this problem, a variable stiffness actuator is proposed. A multi-layer variable stiffness structure is designed to restrain the expanding direction which is perpendicular to the stretch of the actuator. The effect of the variable stiffness structure is validated by the FEM. According to the results of the FEM, the proposed design of the pneumatic actuator can restrain the balloon effect when the chambers of the acutator expand. Due to this design, the non-linearity problems of the kinematics model of the acutator will be improved. In our future work, the kinematics model and the analysis of the bending process will be studied.

References

1. Sun, Y., Song, Y.S., Paik, J.: Characterization of silicone rubber based soft pneumatic actuators. In: 2013 IEEE/RSJ International Conference on Intelligent Robots and Systems, pp. 4446–4453 (2013). https://doi.org/10.1109/IROS.2013.6696995
2. Tolley, M.T., et al.: A resilient, untethered soft robot. Soft Robot. **1**(3), 213–223 (2014). https://doi.org/10.1089/soro.2014.0008
3. Rus, D., Tolley, M.T.: Design, fabrication and control of soft robots. Nature **521**(7553), 467 (2015)
4. Deimel, R., Brock, O.: A novel type of compliant and underactuated robotic hand for dexterous grasping. Int. J. Robot. Res. **35**(1–3), 161–185 (2016)
5. Cianchetti, M., et al.: Soft robotics technologies to address shortcomings in today's minimally invasive surgery: the stiff-flop approach. Soft Robot. **1**(2), 122–131 (2014)
6. Polygerinos, P., Wang, Z., Galloway, K.C., Wood, R.J., Walsh, C.J.: Soft robotic glove for combined assistance and at-home rehabilitation. Robot. Auton. Syst. **73**, 135–143 (2015)
7. Marchese, A.D., Katzschmann, R.K., Rus, D.: Whole arm planning for a soft and highly compliant 2d robotic manipulator. In: 2014 IEEE/RSJ International Conference on Intelligent Robots and Systems, pp. 554–560. IEEE (2014)
8. Katzschmann, R.K., Marchese, A.D., Rus, D.: Autonomous object manipulation using a soft planar grasping manipulator. Soft Robot. **2**(4), 155–164 (2015)
9. Elsayed, Y., et al.: Finite element analysis and design optimization of a pneumatically actuating silicone module for robotic surgery applications. Soft Robot. **1**(4), 255–262 (2014)
10. Moseley, P., Florez, J.M., Sonar, H.A., Agarwal, G., Curtin, W., Paik, J.: Modeling, design, and development of soft pneumatic actuators with finite element method. Adv. Eng. Mater. **18**(6), 978–988 (2016)
11. Luo, M., Agheli, M., Onal, C.D.: Theoretical modeling and experimental analysis of a pressure-operated soft robotic snake. Soft Robot. **1**(2), 136–146 (2014)

Bionic Design and Attitude Control Measurement in a Double Flapping-Wing Micro Air Vehicle

Xuedong Zhang, Huichao Deng$^{(\boxtimes)}$, Shengjie Xiao, Lili Yang,
and Xilun Ding

Space Robot Laboratory, Beihang University, Beijing 100191, China
denghuichao@buaa.edu.cn

Abstract. The interest in flapping-wing Micro Air Vehicles (MAVs) has been rising progressively in the past years, as they can combine high agility manoeuvres with precision hovering flight and can be applied in complex spaces for reconnaissance missions. In this study, we propose a double flapping-wing MAV, which has four wings comprised by two pairs, each pair is driven by one brush motor and one linear servo. The flapping mechanism is composed of a crank-rocker and double rocker mechanism, which can amplify the output angle of wings and used for lift increasing. We take the Rhinoceros beetle as a bionic object and the Weis-Fogh mechanism as the high lift generation principle. The vehicle can actively control 4 degrees of freedom (DOFs), namely, roll, pitch, yaw, and thrust. Compare to the single pair counterpart, our vehicle possess a high thrust-to-weight ratio, which make it possible for more onboard load and beneficial to attitude control, additionally, the 3 rotational DOFs (roll, pitch, and yaw) is completely uncoupled and controlled independently, which is useful for control system design. The currently vehicle weighting 32.8 g (without the battery) and can generate 0.34N thrust at the maximum flapping frequency of approximately 23 Hz.

Keywords: MAV · Flapping-wing · Weis-Fogh mechanism · Thrust-to-weight ratio

1 Introduction

Micro Air Vehicles (MAVs) starts to be part of our daily lives. Apart from military applications they are being utilized more and more by police, fire brigades and other civil field. MAVs with flapping wings have been researched intensively during recent years. Compared with fixed-wing and rotor-wing aircraft, flap-wing aircraft integrates lifting, hovering and propulsion functions, and is more prominent in terms of maneuverability and flexibility. It is more suitable for performing tasks in tight spaces.

The Nano Hummingbird [1] is one of the most advanced tailless flapping-wing MAVs capable of indoor surveillance mission, which has a wingspan of 16 cm and a total flying weight of 19 g, can fly at 5 m/s. Apart from the Nano Hummingbird, there

© Springer Nature Switzerland AG 2019
H. Yu et al. (Eds.): ICIRA 2019, LNAI 11745, pp. 240–254, 2019.
https://doi.org/10.1007/978-3-030-27529-7_22

have been some standalone MAVs developed by academia. TU Delft has introduced a tailless aerial robotic flapper, DelFly Nimble [2–4], it can perform rapid banked turns. Its maximal forward flight speed is 7 m/s, the maximal sideways speed is 4 m/s. The RoboBee [5–9] is developed by Harvard University, weighs 60 mg, has a wingspan of 30 mm, and has a flapping frequency of 110 Hz. Universite´ Libre de Bruxelles introduce a prototype [10–14] has a total mass of 22 g, a wing span of 21 cm and a flapping frequency of 22 Hz. NUS-Roboticbird [15] was proposed by National University of Singapore, the vehicle weighing 31 g and having a wingspan of 22 cm can perform fast forward flight at a speed of about 5 m/s and endure 3.5 min in flight with a useful payload of a 4.5 g onboard camera for surveillance. KUBeetle [16–19] is introduced by Konkuk University, it can successfully perform a vertical climb, then hover and loiter within a 0.3 m ground radius with small variations in pitch and roll body angles. Among these MAVs, they are mainly divided into single flapping wings and double flapping wings. The single flapping wing is smaller in size, but has lower lift efficiency, limited load capacity. In addition, its attitude control is coupled, which results in longer response time and untimely response for each attitude, such as Hummingbird, KUBeetle. RoboBee can only fly under external power supply. Due to the utilization of the Weis-Fogh mechanism, the double flapping-wing MAV can generate greater lift and improve the load capacity. However, the double flapping wing also has the problem of attitude coupling and insufficient utilization of the bionic mechanism.

In this study, We propose a double flapping-wing MAV [20–22], which have a high thrust-to-weight ratio and can produce a high lifting to carry more load for reconnaissance mission required, it can actively control 4 DOFs. We use the Weis-Fogh mechanism [23–26] as a biomimetic principle and design a bionic wing and get the movement picture by the High Speed Camera. Then we analyzed the kinematics of the flapping mechanism, and get the equation between the input angle of crank and output angle of rocker, and make a simulation with ADAMS software. Finally, make an analysis of the attitude control mechanism (pitch, yaw, and roll) and test it by the 3DOFs platform.

2   Design of the Double Flapping-Wing MAV

2.1   Weis-Fogh Mechanism and Bionic Design of Wings

When the insects take off, they quickly flap their wings. Bees and flies's wing frequency is about 200 Hz, mosquitoes and wasps are up to 1000 Hz. This energy comes from the developed muscles in the middle of the body. The wings of insects are not only flapping up and down. When the insects rise, the wings move differently from the wings of most other flying creatures, and they appear as a "8" movement. Insect wings can produce lift when they are swung up and down. This is different from the wings of birds or bats. The lift generated only by the downward flutter.

Weis-Fogh studied the wasp and found that it had different forms of wing-flapping motion from that of bird, which starts faster than birds and proposes the Weis-Fogh mechanism. Figure 1 shows the small wasp using the Weis-Fogh mechanism to generate high lift. The wings of the backrest are rapidly opened during the leading edge of the trailing edge. In fact, the Weis-Fogh mechanism can be divided into four processes, as shown in Fig. 1. First, at the beginning of a stroke, the leading edges of the two wings are gradually closed together, and then the two wings are gradually twisted and separated from the leading edge, at this time, the angle between the two wings increases, forcing air to flow into the gap between the two wings. As the angle between the two wings increases, the air flow causes two rotating vortices to form around the wings, and the surface of the wings quickly forms a circulation. When the equivalent wings are opened, the two wings are separated and flutters, there is a boundary vortex on the surface of the wings, so that the lifting force is as large as possible.

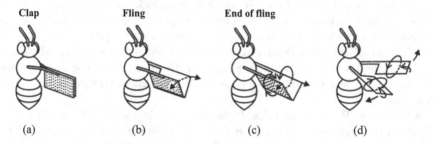

Fig. 1. The process of the small wasp using the Weis-Fogh mechanism to generate high lift.

In this study, we take the Rhinoceros beetle as a bionic object and observed its flight process with a High-Speed Camera. The Rhinoceros beetle belongs to the family of the chafer, which is larger in size. The adult body is 30–50 mm long (excluding the frontal angle), the body width is 20–30 mm, it is one of the largest flying insects. Therefore, it is easier to observe its body and wing structure with the naked eye and examine its flapping-wing motion using a High-Speed Camera. We set it at 2000 frames/s and mainly observe the shape transformation of the wings during the flight of the Rhinoceros beetle to explore the lift and attitude transformation. Through observation, we found that the wings of the Rhinoceros beetle flutter in a way similar to the paddles during the flight, and at the maximum and minimum positions of the flapping angle, the wings are rotated around the wings edge to adapt to the next flap. Through this form of modulation, it is possible to obtain sufficient lift and the torque required for rapid attitude change during flight. In this observation, we obtained the wing shape transformation process in one cycle of the Rhinoceros beetle, and the flapping frequency is about 35 Hz per second, a complete cycle is shown in Fig. 2.

Fig. 2. The flapping process of the Rhinoceros beetle in one cycle (camera shooting speed, 2000 frames, wing flapping frequency 35 Hz).

Fig. 3. Movement and shape changes of the vehicle wings in one cycle (camera shooting speed, 2000 frames, the flapping frequency is approximately 17 Hz).

Similarly, we observed the shape changes of the wings of the double flapping-wing MAV by High-Speed Camera to guide our design. As shown in Fig. 3, the shape of the wing changes in one cycle. We can conclude that the variation of its wings shape is similar to the Rhinoceros beetle flying process. Particularly, during the 0–8 ms, the angle between two wings reaches to minimum gradually, at this period, the shape of the wings change is similar to Rhinoceros beetle at 0–4 ms, which same to a paddle. That is the utilizing of the Weis-Fogh mechanism mentioned above. Hence, the double flapping-wing MAV can generate a large lift.

2.2 Overall Structure of Prototype

The overall structure of the double flapping-wing MAV is shown in Fig. 4. It mainly consists of flapping mechanism, attitude control mechanism, two pairs of wings, control panel, bracket and battery. The main parts are made of nylon material by 3D printing, and the wings are composed of polyimide film and carbon fiber rod. The flapping mechanism is driven by two brush motors and decelerated by two stages of a gear box, the reduction ratio is 13.33. The control mechanism is driven by two linear servos. The vehicle can realize four DOFs movement, namely, lifting movement, front and back, left and right and rotation around its own axis. That is four attitude: lifting, roll, pitch and yaw, where the lifting movement is controlled by the two brush motor in same speed, the roll motion is controlled by the differential brush motor speed on both sides, and the pitch motion is controlled by the same offset of the two linear servo, the yaw motion is controlled by the contrast offset of the two linear servo. The overall weight of the prototype is 32.8 g (without the battery), and the flapping maximum frequency is 23 Hz (measured by the stroboscope), the maximum lift is 34 g (measured by 6 axis sensor).

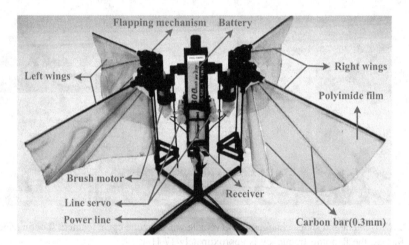

Fig. 4. The overall structure of the vehicle and the compose of each part

2.3 Flapping Mechanism Design and Analysis

Our flapping-wing system aimed to mimic the insect counterpart, namely, Rhinoceros beetle. Here, we briefly summarize the mathematical model of the flapping mechanism and the kinematics simulation based on ADAMS software. We designed a mechanism that can convert the rotary motion of the brush motor into flapping motion of the wing. For that purpose, a crank-rocker-rocker composite mechanism was utilized to transform the rotary motion of the brush motor into the reciprocating motion of the rocker to where the wing is attached. As shown in Fig. 5, the flapping mechanism consists of a crank-rocker ($O_1AB_1O_2$) and a rocker-rocker ($O_2C_1D_1O_3$) mechanism. The original coordinate system is fixed at joint O_1. The input crank angle, θ, is measured from the X-axis around O_1 to O_1A along counterclockwise, and the angle, φ_R, of the right rocker-1 is measured from the x-axis around O_2 to O_2B_1, To calculate the flapping angle, the kinematics of the crank-rocker mechanism $(O_1AB_1O_2)$ is first analyzed for the angle of rocker-1, φ_R, which will then be used in the second analysis of the rocker-rocker mechanism $(O_2C_1D_1O_3)$ for the rocker-2 angle, ψ_R. Using the length of the connecting link, a_R, provides the constrain equation,

$$\overrightarrow{AB_1} \cdot \overrightarrow{AB_1} = a_R^2 \tag{1}$$

where

$$\overrightarrow{OA} = \begin{Bmatrix} r\cos\theta \\ r\sin\theta \end{Bmatrix} \tag{2}$$

$$\overrightarrow{OB_1} = \overrightarrow{OC_1} + \overrightarrow{C_1B_1} = \begin{Bmatrix} m \\ n \end{Bmatrix} + \begin{Bmatrix} b_R\cos\varphi_R \\ b_R\sin\varphi_R \end{Bmatrix} = \begin{Bmatrix} m + b_R\cos\varphi_R \\ n + b_R\sin\varphi_R \end{Bmatrix} \tag{3}$$

then

$$\overrightarrow{AB_1} = \overrightarrow{OB_1} - \overrightarrow{OA} = \begin{Bmatrix} m + b_R\cos\varphi_R - r\cos\theta \\ n + b_R\sin\varphi_R - r\sin\theta \end{Bmatrix} \tag{4}$$

Solving Eq. (1) with the substitution of Eq. (4) obtains the angle of the rocker-1, we can get the Eq. (5),

$$\frac{(m - r\cos\theta)\cos\varphi_R}{\sqrt{m^2 + n^2 + r^2 - 2r(m\cos\theta + n\sin\theta)}} + \frac{(n - r\sin\theta)\sin\varphi_R}{\sqrt{m^2 + n^2 + r^2 - 2r(m\cos\theta + n\sin\theta)}}$$

$$= \frac{a_R^2 - m^2 - n^2 - b_R^2 + 2r(m\cos\theta + n\sin\theta)}{2b_R\sqrt{m^2 + n^2 + r^2 - 2r(m\cos\theta + n\sin\theta)}} \tag{5}$$

finally, the rocker-1 angle, φ_R, is calculated by,

$$\varphi_R = \sin^{-1}\frac{a_R^2 - m^2 - n^2 - b_R^2 - r^2 + 2rk_1}{2b_R\sqrt{m^2 + n^2 + r^2 - 2rk_1}} - \Phi_1 \tag{6}$$

where

$$k_1 = m\cos\theta + n\sin\theta, \quad \Phi_1 = \sin^{-1}\frac{m - r\cos\theta}{\sqrt{m^2 + n^2 + r^2 - 2rk_1}}.$$

Similarly, using the length of the connecting link, d_R, provides the constrain equation,

$$\overrightarrow{C_1D_1} \cdot \overrightarrow{C_1D_1} = d_R^2 \tag{7}$$

where

$$\overrightarrow{O_2D_1} = \overrightarrow{O_2O_3} + \overrightarrow{O_3D_1} = \left\{ \begin{matrix} p \\ q \end{matrix} \right\} + \left\{ \begin{matrix} e_R \cos\psi_R \\ -e_R \sin\psi_R \end{matrix} \right\} = \left\{ \begin{matrix} p + e_R \cos\psi_R \\ q - e_R \sin\psi_R \end{matrix} \right\} \tag{8}$$

$$\overrightarrow{O_2C_1} = \left\{ \begin{matrix} -c_R \cos(\varphi_R + \delta) \\ c_R \sin(\varphi_R + \delta) \end{matrix} \right\} \tag{9}$$

then we can get the vector $\overrightarrow{C_1D_1}$,

$$\overrightarrow{C_1D_1} = \overrightarrow{O_2D_1} - \overrightarrow{O_2C_1} = \left\{ \begin{matrix} p + e_R \cos\psi_R \\ q - e_R \sin\psi_R \end{matrix} \right\} - \left\{ \begin{matrix} -c_R \cos(\varphi_R + \delta) \\ c_R \sin(\varphi_R + \delta) \end{matrix} \right\}$$

$$= \left\{ \begin{matrix} p + e_R \cos\psi_R + c_R \cos(\varphi_R + \delta) \\ q - e_R \sin\psi_R - c_R \sin(\varphi_R + \delta) \end{matrix} \right\} \tag{10}$$

Solving Eq. (7) with the substitution of Eq. (10) obtains the angle of the rocker-2, we can get the Eq. (11) firstly,

$$\frac{[2pe_R + 2c_Re_R \cos(\varphi_R + \delta)] \cos\psi_R}{2e_R\sqrt{p^2 + q^2 + c_R^2}} - \frac{[2qe_R + 2c_Re_R \sin(\varphi_R + \delta)] \sin\psi_R}{2e_R\sqrt{p^2 + q^2 + c_R^2}}$$

$$= \frac{d_R^2 - p^2 - q^2 - e_R^2 + 2c_R[q \sin(\varphi_R + \delta) - p \cos(\varphi_R + \delta)]}{2e_R\sqrt{p^2 + q^2 + c_R^2}} \tag{11}$$

finally, the flapping angle, ψ_R, is calculated by,

$$\psi_R = \Phi_2 - \sin^{-1}\frac{d_R^2 - e_R^2 - k_2^2 + 2c_R(qk_3 - pk_4)}{2e_R\sqrt{k_2}} \tag{12}$$

where

$$k_2 = \sqrt{p^2 + q^2 + c_R^2}, \ k_3 = \sin(\varphi_R + \delta), \ k_4 = \cos(\varphi_R + \delta),$$

$$\Phi_2 = \sin^{-1}\frac{2pe_R + 2c_Re_Rk_4}{2e_R\sqrt{k_2}}.$$

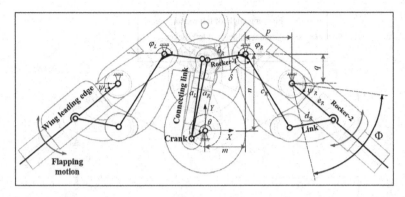

Fig. 5. Flapping mechanism with crank-rocker-rocker mechanism. Wing leading edge is attached to the rocker-2.

After completing the theoretical model of the flapping mechanism, we simulated the kinematics of the flapping mechanism based on the ADAMS software. The simulation model is shown in Fig. 6. Then we get the parameters of the rockers. Figure 7 shows the parameters of the left rocker. The red solid line represents the flapping angle of the rocker, which is divided into two stages, in-stroke and out-stroke, during the in-stroke stage, the angle between the left rocker and right rocker is decrease, the wings on both sides are close to each other, at the end of this stage, the angle between the left wing and right wing is minimum. Then, it is the start of the other stage, out-stroke, and during the transition of these two stages, the wings movement style is similar to the Weis-Fogh mechanism, imitating the insects counterpart, and it can produce greater lift at this stage. The blue line shown is the angular velocity curve of the rocker, and it shows a gentle change. The black dotted line shows the angular acceleration curve of the rocker. Figure 8 shows the parameters of the right wing.

Fig. 6. Flapping mechanism with crank-rocker-rocker mechanism ADAMS simulation model and 3D printed assembly model

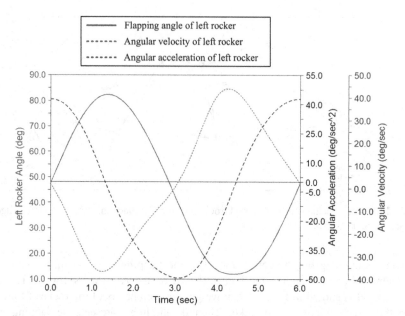

Fig. 7. Flapping angle, angular velocity and angular acceleration of the left wing. (Color figure online)

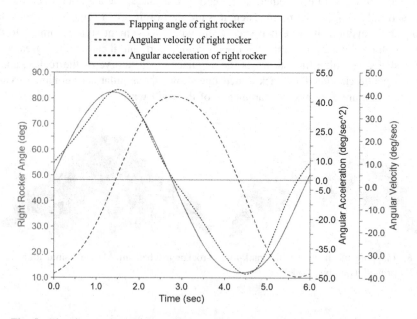

Fig. 8. Flapping angle, angular velocity and angular acceleration of the right wing.

2.4   Attitude Control Mechanism Design

In this study, the vehicle can realize four DOFs, namely, up and down, roll, pitch and yaw, which make it possible to free fly in the three-dimensional space. The yaw, pitch and roll attitude are three rotational motion, which around Z-axis, X-axis and Y-axis respectively, the yaw attitude can change the direction of the MAV, the pitch attitude and control the MAV fly front or back freely, the roll attitude can control the MAV fly left or right side.

Yaw Attitude Control

The yaw torque is created by different offset of two linear servo fixed in two sides, by tilting the left and right wings in contrast direction, due to the asymmetry thrust there will produce a torque around the Z-axis, different linear servo offset combinations will produce a clockwise and anticlockwise yaw direction, as is shown in Fig. 9. The type of linear servo is AFRC-D1015-Pro, the maximum torque is 0.24 kg cm, the sensitivity is 0.15 s/cm, maximum stroke is 9 mm.

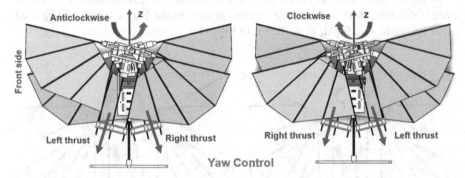

Fig. 9. Yaw attitude test experiment, by tilting the two linear servo in a different direction, the vehicle will rotate around Z-axis.

Pitch Attitude Control

The pitch torque is created by same offset of two linear servo fixed in two sides, by tilting the left and right wings in same direction, there will produce a torque around the X-axis, the combined force of gravity and lift is in the horizontal direction, which can provide the force to fly front and back, as is shown in Fig. 10.

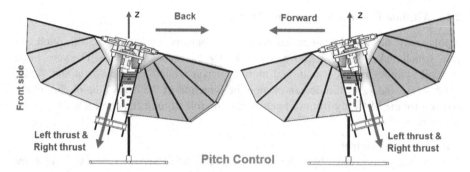

Fig. 10. Pitch attitude test experiment, by tilting the two linear servo in the same direction, the vehicle will rotate around *X*-axis.

Roll Attitude Control
The roll torque is created by two brush motors which driven the two sides of the wings, if two motors rotate in same speed, there will no torque exist, in contrast, if the motor speed is different, there will produce an extra torque around *Y*-axis, which will be used in left and right side flight, as is shown in Fig. 11.

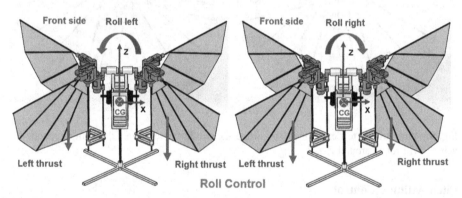

Fig. 11. Roll attitude test experiment, the two brush motors rotate in different speed, the vehicle will rotate around *Y*-axis.

3   Attitude Measurement Based on 3-DOFs Platform

In order to verify the effectiveness of the attitude control structure, we used a 3DOFs platform to test the performance of the three rotating attitudes of the vehicle. As shown in Fig. 12, the platform is mainly composed of three rotational DOFs, which around *X*, *Y*, and *Z*-axis. Corresponding to the roll, yaw and roll attitude of the vehicle. Each DOF of the platform can be rotate separately, and the required DOF can be selected according to the test requirements.

Fig. 12. 3DOFs platform (every DOF can rotate independently)

As shown in Fig. 13, it is the yaw test experiment, where, the platform possess only one DOF which around the Z-axis, by controlling the left linear servo offset forward, control the right linear servo offset backwards, the vehicle can produce a yaw moment in clockwise direction. Figure 14 shows the roll attitude test experiment, where, the platform possess only one DOF which around the Y-axis, by controlling the voltages of the two DC regulated sources, the two brush motors rotate at different speeds, thus the vehicle can produce the roll torque around Y-axis. As shown in Fig. 15, it is the pitch test experiment, where, the platform possess only one DOF which around the X-axis, by controlling the left and right linear servo offset in forward direction, the prototype can generate the tilting moment around the X-axis, the vehicle will tilt to the right side. The 3 DOFs platform verifies the effectiveness of the three rotational attitudes (pitch, yaw, and roll) of the vehicle, and also proves the uncoupling of the three attitudes.

Fig. 13. Yaw attitude test experiment, by tilt the two linear servo in different direction, the vehicle will rotate around its own axis.

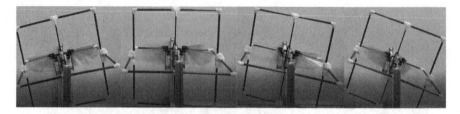

Fig. 14. Roll attitude test experiment, by control the two brush motors in different speed, the vehicle will rotate around Y-axis.

Fig. 15. Pitch attitude test experiment, by tilt the two linear servo in same direction, the vehicle will rotate around X-axis.

4 Conclusion

In this study, we propose a double flapping-wing MAV, and mainly completed the following works:

(1) Firstly, Weis-Fogh mechanism was cited to explain the aerodynamic mechanism by which insects can produce high lift, and make it as our bionic design principles. Then we take the Rhinoceros beetle as a bionic object, it was photographed with a High-Speed Camera platform, and the shape change of the wings in one cycle was obtained to guide our wing structure design. At the same time, we also used the High-Speed Camera to observe the changes of the vehicle's wings shape, which can provide a guidance of the bionic wing shape design.

(2) Secondly, the mathematical model of the flapping mechanism is established, and the equations between the crank input angle and the rocker output angle are obtained. Based on this model, the flapping structure designed by us is simulated based on ADAMS software. Output angle, angular velocity, and angular acceleration data of the rockers on both sides is obtained and as the parameter indicators of vehicle design.

(3) Finally, the attitude control structure is analyzed, and the attitude control structure is tested by the 3 DOFs platform, the attitude constructure is confirmed effective and uncoupled.

Through experiments and analysis, we can get the conclusion that the double flapping-wing MAV has a large thrust-to-weight ratio, the three rotation attitude controls are uncoupled and can control of the three rotate attitude independently. The analysis and the experiment provides a theoretical reference and experiment basis for a high-performance MAV research and development.

Acknowledgments. This research was primarily supported by the National Natural Science Foundation of China (Grant number 73048001), Science & Technology Ministry of China (Grant number 2018YFB1304600).

References

1. Keennon, M., Klingebiel, K., Won, H.: Development of the nano hummingbird: a tailless flapping wing micro air vehicle. In: 50th AIAA Aerospace Sciences Meeting Including the New Horizons Forum and Aerospace Exposition (2012)
2. Karásek, M., et al.: A tailless aerial robotic flapper reveals that flies use torque coupling in rapid banked turns. Science **361**(6407), 1089–1094 (2018)
3. Armanini, S.F., et al.: Modelling wing wake and tail aerodynamics of a flapping-wing micro aerial vehicle. Int. J. Micro Air Veh. **11**, 1756829319833674 (2019)
4. De Croon, G.C.H.E., et al.: Design, aerodynamics, and vision-based control of the DelFly. Int. J. Micro Air Veh. **1**(2), 71–97 (2009)
5. Ma, K.Y., et al.: Controlled flight of a biologically inspired, insect-scale robot. Science **340** (6132), 603–607 (2013)
6. Wood, R.J.: The first takeoff of a biologically inspired at-scale robotic insect. IEEE Trans. Robot. **24**(2), 341–347 (2008)
7. Finio, B.M., Wood, R.J.: Open-loop roll, pitch and yaw torques for a robotic bee. In: 2012 IEEE/RSJ International Conference on Intelligent Robots and Systems. IEEE (2012)
8. Teoh, Z.E., et al.: A hovering flapping-wing microrobot with altitude control and passive upright stability. In: 2012 IEEE/RSJ International Conference on Intelligent Robots and Systems. IEEE (2012)
9. Whitney, J.P., Wood, R.J.: Aeromechanics of passive rotation in flapping flight. J. Fluid Mech. **660**, 197–220 (2010)
10. Karásek, M., et al.: Pitch and roll control mechanism for a hovering flapping wing MAV. Int. J. Micro Air Veh. **6**(4), 253–264 (2014)
11. Karásek, M., et al.: Pitch moment generation and measurement in a robotic hummingbird. Int. J. Micro Air Veh. **5**(4), 299–309 (2013)
12. Karásek, M., Preumont, A.: Flapping flight stability in hover: a comparison of various aerodynamic models. Int. J. Micro Air Veh. **4**(3), 203–226 (2012)
13. Roshanbin, A., et al.: COLIBRI: a hovering flapping twin-wing robot. Int. J. Micro Air Veh. **9**(4), 270–282 (2017)
14. Karasek, M., Preumont, A.: Simulation of flight control of a hummingbird like robot near hover. Eng. Mech. **58**, 322 (2012)
15. Nguyen, Q.-V., Chan, W.L.: Development and flight performance of a biologically-inspired tailless flapping-wing micro air vehicle with wing stroke plane modulation. Bioinspiration Biomimetics **14**(1), 016015 (2018)
16. Phan, H.V., Kang, T., Park, H.C.: Design and stable flight of a 21 g insect-like tailless flapping wing micro air vehicle with angular rates feedback control. Bioinspiration Biomimetics **12**(3), 036006 (2017)
17. Van Truong, T., et al.: Experimental and numerical studies of beetle-inspired flapping wing in hovering flight. Bioinspiration Biomimetics **12**(3), 036012 (2017)

18. Au, L.T.K., Phan, V.H., Park, H.C.: Longitudinal flight dynamic analysis on vertical takeoff of a tailless flapping-wing micro air vehicle. J. Bionic Eng. **15**(2), 283–297 (2018)
19. Truong, T.N., Phan, H.V., Park, H.C.: Design and demonstration of a bio-inspired flapping-wing-assisted jumping robot. Bioinspiration Biomimetics **14**, 036010 (2019)
20. Zhou, W., Deng, H., Ding, X.: Bionic structure design of a flapping wing robot. In: Zhang, X., Wang, N., Huang, Y. (eds.) Mechanism and Machine Science. LNEE, vol. 408, pp. 101–110. Springer, Heidelberg (2016). https://doi.org/10.1007/978-981-10-2875-5
21. Xiao, S., et al.: Optimization design of flapping mechanism of micro air vehicle based on matlab and adams. In: 2018 IEEE International Conference on Robotics and Biomimetics (ROBIO). IEEE (2018)
22. Chen, Z., et al.: Structural integrity analysis of transmission structure in flapping-wing micro aerial vehicle via 3D printing. Eng. Failure Anal. **96**, 18–30 (2019)
23. Weis-Fogh, T.: Quick estimates of flight fitness in hovering animals, including novel mechanisms for lift production. J. Exp. Biol. **59**(1), 169–230 (1973)
24. Lighthill, M.J.: On the Weis-Fogh mechanism of lift generation. J. Fluid Mech. **60**(1), 1–17 (1973)
25. Weis-Fogh, T.: Unusual mechanisms for the generation of lift in flying animals. Sci. Am. **233**(5), 80–87 (1975)
26. Bennett, L.: Clap and fling aerodynamics-an experimental evaluation. J. Exp. Biol. **69**(1), 261–272 (1977)

Design and Simulation of Heavy Load Wheeled Mobile Robot Driving Mechanism

Yang Zhang[1,2,3(✉)], Zhi-gang Xu[1,3], Song-kai Liu[1,3],
and Qing-yun Wang[1,2,3]

[1] Shenyang Institute of Automation Chinese Academy of Sciences,
Shenyang 110016, China
Zhangyang4@sia.cn
[2] University of Chinese Academy of Sciences, Beijing 100039, China
[3] Institutes for Robotics and Intelligent Manufacturing,
Chinese Academy of Sciences, Shenyang 110016, China

Abstract. Facing with the problem of high labor intensity, low standard of automation and low production efficiency, traditional pattern of rocket cabins transportation should be eliminated. The traditional way was still unable to cope with the mixed flow of multiple series and types of rocket cabin. Hence, it is of great significance to design an AGV with good stability, good driving performance and load capacity as the transport equipment of the rocket cabin. A heavy load Omnidirectional AGV for rocket cabin transportation is proposed. A kinematic model of the AGV was set up and analyzed by the software of ADAMS (Automatic Dynamic Analysis of Mechanical Systems). Results of the ADAMS simulation indicate that the driving mechanism of the automatic guide vehicle in this study performs well in most working conditions, and the problem of "locked up" in the transverse working conditions has also been well solved. It is of great reference significance to the research of the heavy-duty automatic guided vehicle for large segment transshipment.

Keywords: AGV · Kinematic · ADAMS · Omni-directional

1 Introduction

The rocket cabin has the characteristics of large volume and large mass. The traditional transfer of the rocket cabin is completed by the truck pushed by workers. This transfer mode has high labor intensity, low degree of automation and poor production efficiency. It is also unable to adapt to the mixed production of multi-series and different types of rocket cabin. Automatic guided vehicle is a common equipment for automatic transfer of rocket cabin, but in the process of transfer of large rocket cabin, it may occur that the automatic guided vehicle cannot operate normally due to improper driving arrangement. Therefore, it is necessary and of great significance to develop an automatic guided vehicle with high stability, good driving performance and capable of carrying both loads as the transport equipment of the rocket cabin.

Many scholars have studied the design layout and kinematics of automatic guided vehicles. Paper [1] systematically carried out a kinematical analysis on the various

© Springer Nature Switzerland AG 2019
H. Yu et al. (Eds.): ICIRA 2019, LNAI 11745, pp. 255–272, 2019.
https://doi.org/10.1007/978-3-030-27529-7_23

types of wheel, paper [2] are analyzed in detail a variety of typical wheel decorate a form, paper [3–6] are introduced in detail for all kinds of wheeled mobile robot, including automatic guided vehicle modeling method, the research provides profound theoretical basis for the study.

This research aiming at the problems that may exist in the operation of the automatic guided vehicle for the transfer of rocket cabin, the walking driving mechanism of the automatic guided vehicle was designed and optimized. In order to test whether the automatic guide vehicle in this study has the ability of omni-directional movement such as horizontal translation, longitudinal translation and rotation, the kinematics of the vehicle is analyzed and the multi-body kinematics simulation software is used to simulate the vehicle. The research on the large heavy-load automatic guided vehicle for rocket docking has important guiding significance for improving the technology level of digital transfer of rocket cabin.

2   Driving System of the Automatic Guided Vehicle

The driving system of an automatic guide vehicle includes a steering part and a driving part, in which the driving part comprises driving wheels and driven wheels. The rocket cabin has the characteristics of large volume, large mass and complex production environment. Due to the low stability of single-wheel, two-wheel and three-wheel layout, it is prone to roll over and tilt, etc., and the four-wheel layout has good structural stability, but the control accuracy is not ideal. Therefore, these are not suitable for the automatic guided vehicle facing the transfer of rocket cabin. The six-wheel layout has good stability, good load capacity and guaranteed control accuracy. Therefore, the six-wheel layout scheme is selected in this research. Among them, the center of two driving wheels in the direction of control is symmetrically arranged in the middle of the frame of the automatic guide truck to improve the control accuracy of the car body, and four small casters are arranged at the four corners as slave wheels to ensure the stability of the car body. The specific wheel arrangement structure of the automatic guide vehicle can be seen in Fig. 1.

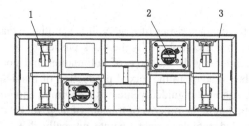

1- driven wheels of the automatic guiding vehicle; 2- driving wheels of the automatic guided vehicle; 3- the frame of the automatic guided vehicle

Fig. 1. Wheel arrangement scheme of walking driving mechanism

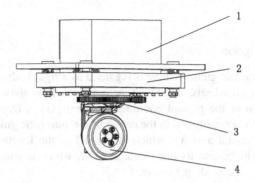

1- electric case of driving wheel; 2- driving mechanism of driving wheel; 3- driving wheel fork; 4 - driving wheel

Fig. 2. Structural design of driving wheel assembly

The structure of the driving wheel assembly is shown in Fig. 2, which includes an electric case integrating a directional control motor and a motion control motor. It is composed of a transmission mechanism composed of a number of gears, a driving wheel frame and a driving wheel. The structure of the slave wheel component is shown in Fig. 3. The vertical rotation axis is combined with the triangular wheel frame and assembled with the slave wheel.

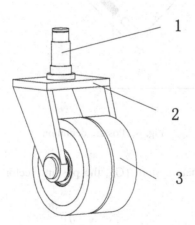

1- Vertical rotation axis of the castor; 2-Castor fork; 3- Castor

Fig. 3. Structural design of driven wheel assembly

3 Kinematic

3.1 Posture Description

The frame of the automatic guide vehicle is regarded as a rigid body, and on the basis of no deformation of all wheels, the AGV car is modeled, as shown in Fig. 2. It is known that the origin of the ground coordinate system {G} is O_G, and AGV fixed coordinate system {A} is established in the center of the automatic guiding vehicle. Let the origin be its horizontal axis X_A, which is parallel to the length direction of the automatic guiding vehicle, and its horizontal axis Y_A, which is parallel to the width direction of the automatic guiding vehicle.

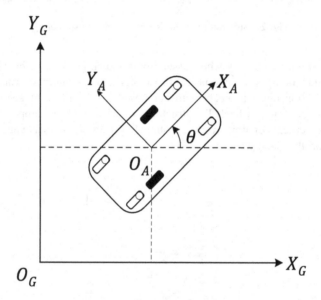

Fig. 4. Posture definition

In the ground coordinate system {G}, the posture vector of the automatic guide vehicle is:

$$\xi_G = [x \quad y \quad \theta]^T \tag{1}$$

Where x and y are respectively the horizontal and vertical coordinates in the ground coordinate system {G}, and θ are the Angle between the horizontal coordinate axis X_G of the ground coordinate system {G} and the horizontal coordinate axis of the fixed coordinate system {A} of the automatic guide vehicle, and the counterclockwise direction is positive and the clockwise direction is negative.

Then the transformation operator matrix of the fixed frame {A} with respect to {G} is written as:

$$R(\theta) = \begin{bmatrix} \cos\theta & \sin\theta & 0 \\ -\sin\theta & \cos\theta & 0 \\ 0 & 0 & 1 \end{bmatrix} \tag{2}$$

3.2 Wheel Constraints

The driving wheel is a standard wheel that can be manipulated and is a type of centering wheel, as shown in Fig. 3. In the process of driving, the contact point between the wheel and the ground along the direction of wheel motion and the velocity component perpendicular to the direction of motion are both zero. In the fixed coordinate system {A} of the automatic guide vehicle, the following equation is established:

Direction of wheel movement:

$$\begin{bmatrix} -\sin(\alpha+\beta) & \cos(\alpha+\beta) & l\cos\beta \end{bmatrix} R(\theta) \begin{bmatrix} x \\ y \\ \theta \end{bmatrix} + r\varphi = 0 \tag{3}$$

Perpendicular to the direction of wheel motion:

$$\begin{bmatrix} -\cos(\alpha+\beta) & \sin(\alpha+\beta) & l\sin\beta \end{bmatrix} R(\theta) \begin{bmatrix} x \\ y \\ \theta \end{bmatrix} = 0 \tag{4}$$

Rolling constraint equation:

$$\begin{bmatrix} \sin(\alpha+\beta) & -\cos(\alpha+\beta) & (-l)\cos\beta \end{bmatrix} R(\theta)\dot{\xi}_G - r\dot{\varphi} = 0 \tag{5}$$

Sliding constraint equation:

$$\begin{bmatrix} \cos(\alpha+\beta) & \sin(\alpha+\beta) & l\sin\beta \end{bmatrix} R(\theta)\dot{\xi}_G = 0 \tag{6}$$

l is the distance from the wheel center to the fixed coordinate system {A} origin of the automatic guide vehicle; α is the Angle between the connecting line between the wheel rotation center and the fixed coordinate system {A} of the automatic guide vehicle and the axis X_A, which is positive counterclockwise and negative clockwise; β is the Angle between the normal line of the plane where the wheel is located and the fixed coordinate system {A} origin line of the wheel center and the automatic guide vehicle, which is a fixed value; r is the radius of the driving wheel; φ is the rolling angle of the wheel, which varies with time.

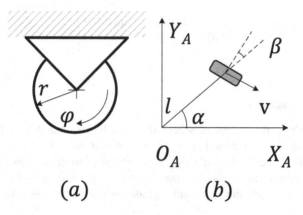

Fig. 5. Centered orientable wheels

The small castor (eccentric universal wheel) serves as the driven wheel, as shown in Fig. 4. The eccentric universal wheel can rotate around a vertical axis that does not pass through the contact point on the ground. The rolling constraint equation is the same as that of the centering wheel, because the offset axis does not work when the motion direction is in coplanar with the wheel. The equation is established as follows:

$$[-\cos(\alpha+\beta) \quad \sin(\alpha+\beta) \quad l\sin\beta]R(\theta)\begin{bmatrix} x \\ y \\ \theta \end{bmatrix} + d\beta = 0 \tag{8}$$

$$[\sin(\alpha+\beta) \quad -\cos(\alpha+\beta) \quad (-l)\cos\beta]R(\theta)\dot{\xi}_G - r'\dot{\varphi} = 0 \tag{9}$$

$$[\cos(\alpha+\beta) \quad \sin(\alpha+\beta) \quad d+l\sin\beta]R(\theta)\dot{\xi}_G + d\dot{\beta} = 0 \tag{10}$$

Where, r' is the radius of the driven wheel; D is the deviation between the ground contact point of the driven wheel and the vertical rotation axis (Fig. 5).

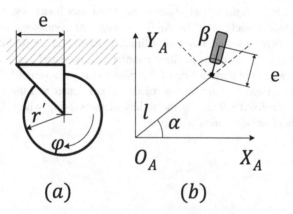

Fig. 6. Off centered orientable wheels

Due to the different degrees of freedom of the internal wheels, only the fixed standard wheels and the controllable standard wheels will impose kinematic constraints on the frame of the automatic guide vehicle. Among the other wheels (Fig. 6),

There are a total of $N = 2$ standard wheels in the automatic guide vehicle, in which, fixed standard wheel, $N_f = 0$, adjustable standard wheel, $N_s = 2$, $\beta_s(t)$ represents N_s variable control angle of the controlled standard wheel, β_f refers to the N_f direction angle of a fixed standard wheel.

In the state of wheel rotation, the fixed and manipulated wheels have rotation positions around the horizontal axis, which changes with time. The rolling Angle of the fixed and manipulated standard wheels is represented by $\varphi_f(t)$ and $\varphi_s(t)$, hence the combination of the two has

$$\varphi(t) = \begin{bmatrix} \varphi_f(t) \\ \varphi_s(t) \end{bmatrix} = \begin{bmatrix} \varphi_{s1}(t) \\ \varphi_{s2}(t) \end{bmatrix} \tag{11}$$

The rolling constraints of all wheels are combined into an expression, then

$$\begin{bmatrix} J_{1f} \\ J_{1s}(\beta_s) \end{bmatrix} \begin{bmatrix} \cos\theta & \sin\theta & 0 \\ -\sin\theta & \cos\theta & 0 \\ 0 & 0 & 1 \end{bmatrix} \dot{\xi}_G - \begin{bmatrix} r & 0 \\ 0 & r \end{bmatrix} \dot{\varphi} = 0 \tag{12}$$

or

$$J_1(\beta_s)R_\theta \dot{\xi}_G - J_2\dot{\varphi} = 0 \tag{13}$$

Represents a matrix with a projection onto the motion of all the wheels along the plane of their respective wheels. For each fixed standard wheel $J_{1f}(\beta_f)$ is a $N_f \times 3$ matrix For each controllable standard wheel, $J_{1s}(\beta_s)$ is a $N_s \times 3$ matrix. In other words, formula (13) expresses the constraint that all standard wheels must rotate around the horizontal axis at an appropriate Angle according to their motion along the plane, so that the rolling occurs at the contact point with the ground. Similarly, all sliding constraints are combined into a single expression:

$$C_1(\beta_s)R(\theta)\dot{\xi}_G = 0 \tag{14}$$

It's a constraint on all the standard wheels, and the components of motion that are orthogonal to the plane of the wheel must be zero. This constraint has the most significant influence on determining the mobility of the frame of the automatic guide vehicle.

$$C_1(\beta_s) = \begin{bmatrix} C_{1f} \\ C_{1s}(\beta_s) \end{bmatrix} \tag{15}$$

$$J_1(\beta_s)R_\theta \dot{\xi}_G - J_2\dot{\varphi} = 0 \tag{16}$$

$$J_1(\beta_s)R_\theta \dot{\xi}_G = J_2 \dot{\varphi} \tag{17}$$

$$C_1(\beta_s)R(\theta)\dot{\xi}_G = 0 \tag{18}$$

Simultaneously, the correlation equation between rolling constraint and sliding constraint in robot motion and wheel speed is obtained as follows:

$$\begin{bmatrix} \sin(\alpha_1+\beta_1) & -\cos(\alpha_1+\beta_1) & (-l)cos\beta_1 \\ \sin(\alpha_2+\beta_2) & -\cos(\alpha_2+\beta_2) & (-l)cos\beta_2 \\ \cos(\alpha_1+\beta_1) & \sin(\alpha_1+\beta_1) & lsin\beta_1 \\ \cos(\alpha_2+\beta_2) & \sin(\alpha_2+\beta_2) & lsin\beta_2 \end{bmatrix} R(\theta)\dot{\xi}_G = \begin{bmatrix} J_2\dot{\varphi} \\ 0 \end{bmatrix} \tag{19}$$

or

$$\begin{bmatrix} J_1(\beta_s) \\ C_1(\beta_s) \end{bmatrix} R(\theta)\dot{\xi}_G = \begin{bmatrix} J_2\dot{\varphi} \\ 0 \end{bmatrix} \tag{20}$$

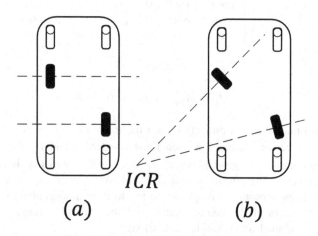

Fig. 7. Instantaneous center of rotation

The degree of mobility is known from formula (18), which imposes a constraint on each wheel to avoid any lateral slip. Therefore, for the driving wheel:

$$C_{1s}(\beta_s)R(\theta)\dot{\xi}_G = 0 \tag{21}$$

The equation of the geometric meaning can use the instantaneous center of rotation (instantaneous center of rotation, ICR) concept to describe. A driving wheel, with no lateral motion due to sliding constraints, can geometrically pass through its axis of horizontal rotation and be perpendicular to the wheel plane to draw a line of zero motion. The intersection point of zero motion line of two driving wheels is the instantaneous rotation center (ICR). In the normal pose, the two driving wheels each provide a constraint or a zero motion line, and a single point will be generated after the combination. In the straight pose, as shown in Fig. 7, the zero motion line of the two driving wheels does not coincide, which will not result in $Rank[C_1(\beta_s)]$

$$rank[C_1(\beta_s)] = 2 \tag{22}$$

Then the degree of mobility of the AGV

$$\delta_m = dimN[C_1(\beta_s)] = 3 - rank[C_1(\beta_s)] = 1 \tag{23}$$

By controlling the speed and direction of the wheel, the change rate of the direction of the autopilot can be controlled and its forward and backward speed can be controlled.

$$\delta_s = rank[C_{1s}(\beta_s)] = 2 \tag{24}$$

In other words, $0 \leq \delta_s \leq 2$ the vehicle has the maximum maneuverability and can put ICR in any position on the ground plane. The degree of maneuverability of an autopilot.

$$\delta_M = \delta_m + \delta_s = 3 \tag{25}$$

In other words, the vehicle can operate a total of three degrees of freedom (translation in the x direction, translation in the y direction, and rotation around the z axis). To sum up, the layout of the walking driving mechanism of the automatic guide vehicle is reasonable.

4 Simulation

4.1 Modeling

The focus of ADAMS software simulation is on the constraint relationship between point position and construction. Therefore, during the modeling process, we simplify each component into the simplest geometric model as far as possible. Parameter setting is carried out in ADAMS. The geometric model design variables set are shown in Table 1. After the design variables are set, geometric modeling is conducted to establish four universal wheels, two driving wheels and their corresponding wheel frames and vehicle frames (Figs. 9, 10, 11 and 12).

When driving, driving wheel frame is regarded as solid even with the frame, applying Fixed vice (Fixed to be), and each driven wheel (eccentric wheels off - centered orientational wheels that Castor wheel) wheel frame and the frame to rotate vice (Revolute be) connection, simulate the relative rotation between the universal wheel frame and the frame, this in the subsequent study is an important link, must ensure that the accurate position, Each driven wheel (eccentric universal wheel), driving wheel and wheel frame are connected with a rotating pair to simulate the rotation of the wheel itself. In addition, as a cuboid on the Ground, Fixed Joint is imposed between the ground. Otherwise, after the simulation starts, the geometric entity will fall under the action of gravity, thus failing to achieve the simulation purpose. In order to accurately position when the motion pair is applied, we establish corresponding marker points on the entity.

Table 1. Design variables for geometric models

Design variables	Value
Radius of the driven wheel	100
Width of the driven wheel	200
Width of the driven wheel fork	200
Frame length	4300
Frame width	1420
Frame hight	1000
Radius of the driving wheel	115
Width of the driving wheel	70
Width of the driving wheel fork	70

After adding the constraint, it is necessary to set the contact parameters between the six wheels and the ground, and add the drive on the basis of the corresponding constraint. According to a series of parameters of the selected wheel, the driving torque of the corresponding driving mechanism applied to the two driving wheels is calculated as a reference. Wheel Contact with the ground, need a Contact TAB, Contact types for the rigid body of rigid body (Solid to Solid), six wheel Contact with the ground Stiffness index (Stiffness), Force (the Force Exponent), Damping (Damping), Penetration Depth, Penetration the Depth), such as at the beginning of the model has been set up corresponding design parameter, simply call the corresponding design parameters, friction type selection of Coulomb friction (Coulomb) (Table 2).

Table 2. Design variables of simulation environment

Design variables	Value
Stiffness	10
Force Exponent	2.2
Damping	10
Penetration Depth	5

Before the dynamics simulation, can initialize first assembly (initial condition the solution) is calculated model of constraint is correct, then check the information window, will choose to Default (the Default), the type of simulation system will be determined according to the circumstance such as degree of freedom of the model itself simulation category, otherwise, if manually choose the wrong type of simulation, system error.

4.2 Simulation Result

The simulation is carried out when the rotation direction of the driving wheel and the axis of the frame are 45°. - as shown in Fig. 13, as shown in Fig. 8 in straight condition, each wheel under the driving moment of the given would be able to start, start, backward, driving wheel and the body axis a 45° condition, such as AGV start smoothly, drive steady, that is to say, in most cases, the selected models of driving wheel can satisfy the power demand of the AGV, but in the ninety - degree traverse, the result is shown in Fig. 16, agency show "lock" (locked up) state, confirm it through the experience in engineering, AGV does not move, In line with the starting point of optimizing the design, finding out the problems at the beginning of the design and solving them, we optimized the steering gait. In the case of lateral movement, first turn the driving wheel to 30°, walk a short distance, and then turn the driving wheel to 90° from the car body, as shown in Figs. 15, 16, 17, 18 and 19. The simulation results show that the vehicle can achieve the goal of lateral movement smoothly after the gait improvement. Therefore, the selected gait optimization method is feasible (Figs. 14, 20 and 21).

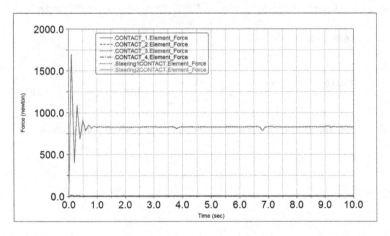

Fig. 8. Friction force in X direction for each wheel in straight direction

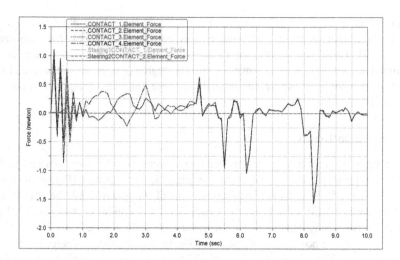

Fig. 9. Friction force in Y direction for each wheel in straight direction

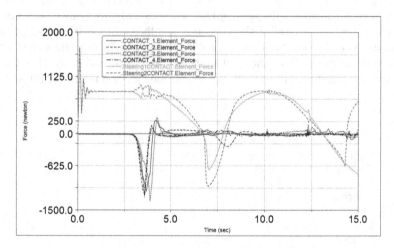

Fig. 10. Friction force in X direction for each wheel during astern

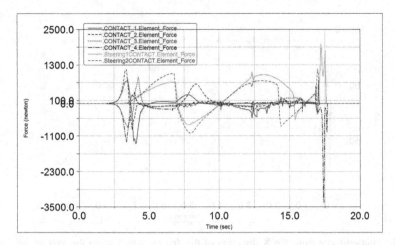

Fig. 11. Friction force in Y direction for each wheel during astern

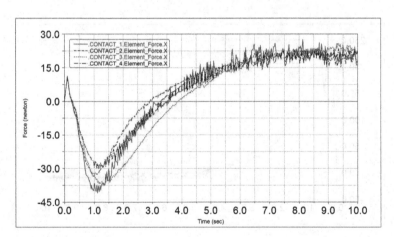

Fig. 12. Friction force from the X direction of the drived wheel when the axis of the driving wheel and the frame is 45°

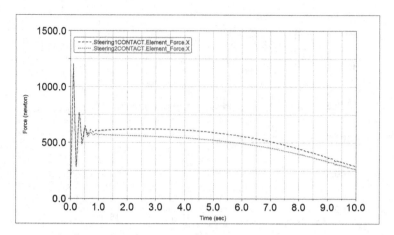

Fig. 13. Friction force from the X direction of the driving wheel when the axis of the driving wheel and the frame is 45°

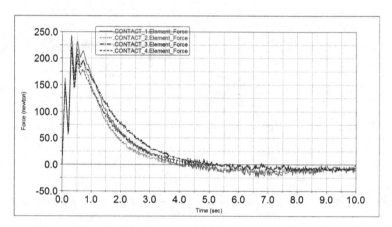

Fig. 14. Friction force from the Y direction of the drived wheel when the axis of the driving wheel and the frame is 45°

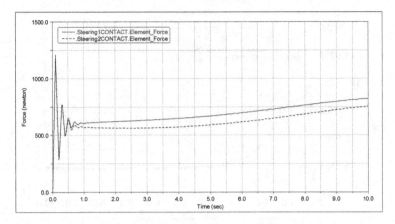

Fig. 15. Friction force from the Y direction of the driving wheel when the axis of the driving wheel and the frame is 45°

```
ERROR:      Time T=2.823888143E+01.
     Adams can not solve the equations of motion because the mechanism has
     "locked up". At least one constraint can no longer be satisfied.
     Adams is unable to satisfy the constraint for:  RevJnt/25 Z Delta.
ERROR:      Simulation failure detected.
ERROR:      Simulation failure detected.
```

Fig. 16. The mechanism "locks up" during traverse

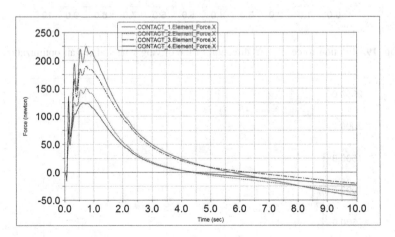

Fig. 17. Friction force from X direction of the drived wheel after gait optimization

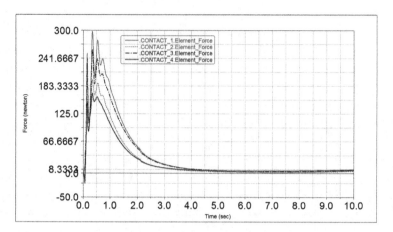

Fig. 18. Friction force from Y direction of the drived wheel after gait optimization

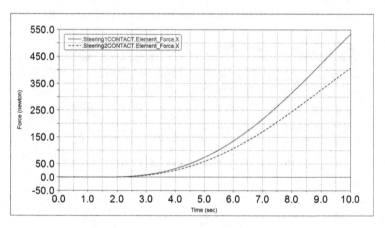

Fig. 19. Friction force from Y direction of the driving wheel after gait optimization

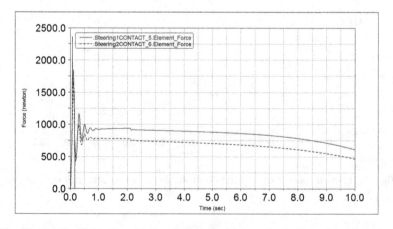

Fig. 20. Friction force from Y direction of the driving wheel after gait optimization

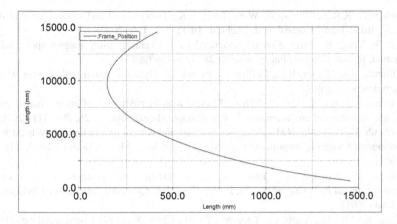

Fig. 21. Path tracking curve after gait optimization

5 Conclusion

This paper with a rocket compartment transit oriented large overload AGV as the research object, the walking wheel driving mechanism of layout scheme were studied, analysis the wheels and AGV frame of kinematic constraint conditions, analyses its mobility, manipulability and mobility, and carry on the modeling and simulation of ADAMS. The ADAMS simulation results show that the walking driving mechanism of the automatic guide vehicle in this study performs well in the straight, 45° and backward working conditions, and the "locking" problem in the transverse working conditions has also been solved and optimized. It is of great reference significance to the drive design and motion research of the automatic guided vehicle for the docking assembly of large heavy-duty segment.

References

1. Campion, G., Bastin, G., D'Andrea-Novel, B.: Structural properties and classification of kinematic and dynamic models of wheeled mobile robots. IEEE Trans. Robot. Autom. **12**(1), 47–62 (1996)
2. Zhao, D., Yi, J., Deng, X.: Structure and kinematic analysis of omni-directional mobile robots. Robot. **25**(5), 394–398 (2003)
3. Siegwart, R., Nourbakhsh, I.R., Scaramuzza, D.: Introduction to Autonomous Mobile Robots. The MIT Press, Cambridge (2012)
4. Jaulin, L.: Mobile Robotics. ISTE Press, London (2015)
5. Niku, S.B.: Introduction to Robotics: Analysis, Control, Applications, 2nd edn. Willey, Hoboken (2011)
6. Craig, J.J.: Introduction to Robotics: Mechanics and Control, 4th edn. Pearson Education, London (2018)
7. Huang, C., Yang, C., Huang, J.Y.: Path tracking of an autonomous ground vehiclewith different paylosds by hierarchical improved fuzzy dynamic sliding-mode control. IEEE Trans. Fuzzy Syst. **26**(2), 899–914 (2018)

8. Kodagoda, K.R.S., Wijesoma, W.S., Teoh, E.K.: Fuzzy speed and steering control of an AGV. IEEE Trans. Control Syst. Technol. **10**(1), 112–120 (2002)
9. Lee, S., Yang, H.: Navigation of automated guided vehicles using magnet spot guidance method. Robot. Comput.-Integr. Manuf. **28**, 425–436 (2012)
10. Williams, R.L., Carter, B.E., Gallina, P., Rosati, G.: Dynamic model with slip for wheeled omnidirectional robots
11. Martínez-Barberá, H., Herrero-Pérez, D.: Autonomous navigation of an automated guided vehicle in industrial environments. Robot. Comput.-Integr. Manuf. **26**, 296–311 (2010)
12. Tahboub, K.A., Asada, H.H.: Dynamics analysis and control of a holonomic vehicle with a continuously variable transmission. ASME J. Dyn. Syst. Meas. Control **124**(3), 118–126 (2002)
13. Wilson, L., Williams, C., Yance, J., et al.: Design and modeling of a redundant omnidirectional RoboCup goalie. In: Proceedings RoboCup 2001 International Symposium, Seattle (2001)
14. Wang, K., Shi, W., Yang, C., Yao, W., Ya, H., Chen, X., et al.: Commercial vehicle cab suspension system vibration modes and transmission characteristics by means of ADAMS. J. Jilin Univ. (Eng. Technol. Ed.) **40**(2), 330–334 (2010)
15. Carter, B., Good, M., Dorohoff, M., et al.: Mechanical design and modeling of an omnidirectional RoboCup player. In: RoboCup AI Conference, Seattle, W A, pp. 1–10 (2001)
16. Paromtchik, I.E., Rembold, U.A.: Motion generation approach for an omnidirectional vehicle. In: Proceedings of the 2000 IEEE International Conference on Robotics and Automation, San Francisco, pp. 1213–1218 (2000)
17. Holmberg, R., Khatib, O.: Development and control of a holonomic mobile robot for mobile manipulation tasks. Int. J. Robot. Res. **19**(11), 1066–1074 (2000)
18. Park, T.B., Lee, J.H., Yi, B.J., et al.: Optimal design and actuator sizing of redundantly actuated omni-directional mobile robots. In: Proceedings of the 2002 IEEE International Conference on Robotics and Automation, San Francisco (2002)
19. Moore, K.L., Flann, N.S.: A six-wheeled omnidirectional autonomous mobile robot. IEEE Control Syst. Mag. **20**(6), 53–66 (2000)
20. Schramm, D., Hiller, M., Bardini, R.: Vehicle Dynamics: Modeling and Simulation, p. 8 (2017)

Dynamics Analysis of the Human-Machine System of the Assistive Gait Training Robot

Tao Qin[1,2(✉)], Xin Meng[1,3], Jinxing Qiu[1], Dingjian Zhu[1],
and Jianwei Zhang[2]

[1] School of Mechanical Engineering, Hubei University of Arts and Science,
Xiangyang 441053, China
heu_qt@163.com
[2] Institute of Technical Aspects of Multimodal Systems (TAMS),
Department of Informatics, University of Hamburg, 22527 Hamburg, Germany
[3] School of Mechanical Automation, Wuhan University of Science
and Technology, Wuhan 430081, China

Abstract. In order to help the patients with lower limb dysfunction to complete gait rehabilitation training, a new assistive gait training robot prototype was developed. The dynamics of the human-machine system of the robot was analyzed comprehensively. The theoretical dynamics model of the human-machine system was established by using the Newton-Euler method, and the dynamic simulation model was established by Matlab/SimMechanics toolbox. The loaded dynamics model of gait mechanism was taken as the controlled object, the influence of gait training with different unloading forces and gait speeds on the driving performance of the system were analyzed. The research results verify the correctness of the theoretical dynamic analysis of the human-machine system, and it also provides a reference for the mechanical system optimization of the gait mechanism and the reasonable selection of the drive motors and lays a theoretical foundation for the research on the control method of the human-machine system.

Keywords: Gait training robot · Human-machine system · Dynamics ·
Simulation analysis

1 Introduction

With the rapid development of robotics technology in the field of rehabilitation, rehabilitation robots have been the first choice for clinical rehabilitation problems. As an effective method for lower limb rehabilitation, assistive gait training robot is better than artificial ground walking training in improving walking and balance ability [1, 2], which has gradually become a research hotspot in the field of robotics.

The human-machine system dynamics is one of the basic technology research problems because of the direct contact between human and robot during the robot-assisted gait training process [3]. The theoretical dynamics modeling methods applied to rehabilitation robots mainly include Lagrange method [4–6], Newton-Euler method [7, 8], Kane method [9], etc. The Newton-Euler method is simple and efficient in

H. Yu et al. (Eds.): ICIRA 2019, LNAI 11745, pp. 273–282, 2019.
https://doi.org/10.1007/978-3-030-27529-7_24

solving the dynamics problem of multi-rigid-body mechanism. It can calculate the torque of each joint and solve the force of each link [9]. The simulation model of the robot mechanism can be established by Admas or Matlab/SimMechanics to simulate and analyze the joint force and torque, which can verify the correctness of the theoretical dynamic model.

The motion constraint equation and dynamic equations of the assistive gait training robot were derived by using the Newton-Euler method, and the theoretical dynamics model of the human-machine system was established. The simulation model was established by using Matlab/SimMechanics toolbox for analyzing the driving performance and the drive motor selection of the human-machine system.

2   Assistive Gait Training Robot

The developed experimental prototype of the assistive gait training robot is shown in Fig. 1. It consists of two parts: the gait training unit and the body weight support system. The body weight support system is equipped to unload partial body weight of the patients who are difficult to support their own body weight during assistive gait training with the gait training unit.

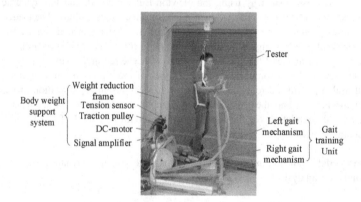

Fig. 1. The experimental prototype of the assistive gait training robot

The gait training unit consists of two sets of symmetrical crank-rocker mechanisms, which are used to control the footplate movement to realize an elliptical training gait. The middle of the footplate is hinged on the linkage, and the tail of the footplate is hinged at the linear slider constrained by the inclined sliding rail to controls the rotational attitude the footplate, to realize the extension and flexion movement of the ankle joint and the metatarsophalangeal joint. The body weight support system adopts a DC motor with worm reducer to control the cable elongation of the cable-pulley mechanism, to control the ensure the vertical motion of patient's center of gravity during assistive gait training. A tension sensor is applied to continuously adjust the vertical displacement and the amount of unloading force to enable the safety and stability of the patient [10]. When the robot system is used to assistive gait training, the human-machine contact points include the human body and the wearable vest, the patient's feet, and the footplates. The human-machine contact forces include the unloading force and the foot reaction force. The unloading force can be thought of as loading directly on the center of gravity of the human body. And the foot reaction forces are applied to the patient's feet by the bilateral footplates.

In order to assess the patient's training status and the rehabilitation effect, and detect the force of the plantar and lower limbs in real time, the gait training unit is equipped with two two-stage and double-layer footplates to detect the foot reaction forces as shown in Fig. 2. Four micro pressure sensors are located at the four main stress areas of the foot bottom in the middle of the double-layer footplate, corresponding to the toe area, the 1-2 phalangeal area, the 4-5 phalangeal area, and the heel area respectively. The toe area pressure sensor is used to detect the pressure of the forefoot, and the other three pressure sensors on the rear-footplate are arranged in an isosceles triangle to detect the pressure of the rearfoot.

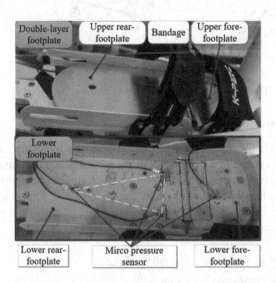

Fig. 2. The double-layer force measurement footplate

3   Human-Machine System Dynamics Modeling

In order to analyze the dynamic characteristics of human-machine systems, the dynamic model of the human-machine system is established by using the Newton-Euler method. Firstly, the motion constraint equation and Newton-Euler equation of human-machine system are written according to the force of each component, the constraint matrix equations of the system, namely the dynamic equations, are derived. The simplified human-machine system model is shown in Fig. 3. Assuming the applied point of the unloading force F_C is at the center of gravity of the human body. The applied point of the rearfoot reaction force f_{GRFRf} is at the foot center of mass, and the forefoot reaction force f_{GRFRf} is at the midpoint of the toe.

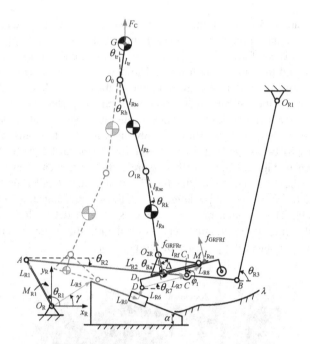

Fig. 3. The simplified human-machine system model

3.1   Motion Constraint Equation

Assuming that both feet are always in contact with the footplates, and the metatar-sophalangeal joints of the feet are always on the hinges of the fore- and rear-footplates (*M* point), and the coordinates of the centroid of each rigid rod body of the lower limb mechanism in the human-machine system can be obtained from the positional relationship as shown in Fig. 3. The centroid acceleration of each rigid rod body can be obtained by deriving the position coordinates twice in succession:

$$
\begin{cases}
\ddot{x}_{Rc1} = -L_{Rc1}\sin\theta_{R1}\ddot{\theta}_{R1} - L_{Rc1}\cos\theta_{R1}\dot{\theta}_{R1}^2 \\
\ddot{y}_{Rc1} = L_{Rc1}\cos\theta_{R1}\ddot{\theta}_{R1} - L_{Rc1}\sin\theta_{R1}\dot{\theta}_{R1}^2 \\
\ddot{x}_{Rc2} = -L_{R1}\sin\theta_{R1}\ddot{\theta}_{R1} - L_{R1}\cos\theta_{R1}\dot{\theta}_{R1}^2 - L_{Rc2}\sin\theta_{R2}\ddot{\theta}_{R2} - L_{Rc2}\cos\theta_{R2}\dot{\theta}_{R2}^2 \\
\ddot{y}_{Rc2} = L_{R1}\cos\theta_{R1}\ddot{\theta}_{R1} - L_{R1}\sin\theta_{R1}\dot{\theta}_{R1}^2 + L_{Rc2}\cos\theta_{R2}\ddot{\theta}_{R2} - L_{Rc2}\sin\theta_{R2}\dot{\theta}_{R2}^2 \\
\ddot{x}_{Rc3} = -L_{R1}\sin\theta_{R1}\ddot{\theta}_{R1} - L_{R1}\cos\theta_{R1}\dot{\theta}_{R1}^2 - L_{R2}\sin\theta_{R2}\ddot{\theta}_{R2} - L_{R2}\cos\theta_{R2}\dot{\theta}_{R2}^2 \\
\qquad - L_{Rc3}\sin\theta_{R3}\ddot{\theta}_{R3} - L_{Rc3}\cos\theta_{R3}\dot{\theta}_{R3}^2 \\
\ddot{y}_{Rc3} = L_{R1}\cos\theta_{R1}\ddot{\theta}_{R1} - L_{R1}\sin\theta_{R1}\dot{\theta}_{R1}^2 + L_{R2}\cos\theta_{R2}\ddot{\theta}_{R2} - L_{R2}\sin\theta_{R2}\dot{\theta}_{R2}^2 \\
\qquad + L_{Rc3}\cos\theta_{R3}\ddot{\theta}_{R3} - L_{Rc3}\sin\theta_{R3}\dot{\theta}_{R3}^2 \\
\ddot{x}_{Rc6} = \ddot{L}_{R0}\cos\alpha \\
\ddot{y}_{Rc6} = -\ddot{L}_{R0}\sin\alpha \\
\ddot{x}_{Rc7} = -L_{Rc7}\sin\theta_{R7}\ddot{\theta}_{R7} - L_{Rc7}\cos\theta_{R7}\dot{\theta}_{R7}^2 \\
\ddot{y}_{Rc7} = L_{Rc7}\cos\theta_{R7}\ddot{\theta}_{R7} - L_{Rc7}\sin\theta_{R7}\dot{\theta}_{R7}^2
\end{cases}
\tag{1}
$$

3.2 Dynamics Model

The separation rigid rod body of the gait mechanism and the lower limb of the human-machine system model are taken for force analysis. The dynamic equations of each rigid rod body are written separately by using Newton's law to form the Newton-Euler equations. The schematic diagram of force analysis of the human-machine system model is shown in Fig. 4. F_{Rmnx}, F_{Rmny} represent the component of the force of the rod body m to the rod body n in the x-axis and y-axis directions, respectively.

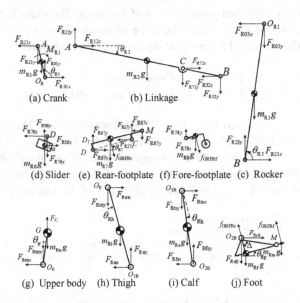

(a) Crank   (b) Linkage

(d) Slider (e) Rear-footplate (f) Fore-footplate (c) Rocker

(g) Upper body (h) Thigh   (i) Calf   (j) Foot

Fig. 4. The schematic diagram of the force analysis of the human-machine system model

Figure 4(a) is a simplified force diagram of the crank. The crank is constrained by the force of the frame F_{R01x}, F_{R01y}, the force of the linkage F_{R21x}, F_{R21y}, the driving torque M_{R1} and the gravity of the crank $m_{R1}g$. The dynamic equations of the crank are:

$$\begin{cases} m_{R1}\ddot{x}_{Rc1} = F_{R01x} - F_{R21x} \\ m_{R1}\ddot{y}_{Rc1} = F_{R01y} - F_{R21y} - m_{R1}g \\ J_{R1}\ddot{\theta}_{R1} = F_{R21x}L_{R1}\sin\theta_{R1} - m_{R1}gL_{Rc1}\cos\theta_{R1} - F_{R21y}L_{R1}\cos\theta_{R1} - M_{R1} \end{cases} \quad (2)$$

Figure 4(b) is a simplified force diagram of the linkage. The linkage is constrained by the force of the crank F_{R12x}, F_{R12y}, the force of the rocker F_{R32x}, F_{R32y}, the force of the connection joint C of the footplate F_{R72x}, F_{R72y}, and the gravity of the linkage $m_{R2}g$. The dynamic equations of the linkage are:

$$\begin{cases} m_{R2}\ddot{x}_{Rc2} = F_{R12x} + F_{R72x} - F_{R32x} \\ m_{R2}\ddot{y}_{Rc2} = F_{R12y} - F_{R72y} - F_{R32y} - m_{R2}g \\ J_{R2}\ddot{\theta}_{R2} = F_{R72x}(L'_{R2} - L_{Rc2})\sin\theta_{R2} - F_{R72y}(L'_{R2} - L_{Rc2})\cos\theta_{R2} - F_{R32x}(L_{R2} - L_{Rc2})\sin\theta_{R2} \\ \quad - F_{R32y}(L_{R2} - L_{Rc2})\cos\theta_{R2} - F_{R12x}L_{Rc2}\sin\theta_{R2} - F_{R12y}L_{Rc2}\cos\theta_{R2} \end{cases}$$

$$(3)$$

Figure 4(c) is a simplified force diagram of the rocker. The rocker is constrained by the force of the frame F_{R03x}, F_{R03y}, the force of the linkage F_{R23x}, F_{R23y}, and the gravity of the rocker $m_{R3}g$. The dynamic equations of the rocker are:

$$
\begin{cases}
m_{R3}\ddot{x}_{Rc3} = F_{R23x} - F_{R03x} \\
m_{R3}\ddot{y}_{Rc3} = F_{R23y} - F_{R03y} - m_{R3}g \\
J_{R3}\ddot{\theta}_{R3} = F_{R23x}L_{R3}\sin\theta_{R3} + m_{R3}gL_{Rc3}\cos\theta_{R3} - F_{R23y}L_{R3}\cos\theta_{R3}
\end{cases}
\tag{4}
$$

Figure 4(d) is a simplified force diagram of the slider. The slider is constrained by the force of the frame F_{R06x}, F_{R06y}, the force of the footplate F_{R76x}, F_{R76y}, and the gravity of the slider $m_{R6}g$. The dynamic equations of the slider are:

$$
\begin{cases}
m_{R6}\ddot{x}_{Rc6} = F_{R06x} - F_{R76x} \\
m_{R6}\ddot{y}_{Rc6} = F_{R06y} - F_{R76y} - m_{R6}g
\end{cases}
\tag{5}
$$

Figure 4(e) is a simplified force diagram of the rear-footplate. The rear-footplate is constrained by the force of the hinge axis of the slider F_{R67x}, F_{R67y}, the force of the connection joint C of the linkage F_{R27x}, F_{R27y}, the force of the hinge joint M between fore- and rear-footplate F_{R87x}, F_{R87y}, the gravity of the rear-footplate $m_{R7}g$, and the rearfoot reaction force f_{GRFRr}. The dynamic equations of the rear-footplate are:

$$
\begin{cases}
m_{R7}\ddot{x}_{Rc7} = F_{R67x} - F_{R27x} - F_{R87x} + f_{GRFRr}\sin\theta_{R7} \\
m_{R7}\ddot{y}_{Rc7} = F_{R67y} + F_{R27y} - F_{R87y} - m_{R7}g - f_{GRFRr}\cos\theta_{R7} \\
J_{R7}\ddot{\theta}_{R7} = F_{R67x}(L_{R7} + L_{R8}\sin\varphi_1)\sin\theta_{R7} - F_{R67y}(L_{R7} + L_{R8}\sin\varphi_1)\cos\theta_{R7} - F_{R27x}L_{R8}\sin\varphi_1\sin\theta_{R7} \\
\quad - F_{R27y}L_{R8}\sin\varphi_1\cos\theta_{R7} + m_{R7}g(L_{R7} + L_{R8}\sin\varphi_1 - L_{Rc7})\cos\theta_{R7} + f_{GRFRr}(L_{R7} + L_{R8}\sin\varphi_1 - L_{Rc7})
\end{cases}
\tag{6}
$$

Figure 4(f) is a simplified force diagram of the fore-footplate. The fore-footplate is constrained by the force of the hinge joint M between fore- and rear-footplate F_{R78x}, F_{R78y}, the gravity of the fore-footplate $m_{R8}g$, and the forefoot reaction force f_{GRFRf}. The dynamic equations of the fore-footplate are:

$$
\begin{cases}
m_{R8}\ddot{x}_{Rc8} = F_{R78x} + f_{GRFRf}\sin(\theta_{R7} + \Delta - \theta_{Rm}) \\
m_{R8}\ddot{y}_{Rc8} = F_{R78y} - f_{GRFRf}\cos(\theta_{R7} + \Delta - \theta_{Rm}) - m_{R8}g \\
J_{RM}\ddot{\theta}_{Rm} = -f_{GRFRf}L_{RM}\cos 2(\theta_{R7} + \Delta - \theta_{Rm}) - m_{R8}gL_{RM}\cos(\theta_{R7} + \Delta - \theta_{Rm})
\end{cases}
\tag{7}
$$

Where, L_{RM} is the distance from the centroid of the fore-footplate to the hinge joint M, and J_{RM} is the moment of inertia of the fore-footplate.

Figure 4(g) is a simplified force diagram of the upper body of the human body. The upper body is constrained by the unloading force F_C, the force of hip joint F_{Rttrx}, F_{Rttry}, and the gravity of the trunk $m_{Rtr}g$. The dynamic equations of the upper body are:

$$
\begin{cases}
m_{Rtr}\ddot{x}_{Rtrc} = -F_{Rttrx} \\
m_{Rtr}\ddot{y}_{Rtrc} = F_C + F_{Rttry} - m_{Rtr}g \\
J_{tr}\ddot{\theta}_{tr} = F_C l_{tr}\cos\theta_{tr} - m_{Rtr}g l_{tr}\cos\theta_{tr}
\end{cases}
\tag{8}
$$

Figure 4(h) is a simplified force diagram of the thigh, the thigh is constrained by the force of hip joint $F_{\text{Rtrtx}}, F_{\text{Rtrty}}$, the force of knee joint $F_{\text{Rstx}}, F_{\text{Rsty}}$, and the gravity of the thigh $m_{\text{Rt}}g$. The dynamic equations of the thigh are:

$$\begin{cases} m_{\text{Rt}}\ddot{x}_{\text{Rtc}} = F_{\text{Rtrtx}} - F_{\text{Rstx}} \\ m_{\text{Rt}}\ddot{y}_{\text{Rtc}} = F_{\text{Rsty}} - F_{\text{Rtrty}} - m_{\text{Rt}}g \\ J_{\text{Rt}}\ddot{\theta}_{\text{Rt}} = F_{\text{Rsty}}(l_{\text{Rt}} - l_{\text{Rtc}})\sin\theta_{\text{Rh}} - F_{\text{Rstx}}(l_{\text{Rt}} - l_{\text{Rtc}})\cos\theta_{\text{Rh}} + F_{\text{Rtrty}}l_{\text{Rtc}}\sin\theta_{\text{Rh}} - F_{\text{Rtrtx}}l_{\text{Rtc}}\cos\theta_{\text{Rh}} \end{cases}$$

$$(9)$$

Figure 4(i) is a simplified force diagram of the calf, The calf is constrained by the force of knee joint $F_{\text{Rtsx}}, F_{\text{Rtsy}}$, the force of ankle joint $F_{\text{Rfsx}}, F_{\text{Rfsy}}$, and the gravity of the calf $m_{\text{Rs}}g$. The dynamic equations of the calf are:

$$\begin{cases} m_{\text{Rs}}\ddot{x}_{\text{Rsc}} = F_{\text{Rtsx}} - F_{\text{Rfsx}} \\ m_{\text{Rs}}\ddot{y}_{\text{Rsc}} = F_{\text{Rfsy}} - F_{\text{Rtsy}} - m_{\text{Rs}}g \\ J_{\text{Rs}}\ddot{\theta}_{\text{Rk}} = F_{\text{Rfsy}}(l_{\text{Rs}} - l_{\text{Rsc}})\sin\theta_{\text{Rk}} - F_{\text{Rfsx}}(l_{\text{Rs}} - l_{\text{Rsc}})\cos\theta_{\text{Rk}} + F_{\text{Rtsy}}l_{\text{Rsc}}\sin\theta_{\text{Rk}} - F_{\text{Rtsx}}l_{\text{Rsc}}\cos\theta_{\text{Rk}} \end{cases}$$

$$(10)$$

Figure 4(j) is a simplified force diagram of the foot, the foot is constrained by the force of ankle joint $F_{\text{Rsfx}}, F_{\text{Rsfy}}$, the force of the fore- and rear-footplate f_{GRFRf} and f_{GRFRr}, the gravity of the forefoot $m_{\text{Rm}}g$ and the rearfoot $m_{\text{Rf}}g$. The dynamic equations of the foot are:

$$\begin{cases} F_{\text{Rsfx}} - f_{\text{GRFRr}}\sin\theta_{\text{Rp}} - f_{\text{GRFRf}}\sin(\theta_{\text{Rp}} + \Delta - \theta_{\text{Rm}}) = (m_{\text{Rf}} + m_{\text{Rm}})\ddot{x}_{\text{Rfc}} \\ f_{\text{GRFRr}}\cos\theta_{\text{Rp}} + f_{\text{GRFRf}}\cos(\theta_{\text{Rp}} + \Delta - \theta_{\text{Rm}}) - F_{\text{Rsfy}} - (m_{\text{Rf}} + m_{\text{Rm}})g = (m_{\text{Rf}} + m_{\text{Rm}})\ddot{y}_{\text{Rfc}} \\ f_{\text{GRFRf}}l_{\text{Rm}}/2 + f_{\text{GRFRr}}l_{\text{Rf}}\sin\Delta + F_{\text{Rfsy}}l_{\text{Rf}}\sin(\theta_{\text{Rp}} + \Delta) - F_{\text{Rfsx}}l_{\text{Rf}}\cos(\theta_{\text{Rp}} + \Delta) + \cdots \\ m_{\text{Rf}}gl_{\text{Rf}}\sin\Delta\cos\theta_{\text{Rp}} - m_{\text{Rm}}gl_{\text{Rm}}\cos(\theta_{\text{Rp}} + \Delta - \theta_{\text{Rm}})/2 = (J_{\text{Rf}} + J_{\text{Rm}})\ddot{\theta}_{\text{Rp}} - J_{\text{Rm}}\ddot{\theta}_{\text{Rm}} \end{cases}$$

$$(11)$$

In the above equations, $\theta_{\text{R4}} = \beta, \theta_{\text{R5}} = \gamma, \theta_{\text{R0}} = -\alpha, \theta_{\text{R6}} = \pi/2 - \alpha, \theta_{\text{Rp}} = \theta_{\text{R7}}$. Equations (2)–(11) constitute the force balance equations of the human-machine system.

The constraint equations and the force balance equations constitute the dynamics equations model of the human-machine system. The constrained matrix equations of the human-machine systems can be obtained simultaneously as follows:

$$A_{\text{R}} \cdot X_{\text{R}} = B_{\text{R}} \qquad (12)$$

X_{R} represents the column vector to be solved of the acceleration and the constrained reaction force of the human-machine system. A_{R} represents a large sparse matrix composed of known amounts of each rod body. B_{R} represents an input matrix composed of angle, angular velocity and angular acceleration of each rod body. Due to the limited space, the matrix $A_{\text{R}}, B_{\text{R}}$, and X_{R} are not listed.

When the inverse of A_{R} exists, the solution of acceleration and reaction force of each rod body in the human-machine system can be obtained as follows:

$$X_R = A_R^{-1} \cdot B_R \tag{13}$$

The subscript R indicates the right gait mechanism model of the human-machine system. Similarly, the dynamic equations of the left gait mechanism model can be obtained as follows:

$$X_L = A_L^{-1} \cdot B_L \tag{14}$$

Therefore, the human-machine system dynamics equations can be rewritten as:

$$\begin{cases} X_L = A_L^{-1} \cdot B_L \\ X_R = A_R^{-1} \cdot B_R \end{cases} \tag{15}$$

The m-function of the human-machine system dynamics model is written by Matlab language to solve $X_\lambda (\lambda = L$ or R). The parameters such as acceleration and constraint reaction force of each rod body in the human-machine system mechanism model can be obtained.

4 Simulation Analysis

The dynamics simulation results of the human-machine system are the theoretical basis for the important parameters of the drive motor selection and the control strategy. Based on the established human-machine system theoretical dynamics model, the dynamics simulation model is established by Matlab/SimMechanics toolbox. The motion planning method in reference [10] is used as the input of the dynamic simulation model. The variation laws of the driving torque of the gait mechanism during assistive gait training under different unloading force are studied, such as no unloading force, 20% unloading force, and 30% unloading force.

The driving torque curves of the bilateral gait mechanism in the case that a tester weights 65 kg and the gait cycle is $T = 10$ s under different unloading force are shown in Fig. 5. The corresponding foot reaction force curves are shown in Fig. 6, where $f_{GRF\lambda v}$ and $f_{GRF\lambda h}(\lambda = L$ orR) represent respectively the vertical and horizontal foot reaction force. The variation laws are consistent with the alternating changing characteristics during the support phase and swing phase of the normal gait cycle. Obviously, the driving torque of the gait mechanism with no unloading force is greater than the driving torque with unloading force. The larger of the load force, the larger of the driving torque, which is in accordance with the actual situation and the gait cycle change. The driving torque curves of the left and the right gait mechanisms change in opposite phases due to the 180° phase relationship of the two cranks.

The driving torque curves of the right gait mechanism under the different speeds, when the gait cycle is $T = 4$ s, $T = 6$ s, and $T = 10$ s respectively in the case of no unloading force, are shown in Fig. 7. The maximum driving torque is about 39 N•m as shown in Fig. 7. The gait cycle has no significant effect on the driving torque required by the gait mechanism. The above dynamics simulation results provide a reference for

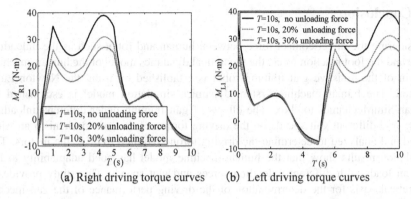

(a) Right driving torque curves   (b) Left driving torque curves

Fig. 5. Driving torque curves of the gait mechanism with different unloading forces

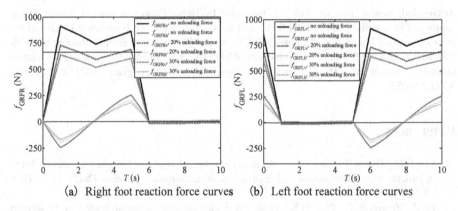

(a) Right foot reaction force curves   (b) Left foot reaction force curves

Fig. 6. Right side foot reaction curve with different gravity reduction

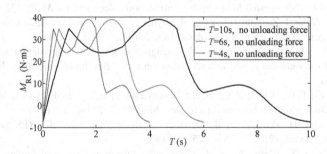

Fig. 7. Driving torque curves of the gait mechanism in different gait cycle

the structural stiffness check of the gait mechanism and the design and calculation of the drive motor. It also provides a theoretical basis for robot control and performance improvement.

5   Conclusion

Considering the direct contact force between human and robot such as the unloading force and the foot reaction force, the theoretical dynamics model of the human-machine system of the assistive gait training robot is established by using the Newton-Euler method. The human-machine system dynamics simulation model is established by Matlab/SimMechanics toolbox. The effects of gait training under different unloading forces and different gait speeds on the driving torque of the gait mechanism are simulated and analyzed to determine the driving torque required to drive the motors. The simulation results show that the human-machine model has good adaptability to the bipedal loads with different unloading forces and gait speeds. This study provides a theoretical basis for the determination of the driving performance of the gait mechanism and the selection of the drive motor. It also laid the foundation for control system design and experimental research.

Acknowledgments. This research was supported by Hubei Provincial Natural Science Foundation of China under grant 2018CFB313, and the German Research Foundation(DFG) and the National Science Foundation of China (NSFC)in project Crossmodal Learning under grant TRR-169, and Xiangyang Science and Technology R&D Project, and Hubei Superior and Distinctive Discipline Group of "Mechatronics and Automobiles" under grant XKQ2019002 and XKQ2019053.

References

1. Lin, H.D., Zhang, T., Chen, Q., et al.: Effect of robot-assisted gait training on walking ability in patients with incomplete spinal cord injury. Acta Automatica Sinica **42**(12), 1832–1838 (2016)
2. Li, J., Zhang, X.F., Pan, G.X.: Design and clinical application of body weight support treadmill training robot. J. Med. Biomech. **27**(06), 681–686 (2012)
3. Meng, W., Liu, Q., Zhou, Z.D., et al.: Recent development of mechanisms and control strategies for robot-assisted lower limb rehabilitation. Mechatronics **31**(4), 132–145 (2015)
4. Chen, W., Wang, L.Z., Zhang, L.Y., et al.: Dynamic analysis and simulation for lower limb exoskeleton rehabilitation robot. J. Mach. Des. **35**(04), 71–77 (2018)
5. Wang, L.L., Hu, X., Cao, W.J., et al.: Design and kinematics simulation and dynamic analysis of the wearable upper-limb rehabilitation robot. Beijing Biomed. Eng. **36**(02), 177–185 (2017)
6. Bian, H., Li, E.W., Chen, Z.Y., et al.: Design and dynamics analysis of a body weight support exoskeleton mechanism. Mach. Des. Manuf. **12**, 251–254 (2017)
7. Liang, C., Gao, H., Peng, Z., et al.: Dynamics analysis and control of 3-RPS parallel robot. Mach. Des. Manuf. (9), 251–253 + 257 (2018)
8. Xia, T., Huan, X., Chen, Y., et al.: Dynamics analysis and study of human lower limb exoskeleton rehabilitation robot. Mach. Des. Manuf. **9**, 258–261 (2018)
9. Dong, Y.H.: Dynamics analysis on pelvis position mechanism of walking aided training robot. Mech. Sci. Technol. Aerosp. Eng. **34**(3), 352–355 (2015)
10. Qin, T., Zhang, L.X.: Motion planning of a footpad-type walking rehabilitation robot considering motion of metatarsophalangeal joint. Robot **36**(3), 330–336 (2014)

Medical Robot

A Noninvasive Calibration-Free and Model-Free Surgical Robot for Automatic Fracture Reduction

Shijie Zhu[1], Yitong Chen[1], Yu Chen[1], Jiawei Sun[1], Zhe Zhao[2], Changping Hu[1], and Gangtie Zheng[1(✉)]

[1] School of Aerospace Engineering, Tsinghua University,
Beijing 100084, China
gtzheng@mail.tsinghua.edu.cn
[2] Department of Orthopaedics, Beijing Tsinghua Changgung Hospital,
Beijing 102218, China

Abstract. Surgical robots for femoral fracture reduction have enjoyed a surge of interest among surgeons recently because robots can avoid problems like over radiation and insufficient accuracy. However, tedious calibration procedures, complicated tissue modeling and hurtful invasive fixation restrict their clinical application. Here we introduce a novel fracture reduction idea based on visual servo to eliminate calibration, kinematics and muscle modeling and invasive markers to finish femoral fracture reduction simply and automatically. It employs images from two perpendicular directions to estimate the mapping from robot movements to displacements of limbs. We also present its satisfactory performance on simulation and skeleton experiments. Our method shows rapid convergence, stable precision and adequate domain of convergence under various circumstances. Hopefully this technique will enable a surgeon to manage several surgeries simultaneously, which offers brand new possibilities for present medical treatment.

Keywords: Calibration-free · Model-free · Noninvasive · Automatic fracture reduction

1 Introduction

The femoral fracture is one of the most common clinical fracture cases. The conventional treatment is that the doctor firstly moves the broken bones to the right positions, which is called "fracture reduction", and executes the fixation such as intramedullary nailing. Therefore, the result of the surgery directly depends on the accuracy of reduction. Obviously, the traditional open reduction brings a great risk of severe injuries and complications to the patients. However, in the more recommended minimal invasive surgeries, doctors can only use plenty of CT, X-ray to identify the positions and orientations of broken bones since femoral bones are covered by skins and

---

S. Zhu and Y. Chen—Contributed equally.

© Springer Nature Switzerland AG 2019
H. Yu et al. (Eds.): ICIRA 2019, LNAI 11745, pp. 285–296, 2019.
https://doi.org/10.1007/978-3-030-27529-7_25

muscles. It leads to two serious problems: (1) over radiation to surgical participants; (2) difficulty to align fragments to correct positions. More than 5–10 min of radiation is quite common during reduction surgeries [1]. A large amount of radiation exposure has already been reported to increase doctors' risks of cancer [2]. Additionally, relocating the bones usually demands great strength because of intricate muscular tension. Flexible muscular tissues and connective tissues also make the positions and orientations difficult to maintain [3, 4].

Accordingly, surgeons and engineers start to introduce computers and robots to assist fracture reduction [5]. There are two main kinds of control methods currently: (1) based on surgeons, such as teleoperation through a joystick [6]; (2) based on visual servo, such as [7]. Few of current commercial surgical robots such as Amigo and THINK Surgical (ROBODOC) [8] can be applied to fracture reduction. Additionally, two critical problems remain: (1) Current methods all require complicated preprocess of calibration which often results in long preparation time and hurtful invasive markers [9]. (2) The strong muscle tension will cause relative displacement between the distal end of the limb and the robot manipulator, which is not considered or compensated in current methods. These two problems prevent those robots from clinical application.

Correspondingly, we propose a novel robot system that performs automatic fracture reduction without complicated calibration, or invasive fixation. It is composed of a Stewart platform to manipulate the broken limb and a G-arm X-ray machine for imaging. We employ visual servo with X-ray images from two perpendicular directions to online estimate the relationship between the robot movement and the limbs' displacement with Kalman filters. The kinematics of the robot platform is also unnecessary. This method significantly simplifies the whole fracture reduction process. Simulations and experiments with femur models demonstrate the convergent and accurate reduction results. The experiments based on the Monte Carlo method also indicate an adequate domain of convergence for normal femoral fracture reduction. We also introduce the interaction with doctors: surgeons can set the value of torsional degree of freedom (DOF) manually before the robot system works, considering a common difficulty in fracture reduction surgery is to control the torsional DOF. Comparison with existing works is discussed in the end.

2   Method

This section introduces the detailed principles and procedures of the automatic fracture reduction performed by our robot system. It includes an overview of our robot system, the complete fracture reduction workflow and the solution of axial torsion control.

2.1   Preoperative Preparations

We employ a G-arm X-ray machine (Fig. 1(a)) as the imaging equipment during surgery according to the demand of fracture reduction. It provides images from two perpendicular directions including both ends of the broken limbs simultaneously. We use a customized six DOF Stewart platform (in parallel) to move the broken limb. The struts of the platform are six customized linear actuators with encoders. It has two

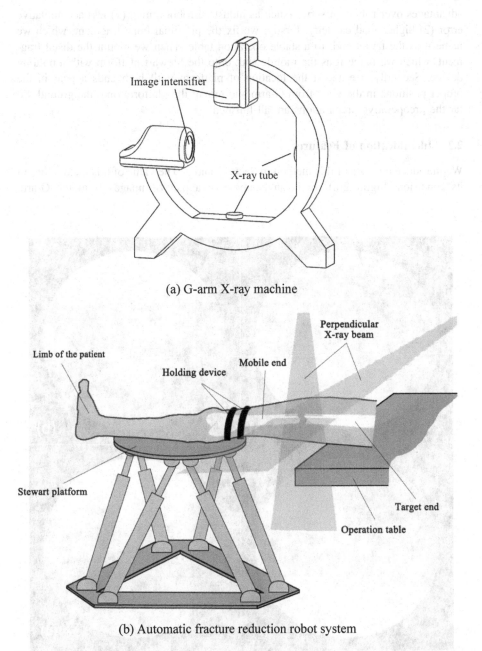

(a) G-arm X-ray machine

(b) Automatic fracture reduction robot system

Fig. 1. Sketches. (a) The imaging equipment used in this study is a G-arm X-ray machine, which has two independent imaging system for different directions. Each imaging system is composed of an X-ray tube producing cone beam X-ray and an image intensifier to receive the X-ray, which works like the pinhole camera. (b) The sketch of the automatic fracture reduction robot system. The mobile end is fixed to the robot platform and the target end is fixed to the operation table.

advantages over robots in series (such as industrial robot arms): (1) less accumulative error (2) higher load capacity. Firstly, we fix the proximal bone fragment, which we name it as the target end, to a stable operation table. Then we mount the distal fragment, which we name it as the mobile end, onto the Stewart platform with a holding device. Secondly, we adjust the location of platform until both ends appear in the proper positions in the view from G-arm and mount the platform onto the ground. So far the preoperative preparations are all finished.

2.2   Identification of Features

We introduce the core of this method in Sects. 2 and 3. The value of this method lies in its concision. Figure 2(a) (b) is an example of a pair of images from the G-arm

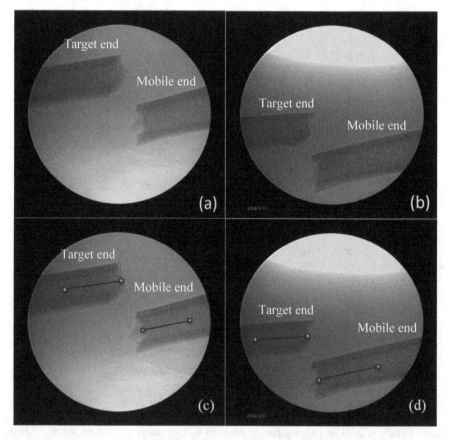

Fig. 2. (a) The lateral view of an example X-ray image acquired by the G-arm. (b) The anteroposterior view of an example X-ray image acquired by the G-arm. (c) (d) Feature points and the lines between them on a pair of X-ray images. Two of the four points are on the cross section of the fragments. (These human femur X-ray images are provided by Beijing Tsinghua Changgung Hospital, Beijing, China)

(anteroposterior (AP) view and lateral (LT) view). We choose two points respectively on each side as features to extract, where two of the four points are on the cross section of the fragments (Fig. 2(c) (d)). Therefore, we can define the vectors of image features:

$$\mathbf{f}_m = (x_m^{AP} \quad y_m^{AP} \quad y_m^{LT} \quad \alpha_m \quad \beta_m)^T$$
$$\mathbf{f}_t = (x_t^{AP} \quad y_t^{AP} \quad y_t^{LT} \quad \alpha_t \quad \beta_t)^T \tag{1}$$

where x, y represent the horizontal and vertical coordinates of the fracture end point in the images, and the subscripts AP and LT denote the AP view and LT view. α, β represent the angles between the midline of the bone fragment and the horizontal direction in the AP and LT image respectively. The subscripts m and t denote the mobile end and the target end respectively. The axial torsional angle γ is eliminated here because it is usually difficult to extract from these two images.

The control error $\mathbf{e}$ is defined as:

$$\mathbf{e} = \mathbf{f}_m - \mathbf{f}_t \tag{2}$$

We assign a threshold of $\mathbf{e}$ as ε_0 according to the accuracy requirement of the reduction surgery. When $\|\mathbf{e}\| < \varepsilon_0$, the accuracy meets the demand and reduction task accomplishes. When $\|\mathbf{e}\| \geq \varepsilon_0$, the program continues to the next loop. The value of the threshold ε_0 is decided based on the current clinical practice standards.

2.3   Trial Motion and Fracture Reduction

The relationship between the robot motion and the image feature is established using the Jacobian matrix. Firstly, we perform a trial motion to initialize the Jacobian matrix [10], that is, we choose one of the six struts of the Stewart platform, change it by a unit length and acquire X-ray images from both AP and LT view again to extract new information of all feature points. Accordingly, we obtain the correlation between the change of certain struts length and image features. This procedure is repeated six times successively until all struts are traversed. Finally, we put the vectors that represent the change of image features to obtain the initial estimation of Jacobian Matrix:

$$\mathbf{J} = (\Delta^{(1)}\mathbf{f}_m \quad \Delta^{(2)}\mathbf{f}_m \quad \Delta^{(3)}\mathbf{f}_m \quad \Delta^{(4)}\mathbf{f}_m \quad \Delta^{(5)}\mathbf{f}_m \quad \Delta^{(6)}\mathbf{f}_m) \tag{3}$$

where $\Delta^{(i)}\mathbf{f}_m$ represents the variation of image feature when changing a unit length of the ith strut of the robot.

According to

$$\Delta\mathbf{r} = -k\mathbf{J}^\dagger\mathbf{e} \tag{4}$$

where k represents a feedback parameter ranging from 0 to 1, $\mathbf{J}^\dagger$ represents the pseudo inverse of Jacobian matrix and $\mathbf{e}$ represents the error vector, we can obtain the ideal change to apply on the length of struts to reduce the error. Using the original Jacobian matrix for every loop performs well in our simulations. We can also update Jacobian Matrix according to real-time images and use the Kalman filter [10, 11] to improve the accuracy. The system keeps moving until it satisfies the accuracy requirement and finish the reduction (Fig. 3).

Fig. 3. An example of the X-ray image when the reduction is finished. (This human femur X-ray image is provided by Beijing Tsinghua Changgung Hospital, Beijing, China)

2.4   Axial Torsion Control

The six DOFs of the broken bones are three translational DOFs and three rotational DOFs. Obviously, the axial torsional DOF is the most difficult one to control by visual servo because we cannot clearly identify it from X-ray images from the G-arm. However, it can be simply determined by the orientation of the patient's foot on the

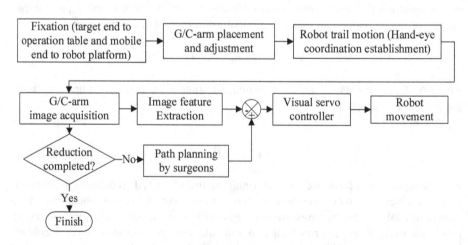

Fig. 4. Block diagram of the surgery workflow

broken limb. The surgeons can assign the axial torsional DOF before the automatic reduction in our system. Otherwise the system will keep it unchanged by default during the surgery with the five-DOF feature vector. According to the definition of image feature in Eq. (1), the torsional rotation will not change the image features. Thus the robot movement $\Delta r_{tortional}$ corresponding to the pure torsional rotation of the mobile end is determined by the null space of the image Jacobian matrix, i.e., $\mathbf{J}\Delta r_{tortional} = 0$ (Fig. 4).

3   Results

This section introduces our simulation and skeleton model experiments to verify the feasibility and stability of our method. The results turn out to be satisfactory under various situations.

3.1   Simulation

We design careful simulation experiments to verify the feasibility of our method. We use the pinhole camera model and kinematics of the Stewart platform to simulate the images from G-arm in each iterative step.

Platform
Figure 5 is a sketch of the Stewart platform we use in simulation and skeleton model experiments (related parameters labeled in the figure). We use the Newton Iterative Method to calculate the position and orientation with length of the six struts (forward kinematics) and calculate the length of the struts with position and orientation (inverse kinematics) [12]. The kinematics is necessary in simulation but unnecessary in practical experiments and surgeries.

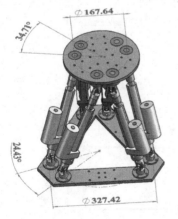

Fig. 5. The sketch of the 6-DOF Stewart platform we use in simulation and skeleton experiments. It is composed of six linear actuators.

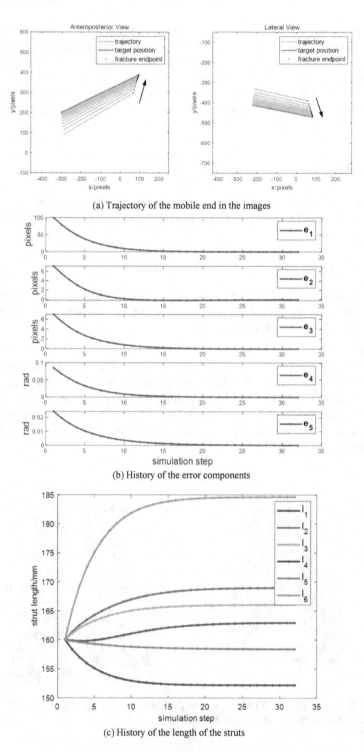

(a) Trajectory of the mobile end in the images

(b) History of the error components

(c) History of the length of the struts

Fig. 6. An example automatic reduction process

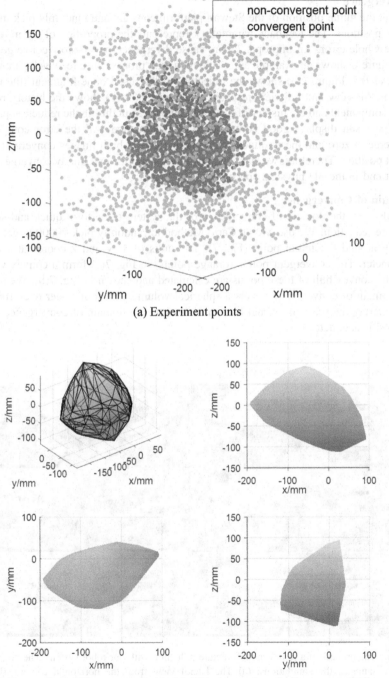

(a) Experiment points

(b) Convex hull of the convergent point (3D view and projections on each direction)

Fig. 7. The result of one of the Monte Carlo Method experiments. (Color figure online)

Convergence

We set the initial position of the Stewart platform constant and randomly pick multiple target positions. The feedback parameter k represents the proportion of the movement in the whole error. An improper k may cause divergence or too-slow convergence.

Figure 6 shows an example automatic reduction process. The feedback parameter k is set as 0.2. Figure 6(a) shows the trajectory of the distal bone fragment (the mobile end) in AP view and LT view respectively. Figure 6(b) (c) shows the history of each error component and the history of the length of each strut during the reduction process.

The result displays good convergence of our method. All the error components converge to zero and the midlines of the mobile end in both images converge to their target position. Therefore, we can conclude that the mobile end finally converges to the target end in the 3D physical space.

Domain of Convergence

We also test the domain of convergence of the system to perform quick and success fracture reduction. We use Monte Carlo Method to randomly pick 20000 target points totally around the initial point (Fig. 7). The units of x, y and z coordinates are all millimeter. The convergent points (orange points) in Fig. 7(a) form a convex volume and the convex hull of these points are calculated and shown in Fig. 7(b). We can see the domain of convergence covers a spherical volume with a diameter over 100 mm. Considering the scale of normal fracture reduction, the domain of convergence of our method is adequate.

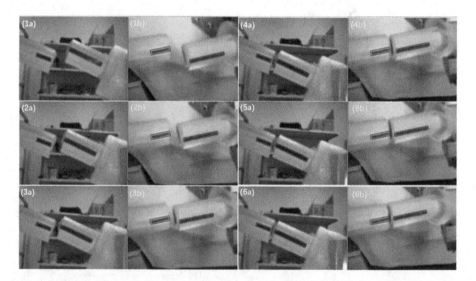

Fig. 8. The process of a femur model fracture reduction with our robot system. The procedures are the same as the simulations. (a) The lateral view from the horizontal camera. (b) The anteroposterior view from the vertical camera.

3.2   Practicality Experiments

Here we demonstrate a simple practicality experiment with a femur model to proof the feasibility of our system as a concept proof. The system succeeds in accurate reduction within five iterations in average (Fig. 8). The system performs efficient and cursory recovering in Fig. 8-1, 2, 3 and fine adjustment in Fig. 8-4, 5, 6. The rapid convergence in this demonstration indicates great potential of our system to reduce the X-ray exposure in future clinical application.

4   Discussion and Conclusion

Our method provides a quick, precise and automatic potential solution for current fracture reduction surgeries. The experiments show promising results of our reduction method. It is rapid, precise and effort-saving.

Compared to similar works proposed by Westphal et al. [5, 13] and Du et al. [14], our method only uses 2D X-ray images and needs no calibration process or 3D imaging methods. Besides, due to the feedback mechanism in the visual servo algorithm our work achieved satisfactory accuracy without any robot kinematics modelling. To mitigate the accuracy loss caused by muscle tension, in many existing works [15–17], metal pins are used to fix the injured limb to the robot, which may cause secondary injury to the patient. While non-invasive fixations are used in our system as the visual servo algorithm can compensate the influence of the muscle tension. However, as a preliminary concept proof, some parts remain to be improved for actual clinical situations: (1) the fractures in clinical cases are more complicated than the demonstration in this paper and a simple proportional controller may not be able to handle all kinds of fractures. (2) we use color bars on the model bone to simplify the feature extraction, while the automatic extraction of the feature points on clinical X-ray images by computer vision is still a challenging but interesting problem.

In conclusion, we proposed a fracture reduction method that doesn't need calibration or robot and muscle modeling. This method mainly has three advantages compared to current clinical fracture reduction methods: (1) much less radiation to surgeons (2) simple and rapid surgery workflow (3) no invasive fixations or markers. These advantages enable one surgeon to be in charge of multiple surgeries simultaneously, which provides a new paradigm for modern medical treatment.

The future works will focus on developing a GUI for the doctor to intervene the reduction procedure when dealing with complicated fractures, and developing a feature extraction algorithm for clinical X-ray fracture images. We will also further test our method with animal and cadaver experiments.

Acknowledgement. We thank Boyuan Deng from TEEP, Tsinghua University and Dr. Yongwei Pan from Tsinghua Changgung Hospital for their help during design and experiments. This research is funded by Tsinghua University.

References

1. Füchtmeier, B., et al.: Reduction of femoral shaft fractures in vitro by a new developed reduction robot system 'RepoRobo'. Inj.-Int. J. Care Inj. **35**(1), 113–119 (2004)
2. Mastrangelo, G., et al.: Increased cancer risk among surgeons in an orthopaedic hospital. Occup. Med. (Lond) **55**(6), 498–500 (2005)
3. Westphal, R., et al.: Automated robot assisted fracture reduction. In: Kröger, T., Wahl, F.M. (eds.) Advances in Robotics Research, pp. 251–262. Springer, Heidelberg (2009). https://doi.org/10.1007/978-3-642-01213-6_23
4. Joung, S., Park, I.: Medical robotics for musculoskeletal surgery. In: Zheng, G., Li, S. (eds.) Computational Radiology for Orthopaedic Interventions. LNCVB, vol. 23, pp. 299–332. Springer, Cham (2016). https://doi.org/10.1007/978-3-319-23482-3_15
5. Westphal, R., et al.: Robot-assisted long bone fracture reduction. Int. J. Robot. Res. **28**(10), 1259–1278 (2009)
6. Suero, E.M., et al.: Improving the human–robot interface for telemanipulated robotic long bone fracture reduction: joystick device vs. haptic manipulator. Int. J. Med. Robot. Comput. Assist. Surg. e1863-n/a
7. Shirai, Y., Inoue, H.: Guiding a robot by visual feedback in assembling tasks. Pattern Recognit. **5**(2), 99–106 (1973)
8. Hoeckelmann, M., Rudas, I.J., Fiorini, P., Kirchner, F., Haidegger, T.: Current capabilities and development potential in surgical robotics. Int. J. Adv. Robot. Syst. **12**, 61 (2015)
9. Du, H., et al.: Advancing computer-assisted orthopaedic surgery using a hexapod device for closed diaphyseal fracture reduction. Int. J. Med. Robot. Comput. Assist. Surg. Mrcas **11**(3), 348–359 (2014)
10. Qian, J., Su, J.: Online estimation of image Jacobian matrix by Kalman-Bucy filter for uncalibrated stereo vision feedback. In: IEEE International Conference on Robotics and Automation, Proceedings, ICRA, vol. 1. pp. 562–567 (2002)
11. Auger, F., et al.: Industrial applications of the Kalman filter: a review. IEEE Trans. Ind. Electron. **60**(12), 5458–5471 (2013)
12. Yang, C., et al.: Forward kinematics analysis of parallel manipulator using modified global Newton-Raphson method. In: International Conference on Intelligent Computation Technology & Automation (2009)
13. Suero, E.M., et al.: Improving the human-robot interface for telemanipulated robotic long bone fracture reduction: Joystick device vs. haptic manipulator. Int. J. Med. Robot. Comput. Assist. Surg. **14**(1), e1863 (2018)
14. Du, H., et al.: Preoperative trajectory planning for closed reduction of long-bone diaphyseal fracture using a computer-assisted reduction system. Int. J. Med. Robot. Comput. Assist. Surg. **11**(1), 58–66 (2015)
15. Kim, W.Y., Ko, S.Y.: Hands-on robot-assisted fracture reduction system guided by a linear guidance constraints controller using a pre-operatively planned goal pose. Int. J. Med. Robot. Comput. Assist. Surg. **15**, e1967 (2018)
16. Abedinnasab, M.H., Farahmand, F., Gallardo-Alvarado, J.: The wide-open three-legged parallel robot for long-bone fracture reduction. J. Mech. Robot.-Trans. Asme **9**(1), 015001 (2017)
17. Li, C.S., et al.: A novel master-slave teleoperation robot system for diaphyseal fracture reduction: a preliminary study. Comput. Assist. Surg. **21**, 163–168 (2016)

Force Modeling of Tool-Tissue Interaction Force During Suturing

Shuai Gao, Shijun Ji, Mei Feng$^{(\boxtimes)}$, Qiumeng Li, Xiuquan Lu,
Zhixue Ni, and Yan Li

Institute of Intelligent Precision Manufacturing, Jilin University,
Changchun, China
fengmei@jlu.edu.cn

Abstract. A proper mechanical characterization of soft biological tissue has a great significance in the medical application, such as virtual reality simulators, surgery preoperative planning and the design of force feedback system for master-slave medical robot. To study the mechanical properties of soft tissue in suture operation, this paper divided the suture into three phases on basis of suture operation process, and conducted experiments to investigate the tool-tissue interactive forces, where the parameters related to suturing operation were considered in experiments design to guarantee the reliability of the experiment, and the force model of each phases was established according to the experimental statistical data. And verification experiments were conducted to evaluate the models by comparing the forces obtained by models with those by sensor. The results showed that the built force model agreed with the experimental data well. The proposed force models can be used to reflect the force variation during suture.

Keywords: Biomechanics · Suture · Tool-tissue interaction force · Mechanical properties

1 Introduction

Measurement of soft tissue mechanical properties plays a significant role in medical diagnosis, organ reconstruction, surgical training and simulation [1, 2]. To investigate the mechanical properties of soft tissue, researchers have performed tissue experiments [3–6]. Fung [7, 8] carried out a series of indentation and tensile experiments on skin and derived the constitutive equations describing the stress and strain relationship of the skin. Brouwer *et al.* [9] developed specialized devices to measure tissue properties under extension and indentation operation. Ottensmeyer *et al.* [10] designed a tool to precisely deform tissues and record the force-displacement response under indentation operation to evaluate the viscoelastic properties of soft tissues [11]. Okamura *et al.* [12] used bovine liver as experimental sample and presented a force model for needle insertion, which was composed by stiffness, friction and cutting forces, and studied the needle geometry effects on the total force. Bao *et al.* [13] conducted systematic experiments to observe the needle insertion force with numerous variables, including insertion velocities, tissue materials and needle types.

© Springer Nature Switzerland AG 2019
H. Yu et al. (Eds.): ICIRA 2019, LNAI 11745, pp. 297–309, 2019.
https://doi.org/10.1007/978-3-030-27529-7_26

The previous researches mainly investigated the tissue biomechanics under the operation with simple step, such as indentation, extension and probing, etc. However, for some common surgical operations consisting of a series of movements, the tool-tissue interaction force is complex and variable and has not been studied. Based on this, in this paper we took the suturing operation [12] as research subject to study the needle-tissue interaction actions, the operation was divided into three phases on the basis of the suture movement process, and tool-tissue interactive force was investigated for each phase. And the variables related to suturing operation were systematically examined for comprehensively investigating suture mechanism. The research work of this paper will provide a foundation for in vivo study of the mechanical characterization of suturing operation.

2   Materials and Methods

There are more than ten kinds of suture methods, such as lock-stitch suture, Cornell suture, Halsted suture, and so on [14]. However, each of suture method contains a group of basic movements: the needle point is pressed into tissue, advanced along the trajectory of the needle's curve until it emerges from the surface of the tissue, afterwards pulled the whole needle through the tissue, as shown in Fig. 1.

Therefore, according to the characteristics of typical suture action, the whole suture process is divided into the following three phases. Phase 1: after the tip contacts the tissue, it penetrates the tissue and advances along the trajectory of the tip curve until the tip is exposed; Phase 2: The needle continues to move through the tissue until the end of the needle passes through the tissue; Phase 3: pulling the suture thread.

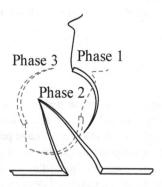

Fig. 1. The schematic diagram for describing suture basic movements

This paper studied the effect of the needle geometries, the sutures and the suturing velocities on the interaction force. For the effect of soft tissue thickness, because the rotation center of the needle during suturing experiment coincides with the center of the circular curve of the needle, there is no lifting or pressing impact on the soft tissue in the suture process, so the effect of the soft tissue thickness should not be considered when observing interaction force between the needle and the soft tissue. According to the shape of the needle tip, suture needles can be classified into round and triangle needles [15]. Because the round needles are mainly used for soft tissue suture, they were selected in our study, including O 1/2 7 × 17, O 1/2 6 × 20, O 1/2 8 × 20, O 1/2 11 × 24, O 1/2 12 × 24, O 1/2 10 × 28, as shown in Fig. 2, where O refers to the cross-section shape of the needle tip which is circular. 1/2 represents that the body of needle is crooked in semicircle, the subsequent expression such as "10 × 28", 10 equals the needle diameter multiplied by 10, which is 10 times of the needle body diameter (unit: mm), 28 is the distance between the needle head and the tail (unit: mm).

The suture threads were non-absorbable sutures: silk (0, 2-0, 3-0, 4-0, 5-0, 6-0), and absorbable sutures: PGA (with needle O 1/2 7 × 17) and PGLA (2-0, 3-0, 4-0, 5-0), as shown in Fig. 3. The label 3-0 is the abbreviation of 000, "3" represents the number of the "0", the suture with less number of '0' has larger diameter, which means the diameter of suture 3-0 is smaller than that of suture 2-0. To investigate the effect of suturing velocities on interaction force, different suture velocities were performed as shown in Table 1, which covered the velocity range of surgeon manual suture operation. Moreover, during the suturing, as the needle tip was usually perpendicular to the stitched surface when penetrating tissue [11], the penetration angle in the experiments was set to 90°. Meanwhile, to guarantee the reliability and repeatability of the experiments, each group of experiments was conducted ten times.

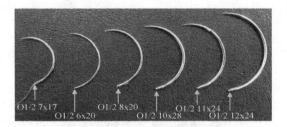

Fig. 2. Suture needles used in the experiments

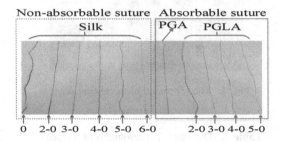

Fig. 3. Sutures used in the experiments

Table 1. The needle velocities in each suturing phase

Phase	Velocity value (mm/min)					
Phase 1	60	90	120	150	180	210
Phase 2	60	90	120	150	180	210
Phase 3	300	500	900	700	1100	1300

The experiment was carried out on our self-developed testing platform, as shown in Fig. 4, The platform has six joints that can move along the X, Y and Z axes and rotate around the three axes. The combination of six joint motions enables the tool to follow a user-defined trajectory, and the ATI industrial automation force sensor Nano 43 is mounted on joint 6 for force and torque measurement. The range and resolution of the sensor are shown in Table 2.

As the needle was mounted on joint by a fixture, the needle suturing velocity can be obtained as follows:

$$v = \omega \frac{D}{2} \tag{1}$$

Where ω is the angular velocity of the needle, D is the diameter of the needlecurve.

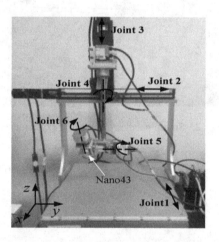

Fig. 4. The schematic of the testing device

Table 2. The range and resolution of the sensor

Axis	Range	Resolution
$F_x/F_y/F_Z$(N)	18	1/256
$T_x/T_y/T_Z$(Nmm)	250	1/20

Using the collected force from the ATI Nano 43 sensor, the interaction force can be obtained as follows:

$$F = \sqrt{F_x^2 + F_y^2 + F_Z^2} \tag{2}$$

Where F_x, F_y and F_z represented the sensor collected forces along x, y, and z directions.

3   Experiments for Force Models Building

The porcine muscle was chosen as experimental sample as the pig had the analogous biomechanical characteristic and morphological structure with human [16]. Several excised fresh porcine muscles were kept in 0.9% normal saline water and transported to laboratory within 4 h postmortem to avoid dehydration. The three-phase experimental processes were shown in Fig. 5.

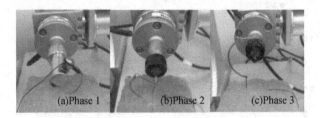

(a)Phase 1   (b)Phase 2   (c)Phase 3

Fig. 5. The experimental pictures of suturing

3.1   Analysis and Modeling of Phase 1

The experimental results of the first phase are shown in Figs. 6 and 7. Figure 6 shows the force-displacement curves of the different velocities at the same needle. Figure 7 shows the force-displacement curves of the different needles at the same velocity.

In this process, when the needle pressed the soft tissue, there was mainly the stiffness force resulting from tissue resistance [17]. Along with the increasing deformation of the tissue, the interaction force presented an increasing trend. Once the pressure reached the tissue split threshold, the needle started to puncture the tissue [18, 19]. Then the needle traveled through the tissue, the needle-tissue interaction force existed as a combination of cutting force, friction force and pulling force. The pulling force occurred because the needle had the pulling effect on the tissue when it moved upward. The cutting force was puncture force acted on the needle tip. The friction force between the needle body and the tissue was resulted from the tissue characterization of inhomogeneity and super viscoelasticity.

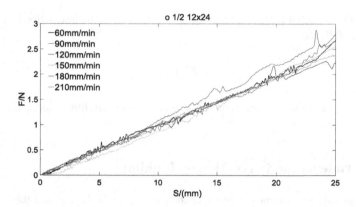

Fig. 6. Force-displacement curves of the same needle at different velocities

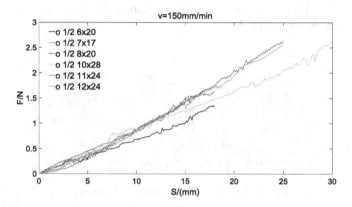

Fig. 7. Force-displacement curves of different needles at the same velocity

Based on the trend of the force-displacement curve, a linear fitted model was derived to describe the needle-tissue interaction force which was related with the needle displacement as follows:

$$F = AS + B \tag{3}$$

According to the experimental data, A and B were fitted as:

$$A = a_1 d^3 + a_2 d^2 + a_3 d + a_4 \tag{4}$$

$$B = a_5 d + a_6 v + a_7 \tag{5}$$

Where v was the suturing velocity, d was the diameter of the needle body. The values of parameters a_1, a_2, a_3, a_4, a_5, a_6, a_7 obtained by polynomial fitting of experimental data were shown in Table 3. Based on the built force model, the suturing velocity had little effect on the interaction force, which was in accordance with the experimental data shown in Fig. 6.

Table 3. The parameter values obtained by data fitting

Parameter	a_1	a_2	a_3	a_4	a_5	a_6	a_7
Value	0.7188	−1.983	1.802	−0.4456	−5.898E−2	−1.891E−2	−2.142E−2

3.2 Analysis and Modeling of Phase 2

The experimental results of the second phase are shown in Figs. 8 and 9. Figure 8 shows the force-displacement curves of the different velocities at the same needle. Figure 9 shows the force-displacement curves of the different needles at the same velocity.

In this process, the needle-tissue interaction forces included the friction force between the needle and tissue, the extrusion force resulting from the variable cross-section area of needle body and the friction force between the suture thread and tissue. The needle-tissue friction force and extrusion force increased because of the increasing in cross-section area of needle body, which resulting in the increase of resultant force (as shown in Fig. 8). Then the suture thread entered the tissue, for the needles O 1/2 6 × 20, O 1/2 7 × 17 and O 1/2 8 × 20, their cross-section of needle ends were almost same as that of the needle body, so that the extrusion force did not change much. The decrease in the needle-tissue friction force was approximately equal to the increase in the suture-tissue friction force, so the resultant force remained a relatively stable state in this segment, as shown in Fig. 9.

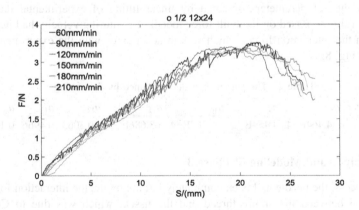

Fig. 8. Force-displacement curves of the same needle at different velocities

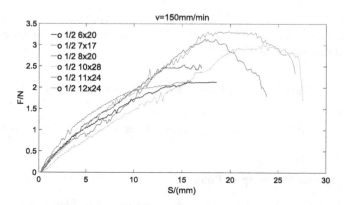

Fig. 9. Force-displacement curves of different needles at the same velocity

Based on the trend of force-displacement curve, the force model in this phase was approximately fit by a third-order polynomial function, so the interaction force was estimated as follows:

$$F = CS^3 + DS^2 + E \cdot S + a \tag{6}$$

According to experimental data, the C, D, E parameters were fitted as:

$$C = a_8 d \tag{7}$$

$$D = a_9 d + a_{10}v + a_{11} \tag{8}$$

$$E = a_{12}d + a_{13} \tag{9}$$

The values of parameters obtained by linear fitting of experimental data were shown in Table 4. Based on the built force model, the suturing velocity had negligible impact on the interaction force, which was in accordance with the experimental data shown in Fig. 8.

Table 4. The parameter values obtained by data fitting

Parameter	a_8	a_9	a_{10}	a_{11}	a_{12}	a_{13}	a
Value	−4.464E−4	4.454E−2	−6.867E−4	−3.686E−2	−0.3063	0.4966	0.1407

3.3   Analysis and Modeling of Phase 3

In this process, the needle had been completely left the tissue, the interaction force was the friction between the suture thread and the tissue, which was due to Coulomb friction, tissue adhesion and damping [14].

To observe the statistics distribution of the experimental data, the Grubbs Criterion [14] was adopted to eliminate the data with large deviation. According to the force range, the forces were divided into thirteen groups based on the principle of the statistics [20], and the percentages of each group were shown in Fig. 10.

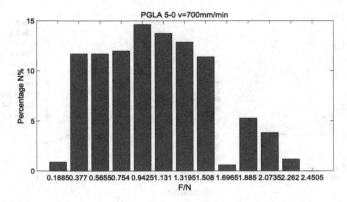

Fig. 10. The force distribution of a suture thread at one pulling velocity

According to distribution of the experimental data (as shown in Fig. 10), it revealed that the interaction force fluctuated in a certain range, thus a weighted average of the forces is used to represent the force of this process, as shown in Eq. 10:

$$F_m = \frac{f_{11} + f_{12} + \cdots + f_{1i}}{i} \times Q_1 + \frac{f_{21} + f_{22} + \cdots + f_{2j}}{j} \times Q_2 + \cdots$$
$$+ \frac{f_{n1} + f_{n2} + \cdots + f_{nk}}{k} \times Q_n \tag{10}$$

Where F_m was the suture-tissue interaction force of phase 3, subscript m was the series number of the experiment, f_{nk} was the force value of group n, Q_n was the percentage of the force group n subscripts $i, j, \cdots k$ represented the series number of the collected force in each group.

To observe the effect of the suture thread type and pulling velocity on the interaction force, the needle-tissue interaction force in certain situation was calculated on the basis of the Eq. (10), as shown in Figs. 11 and 12.

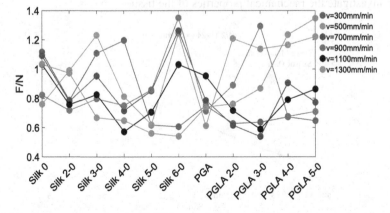

Fig. 11. The interaction forces of different types of suture threads at one pulling velocity

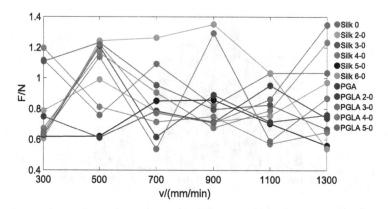

Fig. 12. The interaction forces of a certain suture thread at six pulling velocities

According to the Figs. 11 and 12, the suturing velocity and the type of suture thread had little effect on the needle-tissue interaction force.

4 Result

To verify the effectiveness of the built force models, O 1/2 12 × 24 needle and silk 5-0 suture thread were used to suture a piece of porcine muscle. The sensor collected forces and the model calculated forces of each phase were shown in Figs. 13, 14, and 15. It can be seen that although the force curves formed by sensor collected data are not completely consistent with those formed by built force model, their trend were alike. Applying the built force model to surgery simulation or master-slave force feedback can make surgeon feel the interactive force change in suturing operation, where it is not necessary to know the actual magnitude of the suturing force because of the force scaling for heavy physical operation or delicate surgical operation which need to magnify or reduce the force magnitude. Therefore, the force models proposed in this paper reflecting the variations of the interaction force in suture meet the surgical application requirements, which can be used to investigate the mechanical properties of the tissue.

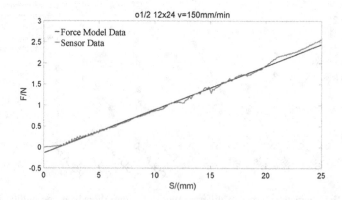

Fig. 13. The experimental results in the first phase were compared with the model curves

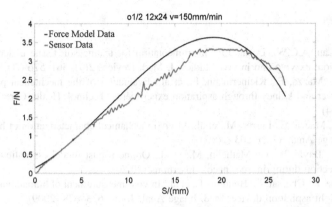

Fig. 14. The experimental results in the second phase were compared with the model curves

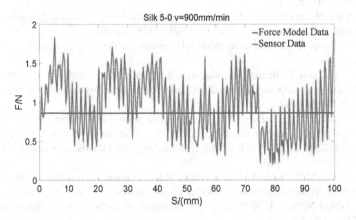

Fig. 15. The experimental results in the third phase were compared with the model curves

5   Conclusion

In order to study the mechanical properties of soft tissue in suture operation, this paper divided the suture process into three phases on basis of suture operation process, and conducted a large number of in vitro suture experiments to investigate the tool-tissue interactive forces, where the parameters related to suturing operation were also considered into experiments design to guarantee the reliability of the experiment. On the basis of the soft tissue properties and the experimental statistical data, the force models were built. Finally, validation experiments were performed to evaluate the effectiveness of the force model, which shown the forces established by models fit the sensor collected forces well. The research of this paper provided a foundation for the in vivo study of the mechanical characterization of the suturing operation, which has a potential application in the surgery preoperative planning, virtual simulation and training.

References

1. Hu, T., Lau, A.C.W., Desai, J.P.: Instrumentation for testing soft tissue undergoing large deformation: ex vivo and in vivo studies. J. Med. Devices **2**(4), 561–576 (2008)
2. Nava, A., Mazza, E., Kleinermann, F., et al.: Evaluation of the mechanical properties of human liver and kidney through aspiration experiments. Technol. Health Care **12**(3), 269–280 (2004)
3. Nava, A., Mazza, E., Furrer, M., et al.: In vivo mechanical characterization of human liver. Med. Image Anal. **12**(2), 203 (2008)
4. Barbé, L., Bayle, B., De Mathelin, M., et al.: Online robust model estimation and haptic clues detection during in vivo needle insertions (2006)
5. Schiavone, P., Chassat, F., Boudou, T., et al.: In vivo measurement of human brain elasticity using a light aspiration device. Med. Image Anal. **13**(4), 673–678 (2009)
6. O'Leary, M.D., Simone, C., Washio, T., et al.: Robotic needle insertion: effects of friction and needle geometry. In: IEEE International Conference on Robotics and Automation, no 2, pp. 1774–1780 (2003)
7. Fung, Y.C.: Biomechanics: Mechanical Properties of Living Tissues, 2nd edn. Springer, New York (1993). https://doi.org/10.1007/978-1-4757-2257-4
8. Tong, P., Fung, Y.C.: The stress-strain relationship for the skin. J. Biomech. **9**, 649–657 (1993)
9. Brouwer, I., Ustin, J., Bentley, L., Sherman, A., Dhruv, N., Tendick, F.: Measuring in vivo animal soft tissue properties for haptic modeling in surgical simulation. Med. Meets Virtual Reality **9**, 69–74 (2001)
10. Ottensmeyer, M.P., Salisbury, J.K.: In vivo data acquisition instrument for solid organ mechanical property measurement. In: Niessen, W.J., Viergever, M.A. (eds.) MICCAI 2001. LNCS, vol. 2208, pp. 975–982. Springer, Heidelberg (2001). https://doi.org/10.1007/3-540-45468-3_116
11. Ottensmeyer, M.P., Kerdok, A.E., Howe, R.D., Dawson, S.L.: The effects of testing environment on the viscoelastic properties of soft tissues. In: Cotin, S., Metaxas, D. (eds.) ISMS 2004. LNCS, vol. 3078, pp. 9–18. Springer, Heidelberg (2004). https://doi.org/10.1007/978-3-540-25968-8_2
12. Okamura, A.M., Simone, C., O'Leary, M.D.: Force modeling for needle insertion into soft tissue. IEEE Trans. Biomed. Eng. **51**(10), 1707–1716 (2004)
13. Bao, X., Li, W., Lu, M., et al.: Experiment study on puncture force between MIS suture needle and soft tissue. Biosurface Biotribology **2**(2), 49–58 (2016)
14. DiMaio, S.P., Salcudean, S.E.: Needle insertion modeling and simulation. In: Proceedings of IEEE International Conference on Robotics Automation, pp. 2098–2105 (2002)
15. Samur, E., Sedef, M., Basdogan, C., et al.: A robotic indenter for minimally invasive measurement and characterization of soft tissue response. Med. Image Anal. **11**(4), 361 (2007)
16. Ahn, B., Kim, J.: Measurement and characterization of soft tissue behavior with surface deformation and force response under large deformations. Med. Image Anal. **14**(2), 138–148 (2010)
17. Xie, A., Fang, C., Huang, Y., et al.: Application of three-dimensional reconstruction and visible simulation technique in reoperation of hepatolithiasis. J. Gastroenterol. Hepatol. **28**(2), 248 (2013)

18. Kataoka, H., Washio, T., Chinzei, K., Mizuhara, K., Simone, C., Okamura, A.M.: Measurement of the tip and friction force acting on a needle during penetration. In: Dohi, T., Kikinis, R. (eds.) MICCAI 2002. LNCS, vol. 2488, pp. 216–223. Springer, Heidelberg (2002). https://doi.org/10.1007/3-540-45786-0_27
19. Podder, T.K., Sherman, J., Messing, E.M., et al.: Needle insertion force estimation model using procedure-specific and patient-specific criteria. In: International Conference of Engineering in Medicine and Biology Society, pp. 555–558 (2006)
20. Ziegel, E.R.: Introduction to the Practice of Statistics. W.H. Freeman, New York (2001)

Minimally Invasive Instrument Joint Design Based on Variable Stiffness of Transmission Efficiency

Longkai Chen[1], Fan Zhang[2(✉)], Guohua Cui[2], Jing Sun[3],
Minhua Zheng[3], and Ruijun Pan[4]

[1] College of Mechanical and Automotive Engineering,
Shanghai University of Engineering Science, Longteng Road No. 333,
Songjiang District, Shanghai 201620, People's Republic of China
[2] Intelligent Robotics Research Center of Shanghai University
of Engineering Science, Shanghai University of Engineering Science,
Longteng Road No. 333, Songjiang District, Shanghai 201620,
People's Republic of China
pdszhangfan@sues.edu.cn
[3] Department of General Surgery, Shanghai Minimally Invasive Surgery Center,
Ruijin Hospital, Shanghai Jiao Tong University School of Medicine,
Shanghai 200025, People's Republic of China
[4] Department of Digestive Surgery, Shanghai Minimally Invasive Surgery Center,
Ruijin Hospital, Shanghai Jiao Tong University School of Medicine,
Shanghai 200025, People's Republic of China

Abstract. In order to improve the posture adjustment ability of the minimally invasive surgical instrument joints, to better adapt to the needs of the surgical environment, the variable stiffness is achieved by changing the transmission efficiency, and the work of the actuated joint in each limb of the parallel mechanism is analyzed, Analysis of work done by main power to each motion pair in parallel Mechanism. Based on the solution of the matrix, the influence of the transmission efficiency on the Jacobian matrix is investigated, and the stiffness matrix of the Jacobian matrix-based mechanism is established. The research results shows that the stiffness can be adjusted by changing the transmission efficiency. Stiffness model analysis of the designed minimally invasive instrument joints was carried out. Through the stiffness calculation of the model, ANSYS static stiffness analysis and model experiment verification, it was finally proved that the variable stiffness based on transmission efficiency is highly practicable.

Keywords: Transmission efficiency · Variable stiffness ·
Redundant mechanism

1 Introduction

Minimally Invasive Surgical Techniques has the advantages of less pain, less bleeding, faster recovery, and lower infection rate [1]. It can minimize iatrogenic trauma and is an inevitable trend in the development of modern surgery. In minimally invasive surgery,

H. Yu et al. (Eds.): ICIRA 2019, LNAI 11745, pp. 310–321, 2019.
https://doi.org/10.1007/978-3-030-27529-7_27

because the surgical instrument enters the patient through the stamp, it prevents the surgical instrument from performing additional damage to the patient's body. It is hoped that the stiffness of the surgical instrument can be adjusted, the flexibility and spatial accessibility of the operating arm of the surgical instrument can be increased, the position and posture of the surgical tool can be adjusted conveniently during the operation, and the damage to the poke point can be reduced [1]. Therefore, the controllable stiffness technology of minimally invasive surgical instruments is of great significance for improving the quality of surgery and reducing complications.

The use of redundant mechanism characteristics is one of the stiffness adjustment techniques, wherein the redundant mechanism refers to a means of reducing the singularity of the parallel mechanism to improve the overall performance of the mechanism, that is, the number of mechanism drives is not equal to the number of degrees of freedom in terminal actuator. Changing the number of passive joints into active joints or increasing the number of active joint branches on a normal basis can make the mechanism redundant. Some scholars have studied this in order to improve the performance of parallel mechanisms by means of redundancy. Literature [2, 3] studied and proved the stiffness of parallel machine tools by introducing redundant drive branches. The literature [4] uses the principle of virtual work to construct the mapping relationship between the end force of the parallel mechanism and the deformation of the moving platform. Based on the screw theory, the literature [5] proposed the ratio of instantaneous power to maximum transmission power as an important indicator to evaluate the motion/force characteristics of the mechanism. In this paper, the research on redundant mechanism is to use the redundant mechanism to have multiple solutions of motion, to change the transmission efficiency through the change of posture and shape of the mechanism, thereby changing the stiffness matrix of the mechanism, and thus realizing the mechanism. The stiffness is adjustable to meet the needs of the surgical joints of the device. In this paper, firstly, the stiffness controllable principle based on transmission efficiency is analyzed, and then the static stiffness of joints is analyzed through ANSYS. Finally, the feasibility of this principle is confirmed through model experiment. The designed joint can be used for the joint part of minimally invasive surgical instruments, which is convenient to realize the controllable stiffness of the mechanism and the locking at any position, easy to realize and easy to control.

2   Controllable Principle of Stiffness Based on Transmission Efficiency

2.1   Main Power

Force Screw Calculation Method for Motion Screw
In general, a screw can represent the torsional motion of a rigid body, the motion of a rigid body relative to the reference coordinate system can be represented as a screw, and in the Plücker coordinate system, it can be expressed as [5]:

$$\widetilde{\$} = w\$ = [L\ M\ N\ P\ Q\ R]^T \tag{1}$$

Where **w** is the intensity of $\$$, the unit screw used to represent the motion, [L M N] the rotation motion of the rigid body, and [P Q R] the movement of a point on the rigid body. In contrast, the inverse screw can be expressed in the Plücker coordinate system as [5]:

$$\widetilde{S} = fS = [P'\ Q'\ R'\ L'\ M'\ N']^T \tag{2}$$

Where f is the intensity of S, S is used to represent the unit screw of force, [P' Q' R'] refers to the moment of the object relative to the reference frame coordinate system, [L' M' N'] refers to the force exerted on the object. According to the theory of screw,

$$\$^T * S = LP' + MQ' + NR' + PL' + QM' + RN' = 0 \tag{3}$$

The operation of the above formula is called the inner product of $\$^T$ and S. Also known as S and $\$$ as a pair of reciprocal screw.

For a n-degree-of-freedom non-redundant parallel mechanism, n input joints transmit motion to the end of the mechanism under the action of their corresponding n transfer forces to achieve n degrees of freedom motion of the terminal actuator of the mechanism, Since the remaining 6-n degrees of freedom of the terminal actuator are constrained by the constraint forces provided by each branch [7]. For a single input joint to the end output motion, assuming that n-1 input joints are locked and only the ith joint is driven, then only the movement of the ith input joint can be transmitted to the terminal actuator, at which time the mechanism changes For a single degree of freedom mechanism, the unit instantaneous motion of the terminal actuator can be expressed in units of output rotation. At this point, it can be considered that only the ith transfer force (Denoted by $\$_{ai}$) can work on the terminal actuator of the mechanism, while the remaining n-1 transfer forces become constraint forces. The work of the force screw on motion can be expressed as: $P = \$_{aj}^T * \$_{0i}(j = 1, 2, \ldots, n; \ i \neq j)$ From the reciprocity of the motion screw and the force screw, we know that $\$_{aj}^T * \$_{0i} = 0$, If the inner product of the force screw and the motion screw is 0, it will not do work, otherwise the force screw will do work for the motion screw.

Main Force at the End of the Branch

For the branch chain of a parallel mechanism with multiple rotating pairs in series in sequence, If all kinds of high pairs are replaced by rotating pair and moving pair, then the high pair is replaced by the rotating pair and the moving pair, the series mechanism can be regarded as C_i single-degree-of-freedom motion pairs connected in sequence. The end-motion system of the mechanism can be equivalent to a linear combination of C_i single-degree-of-freedom motion screws [5], i.e.

$$\$_p = \sum_{j=1}^{C_i} \dot{\theta}_{j,i}\ \$_{j,i}(i = 1, 2, \ldots, m) \tag{4}$$

Where $\$_{j,i}$, represents the unit screw of the jth motion pair on the ith branch, $\dot{\theta}_{j,i}$ indicates the intensity of the jth motion pair input motion. According to the theory of reciprocity, the constraint screw $\$_{r,k,i}$ is satisfied, so there is

$$\$_{r,k,i}^{T} * \$_{p} = 0 \qquad (5)$$

where:

$$\$_{r,k,i} = \{\$_{r,1,i}, \$_{r,2,i}, \ldots, \$_{r,(6-C_i),i}\}$$

Assume there is only one active pair per branch. If the active pair is locked, the number of motion pairs of the branch should be reduced by one, and then the counter screw of the motion is reversed.

$$\$_{r,k,i} = \{\$_{r,1,i}, \$_{r,2,i}, \ldots, \$_{r,(6-C_i),i}, \$_{r,(6-C_i+1),i}\} \qquad (6)$$

At the same time, there is one more constraint force, and the extra force rotation $\$_{r,(6-C_i+1),i}$ is the driving force rotation which is in a dual relationship with the motion rotation.

Main Power Transmission Efficiency

In [8], the transmission efficiency is defined as the absolute value of the ratio of the actual power to the maximum power of each unit of the screw force of each branch, and the transmission efficiency of the mechanism takes the minimum of the efficiency of each branch. In [5], the transmission efficiency is expressed by two performance indicators: the transmission fator (TF) and the manipulability fator (MF). This paper uses the solution method defined in.

The rotation screw corresponding to each motion pair is listed, wherein the rotation amount corresponding to the drive pair (transmission force) is represented by $\$_{I,i}$, The rotation corresponding to the output pair is represented by $\$_{O,i}$, After removing the drive screw and the output screw, the corresponding motion screws are represented by $\$_{1,i}, \$_{2,i}, \ldots, \$_{r,i}$, respectively, and these screws must be linearly independent. The constrained screw system $r = \{\$_{1,i}^{r}, \$_{2,i}^{r}, \ldots, \$_{6-r,i}^{r}\}$ can be obtained by the screw theory [7].

The necessary and sufficient conditions for the mechanism to move are: all the screws on it are linearly dependent, i.e.

$$w_{I,i}\$_{I,i} + \sum_{j=1}^{r_i} w_{j,i}\$_{j,i} + w_{o,i}\$_{o,i} = 0 \qquad (7)$$

Since $\$_{r,(6-C_i+1),i}$ and $\sum_{j=1}^{n} w_{j,i}\$_{j,i}$ inner product is zero, the above formula can be written as

$$\$_{r,(6-C_i+1),i}^{T} *\$_{I,i} w_{I,i} + \$_{r,(6-C_i+1),i}^{T} *\$_{O,i} w_{O,i} = 0 \tag{8}$$

The manipulability factor is: $\quad MF = \left| \$_{r,(6-C_i+1),i}^{T} *\$_{I,i} \right| \tag{9}$

The magnitude of the inner product of the two screws is dependent to the angle between the directions corresponding to the two screws. When the overall size of the mechanism is determined, the transfer efficiency changes only when the pose of the mechanism changes.

2.2 Transmission Efficiency Affects Stiffness

2.2.1 Main Power Jacobian Matrix

As described in the previous section, when the input motion pair is locked, the driving force corresponding to the input motion of each branch is set to $\$_{r,g,(6-C_i+1)}$, $\$_{gi,i}$ indicate that the gi joint of the ith branch is the input motion screw.

$$\$_{r,(6-C_i+1),i}^{T} * \$_{p} = \dot{\theta}_{gi,i} \$_{r,(6-C_i+1),i}^{T} * \$_{gi,i} \tag{10}$$

M branch expressed the form of a matrix:

$$\mathbf{J}_x \$_{p} = \mathbf{J}_q \dot{\mathbf{q}} \tag{11}$$

where:

$$\mathbf{J}_x = \begin{bmatrix} \$_{r,(6-C_1+1),1} \\ \$_{r,(6-C_2+1),2} \\ \vdots \\ \$_{r,(6-C_M+1),M} \end{bmatrix} \quad ;$$

$$\mathbf{J}_q = \begin{bmatrix} \$_{r,6-C_1+1,i}\$_{g1,1} & 0 & \cdots & 0 \\ 0 & \$_{r,6-C_2+1,i}\$_{g2,2} & \cdots & 0 \\ \vdots & \vdots & \cdots & \vdots \\ 0 & 0 & \cdots & \$_{r,6-C_M+1,M}\$_{gM,M} \end{bmatrix}$$

$$\dot{\mathbf{q}} = \begin{bmatrix} \dot{\theta}_{g1,1}, & \dot{\theta}_{g2,2} & \cdots & \dot{\theta}_{gM,M} \end{bmatrix}^{T}$$

Jacobian of actuations:

$$\mathbf{J_a} = \mathbf{J}_X/\mathbf{J}_q = \begin{bmatrix} \$_{r,(6-C_1+1),1}/\$_{r,(6-C_1+1),1}\$_{g_1,1} \\ \$_{r,(6-C_2+1),2}/\$_{r,(6-C_1+1),2}\$_{g_2,2} \\ \vdots \\ \$_{r,(6-C_M+1),M}/\$_{r,(6-C_1+1),M}\$_{g_M,M} \end{bmatrix} \tag{12}$$

2.2.2 Stiffness Matrix

The relationship between the end output force screw and the joint force screw can be derived from the virtual work principle. The work done by the system can be expressed as [7]:

$$W = \int_{t_1}^{t_2} \mathbf{F} \cdot \mathbf{V} dt = \int_{t_1}^{t_2} \mathbf{V}^T \cdot \mathbf{F} dt \tag{13}$$

Where, V is the velocity of the end, F is the output force, and if β is used to express the joint force.

$$W = \int_{t_1}^{t_2} \beta \cdot \dot{\theta} \, dt \tag{14}$$

Where θ indicates the end of the motion can be derived from the above two formulas:

$$\mathbf{V}^T \cdot \mathbf{F} = \dot{\theta}^T \cdot \beta \tag{15}$$

According to the definition of the robot Jacques matrix can be written with:

$$\mathbf{V} = \mathbf{J} \dot{\theta} \tag{16}$$

The relationship between the end output force and the joint force can be written with:

$$\beta = \mathbf{J}^T \mathbf{F} \tag{17}$$

In the parallel mechanism, the driving rotation amount of each branch is expressed as $\beta = (\tau_1, \tau_2, \ldots \ldots \tau_n)^T$, Δq is the deformation of the corresponding joint, and $\varepsilon = \text{diag}(k_1, k_2, \ldots, k_n)$ is set at the same time, and has the following matrix relationship:

$$\beta = \varepsilon \Delta q \tag{18}$$

The velocity Jacques matrix is expressed in differential form and can be written as:

$$\Delta q = J\Delta x \tag{19}$$

In the formula, Δx is a small deformation of the moving platform. definition:

$$F = K\,\Delta x \tag{20}$$

Let $\varepsilon = \mathrm{diag}(k_1, k_2, \ldots, k_n)$. where k_i is the equivalent spring rate coefficient, Stiffness Matrix is:

$$K = \begin{bmatrix} \$_{r,(6-C_1+1),1}/\$_{r,(6-C_1+1),1}\$_{g_1,1} \\ \$_{r,(6-C_2+1),2}/\$_{r,(6-C_2+1),2}\$_{g_2,2} \\ \vdots \\ \$_{r,(6-C_M+1),M}/\$_{r,2,(6-C_M+1)}\$_{g_M,M} \end{bmatrix}^T \varepsilon \begin{bmatrix} \$_{r,(6-C_1+1),1}/\$_{r,(6-C_1+1),1}\$_{g_1,1} \\ \$_{r,(6-C_2+1),2}/\$_{r,(6-C_2+1),2}\$_{g_2,2} \\ \vdots \\ \$_{r,(6-C_M+1),M}/\$_{r,2,(6-C_M+1)}\$_{g_M,M} \end{bmatrix} \tag{21}$$

Combining Eqs. (4) and (14), the above equation can be written as:

$$K = \begin{bmatrix} k_1\$_{r,(6-C_1+1),1}/MF_1^2 \\ k_2\$_{r,(6-C_2+1),2}/MF_2^2 \\ \vdots \\ k_M\$_{r,(6-C_M+1),M}/MF_M^2 \end{bmatrix} \tag{22}$$

Where MF_i ($i = 1, 2\ldots, M$) represents the manipulability factor of the branch; since the parameters in the stiffness matrix are dependent to the manipulability factor, the control of the input parameters of the active pair can be achieved, and the control of the Jacobian matrix can be achieved to achieve the purpose of variable stiffness.

3   Stiffness Controllable Surgical Instrument Joint Design

Based on the joint form of minimally invasive surgical instruments, the upper and lower platforms can be viewed as the upper and lower undersides of the two joints respectively, and the controllable stiffness joints as shown in Fig. 1 are designed. The left side of the mechanism is composed of six rotating pairs connected in sequence, the two ends are connected to the moving platform and static platform in turn, and the right side is a single rotating pair. The two ends are connected to the first and second rotating joints of the moving platform. The axes of the first revolute joint, the third revolute joint and the sixth revolute joint are in common point in space at the initial position.

The axis of the second driving revolute joint, the axis of the fourth revolute joint and the axis of the fifth revolute joint are parallel in space and not parallel to the axis of the seventh revolute join. It can be known from the screw theory that the motion screw of the six joints on the left side not have a linearly dependent screw, and the main power of the branch can be obtained by locking the active pair to find its inverse screw. It is found that the direction of the main power is not in the same plane as the axis of the seventh rotating joint, so the main power is working on the seventh rotating joint, thereby causing the rotational movement of the moving platform.

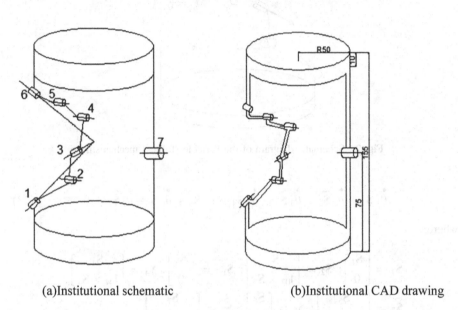

(a)Institutional schematic   (b)Institutional CAD drawing

Fig. 1. Variable stiffness mechanism

4 Stiffness Performance Analysis

4.1 Stiffness Model

As shown in Fig. 2, a coordinate system as shown in the figure is established, and the upper and lower platforms are connected by two branches, wherein the motion screw corresponding to the branches includes $\$_1, \$_2, \ldots, \$_6$, l_{ii} represents a vector of the length direction of the connecting rod between the ith rotating pair and the (i + 1)th rotating pair, l_{oi} Represents the vector diameter of the axis of the rotation pairs, and the branch is a single-degree-of-freedom motion pair.

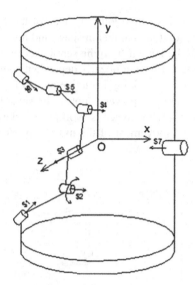

Fig. 2. Schematic diagram of the variable stiffness mechanism

$$\dot{\theta}_1 \,\tilde{\$}_1 + \dot{\theta}_2 \,\tilde{\$}_2 + \dot{\theta}_3 \,\tilde{\$}_3 + \dot{\theta}_4 \,\tilde{\$}_4 + \dot{\theta}_5 \,\tilde{\$}_5 + \dot{\theta}_6 \,\tilde{\$}_6 - \dot{\theta}_7 \,\tilde{\$}_7 = 0 \qquad (23)$$

where:

$$\tilde{\$}_1 = \begin{bmatrix} \mathbf{S}_1 \\ 0 \end{bmatrix}; \ \tilde{\$}_2 = \begin{bmatrix} \mathbf{S}_2 \\ \mathbf{l}_{02} \times \mathbf{S}_2 \end{bmatrix}; \ \widetilde{\$}_{1,3} = \begin{bmatrix} \mathbf{S}_3 \\ 0 \end{bmatrix}; \ \tilde{\$}_4 = \begin{bmatrix} \mathbf{S}_4 \\ \mathbf{l}_{04} \times \mathbf{S}_4 \end{bmatrix}$$

$$\tilde{\$}_5 = \begin{bmatrix} \mathbf{S}_5 \\ \mathbf{l}_{05} \times \mathbf{S}_5 \end{bmatrix}; \ \tilde{\$}_6 = \begin{bmatrix} \mathbf{S}_6 \\ 0 \end{bmatrix}; \ \tilde{\$}_7 = \begin{bmatrix} \mathbf{S}_7 \\ \mathbf{l}_{07} \times \mathbf{S}_7 \end{bmatrix}$$

$\tilde{\$}_1, \tilde{\$}_2, \tilde{\$}_3, \tilde{\$}_4, \tilde{\$}_5, \tilde{\$}_6, \tilde{\$}_7$ are Representing the rotational screw of the rotating pairs rotating pairs on the branch. When the inverse screw is an even amount, only when the even amount is perpendicular to all the line vector axes in the screw system, can it reciprocate with all the line vectors in the screw system. When the inverse screw is a force vector, the force vector must intersect with all the line vectors in the screw system and the line vector perpendicular to all the even quantities in the screw system to reciprocate with all the screws in the screw system. Firstly, the first, third and sixth rotating joints are analyzed. If there is a reverse screw, it must be a force vector. In the analysis of the second, fourth and fifth rotating pairs, if the force vector is not satisfied with all the revolving, it is There is no reverse screw in the branch.

Next, locking the active pair of the first branch adds a reverse screw to $\$_{r,2}$, which is reciprocal with other moving screws.

$$\$_{r,2} = \begin{bmatrix} S_{1,4} \\ 0 \end{bmatrix} \tag{24}$$

is the driving force of the motion branch. Take the inner product on both sides of Eq. (20)

$$\$_{r,2}^T * \$_p = \dot{\theta}_{1,2} \tag{25}$$

Write the above form as a matrix, with:

$$J_a \$_p = \dot{q} \tag{26}$$

where:

$$\dot{q} = \dot{\theta}_{1,2}$$

Let the stiffness corresponding to the branch chain be k, then the stiffness matrix corresponding to the mechanism is:

$$K = \left[\$_{r,2}^T / \$_{r,2}^T \$_{1,7} \right]^T \varepsilon \left[\$_{r,2}^T / \$_{r,2}^T \$_{1,7} \right]$$
$$= \left[k\$_{r,2}^{T2} / MF^2 \right]$$

Therefore, the variability of the stiffness matrix can be further realized by controlling the manipulability factor to change the comparable matrix.

4.2   Experimental Verification

ANSYS Analysis
The 3D model in Solidworks was imported into ANSYS software for analysis. ANSYS Workbench was used as the main analysis software of the joint. In two different postures, a vertical downward 2 N force was applied at the joint of the upper arm and the upper platform. It is found from the strain diagram that the shape variables in the two attitudes are significantly different. The maximum deformation of the left diagram is 0.011 mm, and the maximum deformation of the right diagram is 0.125 mm. Due to the linear relationship between the force and the deformation, it can be concluded In both postures, the stiffness of the mechanism is different (Fig. 3).

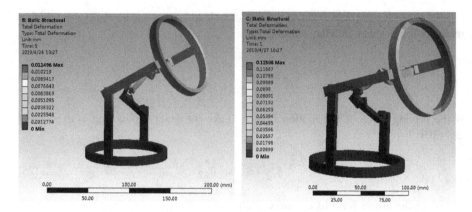

Fig. 3. Mechanism deformation diagram in different poses

Experimental Verification

Through the 3D printing analysis of the Solidworks model, the lower platform is fixed on the experimental platform, and the weight is tied by the rope on the connection between the upper arm of the model and the upper platform, so that the weight naturally hangs under the action of gravity, and the weight-bearing experiment is performed. It can bear a certain load at two different postures, which can prove the stiffness change at the joint and can achieve the locked state. Due to the rigidity and accuracy of the print, it can only withstand a small amount of load (Fig. 4).

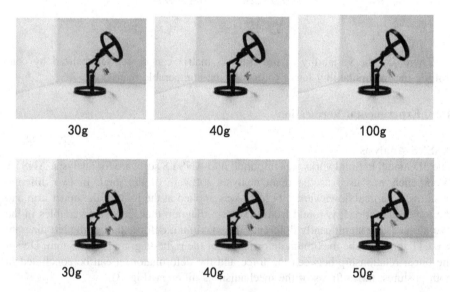

Fig. 4. Load experiment of controllable stiffness joints at different corners

5 Conclusion

In this paper, combined with the variable characteristics of the geometrical characteristics of the redundant mechanism, since the transmission efficiency of the main power has a certain correlation with the geometrical characteristics of the mechanism, the transmission efficiency of the end is further changed by changing the geometric characteristics of the mechanism. At this time, the corresponding Jacobian matrix of the mechanism also changes, which changes the rigidity of the mechanism. Firstly, the theoretical analysis and verification are carried out, and the designed model is analyzed by the example. Finally, the analysis and verification of ANSYS and experiment are carried out, and the effect is obvious. It shows that the variable stiffness can be achieved by the transmission efficiency of the redundant mechanism.

References

1. Li, X: Research and optimal design of the variable stiffness manipulator in single-port surgical instrument. Tianjin University (2017)
2. Bai, Z., Chen, W.: Calculation model of ball joint stiffness and improvement of stiffness of parallel machine tools by redundant branches. Int. J. Mech. Eng. Educ. **42**(10), 142–145 (2006)
3. Qu, H., Liang, Y., Fang, Y., Zhou, Y.: Statics and stiffness analysis of 4-RRS redundant spherical parallel mechanism. J. Mech. Eng. **51**(11), 8–15 (2015)
4. Gosselin, C.: Stiffness mapping for parallel manipulators. IEEE Trans. Robot. Autom. **6**(3), 377–382 (1990)
5. Tsai, M.J., Lee, H.W.: Generalized evaluation for the transmission performance of mechanisms. Mech. Mach. Theory **29**(4), 607–618 (1994)
6. Tsai, L.W., Joshi, S.: Jacobian analysis of limited-DOF parallel manipulators. Trans. ASME J. Mech. Des. **124**(2), 254–258 (2002)
7. Yu, J., Liu, X., Ding, X.: Foundation of Mathematics of Robot Mechanism, 2nd edn. China Machine Press, Beijing (2008)
8. Liu, X., Xie, F., Wang, J.: The Basis of Mechanism of Parallel Robots. Higher Education Press, Beijing (2016)
9. Marquet, F., Krut, S., Company, O., Pierrot, F.: A new redundant parallel mechanism-modeling, control and first results. In: IEEE/RSJ International Conference on Intelligent Robots & Systems. IEEE (2001)
10. Tsai, L., Joshi, S.: Comparison study of architectures of four 3 degree-of-freedom translational parallel manipulators. In: IEEE International Conference on Robotics & Automation. IEEE (2001)
11. Cao, W., Yang, D., Ding, H.: A method for stiffness analysis of over constrained parallel robotic mechanisms with Scara motion. Robot. Comput. Integr. Manuf. **49**, 426–435 (2018)
12. Jun, Z., Yanqin, Z., Jiansheng, D.: Compliance modeling and analysis of a 3-RPS parallel kinematic machine module. Chin. J. Mech. Eng. **27**(4), 703–713 (2014)
13. Xu, Y., Liu, W., Yao, J., Zhao, Y.: A method for force analysis of the over constrained lower mobility parallel mechanism. Mech. Mach. Theory **88**, 31–48 (2015)

Robot Intelligence, Learning and Linguistics

A Hybrid Path Planning Method for Mobile Robot Based on Artificial Potential Field Method

Haiyi Kong[1], Chenguang Yang[1(✉)], Zhaojie Ju[2], and Jinguo Liu[3]

[1] College of Automation Science and Engineering,
South China University of Technology, Guangzhou 510640, China
cyang@ieee.org
[2] School of Computing, University of Portsmouth, Portsmouth PO1 3HE, UK
[3] Institutes for Robotics and Intelligent Manufacturing,
Chinese Academy of Sciences, Shenyang 110016, China

Abstract. This paper proposes a hybrid path planning method based on artificial potential field method (APF) for mobile robot, which combines wall following method (WFM) and obstacles connecting method (OCM) for dealing with local minimum. The environment information is took into consideration to decide the escape direction of WFM. To ensure the success of escaping from local minimum, more reliable switching conditions are designed. OCM is applied to reduce the difficulty of path planning for complex workspace with concave obstacles. Simulation studies have been carried out to verify the validity of the proposed method.

Keywords: Artificial potential field method · Wall following method · Escape direction · Switching conditions · Obstacles connecting method

1 Introduction

In recent years, mobile robot has been drawn much attention in various fields, such as military, rescue and inspection. Since the actual application scenarios are often complex, it puts forward high demands on the path navigation and collision avoidance strategy of mobile robot [1–3].

There have been plenty of researches on the path planning, the typical algorithms are Dijkstra [4], A* [5], RRTs [6] and artificial potential field method [7]. Dijkstra, A*, RRTs are global path planning methods, whose amount of calculation will increase dramatically as the map expands. Comparatively, the artificial potential field method (APF), which has the character of simplicity and low-time consumption, is more suitable for mobile robot real-time path planning. The basic idea of APF is to conduct the robot to move towards the goal by the attractive force, and avoid obstacles by the repulsive force. However, this method is prone to fall into local minimum, leading to the failure of reaching the target [9].

© Springer Nature Switzerland AG 2019
H. Yu et al. (Eds.): ICIRA 2019, LNAI 11745, pp. 325–331, 2019.
https://doi.org/10.1007/978-3-030-27529-7_28

In order to further apply the APF in practice, the local minimum problem has been extensively studied [8–12]. In [8], a gradually expanding search range was proposed to detect the obstacles nearby, therefore the UAV can always move towards the low potential energy direction with no collision. In [10,11], a method combined the wall following method (WFM) with the APF was developed to escape from the local minimum. However, due to the insufficient utilization of the environment information, it may not choose the best escape direction, resulting in the extension of useless path. In [12], to prevent the mobile robot from being trapped by the obstacle groups, the obstacles connecting method (OCM) was employed to connect the obstacles into a whole.

Inspired by the results of [10–12], in this paper, we propose a hybrid path planning method based on the APF, combining the WFM and OCM. Once the mobile robot is trapped in the local minimum, WFM is utilized to escape from the trap. The environment information will be took into consideration to decide the escape direction. The switching conditions from WFM to AFP have been fully studied. For better path planning performance, the OCM is applied to prevent the mobile robot from dropping into the traps consisting of concave obstacles or multiple independent obstacles. The APF will be briefly described in Sect. 2. In Sect. 3, the schemes of dealing with local minimum are discussed. In Sect. 4, the simulation results are given.

2   The Traditional Artificial Field Method

For simplicity, we regard the mobile robot as a mass point, and its position in workspace is denoted by $\mathbf{p} = (x, y)$. In the same way, the position of goal is denoted by $\mathbf{p}_{goal} = (x_{goal}, y_{goal})$.

The attractive potential function is defined as:

$$U_{att}(\mathbf{p}) = \frac{1}{2}\alpha\rho^2(\mathbf{p}, \mathbf{p}_{goal}) \tag{1}$$

where α is a positive constant, $\rho(\mathbf{p}, \mathbf{p}_{goal}) = \|\mathbf{p}_{goal} - \mathbf{p}\|$ represents the Euclidean distance between $\mathbf{p}$ and $\mathbf{p}_{goal}$.

The repulsive potential function takes the form [11]:

$$U_{rep}(\mathbf{p}) = \begin{cases} \frac{1}{2}\beta(\frac{1}{\rho(\mathbf{p}, \mathbf{p}_{obs})} - \frac{1}{\rho_0})^2\rho^2(\mathbf{p}, \mathbf{p}_{goal}) & \rho(\mathbf{p}, \mathbf{p}_{obs}) < \rho_0 \\ 0 & \rho(\mathbf{p}, \mathbf{p}_{obs}) \geq \rho_0 \end{cases} \tag{2}$$

where ρ_0 is the maximum influence distance of obstacles, $\mathbf{p}_{obs} = (x_{obs}, y_{obs})$ denotes the closest point to the robot on the obstacle, $\rho(\mathbf{p}, \mathbf{p}_{obs})$ represents the minimum distance between $\mathbf{p}$ and $\mathbf{p}_{obs}$.

Then, we can obtain the attractive force $F_{att}(\mathbf{p})$ and repulsive force $F_{rep}(\mathbf{p})$ by taking the negative gradient of the corresponding potential. Due to the limited space, it will not be presented here.

The resultant force on the robot can be expressed as:

$$F_{res}(\mathbf{p}) = F_{att}(\mathbf{p}) + \Sigma F_{rep}(\mathbf{p}) \tag{3}$$

where $\Sigma F_{rep}(\mathbf{p})$ is the sum of repulsive forces of all obstacles.

3 Schemes for Coping with Local Minimum

3.1 Escape Direction of Wall Following Method

When the robot is in the local minimum, the attractive force on it is equal to the sum of the repulsive forces. And we can see the phenomenon that the robot stops at a location or hovers around a small area. To judge whether the robot is trapped in the local minimum, we define the following condition:

$$\|\mathbf{p}(t) - \mathbf{p}(t - 2T)\| < \gamma \tag{4}$$

where $\mathbf{p}(t)$ denotes the current position of the robot, T is a cycle time, $\mathbf{p}(t-2T)$ represents the position in the last two cycles, γ is a distance threshold.

Once the robot drops into the local minimum, WFM will be applied to break the deadlock. Then robot can keep moving on along the direction of $\theta_{rep} \pm 90°$, until the switching conditions for converting to APF are satisfied, where θ_{rep} is the direction of the sum of repulsive forces. As to the local minimum generated by concave obstacle or multiple independent obstacles, different escape directions can lead to greatly different path planning results. Figure 1 shows the results of path planning from (6,4) to (2,4) with different escape directions, in which the red arrows represent the direction of θ_{rep} at the local minimum. Since we have obtained the environment information in advance, we can specifically set the escape direction for the complex obstacles to enhance the success rate of path planning. When the robot is trapped in a concave obstacle, if the distance to the goal in the clockwise direction along the obstacle is closer, the escape direction will be set to $\theta_{rep} + 90°$. If the robot moves to the goal closer in the counterclockwise direction, the escape direction will be set to $\theta_{rep} - 90°$. While, if the robot is trapped outside the obstacle, it will get the opposite result. For general obstacles, the escape direction is $\theta_{rep} + 90°$ by default.

3.2 Switching Conditions from Wall Following Method to Artificial Potential Field Method

After escaping from the local minimum using WFM, the movement pattern needs to be converted to APF to approach the goal. The switching conditions from WFM to APF play a key role in the path planning scheme. If the movement pattern is converted to APF too late, the robot will miss the goal, or if the conversion is too early, the robot will remain trapped in the local minimum.

In [11], the robot needs to go a long way around the edge of the obstacles to meet the switching conditions if it is trapped by a local minimum, which is not suitable for practical application. Based on the switching conditions in [11], we have added new switching conditions to improve the performance of path planning:

$$(|\Delta\theta_{att-trap}| > 90° \bigcup |\Delta\theta_{att}| > \theta) \bigcap \theta_{min} < \theta_{res} < \theta_{max} \qquad (5)$$

where $\Delta\theta_{att-trap} = \theta_{att} - \theta_{trap}$ and $0 \leq \Delta\theta_{att-trap} \leq 180°$, θ_{att} is the angle of attractive force, θ_{trap} is the angle of the vector that points to the local minimum from the current position, $\Delta\theta_{att}$ is the angle increment of attractive force since the movement pattern is converted to WFM, θ_{res} is the angle of resultant force, θ, θ_{min} and θ_{max} are angle thresholds, the values of which are shown in Table 1. The first two conditions ensure that the robot has been away for a long enough distance in the WFM mode. The last condition is used to confirm the robot has been escaped from the local minimum successfully. When it is satisfied, the component of the resultant force on the robot is greater in the direction of attractive force, then the robot can move towards the goal under the control of the resultant force. The experiment results compared with the method in [11] are showed in Fig. 2.

Table 1. The values of θ_{max} and θ_{min}

		$|\theta_{att} - \theta_{trap}| < 180°$	$|\theta_{att} - \theta_{trap}| \geq 180°$
$\theta_{att} < \theta_{trap}$		$\theta_{min} = \theta_{att} - 90°$	$\theta_{min} = \theta_{att} - (360° - |\theta_{att} - \theta_{trap}|)/2$
		$\theta_{max} = \theta_{att} + |\theta_{att} - \theta_{trap}|/2$	$\theta_{max} = \theta_{att} + 90°$
$\theta_{att} > \theta_{trap}$		$\theta_{min} = \theta_{att} - |\theta_{att} - \theta_{trap}|/2$	$\theta_{min} = \theta_{att} - 90°$
		$\theta_{max} = \theta_{att} + 90°$	$\theta_{max} = \theta_{att} + (360° - |\theta_{att} - \theta_{trap}|)/2$

3.3 Obstacles Connecting Method

Local minimum is easily formed around the concave obstacles and obstacle groups. When the robot needs to go through those obstacles to approach the

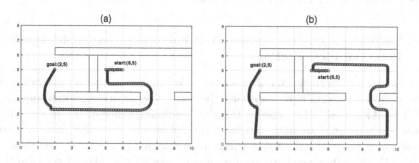

Fig. 1. The escape direction. (a) $\theta_{rep} - 90°$. (b) $\theta_{rep} + 90°$.

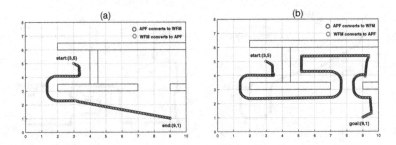

Fig. 2. (a) Switching conditions in proposed method. (b) Switching conditions in [11].

goal, it will spend extra useless costs to bypass the obstacles or escape from the local minimum. According to the environment information, we can connect the concave obstacles and obstacle groups into convex obstacles which can greatly reduce the difficulty of path planning and improve the path planning performance. Figure 3 shows the path planning results of whether the obstacle is connected.

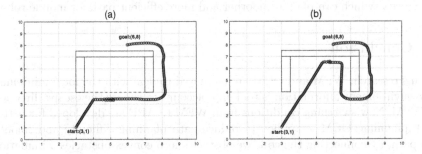

Fig. 3. (a) Connecting obstacles. (b) No disposal.

4 Simulation Results

To verify the rationality and superiority of the proposed method, we carry out a simulation experiment and compare with the method in [11]. The workspace is in the size of the $10m \times 8m$ with concave and convex obstacles. The parameters are set as $\alpha = 1$, $\beta = 0.1$, $\rho_0 = 0.8$, $\gamma = 0.08$, $\theta = 90°$. Suppose the robot is moving at a constant speed of 0.1m/s, and the resultant force on it only determines the direction of its motion. The starting position and the goal are set to $(9.7, 2)$ and $(1, 7)$, respectively.

The comparative experiment results are shown in Fig. 4. It is obvious that the length of the path in (a) is shorter than that in (b). When the robot first falls into the local minimum generated by the concave obstacle, it chooses the escape direction of $\theta_{rep} - 90°$ in (a) and then easily gets away from the trap. Due to the next concave obstacle is connected into a convex obstacle that reduces

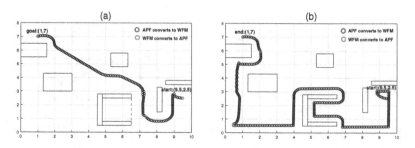

Fig. 4. (a) The proposed method. (b) The method in [11].

the difficulty of path planning, the robot successfully passes through it and reaches the goal at last. However, in (b), the robot chooses the escape direction of $\theta_{rep} + 90°$. It goes a long way under the WFM mode around the boundary of the obstacles before the APF converting conditions are satisfied. Besides, there are many sharp turns in the path, which makes it difficult for the robot to track in practice. It can be seen from the simulation results that the proposed method is effective, which can plan a smoother and more efficient path for mobile robot.

5   Conclusion

In this research, WFM and OCM are employed to deal with the local minimum. The environment information is took into account to choose the escape direction of WFM. New switching conditions from WFM to APF are developed for better path planning. OCM is applied to reduce path planning difficulty and smooth the path, by connecting the concave obstacles into convex obstacles. Simulation results show that the proposed hybrid path planning method can plan a more reasonable path for mobile robot, witch is shorter and smoother.

Acknowledgement. This work was partially supported by National Nature Science Foundation (NSFC) under Grants 61861136009 and 61811530281.

References

1. Rasekhipour, Y., Khajepour, A., Chen, S., Litkouhi, B.: A potential field-based model predictive path-planning controller for autonomous road vehicles. IEEE Trans. Intell. Transp. Syst. **18**(5), 1255–1267 (2017)
2. Wen, G., Ge, S.S., Tu, F., Choo, Y.S.: Artificial potential-based adaptive H∞ synchronized tracking control for accommodation vessel. IEEE Trans. Ind. Electron. **64**(7), 5640–5647 (2017)
3. Wu, X., Wang, S., Xing, M.: Observer-based leader-following formation control for multi-robot with obstacle avoidance. IEEE Access **7**, 14791–14798 (2018)
4. Dijkstra, E.: A note on two problems in connexion with graphs. Numerische Mathematics **1**(1), 269–271 (1959)

5. Hart, P., Nilsson, N., Raphael, B., et al.: A formal basis for the heuristic determination of minimum cost paths. IEEE Trans. Syst. Sci. Cybern. **4**(2), 100–107 (1968)
6. LaValle, S., Kuffner, J.: Randomized kinodynamic planning. Int. J. Robot. Res. **20**(5), 378–400 (2001)
7. Khatib, O.: Real-time obstacle avoidance for manipulators and mobile robots. Int. J. Robot. Res. **5**(1), 396–404 (1986)
8. Liu, Z., Jiang, T.: Route planning based on improved artificial potential field method. In: 2017 2nd Asia-Pacific Conference on Intelligent Robot Systems (ACIRS) (2017)
9. Zhou, L., Li, W.: Adaptive artificial potential field approach for obstacle avoidance path planning. In: 2014 Seventh International Symposium on Computational Intelligence and Design (2014)
10. Zhu, Y., Zhang, T., Song, J: An improved wall following method for escaping from local minimum in artificial potential field based path planning (2009)
11. Ge, S., Cui, Y.: New potential functions for mobile robot path planning. IEEE Trans. Robot. Autom. **16**(5), 615–620 (2000)
12. Zhang, H., Yang, L., Gao, Z., Cao, Y.: The dynamic path planning research for mobile robot based on artificial potential field, **49**(6), 937–940 (2018)

Towards End-to-End Speech Recognition with Deep Multipath Convolutional Neural Networks

Wei Zhang[1,3], Minghao Zhai[1,3], Zilong Huang[1,3], Chen Liu[1,3],
Wei Li[2], and Yi Cao[1,3(✉)]

[1] School of Mechanical Engineering, Jiangnan University, Wuxi 214122,
Jiangsu, China
caoyi@jiangnan.edu.cn
[2] Suzhou Vocational Institute of Industrial Technology, Suzhou 215104,
Jiangsu, China
[3] Jiangsu Key Laboratory of Advanced Food Manufacturing Equipment and
Technology, Wuxi 214122, Jiangsu, China

Abstract. Approaches to deep learning have been used all over in connection to Automatic Speech Recognition (ASR), where they have achieved a high level of accuracy. This has mostly been seen in Convolutional Neural Network (CNN) which has recently been investigated in ASR. Due to the fact that CNN has an increased network's depth on one branch, and may not be wide enough to work on capturing adequate features on signals of human speech. We focus on a proposal for an architecture that is deep and wide in CNN referred to as Multipath Convolutional Neural Network (MCNN). MCNN-CTC combines three additional paths with Connectionist Temporal Classification (CTC) objective function, and can be defined as an end-to-end system that has the ability to fully exploit spectral and temporal structures related to speech signals simultaneously. Results from the experiments show that the newly proposed MCNN-CTC structure enables a reduction in the error rate arising from the construction of end-to-end acoustic model. In the absence of a Language Model (LM), our proposed MCNN-CTC acoustic model has a relative reduction of 1.10%–12.08% comparing to the traditional HMM-based or DCNN-CTC-based models with strong generalization performance.

Keywords: Automatic Speech Recognition (ASR) · Acoustic Model (AM) · MCNN-CTC · Connectionist Temporal Classification (CTC)

1 Introduction

Automatic Speech Recognition (ASR) is an automatic method designed to translate human form speech content into textual form [1]. Deep learning has in the past been applied in ASR to increase correctness [2–4], a process that has been successful. As of late, CNN has been successful in acoustic model [5, 6]. Which is applied in ASR combining with HMMs [5], in a way identical to the regular Deep Neural Networks (DNNs) [7, 8], which in turn lead to a hybrid system. DNN-HMM uses a discriminant

© Springer Nature Switzerland AG 2019
H. Yu et al. (Eds.): ICIRA 2019, LNAI 11745, pp. 332–341, 2019.
https://doi.org/10.1007/978-3-030-27529-7_29

model to replace the GMM-HMM generation model, which takes advantage of DNN's powerful fitting ability to model the posterior probability of each frame. The HMM still handles the operations in temporal modelling and decoding whereas the neural network generates posterior probability of the corresponding state [4].

A large amount of problems arise as a result of this hybrid system, where the modules' training which is done separately for different modules and with a different criteria that may certainly not be optimal in the solution of the final task. Consequently, additional hyperparameters turning throughout all training stages are required and can be not only time consuming but also highly laborious [9]. Contrary to the above system, end-to-end model is proposed recently because of its simplicity of modeling process, and also the recognition accuracy is gradually approaching the hybrid system [10–12]. CTC is a objective function introduced by Graves as a means to simplify this process [13, 14], which infers alignments in speech label automatically leading to an end-to-end system. This has generated promising results that can discovery in Deep Speech [15, 16] and EESEN [10].

We propose the MCNN model and construct the MCNN-CTC acoustic model in combination with the CTC objective function, which obtains a significant recognition results. Based on the CTC loss function, this paper studies the speech recognition of small and medium datasets in detail. The merits of the MCNN-CTC include: (a) The above acoustic model can extract more useful features, both in time dimension and frequency axis; (b) MCNN has wider network structure, which can extract sufficient features of speech, and has stronger nonlinear capability; (c) Thanks to the CTC loss, MCNN-CTC can take an end-to-end training manner [17].

The rest of this paper is organized as follows. Section 2 describes the network architecture of MCNN-CTC. A concise introduction to CTC objective function and decoding algorithm are given in Sect. 3. We represent the experimental results in Sect. 4 and conclude our future work in Sect. 5.

2   Multipath Convolutional Neural Networks

As we can see clearly from Fig. 1, MCNN is an augmentation of the CNN's width, and has the ability to extract additional detailed features from speech in terms of width as compared to the basic extraction of high-dimensional speech features in term of depth. Therefore, MCNN is able to increase the performance of the recognition.

The MCNN's structure is shown in Fig. 1. The full structure of MCNN comprises of a total of three sub-networks, extracting features of speech and concatenating them. The calculation formulas are shown in Eq. (1)–(3):

$$h^{(l)} = \sigma\left(W^{(l)} * h^{(l-1)} + b^{(l)}\right) \tag{1}$$

In formula (1), where $h^{(l-1)}$ and $h^{(l)}$ represent two adjacent feature layers, * represents convolution calculation, and $W^{(l)}$ and $b^{(l)}$ represent weights and bias matrices obtained from network training, respectively; $W^{(l)}$ is convoluted with $h^{(l-1)}$, and $\sigma(\bullet)$ represents the activation function. In formula (2), t_{nl}^{out} represents the output value of the

l'th neuron in the n'th feature map; t_{nq}^{in} represents the input value of the q'th neuron in the n'th feature map; $f_{pool}(\bullet)$ is the pooling function.

$$t_{nl}^{out} = f_{pool}\left(t_{nq}^{in}, t_{n(q+1)}^{in}\right) \tag{2}$$

$$H^l = Concat\left(h_i^l, h_j^l, h_k^l\right) \tag{3}$$

In formula (3), where h_i^l, h_j^l, h_k^l represent the i, j, and k feature maps of three different branches, respectively, and the $Concat(\bullet)$ function represents the spliced feature map to obtain the total feature map H^l of the current layer.

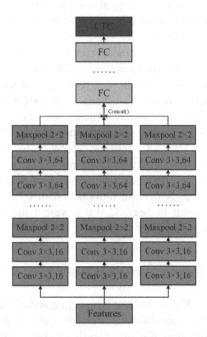

Fig. 1. The structure of multipath convolutional neural network

3 Connectionist Temporal Classification

Connectionist Temporal Classification (CTC) [12, 13] can basically be defined as a target function that maximizes the possibilities of any output sequence [18], which enables this by employing a softmax output layer and summing over all likely input sequences efficiently. It characterizes a separate output circulation $P(k|t)$ throughout every progression t in the input succession and an extra "blank" symbol which is the representation for non-output. The network makes decision on whether to remove any label at each step or not. The probability of removing or emitting the blank or label given T as length, x as input sequence and y_t as output vectors, is given as follow with k and t as index and time respectively:

$$P(k \mid t, x) = \frac{\exp\left(y_t^k\right)}{\sum_{k'}\left(y_t^{k'}\right)} \qquad (4)$$

y_t^k is component k of y_t. Then, π is a length T representing blank indices as well as label indices for a CTC path. $P(\pi|x)$ is the probability representing the emission probabilities' product present at each time interval:

$$p(\pi \mid x) = \prod_{t=1}^{T} p(\pi_t \mid t, x) \qquad (5)$$

There are tons of paths and ways of separating labels using blanks for any given transcription sequence. In order to map all paths to the given transcription, one can apply methods such as a many-to-one map ψ, which can be outlined as a means that removes first the repeated labels. Then, y which is the output interpretation can be determined by including the probabilities of all the paths mapped onto it by ψ:

$$P(y \mid x) = \sum_{\pi \in \psi^{-1}(y)} P(\pi \mid x) \qquad (6)$$

$$\left\{ \begin{array}{l} \psi(a, b, c, -, -) \\ \psi(a, b, -, -, c) \\ \psi(a, b, b, -, c) \\ \cdots \\ \psi(a, -, b, b, c) \end{array} \right\} = (a, b, c) \qquad (7)$$

The "crumbling together" as seen throughout different paths apparently in the similar translation allows the utilization of unsegmented information by CTC. This is as a result of the removal of all requirements needed to know the location in which the input sequence occurs. When given a certain transcription y^*, CTC objective function can be minimized by training the network:

$$CTC(x) = -logP(y^* \mid x) \qquad (8)$$

As a means to generate predictions, the best path decoding algorithm is applied from to a trained model using CTC which in turns generates predictions. The highest probability latent sequence are obtained by removing the most likely at each interval since the model assumes that there is independence between the latent symbols given a frame-wise case in the network. By applying $\sigma(\cdot)$ to the prediction of latent sequence, the predicted sequence can be identified as follows:

$$L \approx \sigma(\pi^*) \tag{9}$$

In this case, π^* becomes the most probable concatenation formalized using $\pi^* = Argmax_\pi P(\pi|x)$. In this situation you have to consider the outcome as it is not really the highest probable output arrangement. This sequence requires search procedures that are approximate such as beam search, and the search for this sequence is not tractable.

4 Experiments

This section focuses on the proposed model, where we evaluate it based on the phonetic recognition in relation to the Thchs30 and ST-CMDS datasets. Figure 1 shows MCNN-CTC architecture.

4.1 Data and Experimental Equipment

In order to verify the superiority of the proposed model, we test on two standard Chinese Mandarin speech datasets, Thchs30 and ST-CMDS. For the sake of ensuring the reliability of the experimental results, we have adopted different methods for the two datasets. In the Thchs30 dataset, the number of training set, validation set and test set are 10000, 893 and 2495 sentences respectively. However, in the ST-CMDS dataset, since the original corpus did not divide the dataset, we referred to the division method of Thchs30 dataset and randomly selected 100000 sentences as the training set, 600 sentences as the validation set, and the remaining 2000 sentences as the test set. For the two previous datasets, there are no overlapping between the corpus. GTX-1080Ti graphics card is used for training to ensure the smooth operation of the experiment.

4.2 Modeling Unit and Feature Extraction

The speech recognition of Chinese speech uses the traditional method of modelling which comprises of characters, state, phoneme, and a few phonetic methods of modeling [19]. As a means of making up for the lack of phonetic modeling research, this paper utilizes experiments with phonetic as the only method of modeling. Two major advantages of phonetic modelling are: (a) With the Chinese dictionary having about 200 phonemes, the phonetics are about 1400; (b) Direct modelling leads to inaccurate classification of networks due to many parameter as words in the dictionary as about 16,000 [20, 21].

We use two different data preprocessing methods for two different datasets. For the Thchs30 dataset and the ST-CMDS dataset, we use a frame length of 25 ms and a frame shift of 10 ms to frame the speech signal. However, it is worth noting that for the Thchs30 dataset, we extract the 200-dimensional spectrogram as the speech feature. Nevertheless, in the ST-CMDS dataset, 120-dimensional FBank are applied to the speech feature with splicing one frame before and after, and the total feature dimension is 360 dimension.

4.3 Training and Evaluation

In order to fully advance the model, we apply Adam [22] with learning rate at 1e−2 in training stage. The stochastic gradient descent is used for fine-tuning and has a learning rate 1e−4. During training, batch size 32 are also used. With a 0.3 probability, dropout [23] is applied to all layers with an exception for the layers of input and output. Applied at the fine-tuning stage is L2 norm with coefficient 1e−5 [24]. The pool size and kernel size are 2*2 and 3*3 respectively [25], where at the same time the predicted sequences are acquired using the best path decoding [26].

4.4 Experimental Results of Thchs30

Table 1 shows the test results that help in determining the influence as a result of the layers of the fully connected layer.

Table 1. The influence of different fully connected layers on phonetic error rate

Fully connected layer	Modeling unit	Number of parameters	Phonetic error rate
512-1422	Phonetic	1.95 M	26.65%
1024-512-1422	Phonetic	2.22 M	26.49%

Table 1: 512-1422 represents the neurons in the fully connected layer as 512 and 1422, and the DCNN model utilizes two layers from the fully connected layers with the quantity of neurons as 512-1422; MCNN makes use of the three layers of the fully connected layer with the quantity of neurons as 512-1024-1422.

The error rate is lowest when the fully connected layer has three layers as shown in Table 1, however, the model's performance does not improve a lot than that of two layers. The network parameters are also improve when the connected layers are three as compared to when they are two. Therefore, DCNN-CTC uses two layers of fully connected layers, but MCNN-CTC uses a three layers fully connected layer to further classify features.

Table 2. Experimental results of different acoustic models

Modeling structure	Modeling unit	Number of parameters	Word error rate	Phonetic error rate
GMM-HMM [27]	Phone	-	30.53%	-
DNN-HMM [27]	Phone	-	25.16%	-
BLSTM-CTC [28]	Phone	-	25.35%	-
DCNN(7)-CTC	Phonetic	1.95 M	-	26.65%
DCNN(8)-CTC	Phonetic	2.20 M	-	25.66%
DCNN(9)-CTC	Phonetic	2.25 M	-	25.42%
MCNN(6)-CTC	Phonetic	4.66 M	-	25.37%
MCNN(7)-CTC	Phonetic	4.77 M	-	**23.43%**
MCNN(8)-CTC	Phonetic	3.61 M	-	24.85%
MCNN(9)-CTC	Phonetic	3.72 M	-	25.18%

Table 2: MCNN(7) represents that we use three paths CNN and convolution layers are seven. Phone and phonetic represent the modeling units of acoustic models, and we use phonetic modeling in this paper. The training and fine-tune loss of MCNN(7)-CTC are shown in Fig. 2(a) and (b) respectively.

The error rate is highly reduced in the testing process with a 23.43% phonetic error rate as compared to the GMM-HMM, DNN-HMM and BLSTM-HMM, and the error rate reduces by a 7.10, 1.73 and 1.92% respectively. It can be clearly seen from Table 2 that depth is very import for CNN, and we can come up with it development has the following main trends: as the number of DCNN layers increases, the error rate decreases gradually.

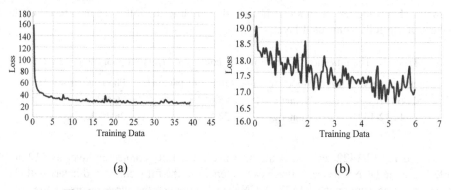

(a)   (b)

Fig. 2. Curve of Thchs30 dataset's loss function in MCNN(7)-CTC

4.5   Experimental Results of ST-CMDS

In the experiment of the ST-CMDS dataset, in order to verify the generalization performance of the models proposed in this paper, we refer to the experimental results of Thchs30 and use DCNN(7)-CTC and MCNN(7)-CTC acoustic model for the experiment. Finally, the experimental results of DCNN-CTC and MCNN-CTC for the acoustic model are shown in Table 3.

Table 3. Comparison of experimental results between DCNN-CTC and MCNN-CTC

Modeling structure	Modeling unit	Number of parameters	Error rate of validation	Error rate of test
DCNN(7)-CTC	Phonetic	7.80 M	23.86%	23.80%
MCNN(7)-CTC	Phonetic	6.74 M	22.92%	22.97%

From Table 3, Compared with the DCNN-CTC acoustic model, the MCNN-CTC has a relative error reduction of 3.94% and 3.45% in the validation set and the test set respectively. Moreover, thanks to the reduction in the number of convolution kernels, the parameter amount of the MCNN-CTC acoustic model is greatly reduced, and the parameter amount are relatively reduced by 14.10%. In view of this, the structure of

MCNN proposed in this paper is applied to acoustic model with remarkable effect and strong generalization performance.

4.6 Experimental Summary

In summary, this paper conducts a detailed study on the end-to-end acoustic model built by combining DCNN with CTC objective function, and proposes MCNN-CTC acoustic model which has a superior performance in the Chinese standard corpus Thchs30 and ST-CMDS datasets. It is worth noting that, based on the experimental results of Tables 2 and 3, we can conclude that the MCNN-CTC proposed in this paper have greatly reduced the error rate of the model compared with the traditional DCNN-CTC acoustic model. The best results for the Thchs30 and ST-CMDS datasets were reduced by 12.08% and 3.45%, respectively, with reasonable experimental parameters. Moreover, it can be vividly seen from the experimental results that the generalization performance of the acoustic model constructed by MCNN-CTC is excellent, and compared with the acoustic model constructed by the traditional GMM-HMM, the error rate is greatly reduced in a exceedingly simple manner.

5   Conclusion and Future Works

In this paper, an end-to-end system for Chinese Mandarin is established, which is based on CNN and CTC objective function. We deeply analyze the influence of different convolution layers, pooling layers and fully connected layers on DCNN-CTC. Based on the above acoustic model, we propose MCNN-CTC, which is combined MCNN with CTC objective function. We can also find that data is very significant and with the increase of data, MCNN-CTC perform much better than DCNN-CTC or hybrid system. Further, as shown by the promising results from Thchs30 and ST-CMDS, the generalization performance of MCNN-CTC is strong.

In the future, an enormous amount of research will be done on MCNN-CTC with the purpose of building a better acoustic model. In the decoding phase, we will incorporate Language Model to further reduce the error rate.

Acknowledgements. This work reported here was supported by the National Natural Science Foundation of China (Grant No. 51375209), 111 Project (Grant No. B18027), the Six Talent Peaks Project in Jiangsu Province (Grant No. ZBZZ-012), the Research and the Innovation Project for College Graduates of Jiangsu Province (Grant No. SJCX18-0630 and KYCX18-1846). Finally, the authors would like to thanks for the support of Thchs30 and ST-CMDS datasets.

References

1. Lecun, Y., Bengio, Y.: Convolutional networks for images, speech, and time series. In: The Handbook of Brain Theory and Neural Networks. MIT Press, USA (1995)
2. Abdel, H.O., Mohamed, A.R., Jiang, H.: Convolutional neural networks for speech recognition. IEEE/ACM Trans. Audio Speech Lang. Process. **22**(10), 1533–1545 (2014)

3. Mohamed, A., Dahl, G.E., Hinton, G.E.: Acoustic modeling using deep belief networks. IEEE Trans. Audio Speech Lang. Process. **20**(1), 14–22 (2012)
4. Hinton, G.E., Deng, L., Yu, D.: Deep neural networks for acoustic modeling in speech recognition: the shared views of four research groups. IEEE Signal Process. Mag. **29**(6), 82–97 (2012)
5. Abdel, H.O., Mohamed, A.R., Jiang, H.: Applying convolutional neural networks concepts to hybrid NN-HMM model for speech recognition. In: International Conference on Acoustics, Speech and Signal Processing, pp. 4277–4280. IEEE, Kyoto, May 2012
6. Sainath, T.N., Mohamed, A.R., Kingsbury, B.: Deep convolutional neural networks for LVCSR. In: International Conference on Acoustics, Speech and Signal Processing, pp. 8614–8618. IEEE, Vancouver, May 2013
7. Zhang, Y., Pezeshki, M., Brakel, P.: Towards end-to-end speech recognition with deep convolutional neural networks. arXiv preprint arXiv:1701.02720, January 2017
8. Qian, Y.M., Woodland, P.C.: Very deep convolutional neural networks for robust speech recognition. In: Spoken Language Technology Workshop, pp. 481–488. IEEE, Berkeley, June 2017
9. Bahdanau, D., Chorowski, J., Serdyuk, D.: End-to-End attention-based large vocabulary speech recognition. In: International Conference on Acoustics, Speech and Signal Processing, pp. 4945–4949. IEEE, Shanghai, March 2016
10. Miao, Y.J., Gowayyed, M., Metze, F.: EESEN: end-to-end speech recognition using deep RNN models and WFST-based decoding. arXiv preprint arXiv:1507.08240, October 2015
11. Zhang, H., Bao, F., Gao, G.: Mongolian speech recognition based on deep neural networks. In: Sun, M., Liu, Z., Zhang, M., Liu, Y. (eds.) CCL 2015. LNCS (LNAI), vol. 9427, pp. 180–188. Springer, Cham (2015). https://doi.org/10.1007/978-3-319-25816-4_15
12. Tan, T., Qian, Y.M., Hu, H.: Adaptive very deep convolutional residual network for noise robust speech recognition. IEEE/ACM Trans. Audio Speech Lang. Process. **26**(8), 1393–1405 (2018)
13. Graves, A., Santiago, F., Gomez, F.: Connectionist temporal classification: labelling unsegmented sequence data with recurrent neural networks. In: International Conference on Machine Learning, pp. 369–376. IEEE, Pittsburgh, June 2006
14. Graves, A., Mohamed, A., Hinton, G.E.: Speech recognition with deep recurrent neural networks. In: International Conference on Acoustics, Speech and Signal Processing, pp. 6645–6649. IEEE, Hong Kong, April 2003
15. Hannun, A., Case, C., Casper, J.: Deep speech: scaling up end-to-end speech recognition. arXiv preprint arXiv:1412.5567 (2014)
16. Amodei, D., Anubhai, R., Battenberg, F.: Deep speech 2: end-to-end speech recognition in English and Mandarin. arXiv preprint arXiv:1512.02595 (2015)
17. Wang, Y., Deng, X., Pu, S.: Residual convolutional CTC networks for automatic speech recognition. arXiv preprint arXiv:1702.07793, February 2017
18. Li, J., Zhang, H., Cai, X.Y.: Towards end-to-end speech recognition for Chinese Mandarin using long short-term memory recurrent neural networks. In: Interspeech 2015, pp. 3615–3619. IEEE, Berlin, September 2015
19. Zhou, S.Y., Dong, L.H., Xu, S., Xu, B.: Syllable-based sequence-to-sequence speech recognition with the transformer in Mandarin Chinese. arXiv preprint arXiv:1804.10752, June 2018
20. Zou, W., Jiang, D.W., Zhao, S.J., Li, X.G.: A comparable study of modeling units for end-to-end Mandarin speech recognition. arXiv preprint arXiv:1805.03832, May 2018
21. Dong, L.H., Xu, S., Xu, B.: Speech-transformer: a no-recurrence sequence-to-sequence model for speech recognition. In: International Conference on Acoustics, Speech and Signal Processing, pp. 4437–4441. IEEE, Calgary, April 2018

22. Kingma, D., Ba, J.: Adam: a method for stochastic optimization. arXiv preprint arXiv:1412. 6980, July 2015
23. Srivastava, N., Hinton, G.E., Krizhevsky, A.: Dropout: a simple way to prevent neural networks from overfitting. J. Mach. Learn. Res. **15**(1), 1929–1958 (2014)
24. Zhou, Z.H.: Machine Learning. Tsinghua University Press, Beijing (2016)
25. Simonyan, K., Andrew, Z.: Very deep convolutional networks for large-scale image recognition. arXiv preprint arXiv:1409.1556 (2015)
26. Awni, Y.H., Andrew, L.M., Daniel, J.: First-pass large vocabulary continuous speech recognition using bi-directional recurrent DNNs. arXiv preprint arXiv:1408.2873, December 2014
27. Wang, D., Zhang, X.: THCHS-30: a free chinese speech corpus. arXiv preprint arXiv:1512. 01882, December 2015
28. Zhang, L.M., Wang, Y.Z., Zhang, B.Q.: Chinese Mandarin recognition and improvement based on CTC criterion. Comput. Eng. (2019)

Robot Intelligent Trajectory Planning Based on PCM Guided Reinforcement Learning

Xiang Teng[1], Jian Fu[1(✉)], Cong Li[1], and ZhaoJie Ju[2]

[1] School of Automation, Wuhan University of Technology, Wuhan 430070, China
fujian@whut.edu.cn
[2] School of Computing, University of Portsmouth,
Portsmouth, London PO1 3HE, UK

Abstract. Reinforcement Learning (RL) was successfully applied in multi-degree-of-freedoms robot to acquire motor skills, however, it hardly ever consider each joints' relationship, or just think about the linear relationship between them. In order to find the nonlinear relationship between each degrees of freedom (DOFs), we propose a Pseudo Covariance Matrix (PCM) to guide reinforcement learning for motor skill acquisition. Specifically it combined Path Integral Policy Improvement (PI^2) with Kernel Canonical Correlation Analysis (KCCA), where KCCA is used to obtain the PCM in high dimensional space and record it as the heuristic information to search an optimal/sub-optimal strategy. The experiments based on robots (SCARA and UR5) demonstrate the new method is feasible and effective.

Keywords: Trajectory planning · Learning from demonstration ·
Kernel Canonical Correlation Analysis ·
Path Integral Policy Improvement · Pseudo Covariance Matrix

1 Introduction

Reinforcement Learning combined with Demonstration Learning was successfully used in robot to acquire new motor skills. It includes three stages: expression stage, imitation stage and optimization stage, above them the optimization stage is the most important stage to obtain the motor skills, which can realize a reinforcement learning from demonstrate trajectory. The classic methods during this stage include Policy Learning by Weighting Exploration with the Returns (PoWER) (Kober and Peters 2011), Relative Entropy Policy Search (REPS) (Daniel et al. 2016), Covariance Matrix Adaptation Evolutionary Strategy (CMA-ES) (Gregory et al. 2015) and PI^2 (Theodorou et al. 2010). These

X. Teng—The author acknowledges the National Natural Science Foundation of China (61773299, 515754112), Excellent Dissertation Cultivation Funds of Wuhan University of Technology (2017-YS-066).

H. Yu et al. (Eds.): ICIRA 2019, LNAI 11745, pp. 342–355, 2019.
https://doi.org/10.1007/978-3-030-27529-7_30

methods all update parameters by decreasing the cost function, but PI^2 is the most efficient method.

PI^2 is an intelligent algorithm to avoid the local optimal problem. However its searching strategy is random. Freek Stulp and Olivier Sigaud proposed an algorithm named Path Integral Policy Improvement with Covariance Matrix Adaptation (PI^2-CMA) (Stulp and Sigaud 2012). It deduces the implicit linear relation among parameters in parameter space based on covariance. In this paper, we coupled each joints, and consider the nonlinear relation of parameters not only in its own joint space.

Based on previous research, we use KCCA to get a PCM which can guide the searching strategy. It can infer the nonlinear model among each joints based on experience as the heuristic information, and it can search the optimal/suboptimal strategy for the new task, we called this method as Path Integral Policy Improvement with Kernel Canonical Correlation (PI^2-KCCA).

2   Demonstration and Reinforcement Learning Based on DMPs-PI^2

Dynamical movement primitives (DMPs) is a parametric kinematics model based on Spring-Damping system, which mainly includes conversion system, model system and forcing component (Ijspeert et al. 2013). The equation shows in (1). DMPs can achieve Supervised learning and RL by changing its forcing component.

$$\begin{cases} \tau \ddot{x}_t = \underbrace{\alpha_x(\beta_x(g - x_t) - \dot{x}_t)}_{\alpha_z} + \underbrace{\Psi_\theta(s_t)s_t(g - x_0)}_{\alpha_f} \\ \tau \dot{s}_t = -\alpha_s s_t \\ \Psi_\theta(s_t) = \frac{\sum_{i=1}^K \psi_i \omega_i}{\sum_{i=1}^K \psi_i} \end{cases} \quad (1)$$

where α_z represents an ideal Spring-Damping system, α_f represents the forcing component, it denotes the error between ideal acceleration and real acceleration, τ is the scaling factor of motion duration, x_t is a demonstrated trajectory of one joints, s_t is a phase variable of time which can be described as $s_t = exp(-\frac{\alpha_s t}{\tau})$, ψ_i is the ith Gaussian function, ω_i is the weight of the ith Gaussian function, g is the goal position, x_0 is the start position and $\alpha_x, \beta_x, \alpha_s$ is a positive constant.

2.1   Learning from Demonstration by LWR

In DMPs model, LWR is an effective way to learn from demonstration. It uses the distance between the query points and sample points as the coefficients of independent variables. LWR is an improved algorithm based on least square fitting, its cost function is:

$$
\begin{cases}
J(\theta) = \sum_{j=1}^{n} \sum_{i=1}^{K} \psi_i^{(j)} (y^{(j)} - h_\theta(x^{(j)}))^2 \\
\psi_i^{(j)} = \exp\left(-\dfrac{(x^{(j)} - c_i)^2}{2\sigma_i^2}\right)
\end{cases}
\tag{2}
$$

Here $y^{(j)}$ denotes the jth sample point, $h_\theta(x^{(j)})$ denotes the jth query point, c_i represents the ith center of clustering, σ_i denotes the width of $i^{(th)}$ cluster. In order to let the $J(\theta)$ approaches zero, (2) can be converted into (3):

$$
y = \frac{\sum_{i=1}^{K} \psi_i \omega_i}{\sum_{i=1}^{K} \psi_i} x
\tag{3}
$$

Obviously, we can get the $\omega = \{\omega_1, \omega_2, \ldots, \omega_K\}$ from (3). When the parameter of model is confirmed, α_f can be calculated by (1), and then it is easily to get the trajectory by α_z and α_f.

2.2   Reinforcement Learning by PI^2

PI^2 uses the Monte Carlo method to spontaneously search the solution which can minimize the cost function in the parameter space (Liu et al. 2017). It avoid the curse of dimensionality by its updating strategy, and the estimate of gradient by using probability weighted average. The main principle of PI^2 is the first principle of random optimal control based on Hamilton-Jacobi-Bellman (HJB) equation (Lions 1983). In order to get the value function and the optimal control strategy, it convert the target cost function into the path integral by using Feynman-Cutts theorem.

In each step of iteration, we produce 10 trajectories with different cost by add random noise ε on the parameter ω. The cost function of kth trajectory is:

$$
\begin{aligned}
S(\tau_{i,k}) = \phi_{t_N,k} + \sum_{j=i}^{N-1} q_{t_j} dt + \tfrac{1}{2} \times \\
\sum_{j=i}^{N-1} \left(\omega + M_{t_j,k}\varepsilon_{t_j,k}\right)^T R \left(\omega + M_{t_j,k}\varepsilon_{t_j,k}\right)
\end{aligned}
\tag{4}
$$

Where Φ_{t_N} represents the end cost at time t_N, R represents the weight control matrix of square cost function, $M_{t_j,k}$ is the projection matrix of the control matrix on the subspace, and it satisfies the equation: $\lambda R^{-1} = \Sigma_\varepsilon$, here Σ_ε is the variance of Gaussian noise, $\varepsilon_{t_j,k}$ is the noise of kth trajectory added on ω in j^{th} time index. q_{t_j} denotes the cost of state in the control system, which is represented by the square of the acceleration, and on the other hand, it can also represent the consumed energy in the system. The probability of the trajectory at time t_i is:

$$
P(\tau_i) = \frac{e^{-\frac{1}{\lambda} S(\tau_{t_i})}}{\int e^{-\frac{1}{\lambda} S(\tau_{t_i})} d\tau_i}
\tag{5}
$$

In (5), the probability is represented by the softmax function, it denotes the discrete probability of each trajectory at time t_i, so the probability is inversely proportional to the cost. λ is used to control sensitivity of the cost.

$$\delta\omega_{t_i} = \sum_{k=1}^{K} [P(\tau_{i,k}) M_{t_i,k} \varepsilon_{t_i,k}] \tag{6}$$

Equation (6) is be used to update the ε at time t_i. The main idea is to compute the average of weighted noise. The cost is decreasing and converging, because the probability is in inverse ratio to the cost.

3 Optimize PI² by Heuristic Information

3.1 Introduction of PCM

According to (5) and (6), the probability of noise added on each joints is equal. The perturbation ϵ depends on its own joint, so the covariance matrix of ϵ can be described as:

$$\Sigma_\epsilon = \begin{bmatrix} \sigma_1^2 & & \\ & \sigma_2^2 & \boldsymbol{0} \\ & & \ddots \\ \boldsymbol{0} & & \sigma_M^2 \end{bmatrix} \tag{7}$$

Here, M denotes the number of DOFs, $\Sigma_\epsilon \in \mathbb{R}^{M \times M}$ is a symmetric matrix whose $\sigma_1^2 = \cdots = \sigma_M^2 = \sigma^2$.

The latest study in cognitive science suggests that the human brain is an organ for statistical analysis and inference. It continually generates hypotheses, and then corrects it based on the sensor. As similar in robot, there is an unknown mode called Heuristic Information between its joints when human given robot a new motor skill. So it would be effective for robot to uses this information to accelerate the learning speed.

Here we consider the nonlinear relationship between each joints as the Heuristic Information. Different from the usual covariance matrix, using kernel method to map ϵ to $\Phi(\epsilon)$ and then (7) converted to (8):

$$\Sigma_{\Phi(\tilde{\epsilon})} = \begin{bmatrix} \Gamma(\tilde{\epsilon}_1, \tilde{\epsilon}_1) & \Gamma(\tilde{\epsilon}_1, \tilde{\epsilon}_2) & \cdots & \Gamma(\tilde{\epsilon}_1, \tilde{\epsilon}_M) \\ \Gamma(\tilde{\epsilon}_2, \tilde{\epsilon}_1) & \Gamma(\tilde{\epsilon}_2, \tilde{\epsilon}_2) & & \\ \vdots & & \ddots & * \\ \Gamma(\tilde{\epsilon}_M, \tilde{\epsilon}_1) & * & & \Gamma(\tilde{\epsilon}_M, \tilde{\epsilon}_M) \end{bmatrix} \tag{8}$$

Where $\Gamma(\tilde{\epsilon}_i, \tilde{\epsilon}_j) = cov(\Phi(\tilde{\epsilon}_i), \Phi(\tilde{\epsilon}_j))$ is the covariance of $\tilde{\epsilon}_i$ and $\tilde{\epsilon}_j$ on a higher dimensional space. It can represent the heuristic information.

However $\Sigma_{\Phi(\tilde{\epsilon})}$ just express the covariance matrix in the same space $\Phi(\cdot)$. Obviously it is not the best way to do the correlation analysis. We can find a local coordinate system to make a proper projection, and then the correlation analysis would be efficient. In this paper using Generalized Rayleigh Quotient to find nonlinear correlation between $\tilde{\epsilon}_i$ and $\tilde{\epsilon}_j$. In (8), if $i \neq j$, let $\Theta(\tilde{\epsilon}_i, \tilde{\epsilon}_j) = cov(Proj\Phi(\tilde{\epsilon}_i), Proj\Phi(\tilde{\epsilon}_j))$ as the heuristic information. The perturbation will be guided by covariance $\Theta(\tilde{\epsilon}_i, \tilde{\epsilon}_j)$. By using this method, (8) can change to (9), which can be called as pseudo covariance matrix(PCM). The process is shown in Fig. 1.

$$\Sigma^+_{\Phi(\tilde{\epsilon})} = \begin{bmatrix} \Gamma(\tilde{\epsilon}_1, \tilde{\epsilon}_1) & \Theta(\tilde{\epsilon}_1, \tilde{\epsilon}_2) & \cdots & \Theta(\tilde{\epsilon}_1, \tilde{\epsilon}_M) \\ \Theta(\tilde{\epsilon}_2, \tilde{\epsilon}_1) & \Gamma(\tilde{\epsilon}_2, \tilde{\epsilon}_2) & & \\ \vdots & & \ddots & * \\ \Theta(\tilde{\epsilon}_M, \tilde{\epsilon}_1) & * & & \Gamma(\tilde{\epsilon}_M, \tilde{\epsilon}_M) \end{bmatrix} \qquad (9)$$

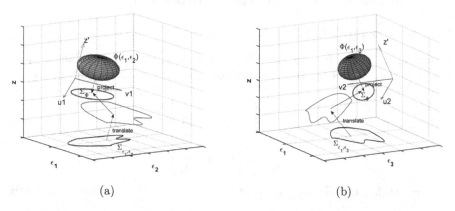

(a)   (b)

Fig. 1. In order to show how it works to change the perturbation's searching strategy, we simply demonstrate the process in ϵ_1, ϵ_2 and ϵ_3. In (a), $\Phi(\epsilon_1, \epsilon_2)$ was project to $[u_1, v_1]$, however, in (b) $\Phi(\epsilon_1, \epsilon_3)$ was project to $[u_2, v_2]$. As a result, we can find the linear relationship under the projection of high dimensional space.

3.2   Get the PCM by KCCA

KCCA is an improved algorithm based on Canonical Correlation Analysis (Cai and Huang 2017), which can get the nonlinear relationship between two sets of data and generate a PCM. In this paper, we using PCM as the heuristic information. After each iteration of PI^2, we set the cost decreasing rate as $Trate$. If $Trate$ is greater than its maximum $Tratemax$, we regard this step of searching strategy is useful and record it as PCM by KCCA. Here considering two joints' perturbation $\tilde{\epsilon}_i = \{\epsilon_i^{(1)}, \epsilon_i^{(2)}, \cdots, \epsilon_i^{(n)}\}$ and $\tilde{\epsilon}_j = \{\epsilon_j^{(1)}, \epsilon_j^{(2)}, \cdots, \epsilon_j^{(n)}\}$, where $\tilde{\epsilon}_i, \tilde{\epsilon}_j \in \mathbb{R}^{k \times n}$, n is the number of time samples, and k is the number of ω in (3), here we set k equals to 10. In order to get the PCM, gauss kernel method is an effective way to map data to high-dimensional feature space (Cai et al. 2016).

After mapping, CCA is a useful algorithm to find the linear relationship between $\Phi(\tilde{\epsilon}_i)$ and $\Phi(\tilde{\epsilon}_j)$. The main principle of CCA is to find two projection vectors $\omega_i \in \mathbb{R}^{N \times 1}$ and $\omega_j \in \mathbb{R}^{N \times 1}$ to maximize the correlation coefficient of u_i and u_j, where $u_i = \omega_i^T \Phi(\tilde{\epsilon}_i)$ and $u_j = \omega_j^T \Phi(\tilde{\epsilon}_j)$. Since the mean of $\Phi(\tilde{\epsilon}_i)$ and $\Phi(\tilde{\epsilon}_j)$ are equal to 0, the mean of u_i and u_j are also equal to 0. Then we can obtain the variance of u_i and u_j as below:

$$
\begin{aligned}
var(u_i) &= \frac{1}{m-1} \omega_i^T \Phi(\tilde{\epsilon}_i) \Phi^T(\tilde{\epsilon}_i) \omega_i \\
var(u_j) &= \frac{1}{m-1} \omega_j^T \Phi(\tilde{\epsilon}_j) \Phi^T(\tilde{\epsilon}_j) \omega_j
\end{aligned}
\tag{10}
$$

The covariance of u_i and u_j is shown as below:

$$
cov(u_i, u_j) = \frac{1}{m-1} \omega_i^T \Phi(\tilde{\epsilon}_i) \Phi^T(\tilde{\epsilon}_j) \omega_j
\tag{11}
$$

Melzer et al. (2003) propose that the projection vectors ω_i and ω_j should be in the space which is generated by $\Phi(\tilde{\epsilon}_i)$ and $\Phi(\tilde{\epsilon}_j)$. So there is $\omega_i = \Phi(\tilde{\epsilon}_i)\alpha$ and $\omega_j = \Phi(\tilde{\epsilon}_j)\beta$ where $\alpha, \beta \in \mathbb{R}^{n \times 1}$. In (9) $\Theta(\tilde{\epsilon}_i, \tilde{\epsilon}_j)$ can be described as follow:

$$
\rho = \frac{\alpha^T K_{\tilde{\epsilon}_i} K_{\tilde{\epsilon}_j} \beta}{\sqrt{\alpha^T K_{\tilde{\epsilon}_i} K_{\tilde{\epsilon}_i} \alpha} \sqrt{\beta^T K_{\tilde{\epsilon}_j} K_{\tilde{\epsilon}_j} \beta}}
\tag{12}
$$

Here we use kernel method to given $K_{\tilde{\epsilon}_i} = \Phi^T(\tilde{\epsilon}_i)\Phi(\tilde{\epsilon}_i)$ and $K_{\tilde{\epsilon}_j} = \Phi^T(\tilde{\epsilon}_j)\Phi(\tilde{\epsilon}_j)$, $K_{\tilde{\epsilon}_i}, K_{\tilde{\epsilon}_j} \in \mathbb{R}^{n \times n}$ are the Gauss Radial Basis Function (Lai and Fyfe 2000).

From (12), you can obviously find that the value of ρ dose not change with α and β. So the main problem is to find the appropriate α and β to maximize $\alpha^T K_{\tilde{\epsilon}_i} K_{\tilde{\epsilon}_j} \beta$ while $\alpha^T K_{\tilde{\epsilon}_i} K_{\tilde{\epsilon}_i} \alpha = 1$ and $\beta^T K_{\tilde{\epsilon}_j} K_{\tilde{\epsilon}_j} \beta = 1$. The Lagrangian function can be constructed as below:

$$
\begin{aligned}
L = &\alpha^T K_{\tilde{\epsilon}_i} K_{\tilde{\epsilon}_j} \beta - \lambda_1(\alpha^T K_{\tilde{\epsilon}_i} K_{\tilde{\epsilon}_i} \alpha - 1) - \\
&\lambda_2(\beta^T K_{\tilde{\epsilon}_j} K_{\tilde{\epsilon}_j} \beta - 1)
\end{aligned}
\tag{13}
$$

The derivative of α and β in (13) is:

$$
\lambda = \alpha^T K_{\tilde{\epsilon}_i} K_{\tilde{\epsilon}_j} \beta
$$

$$
R \times \begin{bmatrix} \alpha \\ \beta \end{bmatrix} = \lambda D \times \begin{bmatrix} \alpha \\ \beta \end{bmatrix}
\tag{14}
$$

where

$$
R = \begin{bmatrix} 0 & K_{\tilde{\epsilon}_i} K_{\tilde{\epsilon}_j} \\ K_{\tilde{\epsilon}_j} K_{\tilde{\epsilon}_i} & 0 \end{bmatrix} \quad D = \begin{bmatrix} K_{\tilde{\epsilon}_i} K_{\tilde{\epsilon}_i} & 0 \\ 0 & K_{\tilde{\epsilon}_j} K_{\tilde{\epsilon}_j} \end{bmatrix}
$$

In order to maximize ρ in (12), $[\alpha^T, \beta^T]^T$ should be the eigenvector corresponding to the maximum eigenvalue of the matrix $D^{-1}R$. Above all, the heuristic information PCM can be obtained.

3.3   Predict the Perturbation by Heuristic Information

During the PI^2 updating, if $Trate$ is lower than its minimum $Tratemin$. We will user the latest PCM to guide the searching strategy. The first joint's perturbation $\tilde{\epsilon}_1$ is generated randomly as usual, but the other joints' perturbations will calculate by using PCM and $\{(\alpha_{1,2}^T, \beta_{1,2}^T), \cdots, (\alpha_{1,M}^T, \beta_{1,M}^T)\}$ according to the following method.

When all of the sample points are different, $K_{\tilde{\epsilon}_i}$ can be regarded as a full rank matrix (Smola 2008). From (14), there is:

$$K_{\tilde{\epsilon}_i} K_{\tilde{\epsilon}_j} \beta = \lambda K_{\tilde{\epsilon}_i} K_{\tilde{\epsilon}_i} \alpha \tag{15}$$

Because $K_{\tilde{\epsilon}_i}$ is an invertible matrix, we can get an equation about $K_{\tilde{\epsilon}_i}$ and $K_{\tilde{\epsilon}_j}$:

$$K_{\tilde{\epsilon}_j} \beta = \lambda K_{\tilde{\epsilon}_i} \alpha \tag{16}$$

According to the first joints' perturbation $\tilde{\epsilon}_1$, we can get its kernel space mapping $K_{\tilde{\epsilon}_1}$, and calculate $K_{\tilde{\epsilon}_2}$ by $(\alpha_{1,2}^T, \beta_{1,2}^T)$ and $\Theta(\tilde{\epsilon}_1, \tilde{\epsilon}_2)$ in PCM, and then deduce the $\tilde{\epsilon}_2$ by $K_{\tilde{\epsilon}_2}$.

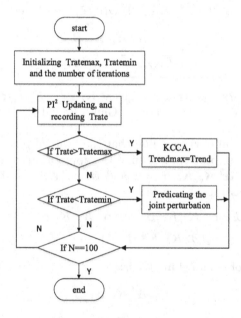

Fig. 2. In the flow chart of PI^2-KCCA, $Trate$ represent the drop rate of cost. $Tratemax$ represents the upper limit of $Trate$, and $Tratemin$ represents the lower limit of $Trate$.

The whole flow chart is shown in Fig. 2. Here $Tratemax$ is setting to 0.4, and $Tratemin$ is setting to 0.2. When $Tratemin <= Trate <= Tratemax$, the perturbations on each joints are randomly generated. During this flow, it generates hypotheses based on maximum likelihood estimation, and modifies it according to the reward.

4   Experiments on SCARA and UR5

4.1   Using SCARA via One Point

In this part, we employ SCARA robot arm to show how PI^2-KCCA works in a new task. SCARA has three revolute joints q_1, q_2, q_3 and one prismatic joint q_4. This experiment can be described as five steps:

1. Set point $(20, 0, 0)^T$cm as the start point of the end-effector. In joint space, the start joint vector is $(0, 0, 0)^T$rad.
2. Set point $(4.5, 16, 0)^T$cm as the end point of the end-effector. In joint space, the end joint vector is $(0.7068, 1.1796, 0)^T$rad.
3. Give SCARA a demonstrated trajectory.
4. Acquire SCARA a via-point $(16.4, 11.2, 0)^T$cm at 0.3 min by using PI^2-CMA and PI^2-KCCA.
5. Compare the result of two method.

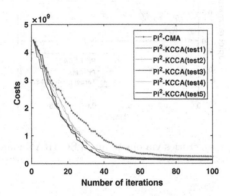

Fig. 3. Comparing the cost trend after one experiment by PI^2-CMA and five experiments by PI^2-KCCA.

In Fig. 3, after 100 times of iteration, we find that PI^2-KCCA's drop speed is faster than PI^2-CMA. Moreover, the terminal cost of PI^2-KCCA is lower. The specific data is shown in Table 1.

Figure 4 describes joints' trajectories in SCARA's joint space. Here q_3 always equals to zero, because q_3 is a revolute joints and it does not affect the position of end-effector. It is easily to find that the green line is more accurate than the black dotted line to pass the specific point in time.

In order to show the performance of PI^2-KCCA in cartesian space, we use robotics toolbox in matlab to simulate the experiment. The result shows in Fig. 5. The green line represents the joint trajectory under PI^2-KCCA, and the black dotted line represents the joint trajectory under PI^2-CMA. The end-effector of SCARA should pass though red mark at 0.3 min, the black mark denotes the real position at 0.3 min under PI^2-CMA, and the green mark represents the real position at 0.3 min under PI^2-KCCA. It is obviously to find that the trajectory under PI^2-KCCA is more closer to the red mark at 0.3 min.

Table 1. Terminal cost comparison of SCARA via one point between PI²-CMA and PI²-KCCA

Experiment	Final cost
PI²-CMA	2.561e+08
PI²-KCCA(test1)	1.229e+08
PI²-KCCA(test2)	1.452e+08
PI²-KCCA(test3)	1.556e+08
PI²-KCCA(test4)	1.758e+08
PI²-KCCA(test5)	1.373e+08

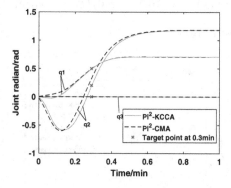

Fig. 4. Comparing the trajectories via one point in SCARA's joint space between PI²-CMA and PI²-KCCA.

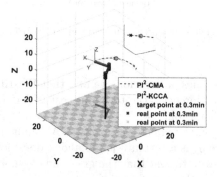

Fig. 5. Comparing the trajectories via one point in SCARA's cartesian space between PI²-CMA and PI²-KCCA.

4.2 Using SCARA via Two Points

In this part, we require SCARA to acquire a new motion skill which is more difficult than before. Two via-points $(17.464, 9.541, 0)^{\mathrm{T}}$cm and $(12.834, 13.215, 0)^{\mathrm{T}}$cm are given at 0.15 min and 0.23 min. The experiment's process is the same as above.

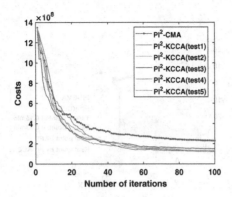

Fig. 6. Comparing the cost trend after one experiment by PI^2-CMA and five experiments by PI^2-KCCA.

Table 2. Terminal cost comparison of SCARA via two points between PI^2-CMA and PI^2-KCCA

Experiment	Final cost
PI^2-CMA	2.284e+08
PI^2-KCCA(test1)	1.207e+08
PI^2-KCCA(test2)	1.297e+08
PI^2-KCCA(test3)	1.491e+08
PI^2-KCCA(test4)	1.296e+08
PI^2-KCCA(test5)	1.269e+08

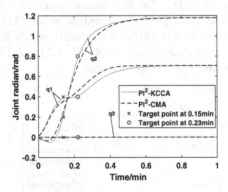

Fig. 7. Comparing the trajectories via two points in SCARA's joint space between PI^2-CMA and PI^2-KCCA.

According to Fig. 6 and Table 2, we conclude that the convergence rate in PI^2-KCCA is higher than that in PI^2-CMA, and under the learning of PI^2-KCCA, we can get a much lower terminal cost than PI^2-CMA.

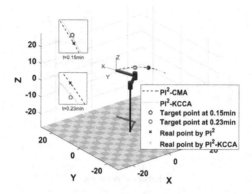

Fig. 8. Comparing the trajectories via two points in SCARA's cartesian space between PI²-CMA and PI²-KCCA. (Color figure online)

Figure 7 describes the trajectories in joint space, and Fig. 8 describes the trajectories in cartesian space which is simulated by Robotics Tool in Matlab. In Fig. 8, blue point represents the first via-point at 0.15 min, and red point represent the second via-point at 0.23 min. The subfigure in Fig. 8 shows that the SCARA in PI²-KCCA is more accurate than that in PI²-CMA.

4.3 Using UR5 via One Point

In this experiment, we use six DOFs robot UR5 to learn new motor skills. Firstly, we set a start point with $(83.88, -175.09, 601.31)^T$mm, and a terminal point with $(91.23, -630.98, -296.22)^T$mm. Secondly, we give UR5 a demonstrated trajectory from start point to terminal point. Thirdly, we choose a via-point $(-325.92, -552.71, 231.54)^T$mm randomly which stays away from the demonstrated trajectory. In the end, we apply PI²-CMA and PI²-KCCA to UR5 respectively, and compare the results of them.

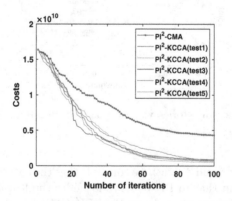

Fig. 9. Comparing the cost trend after one experiment by PI²-CMA and five experiments by PI²-KCCA.

Table 3. Terminal costs comparison of UR5 via one point between PI²-CMA and PI²-KCCA

Experiment	Final cost
PI²-CMA	4.326e+09
PI²-KCCA(test1)	7.627e+08
PI²-KCCA(test2)	5.127e+08
PI²-KCCA(test3)	8.790e+08
PI²-KCCA(test4)	7.310e+08
PI²-KCCA(test5)	6.591e+08

As shown in Fig. 9, the cost's droop rate of PI²-KCCA is higher than that of PI²-CMA. Table 3 describes the terminal costs of PI²-CMA and PI²-KCCA. We can easily find the terminal cost of PI²-KCCA is smaller than that in PI²-CMA. Therefore, the convergence rate of cost under PI²-KCCA is faster than PI²-CMA and PI²-KCCA can get a much lower terminal cost than PI²-CMA.

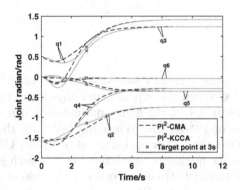

Fig. 10. Comparing the trajectories via one point in UR5's joint space between PI²-CMA and PI²-KCCA.

Figures 10 and 11 describes the trajectory in joint space and cartesian space respectively. In Fig. 10, just PI²-KCCA can reach the specific position in time in its joint space. However by using PI²-CMA, the joint trajectories can not reach the specific position at the same time. In cartesian space, the end-effector of UR5 can pass through the via-point and touch the red cap under PI²-KCCA learning, but under the learning of PI²-CMA, UR5 fails to search the via-point in its workspace.

(a) Reinforcement Learning by PI²-CMA   (b) Reinforcement Learning by PI²-KCCA

Fig. 11. Comparing the trajectories via one point in UR5's cartesian space between PI²-CMA and PI²-KCCA.

Table 4. Optimization effect comparison table

Experiment	Reduction rate (%)		Optimization (%)
	PI²-CMA	PI²-KCCA	
Experiment 1	94.2	96.9	2.7
Experiment 2	83.0	90.5	7.5
Experiment 3	73.6	96.0	22.4

5 Conclusions

According to Table 4, the average cost reduction rate of PI²-KCCA is always higher than PI²-CMA. When the experimental objects are the same, the more complex the new task target is, the higher optimization will be, because of the heuristic exploration of PI²-KCCA. When the tasks are the same, the more DOFs the objects have, the higher optimization of PI²-KCCA will be, because PI²-KCCA considers the nonlinear correlation between each joints.

Recently RL has received strong attention in the field of intelligent robots. Accelerating the iteration speed of RL is important. In this paper, we propose a novel algorithm PI²-KCCA base on PI²-CMA to find the heuristic information as a PCM during the convergence of cost. KCCA is an effective way to establish the nonlinear relationship between each joints, and we use it to recode the relationship as the heuristic information while the convergence rate is greater than the threshold, to learn a appropriate perturbation strategy, and apply this strategy to predict joints' noise when the convergence rate is going down. According to the experiments, PI²-KCCA can not only speed up the convergence rate, but improve the accuracy for new tasks.

References

Theodorou, E., Buchli, J., Schaal, S.: A generalized path integral control approach to reinforcement learning. J. Mach. Learn. Res. **11**, 3137–3181 (2010)

Ijspeert, A.J., Nakanishi, J., Hoffmann, H., Pastor, P., Schaal, S.: Dynamical movement primitives: learning attractor models for motor behaviors. Neural Comput. **25**(2), 328–373 (2013)

Cai, J., Huang, X.: Robust kernel canonical correlation analysis with applications to information retrieval. Eng. Appl. Artif. Intell. **64**, 33–42 (2017)

Cai, J., Tang, Y., Wang, J.: Kernel canonical correlation analysis via gradient descent. Neurocomputing **182**, 322–331 (2016)

Daniel, C., Neumann, G., Kroemer, O., Peters, J.: Hierarchical relative entropy policy search. J. Mach. Learn. Res. **17**, 3190–3239 (2016)

Gregory, M.D., Martin, S.V., Werner, D.H.: Improved electromagnetics optimization: the covariance matrix adaptation evolutionary strategy. IEEE Antennas Propag. Mag. **57**(3), 48–59 (2015)

Kober, J., Peters, J.: Policy search for motor primitives in robotics. Mach. Learn. **84**(1–2), 171–203 (2011)

Lai, P.L., Fyfe, C.: Kernel and nonlinear canonical correlation analysis. In: IEEE/INNS/ENNS International Joint Conference on Neural Networks (IJCNN 2000), Como, Italy (2000)

Lions, P.L.: Optimal-control of diffusion-processes and Hamilton-Jacobi-Bellman equations, 1. Commun. Part.L Differ Eqn. **8**(10), 1101–1174 (1983). The dynamic-programming principle and applications

Liu, J., Qi, Y., Meng, Z., Fu, L.: Self-learning Monte Carlo method. Phys. Rev. B **95**(4), 041101 (2017)

Melzer, T., Reiter, M., Bischof, H.: Appearance models based on Kernel canonical correlation analysis. Pattern Recognit.: J. Pattern Recognit. Soc. **36**(9), 1961–1971 (2003)

Smola, A.J.: Learning with Kernels—support vector machines. Lect. Notes Comput. Sci. **42**(4), 1–28 (2008)

Stulp, F., Sigaud, O.: Path integral policy improvement with covariance matrix adaptation. Comput. Sci. (2012)

Fast Robot Motor Skill Acquisition Based on Bayesian Inspired Policy Improvement

Jian Fu[✉], Siyuan Shen, Ce Cao, and Cong Li

School of Automation, Wuhan University of Technology, Wuhan 430070, China
fujian@whut.edu.cn
http://www.escience.cn/people/fujiane/index.html

Abstract. Learning from demonstration with the reinforcement learning (LfDRL) framework has been successfully applied to acquire the skill of robot movement. However, the optimization process of LfDRL usually converges slowly on the condition that new task is considerable different from imitation task. We in this paper proposes a ProMPs-Bayesian-PI^2 algorithms to expedite the transfer process. The main ideas is adding new heuristic information to guide optimization search other than random search from the stats of imitation learning. Specifically, we use the result of Bayesian estimation as the heuristic information to guide the PI^2 when it random search. Finally, we verify this method by UR5 and compare it with the traditional method of ProMPs-PI^2. The experimental results show that this method is feasible and effective.

Keywords: Motion planning · Path integral · Bayesian estimation · Probabilistic movement primitives

1 Introduction

Researchers in the robot have been desiring to make the robot behave like human. Learning from demonstration (LfD) (Schaarschmidt et al. 2018; Havoutis and Calinon 2018) can make robot learn the similar skills as the demonstration action. But it is impossible to learn more complex and dissimilar to demonstration task. So recently, robot learning from demonstration together with reinforcement learning (RL) has attracted significantly increased attention. By means of LfDRL, researchers can autonomously derive a robot controller from merely observing a human's own performance. Furthermore, the controller could be self-improved ro refine and expand robot motor capability obtained from demonstration to meet with task requirement depicted as a functional criterion. Those advantages indicate that LfDRL might been the promising paradigm to bring the above dream closer to reality.

Usually, LfDRL is built throughout three-phase paradigm sequentially: representation phase, imitation phase and optimization phase. A parametric policy

---

J. Fu—The author acknowledges the National Natural Science Foundation of China (61773299, 515754112).

H. Yu et al. (Eds.): ICIRA 2019, LNAI 11745, pp. 356–367, 2019.
https://doi.org/10.1007/978-3-030-27529-7_31

representation is selected on the first phase. Generally, a dynamic model with flexible adjustment sounds good, for the reason that it is easy to modulate online and exhibit robustness. DS (Khoramshahi and Billard 2019; Salehian et al. 2017) and DMPs (Pervez and Lee 2018; Yang et al. 2018) models are current popular dynamic model. DS represent motion scheduling in the form if a nonlinear autonomous dynamic system, which is time-invariance and global/local asympotic stable. Whereas, DMPs models the movement planning as superimposition of a linear dynamic system and a nonlinear term. And there is time-based model like probabilistic movement primitives (ProMPs) (Paraschos et al. 2018; Kroemer et al. 2018). During the imitation phase, the flexible adjustment of model will learn suitable parameters according to the data from demonstration. Various methods including radial basis function networks, regularized kernel least-square, locally weighted regression (Sigaud et al. 2011) and Gaussian process (Deisenroth et al. 2015; Ben Amor et al. 2014) etc. were proposed to present flexible adjustment.

On the optimization stage, the policy parameters learned from the second phase will be constantly adjusted, chosen and updated with respect to a utility function with reinforcement learning until reach the target task.

Although there are many successful achievements int the LfDRL community, many if the existing studies lay emphasis on the innovation in one phase. In our previous research results in Fu et al. (2015a, b), we have developed an effective policy representation which combines a 2nd order critical damping system and a forcing term in the form of Gaussian Mixture Regression (GMR). In previous we proposed a method named PI^2-GMR for motor skill learning, with which robot could be board applicable for various task and of good quality for given task simultaneously.

This main contribution of this paper is introduction of a method to learning complex task faster. On the basis of previous research we propose a method named Bayesian-PI^2 for the moment, which can improve the efficiency of reinforcement learning on the third stage of LfDRL. Traditional PI^2 can explore all space of parameter, so it has lower efficiency for our task scenario. The Bayesian-PI^2 can narrow the search space of parameter, and we can call this method a heuristic search.

The paper is organized as follow. Section 2 depicted ProMPs for policy representation and imitation learning. In Sect. 3, we can introduce briefly traditional PI^2. At the same time introduce the ProMPs-PI^2. Then the heuristic process of Bayesian estimation for parameter search is introduced in detail in Sect. 4. And we can discussed the method of Bayesian-PI^2 in combination with imitation learning. In Sect. 5, we present in detail the classical benchmark experiment trajectory planning via prior unknown point(s) using the theory of this article. In addition, detailed experimental settings and results are presented and analyzed. Finally, conclusions are given in Sect. 6.

2 Probabilistic Movement Primitives

In the first stage of LfDRL, we use probabilistic movement primitives as parametric policy representation. This is a method based on probability, so this method is data-drived. This section we could introduce basic concepts of ProMPs.

ProMPs represent a distribution over trajectory that are correlated spatially and temporally. For a single DOF, mark the current position of the joint with a symbol q_t. Thus, we denote $y_t = q_t$ as state of joint at time step t, and a trajectory of length T as a sequence $\boldsymbol{y}_{1:T}$. Assuming a smooth trajectory, it can be achieved by linear regression on N Gaussian basis functions, here denoted as ψ. Thus,

$$y_t = q_t = \boldsymbol{\psi}_t^T \boldsymbol{\omega} + \varepsilon_t \tag{1}$$

and,

$$p(y_t|\boldsymbol{\omega}) = \mathcal{N}(y_t|\boldsymbol{\psi}_t^T \boldsymbol{\omega}, \Sigma_t) \tag{2}$$

where ψ_t is a time dependent basis matrix and $\varepsilon_t \sim \mathcal{N}(0, \Sigma_t)$. The probability of observing the whole trajectory is then

$$p(\boldsymbol{y}_{1:T}|\boldsymbol{\omega}) = \prod_1^T \mathcal{N}(y_t|\boldsymbol{\psi}_t^T \boldsymbol{\omega}, \Sigma_t) \tag{3}$$

In order to decouple movement from time, a phase variable is introduced to replace the time in the Eq. (2). For simplicity, in this article we will assume the phase of the model os identical to the timing of the demonstration such that $z_t = t$ and $\psi_{z_t} = \psi_t$.

For probabilistic models, a large amount of data is needed to learn the parameters. So assume M trajectories are obtained via demonstrations. we can obtain a set of parameter of each trajectory denoted $\boldsymbol{\omega}_m$, and there is sign $W = \{\omega_1, \cdots, \omega_m, \cdots, \omega_M\}$. Define a learning parameter $\boldsymbol{\theta}$ to govern the distribution of $\boldsymbol{\omega}_m$ such that $\boldsymbol{\omega} \sim p(\boldsymbol{\omega}; \boldsymbol{\theta})$. A distribution of trajectory is obtained by integrating out $\boldsymbol{\omega}$,

$$p(\boldsymbol{y}_{1:T}; \boldsymbol{\theta}) = \int p(\boldsymbol{y}_{1:T}|\boldsymbol{\omega}) p(\boldsymbol{\omega}; \boldsymbol{\theta}) d\boldsymbol{\omega} \tag{4}$$

In ProMPs, the relationship between parameters is shown in the Fig. 1.

we model $p(\boldsymbol{\omega})$ as a Gaussian with mean $\boldsymbol{\mu} \in \mathbb{R}^N$ and covariance $\boldsymbol{\Sigma} \in \mathbb{R}^{N \times N}$, that is $\boldsymbol{\theta} = \{\boldsymbol{\mu}, \boldsymbol{\Sigma}\}$, computed from the training set $\boldsymbol{W}$. The fidelity with which the distribution of trajectories in Eq. (4) captures the true nature of a task clearly depends on how $\boldsymbol{\theta}$ controls the distribution of weights.

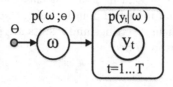

Fig. 1. Relationship between parameters of ProMPs

3   Path Integral

Although imitation learning can effectively replicate and generalize robot demonstration movement, it maybe not a optimal/suboptimal policy for the task. Furthermore, it can not autonomously fulfill the motion different from demonstration criterion. So we combine imitation learning (policy representation) with path integration (policy improvement) (Theodorou et al. 2010) through stochastic optimal control to meet the requirement. Specifically, we apply Feynman-Kac theorem to derive the state value function based on path integral, and then deduce the optimal control policy. In this way, we solve the Hamilton-Jacobian-Ballman (HJB) equation indirectly.

In Sect. 2, we use the method of ProMPs to parameterize the trajectory of robot joint. The ω in Eq. (2) is the parameter representation of trajectory. we can use parameter ω to repeat the demonstration. In this section, we will use a reinforcement learning called Policy Improvement with Path Integrals(PI^2) to make robot obtain skill of complex task like via point(s).

Multiple paths of variation τ_i can be generated by adding random perturbation to the weights(ω), and the optimal control quantity of system is the form of weighted average of the path shown as Eq. (5).

$$
\begin{aligned}
u_{t_i} &= -R^{-1} B_{s_{t_i}}^T \left(\nabla_{x_{t_i}} V_{t_i} \right) \\
&= \int P(\tau_i) u_L(\tau_i) d\tau_i
\end{aligned}
\tag{5}
$$

where $P(\tau_i)$ is a softmax function maping the cost $S(\tau_i)$ of ith trajectory to the interval [0,1] shown as Eq. (6), and there is the higher the cost, the lower the probability which can ensure that PI^2 converges to the lower cost. And $u_L(\tau_i)$ means the local control based on variation path, the form can be seen as Eq. (7).

$$
P(\tau_i) = \frac{e^{-\frac{1}{\lambda} S(\tau_{t_i})}}{\int e^{-\frac{1}{\lambda} S(\tau_{t_i})} d\tau_i}
\tag{6}
$$

$$
u_L(\tau_i) = \frac{R^{-1} B_{s_{t_i}} B_{s_{t_i}}^T}{B_{s_{t_i}}^T R^{-1} B_{s_{t_i}}} (\omega + \varepsilon_{t_i})
\tag{7}
$$

The most important part for the customized task is the cost function in applying PI^2 which limits the convergence direction of algorithm, the form shows as following:

$$
\begin{aligned}
S(\tau_i, k) = &\phi_{t_N,k} + \sum_{j=i}^{N-1} q_{t_j} dt + \\
&\frac{1}{2} \sum_{j=i}^{N-1} \left(\omega + M_{t_j,k} \varepsilon_{t_j,k} \right)^T R \left(\omega + M_{t_j,k} \varepsilon_{t_j,k} \right)
\end{aligned}
\tag{8}
$$

where $\phi_{t_N,k}$ means the terminal reward, q_{t_j} are a state-dependent variable that the acceleration squared is used in this paper, and $bmM_{t_j,k}$ is a projection matrix

---
Algorithm 1. The pseudocode of ProMPs-PI2

1: initialization parameter
2: ProMPs represent movement of joint, result denoted as ω
3: **repeat**
4:      - create K roll-outs from start state ω using stochastic parameters
5:      - using equation (6) (8) (9) (11) (12) to calculate new parameters denoted ω^{new}
6:      - update parameters, $\omega = \omega^{new}$
7:      - if rate of change of cost is less than the set value, break
8: **until** rate of change of cost is less than the set value
9: calculate the final trajectory by using ProMPs

---

that can be seen as following:

$$M_{t_j,k} = \frac{R^{-1} B_{s_{t_i}} B_{s_{t_i}}^T}{B_{s_{t_i}}^T R^{-1} B_{s_{t_i}}} \tag{9}$$

Combining the actual task, the cost of end point present,

$$\phi_{t_N} = K_1 \sum_{i=t_{N'}}^{t_N} \dot{y}^2 + K_2 \sum_{i=t_{N'}}^{t_N} (y - y_{\text{goal}})^2 \tag{10}$$

where the y and $\dot{y}$ are the position and velocity respectively. The cost consists of two part, one can ensure the velocity decay to zero in a very short time which is from $t_{N'}$ to t_N, other make sure that the joint can reach the desired position. K_1 and K_2 are constants which can be adjusted based on the demand.

In order to via point, we add the three part to cost function.

$$R_{\text{viapoint}} = K \sum_{i=1}^{N} \left(y_{i,t_j} - y_{i,t_j}^* \right)^2 \tag{11}$$

where the y_{i,t_j} and y_{i,t_j}^* are the joint current position and desire position respectively. So, we can get the goal parameter which can achieve via point task.

$$\delta\omega_{t_i} = \sum_{k=1}^{K} \left[P\left(\tau_{i,k}\right) M_{t_i,k} \varepsilon_{t_i,k} \right] \tag{12}$$

$$\omega^{new} = \omega^{old} + \frac{\sum_{i=0}^{N-1}(N-i)w_{t_i}\,\delta\omega_{t_i}}{\sum_{i=0}^{N-1} w_{t_i}(N-i)} \tag{13}$$

The way of via point by using ProMPs-PI^2 is shown as the Algorithm 1.

When using the method of ProMPs-PI^2 to make the robot get new skills, we should use Eq. (14) to generate K roll-outs that is shown the line 4 in Algorithm 1.

$$\omega_k = \omega + \varepsilon_k, k = 1 \cdots K \tag{14}$$

where $\omega \in \mathbb{R}^N$, and N is the number of basis. And, $\varepsilon_k \in \mathbb{R}^N$ is the random. ε_k^i that is the ith component obeys the Gaussian that mean is 0 and the variance is proportional to the order of magnitude of the data.

Algorithm 2. The pseudocode of ProMPs-Bayesian-PI2

1: initialization parameter
2: ProMPs represent movement of joint, result denoted as $\boldsymbol{\omega}$
3: **repeat**
4:     - use equation (15) of Bayesian to complete task, result denoted as $\boldsymbol{\omega}^+$
5:     - calculate the direction of perturbation, $\eta = sign(\boldsymbol{\omega}^+ - \boldsymbol{\omega})$
6:     - create K roll-outs from start state $\boldsymbol{\omega}$ using heuristic stochastic parameters
7:     - using equation (6) (8) (9) (11) (12) to calculate new parameters denoted $\boldsymbol{\omega}^{new}$
8:     - update parameters, $\boldsymbol{\omega} = \boldsymbol{\omega}^{new}$
9:     - if rate of change of cost is less than the set value ,break
10: **until** rate of change of cost is less than the set value
11: calculate the final trajectory by using ProMPs

4   ProMPs-Bayesian-PI^2

Random perturbation will be added to the original PI^2 in parameter optimization. In other word, original PI^2 could search the whole parameter space. So, The efficiency of using traditional PI^2 to complete task of via point is relatively lower. In this section, we introduce a method of PI^2 combining the Bayesian estimate to compete the task such that via points faster.

Similar to Sect. 3, we assume the current position of joint at time t is y_t, desired position is y_t^*. Based on ProMPs, we can represent the trajectory as $\theta = \{\boldsymbol{\mu}_\omega, \boldsymbol{\Sigma}_\omega\}$. On the basis of this assumption, we could use Eq. (15) to update the trajectory of via point.

$$
\begin{aligned}
\boldsymbol{\mu}_\omega^+ &= \boldsymbol{\mu}_\omega + \boldsymbol{K}(y_t^* - \boldsymbol{H}_t^T \boldsymbol{\mu}_\omega) \\
\boldsymbol{\Sigma}_\omega^+ &= \boldsymbol{\Sigma}_\omega - \boldsymbol{K}(\boldsymbol{H}_t^T \boldsymbol{\Sigma}_\omega) \\
\boldsymbol{K} &= \boldsymbol{\Sigma}_\omega \boldsymbol{H}_t (\boldsymbol{\Sigma}_y^* + \boldsymbol{H}_t^T \boldsymbol{\Sigma}_\omega \boldsymbol{H}_t)^{-1}
\end{aligned}
\tag{15}
$$

where $\boldsymbol{H}_t = \psi_t$, and the parameter $\boldsymbol{K}$ is called Kalman gain in the algorithm of Kalman filter.

The parameter $\boldsymbol{\theta}^+ = \{\boldsymbol{\mu}_\omega^+, \boldsymbol{\Sigma}_\omega^+\}$ generate trajectory which could via point. This method complete task of via point very fast, because it only needs to be calculated once. But this trajectory isn't smooth, especially near the time t. Too much acceleration is fatal to the joint damage of robots.

In order to make better use of the advantages of Bayesian estimate and PI^2, we can use the results of Bayesian estimate to inspire the parameter search of PI^2. Let's call this method Bayesian-PI^2. To be specific, using Bayesian estimation complete the task quickly. Then which is the result of Bayesian estimation can provide a direction for the PI2 search. It can avoid PI^2 explore in the whole parameter space. At the same time, in order to ensure the effect of PI2, we could inspire the primary weights of the related task.

Compare the pseudocode in Algorithms 1 and 2, the method proposed in this paper adds heuristic search for PI^2 by result target of Bayesian estimate as shown the line 4–6 in the Algorithm 2. The method of heuristic search generate K roll-outs shown in the Eq. (16).

$$\omega_k = \omega + \eta'^T \cdot \varepsilon_k, k = 1 \cdots K$$
$$\eta' = [1, \eta_{i:i'}, 1] \tag{16}$$

where the $\eta' \in \mathbb{R}^N$ and the N is the number of basis. Here we recombine the heuristic factory η' that the part of $\eta_{i:i'}$ is the $[\eta_i \cdots \eta_{i'}]$ and others are the scalar 1. The position of i in the η and η' is the same and the option of parameters of i and i' is related with task. Such as the task of via point in this article, we can select the position of the basis with the largest influence for via-point and its left and right five. The $\varepsilon_{i,i'}$ is the positive random and others is the random which obey Gaussian.

As shown in the Algorithm 2 and the Eq. (16), the parameter η' has been added into heuristic information when PI^2 random search by using the result of Bayesian estimation. It can improve learning speed and ability of PI^2. The use of this method is described in more detail in the next section.

5   Simulation and Experiments

In this section, we would verify the method of preceding part of the text. At the same time, we would also explain the application scenarios of the theory. In the first experiment we verified the validity and rapidity of the algorithm with actual UR5 robot. Later, more complex tasks will be performed using a simulation robot on the V-REP platform by using Bayesian-PI^2.

5.1   Simple Task with Actual UR5

The UR5 is a collaborative robot with six degrees of freedom a repetition accuracy of 0.03 mm. So we can ignore the error of the robot itself in the experiment.

As shown int the table 2, using ProMPs represents the movement of the robot joint firstly. So based on the theory, we do several demonstration actions and record data of joints' trajectory for the same task. When we say the same task, we mean the same starting point and ending point and the general trend of the trajectory is the same.

In the experiment, we use 31 basis function and evenly distribute over the timeline to fit the trajectory.

Then we randomly put a small landmark in the domain, which the robot can reach (excluding the point of demonstrations trajectories). So the robot is supposed to move passing through this via-point (for example strike) from previous start point to end point with the same duration.

We now proceeded to test the performance of traditional PI^2 and Bayesian PI^2. Detail results are shown in Fig. 2. The cost function is in the form of

$$0.5\sum_{j=1}^{6}\sum_{i=1}^{N-1}\left[10^{3}\left(\ddot{x}^{(j)}(i)\right)^{2}+\left(a_{f}^{(j)}(i)\right)^{2}\right]+\sum_{j=1}^{6}10^{10}\left[\left(x^{(j)}(m)-x_{v}^{(j)}\right)^{2}\right]$$

$$+\sum_{j=1}^{6}10^{3}\left[\left(\dot{x}^{(j)}(N)\right)^{2}+\left(x^{(j)}(N)-x_{g}^{(j)}\right)^{2}\right] \tag{17}$$

where i indicates the time index from 1 to N, j indicates the joint index from 1 to 3. Besides, $x_g^{(j)}$ denotes the expected position of point j when the task ends. When the time index equals m, $x^{(j)}(m)$ is the position of joint j which is corresponding to the expected via-point $x_v^{(j)}$ of the joint j. Apparently, $\ddot{x}^{(j)}$ is an arbitrary state-dependent cost value, $a_f^{(j)}(i)$ is the acceleration (forcing term) relevant to joint j at the time index i. $\dot{x}^{(j)}(N)$ is the velocity of joint when time index is N.

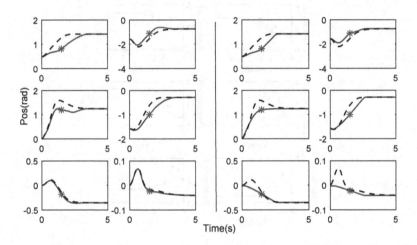

Fig. 2. The curve of Bayesian-PI^2 and tradition PI^2 through via-point in the joint space, Left: Bayesian-PI^2, Right: tradition PI^2, and the red mark(*) is the via point which is set artificial randomization in the joint space (Color figure online)

In this experiment, we set a point which position of joint space is (0.8,-1.14,1.2,-1.0,-0.18,-0.02) and make robot via point at time 1.5s. According to the result as shown in Fig. 2, the traditional PI^2 and Bayesian PI^2 both complete the task of via point with high accuracy. It can explain that the method mentioned in this paper is effective. But in terms of the rate of convergence of cost, as shown in Fig. 3, Bayesian PI^2 has fewer iterations than the methods of traditional PI^2.

On the other hand, we use the same number of iterations to compare the results of two methods. The results are shown in the Fig. 4.

As shown in Fig. 4, dash line is the mean trajectory of multiple demonstration. Dash-dot line and solid line are the curve of traditional PI^2 and Bayesian

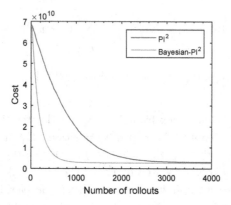

Fig. 3. Compare cost of traditional PI^2 and Bayesian PI^2

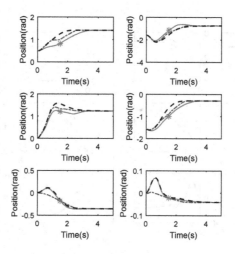

Fig. 4. Compare the trajectory in space of joint when traditional PI^2 and Bayesian PI^2 both have the same number of iterations

PI^2, respectively. In the experiment, we use the UR5 to verify proposed method and the result is shown as Fig. 5.

In this experiment, the result indicate the Bayesian PI^2 of this paper is effective and converges faster than traditional PI^2.

5.2   Complex Task on V-REP Platform

As shown in Fig. 6(a), we set two points in the joint space which the position in the space of joint are $(0.8,1.9,1.2,-1.0,-0.18,-0.22)$ and $(0.55,-1.5,1.34,-0.62,-0.7,0.16)$ denoted as the mark (*) and (+) respectively. In Fig. 6(b), the mark of red and blue are point set int the Cartesian space which calculate by forward kinematics. Using the method of Bayesian-PI^2 make the end

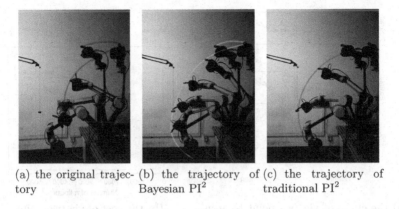

(a) the original trajec- (b) the   trajectory of (c) the   trajectory of
tory   Bayesian PI^2 traditional PI^2

Fig. 5. The actual with UR5, tradition PI^2 and Bayesian-PI^2 both pass the point

of robot via two point at time 1s and 2s, respectively. The result indicates the
method has the ability to perform more complex tasks.

Similar to the experiment in the Sect. 5.1, we compare the method tradition
PI^2 when make robot via two point. The result is shown as Fig. 7. In the Fig. 7(a),
the way of traditional PI^2 can't via points accurately. But the method that this
paper proposed can via points we set randomly. The result shows the method
of Bayesian PI^2 has the better performance for complex task such that via two
points. As shown in Fig. 7(b), the rate of convergence of Bayesian PI^2 is faster
than traditional PI^2 similarly.

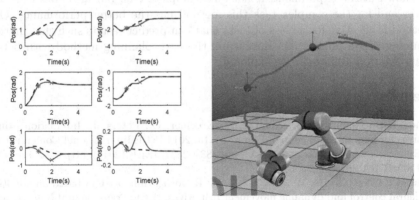

(a) the curve of via two point in space of (b) UR5 via two points on the V-REP
joint by using Bayesian-PI^2 platform

Fig. 6. Via two points by using the method of Bayesian-PI^2 (Color figure online)

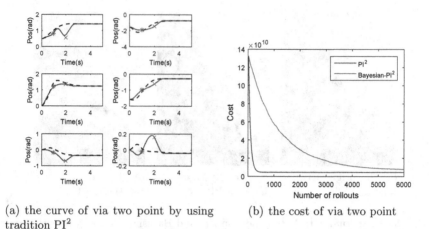

(a) the curve of via two point by using tradition PI^2

(b) the cost of via two point

Fig. 7. The result of tradition PI^2 and compare the cost with Bayesian PI^2

6   Conclusions

This paper present an methods which can make the robot obtain new skills faster on the policy improved stage. The results of Bayesian estimation can provide a heuristic to the search parameters. The search space of policy improved can be reduced by the posterior space of Bayesian estimation. So it can speed up optimization.

At the same time, the article verify the method of Bayesian-PI^2 with UR5. As shown in the experiment, it not only complete task but also does converge faster and for the complex task this method has the better performance. Our method is effective for a class of tasks that can predict results such that motion planning of via point(s). In the future, the path planning method with better generalization ability can be explored.

References

Amor, H.B., Neumann, G., Kamthe, S., Kroemer, O., Peters, J.: Interaction primitives for human-robot cooperation tasks. In: 2014 IEEE International Conference on Robotics and Automation (ICRA), pp. 2831–2837. IEEE (2014). https://doi.org/10.1109/ICRA.2014.6907265

Yang, C., Chen, C., He, W., Cui, R., Li, Z.: Robot learning system based on adaptive neural control and dynamic movement primitives. IEEE Trans. Neural Netw. Learn. Syst. **30**, 777–787 (2018)

Deisenroth, M.P., Fox, D., Rasmussen, C.E.: Gaussian processes for data-efficient learning in robotics and control. IEEE Trans. Pattern Anal. Mach. Intell. **37**(2), 408–423 (2015)

Fu, J., Ning, L., Wei, S., Zhang, L.: A novel DS-GMR coupled primitive for robotic motion skill learning. In: 2015 International Conference on Industrial Informatics-Computing Technology, Intelligent Technology, Industrial Information Integration, Wuhan, China, pp. 111–115 (2015a)

Fu, J., Wei, S., Ning, L., Xiang, K.: GMR based forcing term learning for DMPs. In: 2015 Chinese Automation Congress, Wuhan, China, pp. 437–442 (2015b)

Havoutis, I., Calinon, S.: Learning from demonstration for semi-autonomous teleoperation. Auton. Robots **43**, 1–14 (2018)

Khoramshahi, M., Billard, A.: A dynamical system approach to task-adaptation in physical human-robot interaction. Auton. Robots **43**(4), 927–946 (2019)

Kroemer, O., Leischnig, S., Luettgen, S., Peters, J.: A Kernel-based approach to learning contact distributions for robot manipulation tasks. Auton. Robots **42**(3), 581–600 (2018)

Mirrazavi Salehian, S.S., Figueroa Fernandez, N.B., Billard, A.: Dynamical system-based motion planning for multi-arm systems: reaching for moving objects (2017)

Paraschos, A., Rueckert, E., Peters, J., Neumann, G.: Probabilistic movement primitives under unknown system dynamics. Adv. Robot.: Int. J. Robot. Soc. Jpn. **32**(5–6), 297–310 (2018)

Pervez, A., Lee, D.: Learning task-parameterized dynamic movement primitives using mixture of GMMS. Intell. Serv. Robot. **11**(1), 61–78 (2018)

Schaarschmidt, M., Kuhnle, A., Ellis, B., Fricke, K., Gessert, F., Yoneki, E.: Lift: reinforcement learning in computer systems by learning from demonstrations. Mach. Learn. (2018)

Sigaud, O., Salaun, C., Padois, V.: On-line regression algorithms for learning mechanical models of robots: a survey. Robot. Auton. Syst. **59**(12), 1115–1129 (2011)

Theodorou, E., Buchli, J., Schaal, S.: A generalized path integral control approach to reinforcement learning. J. Mach. Learn. Res. **11**, 3137–3181 (2010)

Control of Nameplate Pasting Robot for Sand Mold Based on Deep Reinforcement Learning

Guiben Tuo, Te Li[(✉)], Haibo Qin, Bin Huang, Kuo Liu,
and Yongqing Wang

Key Laboratory for Precision and Non-traditional Machining of Ministry
of Education, Dalian University of Technology, Dalian 116000, China
teli@dlut.edu.cn

Abstract. In order to solve the problem of low-efficiency in the manual operation process of nameplate pasting for sand mold, an intelligent simulation system based on visual sensing and industrial robot is designed to paste nameplate on sand molds, and a deep reinforcement learning control method is proposed. The simulation system including the robot, visual sensor and sand mold is established in ROS combined with the physical simulation engine Gazebo. Then the task of nameplate pasting for sand molds is expressed as a markov process and the robot is trained by DQN method to learn a strategy to complete the task of pasting the nameplate of sand mold. A multi-level reward function algorithm based on multi-distances and collision information is proposed to improve the train success rate. Finally, the method is verified in the simulation system. The results show that the nameplate can be quickly attached to the sand mold cavity by the industrial robot.

Keywords: Sand mold · Nameplate pasting · Industrial robot · DQN

1 Introduction

In the casting of stainless-steel pipes and complex cavities, the production of sand mold is one of the key processes. In order to complete the product number in the stainless-steel pipe and complex cavity casting, including quality, production date and other information, The nameplate shall be pasted on the sand mold. But in current actual production, the manual pasting way is used in most cases which is low production efficiency and health hazards. Therefore, it is very important to realize the automation and robotization of nameplate pasting for sand mold in the casting process.

Using visual navigation and industrial robot is a feasible way to achieve the task of nameplate pasting. Visual feedback in visual servo control [1] is mainly based on position and image feature [2]. In the control process of position-based visual servo, it is usually necessary to use the image information collected by the camera, the camera model, the structure model of the target object and other information for three-dimensional reconstruction, so as to obtain the pose information of the robot. Finally, the feedback control law will be designed based on the current pose and the set pose,

© Springer Nature Switzerland AG 2019
H. Yu et al. (Eds.): ICIRA 2019, LNAI 11745, pp. 368–378, 2019.
https://doi.org/10.1007/978-3-030-27529-7_32

the servo control is completed [3]. However, the position-based method is sensitive to image noise and camera calibration error [4]. The visual feedback method based on image features uses image information to describe the task, so as to enhance the robustness of the visual system [5]. However, the model is complex, the controller design is difficult and the image-based method is sensitive to image noise and the existing feature extraction methods are not very good in repeatability and accuracy when scale and rotation changes, there are big problems in practical application [6]. The robot control method based on position and image features cannot solve the task of nameplate pasting well.

Therefore, a deep reinforcement learning algorithm based on vision is proposed in this paper to solve the problem of nameplate pasting for sand mold. However, there are many challenges in using deep reinforcement learning for robot arm to accomplish specific tasks. Since the nameplate of sand mold and the groove attached to the sand mold are polygons, in order to successfully complete the sand mold nameplate attachment, it is necessary to consider not only that the sand mold nameplate can reach the exact position with the industrial robot, but also that the sand mold nameplate and the groove posture of the sand mold must correspond to each other. In this paper, a multi-level reward function algorithm based on distance is proposed to overcome the above problems. Finally, the algorithm is demonstrated with UR5 in Robot Operating System (ROS) environment, and the results of the experiment show that the robot arm can learn a good strategy for the task of nameplate pasting.

2 Simulation System Establishing by ROS and Gazebo

The simulation system works as virtual training platform, which is established on the ROS (Robot Operation System) and includes the physical models and control algorithm. In the simulation system, the open source 6-DOF UR5 robotic arm is adopted as the agent, whose design parameters are shown in Table 1. As shown in Fig. 1, the nameplate is fixed to the end of the robot by the negative pressure adsorption fixture, and the sand mold is placed in the operational range of UR5 robot arm. A visual sensor is fixed to catch the figures of the robot and sand mold. All these physical models are built based on Gazebo, which is powerful and open source 3D dynamic physical simulation simulator. The control orders, sensor information and state variables can be transmitted through the special message mechanism between ROS and Gazebo.

As shown in Fig. 1(a), A_1, A_2, and A_3 are the vertices on the nameplate, B_1, B_2 and B_3 are the three vertices on the sand mold groove. The success judgement rule of nameplate pasting by the robot is that the distances of $|A_1B_1|$, $|A_2B_2|$ and $|A_3B_3|$ are all less than 3 mm. In this state, the nameplate can be placed with an acceptable posture, and pasted onto the sand mold with glues.

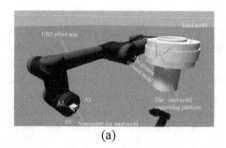
(a)

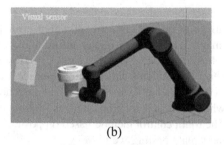
(b)

Fig. 1. The simulation experiment platform for sand mold labeling of mechanical arm. A_1, A_2, and A_3 are the vertices on the nameplate, B_1, B_2 and B_3 are the three vertices on the sand mold groove. The sand mold supporting platform has two degrees of freedom and can move up and down and rotate

Table 1. Parameters of the UR5 robotic arm.

Joint number	a(mm)	α(rad)	d(mm)	θ(rad)
1	0	0.64	89.2	θ_1
2	425	1.40	0	θ_2
3	392	1.14	0	θ_3
4	0	2.31	109.3	θ_4
5	0	0	94.75	θ_5
6	0	π/2	82.5	θ_6

The steps to build the simulation platform are listed as follows:

Step1 Sand mold and sand mold support platform are modeled in Solid works software, then the design files are converted into URDF format files by sw_urdf_exporter plugin, which is supported by the ROS system.

Step 2 Build the camera model in the ROS workspace, set the camera parameters and place it in the appropriate location.

Step 3 Download the corresponding configuration file for the UR5 robot arm on the ROS website.

Step 4 In the ROS system, the sand mold and supporting platform, the open source UR5 robot arm and the camera are placed in the same workspace. That is to complete the construction of sand mold label simulation platform.

3 DQN Control Based on an Improved Reward Function

3.1 Basic Theory of Deep Reinforcement Learning

Reinforcement learning can be described as that the agents learn an optimal strategy to achieve the ultimate goal through dynamic interaction with the environment, combined with continuous trial and error. In other words, in each state, the agent can obtain immediate rewards or punishments by interacting with the environment, and finally maximize the rewards obtained by the agent in each step of action. The process of dynamic interaction between agent and environment can be defined as an Markov Decision Processes, so the optimal strategy can be defined by Eq. (1)

$$Q^*_\pi(s,a) = \max_{\pi^*} E[\sum_{k=0}^{\infty} \gamma^k R_{t+k+1}|s_t = s, a_t = a] \tag{1}$$

where $Q^*_\pi(s,a)$ denotes the optimal action value function, and π^* denotes the optimal strategy, whose cumulative expected return is the greatest. γ denotes the discount factor, $\sum_{k=0}^{\infty} \gamma^k R_{t+k+1}|s_t = s, a_t = a$ denotes the cumulative return of taking action a_t in state s_t.

For the method based on value function [7], when the optional actions are finite discrete, the maximum value is selected in $Q(s,a)$ value by the enumeration. In the case of continuous optional actions, the maximum value is calculated in $Q(s,a)$ value. At this point, the bellman equation can be rewritten as Eq. (2):

$$Q_{i+1}(s,a) = E[r + \gamma \max_{a'} Q(s',a')] \tag{2}$$

The DQN algorithm which can be expressed by Eq. 3 effectively expresses the high-dimensional observations and action value function Q through the neural network and estimates the action value function through a neural network [8]:

$$Q^*_\pi(s,a) = Q(s,a;\theta) \tag{3}$$

It uses a network function with parameter θ as the Q network. Then, when iterating to step i, the loss function of this network can be expressed by Eq. (4) [9]

$$L_i(\theta_i) = E_{s,a,r,s'}[(r_i + \gamma \max_{a'} Q(s',a';\theta_i^-) - Q(s,a;\theta_i))^2] \tag{4}$$

where θ_i is the parameter of the current Q network and θ_i^- is the parameter of the target network.

The architecture of the deep Q network is shown in Fig. 2, including three convolutional layers and two fully connected layers. The network parameters of each layer are shown in Table 2.

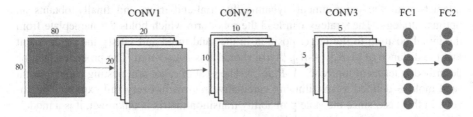

Fig. 2. Deep Q network architecture diagram

Table 2. Parameters of each layer.

Layer	Kernel	Feature	Stride	Activation Function
Input	/	$80 \times 80 \times 1$	/	/
Conv1	$8 \times 8 \times 1 \times 32$	$20 \times 20 \times 32$	4	ReLU
Conv2	$4 \times 4 \times 32 \times 64$	$10 \times 10 \times 64$	2	ReLU
Conv3	$3 \times 3 \times 64 \times 64$	$5 \times 5 \times 64$	2	ReLU
Fc1	1600×512	512	/	Reshape
Fc2	512×729	729	/	ReLU

3.2   Off-Policy

The core idea of reinforcement learning is to approach the optimal strategy through trial and error method in the environment. For this learning algorithm, the maximum reward can be obtained by selecting the optimal action in the current state. But in this case, the resulting strategy is likely to be locally optimal rather than globally optimal. So, it is crucial to explore the whole state space. Therefore, off-policy policy is adopted in this algorithm. It means that the strategy for generating action data is different from the strategy for evaluating and improving the network. $\mu(a|s)$ is used as a strategy of generating action data, which can be expressed by Eq. (5) [10]

$$\mu(a|s) = \begin{cases} 1 - \varepsilon + \frac{\varepsilon}{|A(\varepsilon)|} & \text{if } a = argmax_a Q(s,a) \\ \frac{\varepsilon}{|A(\varepsilon)|} & \text{if } a \neq argmax_a Q(s,a) \end{cases} \tag{5}$$

Evaluation and improvement strategies are denoted as $\pi(a|s)$.

$$\pi(a|s) = \begin{cases} 1 & \text{if } a = argmax_a Q(s,a) \\ 0 & \text{if } a \neq argmax_a Q(s,a) \end{cases} \tag{6}$$

where, $\mu(a|s)$ is obtained by ε-greedy strategy and $\pi(a|s)$ is obtained by greedy strategy. It will balance the relationship between exploration and exploitation. According to these two strategies, the optimal strategy can be found quickly by the agent.

3.3   Markov Model Building for Robotic Pasting of Nameplate

The problem of nameplate pasting for sand mold by robot arm can be considered as a sequential decision problem. Robot arm can be regarded as an agent. It constantly interacts with the environment dynamically, trial-and-error, and finally obtains an optimal strategy. The strategy can lead the robot arm which holds the nameplate from the initial position to the target position in the sand mold and satisfy the requirement that the distance of $|A_1B_1|$, $|A_2B_2|$, $|A_2B_2|$ should less than 3 mm. The procedure can be described in terms of tuples (S, A, P, R, γ). The goal of robot arm pasting nameplate on sand mold is defined as maximizing cumulative returns in every full exploration process. In this task, since the state probability transition matrix is unknown, it is a model-free reinforcement learning model.

In the task of nameplate pasting for sand mold, the state s including robot arm, nameplate and sand mold is the original pixel photo taken by the visual sensor from the virtual simulation system. The raw pixel photo is passed to the neural network to approximate Q-value function (see Fig. 3).

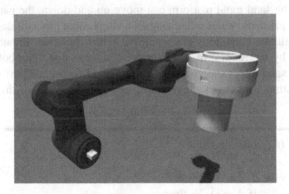

Fig. 3. The original pixel image taken by the camera from the simulation environment is the state input of the neural network.

In order to control the motion of the manipulator arm, the rotation angle of each joint is taken as the output of the neural network. In each movement, six joints move at the same time. Each of the joints can be moved in one of three ways, clockwise by a certain Angle, counterclockwise by a certain Angle or the joint can be kept in its original state. The robot arm has six joints, each of which has three actions, so it has $3^6 = 729$ actions. Agent acquisition strategy is such a sequence of actions.

3.4 Reward Function

Since the state transition matrix is unknown, the robot arm can directly interact with the environment in the current state, select actions, and obtain the next state and reward. In the reinforcement learning, the design of reward function is very important. The reward function has a direct impact on whether an optimal strategy can be converged with fewer exploration steps.

In this task, the return function is affected by two key factors which are the distance factor and the collision factor [11] between the robot arm and the sand mold. On the one hand, the distance can influence the relative posture between the nameplate and the groove of sand mold. On the other hand, the collision between the robot arm and the sand mold is not allowed in the actual operation.

The first key factor is distance. In order to make the sand mold nameplate under the control of the robot arm and the sand mold groove on the posture can be corresponding, the instant reward is given by the difference between the sum of $|A_1B_1|$, $|A_2B_2|$, $|A_3B_3|$ in current time step and the sum in the previous time step. The difference is Δd, the current distance is d_n. In addition, the reward function is graded according to the initial distance and the target distance, so that the strategy of agent can converge faster in the training process. The initial distance is 1.26 m, the target distance is 0.01 m.

The second key factor is the collision between the robot arm and the sand mold. In order to avoid the possibility of collision between the robot arm and the sand mold in the process of exploring the environment, the collision condition is set in the reward function. Since the sand mold platform can move up and down, the parameters of the upper and lower prismatic joints will change when the robot arm collides with the sand mold, so the collision conditions are set in the return function. Finally, the optimal strategy learned by the robot arm is: under the condition that the robot arm does not collide with the sand mold, the goal of the sand mold nameplate pasting task can be achieved. Algorithm 1 describes the reward function mechanism of this task.

Algorithm 1: Reward Function

```
if   collision then
        r=-70
else if  Δd<0 then
     if d_n>1.26 then
            r=+10
        if d_n<1.26 and d_n>0.5 then
            r=+20
        if d_n<0.5 and d_n>0.1 then
            r=+30
        if d_n<0.1 and d_n>0.01 then
            r=+50
        if d_n=0.01 then
            r=+100
else if  Δd==0 then
        if d_n>1.26 then
            r=-20
        if d_n<1.26 and d_n>0.5 then
            r=-15
        if d_n<0.5 and d_n>0.1 then
            r=-10
        if d_n<0.1 and d_n>0.01 then
            r=-5
    else
            r=-40
    end
```

4 Experiment and Results

4.1 Experiment Settings

The simulation experiment is carried out in gazebo. First, the simulation platform is opened in gazebo, and then run the DQN algorithm script file. All the processes in this experiment are run on a computer with Intel Xeon 2650 CPU. Deep neural networks are implemented through TensorFlow.

(1) State Space

We input the state s represented by the original pixel photo obtained from the simulation environment into the neural network. There is a robot arm, a label attached to the end of the arm, and sand mold. The photo is an 80×80 grey-scale image. It goes through three convolutional layers and two fully connected layers. After these processes, it obtains the Q-value of the corresponding actions of the current state. It is a 729×1 matrix and each element of the matrix represents Q-value of an action in its current state.

(2) Action Space

Since UR5 has six joints and each joint has three kinds of actions, including clockwise rotation, counterclockwise rotation and stationary motion, there are $3^6 = 729$ combinations of actions. Adopt the coding method similar to the ternary code, counterclockwise rotation is +1, clockwise rotation is −1, and static is 0. Then multiply that by the step size and you get the rotation angle of each of the joints. The action information is then passed to the robot arm through the ROS topic interface.

(3) Reward Function

The arm initializes at the beginning of each episode. The robot arm explores from its initial position, and when it collides with the sand mold, it receives a −70 penalty. When the robot arm is close to the sand mold groove and the current distance is greater than 1.26 m, it will get a bonus of +10. When the robot arm is close to the sand mold groove and the current distance is less than 1.26 m and greater than 0.5 m, it will get a bonus of +20, When the robot arm is close to the sand mold groove and the current distance is less than 0.5 m and greater than 0.1 m, it will get a bonus of +30, When the robot arm is close to the sand mold groove and the current distance is less than 0.1 m and greater than 0.01 m, it will get a bonus of 50, When the robot arm is close to the sand mold groove and the current distance is equal to 0.01 m, it will get a bonus of +100, When the mechanical arm is far away from the sand mold groove, it will get a minus 40 penalty. When the robot arm is stationary and the current distance is greater than 1.26 m, it will get a minus 20 penalty. When the robot arm is stationary and the current distance is less than 1.26 m and greater than 0.5 m, it will get a minus 10 penalty. When the robot arm is stationary and the current distance is less than 0.5 m and greater than 0.1 m, it will get a minus 5 penalty. When the robot arm is stationary and the current distance is less than 0.1 m and greater than 0.01 m, it will get a minus 1 penalty.

(4) Training

In the experiment, we set the discount factor γ to 0.95, set memory size to 500000, use Adam optimization algorithm to optimize neural network [12], and set learning rate to 6×10^5. In the experiment, we trained the neural network for 1500 episodes, and each of episode has 2000 steps. After 2000 iterations, if it can't to achieve the goal, it means the assignment is failed. Then it will be reset, and begin a new exploration. The mark that mission goal achieves is the distance of $|A_1B_1|$, $|A_2B_2|$, $|A_3B_3|$ less than 3 mm. After 50 training episodes, it will test the neural network. Each test episode has 3000 steps. During the test, we will calculate the success rate of the test and the rate serves as an index to evaluate network performance.

4.2 Simulation Result

After the training, we obtained the experimental results. Figure 4 is the success rate during training process. By analyzing the Fig. 4, we can see that there is a significant increase in training process when it reaches to 600 episodes, and the success rate finally converges to a higher level after 1100 episodes. This indicates that the neural network begins to converge after 1100 episodes. It also means that robot arm has already required an optimal strategy for completing the task through exploring the environment.

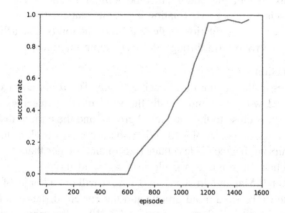

Fig. 4. The success rate during training process.

Figure 5 is four screenshots of a episodes of different iteration timesteps after the strategy convergence. (a) is a screenshot of iteration 0 timestep, (b) is a screenshot of iteration 600 timesteps, (c) is a screenshot of iteration 1200 timesteps, and (d) is a screenshot of the completion of the sand mold labeling task. This indicates that the robot can quickly complete the task of nameplate pasting for sand mold after the strategy convergence.

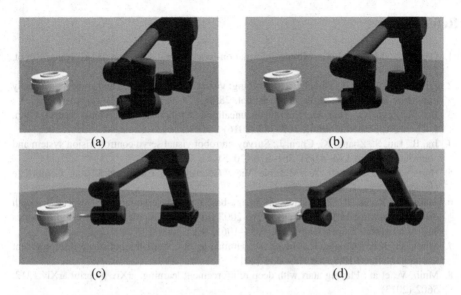

(a)   (b)

(c)   (d)

Fig. 5. Four screenshots of a episodes of different iteration steps after the network convergence.

5   Conclusions

In this paper, a motion control method based on deep reinforcement learning for sand mold labeling of robot arm is proposed. Since the nameplate and groove are polygons, in order to achieve the task of nameplate pasting for sand mold, not only to ensure that the position, but also to ensure the corresponding posture of them. In order to solve this problem, we use the sum of the distances between three vertices on the nameplate and three corresponding vertices in the groove to represent the reward function. When the distance of $|A_1B_1|$, $|A_2B_2|$, $|A_2B_2|$ is 3 mm, the agent can get the biggest reward. Through the reward function, the robot arm can learn an optimal strategy during the exploration to achieve the task of nameplate pasting. Simulation results show that: after a certain time of training, the action strategy of the robot arm converges. The success rate of sand mold labeling reach over 95% during the training process, and It proves that this method has good reliability and stability.

Acknowledgements. This work is partially supported by the National Science Foundation for Young Scientists of China (Grant No. 51805071), the Fundamental Research Funds for the Central Universities (Grant No. DUT18RC(3)073) and Changjiang Scholar Program of Chinese Ministry of Education (No. T2017030).

References

1. Dame, A., Marchand, E.: Mutual information-based visual servoing. IEEE Trans. Robot. **27**(5), 958–969 (2011)
2. Silveira, G., Malis, E.: Direct visual servoing: vision-based estimation and control using only nonmetric information. IEEE Trans. Robot. **28**(4), 974–980 (2012)
3. Bo, T., Zeyu, G., Han, D.: Survey on uncalibrated robot visual servoing control. Chin. J. Theor. Appl. Mech. **48**(4), 767–783 (2016)
4. Jia, B., Liu, S., Zhang, K., Chen, J.: Survey on robot visual servo control: vision system and control strategies. AAS **41**(5), 861–873 (2015)
5. Hartley, R., Zisserman, A.: Multiple View Geometry in Computer Vision. Cambridge University Press, Cambridge (2003)
6. Malis, E., Rives, P.: Robustness of image-based visual servoing with respect to depth distribution errors. In: Proceedings of the 2003 IEEE International Conference on Robotics and Automation, Taipei, China, pp. 1056–1061. IEEE (2003)
7. Mnih, V., Kavukcuoglu, K., Silver, D.: Human-level control through deep reinforcement learning. Nature **518**(7540), 529–533 (2015)
8. Mnih, V., et al.: Playing atari with deep reinforcement learning. arXiv preprint arXiv:1312. 5602 (2013)
9. Zhang, F., Leitner, J., Milford, M., et al.: Towards vision-based deep reinforcement learning for robotic motion control. Comput. Sci. (2015)
10. Sutton, R.S., Barto, A.G.: Reinforcement Learning: An Introduction. 2nd edition in progress. London, England (2017)
11. Xian, G.: The study of robotic arm control policy based on DQN. Beijing Jiaotong University, pp. 41–45 (2018)
12. James, S., Johns, E.: 3D simulation for robot arm control with deep Q-learning. arXiv preprint (2016)

Robot Motor Skill Acquisition
with Learning in Two Spaces

Jian Fu$^{(\boxtimes)}$, Ce Cao, Jinyu Du, and Siyuan Shen

School of Automation, Wuhan University of Technology, Wuhan 430070, China
fujian@whut.edu.cn
http://www.escience.cn/people/fujiane/index.html

Abstract. Motor skill acquisition and refinement is critical for the robot to step in human daily lives, which can endow it with the ability of autonomously performing unfamiliar tasks. However, how does the robot autonomously fulfill the new motion task with preassigned performance based on the demonstration task is still a challenge. We in this paper proposed a novel motor skill acquisition policy to conquer above problem, which is based on improved local weighted regression (iLWR), policy improvement with path integral (PI^2). Besides, the mixture Gaussian regression (GMR) guided self-reconstruction of basis function and the search of weight coefficient in the policy expression are performed alternately in basis function space and weight space to seek the optimal/suboptimal solution. In this way, robot can achieve the gradual acquisition of movement skills from similar tasks which is related to the demonstration to unsimilar task with different criterion. At last, the classical via-points trajectory planning experiment are performed with SCARA manipulator, NAO humanoid robot to verify that the proposed method is effective and feasible.

Keywords: Alternate study in two spaces · GMR-PI^2 · Motor skill acquisition

1 Introduction

It had long been a dream for researchers in the robot communities to endow the robot with motor skill similar to the man. Recently, robot learning from demonstration (LfD) together with reinforcement learning (RL) (Argall et al. 2009; Peters and Schaal 2008; Rombokas et al. 2013; Deisenroth et al. 2013) has attracted significantly increased attention. By means of LfDRL, researchers can derive a robot controller autonomously merely by back-driving or teleoperating it. Furthermore, the controller could be self-improved to refine and expand robot motor capability obtained from demonstration to fulfill the task dissimilar to demonstration task.

J. Fu—The author acknowledges the National Natural Science Foundation of China (61773299, 515754112).

Usually a parametric policy representation is selected firstly for the LfDRL. Generally, a dynamic model with flexible adjustment sounds good, for the reason that it is easy to modulate online and exhibit robustness. DS (Khansari-Zadeh and Billard 2010; 2011) and DMPs (Ude and Gams 2010; Ijspeert et al. 2013) models are current popular dynamic model. DS represents motion scheduling in the form of a nonlinear autonomous dynamic system, which is time-invariance and global/local asymptotic stable. Whereas, DMPs models the movement planning as superimposition of a linear dynamic system and a nonlinear term. The former takes precedence over the latter to guarantee the global convergence at the end of the motion. Then a flexible method to adjust the model is required, including radial basis function networks, regularized kernel least-square, locally weighted regression (Atkeson et al. 1997) and Gaussian process etc.

It is often easier to learn a policy than model a robot with its environment, hence, model-free policy search methods are more popular than model-based policy search methods. Some classic model-free policy search methods were proposed recently, such as Relative Entropy Policy Search (REPS), Covariance Matrix Adaptation-Evolutionary Strategy (CMA-ES). REPS (Parisi et al. 2015; Peters et al. 2010) formulates the policy search problem as an optimization problem in an information theoretic way, meanwhile updates its policy by weighted maximum likelihood estimates. However, CMA-ES is a black-box optimizer. And it uses heuristics to estimate the weight and update the distribution, which often work well in practice but are not founded on a theoretical basis (Gregory et al. 2015).

Aimed to develop a generic method for motor skill learning with good quality for given motion planning task, this paper proposed a DMPs-iLWR policy which learning in two space to search target solution and this paper is organized as follows. Section 2 depicted DMPs-iLWR for policy representation and imitation learning. Section 3 investigates the policy optimization based on GMR-PI^2 from a viewpoint stochastic optimal control. Section 4 describes reconstruction of basis function with auto-encoding and deep iteration process. In Sect. 5, we present in detail the classical benchmark experiment trajectory planning via prior unknown point(s).

2   DMPS-iLWR Based Robot Motor Skill Learning

Classical DMPs model the robot movement in each degree of freedom (DOF) as independent transformation system, which is synchronized in time dimension by a share phase variable. Specifically, it presents a parametric policy in the representation phase, which comprises the transfer system, canonical system and function approximation. Those systems are described as following

$$
\begin{cases}
\tau \ddot{x}_t = \underbrace{\alpha_x \left(\beta_x \left(g - x_t \right) - \dot{x}_t \right)}_{spring-damping.system} + \underbrace{\Psi_\theta \left(s_t \right) s_t \left(g - x_0 \right)}_{forcing.term} & transf.system \\
\tau \dot{s}_t = -\alpha_s s_t & canon.system \\
\Psi_\theta \left(s_t \right) = \frac{\sum_{i=1}^{K} \psi_i w_i}{\sum_{i=1}^{K} \psi_i} & func.approx
\end{cases}
\tag{1}
$$

where τ is the scaling factor for the duration of motion. $x_t = q_{ref}$ is the reference trajectory generated by transformation system for one DOF, s_t is the phase of the movement generated by canonical system, which decays from 1 to 0 over the same duration with transformation system. ψ_i is the Gaussian kernel function with the variance spaced equally across motion duration.

w_i is the weight associated. The goal g is a point attractor and x_0 is the start state. α_x, β_x, α_s are positive constants, by which the spring damping system is modeled as a 2 order critical damping system. θ is the hyper-parameter for basis functions. As we can see, DMPs for each transformation system is a single-input (time) and single-output (joint) (SISO) system. It constructs a time-dependent control reference rather than traditional state dependent one, which dramatically simplifies the learning process.

We in this paper propose an DMPs-iLWR policy representation in which we employ improved Local Weighted Regression (iLWR) to avoid the poor performance of traditional LWR in the imitation learning and employ the data-driven Gaussian Mixture Model to adjust the feature of trajectories adaptively during the PI^2 learning. It is shown in Eq. (2), which comprises a transformation system, a canonical system, a gating system and a weighted basis function.

$$
\begin{cases}
\tau \ddot{x}_t = \underbrace{\alpha_x \left(\beta_x \left(g - x_t \right) - \dot{x}_t \right)}_{a_s} + \underbrace{h_t \bar{\mathbf{B}}_{s_t} \bar{\mathbf{w}}}_{a_f} & \text{transf.system} \\
\tau \dot{s}_t = \begin{cases} \frac{1}{T} & \text{if } t \leq T \\ 0 & \text{otherwise} \end{cases} & \text{canon.system} \\
h_t = \frac{1}{1+e^{\alpha_h(t - \tau T)}} & \text{gatin.system} \\
\bar{\mathbf{w}} = \begin{bmatrix} \bar{w}_1 \cdots \bar{w}_K \ \bar{w}_{K+1} \cdots \bar{w}_{2K} \end{bmatrix}^T & \text{weight} \\
\bar{\mathbf{B}}_{s_t} = \begin{bmatrix} \gamma_1 s_t \ \cdots \gamma_K s_t \ \gamma_1 \cdots \gamma_K \end{bmatrix} & \text{basis.function}
\end{cases}
\tag{2}
$$

where $\bar{\mathbf{B}}$ is the equivalent basis function, and the form of real basis shows as following

$$
\gamma^{(i)} = \frac{exp\left(-\frac{1}{2\sigma_i^2}(s_t - c_i)^2\right)}{\sum\limits_{j=1}^{K} exp\left(-\frac{1}{2\sigma_j^2}(s_t - c_j)^2\right)}
\tag{3}
$$

The revised canonical system can guarantee that the phase is proportional to time in the transient process, and the gating system is used to guarantee the convergence of forcing term, and the transformation system is the important controllable part, and we adopt the form dot product between basis function $\bar{\mathbf{B}}_{s_t}$ and weight $\bar{\mathbf{w}}$ to approximate forcing term a_s, and the trajectories can be adjusted by controlling the weight $\bar{\mathbf{w}}$.

The traditional LWR presents an restrictive effect of imitation learning. Because the default fitting trajectories must cross the origin of coordinates, which means if the phase variable is close to zero, so must be the forcing term. Therefore we revise the controlling term from pattern $(y = Ax)$ to pattern $(y = Ax + B)$ to avoid this restriction. And the new forcing term can be seen as Eq. (4).

$$f(s_t) = \frac{\sum\limits_{i=1}^{K} \psi_i(s_t) \left[A_i \ B_i\right]}{\sum\limits_{i=1}^{K} \psi_i(s_t)} \begin{bmatrix} s_t \\ 1 \end{bmatrix} (g - y_0) \tag{4}$$

$$= \sum_{i=1}^{K} \gamma^{(i)} (A_i s_t + B_i)(g - y_0)$$

Associated with the optimization policy of PI^2, we can learn this two parameters (A and B) simultaneously, which can be seen as the slope and the interception of the linear function respectively. The number of real basis are set to K, naturally the equivalent one are twice and the forms of equivalent basis and weight show as following

$$\bar{\mathbf{B}}_{s_t}^{(m)} = \begin{cases} \gamma^{(i)} s_t \ m = i, m \leq K \\ \gamma^{(i)} \quad m = i + K, K < m \leq 2K \end{cases}$$

$$\bar{\mathbf{w}}^{(m)} = \begin{cases} A_i \ m = i, m \leq K \\ B_i \ m = i + K, K < m \leq 2K \end{cases}$$

Next, LfD can conduct DMPs-iLWR to learn a feasible solution or more in joint space.

3   Policy Improvement Based on iLWR-PI^2

Although DMPs-iLWR can effectively replicate and generalize robot demonstration movement, it maybe not a optimal/suboptimal policy for the task. Furthermore, it can not autonomously fulfill the motion different from demonstration one with a high-quality level, such as the task with additional criterion, though vanilla DMPs-iLWR by which $(g - y_0)$ can be adapt to the goal change and scaling law is an orientation-preserving homeomorphism between the original equations using $g - y_0$ and the scaled differential equation using $k\,(g - y_0)$ (Ijspeert et al. 2013). So we combine DMPs-iLWR (policy representation) with path integration (policy improvement) (Theodorou et al. 2010) through stochastic optimal control to meet the requirement. Specifically, we apply Feynman-Kac theorem to derive the state value function based on path integral, and then deduce the optimal control policy. In this way, we solve the Hamilton-Jacobian-Bellman equation indirectly.

As a reinforcement learning, the cost function shows as the Eq. (5), and we add the constraint associated with tasks.

$$S\left(\tau_i\right) = \phi_{t_N} + \sum_{j=i}^{N-1} q_{t_j} dt + \frac{1}{2} \sum_{j=i}^{N-1} (\mathbf{w} + \varepsilon)^T \frac{\mathbf{B}_{s_{t_j}} \mathbf{B}_{s_{t_j}}^T}{\mathbf{B}_{s_{t_j}}^T R^{-1} \mathbf{B}_{s_{t_j}}} (\mathbf{w} + \varepsilon_{t_j}) + \frac{\lambda}{2} \sum_{j=i}^{N-1} \ln |\boldsymbol{H}|$$

$$\tag{5}$$

where $\frac{\lambda}{2}\sum_{j=i}^{N-1}\ln|\boldsymbol{H}|$ is usually removed given that basis function is fixed. The optimal time-variant policy with value function V_{t_i} shows as

$$\begin{aligned}\mathbf{w}_{t_i} &= -R^{-1}\mathbf{B}_{s_t}^T\left(\nabla_{z_{t_i}}V_{t_i}\right)\\ &= \int P\left(\tau_i\right)u\left(\tau_i\right)d\tau_i,\end{aligned} \tag{6}$$

where

$$\begin{aligned}P\left(\tau_i\right) &= \frac{e^{-\frac{1}{\lambda}S\left(\tau_{t_i}\right)}}{\int e^{-\frac{1}{\lambda}S\left(\tau_{t_i}\right)}d\tau_i}\\ u\left(\tau_i\right) &= \frac{R^{-1}\mathbf{B}_{t_i}\mathbf{B}_{t_i}^T}{\mathbf{B}_{t_i}^T R^{-1}\mathbf{B}_{t_i}}\left(\mathbf{w}+\varepsilon_{t_i}\right)\end{aligned} \tag{7}$$

Specifically, $P\left(\tau_i\right)$ is the path depended probability distribution and $u\left(\tau_i\right)$ is local optimal control derived by value function.

In practical engineering, we usually carry out K roll-outs. And for specific time index i, we gain $P\left(\tau_{i,k}\right)$ similar to softmax function (taking the frequency as probability), where k is the index of K roll-outs.

In this way, we achieve weighted average of adjustment $\delta\mathbf{w}_{t_i} = \mathbf{w}_{t_i}-\mathbf{w}$ across N time index as equivalent time-invariant policy, which could be expressed as

$$\delta\mathbf{w} = \frac{\sum_{i=0}^{N-1}\left(N-i\right)\mathbf{B}_{t_i}\delta\mathbf{w}_{t_i}}{\sum_{i=0}^{N-1}\left(N-i\right)\mathbf{B}_{t_i}} \tag{8}$$

4   Basis Function Auto-Encoding and Alternate Learning in Two Space

Embodiment feature indicates the intelligence what an agent is capable of (from low-level sensory-motor activities to high-level cognitive activities) is closely related to the morphology what the agent is composed of and the way which agent interact with the environment (Pfeifer and Bongard 2006). Therefore, basis function in the policy representation plays an decisive role in determining the feasible coverage of the robot's kinematic intelligent capability. When the robot faces new task which is different from demonstration (for example with additional performance criterion), the new task is less correlative to the experience obtained from demonstration task. In other words, there exists the relative large gap between the experimental basis function from demonstration task and appropriate one for new task. As for new task the minimal return in finite horizon from experimental basis function is ordinarily large than that with appropriate one. We specially draw the Fig. 1 to facilitate the comprehending. Basis function B1 is obtained from demonstration task and blue elliptical region is the projection from space spanned by basis function B1 to feature/measure space. And the location of optimal approximation which associate the optimal weight with basis B1 indicates the distance L3 is relative large. We assume basis function B3 is appropriate basis for the new task and red elliptical region is associated projection. As seen, there are no overlap between two projection regions. That

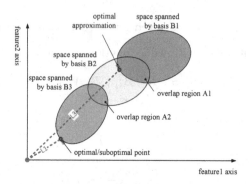

Fig. 1. Diagrammatic sketch of idea for RBAE (Color figure online)

means no correlation between two tasks which is one of the difficulties for the robot skill learning and autonomous skill acquisition.

Since it is unrealistic for the robot to preset the appropriate basis function such as B3 prior to the new task arising in the unstructured scenarios, it is necessary to endow the robot with the capability of gradual learning and skill acquisition. In other words, we can design a sequence of projection zone overlapped each other to join the demonstration task and new task, as yellow elliptical region works shown in Fig. 1. By means of the correlation (overlap) between anteroposterior projection zone in which robot evolving along with, for example form blue zone via yellow zone to red zone shown in Fig. 1, autonomous specific skill improvement could be achieved.

We put forward the alternate learning in two spaces based on above analysis to conduct motion skill acquisition from demonstration to new task. Specifically, reinforcement learning in weight space will gradually drive the candidate elites from blue zone B1 into the overlap region A1 by means of the distance (reward) in feature space. By means of the presentation learning on the data generated from candidate elites, the algorithms can automatically generate the new basis and zone B3 in which the better performance capability is available. In this way, robot can eventually approach the optimal/suboptimal point for the specific new skill by repeating the procedure. So we propose the improved LWR and PI^2 learning in two space to overcome the above challenge. Its main flow is ① →②→③→④→⑤ →⑥→④→⑤→⑥··· shown in Fig. 2. Policy representation (iLWR) for motor skill is firstly constructed based on the principle of maximum entropy. In other words, alike Gaussian functions ψ_i with identical variances are evenly assigned along the phase duration, which can provide the policy the most flexible for learning unknown motion given that the number of basis function is fixed. (①). Then LfD is conducted to seek the appropriate weight to replicate the demonstration(②). Next, for new task (with different performance criterion), we apply RL(iLWR-PI^2) to search the suitable weight until the cost doesn't decrease apparently any more (③④). Usually, the best trajectories so far imply the feature of new task. So K-means++ is applied to cluster classification on the data generated by those candidate elites. Then EM-GMM is adopted to estimates the appropriate parameters μ_k and Σ_k for respective Gaussian distribution component. Next, these parameters will be assign to ψ_i and $r^{(m)}$ to construct the new basis function $\bar{\mathbf{B}}_{s_t}$. In a sense, more appropriate basis functions are constructed adaptively based on data-driven according to the character of targeted task. Also, LfD is performed to seek weights to replicate the best trajectories so far with a posterior maximization.(⑤). Based on them, we again apply DL(iLWR-PI^2) to search the best approximation in the new space(⑥). This procedure repeat again and again (④→⑤→⑥) until a satisfied trajectory is obtained.

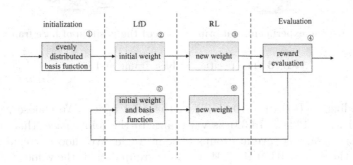

Fig. 2. Algorithm flow for RBAE

5 Simulation Experiment

In this part, we employ NAO robot shown in Fig. 3(a) to verify the effectiveness of the proposed method. This robot is the first humanoid robot of the Aldebaran Robotics company. And it is an interactive companion robot. There are twenty-five joints on the NAO robot. But this experiment only involves five revolute joints with the right arm of NAO: RShulderRoll, RShouderPitch, RElbowRoll, RElbowYaw and RWristYaw.

In this experiment, we fix RShouderPitch and RWristYaw at 0 degree. Experiences are depicted as following. Firstly, man drag the right hand of NAO from starting point to the end point. And at the same time we read the data of three joint angles every 0.05 s. There are 100 sets of data used as the original trajectory. Then we randomly put a small landmark in the domain, which the arm can reach (excluding the start point and the end point). So the arm is supposed to move passing through this via-point (for example strike) from previous start point to end point with the same duration. In addition, the cost which is described in Eq. (9) are met.

In the experiment, we set the start point with (112.62, 62.56, −15.53) in the operation space, which is corresponding to (0.0705, −0.8054, 1.1137) in the joint space. And the coordinates of terminal point is (118.03, 30.59, 214.26)

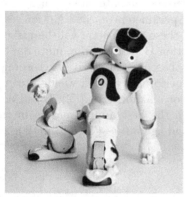
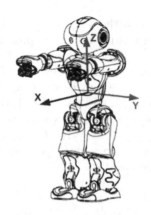

(a) the experiment platform   (b) the position of base frame

Fig. 3. The position of base frame and joints

corresponding to $(-0.15, 0.70, 1.46)$ in the joint space. We choose randomly a point $(157.46, 122.69, 78.30)$ as via point. In the joint space, this via point is with corresponding several groups of joint angle. We choose irregularly and randomly the data $(0.03, 0.15, 1.04)$ in multi group data as the value of via point in the joint space. A clear contrast between our proposed iLWR-PI^2 and classical LWR-PI^2 will be illustrated later.

We now proceeded to test the performance of iLWR-PI^2 and LWR-PI^2. Detail results are listed in Table 1. The cost function is in the form of

$$
S = 0.5 \sum_{j=1}^{3} \sum_{i=1}^{N-1} \left[10^3 \left(\ddot{x}^{(j)}(i) \right)^2 + \left(a_f^{(j)}(i) \right)^2 \right] + \sum_{j=1}^{3} 10^{10} \left[\left(x^{(j)}(m) - x_v^{(j)} \right)^2 \right]
$$
$$
+ \sum_{j=1}^{3} 10^3 \left[\left(\dot{x}^{(j)}(N) \right)^2 + \left(x^{(j)}(N) - x_g^{(j)} \right)^2 \right]
$$
(9)

Where i indicates the time index from 1 to N, j indicates the joint index from 1 to 3. Besides, $x_g^{(j)}$ denotes the expected position of point j when the task ends. When the time index equals m, $x^{(j)}(m)$ is the position of joint j which is corresponding to the expected via-point $x_v^{(j)}$ of the joint j. Apparently, $\ddot{x}^{(j)}$ is an arbitary state-dependent cost value, $a_f^{(j)}(i)$ is the acceleration (forcing term) relevant to joint j at the time index i. $\dot{x}^{(j)}(N)$ is the velocity of joint when time index is N.

According to the result, the proposed iLWR-PI^2 methods execute better than original LWR-PI^2. As for Table 1, we run fifteen times under the same condition. Shown in Table 1 the cost generated by iLWR-PI^2 are remarkably smaller than that of LWR-PI^2, which the overall weighted evaluation include energy consuming, via point and terminal status etc. It indicates that iLWR-PI^2 outperform LWR-PI^2.

Table 1. The final costs when algorithm stop

Times	Cost$_1$ (LWR-PI^2)	Cost$_2$ (iLWR-PI^2)
1st	1.39E+08	2.24E+07
2nd	1.58E+08	2.21E+07
3rd	1.32E+08	2.88E+07
4th	2.00E+08	2.25E+07
5th	2.06E+08	1.74E+07
6th	1.68E+08	1.96E+07
7th	2.03E+08	1.87E+07
8th	2.40E+08	2.03E+07
9th	1.24E+08	2.68E+07
10th	1.79E+08	1.72E+07
Mean	1.75E+08	2.16E+07

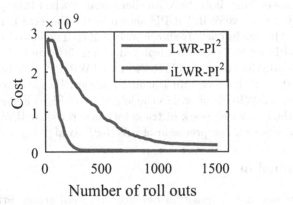

Fig. 4. The red curve shows the cost caused by iLWR-PI^2, The blue curve shows the cost caused by LWR-PI^2(Color figure online)

(a) the origin track   (b) the track of iLWR-PI^2 (c) the track of LWR-PI^2

Fig. 5. The track on the platform

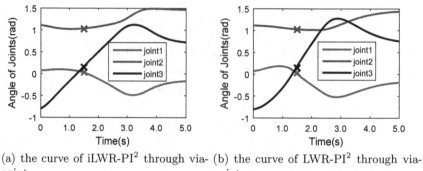

(a) the curve of iLWR-PI^2 through via-point

(b) the curve of LWR-PI^2 through via-point

Fig. 6. The curve of iLWR-PI^2 and LWR-PI^2 through via-point in the joint space

Besides, we compare the learning rate between two methods. As shown in Fig. 4, quicker coverage speed of iLWR-PI^2 is manifest.

And Fig. 6 shows the results of iLWR-PI^2 and LWR-PI^2 through via-point in the joint space. They both have excellent results when they pass the via-point. But clearly, the curve of iLWR-PI^2 shown in the Fig. 6(a) is more smooth than LWR-PI^2. The origin track is shown in Fig. 5(a). The actual track of iLWR-PI^2 and LWR-PI^2 on the robot is displayed in Fig. 5(b) and 5(c). Compared that with Fig. 5(b), the track of iLWR-PI^2 and LWR-PI^2 can go through the via-point. So they all have certain learning abilities. Besides, we can get that the trajectories of iLWR-PI^2 shown in the left figure of Fig. 5 is smoother than LWR-PI^2. And the impact to mark of trajectory generated by iLWR-PI^2 is stronger, which indicates that the precision of iLWR-PI^2 is higher.

6   Conclusion

Recently motor skill acquisition has been received strong attention to, and it is also the highlight for robot learning. However associative dilemma, broad learning and targeted improvement for robot, has still been a challenge. In this paper, we propose a novel GMR-PI^2 motor skill learning based on RBAE to overcome the dilemma throughout the all phases of LfDRL. GMR-PI^2 comprise two parts: DMPs-GMR for LfD, GMR-PI^2 for RL. Besides, affiliated RBAE can extract features discovered so far and perform target-oriented exploration with the basis function generated from previous RBAE. After this process iteratively to a certain depth, robot can obtain the capability to fulfilling unfamiliar task with an optimal/suboptimal criterion.

The most important and prominent part of our work is that we propose general RBAE framework and associated algorithms. Specially, we applied the auto-encoding method into GMR-PI^2, and this promotes the optimization more accurately. There are a few interesting future research directions along this topic. Firstly, how to seek the optimal hyper-parameters such as the noise and number of updating the parameters for PI^2 need to study, since it is somewhat time-consuming to set them suitably. Secondly, we only make uses of the latest information (best trajectories so far) in the algorithms, it is intuitive to allocate and integrate the old/new information which may make the robot more flexible. Thirdly, there are many set of basis functions generated by RBAE which are the features in different proficiency scale. How to utilized them in parallel is a promising research direction.

References

Argall, B.D., Chernova, S., Veloso, M., Browning, B.: A survey of robot learning from demonstration. Robot. Auton. Syst. **57**(5), 469–483 (2009)

Atkeson, C.G., Moore, A.W., Schaal, S.: Locally weighted learning. Artif. Intell. Rev. **11**(1), 11–73 (1997)

Deisenroth, M., Neumann, G., Peters, J.: A survey on policy search for robotics. J. Intell. Rob. Syst. **15**(1), 1–2 (2013)

Gregory, M.D., Martin, S.V., Werner, D.H.: Improved electromagnetics optimization: the covariance matrix adaptation evolutionary strategy. IEEE Antennas Propag. Mag. **57**(3), 48–59 (2015). https://doi.org/10.1109/MAP.2015.2437277

Ijspeert, A.J., Nakanishi, J., Hoffmann, H., Pastor, P., Schaal, S.: Dynamical movement primitives: learning attractor models for motor behaviors. Neural Comput. **25**(2), 328–373 (2013)

Khansari-Zadeh, S.M., Billard, A.: BM: an iterative algorithm to learn stable nonlinear dynamical systems with Gaussian mixture models. In: 2010 IEEE International Conference on Robotics and Automation, Anchorage, USA, pp. 2381–2388 (2010)

Khansari-Zadeh, S.M., Billard, A.: Learning stable nonlinear dynamical systems with Gaussian mixture models. IEEE Trans. Robot. **27**(5), 943–957 (2011)

Parisi, S., Abdulsamad, H., Paraschos, A., Daniel, C., Peters, J.: Reinforcement learning vs human programming in tetherball robot games. In: 2015 IEEE International conference on Intelligent Robots and Systems, Hamburg, Germany, pp. 6428–6434 (2015)

Peters, J., Schaal, S.: Reinforcement learning of motor skills with policy gradients. Neural Netw. Off. J. Int. Neural Netw. Soc. **21**(4), 682 (2008)

Peters, J., Mülling, K., Altun, Y.: Relative entropy policy search. In: 24th AAAI, Atlanta, Westin, USA, pp. 1607–1612 (2010)

Pfeifer, R., Bongard, J.: How the Body Shapes the Way We Think: A New View of Intelligence. MIT Press, Cambridge (2006)

Rombokas, E., Malhotra, M., Theodorou, E.A., Todorov, E., Matsuoka, Y.: Reinforcement learning and synergistic control of the ACT hand. IEEE Trans. Mechatron. **18**(2), 569–577 (2013). https://doi.org/10.1109/TMECH.2012.2219880

Theodorou, E., Buchli, J., Schaal, S.: A generalized path integral control approach to reinforcement learning. J. Mach. Learn. Res. **11**, 3137–3181 (2010)

Ude, A., Asfour, G.T.A.: Task-specific generalization of discrete and periodic dynamic movement primitives. IEEE Trans. Robot. **26**(5), 800–815 (2010)

Motion Control

Way-Point Tracking Control of Underactuated USV Based on GPC Path Planning

Tao Jiang, Yi Yang, Huizi Chen, Xu Wang, and Dan Zhang[✉]

Shanghai University, Shangda Road 99, Shanghai, China
dan.zhang@shu.edu.cn

Abstract. In order to solve the problems of large tracking error and slow error convergence in the tracking process of underactuated asymmetric unmanned surface vehicles (USV) in sharp turns and other extreme paths, an adaptive sliding mode control method based on generalized predictive control (GPC) algorithm (LOS-GPC-SMC) is proposed. Firstly, the path generation part takes into account the mobility constraints of USV, and realizes path generation by GPC combined with Line-of-Sight (LOS). Secondly, due to the asymmetry of the dynamic model of USV, the global homeomorphic differential transformation is used to transform and decouple the state variables of the system. After that, in order to effectively compensate the model uncertainty and external disturbance in the tracking process of USV, the adaptive sliding mode control method is used to design the actual control law to ensure error stabilization and realize path tracking. Finally, the effectiveness of the proposed control strategy is verified by a large number of simulation experiments.

Keywords: Underactuated unmanned surface vehicle · Way-point tracking · Path generation

1 Introduction

Way-point tracking control for underactuated USV includes two aspects: path generation and path tracking for the generated path. The expected trajectory of an underactuated USV is usually obtained by giving the expected position points at each moment, but the usually given trajectory often does not contain the ship's mobility constraints. At the same time, the path tracking control of underactuated USV is also a long-standing control problem, which has been paid attention by the control community for many years [1]. Since the USV has only longitudinal driving force and yaw moment generated by the tail rudder and no lateral driving force, it cannot directly eliminate lateral drift and can only indirectly eliminate lateral error by adjusting yaw angle through yaw moment. Moreover, USV is a typical system with large inertia, nonlinearity and uncertainty of motion model. It is also affected by external environment interference such as wind, wave and current when sailing on the sea surface, which makes accurate path tracking of USV very difficult [2]. Gao et al. presents a predictive optimization-based model reference adaptive control (MRAC) approach for dynamic positioning (DP) of a fully actuated underwater vehicle subject to dynamic uncertainties and actuator saturation [3]. Wu et al. combines GPC with PID control,

© Springer Nature Switzerland AG 2019
H. Yu et al. (Eds.): ICIRA 2019, LNAI 11745, pp. 393–406, 2019.
https://doi.org/10.1007/978-3-030-27529-7_34

and designs GPC-PID cascade controller to control the heading motion and steering motion of USV, indirectly realizing the path tracking control of USV [4]. Yu etc. proposed a sliding mode control law based on surge velocity tracking error and lateral motion tracking error for the robust tracking control of underactuated USV with parameter uncertainty, thus realizing trajectory tracking [5]. Oh et al. designed a model predictive control scheme with LOS path generation capability, and used the three-degree-of-freedom model of USV in the controller design to realize the path following of underactuated surface vehicle with input constraints [1]. Liu et al. proposed a new path following guidance law for underactuated marine surface vessels, and formed a cascade system of tracking error system and prediction error system to realize path tracking [6]. McNinch et al. uses a nonlinear discrete model predictive controller to solve the propulsion and heading control inputs of USV with input saturation and input constraints, and to accomplish specific targets such as minimum error or minimum time, thus realizing trajectory tracking [7]. Wang et al. described ship dynamics using Serreret framework and designed an adaptive path following control law to enable underactuated ships to travel along a predetermined path at a constant forward speed with uncertain parameters [8]. Zhu et al. put forward a sliding mode control method based on upper and lower bounds to solve the problem of model parameter uncertainty and disturbance of external wind waves and currents encountered by underactuated USV in realizing track tracking control of horizontal plane [9]. Zhang et al. combines Kalman filter, disturbance observer and robust constrained model predictive control to propose a new rolling constrained ship path following control method [10]. Soltan et al. proposed a method based on nonlinear sliding mode control, which combines trajectory planning, tracking and coordinated control of USV [11]. Bibuli et al. proposed a linear following guidance scheme for underactuated marine systems, the difference of which is in the definition of the error variables to be stabilized to zero [12]. Tribou et al. proposed a new path following controller that mediates visual control stability [13]. Xu et al. proposed a backstepping adaptive dynamic sliding mode control method for the path following control system of underactuated surface vessel [14]. Pettersen et al. designed the full-state feedback control law by cascade method, and realized the tracking control of ship's way points by yaw torque control [15].

Way-point tracking control usually includes two aspects, path generation and path tracking. The virtual path of most of the above articles is given directly through mathematical expressions, and does not include the maneuvering characteristics constraints of ships. If the given trajectory does not conform to the sailing limit that the hull can reach, especially at the inflection point of the path. If the path includes the physical limitations of the hull, can the ship bend in a more reasonable way? Therefore, how to include the physical properties of the hull in the generated way-points is a focus of this paper. In addition, most of the models used in the above article are based on symmetric models to design controllers, but the model of "jinghai 8-b" has the characteristics of asymmetry. How to realize the tracking control of the virtual trajectory under the interference of the model is also the focus of this article.

2   Problem Description and Model Identification

The dynamic motion of USV is very complicated. Analyzing its motion state involves six degrees of freedom. However, in the actual control analysis, it is often simplified as a three-degree-of-freedom motion analysis, that is, it contains only surge, swaying and yaw motion. The research object of this paper is "jinghai 8-b" USV. When analyzing its motion, only the surge motion, swaying motion and yawing motion are discussed, that is, only the surge velocity u, swaying velocity v and yawing velocity r are concerned [16].

Motion System in Fixed Geodetic Coordinate System:

$$\begin{cases} \dot{x} = v_x \cos\psi - v_y \sin\psi \\ \dot{y} = v_y \cos\psi + v_x \sin\psi \\ \dot{\psi} = r \end{cases} \tag{1}$$

$$\begin{cases} m_{11}\dot{u} - m_{22}vr + d_{11}u = \tau_x + \tau_1 \\ m_{22}\dot{v} + m_{11}ur + d_{22}v = \tau_2 \\ m_{33}\dot{r} + (m_{22} - m_{11})ur + d_{33}r = \tau_r + \tau_3 \end{cases} \tag{2}$$

Where x, y, ψ is the position and heading angle in the fixed coordinate system of the earth. v_x, v_y is the velocity component of the USV in the hull coordinate system, and r is the yaw rate of the USV. $d_{11}, d_{22}, d_{33}, m_{11}, m_{22}, m_{33}$ is the hydrodynamic damping coefficient and inertia parameter including additional mass of the ship system respectively. Control inputs τ_u and τ_r are the longitudinal thrust and steering torque of the ship respectively. τ_1, τ_2, τ_3 is the interference force and moment generated by the external environment.

Since there is no lateral propulsion device and no control input is available in the lateral direction, the ship path tracking problem studied is an underactuated control problem. The problem of way-point tracking control for underactuated USV can be divided into virtual path generation and path tracking control (as shown in Fig. 1. Path generation uses GPC combined with LOS to generate the desired path. The virtual path tracking is realized by designing an adaptive sliding mode controller. How to make the control target drive the USV with asymmetric model to sail along the virtual trajectory by designing feedback control law is also a research focus of the article.

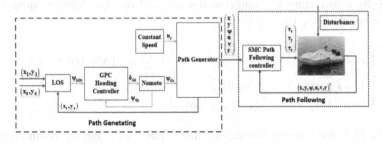

Fig. 1. "Jinghai 8-b" control block diagram.

3   Path Generation and Path Tracking

LOS-GPC is used to generate the desired path. The desired heading angle AA is generated by LOS, and the heading controller is designed by GPC to track AA. The control object is the Nomoto model of USV. So as to generate a path considering the constraint of ship maneuvering characteristics. After the virtual path is generated at the next moment, an adaptive sliding mode control method is adopted to track the virtual path. Because the dynamic model of "jinghai 8-b" USV is asymmetric, the model needs to be preprocessed and decoupled.

3.1   Virtual Path Generation

Design of Virtual Path Generation Controller. The path generation design block diagram is shown in Fig. 1. (x_1, y_1) is the expected way-point in LOS, (x_0, y_0) is the initial point in LOS, δ_{Gr} is the rudder angle value calculated by GPC heading controller at the next moment, ψ_{Gs} is the heading angle that the ship can reach under the action of δ_{Gr}, and also serves as the expected heading angle in the path tracking process. u_r is the desired speed. Through integration and coordinate transformation, the desired position (x_r, y_r) at the next moment can be calculated, thus generating the desired path.

The relevant coefficients $K = 0.1555$ and $T_0 = 0.2214$ in Nomoto model of "jinghai 8-b" are identified through experiments. Therefore, the Nomoto model of "jinghai 8-b" USV is obtained as follows:

$$G(s)_{\delta\psi} = \frac{0.1555}{0.2214s^2 + s} \tag{3}$$

As shown in the following formula, the identified wild model of "jinghai 8-b" is discretized, and the sampling Period is 0.2 s:

$$\psi_{GS}(t) - 1.405\psi_{GS}(t-1) + 0.4052\psi_{GS}(t-2)$$
$$= 0.01062\delta_{GS}(t-1) + 0.007875\delta_{GS}(t-2) \tag{4}$$

$\psi_{GS}(t)$ and $\delta_{GS}(t)$ are the heading angle and virtual rudder angle at time t respectively.

In order to solve the local optimal solution, GPC is the most commonly used method. By constructing an evaluation function and two Diophantine equations for recursive solution [17, 18]:

$$\begin{cases} J = \varepsilon\{ \sum_{j=N_0}^{N_1} (\psi_{GS}(t+j) - \psi_{LOS}(t+j))^2 + \sum_{j=1}^{N_u} \lambda(j)(\Delta\delta_{GS}(t+j-1))^2 \} \\ 1 = E_j(z^{-1})A_1(z^{-1})\Delta + z^{-j}F_j(z^{-1}) \\ E_j(z^{-1})B_1(z^{-1}) = G_j(z^{-1}) + z^{-j}H_j(z^{-1}) \end{cases} \tag{5}$$

Where N_0 is the minimum prediction time domain, N_1 is the maximum prediction time domain, N_u is the control time domain, $\lambda(j)$ is the control weighting sequence.

$A_j, B_j, E_j, F_j, G_j, H_j$ are the polynomial of difference operator $\Delta = 1 - z^{-1}$. At the same time, rudder angle saturation should also be taken as an important factor in solving the optimal deflection angle, namely $-30° \leq \delta_{GS} \leq 30°$.

In order to minimize the evaluation function, J deduces the control law that minimizes the evaluation function as follows:

$$\Delta\delta_{GS}(t) = P^T[\psi_{LOS} - H\Delta\delta_{GS}(t-1) - F\psi_{GS}(t)] \qquad (6)$$

Where P^T takes the first row of $(G^TG + \lambda I)^{-1} G^T$, and the optimal control law at the next moment is:

$$\delta_{GS}(t) = \delta_{GS}(t-1) + \Delta\delta_{GS}(t) \qquad (7)$$

After the design of the heading controller of the virtual ship is completed, the expected heading angle of the actual ship can be generated by combining the identified Nomoto model, and the path is generated at a fixed speed. Through the expected heading angle and speed at each moment, the expected position point (x_r, y_r) at the next moment can be generated. The next problem to be considered is how to track the expected position point (x_r, y_r) at each moment.

3.2 Path Tracking

Because there are non-diagonal elements m_{23} and m_{32} in the inertia matrix $\mathbf{M}$ of the "jinghai 8-b" model, there will be coupling terms after the formula is expanded, so the system model needs to be preprocessed before the controller design.

Model Preprocessing. In order to eliminate the coupling term and facilitate the design of the controller, a homeomorphic differential transformation is carried out on the dynamics model of USV. Design the converted position and velocity state variables $z_i(i = 1, \ldots, 6)$ as follows:

$$\begin{cases} \dot{z}_{1e} = z_4 - v_p \cos(z_{3e}) + z_6 z_{2e} \\ z_1 = x + \frac{m_{23}}{m_{22}}(\cos(\psi) - 1) \\ z_2 = y + \frac{m_{23}}{m_{22}}\sin(\psi) \\ z_3 = \psi \\ z_4 = u \\ z_5 = v + \frac{m_{23}}{m_{22}}r \\ z_6 = r \end{cases} \qquad (8)$$

Carry out the following transformation design on the control input thrust and torque:

$$\begin{cases} f_1 = \dfrac{1}{m_{11}}(\tau_u + m_{22}vr + \dfrac{(m_{23}+m_{32})}{2}r^2 - d_{11}u) \\ f_2 = \dfrac{m_{22}}{m_{22}m_{33}-m_{32}m_{23}}\{\tau_r + (m_{11}-m_{22})uv + \\ \quad [\dfrac{m_{11}m_{32}}{m_{22}} - \dfrac{(m_{23}+m_{32})}{2}]ur + \\ \quad (m_{32}d_{22}-m_{22}d_{32})v/m_{22} - (m_{22}d_{33}-m_{32}d_{23})r/m_{22}\} \end{cases} \tag{9}$$

Similarly, the following transformation design is carried out on the external interference force and moment:

$$\begin{cases} f_{e1} = \dfrac{1}{m_{11}}\tau_1 \\ f_{e2} = \dfrac{m_{23}}{m_{22}m_{33}-m_{32}m_{23}}(\dfrac{m_{33}}{m_{23}}\tau_2 - \dfrac{m_{32}}{m_{22}}\tau_3) \\ f_{e3} = -\dfrac{m_{32}}{m_{22}m_{33}-m_{32}m_{23}}\tau_3 \end{cases} \tag{10}$$

The transformed system can be obtained by derivation as shown in the following formula:

$$\begin{cases} \dot{z}_1 = z_4\cos(z_3) - z_5\sin(z_3) \\ \dot{z}_2 = z_4\sin(z_3) + z_5\cos(z_3) \\ \dot{z}_3 = z_6 \\ \dot{z}_4 = f_1 + f_{e1} \\ \dot{z}_5 = -\alpha z_4 z_6 - \beta z_5 + \gamma z_6 + f_{e2} \\ \dot{z}_6 = f_2 + f_{e3} \end{cases} \tag{11}$$

Where $\alpha = m_{11}/m_{22}$, $\beta = d_{22}/m_{22}$, $\gamma = d_{22}m_{23}/m_{22}^2 - d_{23}/m_{22}$.

The actual position and actual speed of the system are $\mathbf{z} = [z_1, z_2, z_3, z_4, z_5, z_6]^T$. The expected path and expected speed $(x_r, y_r, \psi_r, u_r, v_r, r_r)$ generated by LOS-GPC are transformed according to Eq. (3.5) to obtain the transformed expected pose and expected speed $\mathbf{z}_d = [z_{1d}, z_{2d}, z_{3d}, z_{4d}, z_{5d}, z_{6d}]^T$, and the tracking error is defined as $\mathbf{z}_e = [z_{1e}, z_{2e}, z_{3e}, z_{4e}, z_{5e}, z_{6e}]^T$. The control objective is to design the control inputs τ_u and τ_r so that the tracking error can converge to the initial state field with any small error. At the same time, in order to deal with the uncertainty of the model and external interference, an adaptive term is added to reduce the impact.

Design of Path Tracking Controller. Referring to the design method of adaptive sliding mode control law in article [19], the path tracking error is converted first. Then, longitudinal sliding mode adaptive law, transverse sliding mode adaptive law, steering sliding mode flour and adaptive law are designed respectively.

Transition from Track Tracking to Tracking Error. LOS-GPC generates the desired way-point at the next moment. After (8) transformation, the X-axis and Y-axis can be expressed as z_{1d} and z_{2d} in the fixed coordinate system, and the heading angle is denoted as z_{3d}. Define the position and heading tracking errors under the hull coordinate system as follows:

$$\begin{bmatrix} z_{1e} \\ z_{2e} \\ z_{3e} \end{bmatrix} = \begin{bmatrix} \cos(z_3) & \sin(z_3) & 0 \\ -\sin(z_3) & \cos(z_3) & 0 \\ 0 & 0 & 1 \end{bmatrix} \begin{bmatrix} z_1 - z_{1d} \\ z_2 - z_{2d} \\ z_3 - z_{3d} \end{bmatrix} \qquad (12)$$

$\eta_e = [z_{1e}, z_{2e}, z_{3e}]^T$ is defined as the tracking pose error in the hull coordinate system and $\eta_d = [z_{1d}, z_{2d}, z_{3d}]^T$ is the expected pose in the geodetic coordinate system.

Definition $v_p = \sqrt{\dot{z}_{1d}^2 + \dot{z}_{2d}^2}$.

In order to analyze the position and pose tracking error, the derivative of Eq. (11) is derived:

$$\begin{cases} \dot{z}_{1e} = z_4 - v_p \cos(z_{3e}) + z_6 z_{2e} \\ \dot{z}_{2e} = z_5 + v_p \sin(z_{3e}) - z_6 z_{1e} \end{cases} \qquad (13)$$

In order to stabilize the tracking error of the system, the Lyapunov function of the designed system is:

$$V_1 = \frac{1}{2}(z_{1e}^2 + z_{2e}^2) \qquad (14)$$

Derivation of Lyapunov function V_1 is available:

$$\dot{V}_1 = z_{1e}[z_4 - v_p \cos(z_{3e})] + z_{2e}[z_5 + v_p \sin(z_{3e})] \qquad (15)$$

Then, using the idea of backstepping, in order to make the system satisfy Lyapunov stability, V_1 needs to be set negatively. z_4 and z_3 are selected as virtual control inputs to stabilize tracking errors z_{1e} and z_{2e} respectively. In order to avoid the Euler angle singularity of $z_3 = \psi$, the following virtual velocity variable ϖ_v is selected instead of z_{3e}:

$$\varpi_v = v_p \sin(z_{3e}) \qquad (16)$$

z_4 and ϖ_v are taken as virtual control variables to stabilize the tracking error, and their expected values are respectively selected as follows:

$$\begin{cases} z_{4d} = v_p \cos(z_{3e}) - k_1 z_{1e}/E \\ \varpi_d = -z_5 - k_2 z_{2e}/E \end{cases} \qquad (17)$$

Where $E = \sqrt{1 + z_{1e}^2 + z_{2e}^2}$. k_1 and k_2 are normal numbers.

Based on the expected value of the virtual control quantity, the tracking errors of the virtual control quantities z_4 and ϖ_v are further defined as follows:

$$\begin{cases} z_{4e} = z_4 - z_{4d} \\ \varpi_{ve} = \varpi_v - \varpi_{vd} \end{cases} \qquad (18)$$

$\dot{V}_1$ can be rewritten as:

$$\dot{V}_1 = -(k_1 z_{1e}^2 + k_2 z_{2e}^2)/E + z_{1e} z_{4e} + \varpi_{ve} z_{2e} \tag{19}$$

When the tracking error of the virtual control input tends to zero, $\dot{V}_1$ can reach a negative value. So far, the tracking problem has been transformed into the problem of stabilizing the tracking error of the system. When the tracking error of the virtual control input approaches zero, the system will reach the equilibrium point.

Design of Longitudinal Sliding Mode flour and Adaptive Law. After the trajectory tracking problem is transformed into the tracking error stabilization problem, the is first stabilized according to Eq. (15) as follows:

$$\dot{z}_{4e} = \frac{1}{m_{11}} \left(\tau_u + \tau_1 + m_{22} vr + \frac{(m_{23} + m_{32})}{2} r^2 - d_{11} u - m_{11} \dot{z}_{4d} \right) \tag{20}$$

In Eq. (20), take the uncertainty of the system as:

$$U_1 = \tau_1 + m_{22} vr + \frac{(m_{23} + m_{32})}{2} r^2 - d_{11} u - m_{11} \dot{z}_{4d} \tag{21}$$

The estimated value of the system uncertainty is defined U_1 as $\hat{U}_1$, and the difference between the uncertainty and the estimated value is $\tilde{U}_1$. Select the following Lyapunov equation:

$$V_2 = V_1 + \frac{1}{2} m_{11} z_{4e}^2 + \frac{1}{2} \tilde{U}_1^2 \tag{22}$$

The sliding mode flour of the design control input z_4 is:

$$S_1 = \lambda_1 z_{4e} + \dot{z}_{4e} + \frac{z_{1e}}{m_{11}} - \frac{\tilde{U}_1}{m_{11}} \tag{23}$$

The Lyapunov function of the selected control system is:

$$V_3 = V_2 + \frac{1}{2} m_{11} S_1^2 \tag{24}$$

Derivation of V_3:

$$\dot{V}_3 = -(k_1 z_{1e}^2 + k_2 z_{2e}^2)/E + \varpi_{ve} z_{2e} + m_{11} z_{4e} S_1 - \lambda_1 m_{11} z_{4e}^2 \\ + (z_{4e} - \hat{U}_1) \tilde{U}_1 + S_1 [\lambda_1 (U_1 + \tau_u) + \dot{\tau}_u + \dot{U}_1 + \dot{z}_{1e}] \tag{25}$$

Design $\dot{\tau}_u$:

$$\dot{\tau}_u = -\lambda_1(\hat{U}_1 + \tau_u) - \dot{\hat{U}}_1 - \dot{z}_{1e} - m_{11}z_{4e} - k_{s1}\text{sgn}(S_1) - w_{s1}S_1 \tag{26}$$

k_{s1} and w_{s1} are constants of reaching rate of synovial membrane controller. The adaptive law is designed as follows:

$$\dot{\hat{U}}_1 = z_{4e} + \lambda_1 S_1 \tag{27}$$

Design of Transverse Adaptive Law. Stabilization of virtual control input error ϖ_{ve}:

$$\dot{\varpi}_{ve} = \dot{v}_p \sin(z_{3e}) + v_p \cos(z_{3e})(z_6 - \dot{z}_{3d}) + \frac{U_2}{m_{22}} + Q_1 \tag{28}$$

Where U_2 is an uncertain item and Q_1 is an abbreviated item. The virtual control is selected to stabilize ϖ_{ve}. $\hat{U}_2$ is defined as the estimated value of the system uncertainty U_2, and the difference between U_2 and $\hat{U}_2$ is defined as $\tilde{U}_2$.

The influence of system uncertainty is eliminated by adaptive law. The expected input to define z_6 is:

$$z_{6d} = \dot{z}_{3d} + \frac{-\dot{v}_p \sin(z_{3e}) - \hat{U}_2/m_{22} - Q_1 - k_3\varpi_{ve} - z_{2e}/m_{22}}{v_p \cos(z_{3e})} \tag{29}$$

Where k_3 is a positive number. Definition z_{6e} is:

$$z_{6e} = z_6 - z_{6d} \tag{30}$$

Select Lyapunov function:

$$V_4 = V_3 + \frac{1}{2}m_{22}\varpi_{ve}^2 + \frac{1}{2}\tilde{U}_2^2 \tag{31}$$

The adaptive law defining the system uncertainty estimate $\hat{U}_2$:

$$\dot{\hat{U}}_2 = \varpi_{ve} \tag{32}$$

Derivation V_4 of gives:

$$\dot{V}_4 = -(k_1 z_{1e}^2 + k_2 z_{2e}^2)/E - \lambda_1 m_{11} z_{4e}^2 - k_{s1}|S_1| - w_{s1}S_1^2 - k_3 m_{22}\varpi_{ve}^2 \\ + m_{22}\varpi_{ve}z_{6e}v_p \cos(z_{3e}) \tag{33}$$

Design of Steering Sliding Mode flour and Adaptive Law. The auxiliary virtual control quantity z_6 is introduced above, and then the error of z_6 should be stabilized. Derivation of z_{6e} gives:

$$\dot{z}_{6e} = \frac{1}{\zeta}(\tau_r + U_3) \tag{34}$$

Where $\zeta = (m_{22}m_{33} - m_{32}m_{23})/m_{22}$, U_3 is the uncertainty of the system. $\hat{U}_3$ is defined as the estimated value of the system uncertainty U_3, and the difference between the uncertainty and the estimated value is defined as $\tilde{U}_3$. The stability of r_e is proved by Lyapunov function:

$$V_5 = V_4 + \frac{1}{2}\zeta z_{6e}^2 + \frac{1}{2}\tilde{U}_3^2 \tag{35}$$

The sliding mode flour of Design z_6 is:

$$S_2 = \lambda_2 z_{6e} + \dot{z}_{6e} + \frac{m_{22}\varpi_{ve}v_p\cos(z_{3e}) - \tilde{U}_3}{\zeta} \tag{36}$$

Where λ_2 is a constant, and $Q_2 = m_{22}\varpi_{ve}v_p\cos(z_{3e})/\zeta$.

In order to verify the stability of the sliding mode controller, the following Lyapunov function is taken for the system:

$$V_6 = V_5 + \frac{1}{2}\zeta S_2^2 \tag{37}$$

The design actual control input τ_r is:

$$\tau_r = -\lambda_2(\tau_r + U_3) - \dot{\hat{U}}_3 - \zeta\dot{Q}_2 - \zeta z_{6e} - k_{s2}\text{sgn}(S_2) - w_{s2}S_2^2 \tag{38}$$

The constants k_{s2} and w_{s2} here are constants of the reaching rate of the sliding mode controller and are used to adjust the time when the system approaches the sliding mode flour. An adaptive law is designed:

$$\dot{\hat{U}}_3 = z_{6e} + \lambda_2 S_2 \tag{39}$$

Available:

$$\dot{V}_6 = -(k_1 z_{1e}^2 + k_2 z_{2e}^2)/E - k_3\varpi_{ve}^2 - \lambda_1 z_{4e}^2 - \lambda_2 z_{6e}^2 \\ - k_{s1}|S_1| - w_{s1}S_1^2 - k_{s2}|S_2| - w_{s2}S_2^2 \leq 0 \tag{40}$$

System Stability Analysis. When USV uses the adaptive sliding mode controller designed as above, the tracking error of the control system is assumed to be $\boldsymbol{\varepsilon} = [z_{1e}, z_{2e}, z_{3e}, z_{4e}, \varpi_e, z_{6e}, \tilde{U}_1, \tilde{U}_2, \tilde{U}_3]$. After the system changes from the initial state, the tracking error will tend to zero over a period of time. When ε tends to zero, the tracking error of the system before transformation will also tend to zero, and the system is globally uniformly asymptotically stable.

4 Simulation Experiment

4.1 Tracking Effect

The simulation object is "jinghai 8-b" USV. $K = 0.1555$ and $T_0 = 0.2214$ were identified through experiments, therefore Nomoto model of "jinghai 8-b" USV was obtained. In LOS-GPC-SMC system, two kinds of simulation experiments are carried out:

(1) The tracking effect of two way-points: Starting from (0 m,0 m) to (100 m,100 m) at a constant speed of 1 m/s. The initial heading angle of the ship is 0 rad, and the simulation is carried out in the presence of constant disturbance. The blue line indicates the trajectory points generated by LOS-GPC at each moment, and the red line indicates the tracking situation under the action of the controller. The tracking effect is shown in Fig. 2.

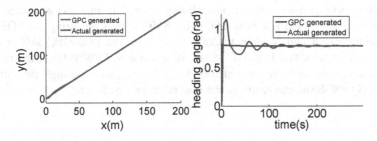

Fig. 2. Path tracking and heading tracking diagram. (Color figure online)

(2) The tracking effect of multiple way-points: Starting from (0 m, 0 m)–(100 m, 100 m)–(300 m, 100 m)–(450 m, 0 m), task is realized at a constant speed of 1 m/s. The initial heading angle of the ship is 0 rad, and the simulation is carried out in the presence of constant disturbance. As shown in Fig. 3, the blue line represents the trajectory points generated by LOS-GPC at each time, and the red line represents the tracking path under the action of the adaptive sliding mode controller. It can be seen from the figure that the USV has reached all the designated way-points, and the trajectory is relatively smooth. Only at (100 m, 100 m) does the trajectory show large amplitude jitter, but it also stabilized the trajectory quickly.

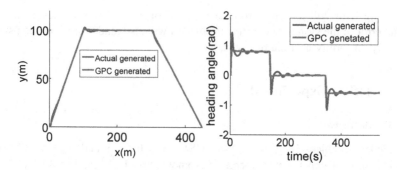

Fig. 3. Path tracking and heading tracking diagram. (Color figure online)

4.2 Comparative Analysis of Simulation

If LOS-GPC is not used to generate the desired trajectory at each moment and LOS guidance is directly used, the actual trajectory will deflect greatly during tracking because the desired trajectory does not consider the physical limitations of its driver. As shown in Fig. 4, the desired trajectory generated by the hull from (0 m, 0 m)–(100 m, 100 m)–(200 m, 0 m)–(300 m, 100 m) blue line; The black line is the desired trajectory generated by LOS, and the path tracking (hereinafter referred to as LOS-SMC system) is directly performed by adaptive sliding mode. The trajectory generated by the actual ship when the red line is in LOS-GPC-SMC state; Comparing the LOS-SMC path tracking result and heading tracking result with the LOS-GPC-SMC tracking result, it can be seen that LOS-GPC-SMC is superior to LOS-SMC in the recovery performance of tracking the desired trajectory. After passing through the inflection point, LOS-GPC-SMC can return to the desired trajectory faster.

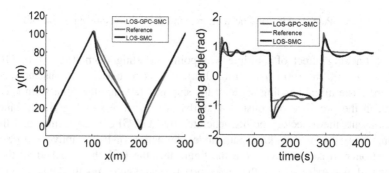

Fig. 4. Path tracking and heading tracking. (Color figure online)

5 Conclusion

In order to solve the problem of how to realize way-point tracking control of an underactuated USV with asymmetric model under the condition of interference, this paper proposes to use LOS-GPC to generate the desired trajectory, decouple the model through homeomorphic differential transformation, and design the hull controller with sliding mode control to design the whole system. In order to simplify the control, the transformation relationship between the virtual rudder angle of "jinghai 8-b" and the double propellers is identified through experiments. In addition, in order to include the physical properties of the hull in the generated virtual path, the Nomoto model of the hull is identified through experiments, and the model is applied to LOS-GPC to generate the desired trajectory. The simulation results show that the whole system has good robustness in the presence of external interference.

References

1. Oh, S., Sun, J.: Path following of underactuated marine surface vessels using line-of-sight based model predictive control. Ocean Eng. **37**(2), 289–295 (2010)
2. Changxi, L., Yuan, F., Li, Y.: Design of a linear track controller for incomplete driving ships based on back stepping method. Ship Eng. **30**(4), 64–67 (2008)
3. Gao, J., Wu, P., Li, T., et al.: Optimization-based model reference adaptive control for dynamic positioning of a fully actuated underwater vehicle. Nonlinear Dyn. **87**(4), 1–13 (2016)
4. Peng, Y., Wu, W., Liu, M.: UAV track tracking GPC - PID cascade control. Control Eng. **21**(2), 245–248 (2014)
5. Yu, R., Zhu, Q., Xia, G.: Sliding mode tracking control of an underactuated surface vessel. IET Control Theory Appl. **6**(3), 461 (2012)
6. Liu, L., Dan, W., Peng, Z.: Predictor-based line-of-sight guidance law for path following of underactuated marine surface vessels. In: Sixth International Conference on Intelligent Control & Information Processing (2016)
7. McNinch, L.C., Muske, K.R., Ashrafiuon, H.: Model-based predictive control of an unmanned surface vessel. In: Proceedings of the 11th IASTED International Conference on Intelligent Systems and Control, pp. 385–390 (2008)
8. Wang, X., Zou, Z., Li, T.: Adaptive path following controller of underactuated ships using Serret-Frenet frame. J. Shanghai Jiaotong Univ. (Sci.) **15**(3), 334–339 (2010)
9. Qidan, Z., Ruiting, Y., Guihua, X.: Sliding mode robust control for track tracking of underactuated ships with wind wave and current disturbance and parameter uncertainty. Control Theory Appl. **29**(7), 959–964 (2012)
10. Zhang, J., Sun, T., Liu, Z.: Robust model predictive control for path-following of underactuated surface vessels with roll constraints. Ocean Eng. **143**, 125–132 (2017)
11. Soltan, R.A., Ashrafiuon, H., Muske, K.R.: State-dependent trajectory planning and tracking control of unmanned surface vessels. In: American Control Conference. IEEE (2009)
12. Bibuli, M., Bruzzone, G., Caccia, M.: Line following guidance control: application to the Charlie USV. In: IEEE/RSJ International Conference on Intelligent Robots & Systems. DBLP (2008)

13. Daly, J.M., Tribou, M.J., Waslander, S.L.: A nonlinear path following controller for an underactuated unmanned surface vessel. In: 2012 IEEE/RSJ International Conference on Intelligent Robots and Systems, pp. 82–87. IEEE (2012)
14. Xu, D., Liao, Y., Pang, Y.: Backstepping control method for the path following for the underactuated surface vehicles. Procedia Eng. **15**(7), 256–263 (2011)
15. Pettersen, K.Y., Lefeber, E.: Way-point tracking control of ships. In: IEEE Conference on Decision & Control (2001)
16. Fossen, T.I.: Handbook of Marine Craft Hydrodynamics and Motion Control. Wiley, Hoboken (2011)
17. Wei, W.: Generalized Predictive Control Theory and Its Application. Science Press, Beijing (1998)
18. Clarke, D.W., Mohtadi, C., Tuffs, P.S.: Generalized predictive control—Part I. The basic algorithm. Automatica **23**(87), 137–148 (1987)
19. Jian, W., Wang, M., Qiao, L.: Dynamical sliding mode control for the trajectory tracking of underactuated unmanned underwater vehicles. Ocean Eng. **105**, 54–63 (2015)

Neural Networks-Based PID Precision Motion Control of a Piezo-Actuated Microinjector

Yizheng Yan and Qingsong Xu[(✉)]

Department of Electromechanical Engineering, Faculty of Science and Technology,
University of Macau, Macau, China
qsxu@um.edu.mo,
https://www.fst.um.edu.mo/en/staff/fstqsx.html

Abstract. Piezoelectric actuators are widely employed in the field of micro-/nanomanipulation. However, hysteresis is the dominant issue in piezoelectric actuators, which leads to a great challenge to achieve high precision micromanipulation. Proportional-integral-derivative (PID) control is an efficient approach to reduce hysteresis effect in piezoelectric actuators. However, its parameter tuning is a time-consuming work for PID motion tracking control implementation. In this work, the neural networks (NN) is adopted to provide a functional model for PID with optimized parameters. It enables an intelligent and adaptive motion tracking process. The effectiveness of the presented NN-based PID control scheme is verified by performing simulation studies.

Keywords: Piezoelectric actuator · Hysteresis · PID control · Neural networks · Precision motion control

1 Introduction

At present, precision micromanipulation systems have attracted increasing interests in various fields such as atomic force microscopy [1] and biological cell micromanipulation [2], etc. Owing to the advantages of fast response speed and high accuracy [3], piezoelectric actuators (PZT) have been employed in many applications, such as bio-cell microinjection [4]. The objective of this research is to achieve precision motion control of a piezo-driven microinjector dedicated to biological cell microinjection.

The current research aims to realize an accurate position tracking of the microinjector for cell manipulation. However, a great challenge has been identified by open-loop test of the microinjector system. That is, the inherent hysteresis exists in PZT, which indicates that there is nonlinearity in the system [5]. It is a tough work to control such systems with hysteresis, because many stand-alone linear control techniques lose their effect.

For the purpose of control design, the piezo-driven microinjector is represented by a second-order dynamics model cascaded with Bouc-Wen hysteresis

© Springer Nature Switzerland AG 2019
H. Yu et al. (Eds.): ICIRA 2019, LNAI 11745, pp. 407–418, 2019.
https://doi.org/10.1007/978-3-030-27529-7_35

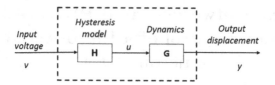

Fig. 1. Hammerstein structure of the piezo-driven microinjector device.

model [6]. System model identification and hysteresis model parameter identification are realized for the controller design. Many approaches have been used to compensate for the drawback of hysteresis, such as sliding mode control [7], model predictive control, etc. These approaches have been applied to suppress the hysteresis phenomenon effectively. However, the controller design based on such approaches is generally a time-consuming process, and the compensation accuracy is limited by the accuracy of the established model.

PID control is a simple and powerful control strategy owing to its ability to handle the problem of disturbance and time delay by providing a feedback control effort [8]. Parameter tuning of the proportional, integral, and derivative coefficients is time-consuming in PID algorithm realization. Trial-and-error method is commonly used in practice [9]. However, it requires certain prior experiences to obtain the optimal values in trial-and-error way. To overcome such issue, neural networks (NN) approach is introduced in this paper to tune the control parameters of PID controller, which makes the parameters tuning process more intelligent and adaptive [10].

In the remaining parts of the paper, the system modeling and model parameter identification are presented in Sect. 2. Then, according to the identified plant model, a PID controller is implemented in Sect. 3 along with optimal PID parameters tuned. In Sect. 4, the NN model is obtained for PID control parameter optimization and extensive simulation studies are carried out. Finally, a summary is made to conclude the work in Sect. 5.

2   System Modeling and Model Identification

The mathematical model of the plant is one of the key requirements for the control system design. In order to describe the dynamic characteristics of the piezoelectric microinjector, the classical Bouc-Wen hysteretic model combined with linear dynamics is developed.

2.1   Modeling of the Piezo-Driven Microinjector System

The general model of the piezo-actuated system can be established as follows [11]:

$$m\ddot{x} + c\dot{x} + kx = k(dv - h) \tag{1}$$

$$\dot{h} = \alpha d\dot{v} + \beta |\dot{v}| h - \gamma \dot{v} |h| \tag{2}$$

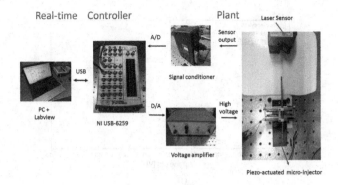

Fig. 2. Experimental setup of the piezo-driven microinjector.

where t is the time variable, x represents the output displacement of the entire piezoelectric-actuated device, parameter m is the mass, c represents the damping coefficient, k and d are stiffness and effective piezoelectric coefficient, respectively. Additionally, v denotes the input voltage of the piezoelectric actuator, h indicates the variable from the hysteresis dynamics in piezoelectric actuators, α, β, γ are the parameters of the hysteresis loop's shape.

Equations (1) and (2) can also be expressed as a Hammerstein structure as shown in Fig. 1, where the model of the entire piezoelectric actuator consists of a nonlinear hysteresis model and a linear dynamic model in cascade.

2.2 Dynamics and Hysteresis Model Identification

By using input and output data of the system, an approximate mathematical model of the physical system is obtained by the system identification method. The experimental setup is shown in Fig. 2. Specifically, the microinjector is driven by a PZT with a high-voltage amplifier. Swept-sine waves with the amplitude of 1–200 V and frequency of 1–1000 Hz are produced to drive the PZT. The position response is measured by the laser displacement sensor [11].

First, the input-output data sets are used to identify the transfer function of the system by System identification Toolbox in MATLAB:

$$G(s) = \frac{1}{s^2 + 7200s + 300000} \tag{3}$$

Based on Eq. (3), the Bode graph can be obtained. The frequency bandwidth below 1000 Hz is mainly discussed in this work.

The Bouc-Wen model has been widely used in describing hysteretic systems, and it is applied to the PZT actuator modeling in this work. The Bouc-Wen model contains both nonlinear damping and nonlinear stiffness, and it can well approximate various hysteresis curves. In this work, the hysteresis parameters α, β, γ are identified as 1.9991, 0.72399, and 0.0328, respectively, by using the particle swarm optimization (PSO) algorithm with MATLAB.

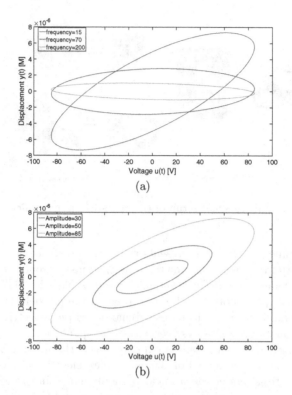

Fig. 3. Output-input relationship. (a) Output displacement versus input voltage with varied frequency; (b) output displacement versus input voltage with varied amplitude.

Combining the dynamic model and hysteresis model into an overall system, we can conduct open-loop test firstly to know more about the system characteristics. Through open-loop test, we find that the nonlinearity is obvious in the system, which is caused by the hysteresis effect of piezoelectric actuator. Moreover, the test results indicate that the complicated nonlinearities are influenced not only by the amplitude but also the frequency of the reference input signals, as shown in Fig. 3(a) (where the hysteresis effect is influenced by the varied frequencies at 15 Hz, 70 Hz, and 200 Hz with the same amplitude of 85 V) and (b) (where the hysteresis effect is influenced by the varied amplitudes of 30 V, 50 V, and 85 V with the same frequency of 50 Hz). The compensation procedures of the hysteretic nonlinearity are carried out in the following sections.

3 PID Control Scheme Design

Although PID controller is one of the earlier control strategies, it still has a wide range of applications due to its easy implementation property. In this work, the PID control is applied to compensate for the nonlinearity caused by hysteresis of PZT.

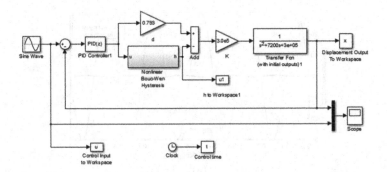

Fig. 4. Block diagram of closed-loop control for the piezo-driven microinjector system.

3.1 PID Controller Design

The PID control scheme is named after its three correcting terms, whose sum governs the control variable. That is, the proportional, integral, and derivative terms are summed to calculate the output of the PID controller. Defining $u(t)$ as the controller output, the final form of the PID algorithm is:

$$u(t) = K_p e(t) + K_i \int_0^t e(\tau)d\tau + K_d \frac{d}{dt}e(t) \tag{4}$$

where K_p is the proportional gain, K_i is the integral gain, and K_d is the derivative gain. In addition, e represents the error, t is time variable, and τ is the variable of integration which takes value from 0 to the present time t.

Considering the system performance in terms of stability, response speed, overshoot, and steady-state accuracy, the tuning roles of K_p, K_i, and K_d are given as follows.

(a) If K_p is too small, it will reduce the steady-state accuracy. The response speed is slow too, and it will extend the settling time and degrade the system performance.

(b) The role of K_i is to eliminate the steady-state error of the system. The static error in the system will be reduced faster when K_i is increased. But if K_i is too big, it will produce larger overshoot amount. If K_i is too small, it is difficult to eliminate the steady-state error, which reduces the accuracy of the control system.

(c) The effect of K_d is to improve the system's dynamic characteristics. It could suppress the change of the error. But if K_d is too big, it will extend the settling time and reduce the robustness of the system.

Using this algorithm, we design the PID controller for the motion tracking control. The general block diagram of the control system is shown in Fig. 4.

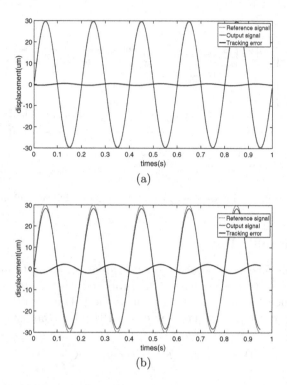

Fig. 5. Sinusoidal trajectory tracking results of PID control. (a) PID with adjusted parameters; (b) PID with unadjusted parameters.

3.2   Simulation Study

The feasibility of the PID controller is tested with the following simulation study. In the controller design process, there are totally three parameters affecting the control performance: proportional coefficient K_p, integral coefficient K_i, and derivative coefficient K_d.

Firstly, a sinusoidal signal with the amplitude of $30\,\mu m$ ($A = 30$) and frequency of $5\,Hz$ ($f = 5$) is used as the system input. Figure 5(a) shows the system response, where the dashed line represents the reference input and solid line represents the output response. The PID controller parameters are adjusted manually by trail-and-error approach. In this way, the PID control parameters K_p, K_i, and K_d are selected as 100, 2, and 2, respectively. It is seen that the system performance is quite good, as the control parameters are adjusted well.

In order to test the performance of the system, different types of input signals are chosen for the microinjector system. As the varying of the amplitudes and frequencies, the overall root mean square (RMS) positioning error is adopted as the major criterion in the simulation study of motion tracking process.

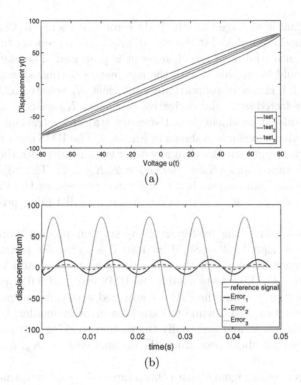

Fig. 6. Control results of PID controller. (a) Hysteresis loop variation with different control parameters; (b) trajectory tracking result with tracking errors.

$$RMS = \sqrt{\frac{1}{n}\sum_{k=1}^{n}[r_{ref}(k) - y(k)]^2} \qquad (5)$$

where $r_{ref}(k)$ represents the reference signal, $y(k)$ is tracking signal output, and n is the total number of data set. $r_{ref}(k)$ and $y(k)$ are stored in every cycle of simulation.

The sinusoidal motion tracking performance of the controller is tested by using sinusoid trajectories with varied amplitudes and frequencies. The function of the reference input signal can be expressed as:

$$r_{ref}(t) = f(A, f, t) = A\sin(2\pi f t + \pi/2) \qquad (6)$$

where A and f represent the amplitude and frequency of sinusoid reference, respectively.

For illustration, the sinusoidal wave trajectory with the amplitude of $A = 30$ and $f = 5$ is used in the motion tracking simulation. When the proportional coefficient K_p is selected as 115, integral coefficient K_i is selected as 2, and derivative coefficient K_d is selected as 3, the trajectory tracking performance is unsatisfactory, as shown in Fig. 5(b). The error between the reference signal and output signal is so large that the RMS error reaches up to 0.739 μm. Trail-and-error method is employed in the overall process of parameter tuning. Varied values are put into trial until the ideal result is produced. The motion tracking performance could be improved with the parameters optimized well.

Finally, with a choice of proportional coefficient K_p selected as 100, integral coefficient K_i selected as 2, and derivative coefficient K_d selected as 2, the PID control is capable of producing a satisfactory trajectory tracking result. The trajectory tracking waveform is shown in Fig. 5(a). The RMS error is reduced to 0.206 μm, which is quite smaller than any other error results with the parameters apart from the tuned ones ($K_p = 100$, $K_i = 2$, $K_d = 2$). The adjustment and selection of optimal parameters is a complicated process, as the PID gains are dependent and coupled with each other in the overall tuning process of PID control.

In order to observe the hysteresis compensation process more efficiently, another reference signal ($A = 80$, $f = 100$) is selected for testing. The hysteresis width becomes smaller as the compensation process conducted better, as shown in Fig. 6. The three tests exhibit the RMS errors of 9.010 μm, 5.501 μm, 1.702 μm, respectively, while the PID are adjusted with different parameters. In the overall simulation tests, while the tracking error is smaller, the hysteresis loop becomes narrower, and eventually the motion tracking performance is better. According to the above procedure, the optimal vectors (K_p, K_i, K_d) can be obtained.

Similarly, reference signals with other amplitudes and frequencies are also tested, and the optimal control parameters (K_p, K_i, K_d) are also tuned manually.

4   Neural Networks Model for PID Tuning

Manually selecting the parameters K_p, K_i and K_d is time-consuming and complicated. In this work, NN is adopted as an efficient tool to establish a model for parameter optimization and selection, which makes the control design more adaptive. The main purpose of this section is to introduce a NN model to represent the relationship between the input data (amplitude and frequency of the reference signal) and target data (optimal parameters K_p, K_i, and K_d of PID controller), as shown in Fig. 7. In particular, the three-layer radial basis function (RBF) network is adopted in this work for illustration.

4.1   Neural Networks Model Development

For different amplitudes and frequencies of the trajectory reference signals, there are corresponding vectors (K_p, K_i, K_d) fitting to the most effective motion tracking result, which is judged with the criterion RMS_{min} (i.e., the minimum root mean square error in Eq. (5)). The following task is to establish a NN model for describing the relation between the input vector (A, f) and the output vector (K_p, K_i, K_d).

$$(K_p, K_i, K_d) = function_{NN}(A, f) \tag{7}$$

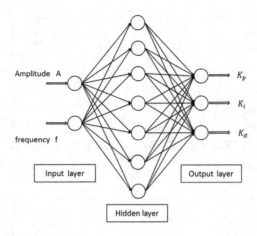

Fig. 7. NN model based on RBF training function.

Neural networks is an efficient tool to establish such a model, which can approximate a nonlinear function associating input vectors with specific output vectors. Generally, three steps are conducted in the training process. Firstly, assembling the training data and determining the network target; secondly, training the network; finally, simulating the network response to new inputs.

In order to establish the model, sufficient sampling data set should be obtained. Here, we totally generate 100 sampling data of reference signals with the amplitude ranging from 2 to 200 μm regularly and frequency ranging from 5 to 500 Hz. Similarly, the tracking simulation under the sinusoid trajectories of incremental amplitudes (2, 4, 6 ... 98, 100, 102 ... 200) and varied frequencies (5, 10, 15 ... 245, 250, 255 ... 500) are placed in one matrix [2, 4, 6 ... 98, 100, 102 ... 200; 5, 10, 15 ... 245, 250, 255 ... 500] as input data for NN training. A set of associated desired output matrix $[K_p, K_i, K_d]$ are used as target data to create a three-layer network with seven neurons selected for the hidden layer.

The data are used to train the network until it learns the function relationship between the sample inputs and targets. Among the data set, 70% of the data are used to train the network and 15% are used to validate how well the network is generalized. The remaining data provide an independent testing of network generalization to data, which the network has never seen. The network is obtained eventually, as illustrated in Fig. 7.

To verify the efficiency of the network, we randomly select a signal (with amplitude of 30 μm and frequency of 75 Hz) as the new input to simulate the network response. Through simulation, we can obtain an output vector (49.730, 10.030, 7.073) as NN optimization result, which is quite similar to the vector (50, 10, 7) in test data during the training.

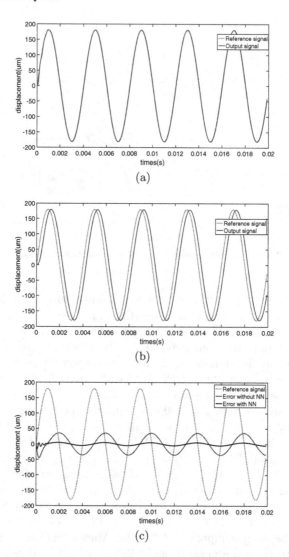

Fig. 8. Sinusoidal motion tracking results of NN-based PID control. (a) PID with NN model; (b) PID without NN model; (c) tracking errors with and without NN model.

4.2 Parameter Verification Using NN Model for PID

The above input parameter vector $(A = 30, f = 75)$ lies within the training sample. In order to verify the effect of the NN further, the vector $(A = 180, f = 250)$ is used as new input. Through simulation with this new input vector, an output vector $(279.210, 30.193, 25.011)$ is obtained as NN optimization result. Taking $279.210 \approx 280$, $30.193 \approx 30$, and $25.011 \approx 25$, the control parameter vector $(280, 30, 25)$ is used for verification. The tracking result is shown in Fig. 8(a), which exhibits that the output tracking signal is close to the reference

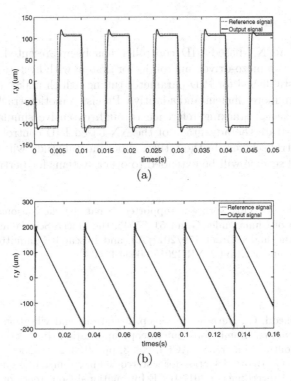

Fig. 9. Tracking results of NN-based PID control for different reference inputs. (a) Trajectory tracking result of rectangular-wave input; (b) trajectory tracking result of sawtooth-wave input.

trajectory. The RMS is only 3.781 μm, which is extremely close to RMS_{min} (3.719 μm). How the tracking performance will be if the output vector is selected without using optimization via NN model? Here, we select (50, 10, 7), i.e., the same as the previous signal ($A = 30, f = 75$), for testing. The tracking result is shown as Fig. 8(b). The tracking errors of the controller without or with NN model are presented in Fig. 8(c).

When other new inputs are presented, the trained RBF network can also give corresponding reasonable results for K_p, K_i, and K_d parameters. In order to verify the effectiveness of the NN model further, we change the sinusoidal signal to rectangular wave and sawtooth wave, respectively. Rectangular wave with the amplitude 110 μm ($A = 110$) and frequency 100 Hz ($f = 100$) is tested, and the tracking performance is shown in Fig. 9(a). In addition, sawtooth wave with the amplitude 200 μm ($A = 200$) and frequency 30 Hz ($f = 30$) is tested, and the tracking performance is shown in Fig. 9(b). The above verifications illustrate the effectiveness of the proposed NN model based PID control scheme.

5   Conclusion

In this paper, an NN-based PID controller has been presented for precision motion control of a piezo-driven microinjector system with hysteresis effect. The NN model is established for PID parameter tuning, which makes the process of controller design more efficient and adaptive. Precision motion tracking has been achieved with varied tracking reference through extensive simulation studies. Results demonstrate the advantage of the NN-based PID control over conventional PID control scheme. In the future, experimental study will be conducted and the control scheme will be extended to other systems for pertinent application.

Acknowledgement. This work was supported in part by the National Natural Science Foundation of China under Grant 51575545, the Macao Science and Technology Development Fund under Grant 179/2017/A3, and Research Committee of the University of Macau under Grant MYRG2018-00034-FST.

References

1. Croft, D., Shedd, G., Devasia, S.: Creep, hysteresis, and vibration compensation for piezoactuators: atomic force microscopy application. In: Proceedings of 2000 American Control Conference (ACC), vol. 3, pp. 2123–2128 (2000)
2. Nan, Z., Xu, Q.: Depth detection for a stereo cell micro-injection system with dual cameras. In: Proceedings of 2017 IEEE International Conference on Robotics and Biomimetics (ROBIO), pp. 1106–1111 (2017)
3. Zhang, X., Xu, Q.: Design and testing of a new 3-DOF spatial flexure parallel micropositioning stage. Int. J. Precis. Eng. Manuf. **19**(1), 109–118 (2018)
4. Xu, Q.: Micromachines for Biological Micromanipulation. Springer, Cham (2018). https://doi.org/10.1007/978-3-319-74621-0
5. Wang, G., Xu, Q.: LuGre model based hysteresis compensation of a piezo-actuated mechanism. In: Chen, W., Hosoda, K., Menegatti, E., Shimizu, M., Wang, H. (eds.) IAS 2016. AISC, vol. 531, pp. 645–657. Springer, Cham (2017). https://doi.org/10.1007/978-3-319-48036-7_47
6. Lin, C.J., Chen, S.Y.: Evolutionary algorithm based feedforward control for contouring of a biaxial piezo-actuated stage. Mechatronics **19**(6), 829–839 (2009)
7. Zhang, Y., Xu, Q.: Adaptive sliding mode control with parameter estimation and kalman filter for precision motion control of a piezo-driven microgripper. IEEE Trans. Control Syst. Technol. **25**(2), 728–735 (2017)
8. Ali, A., Ahmed, S.F., Joyo, M.K., Kushsairy, K.: MPC-PID comparison for controlling therapeutic upper limb rehabilitation robot under perturbed conditions. In: Proceedings of IEEE International Conference on Engineering Technologies and Social Sciences (ICETSS), pp. 1–5 (2017)
9. Zhuang, M., Atherton, D.: Automatic tuning of optimum PID controllers. In: IEE Proceedings D-Control Theory and Applications, vol. 140, pp. 216–224 (1993)
10. Youssef, A.: Optimized PID tracking controller for piezoelectric hysteretic actuator model. World J. Model. Simul. **9**(3), 223–234 (2013)
11. Xu, Q., Tan, K.K.: Advanced Control of Piezoelectric Micro-/Nano-positioning Systems. AIC. Springer, Cham (2016). https://doi.org/10.1007/978-3-319-21623-2

Force/Motion Hybrid Control of Three Link Constrained Manipulator Using Sliding Mode

Sheng Gao[1,2], Wei Zhang[1,2(✉)], Weiguo Kong[1,2], Hucun Ren[1,2], and Bopi Jin[1,2]

[1] State Key Laboratory of Robotics, Shenyang Institute of Automation, Chinese Academy of Sciences, Shenyang 110016, China
{gaosheng,zhangwei,kongweiguo,renhucun,jinbopi}@sia.cn
[2] Institutes for Robotics and Intelligent Manufacturing, Chinese Academy of Sciences, Shenyang 110016, China

Abstract. In order to realize the position control and contact force control of a class of planar three link constrained manipulators end-effector, a hybrid control strategy based on sliding mode controller is proposed. First, the dynamic model of the planar three link constrained manipulator is given. Then, the model order reduction design for the constrained manipulator is proposed with using the constraint condition. Furthermore, a controller based on sliding mode is presented and the tracking error of position and contact force is shown to be globally asymptotically stable via Lyapunov stability theory. Finally, numerical simulations of a planar three link constrained manipulator are performed to illustrate the effectiveness of the proposed control scheme.

Keywords: Three link constrained manipulator · Dynamic model · Sliding mode · Force/Motion hybrid control

1 Introduction

For some industrial robots, in the contact tasks of the end effector and the constrained environment, such as polishing, grinding, assembly and other tasks, not only the position of the robot end effector but also the contact force between the end effector and the restraining surface is controlled. Meet specific requirements and avoid damage to the robot or workpiece due to excessive contact force.

The motion control of the constrained manipulator consists of two aspects: the position control of the manipulator and the contact force control between the end and the restraining face. In general, position control is easier to implement, such as traditional independent joint PD control, etc., and contact force control is relatively difficult. There are many research results related to the force/position mixing control of the manipulator [1–5]. In Ref. [6], a hybrid control strategy based on passive compliant device is proposed in order to realize the position control and contact force control of the polishing robot end-point. In Ref. [7], an adaptive neural network modular force/position control method is proposed for environmentally constrained reconfigurable manipulator systems. In Ref. [8], a method for motion/force control of robot arms with model uncertainties is presented. Ref. [9] present a prioritized, multiple-task

© Springer Nature Switzerland AG 2019
H. Yu et al. (Eds.): ICIRA 2019, LNAI 11745, pp. 419–432, 2019.
https://doi.org/10.1007/978-3-030-27529-7_36

control framework that is able to control forces in systems ranging from humanoids to industrial robots. In Ref. [10], a compliant landing strategy for a trotting quadruped robot on unknown rough terrains based on contact force control is presented. In the paper, we propose a force/motion hybrid control of three link constrained manipulator based on sliding mode control algorithm.

This paper is organized as follow. Section 2 give the dynamic model of the planar three link manipulator, including the dynamic model of the constrained manipulator. Then, the model order reduction is designed in Sect. 3. In Sect. 4, the design of sliding mode controller for three link constrained manipulator is proposed. Furthermore, the designed controller is performed via numerical simulations to verify the effectiveness of the controller. Finally, Sect. 6 summarizes the work of this paper.

2 Manipulator Dynamic Model

In this paper, the Euler-Lagrangian method is used to derive the dynamic model of planar three link manipulator. The structure diagram of planar three link constrained manipulator is shown in Fig. 1.

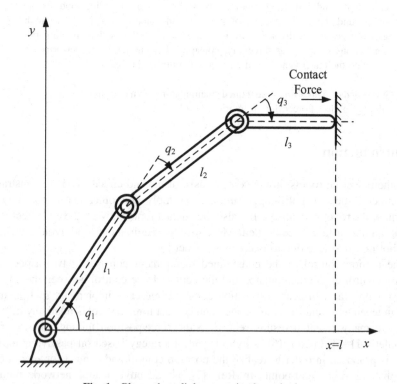

Fig. 1. Planar three link constrained manipulator

where, m_1, m_2 and m_3 are the mass of the three links respectively; l_1, l_2 and l_3 are the length of the three links respectively; q_1, q_2 and q_3 are the rotation angle of the three links respectively.

2.1 Three Link Manipulator Dynamic

Based on the Euler-Lagrangian formulation, the three link manipulator dynamic is derived in joint space, which assumes that the center of mass of the three links is at the end of each link and the absence of friction. It's important to note that because the three links are in series, when the first link rotates, the second link and the third link rotate as well. So, for the first link, the kinetic energy and the potential energy are given as followed.

$$\begin{aligned} K_1 &= \tfrac{1}{2} m_1 l_1^2 \dot{q}_1^2 \\ P_1 &= m_1 g l_1 \sin(q_1) \end{aligned} \tag{1}$$

Then, for the second link, we have

$$\begin{aligned} x_2 &= l_1 \cos(q_1) + l_2 \cos(q_1 + q_2) \\ y_2 &= l_1 \sin(q_1) + l_2 \sin(q_1 + q_2) \\ \dot{x}_2 &= -l_1 \dot{q}_1 \sin(q_1) - l_2 (\dot{q}_1 + \dot{q}_2) \sin(q_1 + q_2) \\ \dot{y}_2 &= l_1 \dot{q}_1 \cos(q_1) + l_2 (\dot{q}_1 + \dot{q}_2) \cos(q_1 + q_2) \end{aligned} \tag{2}$$

In order to simplify formulas, we design $\cos(q_1) = c_1$, $\sin(q_1) = s_1$, $\cos(q_1 + q_2) = c_{12}$, $\sin(q_1 + q_2) = s_{12}$. The following derived process will follow the same abbreviation. So, we have

$$\begin{aligned} v_2^2 &= \dot{x}_2^2 + \dot{y}_2^2 \\ &= l_1^2 \dot{q}_1^2 + l_2^2 (\dot{q}_1 + \dot{q}_2)^2 + 2 l_1 l_2 (\dot{q}_1^2 + \dot{q}_1 \dot{q}_2) c_2 \end{aligned} \tag{3}$$

Then, we can get

$$\begin{aligned} K_2 &= \frac{1}{2} m_2 v_2^2 \\ &= \frac{1}{2} m_2 l_1^2 \dot{q}_1^2 + \frac{1}{2} m_2 l_2^2 (\dot{q}_1 + \dot{q}_2)^2 + m_2 l_1 l_2 (\dot{q}_1^2 + \dot{q}_1 \dot{q}_2) c_2 \\ P_2 &= m_2 g y_2 = m_2 g l_1 s_1 + m_2 g l_2 s_{12} \end{aligned} \tag{4}$$

For the third link, we have

$$\begin{aligned} x_3 &= l_1 c_1 + l_2 c_{12} + l_3 c_{123} \\ y_3 &= l_1 s_1 + l_2 s_{12} + l_3 s_{123} \end{aligned} \tag{5}$$

So, we can get

$$K_2 = \frac{1}{2}m_3 v_3^2$$

$$= \frac{1}{2}m_3 l_1^2 \dot{q}_1^2 + \frac{1}{2}m_3 l_2^2 (\dot{q}_1 + \dot{q}_2)^2 + \frac{1}{2}m_3 l_3^2 (\dot{q}_1 + \dot{q}_2 + \dot{q}_3)^2 + m_3 l_1 l_2 (\dot{q}_1^2 + \dot{q}_1 \dot{q}_2) c_2$$

$$+ m_3 l_1 l_3 (\dot{q}_1^2 + \dot{q}_1 \dot{q}_2 + \dot{q}_1 \dot{q}_3) c_{23} + m_3 l_2 l_3 (\dot{q}_1 + \dot{q}_2)(\dot{q}_1^2 + \dot{q}_2 + \dot{q}_3) c_3$$

$$P_3 = m_3 g y_3 = m_3 g l_1 s_1 + m_3 g l_2 s_{12} + m_3 g l_3 s_{123}$$

$$(6)$$

Furthermore, we have the Lagrangian operator as followed

$$L = K - P$$
$$= K_1 + K_2 + K_3 - P_1 - P_2 - P_3 \tag{7}$$

Substituting the Eq. (7) into the Euler-Lagrangian formulation, we have

$$\frac{d}{dt}\frac{\partial L}{\partial \dot{q}_1} = (m_1 + m_2 + m_3)l_1^2 \ddot{q}_1 + (m_2 + m_3)l_2^2 (\ddot{q}_1 + \ddot{q}_2) + m_3 l_3^2 (\ddot{q}_1 + \ddot{q}_2 + \ddot{q}_3)$$

$$+ (m_2 + m_3)l_1 l_2 (2\ddot{q}_1 + \ddot{q}_2) c_2 + m_3 l_1 l_3 (2\ddot{q}_1 + \ddot{q}_2 + \ddot{q}_3) c_{23}$$

$$+ m_3 l_2 l_3 (2\ddot{q}_1 + 2\ddot{q}_2 + \ddot{q}_3) c_3 - m_3 l_2 l_3 (2\ddot{q}_1 + 2\ddot{q}_2 + \ddot{q}_3) c_3 \tag{8}$$

$$- (m_2 + m_3)l_1 l_2 (2\dot{q}_1 + \dot{q}_2)\dot{q}_2 s_2 - m_3 l_1 l_3 (2\dot{q}_1 + \dot{q}_2 + \dot{q}_3)(\dot{q}_2 + \dot{q}_3)s_{23}$$

$$- m_3 l_2 l_3 (2\dot{q}_1 + 2\dot{q}_2 + \dot{q}_3)\dot{q}_3 s_3$$

$$\frac{\partial L}{\partial q_1} = -(m_1 + m_2 + m_3)g l_1 c_1 - (m_2 + m_3)g l_2 c_{12} - m_3 g l_3 c_{123} \tag{9}$$

So, with using the above equations, we can get

$$\tau_1 = \frac{d}{dt}\frac{\partial L}{\partial \dot{q}_1} - \frac{\partial L}{\partial q_1}$$

$$= [(m_1 + m_2 + m_3)l_1^2 + (m_2 + m_3)l_2^2 + m_3 l_3^2 + 2(m_2 + m_3)l_1 l_2 c_2$$

$$+ 2m_3 l_1 l_3 c_{23} + 2m_3 l_2 l_3 c_3]\ddot{q}_1 + [(m_2 + m_3)l_2^2 + m_3 l_3^2 + (m_2 + m_3)l_1 l_2 c_2$$

$$+ m_3 l_1 l_3 c_{23} + 2m_3 l_2 l_3 c_3]\ddot{q}_2 + [m_3 l_3^2 + m_3 l_1 l_3 c_{23} + m_3 l_2 l_3 c_3]\ddot{q}_3 \tag{10}$$

$$- (m_2 + m_3)l_1 l_2 (2\dot{q}_1 + \dot{q}_2)\dot{q}_2 s_2 - m_3 l_1 l_3 (2\dot{q}_1 + \dot{q}_2 + \dot{q}_3)(\dot{q}_2 + \dot{q}_3)s_{23}$$

$$- m_3 l_2 l_3 (2\dot{q}_1 + 2\dot{q}_2 + \dot{q}_3)\dot{q}_3 s_3 + (m_1 + m_2 + m_3)g l_1 c_1 + (m_2 + m_3)g l_2 c_{12}$$

$$+ m_3 g l_3 c_{123}$$

Moreover, with using above derivation we can also get

$$
\begin{aligned}
\tau_2 &= \frac{d}{dt}\frac{\partial L}{\partial \dot{q}_2} - \frac{\partial L}{\partial q_2} \\
&= [(m_2+m_3)l_2^2 + m_3 l_3^2 + (m_2+m_3)l_1 l_2 c_2 + m_3 l_1 l_3 c_{23} + 2m_3 l_2 l_3 c_3]\ddot{q}_1 \\
&\quad + [(m_2+m_3)l_2^2 + m_3 l_3^2 + 2m_3 l_2 l_3 c_3]\ddot{q}_2 + [m_3 l_3^2 + m_3 l_2 l_3 c_3]\ddot{q}_3 \\
&\quad + (m_2+m_3)l_1 l_2 \dot{q}_1^2 s_2 + m_3 l_1 l_3 \dot{q}_1^2 s_{23} - m_3 l_2 l_3 (2\dot{q}_1 + 2\dot{q}_2 + \dot{q}_3)\dot{q}_3 s_3 \\
&\quad + (m_2+m_3)g l_2 c_{12} + m_3 g l_3 c_{123}
\end{aligned}
\tag{11}
$$

$$
\begin{aligned}
\tau_3 &= \frac{d}{dt}\frac{\partial L}{\partial \dot{q}_3} - \frac{\partial L}{\partial q_3} \\
&= [m_3 l_3^2 + m_3 l_1 l_3 c_{23} + m_3 l_2 l_3 c_3]\ddot{q}_1 + [m_3 l_3^2 + m_3 l_2 l_3 c_3]\ddot{q}_2 + m_3 l_3^2 \ddot{q}_3 \\
&\quad + m_3 l_1 l_3 \dot{q}_1^2 s_{23} + m_3 l_2 l_3 (\dot{q}_1 + \dot{q}_2)^2 s_3 + m_3 g l_3 c_{123}
\end{aligned}
\tag{12}
$$

By making the above equations into the standard matrix form, then we have

$$
M(q)\begin{bmatrix} \ddot{q}_1 \\ \ddot{q}_2 \\ \ddot{q}_3 \end{bmatrix} + C(q,\dot{q})\begin{bmatrix} \dot{q}_1 \\ \dot{q}_2 \\ \dot{q}_3 \end{bmatrix} + G(q) = \begin{bmatrix} \tau_1 \\ \tau_2 \\ \tau_3 \end{bmatrix}
\tag{13}
$$

where, $M(q)$ is inertia matrix; $C(q,\dot{q})$ is the vector of Coriolis and centrifugal torques; $G(q)$ is the vector of gravitational torques.

$$
M(q) = \begin{bmatrix}
\begin{array}{l}(m_1+m_2+m_3)l_1^2 + (m_2+m_3)l_2^2 \\ + m_3 l_3^2 + 2(m_2+m_3)l_1 l_2 c_2 \\ + 2m_3 l_1 l_3 c_{23} + 2m_3 l_2 l_3 c_3 \end{array} &
\begin{array}{l}(m_2+m_3)l_2^2 + m_3 l_3^2 \\ + (m_2+m_3)l_1 l_2 c_2 \\ + m_3 l_1 l_3 c_{23} + 2m_3 l_2 l_3 c_3 \end{array} &
\begin{array}{l} m_3 l_3^2 + \\ m_3 l_1 l_3 c_{23} + \\ m_3 l_2 l_3 c_3 \end{array} \\[2em]
\begin{array}{l}(m_2+m_3)l_2^2 + m_3 l_3^2 \\ + (m_2+m_3)l_1 l_2 c_2 \\ + m_3 l_1 l_3 c_{23} + 2m_3 l_2 l_3 c_3 \end{array} &
\begin{array}{l}(m_2+m_3)l_2^2 + m_3 l_3^2 \\ + 2m_3 l_2 l_3 c_3 \end{array} &
\begin{array}{l} m_3 l_3^2 + m_3 l_2 l_3 c_3 \end{array} \\[2em]
\begin{array}{l} m_3 l_3^2 \\ + m_3 l_1 l_3 c_{23} \\ + m_3 l_2 l_3 c_3 \end{array} &
\begin{array}{l} m_3 l_3^2 + m_3 l_2 l_3 c_3 \end{array} &
\begin{array}{l} m_3 l_3^2 \end{array}
\end{bmatrix}_{3\times3}
$$

$$
C(q,\dot{q}) = \begin{bmatrix}
\begin{array}{l} -2(m_2+m_3)l_1 l_2 \dot{q}_2 s_2 \end{array} &
\begin{array}{l} -(m_2+m_3)l_1 l_2 \dot{q}_2 s_2 - \\ m_3 l_1 l_3 (2\dot{q}_1 + \dot{q}_2 + 2\dot{q}_3)s_{23} \end{array} &
\begin{array}{l} -m_3 l_1 l_3 (2\dot{q}_1 + \dot{q}_3)s_{23} - \\ m_3 l_2 l_3 (2\dot{q}_1 + 2\dot{q}_2 + \dot{q}_3)s_3 \end{array} \\[2em]
\begin{array}{l} (m_2+m_3)l_1 l_2 \dot{q}_1 s_2 + \\ m_3 l_1 l_3 \dot{q}_1 s_{23} \end{array} &
\begin{array}{l} -2m_3 l_2 l_3 \dot{q}_3 s_3 \end{array} &
\begin{array}{l} -m_3 l_2 l_3 (2\dot{q}_1 + \dot{q}_3)s_3 \end{array} \\[2em]
\begin{array}{l} m_3 l_1 l_3 \dot{q}_1 s_{23} + \\ m_3 l_2 l_3 \dot{q}_1 s_3 \end{array} &
\begin{array}{l} m_3 l_2 l_3 (2\dot{q}_1 + \dot{q}_2)s_3 \end{array} &
0
\end{bmatrix}_{3\times3}
$$

$$G(q) = \begin{bmatrix} (m_1 + m_2 + m_3)gl_1c_1 + (m_2 + m_3)gl_2c_{12} + m_3gl_3c_{123} \\ (m_2 + m_3)gl_2c_{12} + m_3gl_3c_{123} \\ m_3gl_3c_{123} \end{bmatrix}_{3\times1}$$

In order to facilitate the design of the control law, some properties of the manipulator model are first given [11]:

Property 1: Inertia matrix $M(q)$ is bounded positive definite symmetric matrix, so for positive M_m and M_M meet $M_m \leq \|M(q)\| \leq M_M$;

Property 2: Given a proper definition of the matrix C, $\dot{M}(q) - 2C(q, \dot{q})$ is skew-symmetric and further meet $C(q, \xi)\varsigma = C(q, \varsigma)\xi$, where ξ and ς are any vector.

2.2 Constrained Manipulator Dynamic

The schematic diagram of a three link manipulator with constraint is shown in Fig. 1. Then, the dynamic model of three link manipulator is rewritten as followed.

$$\begin{aligned} M(q)\ddot{q} + C(q, \dot{q})\dot{q} + G(q) + \tau_f &= \tau \\ \Phi(q) = (\phi_1(q), \cdots, \phi_m(q))^{\mathrm{T}} &= 0 \end{aligned} \tag{14}$$

Where, $q, \dot{q}, \ddot{q}$ represents the position, velocity and acceleration of the manipulator joints. τ_f is the constraining force in joint space. $\Phi(q)$ is the equation of environment constraint in joint space.

Let us define x is the position vector at the end-effector of the manipulator, then the constraint equation is $\phi(x) = 0$. Moreover, we define $x = h(q)$, then the equation of environment constraint in joint space $\Phi(q)$ can be converted to as followed.

$$\Phi(q) = \phi(h(q)) = 0 \tag{15}$$

So, we have

$$J_\phi(q) = \frac{\partial \Phi(q)}{\partial q} = \frac{\partial \phi(x)}{\partial x}\frac{\partial x}{\partial q} = \frac{\partial \phi(x)}{\partial x}\frac{\partial h(q)}{\partial q} \tag{16}$$

$$\tau_f = J_\phi^{\mathrm{T}}(q)\lambda$$

where, $J_\phi(q)$ is the jacobian matrix of environment constraint. λ represents lagrangian multiplier. Finally, we can obtain

$$\begin{aligned} M(q)\ddot{q} + C(q, \dot{q})\dot{q} + G(q) + J_\phi^{\mathrm{T}}(q)\lambda &= \tau \\ \Phi(q) = \phi(h(q)) &= 0 \end{aligned} \tag{17}$$

For the constrained manipulator system, we assume that the following assumptions are satisfied throughout the paper.

Assumption 1: Rigid environmental constraints are fully known, starting with the robot end-effector contact with the restraint surface and ignore the friction between them;

Assumption 2: Select the desired joint trajectory of the robot $q, \dot{q}, \ddot{q}$ and the desired contact force f_d are all bounded;

Assumption 3: $J_\phi^{\mathrm{T}}(q)$ is a full rank matrix.

3 Design of Model Order Reduction

According to the Fig. 1, we can see that because the three link manipulator is constrained by a force, the degree of freedom of the manipulator becomes one degree of freedom. Then, let us define q_1 is the variable that describe constrained motion, q_2 and q_3 are the remaining redundant variables. Therefore, q_2 and q_3 can be represented by q_1.

$$q_2 = \psi(q_1)$$
$$q_3 = \varphi(q_1) \tag{18}$$

Then, we can get

$$\dot{q} = \begin{bmatrix} \dot{q}_1 \\ \dot{q}_2 \\ \dot{q}_3 \end{bmatrix} = \begin{bmatrix} \dot{q}_1 \\ \frac{\partial \psi(q_1)}{\partial q_1} \dot{q}_1 \\ \frac{\partial \varphi(q_1)}{\partial q_1} \dot{q}_1 \end{bmatrix} = L(q_1)\dot{q}_1 \tag{19}$$

$$\ddot{q} = \dot{L}(q_1)\dot{q}_1 + L(q_1)\ddot{q}_1$$

where, $L(q_1) = \begin{bmatrix} 1 & \frac{\partial \psi(q_1)}{\partial q_1} & \frac{\partial \varphi(q_1)}{\partial q_1} \end{bmatrix}^{\mathrm{T}}$.

Substitute the above equation into Eq. (17), we can get

$$M(q)(\dot{L}(q_1)\dot{q}_1 + L(q_1)\ddot{q}_1) + C(q,\dot{q})L(q_1)\dot{q}_1 + G(q) + J_\phi^{\mathrm{T}}(q)\lambda = \tau \tag{20}$$

Moreover, we have

$$M(q)L(q_1)\ddot{q}_1 + (M(q)\dot{L}(q_1) + C(q,\dot{q})L(q_1))\dot{q}_1 + G(q) + J_\phi^{\mathrm{T}}(q)\lambda = \tau \tag{21}$$

Then, by defining $M_1(q_1) = M(q)L(q_1)$, $C_1(q_1,\dot{q}_1) = M(q)\dot{L}(q_1) + C(q,\dot{q})L(q_1)$, $G_1(q_1) = G(q)$ and $J_\phi^{\mathrm{T}}(q_1) = J_\phi^{\mathrm{T}}(q)$, we further have

$$M_1(q_1)\ddot{q}_1 + C_1(q_1,\dot{q}_1)\dot{q}_1 + G_1(q_1) + J_\phi^{\mathrm{T}}(q_1)\lambda = \tau \tag{22}$$

By deriving Eq. (15), we can get $J_\phi(q)\dot{q} = 0$, so we can obtain

$$J_\phi(q_1)L(q_1) = L^{\mathrm{T}}(q_1)J_\phi^{\mathrm{T}}(q_1) \tag{23}$$

Multiply $L^T(q_1)$ by the left and right sides of Eq. (22), we have

$$L^T(q_1)M_1(q_1)\ddot{q}_1 + L^T(q_1)C_1(q_1,\dot{q}_1)\dot{q}_1 + L^T(q_1)G_1(q_1) + L^T(q_1)J_\phi^T(q_1)\lambda = L^T(q_1)\tau \tag{24}$$

By simplifying Eq. (24), we can get

$$M_L(q_1)\ddot{q}_1 + C_L(q_1,\dot{q}_1)\dot{q}_1 + G_L(q_1) = L^T\tau \tag{25}$$

Therefore, Eq. (25) is the three link model by reducing model order, at the same time, Eq. (25) satisfies the following properties [12]:

(1) Defining $M_L(q_1) = L^T(q_1)M_1(q_1)$, then we have $M_L(q_1) = L^T(q_1)D(q)L(q_1)$, $M_L(q_1) > 0$;

(2) Defining $C_L(q_1,\dot{q}_1) = L^T(q_1)C_1(q_1,\dot{q}_1) = L^T(q_1)(M(q)\dot{L}(q_1) + C(q,\dot{q})L(q_1))$, then $M_L(q_1) - 2C_L(q_1,\dot{q}_1)$ is skew-symmetric;

(3) $J_\phi(q_1)L(q_1) = L^T(q_1)J_\phi^T(q_1) = 0$.

Furthermore, we can use Eq. (22) to get the constrained force τ_f in numerical simulations. So we have

$$J_\phi^T(q_1)\lambda = \tau - M_1(q_1)\ddot{q}_1 - C_1(q_1,\dot{q}_1)\dot{q}_1 - G_1(q_1) \tag{26}$$

Remark: It is worth noting that in actual engineering, the value of force τ_f can be measured by force sensor.

Assuming that $q_d(t)$ is the ideal angle command and τ_f^d is the ideal constrained force, at the same time, they satisfy $\Phi(q_d) = 0, \tau_f^d = J_\phi^T(q_d)\lambda_d$. So, the control target is $q(t)$ tracking $q_d(t)$ and τ_f tracking τ_f^d.

4   Design of Sliding Mode Controller

Because $q_2(t)$ and $q_3(t)$ are function of $q_1(t)$, the control target, $q(t)$ tracking $q_d(t)$, becomes $q_1(t)$ tracking $q_{d1}(t)$. therefore, defining

$$\begin{aligned} e_1 &= q_{d1} - q_1 \\ e_\lambda &= \lambda_d - \lambda \\ \dot{q}_{r1} &= \dot{q}_{d1} + \Lambda_1 e_1 + \Lambda_2 e_\lambda \end{aligned} \tag{27}$$

where, $\Lambda_1 > 0$ and $\Lambda_2 > 0$.

So, the sliding surface is designed as followed.

$$s_1 = \dot{q}_{r1} - \dot{q}_1 = \dot{e}_1 + \Lambda_1 e_1 + \Lambda_2 e_\lambda$$
$$s_{L1} = L(q_1)s_1 \tag{28}$$

Then, the sliding controller is designed as

$$\tau = M_1(q_1)\ddot{q}_{r1} + C_1(q_1, \dot{q}_1)\dot{q}_{r1} + G_1(q_1) + K_p r_{L1} + J_\phi^T(q_1)\lambda_r \tag{29}$$

where, $K_p > 0$. λ_r is used for controlling contact force and defined as $\lambda_r = \lambda_d + \Lambda_2 e_\lambda$. So, we have

$$\lambda_r - \lambda = \lambda_d + \Lambda_2 e_\lambda + e_\lambda - \lambda_d = (1 + \Lambda_2)e_\lambda \tag{30}$$

Substitute the Eq. (29) into the Eq. (22), we can get

$$M_1(q_1)\ddot{q}_1 + C_1(q_1, \dot{q}_1)\dot{q}_1 + G_1(q_1) + J_\phi^T(q_1)\lambda =$$
$$M_1(q_1)\ddot{q}_{r1} + C_1(q_1, \dot{q}_1)\dot{q}_{r1} + G_1(q_1) + K_p r_{L1} + J_\phi^T(q_1)\lambda_r$$

Moreover, we have

$$M_1(q_1)\dot{s}_1 + C_1(q_1, \dot{q}_1)s_1 + K_p s_{L1} - J_\phi^T(q_1)(1 + \Lambda_2)e_\lambda = 0 \tag{31}$$

Multiply $L^T(q_1)$ on both sides of Eq. (31) and further according to properties (1)–(3), you can get

$$M_L(q_1)\dot{s}_1 + C_L(q_1, \dot{q}_1)s_1 + L^T(q_1)K_p s_{L1} = 0 \tag{32}$$

To derive the control algorithm, the generalized Lyapunov function is considered

$$V = \frac{1}{2}M_L(q_1)s_1^2 \tag{33}$$

Differentiating V with respect to time yields

$$\dot{V} = s_1(M_L(q_1)\dot{s}_1 + \frac{1}{2}\dot{M}_L(q_1)s_1) \tag{34}$$

Considering is $M_L(q_1) - 2C_L(q_1, \dot{q}_1)$ is skew-symmetric, then substitute the Eq. (32) into the Eq. (34), we have

$$\dot{V} = s_1(M_L(q_1)\dot{s}_1 + C_L(q_1, \dot{q}_1)s_1) = s_1(-L^T(q_1)K_p s_{L1}) = -s_{L1}^T K_p s_{L1} \le 0$$

Because $\dot{V}$ is semi-negative and K_p is positive, then we have $s_{L1} \equiv 0, \dot{s}_{L1} \equiv 0$ when $\dot{V} \equiv 0$, that is, $s_1 \equiv 0, \dot{s}_1 \equiv 0 \rightarrow \dot{e}_1 \equiv 0, e_1 \equiv 0$. According LaSalle theorem, we can see $\dot{e}_1 \rightarrow 0, e_1 \rightarrow 0$ when $t \rightarrow \infty$.

Furthermore, because $s_{L1} \equiv 0, s_1 \equiv 0, \dot{s}_1 \equiv 0$, according to Eq. (31), we can see $\lambda - \lambda_r \equiv 0$. We further use Eq. (30) to get $e_\lambda \equiv 0$. According LaSalle theorem, we can see $\lambda \to \lambda_d$ when $t \to \infty$, that is, $\tau_f \to \tau_f^d$ when $t \to \infty$. The proof is completed.

5 Numerical Simulations

According to the Fig. 1, the position of the end-effector on the constraint surface can be expressed as $x = l_1\cos(q_1) + l_2\cos(q_1 + q_2) + l_3\cos(q_1 + q_2 + q_3) = l$, then the constraint equation can be expressed as

$$\Phi(q) = \phi(h(q)) = \phi(q_1) = l_1\cos(q_1) + l_2\cos(q_1 + q_2) + l_3\cos(q_1 + q_2 + q_3) - l$$

Then, according to the Eq. (16), we have

$$J_\phi(q) = \frac{\partial\Phi(q)}{\partial q} = \begin{bmatrix} -l_1\sin(q_1) - l_2\sin(q_1 + q_2) - l_3\sin(q_1 + q_2 + q_3) \\ -l_2\sin(q_1 + q_2) - l_3\sin(q_1 + q_2 + q_3) \\ -l_3\sin(q_1 + q_2 + q_3) \end{bmatrix}^{\mathrm{T}}$$

Because q_2 and q_3 are function of q_1, in the paper, we have

$$q_2 = \psi(q_1) = \mathrm{acos}(\tfrac{l - l_3 - l_1\cos(q_1)}{l_2}) - q_1$$
$$q_3 = \varphi(q_1) = -q_2 - q_1$$

Moreover, we can get

$$L(q_1) = \begin{bmatrix} 1 & \frac{\partial\psi(q_1)}{\partial q_1} & \frac{\partial\varphi(q_1)}{\partial q_1} \end{bmatrix}^{\mathrm{T}} = \begin{bmatrix} 1 & -2 & -1 \end{bmatrix}^{\mathrm{T}}$$

The specific parameters of the three link manipulator in the paper are set to

$$m_1 = 1.24 \text{ kg}, \ m_2 = 0.92 \text{ kg}, \ m_1 = 0.5 \text{ kg}$$
$$l_1 = 1 \text{ m}, \ l_2 = 1 \text{ m}, \ l_3 = 0.4 \text{ m}, \ l = 1.5 \text{ m}$$

The specific parameters of the sliding mode controller are set to

$$K_p = \begin{bmatrix} 10 & 0 & 0 \\ 0 & 10 & 0 \\ 0 & 0 & 10 \end{bmatrix}, \ \Lambda_1 = 5, \ \Lambda_2 = 0.8$$

The initial state of the simulation is set to

$$q_{1d} = 0.5 + 0.5\sin(t)\text{rad}, \ \lambda_d = 10\text{N}$$
$$q_{10} = 0, \ \dot{q}_{10} = 0$$

The results of the simulation are shown in Figs. 2, 3, 4 and 5. Figure 2 shows position tracking trajectory and tracking error; Fig. 3 shows contact force tracking trajectory and tracking error; Fig. 4 shows control torque of link1, link2 and link3 of manipulator; Fig. 5 shows manipulator pose motion trajectory when end-effector contact constrained surface.

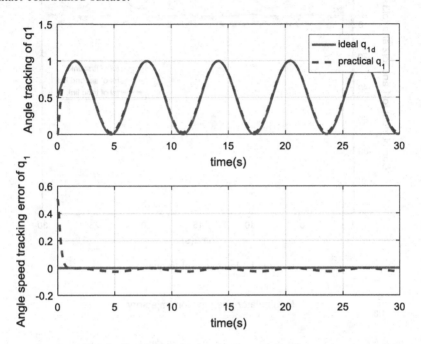

Fig. 2. Position tracking trajectory and tracking error

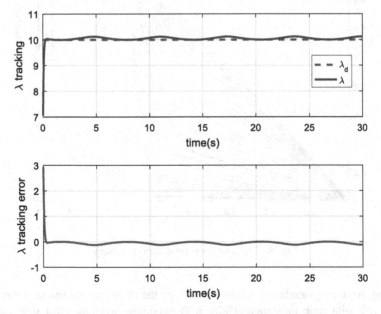

Fig. 3. Contact force tracking trajectory and tracking error

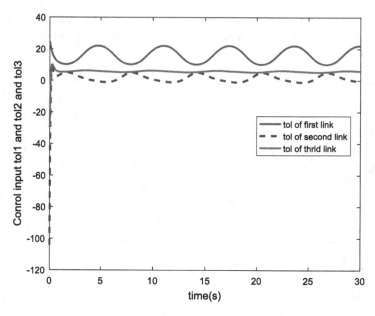

Fig. 4. Joint control torque

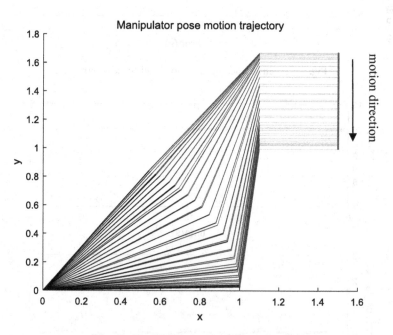

Fig. 5. Manipulator pose motion trajectory

From the above simulation results we can see the three link manipulator can track the desired joint trajectory successfully with maximum tracking error 0.06 rad and root-mean-square of tracking error is 0.016 rad (stabilization stage). At the same time, we can also see the contact force can track the desired force successfully with maximum tracking error 0.12 N and root-mean-square of tracking error is 0.065 N (stabilization stage). These results show that the control objective is achieved successfully.

6 Conclusions

In this paper, a force/motion hybrid control scheme is proposed based on sliding mode control method for the three link constrained manipulator. The dynamic model of the three link manipulator is given and further establish the dynamic model of constrained manipulator. To simplify the design of the controller, we proposed the model order reduction design. Then, a sliding mode control algorithm to achieve trajectory tracking of end-effector on a constrained surface with specified constraint force is presented by using the theory of variable structure system. A three link manipulator and a plane constraint has been used to illustrate the scheme developed in the paper and the simulation results show the control objective is achieved successfully.

Acknowledgments. This work is supported by Foundation of State Key Laboratory of Robotics under Grant 2017-Z011 and 2019-Z06, Strategic Priority Research Program on Space Science, the Chinese Academy of Sciences under Grant XDA1502030505. All the authors are grateful for the funding.

References

1. Shao, Z., Li, S., Yin, H.: Robust sliding-mode position/force set-point control of underactuated constrained manipulator. In: 2017 36th Chinese Control Conference (CCC), Dalian, pp. 1162–1167 (2017)
2. Mai, T., Wang, Y.: Adaptive force/motion control system based on recurrent fuzzy wavelet CMAC neural networks for condenser cleaning crawler-type mobile manipulator robot. IEEE Trans. Control Syst. Technol. **22**(5), 1973–1982 (2014)
3. Chen, C., Liu, Z.: Adaptive motion/force control of robots with input nonlinearities via fuzzy logic system. In: 2014 International Conference on Mechatronics and Control (ICMC), Jinzhou, pp. 11–15 (2014)
4. Fan, X.P., Xu, J.M., Mao, Z.Y., et al.: Robust variable structure hybrid position force control for constrained flexible-link manipulators. Acta Automatica Sinica **26**(02), 176–183 (2000)
5. Su, C.Y., Leung, T.P., Zhou, Q.J.: Force/motion control of constrained robots using sliding mode. IEEE Trans. Autom. Control **37**(5), 668–672 (1992)
6. Huang, T., Sun, L.N., Wang, Z.H., et al.: Hybrid force/position control method for robotic polishing based on passive compliance structure. Robot **39**(6), 776–785 (2017)
7. Li, Y.C., Song, Y., Zhao, B.: Modular position/force control for environmental constrained reconfigurable manipulator. J. Shanghai Jiao Tong Univ. **51**(6), 709–714 (2017)
8. Haifa, M., Olfa, B.: PSO-Lyapunov motion/force control of robot arms with model uncertainties. Robotica **34**(3), 634–651 (2016)
9. Cai, C., Somani, N., Rickert, M., et al.: Prioritized motion-force control of multi-constraints for industrial manipulators. IEEE Int. Conf. Robot. Biomim. IEEE, pp. 952–957 (2015)

10. Lang, L., Wang, J., Wei, Q., et al.: Compliant landing of a trotting quadruped robot based on hybrid motion/force robust control. J. Central South Univ. **23**(8), 1970–1980 (2016)
11. Liu, J.K., Guo, Y.: output feedback dynamic surface control for N link manipulators with actuator saturation. Control Decis. **30**(5), 871–876 (2015)
12. Liu, J.K.: Robot Control System Design and MATLAB Simulation: the Basic Design Method, pp. 282–287. Tsinghua University Press, Beijing (2016)

Computer Integrated Manufacturing

Development of Workshop Management System for Assembly Production Process

Pengfei Zeng[1,2(✉)], Yuyu Hao[1], Changwu Wu[1], Chunjing Shi[1],
and Yongping Hao[2]

[1] School of Mechanical Engineering, Shenyang Ligong University,
Shenyang 110159, China
pfzeng@163.com
[2] R&D Center of CAD/CAM Technology, Shenyang Ligong University,
Shenyang 110159, China

Abstract. In order to meet the requirements of digital production of assembly workshop from an enterprise, a workshop management system is presented for lean production based on the manufacturing execution system (MES). Enterprise assembly production practices and production management requirements are consulted. The requirement of building workshop management system for assembly production process is analyzed. The organization structure of assembly plant is described, and key business processes of assembly production management are modeled. The system functional structure, main use cases and data relationships are established respectively. The system implementation and the work of application investigation are completed based on the J2EE environment. Through the system development, a digital and informatization workshop management platform is set for enterprise assembly production. The intelligent measure of production management is improved, the capacity of resource allocation and production efficiency are promoted in the product assembly process.

Keywords: Workshop management system · Assembly production process · Requirement analysis · Functional structure design · System development

1 Introduction

With the continuous change of customer demands and personalized products come into market, enterprises are facing increasingly fierce market competition [1, 2]. Product functions are more and more complex and product life cycles are gradually shorten [3, 4]. These make enterprises have to adopt multi-variety and small-batch mode of production organization to cope with market challenges, especially in the context that the concept of industrial 4.0 and intelligent factory are proposed [5, 6]. Using information means and networked technology, manufacturing enterprises introduce management ideas and methods related to workshop production to forge information environment and digital capability, to achieve rapid response, so as to gain competitive advantages [7]. The product consists of many parts and components, which are produced through a series of processes and then are assembled to form the final product. Assembly

© Springer Nature Switzerland AG 2019
H. Yu et al. (Eds.): ICIRA 2019, LNAI 11745, pp. 435–446, 2019.
https://doi.org/10.1007/978-3-030-27529-7_37

activities and workshop assembly production are indispensable and necessary links in the product manufacturing process [8].

Assembly production management includes complex enterprise activities. It is necessary to grasp the operation situation of each assembly unit timely and quickly. All kinds of information related to product, process and resource are integrated seamlessly and pushed on-demand. The information flow, data flow and material flow of assembly production process need to be managed integrally. It is necessary to accurately control each operation condition of assembly unit and workstation, the activity state of assembly workers, and the usage of tools and fixtures, etc. Only in this way can improve the quality and efficiency of assembly production management. At present, most Chinese enterprises have implemented manufacturing information engineering, and have made great progress in the application of the product date management (PDM) system and the enterprise resource planning (ERP) system. However, there are still many weak links in the construction of workshop production information system compared with other developed countries. Some manufacturing enterprises are also trying to establish and implement assembly workshop production management system to meet the production characteristics and actual product needs, including electronic and military industries, automobile manufacturing, and shipbuilding or aviation industries [9–12]. At the same time, the research on the workshop management system of enterprise assembly production also shows variety with the participation of academia and industry.

Aiming at the customization requirement of assembly workshop production management from a specific industry company in China, an interactive platform of assembly production information for real-time acquisition and feedback control and management is established based on the MES theory and the application of lean management idea, and combined with the practice of assembly production process. Through the constructed system of assembly workshop production management, many difficult problems that assembly order, production plan, tool and fixture, assembly process and other information can not connect the actual production workshop are improved. Using the system, the errors of information transmission in assembly production process are reduced, the rational resource allocation in assembly production process is improved, and the cost is reduced effectively. This is also the basic work to realize intelligent factory and industrial 4.0 for this company.

2 Manufacturing Execution System

At present, informatization management has become more common in the field of manufacturing industry, and many manufacturing enterprises have also introduced information management system. The purpose of using these systems is to make the whole enterprise operation and management to realize electronic and digital. Generally speaking, these systems will collect data and information from some links such as sales business, production planning, warehouse management, production process, product inspection and final shipment, etc. Enterprise informatization has changed the traditional production and management mode. The AMR Corporation summarized three-tier integration model of manufacturing enterprises: planning layer, execution layer and control layer [13, 14]. As shown in Fig. 1.

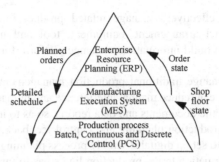

Fig. 1. MES positioning within manufacturing enterprise

(1) Enterprise Resource Planning (ERP): It is at the top level. In general, the business processes of enterprises include production, sale, finance, procurement, and warehouse management. The task of the ERP is to integrate these related systems.
(2) Manufacturing Execution System (MES): It is a production management information system for workshop production control execution, lies in the middle layer.
(3) Process Control System (PCS): It is directly oriented to the production line, real-time detection and control of various data and information from production process, locates at the bottom.

At present, there have been some suppliers for MES solutions, such as Siemens, Rockwell and Honeywell. These MES systems have their own characteristics in function, scalability, system compatibility, and personalized requirement [15, 16]. Moreover, different organizations and research institutes have formed some theories and systems related to MES, including its definition, functional model, location model, data flow model and implementation method. Manufacturing Execution System Association International (MESA) defines MES as: It can optimize the whole production process from order to product completion through information transmission [17]. When a real-time event occurs in a factory, it can respond and report timely and it can use the current accurate data to guide and process them. This rapid response to state change enables MES to reduce internal activities without added value, guide the factory production effectively, so that it can not only improve the timely delivery capacity and material flow performance, but also improve the return on production.

3 Analysis of Assembly Workshop Production Management

3.1 Requirement Analysis of Assembly Production Management

According to the actual enterprise situation, combining the theory and practice of MES with development principle of informatization management system, the enterprise requirement to build workshop management system is summarize for assembly production process.

(1) The system can effectively manage related product information, production planning, personnel arrangement, equipment, tool and fixture, and assembly process, and it can build information exchange platform for assembly production process.

(2) The system can change traditional production management mode and assembly workshop control, can reduce manual interference and human errors, and can fully use various electronic documents and data reports, so as to improve the timeliness and accuracy of production planning and control feedback.

(3) Using the system to set up digital assembly process planning and process card and to push these information to the production line so as to guide assembly activity. At the same time, it can realize the management of parts and components, audit and inspection information needed in the assembly life cycle.

(4) The system can establish some interfaces with product design data, three dimensional assembly process design and other related systems to enable the workshop management system for assembly production process so as to effectively aggregate three dimensional design data and model information, to enhance the ability and practice of crossing system information integration.

3.2   Enterprise Organization Structure Investigation

The enterprise management department consists of some relevant functional departments and offices, such as lean management department, production department, business planning department, party work department, quality safety department, inspection department, process technology department, finance department, human resources department, and group office. Mechanical processing plants and assembly plants are not only the production units of the enterprise, but also important parts of the enterprise. There are three assembly plants in enterprise, each of which is responsible for specific assembly work. The main difference is that the labor division and the assembly object are different. Taking one plant as an example, the personnel composition of assembly plant includes assembly director, technical director, technician, production supervisor, dispatcher, statistician, material worker, production team, comprehensive supervisor and accountant. The production team includes monitor, deputy monitor, quality controller, inspector, safety worker and assembly worker.

The director of the assembly plant is responsible for all the affairs related to the plant. The technical supervisor mainly manages many technicians. The technician is engaged in assembly process planning, fixture design, process training and assessment, etc. The production supervisor is responsible for handling all kinds of problems in the assembly production process. The dispatcher is responsible for decomposing the monthly production plan into specific plans of each team for production scheduling management, and formulating product plans and scheduling matching tables. The statistician is responsible for the statistics of various kinds of information in the assembly production process. The main tasks of the material worker are to get all kinds of materials needed. The inspector completes the inspection of important assembly processes and finished product. The quality control worker manages quality related to assembly process. The safety worker regularly explains safety knowledge and skill, ensures production process safety and specific safety measures implement in place.

3.3   Key Business Analysis of Assembling Production Workshop

Production Planning and Scheduling Management. When the order is received, the enterprise starts the whole production and manufacturing process. The business planning department formulates the production plan of factory level according to the order situation and actual work ability, and sends the plan to the production department. The production department formulates quarterly and monthly production plans and distributes to various plants. The dispatcher of the plant analyses the situation of production team, the degree of urgency, the quantity of production and the production capacity of workshop, and works out specific monthly, weekly and daily production plans in line with the plant internal operation, and distributes these plans to corresponding production teams. According to the monthly production plan and the actual needs of the plant, the material worker gets material from the purchasing department and the production department, and stores them in the transfer warehouse. The monitor will reach every assembly worker under the production plan. After the assembly worker gets production task, they go to the warehouse to collect all kinds of materials needed. The assembly worker proceeds with the planned assembly work. The scheduling process of the production plan is shown in Fig. 2.

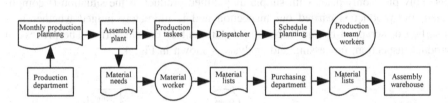

Fig. 2. Production plan scheduling process

Information Management of Process Planning. According to the product technical information, the technology department compiles the general process plan, determines the optimal assembly plan and organization form, and distributes it to the production department. The production department distributes the process plan to the specific plant according to each plant characteristics, work nature and ability. When the corresponding assembly plant gets the assembly process plan, the technician carries out the specific process preparation, improves process design and fixture design. Then, the technician determines the overall process flow, as well as the operation contents and related technical requirements of each assembly procedure and work step, and partitions assembly units. Finally, the technician determines the equipment, tool, fixture, instrument, workplace and related assembly worker. When the assembly process is planned, the assembly plant will audit it. After the audit is qualified, the technical department audit and standardization audit will be required, and the final audit will be conducted by the deputy general manager of the enterprise. After the audit is approved, the assembly process is distributed to related production teams. The audit process of assembly process is shown in Fig. 3.

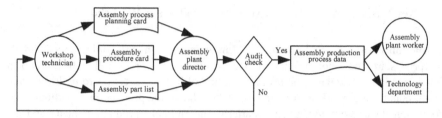

Fig. 3. Assembly process planning data check and issue

Inspection Management of Product Assembly Process. Inspection shall be conducted in accordance with relevant technical requirements during assembly process. Whether each assembly procedure is qualified or not determines the final product is qualified. Therefore, the inspection of each assembly procedure is particularly important. The product or its parts are sent to the inspection room, and the inspector checks whether they are qualified or not. If they are qualified, the inspection leader will sign and they are continued subsequent assembly work. If they are not qualified, they should be temporarily placed in the isolation room, the quality controller shall analyze reasons. The technician will judge whether rework, repair, out-of-tolerance or scrap treatment based on reasons, actual requirements and experiences. In general, the technician of assembly plant only deals with simple unqualified product. If the situation is complicated, the product is carried out inspection and is ultimately judged whether it is qualified or scrapped by the inspection department of the enterprise. The process of product inspection, processing and analysis is shown in Fig. 4.

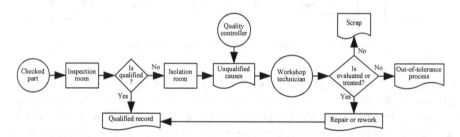

Fig. 4. The inspection process of parts and processing method

Assembly Process Safety Control. Safety control of the assembly process is one of the important links in the enterprise production. It requires not only the safety of the product, but also the safety of the production personnel themselves in the assembly process. Because of the particularity of the assembled product, the production personnel will cause certain injury due to operational errors or other reasons. The enterprise has relevant regulations on safety management, and the specific contents will be mentioned in the annual production and operation responsibility statement. According to the each plant work conditions, the complexity degree of production process and product quality requirements, combined with previous experience to determine overall number of major quality and safety, disabled number and control number, and to divide the corresponding number of plant level. The annual safety table and quarterly safety table are worked out from the time point of view. Safety inspector regularly carries out safety inspections to ensure the safety of all work in the production process without any accidents.

Tool and Fixture Management. The usage range of tool and fixture in assembly workshop covers widely. It includes the whole assembly process and quality inspection process. Meanwhile, the production capacity provided by tools and fixtures also directly affects the process technological documents, assembly production tasks, product quality inspection and timely submission of order formulated by the technology department. The management of tool and fixture includes the inventory information of tool, fixture, mold and tool used in the assembly process, the making and purchasing information of tool, the lending and returning information of tool, the scrapping information of tool and fixture, the measuring tool and other auxiliary tool used in the inspection process.

Work in Process and Inventory Management. Work in process (WIP) management is to plan, coordinate and control the product information being assembled, and to manage the number of finished and semi-finished products that have been assembled, so as to ensure the balance of all aspects of assembly production. Meanwhile, the workshop occupancy of WIP which the assembly workshop simultaneously produces can be effectively reduced, and inventory overstock is reduced. Inventory management is the processing of in-and-out warehouse management and statistical inquiry of products produced by the assembly plant, which makes the inventory keep the best state value in real time and to ensure the assembly production to proceed smoothly and complete order delivery on time.

4 Assembly Workshop Production Management System Design

4.1 System Functional Structure Design

By investigating the management business of enterprise assembly workshop and according to the characteristics of MES, the idea of lean management is integrated into each management link in order to establish a lean integrated production management system for assembly workshop. According to the various aspects analysis for assembly production process, the main functions of the assembly production workshop management system are divided into system management, resource management, planning and scheduling management, process management, quality management, report management and integrated management. The functional structure of the workshop management system is shown in Fig. 5.

(1) System Management: It includes three main contents, namely user information management, system setup and database management. Through the function module, user can be set different roles according to different positions in the system corresponding, different roles corresponding to different access rights,

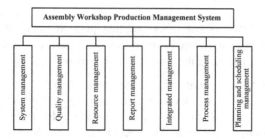

Fig. 5. System function structure map

different permissions corresponding to different authorities for selective processing of information content and data access.

(2) Resource Management: It mainly involves the work staff in the assembly process, the tools and equipments needed in the process, and the corresponding material resources management. In the assembly production process, the most important resource is the personnel, and the work staff of each position is the undertakers to ensure assembly work smooth progress. The requirement for tools, equipments and materials are prerequisites in the whole assembly process.

(3) Planning and Scheduling Management: It mainly includes planning task management, document demand management, planning division management, resource scheduling management, outsourced information management, and dispatching and completion management. Taking production planning as the main line, enterprise, branch and production workshop are connected in series, so that each department is managed as a whole. The production plan may also be changed after it is formulated. It needs to be determined according to the specific production situation and the degree of customer requirement. The function module needs to deal with these changes in time, so as to make the internal resources of workshop more effective adjustment, to ensure the stability of assembly production process.

(4) Process Management: It is mainly responsible for the management of process documents and related information. The assembly process is the method and skill used in the specific assembly process. The assembly process covers process planning, process resource, and process change and assembly route. Only by formulating assembly documents in line with the actual situation of the enterprise can we effectively guide the relevant production activities of the workshop and ensure the correctness and safety of assembly process. The assembly workshop completes parts and components assembly according to the production plan, assembly document and process requirement, and finally a deliverable product is formed.

(5) Quality Management: Its functions include work in process information management, qualified inspection product management, scrap information management and quality report information management. The requirements of assembly production process management for quality management are essential. It is related to the future development of the whole assembly production workshop. The

enterprise has formed certain standardized documents for quality control and needs. The unqualified products are checked through the unqualified product information management. The quality inspection technician shall determine the unqualified reasons, pay special attention to the assembly process and procedure stages and revise the document contents of the quality control process.

(6) Report Management: It is responsible for daily report, monthly report and matched information management in the assembly production process. Daily report processing is the process of statistics, reporting, auditing and publishing the production situation form assembly workshop in a day. Due to the different production conditions, the data of daily report can be entered many times, and the completed data can be modified. The daily data can only be submitted once a day and the submitted data can not be modified. The processing of monthly report is basically the same as that of daily report, only once a month. After the submission of the monthly report, it is also necessary for the management level to confirm, examine and publish the final report. The monthly report is submitted at the end of each month, followed by month reports the following month.

(7) Integrated Management: It is different from other modules. It is mainly responsible for the integrated information management of the non-production directly related to the assembly workshop. It is a specially customized module for assembly plant. Its main functions include daily power management, plant daily affairs management, drawing and document information management, and other affairs management. Through the integrated module, it is convenient to manage and record the daily related production and operation activities or affairs from the assembly plant.

4.2   Database Design

The design of the system database mainly considers two problems, one is data concept modeling, and the other is the establishment of database tables and their related structure relationships. The entity-relationship (E-R) model is used to express relationships between entities. The E-R model of the system is shown in Fig. 6. It is a many-to-one relationship to formulate corresponding process routes according to user needs and production plans, basic information of parts and assembly design drawings. Process route is generated corresponding process documents. Process document corresponds to process information, personnel information corresponds to personnel files, tool and fixture information corresponds to tool specifications, and equipment information corresponds to equipment specifications, and there are one-to-one relationships. Process documents correspond to personnel information, tool information and equipment information, and the corresponding relationship is one-to-many.

Based on the theoretical basis of the system database design, database tables related assembly process mainly include product basic information table, product assembly parts detail information table, product assembly process card information table, product assembly procedure card information table, tool information table, product assembly process planning supported table and product assembly process scheduling supported table. The basic product information table is used as the base table to show the process information management of assembly production through the correlation between tables (Fig. 7).

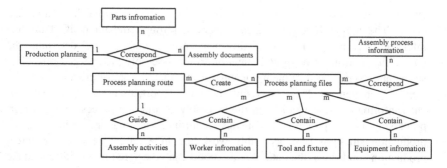

Fig. 6. System E-R model

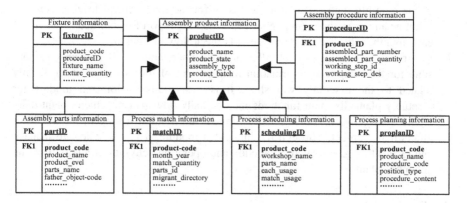

Fig. 7. System database design view

5   System Implementation and Application

Based on the related theory and technology of discrete MES and lean production management, the development of workshop management system for assembly production process is implemented. The design of data model, system function module and business process are completed. The implementation of the assembly workshop production management system is realized under the principle that the use conditions of the system and operating environment are fully considered. The Windows 7 is selected as operation system of application server and data server. Based on the J2EE development environment and the mode-view-controller (MVC) development mode, programming and application test of the system are made through adopting B/S structure. The application server is selected the open source Apache Tomcat 6.0. The database management system is adopted the Microsoft SQL Server 2008. The Internet Explorer and the Google Chrome are used to browsers.

As the Fig. 8 (Left) illustrates, the relevant functional interface and content are displayed after the system is successful login. The login ID is composed of the department and the personnel number. Different users are assigned different roles. User logs in the system according to the assigned ID and password, the background of server verifies these data by database. The system automatically identifies different roles according to the ID to enable the user to enter the corresponding functional interface. The content displayed in the main interface includes public information view and transaction processing panel. User can see the public information that has been published, and handle the corresponding transactions through the to-do item function. As shown in Fig. 8 (Right), it is a query function for production plan of assembly workshop. The production plan management module in the system can make the enterprise production plan, such as annual plan, quarterly plan, monthly production plan of each plant, and includes the formulated production plan and scheduling behavior from the corresponding workshop.

Fig. 8. System application cases. Left is main interface, right is assembly planning view.

6   Conclusion

According to the actual needs of certain enterprise production, a workshop management system is constructed for assembly production process. On the basis of theory and knowledge of MES, the enterprise requirement related to production management system for assembly workshop is analyzed. The investigation work of organization structure is completed. Aim at an assembly plant, main business process is established, and management approach is analyzed. The system function structure design, setup and partition of management function module are realized based on the management idea of the lean production. The E-R graph of concept data model of the developed system is set, and database tables and its relationships are designed. In the Web networked environment, the system realization and the application verification are carried out with the help of the J2EE development environment and the MVC mode. Through the system development, the active needs of digital management of enterprise assembly production workshop are well satisfied. The level and capacity of the enterprise are improved. This laid the foundation to implement smart factory.

Acknowledgements. This work was supported by the Guided Plan Project of Natural Science Foundation of Liaoning Province under Grant No. 20180550932, and the project is sponsored by "Liaoning BaqiQianWan Talents Program".

References

1. Qu, Y., et al.: An integrated framework of enterprise information systems in smart manufacturing system via business process reengineering. Proc. Inst. Mech. Eng. Part B J. Eng. Manuf. 1–15 (2018). https://doi.org/10.1177/0954405418816846
2. Savković, O., et al.: Semantic diagnostics of smart factories. In: Ichise, R., Lecue, F., Kawamura, T., Zhao, D., Muggleton, S., Kozaki, K. (eds.) JIST 2018. LNCS, vol. 11341, pp. 277–294. Springer, Cham (2018). https://doi.org/10.1007/978-3-030-04284-4_19
3. Yin, C., Deng, P., Li, X.: Intelligent manufacturing mode for sophisticated equipment assembly workshop. J. Adv. Manuf. Syst. 17(4), 533–549 (2018)
4. Yu, Y., Sun, G., Huang, N., Lin, G., Qi, Y.: Constraints and resolution strategy of implementation of mes in military electronic industry. Electron. Packag. 18(6), 45–48 (2018)
5. Zeng, P., Ren, K., Zhang, X., Shi, C., Hao, Y.: Development of integrated workshop production management system for lean production. J. Shenyang Ligong Univ. 37(1), 51–57 (2018)
6. Zhang, X., Zeng, P., Hao, Y.: The research of lean production management integrated system for discrete manufacturing. Manuf. Autom. 37(9), 18–21 (2015)
7. Nallusamy, S., Saravanan, V.: Optimization of process flow in an assembly line of manufacturing unit through lean tools execution. Int. J. Eng. Res. Africa 38, 133–143 (2018). http://10.0.15.188/www.scientific.net/JERA.38.133
8. Li, C., Gao, L., Shi, Y., Lei, Z.: Production management system designing of discrete workshop based on MES. Modul. Mach. Tool Autom. Manuf. Tech. 5, 149–151 (2017)
9. Meyer, H., Fuchs, F., Thiesl, K.: Manufacturing Execution Systems (MES): Optimal Design, Planning, And Deployment, 1st edn. McGraw-Hill Professional, New York (2009)
10. Menezes, S., Creado, S., Zhong, R.: Smart manufacturing execution systems for small and medium-sized enterprises. Procedia CIRP 72, 1009–1014 (2018)
11. Dantonio, G., Bedolla, J., Chiabert, P.: A novel methodology to integrate manufacturing execution systems with the lean manufacturing approach. Procedia Manuf. 11, 2243–2251 (2017)
12. Lee, S., Hong, S., Katerattanakul, P., Kim, N.: Successful implementations of MES in Korean manufacturing SMEs: an empirical study. Int. J. Prod. Res. 50(7), 1942–1954 (2012)
13. Cupek, R., Ziebinski, A., Huczala, L., Erdogan, H.: Agent-based manufacturing execution systems for short-series production scheduling. Comput. Ind. 82, 245–258 (2016)
14. Waschull, S., Wortmann, J.C., Bokhorst, J.A.C.: Manufacturing execution systems: the next level of automated control or of shop-floor support? In: Moon, I., Lee, Gyu M., Park, J., Kiritsis, D., von Cieminski, G. (eds.) APMS 2018. IAICT, vol. 536, pp. 386–393. Springer, Cham (2018). https://doi.org/10.1007/978-3-319-99707-0_48
15. Barenji, A.: Cloud-based manufacturing execution system: case study FMS. Int. J. Ind. Syst. Eng. 30(4), 449–467 (2018)
16. Huang, M., Zhou, Q., Bai, A.: Research on smart manufacturing execution system (Smart-MES) for modern numerical control shop floor: functional components and its implementation strategies. Adv. Intell. Syst. Res. 154, 452–456 (2017)
17. MESA International. http://www.mesa.org Accessed 31 Dec 2018

Dynamic Scheduling of Dual-Resource Constrained Blocking Job Shop

Ze Tao[1(✉)] and Xiaoxia Liu[2]

[1] School of Mechanical Engineering, Shenyang Ligong University,
Shenyang 110159, China
taoze@tsinghua.edu.cn
[2] Henan University of Technology, Zhengzhou 450001, China

Abstract. A dynamic scheduling problem of blocking job shop constrained by machines and workers is studied based on genetic algorithm and simulated annealing algorithm (GASA). The problem is characterized by two resources and no storage buffer, and different disturbances. The objective is to minimize the completing time. The static scheduling results are obtained based on GASA, and the dynamic scheduling results are given according to the disturbance type. Judging whether it is rescheduled or minor adjusted according to the influence to the completing time. If it has little influence to the completion time, try not to disorder the original scheduling result, otherwise, it is rescheduled. When these factors are considered, a more effective schedule result can be obtained based on the method proposed in this paper. The performance of the method is proved based on two cases, and the results show that the method proposed in this paper is effective and feasible.

Keywords: Dynamic · Dual-resource · Blocking · Job shop scheduling · Genetic algorithm and simulated annealing algorithm

1 Introduction

The typical job shop scheduling has been studied by many researchers and it was taken as a standard problem in scheduling. However, in practice, the scheduling problems usually cannot be stated as the job shop scheduling model, due to features such as dynamic change constraints, storage-space and resources constraints, parallel processing machines constraints and so on.

Some extension of the typical job shop problem have been studied in the research [1–3], the job shop scheduling with blocking or blocking job shop scheduling(BJSP) is concluded. The job shop scheduling with blocking is a kind of job shop scheduling that there is no intermediate storage space or the storage space is not allowed between two adjacent processing stations. The finished job cannot leave the machine until the next processing machine is available for the job. When the number of machines concluded in the scheduling is more than two, the job shop scheduling problems have been proved to be strongly NP-hard. Therefore, it is very complicated in computation. It is very important to find optimal methods for BJSP in theory and application. Many researcher [4–7] have studied the blocking job shop scheduling problem. Hegera [4] obtained an

© Springer Nature Switzerland AG 2019
H. Yu et al. (Eds.): ICIRA 2019, LNAI 11745, pp. 447–456, 2019.
https://doi.org/10.1007/978-3-030-27529-7_38

optimal solution to the autonomous guided vehicles in a blocking reentrant job shop environment with different jobs based on a mixed integer linear programming (MILP) formulation. Sadaqa [5] proposed Meta-heuristic for randomized priority search method to resolve blocking flow shop scheduling problem. The solution to the job shop problem with limited output buffers was obtained according to an integer nonlinear mathematical programming model [6]. Xie [7] proposed a memetic algorithm based on variable neighborhood search strategy in order to resolve the flow shop scheduling problem with limited buffers. Above researches were BJSP with one resource restraint, and usually the processing system constrained only by machines. Dual-resource constrained blocking job shop scheduling problem(DRCBJSP)is extension of BJSP. Two resources(for example workers and machines) are constrained in the manufacturing process. Dual-resource constrained job shop scheduling problem has proved to better than classical job shop scheduling problem [8], one resource constrained job shop is a special case of two resources constrained job shop, for example, when the number of workers is equal to the number of machines, and one worker can process on his machine and only can process on the machine, then the dual-resource constrained job shop can be simplified to a classical job shop scheduling problem. Dual-resource constrained job shop scheduling has been given more and more attention in recent years [8–11].

In this paper, a dynamic scheduling of dual-resource constrained blocking job shop problem (DDRCBJSP) is studied, and the DDRCBJSP is extension of the classical job shop scheduling concluding three kinds of constraints: (1) Two resources are considered, those are workers and machines, (2) There are no storage space, (3) Dynamic disturbances are considered(machines breakdown, and jobs cancellation). Therefore, DDRCBJSP is very complicated, and it is hard to get optimal or suboptimal solutions. In this paper, the objective is to minimize the completion time of the last processed job (makespan) and select an optimal processing route. The results are obtained based on an improved genetic algorithm and simulated annealing algorithm (GASA), and the results are showed with Gantt graph.

2   Problem Description

DDRCBJSP can be described as follows: h jobs $\{J_1, J_2 \cdots, J_h\}$ are processed on n machines $\{M_1, M_2 \cdots, M_n\}$ by m workers $\{W_1, W_2 \cdots, W_m\}$, where $m < n$. Therefore, at least one worker need process on k ($k \geq 2$) machines, and the flexibility level and processing efficiency of each worker may be different. Each job J_i is processed according the specified processing procedure $\{J_{i1}, J_{i2} \cdots, J_{in_i}\}$, each processing procedure J_{ij} can be processed on multiple machines by different workers, the processing time is decided by the selected worker and machine. The job J_{ij} must remain on the machine M_j till the machine M_{j+1} is available because of no storage buffer. The dynamic scheduling model is studied based on the static scheduling model, it can be constructed with multiple static scheduling models. Two dynamic disturbances are considered: (1) one machine or some machines breakdown (2) one job or some jobs cancellation.

The scheduling objective is:

$$\min Z = \min\{\max C_i\};$$ (1)

Constrained conditions:

1. the last processing procedure of job i

$$T_{ijm_{ij}n_{ij}} \leq Z;$$ (2)

2. the non-last processing procedure of job i

$$T_{ijm_{ij}n_{ij}} - T_{i(j-1)m_{i(j-1)}n_{i(j-1)}} \geq t_{ijm_in_i} \quad \forall i, j, m, n, j \neq 1$$ (3)

$$T_{i(j-1)m_{i(j-1)}n_{i(j-1)}} + R_{i(j-1)m_{i(j-1)}n_{i(j-1)}} = S_{ijm_{ij}n_{ij}}$$ (4)

$$R_{i(j-1)m_{i(j-1)}n_{i(j-1)}} \geq 0$$ (5)

3. For different jobs J_i and J_p, if they both need to be processed on machine n, Operation of job i in the processing route j and operation of job p in the processing routing q

$$T_{ijm_{ij}n} - T_{pqm_{pq}n} \geq t_{ijm_{ij}n};$$ (6)

$$T_{pqm_{pq}n} - T_{ijm_{ij}n} \geq t_{pqm_{pq}n};$$ (7)

4. Any processing procedure j of job i processed by worker m_{ij} on the machine n_{ij}

$$T_{ijm_{ij}n_{ij}} > 0;$$ (8)

Where, C_i is the finishing time of job i $(i = 1, 2, \cdots h)$, Z is the finishing time of the last processed job. m is the total number of workers; n is the total number of machines. M_r represents the rth machine $(r = 1, 2, \cdots n)$, and W_s represents the sth worker $(s = 1, 2, \cdots m)$, $t_{ijm_{ij}n_{ij}}$ and $T_{ijm_{ij}n_{ij}}$ represent processing time and finishing time of job i for the jth processing procedure, and the job is processed by specified worker on corresponding machine. Equation (2) is a natural constraint, it assures the last working procedure will not be finished later than Z; Eq. (3) assures that the former working procedure $(j-1)$ is processed before working procedure j for the same job i. Equation (4) represents that the starting processing time of job J_{ij} is equal to the summation of the finishing time of $J_{i(j-1)}$ and the remaining time of $J_{i(j-1)}$ on the machine because of no storage buffers. (5) denotes the remaining time of $J_{i(j-1)}$ on machine $M_{i(j-1)}$, if the next machine M_{ij} of J_{ij} is available, then $R_{i(j-1)m_{i(j-1)}n_{i(j-1)}} = 0$, otherwise $R_{i(j-1)m_{i(j-1)}n_{i(j-1)}} > 0$. (6) represents J_{ij} is processed before J_{pq}, and (7) represents the opposite processing order, that is, no two operations of J_{ij} and J_{pq} can be overlapped in time on the same machine. (8) is used to assure that any procedure finishing time of J_{ij}.

3 Genetic Algorithm and Simulated Annealing Algorithm

Genetic algorithm and simulated annealing (GASA) combines the characteristics of genetic algorithm and simulated annealing algorithm in optimization mechanism, optimization structure and optimization operation. GASA hybrid algorithm is good for searching for an optimum process, enhancing whole and local search ability and efficiency; it has excellent search ability and high reliability. Moreover, it can effectively control the convergence of the algorithm to avoid premature convergence of the genetic algorithm [12]. Therefore, GASA is easier to obtain the optimal solution than a single genetic algorithm or a single simulation algorithm for job shop scheduling problems. The flow chart of GASA is given is Fig. 1.

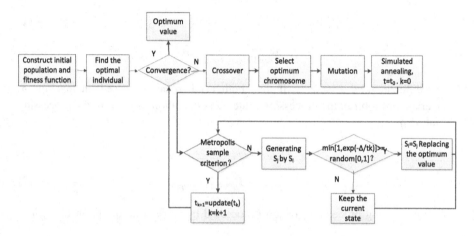

Fig. 1. The flow chart of GASA

4 Dynamic Blocking Job Shop Scheduling

In order to take into account the stability of processing and job completion cycle, different uncertain disturbances are classified to dispose with different methods. Machine breakdown and job cancellation are considered in this paper. Dynamic scheduling depends on the repairing time or the remainder task when disturbance occurs.

4.1 Machine Breakdown

There are two different situations of machine breakdown according to the fault repairing time.

$$t_{m_k}^r \geq N_1 \tag{9}$$

$$(k = 1, 2, \cdots n; \; N_1 > 0)$$

$$0 \leq t^d_{J_i} \leq t^r_{m_k} \tag{10}$$

$$t^r_{m_k} \leq t^b_{J_{ij}} \tag{11}$$

$t^r_{m_k}$ is the fault repairing time of machine m_k; N_1 is the given positive number. Judge whether it is a major or minor fault based on formula (9).

- A mayor fault. When formula (9) is satisfied, then it is a mayor fault, the fault repairing time is long. The machine fault will produce obvious impact on the remainder processing jobs. If the remaining jobs are to be processed after the machine fault is repaired, the completion time will be greatly affected. Therefore, another machine must be selected to replace the faulty machine and the remainder processing jobs are rescheduled.
- A minor fault. When formula (9) is not satisfied, then it is a minor fault, the fault repairing time is short. The remainder processing jobs will not be rescheduled, since it has little effect on the completion time. The remainder jobs continue to be processed according to the initial scheduling results if they are irrelevant to the faulty machine. For the remainder jobs relevant to the faulty machine, the processing procedures will continue to be processed after the fault repairing. The completion time of the relevant jobs will be delayed accordingly. The delayed time is given in (10).

In practice, some delayed procedures do not affect subsequent processes, because there is blocking time between adjacent procedures of the same job, and the relationship between the blocking time and repairing time is given in (11). (11) represents the repairing time is no more than the blocking time.

4.2 Job Cancellation

The job cancellation is classified according to task of order cancelling.

$$\sum_{i=s}^{h} \sum_{j=f}^{g_i} t_{ijm_{ij}n_{ij}} \geq N_2 \quad N_2 > 0 \tag{12}$$

$$\forall i, j; \; 1 \leq f \leq g_i, 1 \leq s \leq h; N_2 > 0$$

Where g_i is the procedure number of job i, the remainder task can be expressed in (12), and the amount of remainder task can be confirmed according to (12). It is rescheduled if the remainder task is heavy, otherwise, the remainder jobs will be processed corresponding to initial scheduling. Some jobs will be completed ahead of initial schedule, because some relevant machines will be free due to job cancellation.

5 Case Study

5.1 Case One

To test the effectiveness and robustness of GASA, one case in [13] is applied. The processing information of jobs and machines is given in Table 1. Run the simulation 10 times and record the results, the results are given in Table 2. One of the optimal results is shown in Fig. 2.

Table 1. The processing information of jobs and machines.

Job	Station 1		Station 2		Station 3		
	M1	M2	M3	M4	M5	M6	M7
1	3	3	6	8	3	4	5
2	5	5	8	10	3	5	6
3	6	6	4	6	6	7	9
4	8	8	6	7	5	6	8
5	4	4	4	7	4	6	7
6	6	6	5	8	5	7	8
7	5	5	4	6	3	4	6
8	3	3	3	5	5	7	9

Table 2. Results of simulation for 10 times.

Time	1	2	3	4	5	6	7	8	9	10
Solution	31	32	31	33	31	31	32	31	31	31

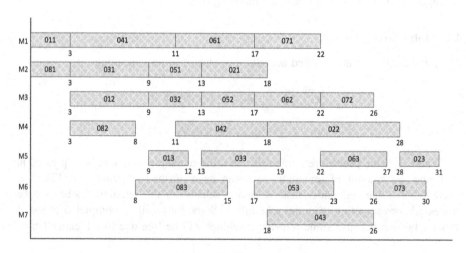

Fig. 2. The optimal scheduling result

From Table 2, it shows that the optimal results are 7 times, and the optimal result is equal to the result in [13]. The results show that non-optimal data fluctuation range are small enough to meet requirement. The validity and the robustness of the algorithm are proved through the results based on GASA.

5.2   Case Two

In this section, the comparison of static scheduling and dynamic scheduling for dual-resource constrained blocking job shop problem is given. The processing information are given in Tables 3 and 4.

Table 3. The relation between worker and machines

	M1	M2	M3	M4	M5	M6
W1	V	V				
W2		V	V			
W3				V	V	
W4					V	V

Table 4. Processing information of jobs

Job	Procedure	Time	Machine	Job	Procedure	Time	Machine
1	1	15	M3/M4	4	1	12	M1/M2
	2	8	M1/M2		2	8	M3/M4
	3	6	M5/M6		3	5	M1/M2
2	1	9	M3/M4	5	1	10	M3/M4
	2	7	M1/M2		2	8	M5/M6
	3	7	M5/M6		3	7	M1/M2
3	1	12	M3/M4	6	1	18	M5/M6
	2	8	M1/M2		2	9	M3/M4
	3	10	M5/M6		3	6	M5/M6

The optimal results of static scheduling and dynamic scheduling are given in Figs. 3, 4 and 5, respectively. The machine 4 fails at 27, the affected job is only job 2, it belongs to a minor machine fault. Therefore, it need not rescheduling, only the job 2 is adjusted. The optimal results is 65, it is longer than the static scheduling result because of the machine 4 breakdown. Another dynamic scheduling result is given in Fig. 6 when job 2 is cancelled. When disturbances occur, not only machines but also workers should be considered. The optimal result is 45, it is shorter than the static scheduling result because of the reduced tasks.

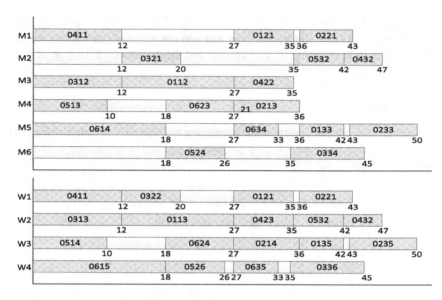

Fig. 3. The static optimal scheduling result

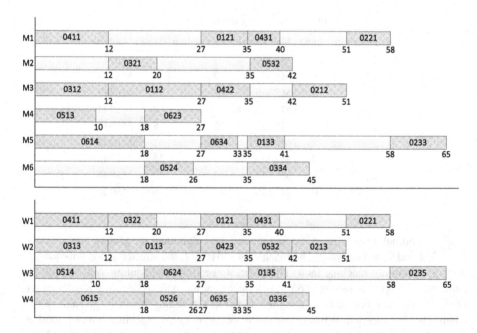

Fig. 4. The dynamic optimal scheduling result of machine 4 breakdown

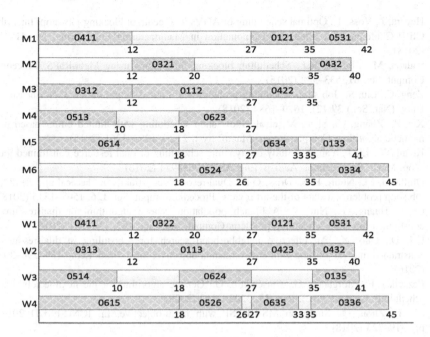

Fig. 5. The dynamic optimal scheduling result of job 2 cancellation

6 Conclusion

Dynamic scheduling problem is more suitable for workshop production than static scheduling problem because of considering the change of processing environment. The optimal results of dynamic scheduling of dual-resource constrained blocking job shop can be obtained based on the static scheduling results. Judging if it is rescheduled again according to the disturbance type and the influence to the completing time. When these factors are considered, a more effective schedule result can be obtained based on the method proposed in this paper. The performance of the method is proved based on two cases and comparisons with some existing algorithms, and the results show that the method proposed in this paper is effective and feasible.

References

1. Lu, T., Chen, P., Wan, X.: Improved cellular genetic algorithm for solving the multi-objective flexible job shop scheduling problem. Mod. Manuf. Eng. **11**, 41–49 (2016)
2. Oulamara, A.: Makespan minimization in a no-wait flow shop problem with two batching machines. Comput. Oper. Res. **34**, 1033–1050 (2007)
3. Yan, S., Shi, Y., Chen, B.: Dynamic jobshop scheduling with personalized customization in intelligent manufacturing. J. Southwest Univ. Sci. Technol. **32**(2), 84–89 (2017)

4. Hegera, J., Voss, T.: Optimal scheduling of AGVs in a reentrant blocking job-shop. In: 11th CIRP Conference on Intelligent Computation in Manufacturing Engineering, pp. 41–45 (2018)
5. Sadaqa, M., Moraga, R.J.: Scheduling blocking flow shops using Meta-RaPS. Procedia Comput. Sci. **61**, 533–538 (2015)
6. Zeng, C., Liu, S.: Job shop scheduling problem with limited output buffer. J. Northeastern Univ. (Nat. Sci.) **39**(12), 1679–1684 (2018)
7. Xie, Z., Zhang, C., Shao, X., et al.: Flow shop scheduling with limited buffer based on memetic algorithm. Comput. Integr. Manuf. Syst. **21**(5), 1253–1261 (2015)
8. Huang, Y., Li, J., Yan, X.: Study on dynamic scheduling of dual resource constrained job shop. Mech. Sci. Technol. Aerosp. Eng. **35**(6), 968–974 (2016)
9. Dhiflaoui, M., Nouri, H.E., Driss, O.B.: Dual-resource constraints in classical and flexible job shop problems: a state-of-the-art review. Procedia Comput. Sci. **126**, 1507–1515 (2018)
10. Li, J., Huang, Y., Niu, X.: A branch population genetic algorithm for dual-resource constrained job shop scheduling problem. Comput. Ind. Eng. **102**, 113–131 (2016)
11. Lei, D., Guo, X.: An effective neighborhood search for scheduling in dual-resource constrained interval jobshop with environmental objective. Int. J. Prod. Econ. **159**, 296–303 (2016)
12. Pezzellaa, F., Morgantia, G., Ciaschettib, G.: Genetic algorithm for the flexible job shop scheduling. Comput. Oper. Res. **35**, 3202–3212 (2008)
13. Ze, T., Zhou, Q.: Study on MS-BHFSP with multi-objective. In: ICNC-FSKD 2017, pp. 319–323 (2018)

Study on No-Wait Flexible Flow Shop Scheduling with Multi-objective

Ze Tao[1(✉)] and Xiaoxia Liu[2]

[1] School of Mechanical Engineering, Shenyang Ligong University,
Shenyang 110159, China
taoze@tsinghua.edu.cn
[2] Henan University of Technology, Zhengzhou 450001, China

Abstract. A multi-objective flexible flow shop scheduling model is constructed inclusive of production period, total expense, and mean flow time, which is based on the characteristics of dual-resource constrained no-wait flow shop scheduling problem with unrelated parallel machines. A genetic algorithm based on Pareto is proposed to solve the multi-objective scheduling problem. Then, consider the machine and worker constraints, and unrelated parallel machines and the successive processing, the production period is given through pushing reversely from the operation. The starting time of some jobs will be delayed and the spare time of machines will be increased in order to ensure the consecutive operations of the same job. Considering three objectives, an optimal set is given, and compared to other algorithms, simulation results show that the method is effective and feasible. At last, a comparative analysis of the same case is made from no-wait flow shop scheduling and flow shop scheduling with non-consecutive operation.

Keywords: No-wait · Multi-objective · Flexible flow shop · Dual-resource

1 Introduction

In the traditional flow shop scheduling model, it is usually assumed that the storage buffer between machines is infinite, and the processed job can remain in the storage buffer until the next procedure machine is available for processing. For some flow shop scheduling problems, the operations of a job have to be processed continuously from start to end without interruptions either on or between machines because of the limitation of processing, equipment and other factors. Otherwise, the products quality will be affected or significant economic losses will be caused. This means, when necessary, the starting time of a job on a given machine is delayed in order that the operation completing time is equal to the starting of the next operation on the subsequent machine. Such flow shops are called no-wait flow shops [1]. The no-wait flow shops are widely applied in plastic, chemical, and food industries. So, the no-wait hybrid flow shop scheduling problems (NWFSP) are studied by many researchers [1–7]. Orhan Engin proposed an effective new hybrid ant colony algorithm for no-wait flow shop scheduling with the criterion to minimize the makespan in [2], and the validity and feasibility of the proposed method was proved. A hybrid biogeography-based optimization with variable

© Springer Nature Switzerland AG 2019
H. Yu et al. (Eds.): ICIRA 2019, LNAI 11745, pp. 457–468, 2019.
https://doi.org/10.1007/978-3-030-27529-7_39

neighborhood search (HBV) is used to resolve NWFSP in [3]. Khalili [4] proposed a multi-objective hybrid NWFSP, the make-span and total tardiness are both considered, and a novel multi-objective electromagnetism algorithm equipped with three types of local search engine is proposed to resolve this problem. Song et al. [5] studied a NWFSP, and for the no-wait constraint between two sequential operations of a job, designing the no-wait algorithm of grading, and the number restriction of machines was embedded into this algorithm. Wang et al. [6] Proposed a heuristic algorithm based on the deep discussion of the duration time between two adjacent jobs in one job permutation and the relation of its upper and lower bound for permutation flow shop scheduling with limited waiting time constraints. Pan et al. [7] proposed a discrete particle swarm optimization algorithm for NWFSP with make-span criterion. Zhang et al. [8] proposed a particle swarm optimization algorithm for the bi-directional no-wait hybrid flow shop problem.

Although most scheduling problems are multi-objective in practice, most research methods for scheduling problems are single objective over the last few years [9]. In recent years, efforts have been made to study scheduling problems with multi-objective and develop algorithm in order to obtain a set of Pareto-optimal solution [9–11]. Due to the complexity of the multi-objective optimization problem, it seems that using a heuristic algorithm is the best way to get effective solutions. Genetic algorithms (GA) are widely used for the multi-objective scheduling problems [10, 11].

The ultimate target of a multi-objective optimization algorithm is to find practical solutions in the Pareto optimal set. It is almost impossible to find the entire Pareto optimal set for most of multi-objective problems. It is common to obtain a set of non-dominated or efficient solutions. In these solutions, at least there is one solution is superior to any other given solutions not included in the set.

In this paper, a genetic algorithm based on Pareto is proposed and applied to a no-wait flexible flow shop scheduling problem (NWFFSP), and the scheduling problem are constrained by machines and workers, and there are unrelated parallel machines in some stages. The objectives are to minimize the completion time, the total expense and mean flow time. At last, the validity and feasibility of the proposed method was proved through two cases.

2   Multi-objective Optimization

If more than one objective is to be treated simultaneously, then it is a multi-objective optimization problem. A single objective optimization algorithm can obtain an optimal or suboptimal solution. However, for multi-objective optimization problem, sometimes there are conflicts among these objectives, so, optimizing one single objective often results in worse solutions with respect to the other objectives. It is always difficult to find a solution that multiple objectives can attain superior at the meantime. It is usually to find a set of solutions, each of which satisfies the objectives at an acceptable level.

Comparing two solutions shown in Fig. 1, if all objectives of one solution (x_0) are superior to the others' $(x_1^1$ or $x_1^2)$, the solution x_0 is called dominate another solution x_1^1(or $x_1^2)$, x_0 is to be preferred solution. If one (x_1^1) or more objectives of solution are inferior to the others' (x_1^2), x_1^1 and x_1^2 are called non-dominated solutions. No solution is dominating the other one, any one of the two is preferable. In Fig. 1, x_0 is called the Pareto optimal solution or non-dominated solution, because it is not dominated by any other solutions (x_1^1 and x_1^2) in the solution space.

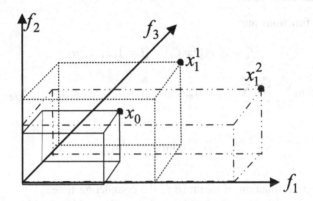

Fig. 1. Dominating and dominated solutions

2.1 Problem Description

In no-wait flexible flow shop scheduling problem with multi-stage unrelated parallel machines (NWFFSP), there is a set of n jobs to be processed through a set of m stages by u workers, and each job has the same m operations. Each operation is specified by the required machines and the processing time. Each stage involves p_j machines, and the job processing time is unrelated on different machines of the same stage. The operations of a job have to be processed continuously from start to the end without pause either on or between stages. NWFFSP is considered under the following assumptions:

- All jobs have no priority and can be processed at the initial time.
- All the machines are available at time 0;
- Job processing cannot be interrupted at any time;
- Machines are available for processing at a stage immediately after processing completion at the previous stage;
- At least one stage exists parallel machines;
- Parallel machines on the same stage are unrelated in capability and processing rate, but they have the same function;
- Each machine can only process one job at any time;
- Each job must be processed on each stage, but the processing machine can be selected according to the optimized objectives;
- A job only can be processed on one machine at the same stage;
- The processing time of each job operation is pre-specified, and the processing time on the parallel machines can be different;

- A job cannot be processed on more than one machine at the same time;
- Jobs cannot wait between two successive stages and intermediate storage does not exist.

2.2 Mathematical Model

The objective functions are:

$$f_1 = \min(\max C_i) \quad (i = 1, 2, \ldots, n) \tag{1}$$

$$f_2 = \min \sum_{i=1}^{n} \sum_{j=1}^{n_i} \sum_{k=1}^{m} (e_k + w_{q_k}) t_{ijk} \quad (j = 1, 2, \ldots, n_i; k = 1, 2, \ldots, m) \tag{2}$$

$$f_3 = \min(\sum_{i=1}^{n} C_i/n) \tag{3}$$

f_1: the objective function of minimizing the completing time;
f_2: the objective function of minimizing the expense of all machines and workers;
f_3: the objective function of minimizing the mean flow time of machines;
i: the index of jobs;
j: the index of operations;
k: the index of machines;
p: the total number of stage;
m: the number of machines;
n: the number of jobs;
O_{ij}: the jth operation number of job i;
C_i: the completion time of job i;
t_{ijk}: processing time of operation O_{ij} on machine k;
q_k: worker q processing operation O_{ij} on machine k;
e_k: hourly rate of machine k;
w_{q_k}: hourly wage rate of worker q.
c_{ijkq_k}: the finishing time of operation O_{ij} on machine k processed by worker q_k;
s_{ijgq_g}: the starting time of operation O_{ij} on machine g processed by worker q_g;

For the no-wait flow shop scheduling problem (NWFS), if there is no parallel machine, then the completing time can be given [6] as follow:

$$d_{is} = \max \left\{ \max_{2 \leq j \leq p} \left[\sum_{x=2}^{j} p_{ix} - \sum_{x=1}^{j-1} p_{sx} \right], 0 \right\} \tag{4}$$

$$\max C_i = \sum_{i=2}^{n} (p_{i-1,1} + d_{i-1,i}) + \sum_{x=1}^{p} p_{n,x} \tag{5}$$

Where d_{is} is the minimum delay between the starting of job i and job s on the first machine with respect to the no-wait restriction, where the job s is processed immediately after the job i in the sequence.

For the single resource constrained NWFFSP, the minimum delay is no longer than the delay of NWFFSP with worker and machine constraints. The difference of delay between single resource constraint and dual-resource constraint is shown in Figs. 2 and 3. For the dual-resource constrained NWFFSP, the minimum delay can be given as follow:

$$d_{is} = \min_{1 \leq L \leq m} \left\{ \max \left[\max_{2 \leq j \leq p} \left(\sum_{x=2}^{j} p_{ixLq_L} - \sum_{x=1}^{j-1} p_{sxLq_L} \right), 0 \right] \right\} \quad (6)$$

Where p_{ixLq_L} is the job i on the stage x, and its processing time on the parallel machine L processed by worker q_L, m_j ($j = 1, 2, \ldots p$) is the parallel machine number of each stage. The processing time on unrelated parallel machines maybe different, so the parallel machines cause mass computation in formula (6). For the first processed job, the parallel machine will be selected on which the processing time of the job is not longer than the other parallel machines and the corresponding worker with less expense is selected. If the job is not the first processed, then the parallel machine is selected according to formula (6).

The calculating steps for completing time are given in details as follow:

Step 1 On stage 1, confirm the first starting machine, if there are the parallel machines, then choose the machine that its processing time is not longer than the other machines on stage 1. After choosing the machine, choosing the worker, if the corresponding worker is free, then the machine is confirmed, otherwise analyzing the next machine.

Step 2 After confirming the first machine and worker on stage 1, then in the last stage, searching for the finishing time of the job.

Step 3 Set $i=1$

Step 4 Calculate the starting time of the job reversely pushing from the finishing time of last stage.

Step 4.1 If $c_{i(j-1)kq_k} \leq s_{ijgq_g}$;

then $c_{i(j-1)kq_k} = s_{ijgq_g}$; ($j = p, p-1, \cdots, 1$)

Repeat step 4.1, confirm the starting time of job i from stage p to stage 1.

Step 4.2 If $c_{i(j-1)kq_k} > s_{ijgq_g}$ when $j = h$; ($2 \leq h \leq p$)

then $s_{ijgq_g} = c_{i(j-1)kq_k}$; ($j = h, \cdots, p$)

Repeat step 4.2 until s_{ihgq_g} to s_{ipgq_g} are all replaced, then go to step 4.1.

Step 5 Update $i=i+1$, if $i > n$, go to step 6; otherwise, in stage 1, select the next starting job, if there are the parallel machines, then choose the machine with shorter processing time and the corresponding worker is free in first, and go to step 2. If there are some workers are available, then select the worker with less expense.

Step 6 Stop and output the final sequence and starting time and the completing time.

where k and g are the parallel machines or the same machine in the same stage.

For each sequence, after calculating the completing time, the function f_2 and f_3 can be obtained easily according to formulas (2) and (3).

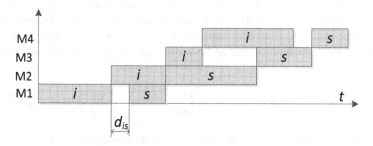

Fig. 2. The delay in NWFSP

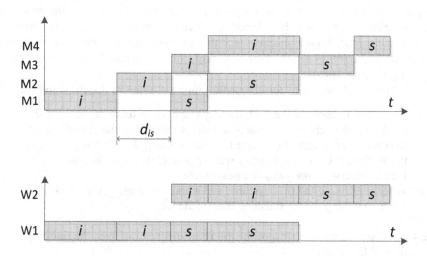

Fig. 3. The delay in dual-resource constrained NWFSP (NWFFSP)

3   Genetic Algorithm Based on Pareto

GA is a kind of evolutionary algorithm that can be defined as a stochastic process based on a population of individuals. Each population expresses a possible solution. For NWFFSP with single objective, the optimal solution is one, but for NWFFSP with multi-objective, the optimal solutions are a set of Pareto-optimal solutions, because in real-life, the multiple objectives are conflicted with other. The decision maker can select one optimal solution from the set at acceptable level according to the practical situation. In this paper, the more concerned objectives are completing time and expense.

The details are as follows:

- Encoding scheme. The encoding scheme is a simple permutation of jobs as a chromosome. The order of jobs in the chromosome represents the processing order on the stage. One chromosome represents one operation sequence, and one operation sequence corresponds to one or more feasible solutions because of the unrelated parallel machines.

- Create initial population and fitness function. The more the populations are, the better solutions they produce. But if they are plenty of populations, the calculating time will be long. Each individual is evaluated for the three objectives.
- Crossover operation: The crossover operation is the very important part in the genetic algorithm. It will produce new individuals through crossover operation, so better solutions can be produced. In this paper, 4 different crossover methods are applied in order to obtain the better solutions easily.
- Mutation.
- Pareto-ranking approach. Before selection, all individuals in current population are ranked by means of their non-domination level considering the three objectives. Therefore, a lower rank corresponds to a better solution (Fig. 1). Compared all the solutions in the population with respect to the three objectives, and a solution is rank 0 if it is superior to the other solutions in at least one objective, and then remove it from the current population. Compared the remainder solutions, and a solution is rank 1 if it is superior to the other solutions in at least one objective, and then remove it from the current population. All solutions can be ranked according the same method. This method can make individuals in the same rank have the same selection probability.
- Selection. Select high-ranking chromosomes to produce offspring by crossover, and rank 0 is the most high rank. If the ranks are equal between two chromosomes, and then both of them are selected or selecting one randomly if the chromosome number is more than the number of initial population.
- Pareto Filter: In order to retain the optimal solutions in the current populations, save the current optimum solution through adding Pareto filter. Through each generation, the solutions with 0 ranking are put into Pareto filter. The size of Pareto filter can be set in advance. Removing the same or similar solutions when optimal solutions amount exceeds the size.
- Termination criterion: Set the eras T, stop searching if the searching eras are equal to T, and the optimum value set in the Pareto Filter are the solutions.

4 Case Study

4.1 Case 1

Performance of the developed method in this paper for NWFFSP is compared with method GASA [12] with respect to three objectives, and the processing information is given in Tables 1 and 2. There are three stages in the processing, and the parallel machines are 3, 2, 4 in each stage, respectively. Set the population size 200, and 0.85 is crossover rate, and mutation rate is 0.01. The compared results are shown in Tables 3 and 4.

The compared results with respect to make-span of GASA and GA proposed in this paper are given in Table 3. From Table 3, it shows that the results obtained based on

GA are close to GASA, and the method is stable. The optimal set is given in Table 4, There are 4 solutions in the optimal set. For r1, the solution with respective to expense is superior to that of r2, but for r2, the objective with respective to expense is superior to that of s1, so there are the same rank between r1 and r2, both of them are rank 0, and it is to be the same rank 0 with r3. Due to the three objectives of r3 are all superior to that of r4, so, r1, r2, and r3 are non-dominated solutions and r4 are dominated solutions. The three objectives of r1 are 23, 2001, and 17.1 corresponds to make-span, expense and mean flow time, respectively. When the make-span is optimal, the expense is a bit higher. Another result r3, although the make-span is 25, the expense is least. It shows that there are conflicts among the three objectives, and it is almost impossible to get results that the three objectives are optimal simultaneously. The Gantt graph is given in Fig. 4.

Table 1. Processing information of jobs.

Job	Station 1		Station 2			Station 3			
	M1	M2	M3	M4	M5	M6	M7	M8	M9
1	2	2	3	4	5	2	3	2	3
2	4	5	4	3	4	3	4	5	4
3	6	5	4	4	2	3	4	2	5
4	4	3	4	6	5	3	6	5	8
5	4	5	3	3	1	3	4	6	5
6	6	5	4	2	3	4	3	9	5
7	3	2	4	4	6	3	4	3	5
8	3	5	4	7	5	3	3	6	4
9	2	5	4	1	2	7	8	6	5
10	3	6	4	3	4	4	8	6	7
11	5	2	4	3	5	6	7	6	5
12	6	5	4	5	4	4	4	7	5

Table 2. Machine cost rate (yuan per hour).

Machine	1	2	3	4	5	6	7	8	9
Cost rate	7	13	6	20	20	30	13	10	30

Table 3. Comparisons of make-span criterion

No.	1	2	3	4	5	6	7	8	9	10
GA	24	24	23	24	25	24	24	25	25	24
GASA	23	23	23	24	24	23	24	24	23	23

Table 4. The optimal set

Solution	Make-span	Expense	Mean flow time
r1	23	2001	17.1
r2	24	1998	17.5
r3	25	1990	17.75
r4	25	1995	17.8

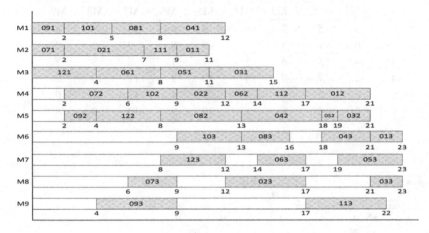

Fig. 4. Gantt graph of r1

4.2 Case 2

In order to further verify the effectiveness and feasibility of the proposed method, a dual-resource constrained scheduling case of NWFFSP is applied. The processing information provided in Tables 2, 5, 6 and 7. The jobs are processed on four different stations. On each station, the machines are 2, 2, 2, 3 respectively. Although machines on the same station have similar processing performance, the processing time may be different for parallel machines. One of the optimal results s1 is given in Fig. 5, the three objectives are 62, 7454, and 43.2 corresponds to make-span, total expense and mean flow time, respectively. If the processed operation can remain in the storage buffer, then one of the scheduling results s2 is given in Fig. 6. The three objectives are 51, 7414, and 40.2.

Table 5. Relation between machines and workers

	M1	M2	M3	M4	M5	M6	M7	M8	M9
W1	V	V							
W2		V	V						
W3			V	V					
W4				V	V				
W5					V	V	V		
W6	V							V	V

Table 6. Worker cost rate (yuan per hour).

Worker	1	2	3	4	5	6
Cost rate	20	30	20	22	25	23

Table 7. The processing information of jobs

Job	Station 1		Station 2		Station 3		Station 4		
	M1	M2	M3	M4	M5	M6	M7	M8	M9
1	4	5	7	6	8	8	10	9	8
2	6	7	8	7	9	8	9	9	8
3	4	5	6	5	7	7	8	8	7
4	8	7	9	9	10	9	11	10	10
5	6	5	7	8	9	8	12	11	10
6	5	6	8	8	10	9	10	9	8

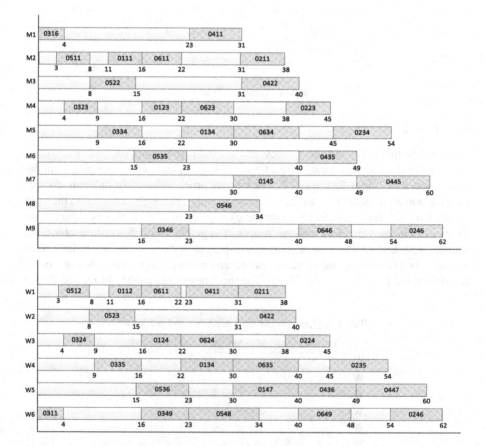

Fig. 5. Gantt graph of s1 (NWFFSP)

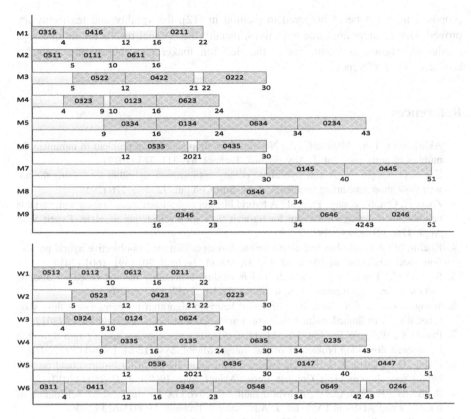

Fig. 6. Gantt graph of s2

For s1, the solution with respective to workers expense is superior to that of s2, but for s2, the objective with respective to completing time and machines expense are superior to that of s1. One hand NWFFSP will cause longer completing time compared to traditional job shop scheduling because of the no-wait operation processing. Compared Figs. 5 and 6, it shows that the starting time of some jobs in Fig. 5 are delayed in order to ensure the continuity of each operation for the same job. In Fig. 5, there is longer spare time than that in Fig. 6. On the other hand, due to there are worker and machine constraints, and the number of workers is less than the number of machines. Workers may not be idle when machines are idle, so it will cause longer spare time on machines.

5 Conclusion

In this paper, a multi-objective no-wait hybrid flow shop scheduling problem with multi-stage unrelated parallel machines is studied. The make-span, expense and mean flow time are considered simultaneously, and the scheduling are constrained by machines and workers, the scheduling results are obtained based on the method proposed in this paper. Compared to method in [12], the validity and feasibility are proved. Due to there are three objectives, usually the optimal results are unique. The results are shown as Gantt charts, the decision maker can choose one sequence according his preference.

References

1. Aldowaisan, T.A., Allahverdi, A.: No-wait flow shop scheduling problem to minimize the number of tardy jobs. Int. J. Adv. Manuf. Technol. **61**, 311–323 (2012)
2. Engin, O., Güçlü, A.: A new hybrid ant colony optimization algorithm for solving the no-wait flow shop scheduling problems. Appl. Soft Comput. **72**, 166–176 (2018)
3. Zhao, F., Qin, S., Zhang, Y., et al.: A hybrid biogeography-based optimization with variable neighborhood search mechanism for no-wait flow shop scheduling problem. Expert Syst. Appl. **126**, 321–339 (2019)
4. Khalili, M.: A multi-objective electromagnetism algorithm for a bi-objective hybrid no-wait flow shop scheduling problem. Int. J. Adv. Manuf. Technol. **70**, 1591–1601 (2014)
5. Song, J.W., Tang, J.F.: No-wait hybrid flow shop scheduling method based on discrete particle swarm optimization. J. Syst. Simul. **22**(10), 2257–2261 (2010)
6. Wang, B.L., Li, T.K., Sun, B.: TSP-based heuristic algorithm for permutation flow shop scheduling with limited waiting time constraints. Control Decis. **27**(5), 768–772 (2012)
7. Pan, Q.K., Wang, W.H., Zhu, J.Y.: Modified discrete particle swarm optimization algorithm for no-wait flow shop problem. Comput. Integr. Manuf. Syst. **13**(6), 1127–1130 (2007)
8. Zhang, Q.L., Chen, Y.S.: Particle swarm optimization algorithm for bi-directional no-wait hybrid flow shop problem. Comput. Integr. Manuf. Syst. **19**(10), 2503–2509 (2013)
9. Reddy, B.S.P., Rao, C.S.P.: A hybrid multi-objective GA for simultaneous scheduling of machines and AGVs in FMS. Int. J. Adv. Manuf. Technol. **31**, 602–613 (2006)
10. Deva Prasad, S., Rajendran, C., Krishnaiah Chetty, O.V.: A genetic algorithm approach to multi-objective scheduling in a Kanban-controlled flow shop with intermediate buffer and transport constraints. Int. J. Adv. Manuf. Technol. **29**, 564–576 (2006)
11. Huang, H.J., Lu, T.P.: Solving a multi-objective flexible job shop scheduling problem with timed Petri nets and genetic algorithm. Discrete Math. Algorithms Appl. **2**(2), 221–237 (2010)
12. Tao, Z.: Study on examination center scheduling problem based on genetic algorithm and simulated annealing algorithm. Bio Technol. (23), 14354–14361(2014)

Dynamic Behavior Analysis and Multi-sensor Modal Information Fusion for Robotic Milling System

Daxian Hao[1(⊠)], Wei Wang[1], Gang Zhang[2], Qilong Wang[1], and Chao Yun[1]

[1] Beihang University, Beijing 100191, China
haodaxian@buaa.edu.cn
[2] HUST-Wuxi Research Institute, Wuxi 214100, China

Abstract. Industrial robots have been proven to be more widely suitable for machining than CNC machines in many applications. However, their lack of rigidity and precision is still a limit for precision tasks. The dynamic behavior of robotic milling system has a significant effect on machining quality. The main difference of dynamic behavior between robot and CNC is that the robot's modes greatly shift, depending on its varying dynamic parameters and joint configurations. Therefore, it is of great significance to study the dynamic characteristics of the robot to suppress the machining chatter and improve the machining accuracy of the robot. Firstly, a series of modal tests are conducted on a milling robot Considering that the robotic milling system is a time-varying system. The improving accuracy FRFs (frequency response function) are obtained by the low-frequency sensitive accelerometer and high-frequency sensitive accelerometer. The accelerometers are used to conduct corresponding modal tests on robot structure and tool-spindle of the system respectively. Then, in order to smooth the curve and splice the data of the two FRFs, a new method for multi-sensor modal information fusion using moving average method and weighted average method is presented. The experimental support for chatter-free prediction in robot high-speed milling by the regenerative chatter theory. The dynamic behavior for Robotic Milling System is analyzed at last.

Keywords: Robotic milling system · Dynamic · Experimental modal analysis · MSIF (Multi-sensor Information Fusion)

1 Introduction

The latest application of robotics technology involves robotic milling/machining and detection [1]. The advantages of robotic machining lie in its ability for offering large working spaces and being used in advanced manufacturing field such as machining of high-speed rails, wind turbine blades and aerospace products.

As for robotic milling operations, many believe that many difficulties need be overcome before it could be readily applied to practical production. Recent researches on machining robot focus on robot stiffness [2], path tacking and compensation [3], and dynamics characterization [4], and stability analysis [5–7]. One of the major hurdles

© Springer Nature Switzerland AG 2019
H. Yu et al. (Eds.): ICIRA 2019, LNAI 11745, pp. 469–481, 2019.
https://doi.org/10.1007/978-3-030-27529-7_40

preventing the adoption of robot for milling process is dynamic behavior of robotic milling system belong to [8].

Extensive research on dynamic modeling of a robot machining system has been done, including rational modeling and dynamic parameter identification. Mousavi et al. [9, 10] conducted a intensive study on the dynamics model of the robot. The dynamic model of ABB IRB 6660 was established by using matrix structure analysis (MSA), but the elasticity and damping parameters need to adjust due to the robot model error. Rafieian et al. [11] built the dynamic model to study chatter vibration in robotic grinding process using a portable special-purpose robot manipulator for rectifying the surfaces of hydro-electric equipments.

It is well known that parameter identification is more accurate for obtain dynamic parameters than dynamic modeling. Some experimental studies on investigation of dynamic characteristics of robot have been done. Mejri et al. [12] conducted modal experiments on ABB IRB 6660, and the dependency of dynamic behavior of robot on its joint configuration is studied. Tunc et al. [13] studied the dynamics of a hexapod platform for robot milling, and found out the dynamic characteristics are different under different robot positions. Dynamics characteristics of a robot machining system have significant modal coupling and dependency on the position. Only by getting reasonable and accurate machining system dynamics characteristics of robot system, can we investigate and reveal the stability of the robot machining system and mechanism of cutting chatter.

This paper aims at getting the accurate dynamic parameters of the robot machining systems in order to analysis the dynamic behavior of the systems in the Cartesian space. The rest of the paper is organized as follows. The Modal test equipment and robotic milling system is introduced in Sect. 2. The FRF (frequency response function) of robotic milling system is identified in Sect. 3 through modal tests. Section 4 presents a new method for multi-sensor modal information fusion using moving average method and weighted average method. The predictability of the model is verified in Sect. 5 through robotic milling experiments. The paper concludes with a brief summary of the present study.

2 Modal Test Equipment for Robotic Milling System

The dynamic characteristics of a structure can be obtained by modal test. Due to the dynamic characteristics at the tip point directly affect the machining quality of workpiece. The researchers usually pay attention to the modal at the tip point, when they investigate the dynamic characteristics of machine tools. The mode at the tip point is usually determined by the tool-spindle system. Therefore, modal test is usually carried out only on the tool tip point. Since the stiffness of the machine tool structure are much higher than that of the tool-spindle. It is difficult to excite the vibration of machine tools in the process of machining, so it can be ignored. However, The stiffness of the robot structure is in the same magnitude as that of the tool-spindle system. The dynamic characteristics of the robot milling system are affected not only by the tool-spindle system but also by the robot structure. Therefore, it is necessary to conduct modal test on the robot milling system to analyze its dynamic characteristics.

The modal test equipment for robotic milling system includes the industrial robot, the data acquisition equipment, as well as the milling tool. All equipment is listed in Table 1. The robot, ABB IRB 6660, is a pre-machining robot with high accuracy and rigidity, and a high-speed motorized spindle is attached to its end. The data acquisition includes a Kistler low-frequency sensitive accelerometer and a high-frequency sensitive accelerometer, as well as a data acquisition card which is used to collect signals and send the digital data into Labview software.

Table 1. Hammer test equipment for robotic milling system

Item	Model
Robot	ABB IRB 6660
Spindle	Jager F100-H530.02 S11W2
End mill type	PCD + carbide
PCB hammer	086C03
Accelerometer	Kistler accelerometer 8776A50 Kistler 8640A
Data acquisition	NI 9234
Cabinet	CompactDAQ-9174
PC	Thinkpad E550
Driver	NI MAX
Software	Labview 2016

Through the pre-experiment of the robot milling system, the suitable modal test equipment can be determined. Experimental modal analysis using accelerometer is a low-cost and simple method. However, two problems need to be solved when it is applied to the robot milling system. Firstly, the accelerometer is usually insensitive to low-frequency responses, so the measurement of low-frequency modes include a considerable error. Secondly, the energy input to the hammer tip usually can only excite the modes of the tool-spindle system. Due to the force at the tip of the hammer is usually small, it is had to excite the modes of the robot structure. Furthermore, the greater hammer force may damage the tool.

In order to solve the above two problems, two types of accelerometers are selected in the modal test. High-frequency sensitive accelerometer is used to test the mode of the tool-spindle system, and low-frequency sensitive accelerometer is used to test the mode of the robot structure. The low-frequency sensitive accelerometer is arranged at the end of the robot's wrist. Selecting the appropriate hammer tip and force can excite the robot structure modes. It can also use greater force to hammer the robot structure in addition. Then the modal test can be operated after appropriate experimental equipment is selected.

3 Hammer Tests and Frequency Domain Signal Process

Different from machine tool, the dynamic behavior of robot system has obvious dependence on its pose and position. Therefore, the multi-point modal tests need to be carried out on the machining trajectory to obtain the dynamic characteristics of the robot on the whole trajectory. The robot's milling path is a straight line along the X axis, as shown in Fig. 1. The length of the milling path is 400 mm. The starting position coordinates of robot milling are (X 0 mm, Y 50 mm, Z 30 mm), and the end point coordinates (X 400 mm, Y 50 mm, Z 30 mm). Other three via TCPs are well distributed between the starting position and the end position at 100 mm intervals.

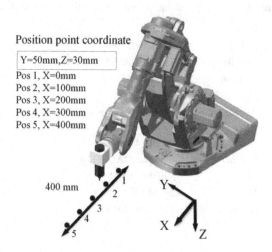

Fig. 1. Positions along the path for modal test.

A single axis accelerometer Kistler 8776A50 is used to collect the high-frequency acceleration signals. The milling tool tip is hammered in the direction of the X-axis, as shown in Fig. 2. The accelerometer and the force hammer signal are collected in the same direction to obtain the FRF of $\Phi_{xx}(i\omega)$. In the same manner, FRF of $\Phi_{yy}(i\omega)$ is obtained along the Y-axis.

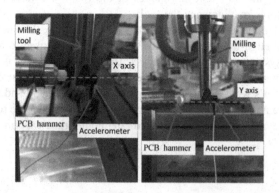

Fig. 2. Tool-spindle accelerometer arrangement for hammer tests.

FRF of the Pos1 is used to diagram the amplitude-frequency plots along both the X- and the Y-axis, respectively, as shown in Figs. 3 and 4. The SNR (Signal to Noise Ratio) of the FRF as shown in the Figs. 3 and 4 in high frequency band is acceptable. The data in the low frequency band below 100 Hz is difficult to identify which contains a lot of noise and random error.

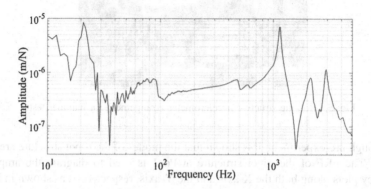

Fig. 3. Amplitude-frequency of robot milling system on the X-axis.

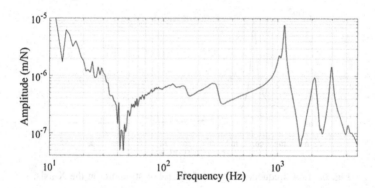

Fig. 4. Amplitude-frequency of robot milling system on the Y-axis.

Therefore, it is necessary to conduct modal experiments on the robot structure to obtain more accurate low-frequency modes as shown in Fig. 5. The low-frequency sensitive accelerometer Kistler 8640A is attached to the wrist end of the robot. A soft rubber hammer tip is used, which can concentrate more energy in the low-frequency band. A larger hammer force can be used to excite the modes of the robot structure.

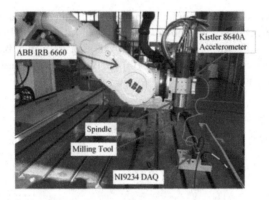

Fig. 5. Robotic structure accelerometer arrangement for hammer tests.

Through pre-experiment, it is shown that the modes of the robot structure are below 100 Hz. The FRF of the robot structure at Pos1 is used to diagram the amplitude-frequency plots along both the X-axis and the Y-axis, respectively, as shown in Figs. 6 and 7. The SNR of the FRF as shown in the Figs. 6 and 7 in low-frequency is acceptable.

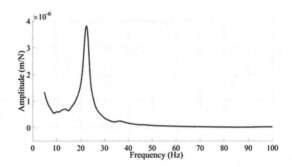

Fig. 6. Low frequency modes of the robot structure on the X-axis.

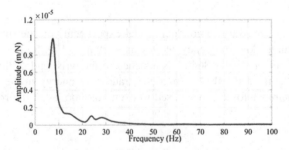

Fig. 7. Low frequency modes of the robot structure on the Y-axis.

4 Multi-sensor Modal Information Fusion

The signal collected by the data acquisition often including noisy signal. In order to filter the interfering signal, it need to improve the FRF curve smoothness. After obtaining the FRF of the robot structure and the tool-spindle system, it also is necessary to fit these data into a curve. Firstly, the five-point smoothing method is used to smooth the data and filter out the high-frequency noise.

Then, in order to splice and combine the FRF data of low frequency sensitive accelerometer and high frequency sensitive accelerometer, the weighted average method is adopted. The two sets of data are spliced and fitted by weighted average algorithm. The FRF of the robot structure is spliced with the FRF of the tool spindle system in the range of 50–100 Hz. The closer it is to 50 Hz, the greater the weight of the low-frequency sensitive accelerometer will be. The closer to 100 Hz, the higher the weight of the high-frequency sensitive accelerometer will be, and the weight at 100 Hz will be 1.

Through the corresponding multi-sensor modal information fusion algorithm, the data is fitted together to obtain the overall modal parameters of the robot. The FRFs of Pos. 1–5 have been plotted in Figs. 8 and 9. It can been found out that the low frequency modes of the robot structure greatly depend on the robot pose. The low frequency band mainly reflects the modes of the robot structure. The frequency of the low frequency FRF can be as low as 5 Hz, and the modal parameters can still be identified. While along the milling path, FRF remain nearly constant in the high frequency region, regardless of the TCP position.

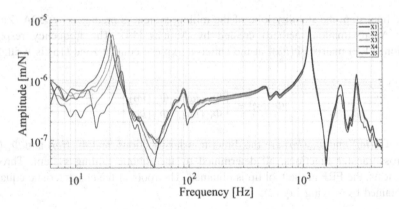

Fig. 8. Amplitude-frequency plot of robot milling system on the X-axis.

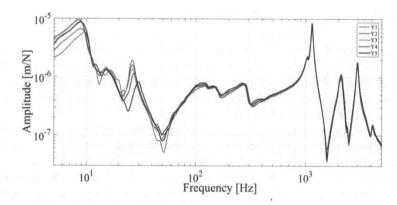

Fig. 9. Amplitude-frequency plot of robot milling system on the Y-axis.

With the extension of the robot cantilever, the dynamic stiffness of robot structure in the X-axis direction increases obviously. While in the Y-axis direction, it show a downward trend. In the process of milling, the path deviation caused by milling force can be reduced by reasonably arranging the milling path. For example, when the robot cantilever is long, the direction of the max milling force should be in the direction of the X-axis of the robot.

5 Robot Milling Tests and Verification

At the final step, the stability lobe of the milling system is predicted by ZOA (Zeroth Order Approximation method) created by Altintas [14]. The frequency response function (FRF) matrix $[\Phi(i\omega)]$ at the cutter-workpiece contact zone [15] is written as Eq. (1):

$$[\Phi(i\omega)] = \begin{bmatrix} \Phi_{xx}(i\omega) & \Phi_{xy}(i\omega) \\ \Phi_{yx}(i\omega) & \Phi_{yy}(i\omega) \end{bmatrix} \tag{1}$$

where $\Phi_{xx}(i\omega)$ and $\Phi_{yy}(i\omega)$ are the direct transfer functions, and $\Phi_{xy}(i\omega)$ and $\Phi_{yx}(i\omega)$ the cross-transfer functions, all determined by the robotic milling system. Through modal tests, the FRF at the tool tip is obtained. The roots of the characteristic equation are obtained by solving Eq. (2):

$$\det|[I] + \Lambda[\Phi(i\omega)]| = 0 \tag{2}$$

where $\Lambda = -\frac{N}{4\pi} a K_t (1 - e^{-i\omega T})$.

Then, the chatter-free depth of cut can be calculated by Eq. (3):

$$a_{\lim} = -\frac{2\pi \Lambda_R}{N K_t}\left(1 + \left(\frac{\sin \omega_c T}{1 - \cos \omega_c T}\right)^2\right) \tag{3}$$

where Λ_R is the real part of Λ, and ω_c represents the chatter frequency, and T is the tool passing period. The critical axial depth a_{lim} is calculated according to Eq. (3), and the lobe of the chatter stability is predicted by ZOA.

By Fig. 10, the stable milling parameters of the robot are predicted. Five sets of milling parameters marked by crossings in the lobe diagrams shown in Fig. 10 are selected and listed in Table 3. Milling tests are carried out to verify the prediction results. During the milling test, a microphone and an accelerometer are used to record vibration signals.

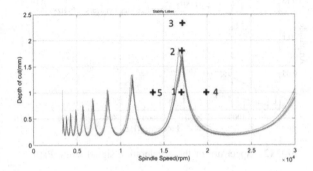

Fig. 10. Lobe superposition diagram from Pos. 1 to Pos. 5.

The slotting results are shown in Fig. 11. The best surface quality is found on Path 1, predicted in the stable area, the worst marks are recorded on Path 3, predicted to be unstable, and on Path 2, the critical condition, moderate milling chattering happened. The surface is measured by a surface roughness tester, results showing on the paths in Fig. 11. Path 1 takes the best surface quality while Path3 takes the lowest.

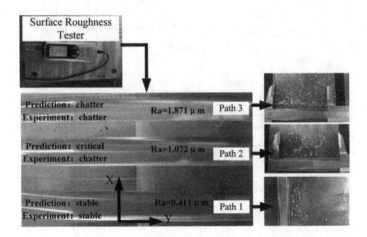

Fig. 11. Comparison of slotting results

FFT (Fast Fourier Transform) is performed on the three paths according to the time domain signal collected by the microphone. In the frequency-amplitude diagram shown in Fig. 12, the frequency at the peak amplitude domain signal is 1115 Hz, two times of the milling frequency. The spectrum indicates that there is no chatter vibration along this path and the vibration is dominated by the forced vibration at the tool passing frequency.

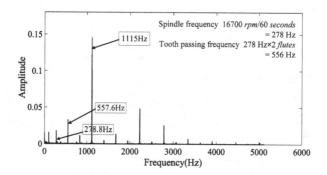

Fig. 12. Spectrum of the acceleration signal along Path 1

On the spectrum of the signal acquired along Path 2 shown in Fig. 13, the frequency at the peak amplitude is 1060 Hz, which is a synchronous frequency of the tool passing. Hence the chattering occurred and are also ascertained by the discontinuous chips shown in Fig. 11.

On the spectrum of the signal acquired along Path 3 shown in Fig. 14, the peak appears at 1042 Hz, which is an asynchronous frequency of the tool passing. Hence the chatter happens on Path 3, as evidenced by the discontinuous chips shown in Fig. 11.

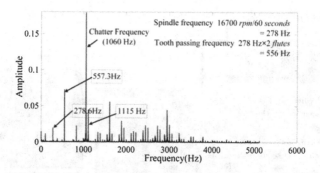

Fig. 13. Spectrum of the acceleration signal along Path 2

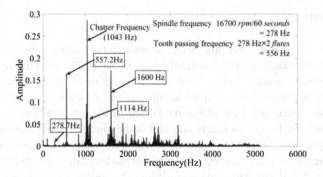

Fig. 14. Spectrum of the acceleration signal along Path 3

When the spindle speed *n* is 13700 rpm, the spindle frequency is 228 Hz, and the tool passing frequency of the double-edged cutter is 456 Hz. The frequency domain graph of Path 4 is shown in Fig. 15. When the spindle speed *n* is 19000 rpm, the spindle frequency is 317 Hz, and the tool passing frequency is 634 Hz. In the frequency domain graph of Path 5 shown in Fig. 16, both of the frequency signals with the peak amplitude show no doubling of the tool passing frequency. Hence, milling on Path 4 and Path 5 is unstable.

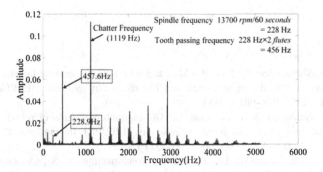

Fig. 15. Spectrum of the acceleration signal along Path 4

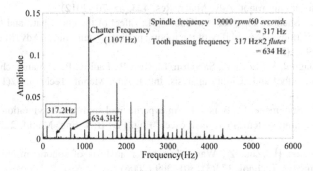

Fig. 16. Spectrum of the acceleration signal along Path 5

6   Conclusions

In order to investigate the dynamic behavior for robotic milling system, a number of experimental validations are provided in the present paper. The pose dependence of the robot's dynamic characteristics is analyzed, and the trend of the robot's dynamic characteristics is pointed out. It can be summarized as follows:

It provides guidance for the global modal test of the robot milling system. Along the milling path, FRFs remain nearly constant in the high frequency region, regardless of the TCP position. Since the modes of tool-spindle system does not shift with the pose, only one modal test is needed. The obtained modes of the tool-spindle system can be applied to the global path trajectory. While the modes of the robot structure is dependent on its pose, discrete modal experiments need to be carried out on the processing path to obtain the corresponding modal parameters under the pose.

A new method for multi-sensor modal information fusion by using moving average method and weighted average method is presented. The algorithm has good curve smoothing and splicing effect for FRF. The FRF of the robotic milling system which obtained by the algorithm is analyzed. It provides a foundation for the research of vibration suppression and chatter-free stability region in robotic milling.

In summary, the milling stability lobes obtained by the regenerative chatter model are verified by the high-speed robotic slotting tests. Therefore the method is applicable to predicting stability of robotic milling.

References

1. Axinte, D., Shirinzadeh, B.: MiRoR—Miniaturized robotic systems for holistic in-situ repair and maintenance works in restrained and hazardous environments. IEEE/ASME Trans. Mechatron. **23**(2), 978–981 (2018)
2. Tyapin, I., Kaldestad, K.B., Hovland, G.: Off-line path correction of robotic face milling using static tool force and robot stiffness. In: IEEE/RSJ International Conference on Intelligent Robots and Systems, pp. 5506–5511 (2015)
3. Makhanov, S.S., Batanov, D., Bohez, E., Sonthipaumpoon, K., Anotaipaiboon, W., Tabucanon, M.: On the tool-path optimization of a milling robot. Comput. Ind. Eng. **43**(3), 455–472 (2002)
4. Bisu, C., Cherif, M., Gerard, A., K'Nevez, J.Y.: Dynamic behavior analysis for a six axis industrial machining robot. Adv. Mater. Res. **423**, 65–76 (2012)
5. Li, J., Li, B., Shen, N.Y., Qian, H., Guo, Z.M.: Effect of the cutter path and the workpiece clamping position on the stability of the robotic milling system. Int. J. Adv. Manuf. Technol. **89**, 2919–2933 (2016)
6. Mejri, S., Gagnol, V., Le, T.P., Sabourin, L., Ray, P., Paultre, P.: Dynamic characterization of machining robot and stability analysis. Int. J. Adv. Manuf. Technol. **82**(1–4), 351–359 (2016)
7. Zaghbani, I., Songmene, V., Bonev, I.: An experimental study on the vibration response of a robotic machining system. Proc. Inst. Mech. Eng. Part B: J. Eng. Manuf. **227**(6), 866–880 (2013)
8. Pan, Z., Zhang, H., Zhu, Z., Wang, J.: Chatter analysis of robotic machining process. J. Mater. Process. Technol. **173**(3), 301–309 (2006)

9. Mousavi, S., Gagnol, V., Bouzgarrou, B.C., Ray, P., Mousavi, S., Gagnol, V., et al.: Stability optimization in robotic milling through the control of functional redundancies. Rob. Comput.-Integr. Manuf. **50**(2018), 181–192 (2017)
10. Mousavi, S., Gagnol, V., Bouzgarrou, B.C., Ray, P.: Dynamic modeling and stability prediction in robotic machining. Int. J. Adv. Manuf. Technol. **88**, 3053–3065 (2017)
11. Rafieian, F., Liu, Z., Hazel, B.: Dynamic model and modal testing for vibration analysis of robotic grinding process with a 6DOF flexible-joint manipulator. In: International Conference on Mechatronics and Automation, vol. 47, pp. 2793–2798 (2009)
12. Mejri, S., Gangol, V., Le, T.P., Sabourin, L., Ray, P., Paultre, P.: Experimental protocol for the dynamic modeling of machining robots. In: Congrés Français De Mécanique, CFM (2013)
13. Tunc, L.T., Stoddart, D.: Tool path pattern and feed direction selection in robotic milling for increased chatter-free material removal rate. Int. J. Adv. Manuf. Technol. **89**(9), 2907–2918 (2017)
14. Altintas, Y.: Manufacturing Automation, 2nd edn. Cambridge University Press, Cambridge (2012)
15. Tunc, L.T., Shaw, J.: Experimental study on investigation of dynamics of hexapod robot for mobile machining. Int. J. Adv. Manuf. Technol. **84**(5–8), 817–830 (2016)

Adaptive Impedance Control for Robotic Polishing with an Intelligent Digital Compliant Grinder

Qianlong Xie, Huan Zhao$^{(\boxtimes)}$, Tao Wang, and Han Ding

State Key Laboratory of Digital Manufacturing Equipment and Technology,
Huazhong University of Science and Technology, Wuhan 430074,
Hubei, People's Republic of China
huanzhao@hust.edu.cn

Abstract. Aircraft-engine blade has a free-form surface in space, which is extremely complicated. And the surface milling must be polished completely to eliminate the surface residual texture and stress concentration. To solve this problem, an intelligent digital compliant grinder with active and passive compliance, double-end floating and multi-station polishing is independent-designed. Besides, a novel impedance controller based on particle swarm optimization algorithm is proposed, which can realize adaptive adjustment of the impedance parameters. And it can maintain the contact force between the grinding tool and the workpiece to a constant value. The experimental results show that the proposed method works well and the surface roughness and the machining consistency of the blade are greatly improved with the intelligent digital compliant grinder for active contact force. Specifically, the surface roughness of the blade reduces from 0.730 μm to 0.065 μm, and the force fluctuation is less than 1 N, therefore, leading to a better surface quality.

Keywords: Complex blade · Robotic polishing ·
Intelligent digital compliant grinder · Particle swarm optimization ·
Adaptive impedance control

1 Introduction

Blades are the key parts of the aero-engine, its manufacturing quality and machining precision have important influence on the aero-engine performance. The aero-engine blades have complex structure and are easy to deform under tremendous pressure, and the remaining texture lines on blades after milling may have tremendous consequences for the aero-dynamic performance of compressing gases. Meanwhile, it may result in the machining accuracy of intake and exhaust edges of the blades are difficult to guarantee [1, 2].

At present, the grinding technology of the blades includes abrasive flow grinding, multi-axis CNC machine grinding and manual grinding [3]. The manual grinding process is mainly completed by workers who hold the grinding tool to polish the blades. It becomes more and more difficult to improve the processing efficiency and obtain a surface with high-quality. To improve the production efficiency and the

© Springer Nature Switzerland AG 2019
H. Yu et al. (Eds.): ICIRA 2019, LNAI 11745, pp. 482–494, 2019.
https://doi.org/10.1007/978-3-030-27529-7_41

surface quality, industrial robots are used in the blades grinding system in recent years [4]. Robotic grinding is a good choice for polishing the blades, because it is much cheaper and more and more flexible than a five-axis machine tool. However, because of complex structure of the blades, the contact force fluctuations greatly limit the achievable surface quality of the blades during the robotic polishing process. Therefore, in order to obtain a good robotic polishing quality of the blades, the contact force needs to be accurately controlled [5]. In order to control the contact force to get the achievable surface quality, different force control methods have been proposed by researchers [6]. Dai et al. [7] propose a parametric modelling controller to guarantee the robotic grinding process is well-controlled. The purpose of the controller is to regulate the normal grinding force accurately. The results of the experiment demonstrate effective-controlled under various grinding conditions. Liu et al. [8] propose a hybrid active/passive force control scheme for grinding with an industrial robot which can effectively reduce the fierce mechanical shock by passive force control and acquire preferable force accuracy by active force control [9–12]. All the above methods for the active force control is by the robot and greatly limits the force control accuracy because of the low positioning accuracy of the industrial robot. Different methods have been presented by researchers to estimate and compensate the positioning error of the industrial robot [13–15].

To solve this problem, a different thought is proposed, that is an intelligent digital compliant grinder would be designed to control the contact force directly instead of applying the active force through the industrial robot. In this way, the problem caused by the low positioning accuracy of the robot can be compensated through applying contact force control with an independent-designed intelligent digital compliant grinder. In this paper, a novel blade polishing method and an independent-designed intelligent digital compliant grinder applied in the robotic polishing process will be detailed analysed. The structure of the intelligent digital compliant grinder is shown in Fig. 1. Because the contact force is a quite important factor during the overall grinding process of the blade and it must stay a constant value to get the better surface quality, a

red nylon belt Drive wheel Transition wheel Force sensor Polishing motor

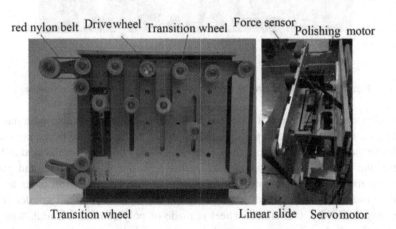

Transition wheel   Linear slide   Servo motor

Fig. 1. An independent-designed intelligent digital compliant grinder.

special intelligent digital compliant grinder with a novel parameters optimization algorithm is presented to control the contact force between the polishing tool and the workpiece directly instead of through the industrial robot.

The remainder of this article is structured as follows. In Sect. 2, the intelligent digital compliant grinder is detailed introduced. Section 3 discusses the original position-based impedance control, a optimization method for the controller parameters and the experiment program design. Section 4 provides some experiment results and some conclusions about this paper are exhibited in Sect. 5.

2 Intelligent Digital Compliant Grinder

This paper presents a novel intelligent digital compliant grinder in order to achieve normal contact successfully between the polishing tool and the workpiece, and the robotic polishing system for complex blades is shown in Fig. 2. The intelligent digital compliant grinder is mainly composed of force sensor, transition wheel, polishing motor, servo motor, red nylon belt, driver wheel, coupling, linear slide. The most important component of the digital compliant grinder is the force sensor, because the actual contact force measured by force sensor must be kept constant with the effect of impedance controller.

Developed Digital
Compliant Grinder   Blade   Rotating Table   Comau robot

Fig. 2. Robotic polishing system for complex blade. (Color figure online)

In addition, the independent-designed intelligent digital compliant grinder has some advantages. Firstly, the intelligent digital compliant grinder can use different positions to achieve the grinding for the concave, the convex and other parts of the blades, that is achieve the whole blade grinding successfully. Secondly, the active and passive compliant mechanism is designed for the digital compliant grinder, in order to avoid the force overshoot which may cause damage to the digital compliant grinder and the force sensor. Thirdly, the contact wheel is made of polyurethane material, which not only can absorb the vibration generated during the polishing process greatly, but also can avoid the impact caused by the stiff contact between the intelligent digital compliant grinder and the blade. Fourthly, the advantage of the tensioning mechanism is that when the tensioning force exceeds the maximum value set by us, the contact wheel and the tensioning wheel move together along the sliding pair in order to make the tensioning force stay constant. Fifthly, the tensioning mechanism is set at the loose side of the belt to achieve internal tension, through this tensioning type, not only the wear of the abrasive belt can be effectively reduced, but also the abrasive belt can be fully tightened and achieve the sufficient contact. Besides, the contact wheel package is not affected whether the abrasive belt is in a stretched state or not. Besides, the circumference of the belt remains basically unchanged and can maintain the fully tension during the whole polishing process, thus ensuring the polishing quality.

3 Constant Contact Force Polishing Method

3.1 Overview of the Impedance Control

Since impedance control method has been investigated extensively over the past years and it is a typical force tracking control method. Through establishing virtual mass-damping-stiffness model, impedance control regulates the dynamic relationship between the polishing tool position of digital compliant grinder and the contact force. Generally speaking, the position-based impedance control is composed of an outer force control loop and an inner position control loop. The position-based impedance control strategy is illustrated in Fig. 3.

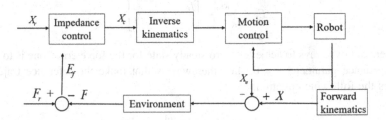

Fig. 3. The position-based impedance control strategy.

Specially, F_d and F_e represent the desired force and actual contact force, so the force error can be expressed as $E_f = F_d - F_e$, and X_r, X_c, X_e, X represent reference trajectory, commanded trajectory, environment location, the real digital compliant grinder position respectively, and K_e is the environment stiffness.

The impedance control algorithm control schematic is shown in Fig. 4 and the actual contact position of the digital compliant grinder X_c satisfies the following equation:

$$M(\dot{X}_c - \dot{X}_r) + B(\dot{X}_c - \dot{X}_r) + K(\dot{X}_c - \dot{X}_r) = E_f \tag{1}$$

Impedance controller

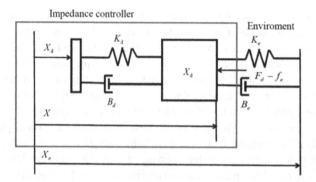

Fig. 4. The one dimension physical interaction model of impedance controller and environment.

where M, B, K represent diagonal mass, damping and stiffness matrices respectively. Obviously, the impedance control model can be seen as a linear second-order system. The commanded reference trajectory satisfies $X_c = X_r + E$, where E represents position modification generated by the impedance controller. Considering (1) result in:

$$E_f = F_d - F_e = M\ddot{E} + B\dot{E} + KE \tag{2}$$

For simplicity of presentation, cartesian variables X and F are decoupled independently to each dimension so that one dimensional variables x and f are considered. Then the force tracking error can be expressed furtherly as following:

$$E_f = \frac{kk_e}{k+k_e}\left[\frac{f_r}{k_e} + x_e - x_r\right] \tag{3}$$

There are two ways to achieve a zero steady state for the force error, one is to make the impedance parameter $k = 0$, the other way is that make the reference trajectory satisfies the following equation:

$$x_r = x_e + \frac{f_d}{k_e} \tag{4}$$

where x_e can be identified when the digital compliant grinder begins to contact with the blade. Then, Eq. (1) can be expressed as:

$$m\ddot{x}(t) + b\dot{x}(t) + (k+k_e)x(t) = (1 + \frac{k}{k_e})f_r + (k_e + k)x_e \tag{5}$$

Considering $(k_e + k)x_e$ is a stable closed-loop reference when k is given, any instability in the Eq. (5) could only arise from f_r. The force tracking transfer function G (s) is then expressed as:

$$G(s) = \frac{x(s)}{f_r} = \frac{1}{k_e} \frac{k + k_e}{ms^2 + bs + k + k_e} \quad (6)$$

3.2 Optimization Method for the Controller Parameters

This paper presents a novel method of particle swarm optimization algorithm and it has the character of simple concept, easy operation, good robustness, which is suitable for the determination and optimization of impedance control parameters. In the process of optimization, the particle swarm algorithm needs to determine the fitness of each particle according to the objective function. In general, the objective function uses the quadratic model to select the minimal direction for optimization control error and output energy. For impedance control algorithm, to ensure that the end of the system reaches the expected value when the system reaches steady state, it must also consider the transition of the system to the steady state and the force peak value should not be too large. If it exceeds a certain range value during the transition, it will definitely damage the machine structure and the force sensor, so this situation must be avoided. The peak of the force feedback as part of the fitness function:

$$min(J) = \sqrt{(E_f)^2 + a_1 m^2 + a_2 F_m} \quad (7)$$

where E_f represents control error and u is controller output corresponding the E. Besides, α_1 is a constant value which ranging from 0 to 1, α_2 is weight coefficient and F_m is the peak of contact force.

The algorithm is carried out as follows: firstly, to update the velocity and position of each particle, we use Y to record the optimal solution searched by the individual, and Z to record the optimal solution that the entire group searches in one iteration. The formula for updating the velocity and the position of each particle is as follows:

$$X(i) = aX(i) + c_1 \cdot rand() \cdot (Y(i) - Z(i)) + c_2 \cdot rand() \cdot (Y - Z(i)) \quad (8)$$

$$Z(i) = Z(i) + X(i) \quad (9)$$

Where $X(i)$ represents the velocity of the i-th particle, a represents the inertia weight, c_1 and c_2 represent the learning parameters, $rand()$ represents the random number between 0 and 1, and $Y(i)$ represents the i-th particle search.

In order to get the optimal value, the Y represents the optimal value searched by the entire cluster, and $Z(i)$ represents the current position of the i-th particle. Then, calculating the fitness according to the objective function mentioned above. In the adaptive impedance control algorithm, the purpose is to make the contact force close to an expect constant value, so the objective function should be minimized. Comparing the contemporary fitness of each particle with the previous value, if the contemporary particle is more adaptive, that is, the value of the fitness function is much smaller in the adaptive impedance control algorithm, then the previous generation particle is replaced. Select the most adaptable individuals in this generation of particles as the global fitness of this generation after comparing each other. If the global fitness of this generation is better than the previous generation, then update the contemporary global fitness. Finally, the termination condition is to achieve the optimal objective function value, if the termination condition is not met, repeat the Eqs. (8) and (9). Instead, when the termination condition is met, the algorithm is exited and the optimal solution is obtained. If it is never reached the termination condition, then the algorithm is exited when the maximum number of iterations is reached, and the procedure of particle swarm optimization is simplify presented in Algorithm 1.

Algorithm 1 Particle swarm optimization scheme

1: **Initialize**: Initializes the position and velocity of the particle swarm randomly
2: **do**
3: **for** Each particle **do**
4:      Calculate its fitness
5:      **If** (its fitness is better than the best value in history)
6:          Renew the best individual $Y(i)$ with $Z(i)$
7: **end for**
8: Select the best particle in the current particle swarm
9: **If** (The current particle is better than the best particle in the history of swarm)
10: Updating Y with the best particle of the current group
11: **for** Each particle **do**
12:      Updating particle velocity using: $X(i) = a \cdot X(i) + c1 \cdot rand() \cdot (Y(i) - Z(i)) + c2 \cdot rand() \cdot (Y - Z(i))$
13:      Updating particle position using: $Z(i) = Z(i) + X(i)$
14:      Renew the best individual $Y(i)$ with $Z(i)$
15: **end for**
16: **while** (The maximum number of iterations is not reached)

3.3 Experiment Program Design

Figure 5 is the block diagram of the experimental program. The entire experimental procedure is carried out through the designed intelligent digital compliant grinder and it is mainly composed of the two sections, including protection program and impedance control section. The impedance control section produces corresponding voltage to control the movement of the servo motor to obtain the command constant contact force. We can adjust the adaptive impedance control parameters (M, B, K) by the particle swarm optimization algorithm in real time during the polishing process of the program to get the ideal grinding effect. After the polishing experiment, M (mass coefficient) is finally selected to be 1, B (damping coefficient) is 50, K (stiffness coefficient) is 625.

The protection program is designed to protect the intelligent digital compliant grinder from being damaged. That is, we set the procedure to limit the polishing tool of digital compliant grinder move less than 25 mm. In addition, during the polishing process, the actual contact force must be less than 20 N. Once one of these conditions

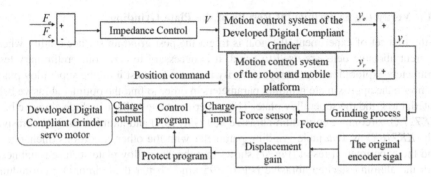

Fig. 5. Block diagram of the experimental program.

is not met, the protection procedure will stop immediately to protect the digital compliant grinder and the force sensor from being damaged.

4 Experimental Verification

This section will design the polishing experiments based on the intelligent digital compliant grinder and the impedance controller. According to the relevant experience of the belt grinding of CNC machine, it is quite important to figure out the relationship between the surface roughness of the workpiece and the polishing parameters such as the abrasive belt type, the abrasive belt velocity and the polishing force. Finally, the roughness measuring instrument (Fig. 6) is used to detect the polished workpiece surface and judge whether the roughness value meets the industrial requirements through it.

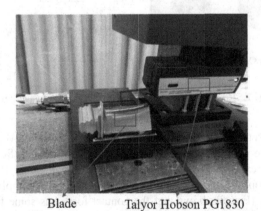

Blade   Talyor Hobson PG1830

Fig. 6. Roughness machine of Taylor Hobson FORM TALYSURF PG1830.

4.1   Verify the Experimental Results of the Plate Grinding

In the first set of experiment, the goal is to get the best grinding surface quality when different abrasive belts are used to grind. It is necessary to carry out preliminary test parameters exploration experiment to verify it, so we first test it on the superalloy plate to choose the approximate grinding parameters in order to find the optimal abrasive belt material to grind the superalloy plate. This experiment uses silicon carbide abrasive belt *(CK721X)*, zirconium corundum abrasive belt *(ZK713X)* and alumina stacked abrasive belt *(KK718X)* as a variable grinding parameter with the other conditions unchanged. And the experimental result (Fig. 7) shows that the superalloy plate surface roughness with the alumina stacked abrasive belt (0.195 µm is better than zirconium corundum abrasive belt (0.300 µm) and silicon carbide abrasive belt (0.229 µm) after grinding. For this reason, in order to improve the surface roughness of the blade made by superalloy, a alumina stacked abrasive belt is chose to complete the blade surface polishing.

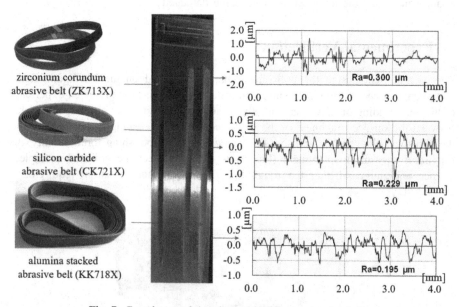

Fig. 7. Roughness of the plate with different abrasive belt.

In the second set of experiment, the aim is to test the adaptive impedance force control performance with the intelligent digital compliant grinder. So we carry out the impedance control experience on the superalloy plate with 3, 5, 10 N to verify the effective of the proposed method and the intelligent digital compliant grinder. The experimental result (Fig. 8) shows that the contact force has some fluctuations when the digital compliant grinder comes into contact with the plate, but there is no significant difference in the condition of the different contact force for the surface roughness of the superalloy plate. When the grinding contact force becomes basically stable, the amount of grinding and polishing removal is kept constant ideally, and the

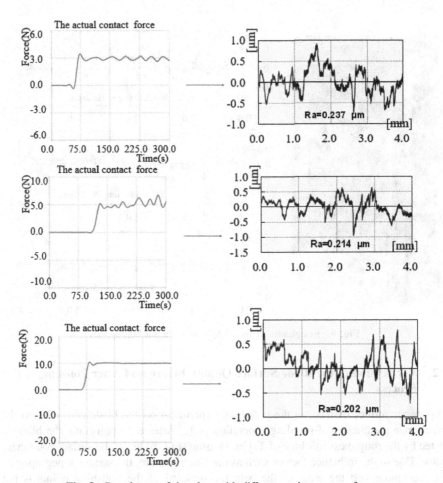

Fig. 8. Roughness of the plate with different active contact force.

sound produced during grinding process becomes smooth and soft. When the grinding force is reduced, the sound during the grinding process is also reduced. To some degree, the greater contact force, the smaller the superalloy plate roughness. However, as the grinding force increases, the sound produced by the abrasive belt rubs against the workpiece significantly increased and it may cause over-grinding if the actual grinding contact force is too large.

In the third set of experiment, this test is designed with different belt grinding speeds (1000 rpm, 2000 rpm, 3000 rpm) with the other conditions unchanged. From Fig. 9, we can see that there is no obvious difference under different belt speeds for the surface roughness of the superalloy plate. As the speed of the belt increases, the amount of metal entering the grinding per unit time increases, the amount of material removed increases, and the surface roughness decreases. To some degree, during the grinding process, the greater the speed, the higher the surface accuracy and the greater the material removal per unit time. However, it may cause the workpiece to be scrapped and over-grinding if the belt grinding speed is too high.

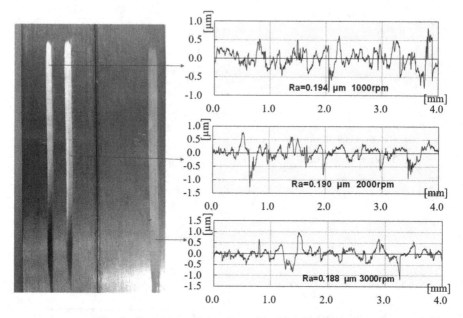

Fig. 9. Roughness of the plate with different belt speeds

4.2 Verification of the Blade Surface Quality Before and After Polishing Process

This paper further carries out the polishing experiment on the blade according to the experience parameters of grinding superalloy plate. After each polishing, the blade is tested by the roughness machine of Taylor Hobson (Fig. 6) to get the surface roughness value. Due to the influence factors such as the touch posture, the surface topography of the workpiece and the wear of the belt, the removal of the polishing points is not uniform when the belt is polished combined with the easy-polishing characteristics of the blade superalloy material. In the polishing process, the blade needs to be polished according to the superalloy plate prior knowledge. Furtherly, two experiments are carried out on blades between force controlled polishing and the case without force controlled. Both experiments are carried out with the 3000 rpm belt speed under the other conditions unchanged.

The experiment result, that is the blade surface appearance and the roughness before and after polishing process is shown in Fig. 10, and it is obvious that the milling mark is effectively removed. Figure 10-b shows that the roughness of the blade without force controlled has been improved but cannot meet the blade surface roughness requirements. Moreover, Fig. 10-c shows that the roughness of the blade with force controlled has been improved a lot and the surface roughness is 0.065 μm. The surface is smooth with good consistency which significantly meets the blade surface roughness requirements.

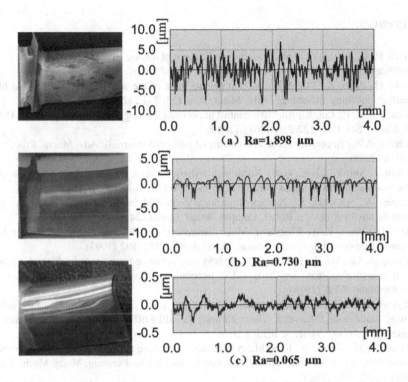

Fig. 10. Roughness test results of different process on the blade (a) before the polishing process (b) polishing without force controlled (c) polishing with force controlled.

5 Conclusions

In order to remove the milling mask of the blade and improve the surface roughness, this paper presents a novel intelligent digital compliant grinder for active force control in robotic polishing, and the contact force during the polishing process can keep constant with the proposed algorithm. The basic experiment is carried out on the superalloy plate to choose the optimal polishing parameters and then the robotic blade polishing experiment is further carried out to verify the effectiveness of the proposed method. When the active contact force under impedance control algorithm works, the surface roughness of the blade reduces from the original 1.898 μm to force controlled 0.065 μm, which is much lower than the case without the force controlled 0.730 μm and the fluctuation of polishing contact force is always stay within 1 N. The results prove that the surface roughness and machining consistency are significantly improved with the proposed intelligent digital compliant grinder and the robotic blade polishing algorithm.

Acknowledgements. This work was supported by the National Key Research and Development Program of China under Grant No. 2017YFB1303401, the National Natural Science Foundation of China under Grant Nos. 91748114 and 51535004.

References

1. Tian, F., Lv, C., Li, Z., et al.: Modeling and control of robotic automatic polishing for curved surfaces. CIRP J. Manufact. Sci. Technol. **14**, 55–64 (2016)
2. Gao, H., Zhao, Z., Sun, Y.W.: Recent development of the aero-engine impeller and blade surface polishing technology. Adv. Mater. Res. **135**, 7–12 (2010)
3. Liao, L., Xi, F., Liu, K.: Adaptive control of pressure tracking for polishing process. ASME. J. Manuf. Sci. Eng. **132**(1), 011015 (2010)
4. Zhong, Z.W.: Recent advances in polishing of advanced materials. Adv. Manuf. Process. **23**(5), 8 (2008)
5. Duan, J., Shi, Y., Li, X., et al.: Adaptive polishing for blisk by flexible grinding head. Acta Aeronautica et Astronautica Sinica **32**(5), 934–940 (2011)
6. Lopes, A., Almeida, F.: A force-impedance controlled industrial robot using an active robotic auxiliary device. Robot. Comput. Integr. Manuf. **24**(3), 299–309 (2008)
7. Dai, H., Yuen, K.M., Elbestawi, M.A.: Parametric modelling and control of the robotic grinding process. Int. J. Adv. Manuf. Technol. **8**(3), 182–192 (1993)
8. Zhang, J., Liu, G., Zang, X., et al.: A hybrid passive/active force control scheme for robotic belt grinding system. In: 2016 IEEE International Conference on Mechatronics and Automation. IEEE (2016)
9. Tyapin, I., Kaldestad, K.B., Hovland, G.: Off-line path correction of robotic face milling using static tool force and robot stiffness. In: IEEE/RSJ International Conference on Intelligent Robots Systems. IEEE (2015)
10. Straub, B.M., Gerke, M., Pahl, M.: A systematic technique to estimate positioning errors for robot accuracy improvement using laser interferometry based sensing. Mech. Mach. Theory **40**(8), 879–906 (2005)
11. Klimchik, A., Pashkevich, A., Chablat, D., et al.: Compliance error compensation technique for parallel robots composed of non-perfect serial chains. Robot. Comput.-Integr. Manuf. **29**(2), 385–393 (2012)
12. Dumas, C., Caro, S., Garnier, S., et al.: Joint stiffness identification of six-revolute industrial serial robots. Robot. Comput.-Integr. Manuf. **27**(4), 881–888 (2011)
13. Klimchik, A., Ambiehl, A., Garnier, S., et al.: Efficiency evaluation of robots in machining applications using industrial performance measure. Robot. Comput.-Integr. Manuf. **48**, 12–29 (2017)
14. Huang, H., Gong, Z.M., Chen, X.Q., et al.: Robotic grinding and polishing for turbine-vane overhaul. J. Mater. Process. Technol. **127**(2), 140–145 (2002)
15. Liu, L., Ulrich, B.J., Elbestawi, M.A.: Robotic grinding force regulation: design, implementation and benefits. In: Proceedings of the IEEE International Conference on Robotics and Automation, pp. 258–265. IEEE (1990)

Robot Cooperation

Path Planning of UAV-UGV Heterogeneous Robot System in Road Network

Mengqing Chen[1], Yang Chen[1,2(✉)], Zhihuan Chen[1,2],
and Yanhua Yang[2]

[1] Institute of Robotics and Intelligent Systems,
Wuhan University of Science and Technology, Wuhan 430081, China
chenyag@wust.edu.cn
[2] Engineering Research Center for Metallurgical Automation
and Measurement Technology of Ministry of Education, Wuhan 430081, China

Abstract. The previous research on path planning of the UAV-UGV heterogeneous robot system plan paths for both UAV and UGV without considering the UGV's moving range or plan only the UAV's path based on the given UGV's path. In reality, the UGV should be restricted to drive in the road network, and the given UGV's path is not necessarily the best UGV's path. In the heterogeneous package delivery system considered in this paper, the UGV's path was restricted to the road network and the UAV's and UGV's paths were optimized simultaneously to get the optimized paths. This paper proposed a two-stage strategy to solve the path planning problem by a hybrid algorithm of modified ant colony optimization and genetic algorithm. The simulation results show that the proposed method is feasible.

Keywords: Heterogeneous robot system · Path planning · Two-stage strategy · Road network

1 Introduction

In heterogeneous robot systems, path planning for unmanned aerial vehicles (UAVs) and unmanned ground vehicles (UGVs) is so important that they can coordinate to perform tasks. At present, the researches on path planning of heterogeneous robot systems have appeared in many applications, such as maritime rescue [1, 2], investigation [3], logistics and distribution [4]. There are two types of the previous study about the path planning of the heterogeneous robot system. The first one is to plan the UAV's and UGV's paths simultaneously, but without considering the moving range of the UGV, that is, the UGV is allowed to move anywhere on the ground. The second one considers the moving range of the UGV, but the UGV's moving is limited to a given road and only the UAV's path is planned.

Most of the current studies are the first type. Klaučo et al. [1] and Garone et al. [2] studied the path planning of the heterogeneous system composed of a ship and a drone in the marine rescue, Klaučo et al. [1] allowed the UAV to visit one rescue point at a time, and Garone et al. [2] allowed the UAV to visit multiple rescue points at a time. Li et al. [5] studied the automatic ground map building and path planning in UAV-UGV

© Springer Nature Switzerland AG 2019
H. Yu et al. (Eds.): ICIRA 2019, LNAI 11745, pp. 497–507, 2019.
https://doi.org/10.1007/978-3-030-27529-7_42

cooperative system, where the ground image is obtained by the UAV from an aerial view, and then the ground map is automatically constructed, and the UGV's path was planned based on the map. Martin et al. [6] allowed the UAV to access multiple target points at a time. Chen et al. [7] considered the neighborhood constraint of the target points on the basis of [6], so that the aircraft only needs to go to the neighborhood of targets and is allowed to access multiple target points at a time. Freitas et al. [8] proposed the Flying Sidekick Traveling Salesman Problem (FSTSP), and used a hybrid heuristic method to solve the path planning problem.

In the above researches on heterogeneous robot systems, the UGV's constraints of moving range were completely not considered. In reality, the ground environment is complex, the roads are fixed, and the UGV's movement should be limited to the roads. Therefore, some studies have been conducted to limit the moving range of UGV, also the second type. Yu et al. [9] studied the target tracking of the UAV and UGV cooperation system in urban environments. Maini et al. [10] studied the application of heterogeneous robotic systems in surveying and mapping in complex environments, in which the ground roads are intricate, and a road was selected for the UGV in advance. Some researchers studied the path planning of the heterogeneous robotic system in package delivery, and the path of the UGV was fixed on a known road. Carlsson et al. [11] studied the path planning problem of package delivery in heterogeneous robot systems, in which the path of the UGV was given in prior and a heuristic method was proposed to obtain the route of the UAV so that the UAV can access all the target points. Mathew et al. [4] restricted the route of the UGV to a given road, selected some fixed points for the UAV on the road, and selected the take-off points and landing points of the UAV at these fixed points to obtain the UAV's route.

There are constraints of road network in city environment, and the UGV should be limited to drive on the roads. Although the researches of Yu et al. [9], Maini et al. [10], Carlsson et al. [11] and Mathew et al. [4] considered the constraint of roads, they only limited the UGV's driving to a given road. But the prior given road is not necessarily the best UGV's route for the system. Therefore, this paper allowed the UGV automatically select a path in the road network, that is to say, not only the UAV's path was planned, but also the UGV's path was optimized, so that the best paths of the system was obtained.

The paper is organized as follows: The description of the path planning problem of the UAV-UGV heterogeneous robot system was given in the Sect. 2. The Sect. 3 showed the model of the problem. The implementation of the hybrid algorithm of the modified ant colony optimization and genetic algorithm for the problem was presented in the Sect. 4. The Sect. 5 was the simulation experiments of the method proposed in this paper, and the Sect. 6 presented the conclusions and future works.

2   Problem Statement

Consider a heterogeneous robot system consisting of an UGV and an UAV to deliver packages to specific customers. The UGV is restricted to drive in the road network while the UAV can be carried by the UGV or fly out to deliver packages to customers. The UGV carries the UAV and the packages setting off from the starting point, and selects a suitable path without duplicate path segments in the road network to move to the end point. During the movement from the starting point to the end point, the UGV always travels on the road with the constant speed v_c, while the UAV will take off from the UGV to the customers to deliver packages with the constant speed v_h. Due to the ability to carry only one cargo each time and limited battery life of the UAV, the UAV visits only one customer each time it separates from the UGV and then rendezvous with the UGV. During the UAV's departure from the UGV to access customer, the UGV will continue to advance. After the UAV has accessed a customer and delivered a package, it will land on the UGV to load a package and then advance with it or swap battery [12, 13] on it, and take off at the next appropriate takeoff point to deliver the package to the next customer. After all the target points have been visited, the UAV returns to the UGV and moves to the end point.

As our example, the scene is shown in Fig. 1(a). It consists of a road network and some specific locations. The blue lines are roads, the locations marked with red positioning marks are customers. The topology of Fig. 1(a) is shown in Fig. 1(b), in which the customers are marked as our target set $\Omega = [q_1, q_2, q_3, \cdots, q_N]$, where $q_j \in R_{2 \times 1}$, $j = 1, 2, \cdots, N$, N is the number of the targets, S is the starting point and E is the end point.

Assuming that UAV and UGV can accurately recognize each other, the path planning goal in this study is to search a suitable path for the UGV in the road network, and to plan the corresponding flight route for the UAV, so that the UAV can access all the targets and the flight distance is the shortest.

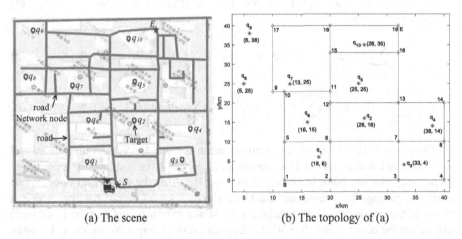

(a) The scene   (b) The topology of (a)

Fig. 1. A heterogeneous robot system to deliver goods to customers. (Color figure online)

3   Path Planning Model

Since there is a strong coupling between the UGV's and UAV's paths, it is difficult to solve the UAV's and UGV's paths simultaneously without any prior knowledge. In this section, the model was established on the basis that the UGV's path had been searched (more details can be seen in the Sect. 4.1). Because of the complexity of the UGV's route, it's difficult to represent it with a continuous function, but it is easier to represent it by discretizing the path to sequentially connected points. Assuming that the discretization accuracy is d, and the coordinates of discrete points are stored in $\mathbf{D} \in R^{M \times 2}$, where M is the number of the discrete points. The UAV will select its takeoff and landing points in $\mathbf{D}$. If UGV's path $\mathbf{D}$ is known, once the takeoff and landing points have been determined, the path of the UAV is also determined.

In order to choose the takeoff and landing points in $\mathbf{D}$, we introduce two 0–1 matrix $\mathbf{A}$ and $\mathbf{B}$, where $A_{i,j} = 1$ $(1 \le i \le M, 1 \le j \le N)$ means that the UAV takes off at the ith point in $\mathbf{D}$ to visit the target q_j. $B_{i,j} = 1$ means that the UAV visits the target q_j and then lands at the ith point in $\mathbf{D}$. The model is presented as follows.

$$\sum_{i=1}^{M} A_{i,j} = 1, \ j = 1, 2, \ldots, N \tag{1}$$

$$\sum_{i=1}^{M} B_{i,j} = 1, \ j = 1, 2, \ldots, N \tag{2}$$

$$\sum_{j=1}^{N} \left(A_{i,j} + B_{i,j} \right) \le 1, \ i = 1, 2, \ldots, M \tag{3}$$

$$\sum_{i=1}^{n} \left(B_{i,j} - A_{i,j} \right) \le 0, \ n = 1, 2, \ldots, M, \ j = 1, 2, \ldots, N \tag{4}$$

$$\sum_{i=1}^{n} \left(A_{i,j+1} - B_{i,j} \right) \le 0, \ n = 1, 2, \ldots, M, \ j = 1, 2, \ldots, N-1 \tag{5}$$

$$\frac{1}{v_h} \left(\left\| \sum_{i=1}^{M} A_{i,j} D_i - q_j \right\| + \left\| \sum_{i=1}^{M} B_{i,j} D_i - q_j \right\| \right) = \frac{1}{v_c} l \sum_{i=1}^{M} \left(i B_{i,j} - i A_{i,j} \right), \ j = 1, 2, \cdots, N \tag{6}$$

The constraints (1) and (2) respectively mean that the UAV has only one takeoff point and one landing point in $\mathbf{D}$ while sending a package to a customer. The constraint (3) presents that any point in $\mathbf{D}$ only allows the UAV to take off or land once. While sending a package to a customer, the UAV should take off before landing, which is shown in the constraint (4). Similarly, the constraint (5) illustrated that the UAV can't take off for the next target before it's landing for previous target. When the UAV takes off from the UGV for a target, the UGV continues to move forward, and they simultaneously arrive at the next rendezvous point. In another word, the UAV and UGV have the same time consumption between the takeoff point and the landing point of each target, shown as the constraint (6), in which D_i indicates the ith row of the matrix $\mathbf{D}$, and q_j is the jth target.

Because the UAV's battery lifetime is limited and the UGV has sufficient energy, the shorter the UAV's flight distance, the less battery the UAV consumes. The objective function is established based on the shortest total flight distance of the UAV to access all targets.

$$f = \sum_{j=1}^{N} \left(\left\| \sum_{i=1}^{M} A_{i,j} D_i - q_j \right\| + \left\| \sum_{i=1}^{M} B_{i,j} D_i - q_j \right\| \right) \tag{7}$$

4   Hybrid Algorithm for the Problem

A two-stage strategy is adopted to solve the problem. In each iteration, in the first stage, the modified ant colony optimization was used to search the path set P_1 along whose paths the UGV can reach the end point and make the UAV visit all the targets. The shortest path P_s in P_1 was selected. In the second stage, after the path P_s was discretized, the genetic algorithm is used to solve the flight path of the UAV corresponding to the UGV's path P_s, and the obtained flight path length is transferred to the modified ant colony optimization to update the pheromone, thereby affecting the selection of the UGV's path in the next iteration. After all the iterations of the modified ant colony optimization are completed, the UGV's path with the shortest UAV's flight distance and the corresponding UAV's flight route were selected.

4.1   The Modified Ant Colony Optimization (MACO)

The pheromone update function and heuristic function were modified based on the traditional ant colony optimization. The pheromone update function and heuristic function of the MACO are shown in Eqs. (8) and (10) respectively.

$$\tau_{ij}(t+1) = (1-\rho)\tau_{ij}(t) + \Delta\tau_{ij}(t) + \Delta\tau_{ij}^{bs}(t), \ 0 < \rho < 1 \tag{8}$$

The first two terms have the same definition as the traditional ACO [14], and the addition item $\Delta\tau_{ij}^{bs}(t)$ indicates that if the UAV's flight distance corresponding to the UGV's path obtained in current iteration is the shortest flight distance so far (we call it condition Θ), the ant that gets this route of the UGV will additionally release pheromone on the path it passes. $\Delta\tau_{ij}^{bs}(t)$ is defined as

$$\Delta\tau_{ij}^{bs}(t) = \begin{cases} \frac{x \cdot E}{L^{bs}}, & \text{condition } \Theta \text{ is satisfied} \\ 0, & \text{otherwise} \end{cases} \tag{9}$$

where x is a constant, and L^{bs} is the flight length of the UAV obtained in the current iteration.

After the modification as Eq. (8), a UGV's path that enables the UAV to access all the targets with shortest distance will be obtained by the MACO. If the UGV's path is shorten as possible simultaneously, the energy will be saved. Thus in each stage of selecting next node, if the ant prefers to select a road connected the current node and the next node that not only with shorter distance but also enables the UAV to access more targets, the whole mission will be completed with shorter UGV's whole distance and thus with less energy. The heuristic function of the MACO is

$$\eta_{ij}(t) = \frac{n_{ij}}{l_{ij}} \tag{10}$$

where l_{ij} is the length of the path connecting the road network node i and j, and n_{ij} is the number of targets that the UAV can access on the path connecting the road network node i and j. The product of n_{ij} makes ants select the roads that can access as many targets as possible. The probability of ants moving from one node to the connected node is the same as the traditional ACO [14].

4.2   The Genetic Algorithm (GA)

Coding. If the matrix A and B have been solved, the path of the UAV is determined. In order to represent the relationship of the takeoff and landing numbers in **D**, we code each chromosome arranged alternately by element in **A** and **B**, and the length of each chromosome is 2 * N. All the chromosomes in *code* satisfy the following conditions at initialization, (i) each gene in a chromosome ranges from 1–M, (ii) the genes in every chromosome are not repeated, and (iii) the genes in each chromosome are ascending. Taking $M = 600$, $N = 4$ as example, an example of the coding is (18, 50, 95, 152, 189, 269, 483, 562), the meaning of whose each gene is: $A_{18,1} = 1$, $B_{50,1} = 1$, $A_{95,2} = 1$, $B_{152,2} = 1$, $A_{189,3} = 1$, $B_{269,3} = 1$, $A_{483,4} = 1$, $B_{562,4} = 1$, and more specifically, it means that the UAV takes off at the location of the 18th point in **D** to visit q_1 and then lands at the location of the 50th point in **D,** and then takes off at the location of the 95th point in **D** to visit q_2 and then lands at the location of the 152th point in **D**, et al.

Genetic Operators. Three genetic operators are adopted in this paper: selection, crossover and mutation. Selection: In each generation, individuals with large fitness value are retained with a certain probability, while individuals with small fitness value are eliminated. Crossover: If a pair of chromosomes is selected to perform the crossover operation, the genes are searched one by one from the first gene of the two chromosomes, and if the conditions (i), (ii) and (iii) are satisfied, the one-point crossover is performed. Mutation: Arbitrarily determining two adjacent takeoff and landing points for mutation, randomly reselecting two new points to replace them. The chromosomes after being crossed and mutated should satisfy conditions (i), (ii) and (iii).

Fitness Evaluation. According to the above coding and genetic operators, only the constraint (6) may be violated. The violation of constraint (6) was converted into a penalty term and added to the objective function (7). The penalty is

$$p = \sum_{j=1}^{N} \left| \frac{1}{v_c} d \sum_{i=1}^{M} \left(iB_{i,j} - iA_{i,j} \right) - \frac{1}{v_h} \left(\left\| \sum_{i=1}^{M} A_{i,j} D_i - q_j \right\| + \left\| \sum_{i=1}^{M} B_{i,j} D_i - q_j \right\| \right) \right| \tag{11}$$

The individual's cost will be calculated by accumulating the above penalty p on the objective function (7). The new cost is f_p as shown in Eq. (12).

$$f_p = f + \gamma p \tag{12}$$

Where γ indicates the weight of the penalty which can be tuned manually. The fitness is built on the inverse of the distance which brings to the optimization more straightforward. It is $fitness = 1/f_p$.

5 Simulation Experiments

5.1 Simulation Results

Some common parameters including main parameters of the MACO, such as maximum iteration ($iter1$), the ants number (m) and main parameters of genetic algorithm, maximum generation ($iter2$), such as population size (Pz), crossover probability (CP), mutation probability (MP), and selection probability (SP) are as follows: $iter1 = 30$, $m = 300$, $iter2 = 800$, $Pz = 800$, $CP = 0.3$, $MP = 0.1$, $SP = 0.1$. The values of other parameters are as follows: $v_c = 18$ (km/h), $v_h = 54$ (km/h), $d = 0.2$ (km), $\gamma = 500$, U (Life time of battery) $= 20$ min, $\alpha = 1$, $\beta = 1$, $\rho = 0.3$, $E = 1$, $x = 5$.

The scene used to simulate is shown as in Fig. 1, and it's topology graph is shown in Fig. 2, in which the red stars are target points. The paths of UGV and UAV are shown in Fig. 2(a), in which the blue thick solid line is the UGV's path and the black dotted lines are the paths of UAV, t_i and l_i ($i = 1, 2, \cdots, 10$) are respective the takeoff and landing points of UAV's visiting each target point. Figure 2(a) shows the driving distance of the UGV is 104.654 km. Figure 2(b) shows the UAV's drive distance in each iteration of the MACO, the generation that gets the best UAV's path was marked by a black solid circle and it is in the 20th generation of the MACO that the shortest flight distance has been obtained. So it is meaningful to study the UAV's curve in the 20th generation of MACO. In the 20th generation of MACO, the penalty curve with penalty term and the result curve of the objective function without penalty term (the total flight distance of the UAV) are shown in Fig. 2(c).

Figure 2(c) shows that the two curves of the drive distance and the cost of the UAV are not completely equal after convergence, the reason is that the cost curve adds the product of γ and the violation on the basis of the flight distance, and γ is a large number, as here, 500. So, although the two curves are not equal, the actual violation is small. The locations of the takeoff t_i and landing l_i ($i = 1, 2, \ldots, 10$) are illustrated in Table 1. Because there are some constraints should be satisfied, and according to the above analysis, only constraint (6) will be violated, so in order to illustrate the violation of the constraints (6), the two columns (TD) of Table 1 has been shown added. The largest violation is the visiting of q_9 and it is 0.0014 h, i.e. 5.04 s. The violations are all very small and it's acceptable.

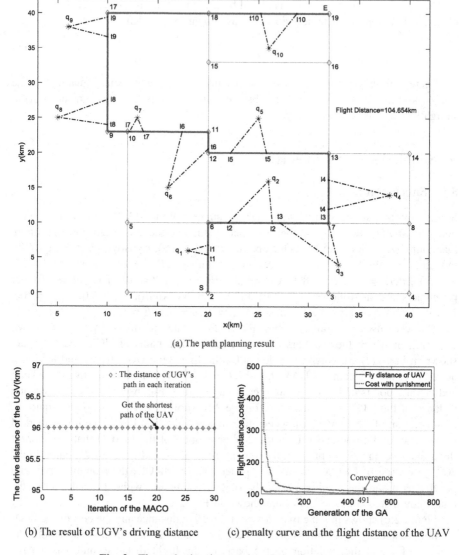

(a) The path planning result

(b) The result of UGV's driving distance   (c) penalty curve and the flight distance of the UAV

Fig. 2. The path planning results. (Color figure online)

5.2   UAV's Path Smoothing

In real applications, considering the kinematics and dynamic constraints of the UAV, the trajectory of the UAV should be a smooth curve with limited curvature. In this paper, a piecewise polynomial curve proposed by Oravec et al. [15] is used to smooth the path of UAV. The order of the piecewise polynomial curve of the UAV is 2nd order. A smooth and feasible UAV's trajectory is obtained as shown in Fig. 3, in which the red solid curves are the UAV's smoothing path.

Table 1. Coordinates of the takeoff location and landing locations

Targets no.	t_i (km)	l_i (km)	TD (h)	Targets no.	t_i (km)	l_i (km)	TD (h)
q_1	(20, 5.4)	(20, 6.8)	7.80e−4	q_6	(20, 20.6)	(17.4, 23)	6.36e−5
q_2	(22, 10)	(26.4, 10)	4.52e−4	q_7	(13.6, 23)	(12.2, 23)	7.80e−4
q_3	(27.2, 10)	(32, 10)	5.15e−4	q_8	(10, 24)	(10, 27.6)	0.0012
q_4	(32, 12)	(32, 16.2)	0.0021	q_9	(10, 36.6)	(10, 39.4)	0.0014
q_5	(25.8, 20)	(22.2, 20)	1.07e−4	q_{10}	(25.2, 40)	(28.8, 40)	1.07e−4

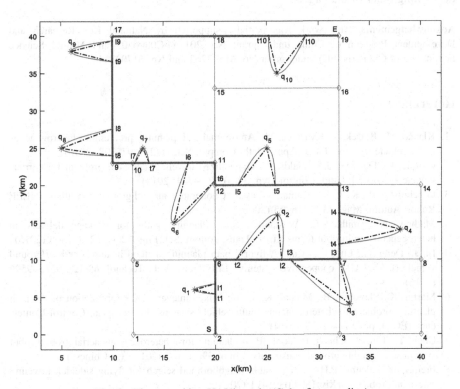

Fig. 3. The smoothing UAV's path. (Color figure online)

6   Conclusion and Future Work

Distinguish from the previous researches that no limitation is added to the moving range of the UGV or only UAV's path is planned on the basis of a given UGV's path, this paper studied the package delivery problem of UAV-UGV heterogeneous robot system with ground road network restrictions. Not only the UAV's path was planned, but also the UGV's path was optimized to get the optimal paths of completing the mission thus saving energy. A hybrid of the modified ant colony optimization and the genetic algorithm was used to solve the path planning problem. Firstly, the modified ant colony optimization is used to search for the feasible path of UGV that can make the UAV visit targets as many as possible, and then the genetic algorithm was used to plan the corresponding UAV's path and the UAV's flight distance was then transferred to the modified ant colony optimization to affect the pheromone update, so that the ants prefer to choose a path that makes the flight distance of the UAV shorter in the next iteration.

This paper planned paths for the UAV-UGV heterogeneous robot system based on the given visiting order of targets. In practice, because of the complexity of the road network, the given order may not be the best. So in the future work, we will optimize the visiting order of the targets.

Acknowledgements. This work was partially supported by National Key Research and Development Program of China under grant No. 2017YFC0806503 and Natural Science Foundation of China (NSFC) under grant No. 61573263 and No. 61703314.

References

1. Klaučo, M., Blažek, S., Kvasnica, M.: An optimal path planning problem for heterogeneous multi-vehicle systems. Int. J. Appl. Math. Comput. Sci. **26**(2), 297–308 (2016)
2. Garone, E., Determe, J.F., Naldi, R.: Generalized traveling salesman problem for carrier-vehicle systems. J. Guid. Control Dyn. **37**(3), 766–774 (2014)
3. Grocholsky, B., Keller, J., Kumar, V., et al.: Cooperative air and ground surveillance. IEEE Robot. Autom. Mag. **13**(3), 16–25 (2006)
4. Mathew, N., Smith, S.L., Waslander, S.L.: Planning paths for package delivery in heterogeneous multirobot teams. IEEE Trans. Autom. Sci. Eng. **12**(4), 1298–1308 (2015)
5. Li, J., Deng, G., Luo, C., et al.: A hybrid path planning method in unmanned air/ground vehicle (UAV/UGV) cooperative systems. IEEE Trans. Veh. Technol. **65**(12), 9585–9596 (2016)
6. Martin, K., Slavomir, B., Michal, K., et al.: Mixed-integer SOCP formulation of the path planning problem for heterogeneous multi-vehicle systems. In: European Control Conference (ECC), pp. 1474–1479 (2014)
7. Chen, Y., Tan, Y., Cheng, L., et al.: Path planning for a heterogeneous aerial-ground robot system with neighbourhood constraints. Robot **39**(1), 1–7 (2017). (in Chinese)
8. Freitas, J.C., Penna, P.H.V.: A variable neighborhood search for flying sidekick traveling salesman problem. arXiv:1804.03954v1 (2018)
9. Yu, H., Meier, K., Argyle, M., et al.: Cooperative path planning for target tracking in urban environments using unmanned air and ground vehicles. IEEE/ASME Trans. Mechatron. **20**(2), 541–552 (2014)
10. Maini, P., Sundar, K., Rathinam, S., et al.: Cooperative planning for fuel-constrained aerial vehicles and ground-based refueling vehicles for large-scale coverage. arXiv:1805.04417v1 (2018)
11. Carlsson, J.G., Song, S.: Coordinated logistics with a truck and a drone. Manag. Sci. **64**(9), 1–31 (2017)
12. Koji, A.O.S., Paulo, K.F., James, R.: Automatic battery replacement system for UAVs: analysis and design. J. Intell. Rob. Syst. **65**(1–4), 563–586 (2012)

13. Swieringa, K.A., Hanson, C.B., Richardson, J.R., et al.: Autonomous battery swapping system for small-scale helicopters. In: IEEE International Conference on Robotics & Automation, pp. 3335–3340 (2010)
14. Gu, P., Xiu, C., Cheng, Y., et al.: Adaptive ant colony optimization algorithm. In: International Conference on Mechatronics and Control, pp. 95–98 (2014)
15. Oravec, J., Klaučo, M., Kvasnica, M., et al.: Optimal vehicle routing with interception of targets' neighbourhoods. In: IEEE European Control Conference (ECC), pp. 2533–2538 (2015)

Automatic Programming for Dual Robots to Grinding Intersecting Curve

Shibo Han, Xingwei Zhao, Qi Fan, and Bo Tao[✉]

School of Mechanical Science and Engineering,
Huazhong University of Science and Technology, Wuhan 430074, China
taobo@mail.hust.edu.cn

Abstract. In this paper, automatic programming for dual robots is proposed to realize autonomous robotic grinding of intersecting curves. Compared to grinding with a single robot, dual robots provide more degree-of-freedom to optimize the grinding path. In this paper, a special grinding path, named as intersecting grinding curve, will be realized by the dual robots. Since the intersecting curve is generated by two motions, the dual robots can decouple the motion and finish this task much easier and more effective than a single robot. Also, the motion of each joint becomes smoother, which will benefit for robotic grinding.

Keywords: Dual robots · Motion planning · Intersecting curve grinding

1 Introduction

The robot is an advanced manufacturing equipment with a high degree of flexibility. With the advent of high-end manufacturing scenarios, single-robot processing has been unable to meet the processing quality and efficiency requirements, and the necessity and importance of dual-robot collaborative processing have become increasingly prominent. Compared with single-robot system, the advantages of dual-robot system are obvious, including to achieve a larger workspace and more flexibility [1]. For instant, it is hard to realize the robotic path following through an intersecting line with a single robot, while it is much easier for a dual robot.

There are many studies on the planning of the dual-robot system. Gan et al. designed an effective calibration procedure for coordinated robots based on a series of handclasp manipulations [2]. Lu et al. analyzed the dual-robot transformation and kinematic constraints to get the proper trajectory for curved-surface nondestructive testing [3]. Caccavale et al. presented a quaternion-based impedance control framework, which is applied for cooperative control of dual robots [4]. Those researches provide theoretical foundations for the application of dual-robot system. Welding is one of the most common applications of the dual-robot system. Shi et al. developed an automatic programming for an industrial robot cooperated with a one DOF positioner to weld intersecting pipes, where the posture of the welding torch was considered [5]. Chen et al. established the parametric equation of the intersecting curve and proposed a path planning method to deal with the tube–sphere intersection welds [6]. Tie and Fan

© Springer Nature Switzerland AG 2019
H. Yu et al. (Eds.): ICIRA 2019, LNAI 11745, pp. 508–516, 2019.
https://doi.org/10.1007/978-3-030-27529-7_43

realized offline motion planning of the dual-robot welding coordination for the steel curved pipe which has been testified by a simulation platform [1].

Even though a mass of references is related to the path planning for robotic welds, only few references are concentrated on the robotic complex curve grinding, who faces more complicated dynamic issues. Therefore, in this paper, automatic programming for dual robot to complete intersecting curve grinding tasks will be studied in detail. The intersecting curve is described in the cylindrical coordinate and the method to get the position and the rotation is also presented. After that, simulation and experiments are carried out to compare the performances of the single robot and the dual-robot system.

2   Cooperation Path Planning Method of Dual Robots

2.1   The Geometrical Model of Intersecting Curves

Firstly, we focus on the description and the cooperation path planning of the intersecting curve. The Fig. 1 shows a general intersecting curve on a pipe. Two orthogonal cylinders with the radiuses R_0 and r_0 intersect while the distance between the two axes is h_0. Cylindrical coordinate is established with z-axis along the axis of the larger cylinder and x-axis along the axis of the smaller cylinder. The axis directions are shown above.

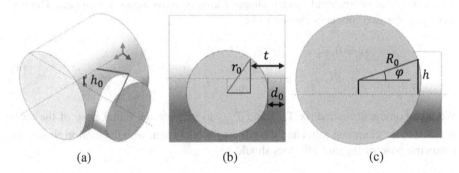

(a)   (b)   (c)

Fig. 1. The intersecting curve. (a) The intersection curve occurs when two cylinders intersect each other, which is described in the cylindrical coordinate. The distance between the two axes is h_0. A point on the intersection curve and the vertical lines to the axes are showed. (b) and (c) show the front view and the left view of the workpiece. (Color figure online)

As the intersection curve occurs when two cylinders intersect each other, we can describe it in the cylindrical coordinate. Points are designated by $[r \quad \varphi \quad z]$, which represents the distance from the z-axis, the rotation about the z-axis and the displacement along the z-axis.

The curve with $t \in [d_0 \quad d_0 + r_0]$ and $h \geq 0$ is discussed. Every point on the curve locates on the surface of the larger cylinder with $r = R_0$. The z coordinates of the points on the curve range from d_0 to $d_0 + r_0$. The point on the curve satisfies the geometric constraints as shown in Fig. 1. The φ coordinate is $\arcsin \frac{h - h_0}{R_0}$, where $h = \sqrt{r_0^2 - (r_0 - t + d_0)^2}$. Therefore, the curve can be described as

$$r = R_0, \varphi = \arcsin\frac{h - h_0}{R_0}, z = t, t \in (d_0, d_0 + r_0) \tag{1}$$

To obtain this curve, the clamping robot and the grinding robot execute the following trajectories

$$r_i = f_{r,i}(t), \varphi_i = f_{\varphi,i}(t), z_i = f_{z,i}(t), i = 1, 2 \tag{2}$$

$i = 1$ indicates the trajectory of the end effect of the clamping robot and $i = 2$ for end effect of the grinding robot. r, φ, z represent the movement along the direction from the current point on the curve to the axis of the larger cylinder, the rotation about the z-axis and the movement along the z-axis respectively.

An intersection trajectory is supposed to be generated by the relative motion between the end effectors in the grinding robot and in the clamping robot. The physical model of the relative movement between the two end effector is

$$r = f_{r,2}(t) - f_{r,1}(t) = R_0, \varphi = f_{\varphi,2}(t) - f_{\varphi,1}(t) = \arctan\frac{h - h_0}{R_0}$$
$$z = f_{z,2}(t) - f_{z,1}(t) = t, t \in (d_0, d_0 + r_0) \tag{3}$$

To simplify the geometrical model, simple forms of movements are chosen. The trajectory of the two robots is chosen to be

$$r_1 = 0, \varphi_1 = f_{\varphi,1}(t), z_1 = f_{z,1}(t)$$
$$r_2 = R_0, \varphi_2 = \arctan\frac{h - h_0}{R_0} + f_{\varphi,1}(t), z_2 = t + f_{z,1}(t) \tag{4}$$

We take homogeneous matrix $T_{c,t,0}$ and $T_{g,t,0}$ to indicate the initial pose of the tools attached to the clamping robot and the grinding robot. Then, with the motion above, the following pose of the end effectors should be

$$T_{c,t,t}^{c,t,0} = T_{c,t,0}^{c,t,0} \cdot \text{trans}(0, 0, z_1) \cdot \text{rot}(z, \varphi_1)$$
$$T_{g,t,t}^{c,t,0} = T_{g,t,0}^{c,t,0} \cdot \text{trans}(0, 0, z_2) \cdot \text{rot}(z, \varphi_2) \tag{5}$$

It is noteworthy that only the position vector makes sense. By now, we can generate the trajectory with the initial pose and the simple movements of one end effector.

Actually, this method provides a practical way to generate the intersection curve in the scenario where the position is requested only. After getting the initial position, the clamping robot and the grinding robot are supposed to execute movements in the tool coordinate, which is the basic function of most robots. Then there is no longer need to carry out calibration of the two robots' relative base coordinate system, providing more convenience to the planning progress of the dual-robot system.

2.2 Cooperation Rotation Planning Based on Geometric Constrain

Meanwhile, the posture makes a lot of sense in the grinding process and ought to be determined. The axis of the tool can be determined with respect to the law vectors of the two cylinders at the current point on the intersection curve. In Fig. 1, the red and the blue lines go in the directions of the two law vectors respectively. Thus it is convenient to get the two law vectors, which are $l_1 = (\, R_0 \quad \varphi \quad 0\,)$ for the red line and $l_2 = (\, h \quad \frac{\pi}{2} \quad t - r_0 - d_0 \,)$ for the blue one, both in the cylindrical coordinate.

It will be easy to transform the two into the descriptions in the Cartesian coordinates and get the rotation matrixes. However, subsequent transformations will be coupled and complex if the clamping robot acts but not along or around the z-axis. Hence, some simple forms of movements have been chosen above as (4). Only the motion about the z-axis makes a difference to l_1 and l_2. Thus, the two vectors should be $l_1 = (\, R_0 \quad \varphi + f_{\varphi,1}(t) \quad 0\,)$ and $l_2 = (\, h \quad \frac{\pi}{2} + f_{\varphi,1}(t) \quad t - r_0 - d_0 \,)$, piled up by the motions of clamping robot.

Next, it is an essential step to convey the representative form in the cylindrical coordinate to the form in the Cartesian coordinate. A vector of $(\, r \quad \theta \quad z\,)$ in cylindrical coordinate is equivalent to $(\, r\cos\theta \quad r\sin\theta \quad z\,)$ in Cartesian coordinate. Thus in the Cartesian coordinates, the two vectors can be represented as

$$
\begin{aligned}
l_1 &= \big(\, R_0 \cos\big(\varphi + f_{\varphi,1}(t)\big) \quad R_0 \sin\big(\varphi + f_{\varphi,1}(t)\big) \quad 0\,\big) \\
l_2 &= \big(\, h\cos\big(\tfrac{\pi}{2} + f_{\varphi,1}(t)\big) \quad h\sin\big(\tfrac{\pi}{2} + f_{\varphi,1}(t)\big) \quad t - r_0 - d_0 \,\big)
\end{aligned}
\tag{6}
$$

As for the tool attached to the grinding robot, its z-axis is determined by l_1 and l_2. A general way to get the direction of Z-axis is

$$
l_z = a l_1 + b l_2 + c l_1 \times l_2
\tag{7}
$$

a and b represent the distance of the tool to the two cylinders, while c is chosen to follow the curve direction and avoid collision. There are obvious physical implications of the three parameters. l_x is determined according to the tool structure, which, if there are no special constraints, can be solved by restricting the axis to have no projection on global y-axis. l_y can be obtained by evaluates the cross product of z-axis and x-axis. The rotation matrix is thus $R_{g,t,t}^{c,t,0} = \begin{bmatrix} l_x^T & l_y^T & l_z^T \end{bmatrix}$.

By now, we have the movements and directions of the two robots determined in the cylindrical coordinate and the trajectory in the Cartesian coordinates can be determined accordingly.

2.3 The Motion Planning of the Dual Robots

In Sects. 2.1 and 2.2, the position and the rotation with respect to the initial tool coordinate are obtained respectively and the trajectory is completely determined thus. To carry out the trajectory planning in the joint space of the robot, it is essential to carry out coordinate transformation. A general dual-robot system is shown in Fig. 2.

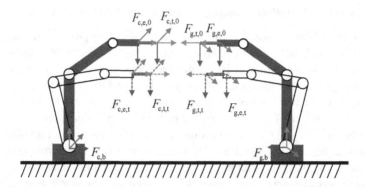

Fig. 2. The Dual robot grinding system. Some significant coordinate systems are indicated. T_j^i indicates the transformation matrix from $\{i\}$ to $\{j\}$. Here, 'c' means 'clamping robot', 'g' means 'grinding robot', 'e' means 'end effect', 't' means 'tool'. '0' indicates the initial position and 't' indicates the immediate position at time 't'.

On the base of previous work, we can obtain $T_{g,t,t}^{c,t,0}$ and $T_{c,t,t}^{c,t,0}$, which mean the descriptions of the tool of the grinding robot and the tool of the clamping robot in the initial tool coordinate of the clamping robot at time 't'. Then, the $T_{c,e,t}^{c,b}$ and $T_{g,e,t}^{g,b}$ can be obtained by Eq. (8) and (9)

$$T_{c,e,t}^{c,b} = T_{c,t,0}^{c,b} T_{c,t,t}^{c,t,0} T_{c,e,t}^{c,t,t} \tag{8}$$

$$T_{g,e,t}^{g,b} = T_{c,b}^{g,b} T_{c,t,0}^{c,b} T_{g,t,t}^{c,t,0} T_{g,e,t}^{g,t,t} \tag{9}$$

For (8) and (9), $T_{c,t,0}^{c,b}$ is given by the initial pose, $T_{c,e,t}^{c,t,t}$ and $T_{g,e,t}^{g,t,t}$ are constant and determined by the structure of the tool, $T_{g,t,t}^{c,t,0}$ and $T_{c,t,t}^{c,t,0}$ are determined by (5) and the method to calibrating $T_{c,b}^{g,b}$ has been widely researched. Finally, the inverse kinematics are employed to calculate the joint displacements.

3 Comparison Study of Single Robotic Grinding and Dual Robotic Grinding

This paper uses Matlab Robotic Toolbox as the tool to verify the validity of the method and provides the comparison of the single robot and the dual robots system in performing the grinding test. A dual-robot system with two UR5 robots are established to execute the task and the DH parameters are listed in Table 1. The single-robot system and the dual-robot system are shown in Fig. 3 with an intersection curve presented as well.

Table 1. The DH parameters of UR5.

Joint i	α_i (rad)	a_i (m)	d_i (m)	θ_i (rad)
1	$\pi/2$	0	0.08920	θ_1
2	0	-0.42500	0	θ_2
3	0	-0.39243	0	θ_3
4	$\pi/2$	0	0.10900	θ_4
5	$-\pi/2$	0	0.09300	θ_5
6	0	0	0.08200	θ_6

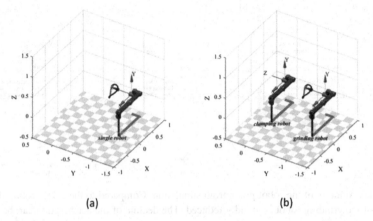

(a)   (b)

Fig. 3. The single-robot system and the dual-robot system. An intersection curve is presented as well of which the red part is planned in the previous chapters. (Color figure online)

In the simulation, the intersection curve is generated by the intersection of two cylinders, whose radiuses are 37.5 mm and 25 mm. The distance between the axes is 5 mm. The initial positions of the workpiece and the duration remain unchanged in the single-robot simulation and the dual-robot simulation. Other system parameters, such as the transformations of the two robot base coordinate system, are determined according to the actual experimental platform. The intersection curve is generated and the joint value is recorded. In the dual robot system, the movements of the clamping robot and the grinding robot are chosen to be

$$r_1 = 0, z_1 = 0, \varphi_1 = -\arctan\frac{h - h_0}{R_0}$$
$$r_2 = 0, z_2 = t, \varphi_3 = 0 \tag{10}$$

The velocity of the joint is shown in Fig. 4. As the figure indicates, the joint velocity is grandly reduced especially for the first joint, with a maximal reduction of 74.31%. Velocity is a key factor affecting the robot performance, especially for the power consumption and the stability. Excessive joint velocity can also lead to heat and additional energy consumption. Damages and danger may be caused to the robot and users, even. Thus, the dual-robot system, with proper collaboration and planning, can be more efficient and safer than a single robot when performing tasks. Additionally, the maximum acceleration is reduced for most joint, with a maximal reduction of 76.68%, which enhances the system stability and is essential to reduce machining vibration and improve machining quality.

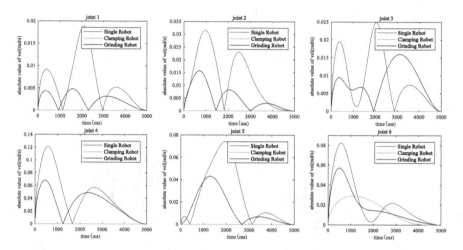

Fig. 4. The velocity of the robot joints from simulation. Compared to the single robot, the joint velocity of the grinding robot is grandly reduced. The decline of the acceleration can be figured out obviously.

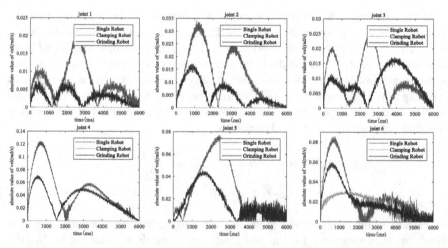

Fig. 5. The velocity of the robot joints from experiments. The simulation and the experiment provide nearly the same positive results, demonstrating the advantage of the dual-robot system and the validity of the proposed planning method.

An experiment was also conducted in our laboratory. The emulation system above shares the same configuration with the dual-robot system. As shown in Fig. 6, an off-line planning is carried out. Though the workpiece were not actually machined, an intersection curve is obviously generated on the surface. The velocity was recorded and illustrated in Fig. 5 after filtered. The simulation and the experiment provide nearly the same positive results, demonstrating the advantage of the dual-robot system and the validity of the proposed planning method. However, dual-robot system requires twice the cost and additional work such as the calibration procedure for the two robots, which bring limits to the widespread use of the advanced system. The robot joints vibrated somehow because we took position control by imputing discrete position points in the experiment. Further, velocity control can be employed to eliminate the vibration.

Fig. 6. Dual robotic machining system. One UR5 holds a pipe and a grinding tool is attached to the end effector of the other.

4   Conclusion

This paper has proposed an automatic programming method for the dual-robot system to complete the intersection curve grinding task, where the two robots perform simple motion simultaneously. Simple movement can be chosen for the clamping robot or the grinding robot and the movement of the other can be automatically generated. The methods to calculate the rotation matrix with the law victories of the two cylinders are raised. A simulation and experiments are carried out to verify the validity of the method.

The proposed method makes full use of the flexibility of dual-robot system, presenting a new method for cooperative planning, which improves the performance of the robot system. The intersection curve is described in the cylindrical coordinate and spited into two motions, which are performed by the two robot respectively. As a result, trajectories of the two robots become smoother and more simple compared to that of the single robot. The velocity is grandly reduced and the acceleration becomes much more smooth, which leads to the enhancement of efficiency and stability. The simulation and the experiment results confirm that conclusion with the joints acting in a smooth and steady way.

The dual-robot system can be useful for other complex curves due to its excellent flexibility and the automatic programming method presented provides the foundation for dual-robot system with more convenience in motion planning. Additionally, other issues such as force controlling and error compensation should be taken into account in future research.

Acknowledgements. Research supported by the National Key Research and Development Program of China under Grant 2017YFB1301504 and the National Science Foundation of China under Grant 91748204.

References

1. Tie, Z., Fan, O.: Offline motion planning and simulation of two-robot welding coordination. Front. Mech. Eng. **7**(1), 81–92 (2012)
2. Gan, Y., Dai, X.: Base frame calibration for coordinated industrial robots. Robot. Auton. Syst. **59**(7–8), 563–570 (2011)
3. Lu, Z., Xu, C., Pan, Q., et al.: Kinematic constraint analysis in a twin-robot system for curved-surface nondestructive testing. Ind. Robot Int. J. **43**(2), 172–180 (2016)
4. Caccavale, F., Natale, C., Siciliano, B., Villani, L.: Quaternion-based impedance control for dual-robot cooperation. In: Hollerbach, J.M., Koditschek, D.E. (eds.) Robotics Research, pp. 59–66. Springer, London (2000). https://doi.org/10.1007/978-1-4471-0765-1_8
5. Shi, L., Tian, X., Zhang, C.: Automatic programming for industrial robot to weld intersecting pipes. Int. J. Adv. Manuf. Technol. **81**(9–12), 2099–2107 (2015)
6. Chen, C., Hu, S., He, D., Shen, J.: An approach to the path planning of tube-sphere intersection welds with the robot dedicated to J-groove joints. Robot. Comput. Integr. Manuf. **29**(4), 41–48 (2013)

Virtual and Augmented Reality

A HoloLens Based Augmented Reality Navigation System for Minimally Invasive Total Knee Arthroplasty

Li Wang[1], Zewen Sun[2], Xiaohui Zhang[1], Zhen Sun[1],
and Junchen Wang[1,3] (✉) iD

[1] School of Mechanical Engineering and Automation, Beihang University,
Beijing 100191, China
wangjunchen@buaa.edu.cn
[2] Knee Surgery Department of the Institute of Sports Medicine,
Peking University Third Hospital, Beijing 100191, China
[3] Beijing Advanced Innovation Center for Biomedical Engineering,
Beihang University, Beijing 100191, China

Abstract. In minimally invasive total knee arthroplasty (MIS-TKA), it is difficult to obtain a global vision of the surgical site in the course of surgery without using X-ray imaging, which brings radiation hazard. To provide the surgeon with accurate image guidance, a Microsoft HoloLens Head-Mounted Display (HMD) based augmented reality approach is proposed. This approach mixes the patient's virtual models with the reality by obtaining the spatial transformations via HoloLens calibration and image registration. It employs the HoloLens and a custom-made binocular camera to overlay the patient's pre-operative CT image onto the physician's field of view by combining a hand-eye calibration method and a Sample Consensus Initial Alignment (SAC-IA) based Iterative Closest Point (ICP) registration algorithm. Using the methods above, the preoperative anatomical model of the patient's knee together with the virtual surgical tool's path can be displayed at correct location in the view of HoloLens. Experiments show that the final overlay error was evaluated to be within 3 mm. The results have shown the potential use of the HoloLens to provide minimally invasive total knee arthroplasties with real-time intuitive surgical visualization without introducing any X-ray radiation.

Keywords: Augmented reality · Surgical navigation · HoloLens ·
Minimally invasive total knee arthroplasty

1 Introduction

With the development of medical image processing technology, in the image guided surgery (IGS) [1], augmented reality (AR) technology has gradually been applied as a new navigation means. Augmented reality navigation can help doctors get accurate

L. Wang and Z. Sun—Equal contributors.

image information of the surgical site without introducing harmful X-ray radiation. In 2010, Sugimoto et al. [2] projected the patient's preoperative medical image onto the patient's body surface to help the doctor obtain the patient's anatomical information. However, this method limits the scope of the surgery and has occlusion problems. At present, the research and experiments on augmented reality surgery navigation are basically based on the Microsoft HoloLens. In 2018, Gregory et al. [3] demonstrated the feasibility of HoloLens for surgical navigation with a shoulder surgery. Pratt et al. [4] used the interactive functions provided by HoloLens to superimpose the virtual model obtained by preoperative scanning on the surgical site and completed 6 limb reconstruction operations. However, they did not propose a reliable method of spatial registration to ensure that the virtual data was aligned with the actual surgical site of the patient. Microsoft has also developed several HoloLens applications for medical treatment [5, 6]. However, they are basically placed in space for educational instructional purposes.

Total knee arthroplasty (TKA) is currently one of the most efficient ways to treat knee joint diseases. Traditional surgery has a problem of large trauma. In contrast, minimally invasive total knee arthroplasty (MIS-TKA) has a tendency to develop muscle vascular damage to patients [7] and gradually become a development trend. However, the difficulty and risk of surgery are increased due to the narrow field of view of the surgical site. In this regard, augmented reality navigation is a very suitable solution.

In this paper, we present an augmented reality navigation system for MIS-TKA based on Microsoft HoloLens. The system can overlay the virtual model in the field of view accurately via holographic space calibration and image registration.

2 Method

2.1 System Overview

Figure 1 illustrates the overall of the system. The system consists of three steps: the calibration of the holographic space, the alignment between medical images and dummy models and the visualization based on augmented reality. In the calibration procedure, multiple groups of the poses, i.e., HoloLens relative to the holographic spatial coordinate system and a vision marker attached to the HoloLens relative to the binocular camera, are simultaneously collected. The transformation matrix between the holographic spatial coordinate system of the HoloLens and the binocular camera system can be obtained by solving a least squares problem. In the alignment procedure, the spatial relationship between the CT image space and the binocular camera system can be obtained using a SAC-IA based ICP algorithm. Due to the weak computing power of HoloLens' CPU, all work involving large amount of computation, such as corner detection and image registration, was done on a desktop computer. The computer transmits the final calculation results to HoloLens via network communication. At last, the results were used to overlay virtual models in the correct positions and orientations respectively in the view of HoloLens.

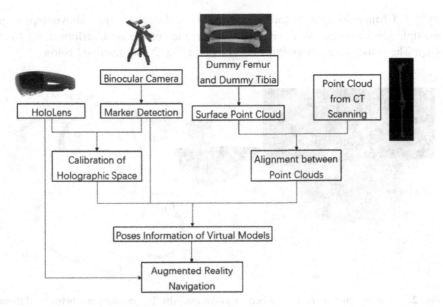

Fig. 1. System overview.

2.2 Calibration of the Holographic Space

There is a global coordinate system, C_{HG}, of holographic space for a holographic application in HoloLens and a local coordinate system, C_{HL}, representing the pose of HoloLens itself. In order to overlay the virtual model in the correct position and orientation in holographic space, it is necessary to obtain a conversion transform relationship between the holographic space and the real space, which is actually represented by a binocular camera coordinate system in this study. In 2018, Wu et al. [8] used the HoloLens camera and the RGB-D sensor to acquire the same QR-Code Marker image and identify its pose respectively, obtaining the relationship between the coordinate systems of the HoloLens camera and the RGB-D sensor. However, the position and orientation of the resulting superimposed virtual model simply appears to be correct in the image captured by the HoloLens camera. Due to the insufficient of HoloLens, the pose of the virtual model is not accurate for users wearing HoloLens.

In this study, a vision marker and a binocular camera were used to calibrate the holographic coordinate system. The marker consisting of several X points is attached to HoloLens (see Fig. 2). The X points in the picture captured by the binocular camera can be located in the three-dimensional space in real time, using a machine learning approach proposed by our previous work [9]. Furthermore, the pose of the marker coordinate system described by the X points relative to the binocular camera coordinate system can also be obtained.

The calibration steps are described as follows: First, place the HoloLens in the field of view of the binocular camera. The pose of the marker coordinate system, C_{HM}, relative to the binocular camera coordinate system, C_C, is recorded and denoted by $^{HM}_C T$. At the same time, record the pose of C_{HL} relative to C_{HG}, which is denoted by $^{HG}_{HL}T$. Change the position and orientation of HoloLens and repeat above steps to get multiple sets of poses. What we need to get is the conversion transform from C_C to C_{HG}. The conversion relationships are shown in Fig. 2 and described below:

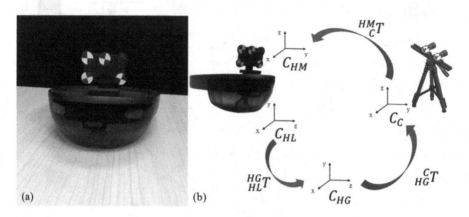

(a)   (b)

Fig. 2. (a) A vision marker is attached to HoloLens. (b) The conversions between different coordinate systems in the calibration procedure.

$$^{HG}_{HL}T^{-1}_i \cdot {}^{HG}_{HL}T_j \cdot {}^{C}_{HG}T = {}^{C}_{HG}T \cdot {}^{HM}_{C}T_i \cdot {}^{HM}_{C}T^{-1}_j \tag{1}$$

where $^{HG}_{HL}T_i$ and $^{HG}_{HL}T_j$ are the $^{HG}_{HL}T$ in the group i and group j respectively. $^{HM}_{C}T_i$ and $^{HM}_{C}T_j$ are interpreted in a similar manner. Then a nonlinear optimal robot hand-eye calibration method proposed by our previous work [10] is used to calculate the $^{C}_{HG}T$.

For some reasons we will discuss later, the result obtained from the calibration is inaccurate. We correct the error by aligning virtual cross models with the x points of a visual marker in the view of HoloLens via network communication between the desktop computer and HoloLens (see Fig. 3). It brings a small change to the translation part of $^{C}_{HG}T$ and only costs dozens of seconds.

2.3 Surface Data Alignment

In our experiment, a dummy femur and a dummy tibia were used to simulate the knee joint of a patient. The dummy models were made by 3D printing using data from a CT scan of a patient. The medical image from CT data are also used for augmented reality visualization. Therefore, the CT coordinate system, C_{CT}, should be integrated with C_{HG} or C_C by image registration. The traditional registration method, the Iterative Closest Point (ICP) algorithm, was proposed by Besl and McKay [11], and Zhang [12], using rigid transformations and iterative calculations to find the best conversion transform from one coordinate system to another. However, the ICP algorithm often relies on a good initial pose estimation to prevent the solution from getting trapped in local minima. It is necessary to choose a coarse registration algorithm in conjunction with ICP algorithm. In addition to the distance-based method represented by the traditional ICP algorithm, there are some classical algorithms including the feature descriptor-based methods represented by Fast Point Feature Histogram (FPFH) descriptor [13] and the geometry-based methods represented by Super 4PCS [14]. In this paper, the Sample Consensus Initial Alignment (SAC-IA) algorithm is used for initial alignment, and the result is used as the initial pose estimation of ICP to improve its performance. The SAC-IA algorithm finds the matching point pairs by comparing the FPFH feature descriptors of the points from the two point clouds. FPFH is an improved version of the Point Feature Histogram (PFH) [15], which uses normal information to calculate the quad consisting of angles and distance information between each pair of points within a specified range of a specified point as the feature descriptor of the point. As a simplified and improved version of PFH, only the tuple features between one point and its neighbors need to be calculated and the FPFH descriptor of the specified point is the weighted sum of its neighbors' tuples. The Super 4PCS algorithm searches for points matching the four points in the source point cloud in the target point cloud according to the affine invariance to calculate the rigid transformation between the point clouds. In the experimental part of this paper, the performance of the registration method based on the PFH feature descriptor and the Super 4PCS algorithm are also examined.

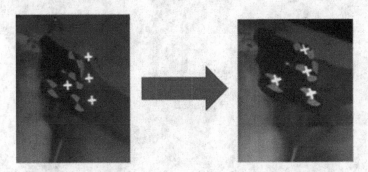

Fig. 3. The process of correcting error of the calibration result.

A vision probe and two vision markers were used to separately acquire the surface point cloud of the dummy femur and the dummy tibia near the joint (see Fig. 4). Taking the alignment of the femur as an example, the tibia is basically the same, a marker is first attached to the femur. In the field of view of the binocular camera, the point cloud of the femur is collected by using the tip of the probe to scribe on the femur's surface [16]. The three-dimensional coordinates of the point cloud are described in the marker coordinate system, denoted by C_{FM}. The real scene and the collected point cloud rendered using OpenGL [17] are shown in Fig. 4.

The point cloud of the dummy femur is used as the source point cloud while the point cloud of the medical image from CT data is used as the target point cloud in the process of the registration. In the SAC-IA procedure, the normal information of each point in the source point cloud and the target point cloud is calculated first according to the three-dimensional information of its all neighbors. The normal information is used to calculate the FPFH descriptors for several selected points in the source point cloud. Then we can find the corresponding points in the target point cloud according to FPFH descriptors and use these matching point pairs to calculate the transformation between the source point cloud and the target point cloud. Using the conversion transform from SAC-IA as the initial pose estimation for the ICP iterations, a satisfying result, $_{CT}^{FM}T$ for the femur or $_{CT}^{TM}T$ for the tibia, will be obtained finally.

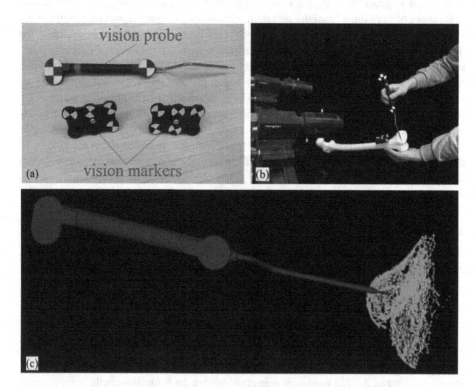

Fig. 4. (a) The vision probe and vision markers. (b) Scene of collecting surface point cloud of the dummy femur. (c) Vision probe model and point cloud rendered using openGL.

2.4   Overlaying Virtual Models

In our study, a virtual femur and a virtual tibia from CT data were overlaid in the view of HoloLens along with the virtual surgical guide model. The relationships between coordinate systems are shown in Fig. 5. Taking the femur as an example, when the two steps above are completed, the virtual model can be transformed into the world coordinate system of HoloLens in the holographic space by the equation as follows:

$$P_{HG} = {}_{HG}^{C}T \cdot {}_{C}^{FM}T \cdot {}_{CT}^{FM}T^{-1} \cdot P_{CT} \qquad (2)$$

where P_{HG} and P_{CT} are the poses of the virtual femur in the holographic world coordinate system and the CT coordinate system respectively. The P_{HG} is used to set the pose of the virtual models with APIs. Then they can be overlaid in the way we want.

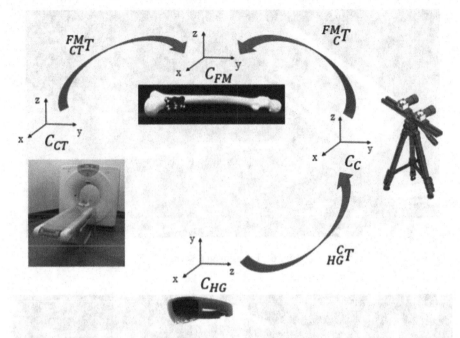

Fig. 5. The conversions between different coordinate systems in the overlay procedure.

3 Experiments and Results

The hardware devices used in the study consisted of a desktop computer, a Microsoft HoloLens and a binocular camera system. The computer is configured with Windows 10 OS, a 64-bit Intel(R) Core(TM) i7-8700 CPU and a Nvidia GTX 1060 GPU while the binocular system consists of two monocular cameras (GS3-U3-41C6M-C) produced by FLIR System. The alignment algorithms were written in C++ using Point Cloud Library (PCL) [18] while the augmented reality application in HoloLens was developed with Unity [19]. The experimental scene is shown in Fig. 6.

3.1 Alignment Evaluation

The SAC-IA algorithm is a parameter-sensitive algorithm. So are the registration method using PFH descriptor and the Super 4PCS algorithm. During the process of alignment, the normal and FPFH information of several selected points in the source point cloud and points in the target point cloud are calculated, according to the coordinates of all neighbor points within a given radius respectively. In our experiment, the final RMSE and time consuming were evaluated given different radius parameters. We stipulate that the search radius parameter used in the process of normal calculations denoted by R_N while in the process of FPFH calculation it is denoted by R_F. For the sake of convenience, we set the two parameters to be equal in our experiment.

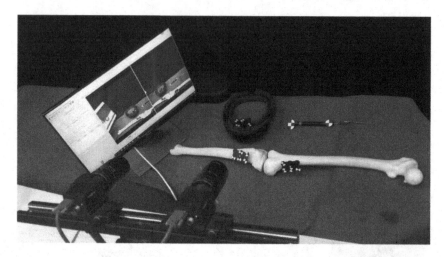

Fig. 6. Experimental scene.

Fig. 7. Example alignment result.

In our experiment, the size of the source point cloud and the target point cloud for the dummy femur are 14704 and 116013 respectively while they are 12791 and 70022 respectively for the dummy tibia. To accelerate the process of alignment, we down-sampled the source point cloud and target point cloud using a 0.3 mm × 0.3 mm 0.3 mm and 0.5 mm × 0.5 mm × 0.5 mm box filter respectively. When the SAC-IA registration is completed, iterative calculations continue using the ICP algorithm until the root mean square error (RMSE) is less than a given threshold, 0.01 mm, or the number of iterations reaches 100. The results of trials for the dummy femur and the dummy tibia, given some groups of radius parameters, are shown in Tables 1 and 2 respectively. Example result is shown in Fig. 7.

The accuracy and time consuming when the PFH-based alignment method and Super 4PCS algorithm are respectively used as the initial alignment method. Table 3 shows the results of two methods in their best performance for the alignment of the femur point clouds.

Table 1. RMSE and time consuming of the alignment for the dummy femur using SAC-IA.

R_N and R_F (mm)	RMSE (mm)	Time (s)
5	18.30	94.8
6	1.08	95.9
9	1.08	105.0
12	1.08	109.4
15	1.08	149.0
18	1.08	207.3
21	1.08	273.5
22	57.95	302.5

Table 2. RMSE and time consuming of the alignment for the dummy tibia using SAC-IA.

R_N and R_F (mm)	RMSE (mm)	Time (s)
4	48.02	53.7
5	1.78	54.0
7	1.78	58.1
9	1.78	65.0
11	1.78	73.2
13	1.78	84.1
14	14.15	89.5

Table 3. RMSE and time consuming of the alignment for the dummy femur using PFH-based method and Super 4PCS respectively.

Methods	RMSE (mm)	Time (s)
PFH-based method	19.07	1311.5
Super 4PCS	14.32	875.4

From Tables 1 and 2 we can see that the available R_N and R_F for SAC-IA range from about 6 to 21 mm for dummy femur and about 5 to 13 mm for dummy tibia. The range is large and the parameters can be slightly adjusted within this range according to the corresponding size of the patient's knee joint. When the parameters are within available range, the alignment method showed good stability and the mean square error were within 2 mm for both femur and tibia. Time consumption is also within acceptable limits. From Table 3 we can see that the performance of PFH-based method and Super 4PCS are far worse than the SAC-IA algorithm, both in terms of accuracy and speed.

3.2 Overlay Accuracy

When all the coordinate systems are integrated, the computer transmits the final poses of the femur, the tibia and their surgical guides, which is used to determine the surgical plane, to HoloLens via telecommunication to overlay virtual models. In our experiment, the accuracy of overlay was evaluated. The distances between the true osteotomy planes and the position of the overlaid virtual surgical guides were measured to evaluate the accuracy of overlay. The overlay errors for the femur and tibia are both about 2.5 mm, which meets the clinical surgical requirement. The results are shown in Fig. 8.

4   Discussion

In MIS-TKA, the wound area of the operation is small. In addition, the occlusion caused by ligament is also a problem. These factors were fully considered in this experiment, and surface point clouds of the femur and tibia were obtained as much as possible according to the actual surgical criteria. However, the problems that may be encountered in actual surgery are multifaceted and difficult to predict and the evaluation of the methods used in this experiment needs further verification in clinical surgery. At the same time, limited by the processing frequency of the image on the computer, the process of collecting the point cloud often takes several minutes to ensure that the density of the point cloud is large enough. Switching to a better performing computer may help.

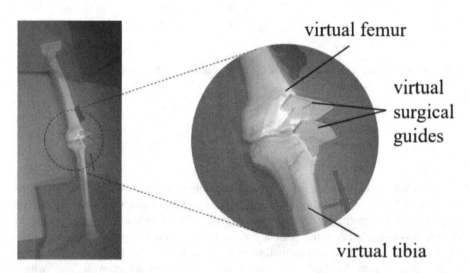

Fig. 8. Overlay result.

On the other hand, HoloLens uses Simultaneous Localization and Mapping (SLAM) to dynamically recognize the surrounding environment. As a result, the world coordinate system of the holographic space may drift when HoloLens' perception of the environment is refreshed. Even if a virtual model is statically overlaid in the view of HoloLens, its position may change over time. A solution is to add a world anchor to the virtual model, using provided functional interfaces. Once the model is added to a world anchor, it will no longer moves unless the space anchor is removed first. Since the patient's legs are fixed during the surgery, it is a viable solution.

5 Conclusion

This paper presents an augmented reality navigation system based on Microsoft HoloLens for MIS-TKA. The system can provide the doctor with accurate location information when the field of view at the surgical site is narrow. The main methods used in the system, including calibration, registration, and augmented reality visualization, are introduced. Experiments were performed to evaluate the system in terms of accuracy. Experiment results show the effectiveness of the system. The surgical robot will be integrated into the system in further research.

Acknowledgement. This work was partially supported by National Key R&D Program of China (Grant No. 2017YFB1303004).

References

1. Traub, J., Sielhorst, T., Heining, S.M., et al.: Advanced display and visualization concepts for image guided surgery. J. Disp. Technol. **4**(4), 483–490 (2008)
2. Sugimoto, M., Yasuda, H., Koda, K., et al.: Image overlay navigation by markerless surface registration in gastrointestinal, hepatobiliary and pancreatic surgery. J. Hepato-Biliary-Pancreat. Sci. **17**(5), 629–636 (2010)
3. Gregory, T.M., Gregory, J., Sledge, J., et al.: Surgery guided by mixed reality: presentation of a proof of concept. Acta Orthop. **89**(5), 480–483 (2018)
4. Pratt, P., Ives, M., Lawton, G., et al.: Through the HoloLens looking glass: augmented reality for extremity reconstruction surgery using 3D vascular models with perforating vessels. Eur. Radiol. Exp. **2**(1), 2 (2018)
5. HoloLens Mixed Reality Surgery, Holographic Augmented Mixed Reality Navigation. https://www.youtube.com/watch?v=qLGD570I1OE. Accessed 20 Apr 2019
6. Holographic Assisted Spine Surgery with HoloLens. https://www.youtube.com/watch?v=zC5097mA9f4. Accessed 20 Apr 2019
7. Tzatzairis, T., Fiska, A., Ververidis, A., et al.: Minimally invasive versus conventional approaches in total knee replacement/arthroplasty: a review of the literature. J. Orthop. **15**(2), 459–466 (2018)
8. Wu, M.L., Chien, J.C., Wu, C.T., et al.: An augmented reality system using improved-iterative closest point algorithm for on-patient medical image visualization. Sensors **18**(8), 2505 (2018)
9. Wang, J., Ji, X., Zhang, X., et al.: Real-time robust individual X point localization for stereoscopic tracking. Pattern Recogn. Lett. **112**, 138–144 (2018)
10. Wang, J., Wang, T., Yang, Y., Hu, L.: Nonlinear optimal robot hand-eye calibration. J. Xian Jiaotong Univ. **45**(9), 15–10 (2011)
11. Besl, P.J., Mckay, N.D.: A method for registration of 3-D shapes. IEEE Trans. Pattern Anal. Mach. Intell. **14**(2), 239–256 (2002)

12. Zhang, Z.: Iterative point matching for registration of free-form curves and surfaces. Int. J. Comput. Vis. **13**(2), 119–152 (1994)
13. Radu, R.B., Nico, B., Michael, B.: Fast Point Feature Histograms (FPFH) for 3D registration. In: 2009 IEEE International Conference on Robotics and Automation, Kobe, pp. 3212–3217. IEEE (2009)
14. Nicolas, M., Dror, A., Niloy, J.M.: Super 4PCS fast global pointcloud registration via smart indexing. Comput. Graph. Forum **33**(5), 205–215 (2014)
15. Rusu, R.B., Blodow, N., Marton, Z.C., Beetz, M.: Aligning point cloud views using persistent feature histograms. In: 2008 IEEE/RSJ International Conference on Intelligent Robots and Systems, Nice, pp. 3384–3391. IEEE (2008)
16. Hu, Y., Wang, T.-M., Wang, J.-C., et al.: A video-based anterior cruciate ligament reconstruction navigation and evaluation system. Chin. J. Biomed. Eng. **28**(2), 231–237 (2009)
17. OpenGL. https://www.opengl.org. Accessed 22 Apr 2019
18. PCL-Point Cloud Library, http://pointclouds.org. Accessed 24 Apr 2019
19. Unity. https://unity.com. Accessed 24 Apr 2019

R-3RPS Robot-Based Mathematical Modeling for a Military Flight Simulator

Cristhian Guerrón[1], Wilbert G. Aguilar[1,2,3(✉)],
Rolando P. Reyes Ch.[1], Nicolás Pinto[1], Santiago Chamorro[1],
and Manolo Paredes[1]

[1] CICTE, Universidad de las Fuerzas Armadas ESPE, Sangolquí, Ecuador
wgaguilar@espe.edu.ec
[2] FIS, Escuela Politécnica Nacional, Quito, Ecuador
[3] GREC, Universitat Politècnica de Catalunya, Barcelona, Spain

Abstract. In the present article we explain the analytical deduction of the kinematic model of a flight simulator, based on a 3 RPS parallel robot with rotation of its lower base, through the resolution of the inverse and direct kinematic problems. The trajectories of the illusions of the simulator were generated with the use of interpolation of speeds and angular accelerations of the final effector, in addition to the operating specifications of the manipulator. For the verification of results, an interface was implemented with the use of MATLAB to simulate the trajectories generated in the obtained model and to verify the analytical kinematic relations proposed together with the simulation in ANSYS. The results obtained from the interface in comparison to the mechanical simulation showed a minimum margin of error between them that reached 0.1% in the worst case at the position of the upper vertices of the simulator.

Keywords: Kinematic model · 3D simulation · Human computer interaction

1 Introduction

The flight simulators have remained for several years in the field of aeronautics [1]; the use of them became an integral part of all airline business operations, for the safety and effectiveness of pilot training before sailing on aircraft real [2]. The designs of flight simulators have advanced from ground-based devices capable of reacting to aerodynamic forces [3], such as the Sanders master device developed in 1910 [4] to virtual reality environments based on the use of parallel manipulators of 3 or 6 degrees of freedom [5]. The function of flight simulators is to recreate visual and vestibular illusions that allow the training of pilots of airlines or armed forces the spatial disorientation produced in real flights [6]. For the development of the simulators are based on parallel manipulators of 3 to 6 degrees of freedom (DoF) [7]. The spatial parallel

This paper is part of the project "Simulador de desorientación espacial para seguridad aérea y entrenamiento de pilotos de las FF.AA" which belongs exclusively to Universidad de las Fuerzas Armadas ESPE. The affiliations of the Universitat Politècnica de Catalunya and Escuela Politècnica Nacional are exclusively of the corresponding author Dr. Wilbert G. Aguilar. The payment of the paper registration was funded exclusively by Universidad de las Fuerzas Armadas ESPE.

© Springer Nature Switzerland AG 2019
H. Yu et al. (Eds.): ICIRA 2019, LNAI 11745, pp. 531–541, 2019.
https://doi.org/10.1007/978-3-030-27529-7_45

robot of 6 DoF is convenient due to the possibility of complete movement and the most used is the Stewart-Gough platform [8], which is based on 6 chains with universal, prismatic and spherical joints, respectively [9], which was developed to be used as a full flight simulator. This work deals with another type of 4 DoF manipulator configuration (3 RPS with rotation) that allows recreating the illusions of a complete flight simulator, which is part of the project with the aim of implementing the simulator with virtual reality [10–14].

The study of kinematics has become an important factor for the analysis of the movement of this type of manipulators, several works reference the inverse kinematic model of the Stewart-Gough platform [15], in which they use the Euler angles method (roll, pitch, yaw) [16], because this methodology facilitates the positioning of a real aircraft together with aerodynamic equations [17]. For this reason in this work, reference is makes to this method to find the inverse kinematics.

The direct kinematics in this application is aimed at calculating the velocities and accelerations of the actuators by setting parameters of these magnitudes in the vertices of the upper base, with the direct geometric method. For the simulation of movements, the trajectories of spatial disorientation illusions are generated by operating specifications of the simulator such as limit positions, maximum velocities and accelerations in the end effector. The need to find this model is bases on the simulation in ANSYS that presents the option of entering parameters of the movement joints of the robot.

2   Related Works

In flight simulators, several works refer to the Stewart-Gough platform and the manipulator 6 RUS [1], which are the most used robots for this type of application, to solve the problem of kinematics in this type of manipulators have used techniques [18] such as of the matrix of rotation by angles of Euler [19], quaternions [20] and the theory of screws [21]. The methods the most used in the literature of kinematic models [22–24] of aircraft is the angles (roll, pitch and yaw), because it allows the positioning of the center of mass of the aerial vehicle by means of rotations and translations through the Cartesian axes [25]. In others documents references are made to the theory of screws because the methodology relates velocities with forces that correlate kinematics with dynamics [26].

For the 3 RPS robots, the researched literature prioritizes the movement restrictions to determine the independent and dependent variables of the input data such as the orientation and coordinates of the final effector point [27], this type of manipulators is limited in comparison to the serial ones [28]. However, for the developed application it fulfills the necessary requirements to recreate the illusions of spatial disorientation. In the case of direct kinematics, the works clearly refer to a particular method, which is of the homogeneous transformations, terminology on which Denavit-Hartenberg [29], is based, in other cases reference is made to the vector formulation [30] that details vector algebra as motion analysis. There are also works that combine the mentioned methods with the kinematic equations typical of the movement of an aircraft.

In this article, the kinematic model is presented in an analytical way by the vector formulation methods in the direct kinematics and the Euler angles for the inverse, in addition to an interface in MATLAB that represents the model obtained to corroborate the simulation in ANSYS [31].

3 Inverse Kinematic Model

The arms of the robot have passive joints that correspond to the spherical and active prismatic, rotational, for the analysis is not taken into account to the passive joints because the position and orientation of these depend on the movement of the active joints that are the ones in charge of the movement in general of the robot. For this reason, the joints taken for the development of the kinematic model are the prismatic and rotational ones located along the arms, in addition to the rotational actuator of the lower base of the simulator [32].

For the analysis the simulator was divided into two parts, one is the robot 3 rps and the other is the lower rotating base, because the transformations made as a function of the angles of roll and pitch cause an angle yaw in the 3-RPS robot. But it is not the yaw that is required in the simulator, the required angle is produced by the rotation of the lower base, reason to solve by means of the subdivision of manipulators the one parallel (3-RPS), while the other is a rotating joint. The same coordinates of the vertices of the triangles of the upper and lower base are defined for both manipulators [32].

Figure 1 shows the location of the lower base vertices (rotating platform) and the upper base (mobile base for the cabin).

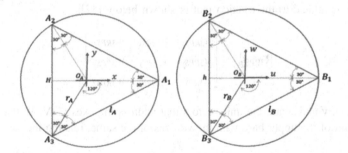

Fig. 1. Coordinates of (a) rotating platform (b) mobile base for the cabin

For the lower base we work with an equilateral triangle inscribed in a circle, for this reason the vertices of this base equidistant to a distance r_A from the center of the circumference (OA) and separated at an angle of 120° between each vertex. For the upper base, we work with an equilateral triangle whose vertices equidistant to a distance r_B from the central point (O$_B$) of this geometric figure and separated at an angle of 120° between each vertex.

As mentioned above, the simulator is divided into two parts: the 3RPS robot and the lower rotating base, as shown in Fig. 2.

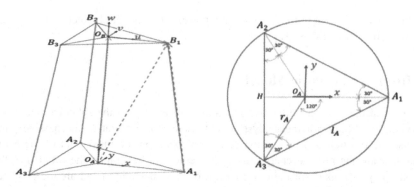

Fig. 2. Robot 3RPS (left), rotating platform (right)

3.1 Inverse Kinematic Modeling of the Robot 3 RPS

For the development of this point, the Euler rotation matrix defined by the angles roll (ϕ), pitch (Θ), yaw (ψ) was used, giving as product the following expression [32]:

$$R_{3RPS}{}_B^A = \begin{bmatrix} c\psi c\theta & c\psi s\theta s\phi - s\psi c\phi & c\psi s\theta c\phi + s\psi s\phi \\ s\psi c\theta & s\psi s\theta s\phi + c\psi c\phi & s\psi s\theta c\phi - c\psi s\phi \\ -s\theta & c\theta s\phi & c\theta c\phi \end{bmatrix} \tag{1}$$

Where c and s represent the trigonometric functions cosine and sine. The proposed expression is related to the rotation matrix shown below [32]:

$$R_{3RPS}{}_B^A = \begin{bmatrix} u_{3RPSx} & v_{3RPSx} & w_{3RPSx} \\ u_{3RPSy} & v_{3RPSy} & w_{3RPSy} \\ u_{3RPSz} & v_{3RPSz} & w_{3RPSz} \end{bmatrix} \tag{2}$$

Where u, v and w are the unit vectors that address the axes U, V, W that join the central point of the upper base with the vertices of the same, relating the two matrices described.

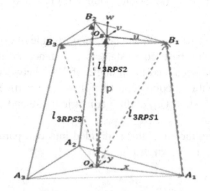

Fig. 3. Vectors for the position of vertices 3RPS

The position of the vertices of the upper base is defined by the vector sum of the vectors of Fig. 3, the expression obtained is shown below:

$$l_{3RPSi} = p + R_{3RPS}{}_{B}^{A} * B_i \tag{3}$$

Where i is the subscript that indicates the vertex number that is worked for this case there are three vertices, l_{3RPSi} is the resulting vector between each vertex B_i with the central point O_A of the lower base, p is the vector between the central points of the lower and upper bases, Bi are the vertices of the upper base.

Resolving (3) the following expressions are reached:

$$l_{3RPS1} = \begin{bmatrix} l_{3RPS1x} \\ l_{3RPS1y} \\ l_{3RPS1z} \end{bmatrix} = \begin{bmatrix} p_x + r_B * u_{3RPSx} \\ p_y + r_B * u_{3RPSy} \\ p_z + r_B * u_{3RPSz} \end{bmatrix} \tag{4}$$

$$l_{3RPS2} = \begin{bmatrix} l_{3RPS2x} \\ l_{3RPS2y} \\ l_{3RPS2z} \end{bmatrix} = \begin{bmatrix} p_x - \frac{1}{2}r_B * u_{3RPSx} + \frac{\sqrt{3}}{2}r_B * v_{3RPSx} \\ p_y - \frac{1}{2}r_B * u_{3RPSy} + \frac{\sqrt{3}}{2}r_B * v_{3RPSy} \\ p_z - \frac{1}{2}r_B * u_{3RPSz} + \frac{\sqrt{3}}{2}r_B * v_{3RPSz} \end{bmatrix} \tag{5}$$

$$l_{3RPS3} = \begin{bmatrix} l_{3RPS3x} \\ l_{3RPS3y} \\ l_{3RPS3z} \end{bmatrix} = \begin{bmatrix} p_x - \frac{1}{2}r_B * u_{3RPSx} - \frac{\sqrt{3}}{2}r_B * v_{3RPSx} \\ p_y - \frac{1}{2}r_B * u_{3RPSy} - \frac{\sqrt{3}}{2}r_B * v_{3RPSy} \\ p_z - \frac{1}{2}r_B * u_{3RPSz} - \frac{\sqrt{3}}{2}r_B * v_{3RPSz} \end{bmatrix} \tag{6}$$

The expression is not yet complete because the part of the rotation of the lower base that is increased at the next point is missing, but the movement restrictions of the robot are defined to define the dependent and independent variables.

3.1.1 Restriction Equations

The movement of this robot has restrictions that limit its mobility, mainly in the arms c_1, c_2, c_3 that connect the vertices A_1B_1, A_2B_2, A_3B_3, which only have mobility along the XZ plane. The arms have a rotated angle of 120° between them.

The restrictions are defined by the following expressions:

$$p_y = -r_B * u_{3RPSy} \tag{7}$$

$$p_x = \frac{1}{2}r_B * \left(u_{3RPSx} - v_{3RPSy}\right) \tag{8}$$

$$v_{3RPSx} = u_{3RPSy} \tag{9}$$

From the expression (9), you can clear the angle yaw (ψ) as a function of the angles roll (Φ) and pitch (θ), leaving as follows:

$$\psi = \text{atan}\left(\frac{sen(\theta) * sen(\phi)}{cos(\phi) + cos(\theta)}\right) \quad (10)$$

3.2   Inverse Kinematic Model of the Rotation of the Lower Base

To complete the inverse kinematic model it is required to increase the rotation around the z axis generated by the rotational articulation movement placed in the center O_A of the lower base, for this expression the same Euler rotation matrix is used but with the use only of the angle of rotation (γ), the matrix is as follows:

$$R_{rB}^A = \begin{bmatrix} cos\gamma & -sen\gamma & 0 \\ sen\gamma & cos\gamma & 0 \\ 0 & 0 & 1 \end{bmatrix} \quad (11)$$

The matrix (11) will multiply the expressions (4), (5), (6) yields the following expressions:

$$l_1 = \begin{bmatrix} l_{1x} \\ l_{1y} \\ l_{1z} \end{bmatrix} = \begin{bmatrix} l_{3RPS1x} * \cos(y) - l_{3RPS1y} * sen(\gamma) \\ l_{3RPS1x} * sen(y) + l_{3RPS1y} * \cos(\gamma) \\ p_z + r_B * u_{3RPSz} \end{bmatrix} \quad (12)$$

$$l_2 = \begin{bmatrix} l_{2x} \\ l_{2y} \\ l_{2z} \end{bmatrix} = \begin{bmatrix} l_{3RPS2x} * \cos(y) - l_{3RPS2y} * sen(\gamma) \\ l_{3RPS2x} * sen(y) + l_{3RPS2y} * \cos(\gamma) \\ p_z - \frac{1}{2} r_B * u_{3RPSz} + \frac{\sqrt{3}}{2} r_B * v_{3RPSz} \end{bmatrix} \quad (13)$$

$$l_3 = \begin{bmatrix} l_{3x} \\ l_{3y} \\ l_{3z} \end{bmatrix} = \begin{bmatrix} l_{3RPS3x} * \cos(y) - l_{3RPS3y} * sen(\gamma) \\ l_{3RPS3x} * sen(y) + l_{3RPS3y} * \cos(\gamma) \\ p_z - \frac{1}{2} r_B * u_{3RPSz} - \frac{\sqrt{3}}{2} r_B * v_{3RPSz} \end{bmatrix} \quad (14)$$

For the calculation of the lengths of the arms, it is necessary to apply the equation of distance between two points that are the vertices of the bases superior l_i and inferior a_i expressing in the following way:

$$c_1 = \sqrt{d_1 + 2d_2 - 2r_A p_x - 2r_A r_B u_{3RPSx}} \quad (15)$$

$$c_2 = \sqrt{d_1 - d_2 + d_3 + r_A\left(p_x - \sqrt{3}p_y\right) - d_6(d_4 - d_5)} \quad (16)$$

$$c_3 = \sqrt{d_1 - d_2 - d_3 + r_A\left(p_x + \sqrt{3}p_y\right) - d_6(d_4 + d_5)} \qquad (17)$$

Being the constants:

$$d_1 = p_x^2 + p_y^2 + p_z^2 + r_A^2 + r_B^2 \qquad (18)$$

$$d_2 = r_B\left(p_x u_{3RPSx} + p_y u_{3RPSy} + p_z u_{3RPSz}\right) \qquad (19)$$

$$d_3 = \sqrt{3}r_B\left(p_x v_{3RPSx} + p_y v_{3RPSy} + p_z v_{3RPSz}\right) \qquad (20)$$

$$d_4 = u_{3RPSx} + 3v_{3RPSy} \qquad (21)$$

$$d_5 = \sqrt{3}v_{3RPSx} + \sqrt{3}u_{3RPSy} \qquad (22)$$

$$d_6 = \frac{1}{2}r_A r_B \qquad (23)$$

The values of c_1, c_2, c_3 are the total lengths of the arms 1, 2, 3, respectively, but the required length is of the prismatic actuator, so the obtained values are subtracted from the fixed value of the actuators, which is 1191.2 mm as follows:

$$e_i = c_i - 1191.2 \qquad (24)$$

For the calculation of the angles of the lower part of the arms, the law of cosines between the upper and lower vertices is used with the lower center point as follows:

$$\alpha_1 = \mathrm{acos}\left((l_1^2 - c_1^2 - a_1^2)/-2a_1c_1\right) \qquad (25)$$

$$\alpha_2 = \mathrm{acos}\left((l_2^2 - c_2^2 - a_2^2)/-2a_2c_2\right) \qquad (26)$$

$$\alpha_3 = \mathrm{acos}\left((l_3^2 - c_3^2 - a_3^2)/-2a_3c_3\right) \qquad (27)$$

In this case, we work with temporal velocities and accelerations that are obtained from the first and second derivatives as a function of the time of the expressions (12), (13), (14), denoted as $\dot{l}_1, \dot{l}_2, \dot{l}_3, \ddot{l}_1, \ddot{l}_2, \ddot{l}_3$. These are data are inputs for direct kinematics.

4 Direct Kinematic Model

This model is used to obtain the speeds and accelerations of the active actuators of the simulator, from the inverse kinematic magnitudes, for this, it requires expressions that describe the position of the vertices of the upper base as a function of translations and rotations, of the actuators, reaching the following expressions:

$$l_1 = \begin{bmatrix} l_{1x} \\ l_{1y} \\ l_{1z} \end{bmatrix} = \begin{bmatrix} (r_A - l_1\cos(\alpha_1)) * \cos(y) \\ (r_A - l_1\cos(\alpha_1)) * \sin(y) \\ l_1\sin(\alpha_1) \end{bmatrix} \tag{28}$$

$$l_2 = \begin{bmatrix} l_{2x} \\ l_{2y} \\ l_{2z} \end{bmatrix} = \begin{bmatrix} (r_A - l_2\cos(\alpha_2)) * \cos(y + 120°) \\ (r_A - l_2\cos(\alpha_2)) * \sin(y + 120°) \\ l_2\sin(\alpha_2) \end{bmatrix} \tag{29}$$

$$l_3 = \begin{bmatrix} l_{3x} \\ l_{3y} \\ l_{3z} \end{bmatrix} = \begin{bmatrix} (r_A - l_3\cos(\alpha_3)) * \cos(y + 240°) \\ (r_A - l_3\cos(\alpha_3)) * \sin(y + 240°) \\ l_3\sin(\alpha_3) \end{bmatrix} \tag{30}$$

Deriving the obtained expressions, $\dot{l}_1, \dot{l}_2, \dot{l}_3, \ddot{l}_1, \ddot{l}_2, \ddot{l}_3$ are obtained, which are equated with the resultants of the inverse kinematics and forming a system of equations that allows finding the velocities and accelerations of the actuators.

With the results obtained you can find operating parameters of the actuators from data of the final effector, the next step is to generate the trajectories of the illusions of the simulator, with the specifications of each one. With the generated illusions, an interpolation is made through the following polynomials to find several calculation points and obtain as a result trajectories of position, velocity and acceleration of the actuators during the simulation of the illusions.

$$\theta_{angular}(k + 1) = \theta_{angular}(k) + w * t \tag{31}$$

$$w = w_o + a * t \tag{32}$$

$$\theta_{angular}(k + 1) = \theta_{angular}(k) + w_o * t + 0.5 * a * t^2 \tag{33}$$

Where t is the interpolation time, w the angular velocity of roll, pitch, yaw in the final effector, $\theta_{angular}$ is the interpolated angular displacement, a is the angular acceleration. The expression (31) is for illusions of constant velocity, while the (32) is used to find the time of illusions with variable velocity.

5   Results and Discussion

The results was divided into two parts: (a) comparison MATLAB with ANSYS by l_1 point and, (b) leans trajectory.

For the first part a comparison of results is made, by obtaining the coordinates of point l_1, because the cabin will be located in that place, the error is estimated using the following formula:

$$e\% = \frac{l_{MATLAB} - l_{ANSYS}}{l_{MATLAB}} \times 100 \qquad (34)$$

Table 1. Roll variable, pitch variable, yaw = 120°

Roll	Pitch	l_i	MATLAB (mm)	ANSYS (mm)	Error %
5°	10°	x	−255.41	−255.4	−0.01
		y	442.38	442.4	0.04
		z	1744.5	1744.5	0
15°	20°	x	−231.89	−232	−0.01
		y	401.65	401.67	0.04
		z	1831.6	1831.6	0
25°	30°	x	−193.41	−193.4	−0.01
		y	335	335	0
		z	1912.8	1912.8	0
35°	40°	x	−151.35	−151.33	0.01
		y	262.15	262.17	0.04
		z	1984.6	1984.6	0

Table 1 shows a rotation in the x-axis and due to the action of the angle yaw, in the other two arms the same thing happens but with the respective rotation of 120° between them. The margin of error of the data shown varies from −0.04 to 0.04, which shows the accuracy of the method developed. For the second part the test was performed with the illusion of tilting that specifies only one displacement in roll and the other angles are 0, in the Fig. 5 the velocity and acceleration of the actuators of the first arm is observed.

6 Conclusions and Future Work

The results of the simulation were verified in ANSYS, using reverse kinematics and MATLAB methods, for which the limitations of movement were considered from the restriction equations, but this data has been verified with the real simulator implemented. Our model has a higher performance than [33]. In this case, the real mechanical restrictions of the plant must be considered, as well as dynamic limitations at the time of control. In the part of generation of accelerations in the actuators of the arms, from constant velocities is defined in the model at the moment of deriving the position in the accelerations part is left multiplication terms of angular velocities for this reason the change in the results. The recreated illusions are tested in MATLAB with the model obtained by reviewing the coherence of results.

References

1. Campos, A., García, A.: Inverse kinematics for general 6-RUS parallel robots applied on UDESC-CEART flight simulator. In: 22nd International Congress of Mechanical Engineering (COBEM 2013), Ribeirão Preto, Brazil (2013)
2. Salehinia, Y., Salehinia, S.: Solving forward kinematics problem of stewart robot using soft computing. In: RSI/ISM International Conference on Robotics and Mechatronics, Tehran, Iran (2013)
3. Caetano, J.V., de Visser, C.C., Mulder, M., Remes, B.: Linear aerodynamic model identification of a flapping wing MAV based on flight test data. Int. J. Micro Air Veh. 5(4), 273–286 (2013)
4. Oliveira, T., Encarnação, P.: Ground target tracking control system for unmanned aerial vehicles. Springer Sci. 69, 373–387 (2012)
5. Aguilar, W.G., Angulo, C.: Real-time model-based video stabilization for microaerial vehicles. Neural Process. Lett. 43(2), 459–477 (2016)
6. Aguilar, W.G., Angulo, C.: Real-time video stabilization without phantom movements for micro aerial vehicles. EURASIP J. Image Video Process. 1, 1–13 (2014)
7. Staicu, S.: Dynamics of the 6-6 Stewart parallel manipulator. Robot. Comput. Integr. Manuf. 27, 212–220 (2011)
8. Bingul, Z., Oguzhan, K.: Dynamic Modeling and Simulation of Stewart Platform, no. 1, pp. 1–26. Intech (2012)
9. Sabbavarapu, R., Vegesina, R., Koona, R.: Design for optimal performance of 3-RPS parallel manipulator using evolutionary algorithms. Trans. Can. Soc. Mech. Eng. 37(2), 1–26 (2013)
10. Aguilar, W.G., Abad, V., Ruiz, H., Aguilar, J., Aguilar-Castillo, F.: RRT-based path planning for virtual bronchoscopy simulator. In: De Paolis, L.T., Bourdot, P., Mongelli, A. (eds.) AVR 2017. LNCS, vol. 10325, pp. 155–165. Springer, Cham (2017). https://doi.org/10.1007/978-3-319-60928-7_13
11. Zhao, Z., Qui, Y.: Design and kinematic analysis of a novel variant 3-RPS micromotion parallel manipulator. J. Residuals Sci. Technol. 13(5), 10–18 (2016)
12. Aguilar, W.G., Morales, S.: 3D environment mapping using the kinect V2 and path planning based on RRT algorithms. Electronics 5(4), 70 (2016)
13. Aguilar, W.G., et al.: Statistical abnormal crowd behavior detection and simulation for real-time applications. In: Huang, Y., Wu, H., Liu, H., Yin, Z. (eds.) ICIRA 2017. LNCS (LNAI), vol. 10463, pp. 671–682. Springer, Cham (2017). https://doi.org/10.1007/978-3-319-65292-4_58
14. Aguilar, W.G., et al.: Real-time detection and simulation of abnormal crowd behavior. In: De Paolis, L.T., Bourdot, P., Mongelli, A. (eds.) AVR 2017. LNCS, vol. 10325, pp. 420–428. Springer, Cham (2017). https://doi.org/10.1007/978-3-319-60928-7_36
15. Krause, G., Zapico, E., Gonzales, S.: Simulador de vuelo de vehículos aeroespaciales de seis grados de libertad. Mecánica Computacional 31, 2961–2977 (2012)
16. Matlalcuatzi, R., Alexandrov, V.V.: Diseño del simulador dinámico para pilotos como un sistema biomecatrónico. In: Memorias del XVI Congreso Latinoamericano de Control Automático, Cancún, Mexico (2014)
17. Condomines, J.-P.: Experimental wind field estimation and aircraft identification. In: Researchgate, France (2015)
18. Izaguirre, E.: Control Desacoplado de Plataforma Neumática de 3-GDL utilizada como Simulador de Movimiento. Revista Iberoamericana de Automática e Informática Industrial 8, 143–159 (2011)

19. Mintenbeck, J., Estaña, R.: Design, modelling and control of a hyper-redundant 3-RPS parallel mechanism. In: International Conference on Robotics and Biomimetics, Tianjin, China (2010)
20. Chablat, D., Jha, R., Rouillier, F., Moroz, G.: Non-singular assembly mode changing trajectories in the workspace for the 3-RPS parallel robot. In: Lenarčič, J., Khatib, O. (eds.) Advances in Robot Kinematics, pp. 149–159. Springer, Cham (2014). https://doi.org/10.1007/978-3-319-06698-1_17
21. Gallardo, J.D., Orozco, H.: Acceleration analysis of 3-RPS parallel manipulators by means of screw theory. Department of Mechanical Engineering, Instituto Tecnológico de Celaya, México (2014)
22. Orbea, D., Moposita, J., Aguilar, W.G., Paredes, M., León, G., Jara-Olmedo, A.: Math Model of UAV multi rotor prototype with fixed wing aerodynamic structure for a flight simulator. In: De Paolis, L.T., Bourdot, P., Mongelli, A. (eds.) AVR 2017. LNCS, vol. 10324, pp. 199–211. Springer, Cham (2017). https://doi.org/10.1007/978-3-319-60922-5_15
23. Aguilar, W.G., Salcedo, V.S., Sandoval, D.S., Cobeña, B.: Developing of a video-based model for UAV autonomous navigation. In: Barone, D.A.C., Teles, E.O., Brackmann, C. P. (eds.) LAWCN 2017. CCIS, vol. 720, pp. 94–105. Springer, Cham (2017). https://doi.org/10.1007/978-3-319-71011-2_8
24. Aguilar, W.G., Casaliglla, V.P., Pólit, J.L.: Obstacle avoidance based-visual navigation for micro aerial vehicles. Electronics 6(1), 10 (2017)
25. Ruiz, N., Blanco, A.: Dinámica y control de un robot paralelo 3-RPS. Pistas Educativas 39 (125), 1–25 (2000)
26. Quiang, Y., Bin, L.: Kinematics comparative study of two overconstrained parallel manipulators. Math. Probl. Eng. 2016, 1–12 (2016)
27. Arahashi, H.: Mathematical Problems in Engineering. MtlabSite.com (2014)
28. Asif, U.: Design of a parallel robot with a large workspace for the functional evaluation of aircraft dynamics beyond the nominal flight envelope. Int. J. Adv. Robot. Syst. 9(2), 51 (2012)
29. Kvrgic, V., Visnjic, Z., Cvijanovic, V.B., Divnic, D., Mitrovic, S.: Dynamics and control of a spatial disorientation trainer. Robot. Comput. Integr. Manuf. 35, 104–125 (2015)
30. Lukanin, V.: Inverse kinematics, forward kinematics and working space determination of 3D of parallel manipulator with S-P-R joint structure. Period. Polytech. Ser. Mech. 49, 31–69 (2004)
31. Gouasmi, M., Ouali, M.: Kinematic modelling and simulation of a 2-R robot using solidworks and verification by MATLAB/Simulink. Intech 9, 245 (2012)
32. Ospina, D.: Cinematica y simulacion de una plataforma robotica paralela 3-RPS. In: III Congreso Internacional de Ingeniería Mecatronica, Cali, Colombia (2012)
33. Villacís, C., et al.: Mathematical models applied in the design of a flight simulator for military training. In: Rocha, Á., Guarda, T. (eds.) MICRADS 2018. SIST, vol. 94, pp. 43–57. Springer, Cham (2018). https://doi.org/10.1007/978-3-319-78605-6_4

Education in Mechatronics Engineering

Innovation Ability Cultivation Quality Evaluation Model of Postgraduate Students Majoring in Mechatronics Engineering

Diankui Gao, Kexin Li, Bin Zhao$^{(\boxtimes)}$, and Lizhi Xu

School of Mechanical Engineering, Liaoning Shihua University,
Fushun 113001, Liaoning, China
Gaodiankui1975@sina.com, zbzbz0203288@163.com

Abstract. In order to improve the innovation ability cultivation quality of machinery postgraduates, the mechatronics engineering is introduced to innovation ability cultivation system. Firstly, main measurements of training the innovation ability of machinery postgraduates based on mechatronics engineering are discussed. Secondly, the innovation ability cultivation quality evaluation model of machinery postgraduates based on mechatronics engineering is constructed, the fuzzy wavelet neural network trained by improved pollen algorithm is applied to evaluate the innovation ability cultivation quality of machinery postgraduates based on mechatronics. The evaluation index system is constructed, and the simulation analysis is carried out, results show that the proposed evaluation model can effectively evaluate innovation cultivation quality of the postgraduates majoring in mechatronics engineering.

Keywords: Mechatronics engineering · Innovation ability cultivation ·
Fuzzy wavelet neural network

1 Introduction

The mechatronics engineering is a cross discipline which involves mechanical engineering, sensor technology, testing technology, electronic technology, control theory and information technology. Most postgraduates have difficulty in mastering this course due to the lack of background knowledge.

With the enlargement of postgraduate recruit students, the demand of society for machinery postgraduates is also changing, how to foster the innovative talents is a major problem for machinery postgraduate educators. With rapid development of electronics, computer and control technology, the electromechanical system is developing towards informatization, intellectualizationn and integration. Currently the pure machinery without penetration of electronics, control and computer technology in key sectors of national economy has difficult to be found. Therefore the machinery postgraduates should comprehensively grasp the machinery, electricity, control and computer technology. Learning time of theoretical courses for postgraduates is one year,

H. Yu et al. (Eds.): ICIRA 2019, LNAI 11745, pp. 545–554, 2019.
https://doi.org/10.1007/978-3-030-27529-7_46

Classroom learning and experiment is an important process of expanding knowledge on mechatronics engineering. Machinery postgraduates should be paid to linking theory with practice. The optimal system of theoretical course, practice course, and technological innovation course should be constructed to provide the innovative talents for research and development of research and development of complex mechanical system [1].

2 Main Measurements of Training the Innovation Ability of Machinery Postgraduates Based on Mechatronics Engineering

Firstly, the theoretical courses system should be optimized. The life cycle management system can be used as the course content. The initial course contents can be re-organized, and reasonable layout of the knowledge and ability elements is carried out. Some frontier technologies can be introduced into the teaching content. The technical frontier lectures on mechatronics engineering should be carried out to improve the innovation ability of postgraduates. The well-known foreign scholars can be invited to teach the latest international developments to develop the international outlook of machinery outlook for machinery postgraduates [2].

Secondly, the practice course system should be improved for matching with construction of theoretical courses. Integrated autonomous test system on mechatronics engineering should be developed for improving practical ability. The postgraduate can independently design the system structure of experimental system, and select the various controlling and driving methods. The experimental results can verify the correctness of theoretical knowledge. Construction of experimental teaching system should be combined with the discipline construction, postgraduate training and scientific research. The practice course system should play a role in competence education, The experiment content and method should focus on the cultivation of postgraduates' creative thinking [3].

Thirdly, the technological innovation course system is also be optimized, the practical platform for scientific and technological innovation can be built for mechatronics engineering. The postgraduates can participate the national science and technology competition relying on the constructed innovation platform. The technological innovation platform should be combined with engineering practice, which starts from solving engineering problems [4].

The system reform of theoretical course, practice course, and technological innovation course should long survive in such a storm, which is a process of accumulation, and reform content should be continuously updated. The comprehensive courses system should be improved according to the comments suggested by experts and postgraduates, which will be more rational.

3 Innovation Ability Cultivation Quality Evaluation Model of Postgraduates Majoring in Mechatronics Engineering

In process of evaluating the innovation ability of postgraduates majoring in mechatronics engineering, it is difficult to give the relational function between the all kinds of affecting factors and innovation ability cultivation quality. The BP neural network can solve the evaluation problems in many fields, however it also has several unavoidable defects, such as over-study, local extreme and poor generalization ability. The wavelet neural network has been applied in many fields such as fault diagnosis, signal inspection and evaluation. The wavelet neural network can only cope with certain information, and can not solve the uncertain information. For innovation ability cultivation process of postgraduates majoring in mechatronics engineering has many uncertain affecting factors, the fuzzy neural network can solve the fuzzy and uncertain problems, however the fuzzy neural network also has some disadvantages, such as poor anti-interference, insufficient promotion capacity and relying on prior knowledge. Therefore the fuzzy wavelet neural network can be constructed through combing with fuzzy neural and wavelet neural network, the advantages of the two methods can be used [5]. The fuzzy wavelet neural network can be applied to evaluate the innovation ability cultivation quality of postgraduates majoring in mechatronics engineering, the stability of algorithm can be improved, the convergence speed can be quickened, and the generalization ability can be improved. The basic structure of the fuzzy wavelet neural network is shown in Fig. 1.

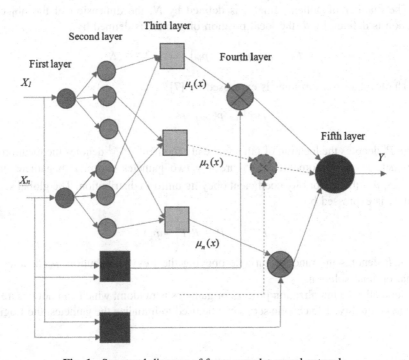

Fig. 1. Structural diagram of fuzzy wavelet neural network

The fuzzy wavelet neural network concludes five layers. First layer is input layer, Second layer is membership degree layer, the third layer is fuzzy rule layer. The fourth layer is wavelet function layer, the Gabor wavelet is used as the mother wavelet function, which is expressed by

$$\varphi(x) = \frac{1}{\sqrt[4]{\pi\sigma^2}} e^{-\frac{x^2}{2\sigma^2}} \tag{1}$$

The result obtained after translation and expansion of the mother wavelet function can be used as the exited function.

The fifth layer is the output layer, and the output result is expressed by [6]

$$Y = \sum_{j=1}^{n} \hat{\mu}_j(x) \cdot v_j \tag{2}$$

where $\hat{\mu}_j(x) = \frac{\mu_j(x)}{\sum_{j=1}^{n} \mu_j(x)}$, v_j is the output value of j th Gabor wavelet function.

The parameters of fuzzy Gabor wavelet neural network should be updated in training process, and the pollen algorithm is a novel meta-heuristic method that needs less parameters and is easy to implement. Therefore the pollen algorithm is applied in optimization of parameters for the fuzzy Gabor wavelet neural network. The mathematical model of the pollen algorithm is listed as follows:

The number of pollen gametes is defined by N, the dimension of the objective function is defined by d, the local position of gamete is defined by

$$P_i = [p_{i1}, p_{i2}, \cdots, p_{id}], i = 1, 2, \cdots, N \tag{3}$$

The local search formulas is expressed by [7]

$$P_i^{t+1} = P_i^t + \mu(P_j^t - P_k^t) \tag{4}$$

where P_i^t denotes the location of i th gamete at t moment, P_i^{t+1} denotes the location of i th gamete at $t+1$ moment, P_j^t, P_k^t are any two gametes except i th gamete in all gametes, μ is the uniformity coefficient obeying uniform distribution. The global search formula is expressed by

$$P_i^{t+1} = P_i^t + R(P_i^t - p_g) \tag{5}$$

where R denotes the random variable obeying the Levy distribution, p_g denotes the global optimal solution.

Generally the initialization process of gametes is random, which can not ensure the individual quality. The chaotic series can be used to initialize the gametes, the Logistic chaotic mapping is used in this research, and the corresponding expression is listed as follows [8]:

$$g(k+1) = \kappa g(k) \cdot (1 - g(k)) \tag{6}$$

where $g(k)$ denotes the real number sequence, κ is chaotic parameter.

4 Innovation Ability Cultivation Quality Evaluation Index System of Postgraduate Students Majoring in Mechatronics Engineering

A complete set of index system is built on the basis of investigation, and the demonstration and research are carried out for the index system. At same time, the indexes are screened through collecting document literature and questionnaire investigation. The final innovation ability cultivation quality evaluation index system of postgraduates majoring in mechatronics engineering is listed in Table 1.

Table 1. Innovation ability cultivation quality evaluation index system of machinery postgraduates

First level index	Second level index
Theoretical course (I_1)	Frontier lectures on mechatronics engineering (I_{11})
	Teaching route on mechatronics engineering (I_{12})
	Latest international developments on mechatronics engineering (I_{13})
Practice course (I_2)	Integrated autonomous test system on mechatronics engineering (I_{21})
	discipline construction (I_{22})
	postgraduate training (I_{23})
	scientific research (I_{24})
Technological innovation course (I_3)	Practical platform for scientific and technological innovation (I_{31})
	Participate national science (I_{32})
	Participate technology competition (I_{33})
	Engineering practice based on mechatronics engineering (I_{34})

The data processing method of the normalization is used to divide the innovation ability cultivation quality into five grades, which are listed in Table 2.

Table 2. Innovation ability cultivation quality grade

Grade	Evaluation value	Feature
I	[0.8, 1)	Excellent
II	[0.6, 0.8)	Good
III	[0.4, 0.6)	Normal
IV	[0.2,0.4)	Poor
V	(0, 0.2)	Very poor

The 20 experts are invited to score the innovation ability cultivation quality evaluation index system, and the postgraduates from 30 mechanical specialties are used as the research objects, the postgraduates from top 20 mechanical specialties are used as training samples, the postgraduates from the other 10 mechanical specialties are used as testing samples.

The number of input nodes of fuzzy wavelet neural network is taken as three, the input variables conclude theoretical course (I_1), practice course (I_2) and technological innovation course (I_3). The number of hidden layer of fuzzy wavelet neural network is taken as 11.

The parameters of pollen algorithm are set as follows: the number of gametes is 25, $\mu = 0.8$, the transition probability between the global and local searches is taken as 0.8. The error requirement is taken as 0.001, the iteration times is taken as 1000. In order to verify the effectiveness of the proposed algorithm, the fuzzy neural network trained by particle swarm algorithm is also applied to train the same samples. The simulation program is compiled by MATLAB software. The convergence curves are shown in Fig. 2.

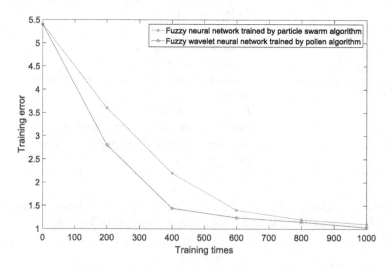

Fig. 2. Convergence curves of the two evaluation models

As seen from Fig. 2, the fuzzy wavelet neural network trained by pollen algorithm reaches to the 0.001 after 600 iteration times, while the fuzzy neural network trained by particle swarm algorithm reaches to the 0.001 after 900 iteration times, therefore the proposed in this research has higher convergence speed, which can improve the evaluation efficiency.

The training samples are trained by the fuzzy wavelet neural network, and the trained fuzzy wavelet neural network is used to evaluate the testing samples, and the final evaluation results are listed in Table 3.

Table 3. Innovation ability cultivation quality of machinery postgraduates

Mechanical specialty	Evaluation value	Evaluation grade	Real grade
1	0.76	II	Good
2	0.64	II	Good
3	0.88	I	Excellent
4	0.48	III	Normal
5	0.69	I	Good
6	0.36	IV	Poor
7	0.71	II	Good
8	0.66	II	Good
9	0.94	I	Excellent
10	0.59	III	Normal

As seen from Table 2, the fuzzy wavelet neural network can obtain the correct evaluation results that are agree wit the real evaluation results. Therefore the fuzzy wavelet neural network trained by pollen algorithm has high evaluation precision, and the evaluation results can offer favorable theoretical basis for making proper reform measurements of innovation ability cultivation of postgraduates majoring in mechatronics engineering.

In order to further verify the effectiveness of the proposed evaluation model, validation error is used to measure the precision of evaluation model, the mechatronics engineering specialty in a university is used as researching object to carry out empirical study. The mechatronics engineering specialty in a university has twenty years history, which is a earliest postgraduate specialty of this university. The mechatronics engineering specialty is the key and brand characteristic specialty. For a long time, the mechatronics engineering specialty carries out teaching and research works on mechatronics products, systems and manufacturing methods, and actively carries out the teaching reform, which has formed the distinctive petrochemical equipment characteristics.

After a few years of accumulation and inheritance, mechatronics engineering specialty has formed a teaching team with high teaching level, strong scientific research ability, and high education level. At present, mechatronics engineering teaching team concludes twenty-four teachers, which has proper age and professional title structure. The age structure of teaching team is listed in Table 4. The professional title structure of teaching team is listed in Table 5. The age and professional title structure can reflect the level of teacher of mechatronics engineering specialty.

Table 4. Age structure of mechatronics engineering teaching team

Age range	Over 50 years	40–49 years	30–39 years	Below 30 years
Number of teachers	2	8	12	4

Table 5. Professional title structure of mechatronics engineering teaching team

Title	Professor	Associate professor	Lecturer	Assistant
Number of teachers	6	7	9	2

The mechatronics engineering specialty gets some excellent scientific research and academic achievements, and in the past five years, teaching team has published 612 papers in some important journals and academic conferences at home and abroad, has obtained eight provincial and ministerial level scientific and technological progress award, and fifteen achievements have been adopted, the cumulative economic benefits are 48 million Yuan,

After many years of development, the mechatronics engineering specialty has formed stable research directions with the petrochemical characteristics, which conclude driving and simulation technology, machinery and equipment, robotic technology and its motion system, sensor and actuator technology, functional groups of measurement technology and image processing, micro-electromechanical system, micro and precision instruments, measurement technology of micro-system, robot technology, biological system, bionic execution technology, control and design and so on. The mechatronics engineering specialty has been listed in the second batch excellence engineer program in China, which is earliest specialty in a university. Based on real characteristics of mechatronics engineering specialty, the talent training framework of engineer of mechatronics engineering specialty is designed.

The proposed evaluation model is applied to evaluate the innovation ability cultivation quality of postgraduates majoring in mechatronics engineering, the innovation ability cultivation quality of postgraduates from 2015 to 2018 is evaluated, and the comparing results are listed in Table 6.

Table 6. Evaluation comparing results of innovation ability cultivation quality of postgraduates from 2015 to 2018

Year	Real value	Evaluation value	Validation error
2013	0.55	0.58	3.64%
2014	0.62	0.66	2.23%
2015	0.68	0.73	4.41%
2016	0.77	0.82	2.60%
2017	0.84	0.86	2.38%
2018	0.85	0.88	3.53%

As seen from Table 5, the proposed model can correctly evaluate the innovation ability cultivation quality of postgraduates majoring in mechatronics engineering, the evaluation results can offer effective measurements for ensuring innovation ability cultivation quality of postgraduates.

The practical teaching system of mechatronics engineering specialty is a critical part of enhancing the ability and quality of postgraduate students, the construction and updating of the practice teaching system should satisfy the actual demand of postgraduates education and mechatronics engineering industry. In addition, construction of practical teaching system not only considers the combination between theory and practice teaching, but also focuses on the internal connection between links and the ability training continuation based on discipline knowledge system and professional course characteristics.

In the new development situation, the practice teaching system and mode of mechatronics engineering specialty can be constructed through using the cultivation and enhancing of mechatronics engineering ability as the main line, which carry out hierarchical and gradient training and education of engineering practical basis cognitive ability, professional engineering and technical ability, professional comprehensive engineering ability and engineering innovation ability.

Engineering professional practical cognitive ability can be cultivated through practice teaching courses. When the postgraduate students just enter into the university or are low junior, the main teaching and learning process is the transformation of learning environment, ideological understanding and basic course. It is the critical period of target positioning, which can affect learning enthusiasm of students and quality of engineering capability finally.

Professional oriented reorganization practical teaching should be carried out, the students should have sound sensory perception for specialty situation, specialty developing trend, industry requirement, specialized characteristics and position, achievements and advantage resources obtained, at same time specialty should cultivate the reasonable locating target of excellence engineer. The experimental teaching of basic courses should be concerned, such as university physics, mathematical experiment, and engineering ethics and other courses, the corresponding teaching may not be carried out by mechatronics engineering professional teachers, however these basic courses can provide important basis for later major teaching, and experiment training can cultivate the engineering awareness of students. The self professional practice in vacation is also concerned, the social practice learning part should be assigned in vacation for the junior students, and needs of students with preliminary practice reorganization for mechatronics engineering specialty, and students should find out professional problems through practice.

5   Conclusions

The mechatronics engineering plays an important role in innovation ability cultivation of machinery postgraduates. The proper teaching method should be used to improve the innovation ability cultivation quality. The fuzzy wavelet neural network is used to evaluate the innovation ability cultivation quality of machinery postgraduates, the evaluation efficiency and precision can be improved effectively through simulation analysis.

Acknowledgments. The research is supported by "Research Project of Postgraduate Education and Teaching Reform in Liaoning Shihua University (No. 2018Y14)".

References

1. Li, X.Y., Wan, L.R., Zhang, X.: Innovation ability training mode of postgraduates in the mechanical discipline based on simulation technology. Int. J. Emerg. Technol. Learn. **12**(9), 168–176 (2017)
2. Zhou, J., Liu, Y., Lei, L., Hu, J.S.: Thinking of expanding practice and remember capacity of postgraduates. J. Chem. Pharm. Res. **6**(9), 185–188 (2014)
3. Verma, P., Sood, S.K., Kalra, S.: Smart computing based student performance evaluation framework for engineering education. Comput. Appl. Eng. Educ. **25**(6), 977–991 (2017)
4. Purzer, Ş., Fila, N., Nataraja, K.: Evaluation of current assessment methods in engineering entrepreneurship education. Adv. Eng. Educ. **5**(1), 1–24 (2016)
5. Zhou, M.L., Yang, P., Zhang, Q., Zhao, Y.: Teaching methods for the course artificial neural networks and applications. World Trans. Eng. Technol. Educ. **12**(3), 507–512 (2014)
6. Dou, L.Q., Ji, R., Gao, J.Q.: Identification of nonlinear aeroelastic system using fuzzy wavelet neural network. Neurocomputing **214**, 935–943 (2016)
7. Solgi, Y., Ganjefar, S.: Variable structure fuzzy wavelet neural network controller for complex nonlinear systems. Appl. Soft Comput. J. **64**, 674–685 (2018)
8. Dias, L.G., Veloso, A.C.A., Sousa, M.E.B.C., Estevinho, L., Machado, A.A.S.C., Peres, A.M.: A novel approach for honey pollen profile assessment using an electronic tongue and chemometric tools. Anal. Chim. Acta **900**, 36–45 (2015)

DOREP: An Educational Experiment Platform for Robot Control Based on MATLAB and the Real-Time Controller

Guanghui Liu[1,3]([✉]), Bing Han[1,2], Qingxin Li[1,2], Shuai Wang[3], and Hualiang Zhang[1,2]

[1] Key Laboratory of Industrial Control Network and System, Shenyang Institute of Automation, Chinese Academy of Sciences, Shenyang, China
ghliu@ks.sia.cn
[2] Institutes for Robotics and Intelligent Manufacturing, Chinese Academy of Sciences, Shenyang, China
[3] Faculty of Robot Science and Engineering, Northeastern University, Shenyang, China

Abstract. The Deep Open Robot Experiment Platform (DOREP) is an experimental system for robot universal control, developed to offer an intuitive and high-level programming interface to the user. It includes a robotic toolbox, a Linux-based real-time controller and corresponding environment deployment tools. It is more open and more comprehensive than other toolboxes. The toolbox includes more than 30 functions, spanning operations such as forward and inverse kinematics computation, point-to-point joint and Cartesian control, trajectory generation, graphical display, 3-D animation and diagnostics. The DOREP which is compatible with many varieties of 6 DOF small and low payload universal robots that include ROKAE robots, Universal robots, ABB robots, AUBO robots and so on, runs on a remote computer connected with the robot controller via TCP/IP.

Keywords: Robot control · Experiment Platform · MATLAB/Simulink

1 Introduction

This rapid growth of robotic automation in all sectors of industry will require an enormous number of technically sound specialists with the skills in industrial robotics and automation to maintain and monitor existing robots, enhance development of future technologies, and educate users on implementation and applications [1]. Many manufacturers are unwilling to publish internal details regarding system architecture due to the high levels of competition in the robot market [2]. MATLAB [3] is a powerful and

This work was partially supported by National Natural Science Foundation of China under Grant (NO. 91648204) and National Key Research and Development Program of China under Grant (NO. 2017YFB1301103).

H. Yu et al. (Eds.): ICIRA 2019, LNAI 11745, pp. 555–565, 2019.
https://doi.org/10.1007/978-3-030-27529-7_47

widely used commercial software environment and there are many MATLAB-based robot control systems, such as the KUKA Control Toolbox (KCT) for motion control of KUKA robot manipulators [4]. The KUKA Sunrise Toolbox (KST), a MATLAB toolbox that interfaces with KUKA Sunrise OS. It contains soft control in real time [5]. However, these tools mainly for robot motion control, lack of force control interface, and for a given robot, which are lack of universality. The robot toolbox of DOREP is a collection of MATLAB functions for motion control of robot manipulators, developed to offer an intuitive and high-level programming interface to the user. It includes more than 30 functions, spanning operations such as forward and inverse kinematics computation, point-to-point joint and cartesian control, trajectory generation, graphical display, 3-D animation and diagnostics.

A brief introduction to the composition and operational flow of DOREP at the begin of this paper. The rest of this paper is organized as follows: Sect. 2 provides a comprehensive overview of the functions of DOREP and several typical control modules. Two examples are reported in Sect. 3 to show the flexibility of the platform in real scenarios. In Sect. 4, conclusions and future research directions are highlighted.

2 Overview of the DOREP

2.1 DOREP Components and Operational Procedures

In this section the constitutes of DOREP will be briefly described.

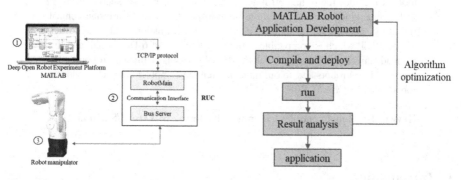

Fig. 1. Communication scheme between DOREP and the manipulator

Fig. 2. DOREP operational procedures

Figure 1 illustrates the communication scheme between DOREP and the robot manipulator. It consists of three parts:

- A remote computer running DOREP under MATLAB,
- The Robot Universal Controller (RUC) based on real-time Linux operating system,
- The robot manipulator.

To establish a connection between the remote computer and the robot controller, DOREP provides RobotMain, a C multi-thread server running on the RUC. RobotMain communicates via Communication Interfaces with bus server, an bus server supports a variety of industrial bus implementations including EtherCAT, Canopen, UDP running on the RUC and managing the information exchange with the robot manipulator in a soft real-time loop 1 ms.

Figure 2 illustrates the DOREP operational procedures. Step1 is the MATLAB Robot program development, after that compile the program and deploy it to the RUC. It can be run after the program is deployed. The algorithm is optimized according to the output result, and the application can be applied if the result is correct.

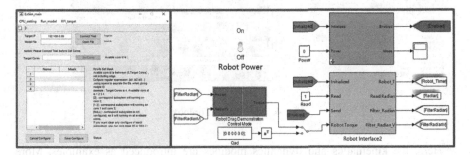

Fig. 3. DOREP system view

The DOREP system view is shown in Fig. 3. It includes the Engineer view required for the real-time control system, and the MATLAB/Simulink programming view. The Engineer view is used to manage some of the properties of MATLAB when deployed to a real-time control system, including the IP address of the controller and the path of some necessary configuration files.

2.2 Synchronization Between MATLAB and Bus Server

Using MATLAB as the development tool, we need to solve the control cycle delay [6]. The period of the communication between bus server and robot manipulator is 1 ms. In order to ensure that the calculation cycle of MATLAB can be synchronized with the bus, the operation of MATLAB is required to be completed within 1 ms. The pulse trigger is set in the bus communication module to ensure the synchronization of operation and communication.

2.3 SIA Robot Toolbox

SIA Robot Toolbox is part of DOREP and is a robotics toolbox based on MATLAB developed by the Shenyang Institute of Automation. As shown in Fig. 4, the SIA Robot Toolbox includes Robot Axis Interface module, Robot Base Control module, Robot Interface module, Robot System Tool module, Robot VR module, Sensor module and so on. These modules are consisted of some functional submodules.

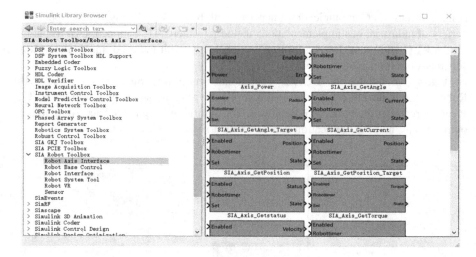

Fig. 4. SIA Robot Toolbox

Here, the kinematics and dynamics modules are introduced as examples. More information about the SIA Robot Toolbox modules are listed in Table 1 (Fig. 5).

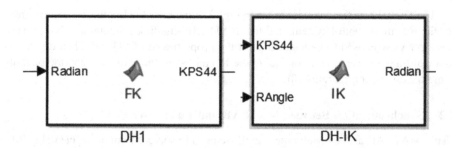

Fig. 5. Forward kinematics module and inverse kinematics module

Kinematics module including two modules, Kine_Forward module and Kine_Inverse module. The input to the Kine_Forward module are the joint angles (in radians) and its output is the End-effector's position and posture vector. To the opposite, the Kine_Inverse module's input is the End-effector's position and posture vector and the output are joint angles of the robot. The module's parameters are the robot Denavit-Hartenberg parameters and this module uses the general solution of robot kinematics to support the kinematics solution of 6 and 7 degrees of freedom robots, and also supports the kinematics solution of the 3 and 4 joint robots.

As shown in Fig. 6, the left figure is the Dyn_Forward which means forward dynamic of robot, and its input consists of a joint position vector, a velocity vector, and an acceleration vector. The output of the module is the joint moment vector solved from the dynamic equation. The right side of Fig. 6 shows the dynamic parameters of the robot linkage, including the mass of each joint of the robot, the position of the centroid of each joint, and the inertia matrix of each joint. These parameters can be obtained by means of robot dynamics parameter identification or by mechanical structure estimation. The DOREP provides a module for kinetic parameter estimation that can be used to derive kinetic parameters.

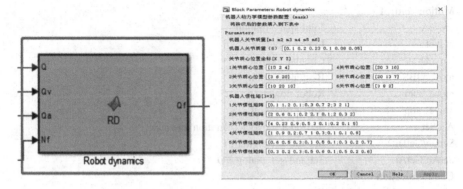

Fig. 6. Dynamics module and parameter configuration

The SIA Robot Toolbox modules are partly listed in Table 1.

Table 1. SIA Robot Toolbox modules

Module name	Explanation
Initialization	
rob_initialization	Load configuration files, set system operation parameters. Such as selected robot, set grip and sensor information, robot mode parameters, and so on
Networking	
SocketCreate	Create tcp/ip server
ClientCreate	Create tcp/ip client
SocketClose	Close tcp/ip server or client
UDPServerCreate	Create udp server
UDPClientCreate	Create udp client
UDPClose	Close udp server or client
Kinematics	
Kine_Forward	Compute the forward kinematics
Kine_Inverse	Compute the inverse kinematics
getrobjoint	Get current robot joints
getrobpose	Get current robot end position and pose
Dynamics	
Dyn_Forward	Compute the forward dynamics
Dyn_Inverse	Compute the inverse dynamics

(continued)

Table 1. (*continued*)

Module name	Explanation
Dyn_Inertia	Compute the inertia matrix
Dyn_Coriolis	Compute the coriolis matrix
Dyn_Gravity	Compute the gravity
Dyn_Friction	Compute the firction
Motion control	
moveA	Joint space motion
moveL	Linear motion
moveC	Circular motion
moveAJBS	B-spline motion
move_start	Robot power
move_stop	Robot poweroff
AccSet	Set robot move acceleration ane jeck
SetDo/GetDi	Set and get digital I/O
SetAo/GetAi	Set and get analog I/O
Communication	
robot_getposition_angle	Get robot joints angle
robot_gettorque_torque	Get robot joints torque
robot_setposition_angle	Set robot target angle
robot_settorque_torque	Set robot target torque
Trajectory planning	
getTrajectory_Line	Plan line path
getTrajectory_Circle	Plan circle path
getTrajectory_BSpline	Plan B-spline path
getVelocityProfile	Plan trajectory of velocity
External device	
grip_position	Grip control
get_torqueSensor	Get torque sensor data

3 Applicative Examples

3.1 Development of Robot Inverted Pendulum Experiment

In this section, the application process of DOREP is illustrated by introducing an experiment in which the robot drags the inverted pendulum to verify the flexibility, convenience, openness and stability of the platform. The experimental equipment includes a ROKAE BX7 manipulator, a DOREP controller, an encoder that supports the EtherCAT bus and a pendulum.

The specific methods to achieve the following:

Step 1: Use a network cable to connect the inverted pendulum encoder with the robot driver to form a unified communication network.

Step 2: Create a new project in the DOREP system programming view and add the Dyn_Forward module, and let the joint position vector of the robot read by the bus module as the input.

Step 3: The selected robot inverted pendulum control scheme is a linear quadratic method [7], and the detailed scheme of the robot dragging the inverted pendulum in [8]. The control module is encapsulated by the S-Function template, the specific packaging process is shown in [9].

Step 4: Add the Kine_Inverse module to solve the joint velocity and send it to each joint using the linear velocity of the robot end solved by the linear quadratic control module. Add the EtherCAT write module and send the calculated joint values to each joint. Add a VR module to display virtual robot.

Step 5: Use DOREP's engineer view to compile and deploy the control plan to the URC and run it.

As shown in Fig. 7, the left side is the block diagram of the inverted pendulum control system developed by the DOREP, including the common control module of the robot and the linear quadratic control module developed by the user module. On the right is the robot 3D rendering window loaded by the 3D rendering module. Figure 8 is a physical diagram of the robotic inverted pendulum experiment system, which uses the DOREP to complete the control of the inverted pendulum of the robot. The simulation interface and the actual position and posture of the robot are exactly the same which means the timeliness of the communication.

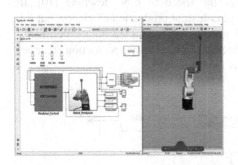

Fig. 7. Robot inverted pendulum and 3D simulation

Fig. 8. Robot inverted pendulum system

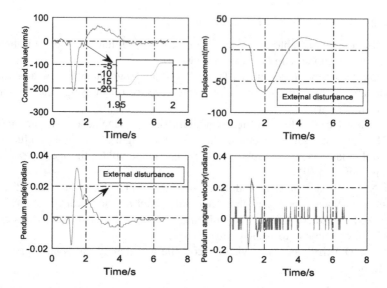

Fig. 9. Robot inverted pendulum and experimental data

The results of the operational data can be observed by the oscilloscope with Simulink, as shown in Fig. 9, which are the curve of control command value, robot end displacement, swing angle and pendulum angular velocity. The openness and practicability of DOREP have been proved by this experiment.

3.2   Direct Robot Teaching Experiment

Direct robot teaching scheme has improved the speed of robot teaching [10]. Its realization is conducive to the improvement of industrial production efficiency, but it is difficult to achieve, and it is of great significance to use it as a teaching experiment.

As shown in Fig. 10, the Coriolis and Inertia force, gravity and friction force are compensated, and the speed is introduced as feedback [11].

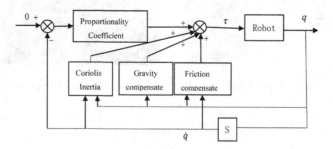

Fig. 10. Direct robot teaching control scheme

The direct robot teaching scheme shown in Fig. 10 is implemented in DOERP as shown in Fig. 11, and more details are encapsulated in the Real Robot Dynamics.

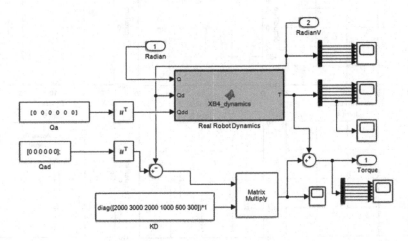

Fig. 11. Direct robot teaching control scheme

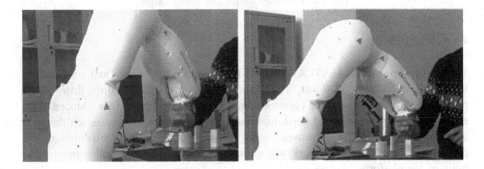

Fig. 12. Direct robot teaching

Compile and deploy it to the RUC and run. As shown in Fig. 12, using the direct robot teaching algorithm developed by DOPRE, the experimenter completed the development and experiment of drag teaching. The experimental data in the drag teaching is shown in Fig. 13. The error actual torque value and the estimated value are small, which proves the validity of the selected algorithm.

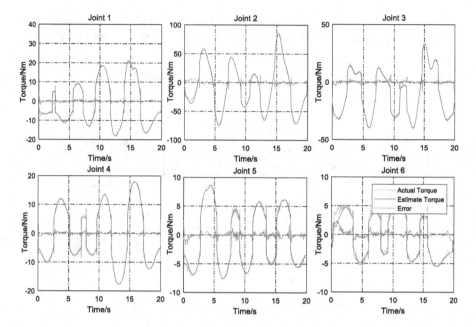

Fig. 13. Estimated torque and actual torque

4   Conclusions

This paper introduces a MATLAB toolbox for general robot control and a supporting research and teaching platform. The main components and operation flow of the platform are discussed, and the corresponding robot motion library is introduced. Two experiments of robot inverted pendulum and direct robot teaching based on the platform are introduced, which proves the rapidity, convenience and reliability of the platform. The next research work will enrich the library functions and general reliability of the platform.

References

1. Gattringer, H., Riepl, R., Neubauer, M.: Optimizing industrial robots for accurate high-speed applications. J. Ind. Eng. **2013**, 12 (2013)
2. Matthias, N., Hubert, G.: A persistent method for parameter identification of a seven-axis manipulator. Robotic **33**, 1099–1112 (2015). https://doi.org/10.1017/S0263574714001465
3. MATLAB and Simulink for Technical Computing. http://www.mathworks.com/
4. Francesco, C., Stefano, S.: KCT: a MATLAB toolbox for motion control of KUKA robot manipulators. IEEE Robot. Autom. Mag. (2010)
5. Mohammad, S., Pedro, N.: Interfacing collaborative robots with MATLAB. IEEE Robot. Autom. Mag. (2019)
6. Francesco, C., Stefano, S.: The KUKA Control Toolbox: motion control of KUKA robot manipulators with MATLAB. IEEE Robot. Autom. Mag. (2010)

7. Tao, Z., Guanghui, L.: Construction of three-dimensional simulation platform for linear inverted pendulum base on model. In: 2018 International Conference on Modeling, Simulation and Optimization (MSO 2018) (2018)
8. Kwon, T., Kwon, J.K.: Momentum-mapped inverted pendulum models for controlling dynamic human motions. ACM Trans. Graph. **36**(1), 1–14 (2017)
9. Chapman, S.J.: Essentials of MATLAB Programming, 3rd edn. China Machine Press, Beijing (2018)
10. Fangming, Y., Toshiyuki, M.: Sensorless force control of direct drive manipulator. In: Proceeding of the IEEE International Symposium on Industrial Electronics (1992)
11. Sang-Duck, L., Kuk-Hyun, A., Song, J.-B.: Torque control based sensorless hand guiding for direct robot teaching. In: IEEE/RSJ International Conference on Intelligent Robots and Systems, 9–14 October 2016 (2016)

Robotic Drilling and Sampling Technology

Design and Analysis of Motor Control System for Drilling Fluid Continuous Wave Generator Based on Improved Active Disturbance Rejection Control and Hysteresis Current Control

Botao Zhou[1,2], Jiafeng Wu[1,2(✉)], Ning Han[1,2],
and Mwelango Martin[1,2]

[1] Key Laboratory of Unconventional Oil & Gas Development (China University of Petroleum (East China)), Ministry of Education, Qingdao 266580, People's Republic of China
wujiafeng@upc.edu.cn
[2] School of Petroleum Engineering, China University of Petroleum (East China), Qingdao 266580, People's Republic of China

Abstract. Large load torque acting on the output of the motor and the internal parameters changing with the surrounding environment will lead to low control precision and drilling fluid continuous wave signal which is unable to meet the requirements. Therefore, it is necessary to design a motor position tracking control system with strong robustness. In this paper, the load torque acting on the output of the motor is firstly analyzed and its alternating characteristic is pointed out. With theoretical model and simulation, the continuous wave generator control system with the speed-current double loop is designed based on the load torque characteristic and verified. In the control system, improved active disturbance rejection controller is used as the controller in the speed loop and the hysteresis current controller is applied as the controller in the current loop. The simulation result shows that the designed motor control system has a very small overshoot and a fast response speed and speed tracking and position tracking control can be achieved.

Keywords: Continuous wave generator · Motor control · Load torque ·
Hysteresis current control · Improved active disturbance rejection control ·
Position track

1 Introduction

In recent years, drilling technology has entered the stage of automated drilling characterized by informationization and intelligence [1]. It is necessary to obtain as much underground information as possible in real time, making the underground information transmission technology the key to realize automatic drilling. As an advanced underground information transmission technology, the drilling fluid continuous wave

H. Yu et al. (Eds.): ICIRA 2019, LNAI 11745, pp. 569–579, 2019.
https://doi.org/10.1007/978-3-030-27529-7_48

technology with the characteristics of high transmission rate good robustness has broad application prospects.

The core component that generates the drilling fluid continuous pressure wave is the continuous pressure wave generator, which is mainly composed of a rotary valve, a shaft, a coupling, a motor and a resolver. When the continuous pressure wave generator is operating, the rotor rotates with the motor driving to periodically change the flow path between the stator and rotor in order to form the continuous pressure disturbance in the wellbore. In order to generate a specific pressure wave that can carry downhole information, the rotary valve needs to reach a prescribed position at a prescribed time. In the environment of high temperature, high pressure and strong fluid impact, the hydraulic torque acting on the rotary valve makes the motor control difficult [2]. At the same time, the factors, such as the change of moment of inertia and stator resistance, have a great influence on the motor control [3, 4], which reduces the precision of the motor control and makes the generated continuous wave signal difficult to meet the requirements. Therefore, in order to improve the control precision to produce the continuous wave signal that meets the requirements, a position tracking control system with strong robustness is required.

At present, the theme of only a small amount of literature is about the method for designing the continuous wave generator motor control system [5–8] and the double loop control system based on the classic PI controller is used to realize the control of the continuous wave generator motor in most of the literature. Wang [5] designed the control systems based on speed-current loop and position-current loop using vector control method in permanent magnet synchronous motor and the control strategy of $i_d = 0$. The classic PI controller is used in each loop of the two control systems and the parameters of PI controller are determined by formulas. Then some scholars proposed that it can be used to improve the accuracy of PI controller by using engineering setting method to determine the parameters of PI controller [6]. Yan [7] analyzed the influence of the hydraulic torque acting on the output of motor on the motor control system and designed the dual-loop control system based on speed-current loop. At the same time, it is pointed out that the continuous wave signal generated by the traditional PID control will be interfered by the noise in the drilling fluid channel and the sliding mode control is used in the speed loop instead of PI control with the controller in current loop unchanged. Lei [8] proposed it can get a good control result by combining the triple-loop control method based on position-speed-current loop with PI controller in each loop and using vector control method in permanent magnet synchronous motor when shear valve continuous wave generator motor control system.

It can be found from the literature that PI controller is used in most of the continuous wave generator motor control system, but the way the controller generates the error signal and the differential of the error signal is not reasonable [9–11] and the control strategy with $i_d = 0$ does not eliminate the coupling relationship between the shaft voltages. During the speed-up and speed-down of the motor, the current accuracy of the d–q axis decreases due to the limitation of the current loop bandwidth, resulting in poor motor control dynamic characteristics [12]. At the same time, the influence of the change of the load torque on the motor control is not considered, which leads to the low precision of the motor control.

Since the position can be obtained by speed integration and position control is implemented, a speed-current based double loop control system will be designed in this paper. The structure of this paper is as follows: the characteristics of load torque acting on the motor output is analyzed in the second section, the motor control system based on the load torque characteristics is designed in the third section, and finally the performance of the motor control system is analyzed by simulation based on MATLAB/Simulink.

2   Characteristics of Load Torque Acting on the Motor Output of Drilling Fluid Continuous Wave Generator

In order to ensure the control accuracy of the motor control system, it is necessary to analyze the load torque acting on the motor output. The load torque mainly includes the hydraulic torque acting on the rotary valve and the friction torque acting on the rotating system of the continuous wave generator. For the study of the hydraulic torque acting on the rotary valve, the CFD simulation method is combined with the hydraulic torque theory of the hydraulic machine to analyze the influencing of rotary valve parameters (such as the rotational speed, stator and rotor spacing) and the external environment (such as drilling fluid flow, Density) on the hydraulic torque. The results show that the hydraulic torque is in an alternating state and the solid in the drilling fluid has no significant effect on hydraulic torque [13–17]. There is no publicly available literature on the study of friction torque acting on the rotating system. In this section, a rotary valve will be firstly designed and CFD simulation method will be used to analyze the load torque acting on the motor output.

Wu et al. [18] proposed a rotary valve design method for continuous wave generators. Based on this method, a three-dimensional model of the rotary valve as shown in Fig. 1 was designed, and the dimensions of each part are shown in Table 1.

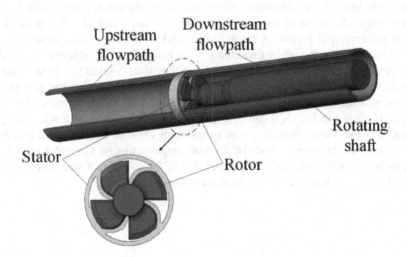

Fig. 1. Rotary valve model of continuous wave generator

Table 1. Size of rotary valve model for low power continuous wave generator.

Component	Upstream flowpath	Downstream flowpath	Gap	Rotor	Stator
Axial size/mm	299	381	2	5	20
Radial size/mm	80 (Inner diameter) 88 (Outer diameter)	80 (Inner diameter) 88 (Outer diameter)	–	76	80

Then load torque analysis is carried out, and the mesh model of the rotary valve is established by using the Mesh module in ANSYS/CFX, as shown in Fig. 2. In the established mesh model, hexahedral mesh is used in all regions. In the model, the gap between the rotor and the stator is 2 mm and the initial rotation angle of the rotor is 0°. In the coordinate system employed, the Z axis is the rotation axis of the rotor and the hydraulic torque acting on the rotor wall is monitored.

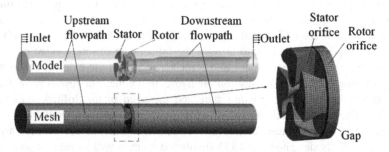

Fig. 2. Mesh model of rotary valve and boundary condition setting.

The k–ε model was used for the simulation, and the outlet type was set to a constant pressure outlet with a pressure value of 1.6 MPa. The inlet type is set to the speed inlet and the flow rate is 4 m/s. The rotary valve rotor is set to a rotating range with a speed of 4 r/s. All walls are set to have no slip boundaries and standard wall equations are used in the near wall region. A second-order backward Euler format is used as the solution method. For the scaling residuals of all parameters, the absolute standard of convergence is set to 10^{-4}. The density of the drilling fluid is set to 997 kg/m^3, and the dynamic viscosity is about 8.9×10^{-4} Pa·s. The system friction torque was experimentally measured as 1 Nm, and the load torque and load torque fitting curves were obtained as shown in Fig. 3. It can be seen from Fig. 3 that the load torque acting on the output of the motor alternates, with a maximum value of 2.8 Nm and a minimum value of 1.3 Nm. In order to describe the load torque acting on the motor output, the curve fitting method is adopted in this paper, that is, the equation of load torque is fitted by MATLAB, and it is used as the basis of motor control.

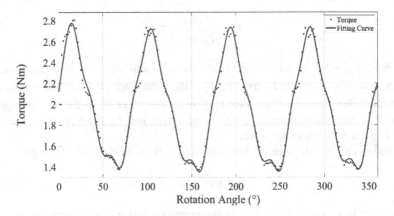

Fig. 3. Load torque and its fitting curve.

3   Continuous Wave Generator Motor Control System Design

3.1   Mathematical Model of Permanent Magnet Synchronous Motor

Since the permanent magnet synchronous motor has the advantages of high power density, high efficiency, large torque inertia ratio, and simple control [19], the permanent magnet synchronous motor is used as the control object in this section. The stator of the permanent magnet synchronous motor adopts three-phase symmetrical winding. The rotor is a permanent magnet, and the stator and rotor interact through the air gap magnetic field, and there is electromagnetic coupling relationship. In order to obtain the mathematical model of the permanent magnet synchronous motor, the permanent magnet synchronous motor is assumed as follows: the core saturation is ignored; the hysteresis and eddy current loss in the motor are not counted; the current of the motor is symmetrical three-phase sinusoidal alternating current; there is no damper winding on the rotor. Rotor field oriented vector control is used and it is defined that the d-axis coincides with the direction of the magnetic field of the rotor, and the q-axis advances by 90° counterclockwise. The mathematical model of the permanent magnet synchronous motor in the d–q axis coordinate system is as follows [20–22]:

$$U_d = p\psi_d - \omega\psi_q + R_s i_d \tag{1}$$

$$U_q = p\psi_q + \omega\psi_d + R_s i_q \tag{2}$$

$$\psi_d = L_d i_d + \psi_f \tag{3}$$

$$\psi_q = L_q i_q \tag{4}$$

$$T_e = P_n(i_q\psi_d - i_d\psi_q) \tag{5}$$

$$T_e = \frac{J}{P_n}\frac{d\omega}{dt} + T_L \qquad (6)$$

Where: ψ_d, ψ_q is the flux linkage of d axis and q axis, R_s is the stator resistance, i_d, i_q is the current of d axis and q axis, L_d, L_q is the inductance of d axis and q axis, ψ_f is the coupled flux linkage of the rotor magnet on the stator, T_e is the electromagnetic torque, P_n is the pole logarithm, T_L is the load torque, and J is the moment of inertia, ω is the angular velocity of the rotor.

Another expression of electromagnetic torque is available from (1) to (6):

$$T_e = P_n[i_q\psi_f + (L_d - L_q)i_d i_q] \qquad (7)$$

In order to facilitate the design of the improved active disturbance rejection controller, the mathematical model of the permanent magnet synchronous motor is written as follows:

$$\frac{d\omega}{dt} = -\frac{B}{J}\omega - \frac{T_L}{J} + \frac{1.5P_n\psi_f}{J}i_q \qquad (8)$$

Where: B is the friction coefficient.

3.2 Current Loop Design

The current hysteresis control does not depend on the motor parameters, and has a simple structure, which can speed up the dynamic adjustment and suppress the intra-loop regulation. It also has strong robustness [23], and does not adopt the SVPWM method [24], which reduces the complexity of the system. The lower complexity of the system is of great significance for the narrow space in the well. Therefore, the current loop of the continuous wave generator motor control system will be designed based on the hysteresis control method in this section.

In the design of current hysteresis controller, the d–q axis reference current and the rotor position angle θ_m is firstly converted into the reference value of phase current. The transformation process is as follows24:

$$\begin{bmatrix} i_{a\_ref} \\ i_{b\_ref} \\ i_{c\_ref} \end{bmatrix} = \begin{bmatrix} \cos\theta_m & \sin(-\theta_m) \\ \cos(\theta_m - 120°) & \sin(120° - \theta_m) \\ \cos(\theta_m - 240°) & \sin(240° - \theta_m) \end{bmatrix} \begin{bmatrix} i_{d\_ref} \\ i_{q\_ref} \end{bmatrix} \qquad (9)$$

Where: i_{a_ref}, i_{b_ref}, i_{c_ref} is the reference current of phase a, b, c, θ_m is the rotation angle of the rotor, i_{d_ref}, i_{q_ref} is the reference current of d axis and q axis.

Then the reference value of three-phase current is compared with the measured value of the three-phase current to obtain the three-phase switching signal S_{abc}, and the three-phase switching signal S_{abc} is sent to the inverter to control the permanent magnet synchronous motor. The hysteresis comparison principle is as follows:

$$S_k = \begin{cases} 1 & i_{k\_ref} - i_{k\_m} > H \\ 0 & i_{k\_ref} - i_{k\_m} < -H \end{cases} \tag{10}$$

Where: S_k is a three-phase switching signal, i_{k_ref}, i_{k_m} are respectively the reference signal of three-phase current and the measured signal of three-phase current, k = a, b, c. H is the loop width of the hysteresis comparator, and when $H > 0$, $S_k = 1$, which indicates that the upper arm of the inverter is turned on, the lower arm is turned off; It means that the upper arm is turned off, and the lower arm is turned on when $S_k = 0$.

3.3 Speed Loop Design

The active disturbance rejection controller (ADRC) has the characteristics of clear structure, simple algorithm, fast response, high control precision, excellent adaptability and robustness to the uncertain factors and external disturbances of the controlled object model11. However, the non-linear combination of its control part increases the cost of the system hardware and the parameters to be adjusted. Due to the limitation of underground space, the hardware resources are insufficient. Therefore, a linear combination is adopted instead of a nonlinear combination in this section, and the speed loop of the continuous wave generator motor control system is designed based on the improved ADRC.

The improved ADRC controller includes a differential tracker, an extended state tracker, and a linear feedback control law. The differential tracker arranges a transition process for the reference input and provides a differential signal with a high signal-to-noise ratio [11], which improves the stability of the system. The expression is as follows:

$$\begin{cases} \omega_{ref}(t+1) = \omega_{ref}(t) + h\dot{\omega}_{ref}(t) \\ \dot{\omega}_{ref}(t+1) = \dot{\omega}_{ref}(t) + hfst(\omega_{ref}(t) - \omega^*(t), \dot{\omega}_{ref}(t), r, h) \end{cases} \tag{11}$$

Where: ω_{ref} is the tracking signal of the motor's reference speed, $\dot{\omega}_{ref}$ is the differential of the motor reference speed signal, $\omega^*(t)$ is the motor reference speed input, r, h are the parameters to be adjusted for the system, fst is the optimal control function for fast control [9].

The extended state observer can be used to track the state variables of the system and estimate the uncertainties of the system model and the real-time values of the disturbances [9]. It can be used to obtain the tracking value of the measured speed signal and its differential signal. The expression is as follows:

$$\begin{cases} e_1 = x_1(t) - \omega(t) \\ x_1(t+1) = x_1(t) + h(x_2(t) - \beta_{01}e_1) \\ x_2(t+1) = x_2(t) + h(w(t) - \beta_{02}fal(e_1, a_1, \delta) + bu(t)) \\ w(t+1) = w(t) - h\beta_{03}fal(e_1, a_2, \delta) \end{cases} \tag{12}$$

Where: x_1 is the tracking signal for measuring the speed; ω is the measured speed signal; x_2 is the differential signal of the measuring speed; w is the tracking signal of the disturbance; u is the reference current value of the input motor; β_{01}, β_{02}, β_{03}, b, a_1, a_2 are the parameters to be adjusted; fal is the system function [9].

The linear feedback control law produces the required current value i_{ref} by the combination of the error signal and the differential of the error signal. The expression is as follows:

$$\begin{cases} e_3 = \omega_{ref}(t) - x_1(t) \\ e_4 = \dot{\omega}_{ref}(t) - x_2(t) \\ i_{ref}(t) = K_1 e_3 + K_2 e_4 \end{cases} \tag{13}$$

Where: e_3 is the error value of the speed signal, e_4 is the error value of the differential signal of the speed signal, K_1, K_2 are the parameters to be adjusted.

4   Simulation and Analysis

The MATLAB/Simulink platform is used for simulation in this section. The parameters used in the simulation are as follows: The pole pair $P_n = 4$, the stator inductance $L_d = L_q = 8.5$ mH, the stator resistance $R_s = 2.875\ \Omega$, the flux linkage $\psi_f = 0.175$ Wb, the moment of inertia $J = 0.0008$ kg·m^2 damping coefficient $B = 0$. In the speed loop controller, $h = 0.01$, $r = 6000$, $\beta_{01} = \beta_{02} = \beta_{03} = 100$, $b = 1$, $a_1 = 0.5$, $a_2 = 0.25$, $K_1 = 1.5$, $K_2 = 0.1$. The switching point of the current loop controller is $[0.05\ -0.05]$, and the output is $[150\ -150]$. The simulation model is shown in Fig. 4. Ode23tb algorithm with a simulation time of 0.25 s and a maximum time step of 0.00125 s in this simulation.

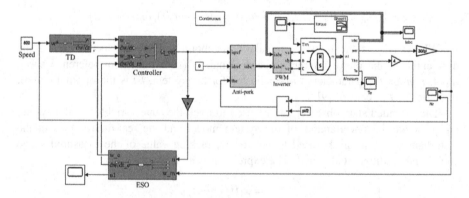

Fig. 4. Simulation model in Simulink.

When the motor speed is set to 800 r/min and the load torque changes according to the law shown in Fig. 3, the actual motor speed changes as shown in Fig. 5. It can be seen from the figure that the motor reaches a given speed after 0.019 s, and the overshoot is almost 0, and the motor can achieve speed following better.

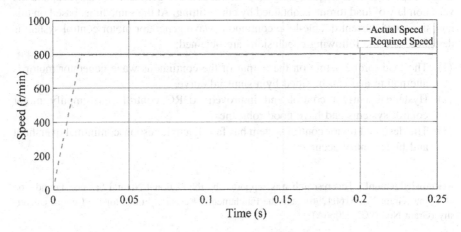

Fig. 5. Actual motor speed and given constant speed.

When the motor speed is set to cosine change and the load torque changes according to the law shown in Fig. 3, the actual motor speed changes as shown in Fig. 6. It can be seen from the figure that the difference between the motor speed and the given speed is small. When the speed decreases, a small overshoot occurs. The maximum overshoot is 12.8 r/min and the duration is 0.0184 s. It can be seen that the motor can be compared. The motor can achieve speed following better.

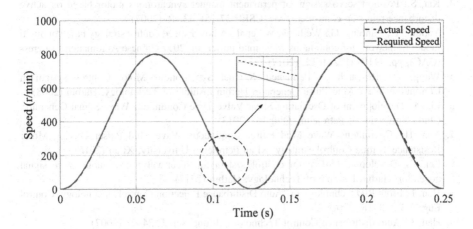

Fig. 6. Actual motor speed and given cosine change speed.

5 Conclusion

In this paper, the load torque acting on continuous wave generator is analyzed, and the variation law of load torque is obtained by curve fitting. At the same time, based on this law, the speed-current double-loop continuous wave generator motor control system is designed, and the following conclusions are obtained:

(1) The load torque acting on the output of the continuous wave generator motor is alternating and can be fitted by a sinusoid curve.
(2) Hysteresis current control and improved ADRC control can simplify motor control systems and have good robustness.
(3) The designed motor control system has fast dynamic response, minimal overshoot and high control accuracy.

Acknowledgement. This research was supported by the National Natural Science Foundation of China (Grant No. 51604296) and the Fundamental Research Funds for the Central University (Grant No. 19CX02066A).

References

1. Klotz, C., Wassermann, I., Hahn, D.: Highly flexible mud-pulse telemetry: a new system. In: SPE Indian Oil and Gas Technical Conference and Exhibition. Society of Petroleum Engineers (2008)
2. Peng, J.: Experimental study on design and signal transmission characteristics of drilling fluid continuous wave generator. China University of Petroleum (East China) Ph.D. thesis, p. 38 (2010)
3. Kai, S.: Position servo system of permanent magnet synchronous motor based on active disturbance rejection controller. Proc. CSEE **27**(15), 43–46 (2007)
4. Yaobin, Y., Yanfeng, G., Weiliang, W., et al.: A noval speed control strategy based on multi model framework for continuous wave mud pulser. In: 2017 Chinese Automation Congress (CAC), pp. 4119–4122. IEEE (2017)
5. Wang, W.: Research on Permanent Magnet Synchronous Motor Control System in Continuous Wave Mud Pulse Generator. Harbin Institute of Technology, Harbin (2008)
6. Li, M.: Development of Oscillating Shear Valve Type Continuous Wave Signal Generator. China University of Petroleum, Qingdao (2013)
7. Yan, H.: Continuous Wave Mud Pulser Continuous Wave Mud Pulser Driving Motor Resistance Torque Control Strategy. Xi'an Petroleum University, Xi'an (2016)
8. Lei, C.: Development of motor control system for shear valve continuous wave signal generator. Harbin Institute of Technology, Harbin (2017)
9. Han, J.: From PID technology to "Auto Disturbance Rejection Control" technology. Control Eng. **9**(3), 13–18 (2002)
10. Han, J.: Auto-disturbance Control Technology. Front. Sci. **1**, 24–31 (2007)
11. Liu, J., Xur, B., Zheng, J.: Analysis and design of active disturbance rejection controller. Inf. Technol. Informatization **2008**(3), 106–108 (2008)
12. Qi, L.: Research and application of permanent magnet synchronous motor control based on sliding mode variable structure method. East China University of Science and Technology (2013)

13. Jia, P., Fang, J., Li, L.: Analysis of erosion performance of series continuous wave signal generator in throttle. Petrol. Mach. **38**, 11–14 (2010)
14. Jia, P., Fang, J., Su, Y., et al.: Hydraulic torque analysis of rotating fluid continuous wave signal generator turning valve. J. China Univ. Petrol. Natural Sci. Ed. **34**(1), 99–104 (2010)
15. Wang, Z., Xiao, J., Zhai, Z.: Research on hydraulic characteristics of rotary valve mud pulser rotor. Pet. Mine Mach. **41**(3), 1–3 (2012)
16. Ye, C., Wang, Z., Lu, Q., Qi, F., Wang, C.: Hydraulic torque of reciprocating mud pulse generator rotor. Ed. Off. Acta Petrol. Sinica **35**(2), 385–389 (2014)
17. Ye, C.: Research on hydraulic characteristics of reciprocating pulser rotor. Hangzhou: Zhejiang University Master's thesis (2014)
18. Wu, J., Rui, Z., Wang, R.: Mathematical model and optimum design approach of sinusoidal pressure wave generator for downhole drilling tool. Appl. Math. Model. **47**, 587–599 (2017)
19. Xia, C.: Numerous DC Motor Control Systems. Science Press, Beijing (2009)
20. Chen, X.: Research and development of high performance AC servo system. Doctoral thesis of Zhejiang University, pp. 33–36 (1996)
21. Pillay, P.: Modeling of permanent magnet motor drives. IEEE Trans. Ind. Electron. **35**(4), 537–540 (1988)
22. Cui, B., Zhou, J., Ren, Z.: Modeling and simulation of Permanent magnet synchronous motor Drives? In: Proceedings of the Fifth International Conference on Electrical Machines and Systems, ICEMS, Shenyang, China, pp. 905–908 (2001)
23. Tiwari, A.N., Agarwal, P., Srivastava, S.P.: Performance investigation of modified hysteresis current controller with the permanent magnet synchronous motor drive. IET Electr. Power Appl. **4**(2), 101–108 (2010)
24. Wei, W., Ming, C., Zhang, B., et al.: Fault tolerant control of phase current sensor in current hysteresis permanent magnet synchronous motor drive system. Proc. CSEE **32**(33), 59–66 (2012)

Trajectory Planning Based on Optimal Control and Exact Derivatives

Xiaodong Zhang[1]([✉]), Ling Tu[1], Jiafeng Wu[2]([✉]), and Shurong Li[3]

[1] College of Information and Control Engineering,
China University of Petroleum (East China), Qingdao 266580, China
{zhangxd,tuling}@upc.edu.cn
[2] Key Laboratory of Unconventional Oil & Gas Development,
China University of Petroleum (East China), Ministry of Education,
Qingdao 266580, China
hitwu@163.com
[3] College of Automation, Beijing University of Posts and Telecommunications,
Beijing, China

Abstract. To solve the trajectory planning problem, a path constrained optimal control model is established and is solved by gradient-based numerical method. Since it is very computationally expensive for the adjoint equation method to calculate the gradients of path constraints, an exact derivative method is used to calculate the gradients of objective and path constraints accurately and efficiently. The method is achieved by regarding the objective and path constraints as explicit functions of the parametrized controls. Then the gradient can be calculated in reverse mode of automatic differentiation which requiring Jacobian information of the integrator for solving state equation. The Jacobian matrix of the new states with respect to current states and controls is analytically derived for the 4th-order Runge-Kutta method and is calculated and stored when integrating the state equation. From a study case, an OCP with inequality path constraints was discretized to nonlinear programming problem by control vector parameterization (CVP) and was solved by sequential quadratic (SQP) method. The simulation case for a differential drive robot demonstrates the efficiency of the proposed method.

Keywords: Optimal control · Path constraint · Gradient · Automatic differentiation

1 Introduction

For trajectory planning problem, a robot should be driven to a position with finite time and low energy consumption, the problem can be formulated to an optimal control model. To avoid obstacles, path constraints should be add to the optimal control model, which should be satisfied at any time. To solve the optimal control problem numerically, the original dynamic optimization problem

© Springer Nature Switzerland AG 2019
H. Yu et al. (Eds.): ICIRA 2019, LNAI 11745, pp. 580–591, 2019.
https://doi.org/10.1007/978-3-030-27529-7_49

is often discretized to a static optimization problem which can be solved by non-linear programming (NLP). The discretization is performed by approximating the states and controls with functions of time on a specified time grid, so the performance and constraints can be calculated from the discretized states and controls. If the states and controls are simultaneously parameterized, the derived static optimization problem is a nonlinear programming with large scale equality constraints, because of the discretization form of state equation must be satisfied on each time node [1,2]. Piecewise polynomials and Gauss pseudospectral [3] are often chosen to discrete the states and controls. If only the control vectors are parameterized [4], the state vectors can be obtained by integrating the state equation. The NLP problem discretized from OCP can be solved by gradient based algorithms or evolutionary optimization algorithms such as genetic algorithm [5], immune-based algorithms [6] and differential evolution [7,8]. For gradient based method, the derivatives of performance index and constraints with respect to the parameters can be obtained by adjoint equation method [9] or sensitivity method [10]. During the procedure of adjoint method, the state equation of optimal control problem is often solved by numerical integration methods such as Euler method and Runge-Kutta method. And the continuous adjoint equation should also be integrated numerically but for the backward time direction. The integration methods should be chosen carefully, otherwise the gradients computed from adjoint variables may differ from its exact value [9,11]. For the gradients of equality and inequality path constraints, it is a tedious and time consuming work to calculate the gradients at each time node by adjoint or sensitivity method. So the penalty function method [12,13] and constraint aggregation method [14,15] were developed to convert the original OCP to an unconstrained problem. But the approximation of path constraints may affect the convergence of the NLP solving procedure [16]. For solving the state equation, the explicit integral methods are often used, the procedure of which can be regarded as a series function calculation. The computing of performance and path constraints can also be regarded as functions of the discretized states and controls. So the gradient needed in NLP method can be derived by chain rule of derivative. The AD (Automatic Differentiation) method has already been applied to solving optimal control problem. Walther [17,18] discuss the relationship for adjoint method and AD method for solving OCP. Birgina [19] calculate the gradient of performance by AD, and solve the OCP by spectral projected method. Chen developed a software packages named RIOTS [20] which using AD to calculate the derivative of states. We also investigated the gradient calculation problem but only considering the gradient of performance index [21]. In order to compute the gradients of both performance and path constraints, an efficient exact derivative method is proposed based on the idea of AD. The Jacobian matrix of RK4 method are calculated and stored in the procedure of solving state equation, which are used for computing gradients.

2   Path Constrained OCP

Trajectory planning can be formulated as the following optimal control problem,

$$\min \ J(u) \ = \ \theta(x(t_f)) + \int_0^{t_f} L(x(t), u(t))dt \tag{1}$$

$$\text{s.t.} \ \dot{x}(t) \ = \ f(x(t), u(t)) \tag{2}$$

$$g(x, u, t) \ \leq \ 0 \tag{3}$$

$$x(0) \ = \ x^0 \tag{4}$$

$$u_L \leq u(t) \leq u_H \tag{5}$$

where $x(t) \in R^n$ is the state of the ODE system, $u(t) \in R^m$ is bounded control vector, $g(x, u, t) \in R^{n_g}$ is path constraint. $\theta(x(t_f))$ is final time performance index and $L(x(t), u(t))$ is instant performance. The initial states of the control system is x^0.

2.1   Discretization

To get the objective value of the optimal control problem, the state equation should be integrated to get states at all time nodes. Explicit integral methods are usually used to solve the state equation, Euler method and 4th-order Runge-Kutta method are adopted in this paper. Let the time span $[0, t_f]$ be divided into N parts, and $\{t_k\}, (k = 0, 1, ..., N)$ denote all the time nodes from $t_0 = 0$ to $t_N = t_f$. The step length at the k-th step is noted as $h^k = t_{k+1} - t_k$. The step length is often chosen as constant for solving optimal control problem, so we use h instead. Let x^k and u^k denote the state and control vector at time grid t_k. If the initial state x^0 and $u^k (k = 0, 1, ..., N-1)$ are given, after solving the state equation, all the state value at time node t_k can be obtained. And the performance and path constraint can be calculated from x^k and u^k. The performance is often discretized as

$$J = \theta(x^N) + \sum_{k=0}^{N-1} hL(x^k, u^k) = J^N + \sum_{k=0}^{N-1} J^k \tag{6}$$

where J^k represents the instant performance at t_k. The path constrain at time t_k is,

$$g^k(x^k, u^k, t_k) \leq 0 \tag{7}$$

In control vector parameterization method, the continuous control variable is piece wisely approximated by a function of time. Usually the time grids for discretizing control are equally divided, and all the control variables have the same time grids. Let N_{cvp} denotes the count of time pieces, and $\{\tau_k\}, (k = 0, 1, ..., N_{cvp})$ denotes the control time nodes from $\tau_0 = 0$ to $\tau_{N_{cvp}} = t_f$. The j-th control variable can be expressed as

$$u_j(t) = \phi_{j,k}(t, \alpha_{j,k}), t \in [\tau_{k-1}, \tau_k]. \tag{8}$$

where $\phi_{j,k}$ is usually chosen as a polynomial function of time t, and $\alpha_{j,k}$ is a vector consist of the coefficients of the polynomial. $\phi_{j,k}$ can also be chosen as a function consists of some basis function, such as wavelet, Chebyshev polynomials, etc. If $\alpha_{j,k}$ for each control variable at all the time intervals are determined, the control $u(t)$ can be obtained. Let denote all of parameters as a vector α, then the problem of finding optimal control is transferred to a NLP problem, which searching the optimal decision variables α to extreme the performance while satisfying the state equation, path constraints, bounded constraint and initial conditions.

2.2 Solving NLP

The NLP problem discretized from OCP by CVP method can be formulated as

$$
\begin{aligned}
\min_{\alpha} \ & J(\alpha) \\
\text{s.t.} \ & g(\alpha) \le 0
\end{aligned}
\tag{9}
$$

The objective function can be computed from Eq. (6), and the inequity constraints includes two parts. One is the path constraints from Eq. (7), the other is bounded constraints of controls. If piece wise constant is chosen for discretizing control, the constraint in Eq. (4) is transferred to bounded constraint of α. For a given α, the control $u(t)$ is determined, then the objective function and constraint can be calculated after solving the state equation. Many approaches can be used to solve the NLP problem. Because it is time consuming for solving the state equation to get the objective and constraint function of the NLP, gradient based algorithms are often adopted, such as SQP, penalty function method and augmented Lagrangian methods [22]. If only the gradient of objective is calculated, one adjoint problem need to be integrated backward time. But for path constraints, the gradient of each constraint at all discretized time nodes are needed. Since the count of adjoint problem to be solved is the number of path constraints multiply by the count of time nodes, it is time consuming for computation and is a tedious work to derive the separated adjoint system for each constraint. So the exact derivative method is proposed for calculating the gradient of objective and path constraints.

3   Exact Derivative

When solving the NLP problem derived from the OCP, the procedure of solving state equation together with the calculation of objective and constraints can be regarded as a series of mathematical operations. So the objective and constraints are the function of initial states and decision variables of NLP problem. Although the calculation is computing intensive, the gradient of objective and constraints with respect to decision variables can be obtained by derivative chain rule. So the automatic differentiation technique can be used. But there is an integration procedure, it is hard to use AD directly. But if the gradients are obtained by AD method, they are exact values. So in this part we will analyze the procedure of objective and path constraint procedure to find the exact gradient.

3.1   Derivative of Objective Function

The objective function is the discretize performance referring to Eq. (6). The calculation procedure can be illustrated as the following figure.

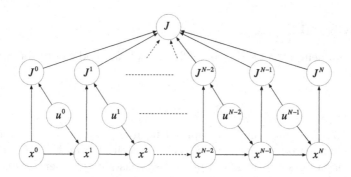

Fig. 1. Calculation procedure of the performance.

From Fig. 1, it is shown that the instant performance J^{N-1} is a function of u^{N-1} and x^{N-1}, and the J^N is a function of x^N. If explicit integration method is used for solving the state equation, x^k can be expressed as a explicit function formulated by

$$x^{k+1} = \varphi(x^k, u^k, h). \tag{10}$$

So x^N is explicit function of u^{N-1} and x^{N-1}, and the derivative of J with respect to u^{N-1} is

$$\frac{\partial J}{\partial u^{N-1}} = \frac{\partial J^{N-1}}{\partial u^{N-1}} + \frac{\partial J^N}{\partial x^N} \frac{\partial x^N}{\partial u^{N-1}}. \tag{11}$$

Similarly, the derivatives of J with respect to u^{N-p} $(p = 2, 3, ..., N)$ is

$$\frac{\partial J}{\partial u^{N-p}} = \frac{\partial J^{N-p}}{\partial u^{N-p}} + \left(\sum_{i=1}^{p-1} \frac{\partial J^{N-i+1}}{\partial x^{N-i+1}} \prod_{j=N-i}^{N-p+1} \frac{\partial x^{j+1}}{\partial x^j} + \frac{\partial J^{N-p+1}}{\partial x^{N-p+1}} \right) \frac{\partial x^{N-p+1}}{\partial u^{N-p}}. \tag{12}$$

Let $k = N - p, (k = 0, 1, .., N - 2)$, the Eq. (12) can be expressed as

$$\frac{\partial J}{\partial u^k} = \frac{\partial J^k}{\partial u^k} + \left(\sum_{i=1}^{N-k-1} \frac{\partial J^{N-i+1}}{\partial x^{N-i+1}} \prod_{j=N-i}^{k+1} \frac{\partial x^{j+1}}{\partial x^j} + \frac{\partial J^{k+1}}{\partial x^{k+1}} \right) \frac{\partial x^{k+1}}{\partial u^k}. \tag{13}$$

In the above equations, the derivatives of instant performance index J^k with respect to x^k and u^k can be analytically derived as

$$\frac{\partial J^k}{\partial x^k} = h\frac{\partial L(x^k, u^k)}{\partial x^k}, \quad \frac{\partial J^k}{\partial u^k} = h\frac{\partial L(x^k, u^k)}{\partial u^k} \tag{14}$$

The derivatives of x^{k+1} with respect to x^k and u^k are Jacobian matrix derived from Eq. (10) which are

$$\frac{\partial x^{k+1}}{\partial x^k} = \frac{\partial \varphi(x^k, u^k, h)}{\partial x^k}, \quad \frac{\partial x^{k+1}}{\partial u^k} = \frac{\partial \varphi(x^k, u^k, h)}{\partial u^k} \tag{15}$$

Since the x^{k+1} is calculated by numerical integration method, $\varphi(x^k, u^k, h)$ is expressed as a series formulas instead of a single analytical form. But the Jacobian matrix can be calculated numerically while solving the state equation. If the Jacobian matrix is stored at every integration step, the exact derivatives of J are can be achieved.

3.2   Derivative of Path Constraint

After getting the discretized state x^k and u^k by solving state equation, the values of path constraint at time t_k can be obtained. The partial derivative of constraint g^k with respect to u^k is $\partial g^k / \partial u^k$ and can be analytically calculated from Eq. (7). The partial derivative of constraint g^k with respect to u^{k-1} is

$$\frac{\partial g^k}{\partial u^{k-1}} = \frac{\partial g^k}{\partial x^k}\frac{\partial x^k}{\partial u^{k-1}}. \tag{16}$$

So the derivative of g^k with respect to $u^i, (i = 0, 1, ..., k-2)$ is

$$\frac{\partial g^k}{\partial u^i} = \frac{\partial g^k}{\partial x^k}\prod_{j=k}^{i+2}\frac{\partial x^j}{\partial x^{j-1}}\frac{\partial x^{i+1}}{\partial u^i}. \tag{17}$$

For $i > k$, $\partial g^k / \partial u^i = 0$. Thus the partial derivatives of g^k with respect to all $u^k, (k = 0, 1, ..., N-1)$ can be calculated, then the gradient of path constraint to decision variables $\nabla g^k(\alpha)$ can be achieved. If the Jacobian matrix of x^{k+1} with respect to x^k is stored from integration procedure, the computation cost will be reduced a lot for gradients calculation at all-time nodes.

3.3   Implementation of Exact Derivative Algorithm

After discretizing the optimal control problem, many NLP algorithms can be used to solve the converted NLP. Thus the procedure of solving the OCP is the iterations of NLP solving methods. In each iteration, the objective, constraints and gradients for both of them should be provided. So the exact derivative algorithm is executed at each iteration of the NLP method. The calculation procedure is given as follows.

Step 1: For a set of parameters α, get the $u(t_k)$ at each time node t_k, solve the state equation for the time from 0 to t_f and save the Jacobian matrix Eq. (15) for each step k.

Step 2: Let $k = N$, calculate J^N and $\partial J^N / \partial x^N$.

Step 3: Let $k = k - 1$ until $k = 0$, calculate $J^k, \partial J^k / \partial x^k, \partial J^k / \partial u^k$. According to Eqs. (11)–(13), compute $\partial J / \partial u^k$ by using the Jacobian matrix provided in step 1.

Step 4: Get the objective value by summarizing J^k for $k = 0$ to N, get the gradient of objective $\nabla J(\alpha)$ by $\partial J^k / \partial u^k$ and Eq. (8).

Step 5: Let $k = N$, calculate the path constraint at time node t_N.

Step 6: Compute g^k and $\partial g^k / \partial u^i$ for all $0 \leq i < k$ by Eqs. (7) (16) and (17).

Step 7: Let $k = k - 1$ go to step6 until $k = 0$.

Step 8: Get the gradient $\nabla g^k(\alpha)$ for all $k = 1, 2...N$ by $\partial g^k / \partial u^i$ and Eq. (8).

4 Jacobian Calculation

For gradient calculation of objective and path constraints, if the Jacobian of integration is provided there is no need to calculate the derivatives inside the integration repeatedly. The explicit integration methods are often used in solving the state equations of an OCP, such as Euler method and Runge-Kutta method. For a given time interval $[t_k, t_{k+1}]$, the state x^{k+1} on t_{k+1} can be calculated from the state x^k, step length h and control u in $[t_k, t_{k+1}]$. The value of control can be treated as constant or varying value during the time interval. In this paper we consider control u is constant and denoted by u^k, so the state x^{k+1} can be express as a explicit function of x^k, u^k and h. But if u is varying and expressed as a function of t, such as interpolation function, additional parameters should be considered. Then the state x^{k+1} may be a function of u^k, u^{k+1} and other parameters, which depend on how to formula the controls in $[t_k, t_{k+1}]$. And the u at grids and all the parameters related to $u(t)$, $t \in [t_k, t_{k+1}]$ can be regarded as augmented controls $\bar{u}^k$ to replace u^k in the previous section. In optimal control problem, the integration step length h is determined by the precision requirement of solving state equations and not a decision variable, so the state x^{k+1} is a function of x^k, u^k. The calculation of Jacobian matrix of x^{k+1} for Runge-Kutta method will be given in the following part.

It is assumed that the control is constant in time interval $[t^k, t^{k+1}]$, then the 4th-order Runge-Kutta method for solving the state equation is shown as follows,

$$
\begin{aligned}
k_1 &= f(x^k, u^k), \\
k_2 &= f(x^k + hk_1/2, u^k), \\
k_3 &= f(x^k + hk_2/2, u^k), \\
k_4 &= f(x^k + hk_3, u^k), \\
x^{k+1} &= x^k + h(k_1 + 2k_2 + 2k_3 + k_4)
\end{aligned}
\tag{18}
$$

In RK4 method, x^{k+1} is an explicit function of x^k, u^k, the Jacobian of x^{k+1} can be derived analytically as follows:

$$\frac{\partial k_1}{\partial x^k} = \frac{\partial f}{\partial x^k}, \quad \frac{\partial k_1}{\partial u^k} = \frac{\partial f}{\partial u^k} \tag{19}$$

$$\frac{\partial k_2}{\partial x^k} = \frac{\partial f}{\partial x}\left(I + \frac{h}{2}\frac{\partial k_1}{\partial x^k}\right), \quad \text{at } x = x^k + \frac{h}{2}k_1 \tag{20}$$

$$\frac{\partial k_2}{\partial u^k} = \frac{h}{2}\frac{\partial f}{\partial x}\frac{\partial k_1}{\partial u^k} + \frac{\partial f}{\partial u^k}, \quad \text{at } x = x^k + \frac{h}{2}k_1 \tag{21}$$

$$\frac{\partial k_3}{\partial x^k} = \frac{\partial f}{\partial x}\left(I + \frac{h}{2}\frac{\partial k_2}{\partial x^k}\right), \quad \text{at } x = x^k + \frac{h}{2}k_2 \tag{22}$$

$$\frac{\partial k_3}{\partial u^k} = \frac{h}{2}\frac{\partial f}{\partial x}\frac{\partial k_2}{\partial u^k} + \frac{\partial f}{\partial u^k}, \quad \text{at } x = x^k + \frac{h}{2}k_2 \tag{23}$$

$$\frac{\partial k_4}{\partial x^k} = \frac{\partial f}{\partial x}\left(I + h\frac{\partial k_3}{\partial x^k}\right), \quad \text{at } x = x^k + hk_3 \tag{24}$$

$$\frac{\partial k_4}{\partial u^k} = h\frac{\partial f}{\partial x}\frac{\partial k_3}{\partial u^k} + \frac{\partial f}{\partial u^k}, \quad \text{at } x = x^k + hk_3 \tag{25}$$

With above equations, the Jacobian of x^{k+1} can be finally achieved as,

$$\frac{\partial x^{k+1}}{\partial x^k} = I + \frac{h}{6}\left(\frac{\partial k_1}{\partial x^k} + 2\frac{\partial k_2}{\partial x^k} + 2\frac{\partial k_3}{\partial x^k} + \frac{\partial k_4}{\partial x^k}\right) \tag{26}$$

$$\frac{\partial x^{k+1}}{\partial u^k} = \frac{h}{6}\left(\frac{\partial k_1}{\partial u^k} + 2\frac{\partial k_2}{\partial u^k} + 2\frac{\partial k_3}{\partial u^k} + \frac{\partial k_4}{\partial u^k}\right) \tag{27}$$

5   Differential Drive Robot Case

5.1   Optimal Control Model

The motion of two wheeled car robot can be described by the dynamic model (see [23,24]) as follows,

$$\dot{x}_1 = x_4 \cos x_3 \tag{28}$$

$$\dot{x}_2 = x_4 \sin x_3 \tag{29}$$

$$\dot{x}_3 = x_5 \tag{30}$$

$$\dot{x}_4 = \frac{-2(B_e + K_a K_b/R_a)}{mr^2 + 2I_e}x_4 + \frac{rK_a}{R_a}\frac{1}{mr^2 + 2I_e}(u_r + u_l) \tag{31}$$

$$\dot{x}_5 = \frac{-4a^2(B_e + K_a K_b/R_a)}{Ir^2 + 4a^2 I_e}x_5 + \frac{rK_a}{R_a}\frac{2a}{Ir^2 + 4a^2 I_e}(u_r - u_l) \tag{32}$$

where x_1, x_2 denotes the coordinates of the midpoint of the car in the global reference frame, x_3 is the angular of forward direction, x_4 is the velocity in forward direction, and x_5 is the angular velocity, u_r, u_l denotes currents of the right and left motor. The coefficients of the model are given in the Table 1.

Table 1. Parameters of the car robot

Parameter	Description	Nominal value
K_a	Torque constant	$0.0487\,\mathrm{Nm/A}$
L_a	Armature inductance	$0.6410^3\,\mathrm{H}$
R_a	Armature resistance	$0.267\,\Omega$
r	Wheel radius	$0.1\,\mathrm{m}$
m	Mass	$30\,\mathrm{Kg}$
I	Inertia	$0.83\,\mathrm{Kgm}^2$
a	Half distance between the wheels	$0.25\,\mathrm{m}$
K_b	Back EMF constant	$0.0487\,\mathrm{V/(rad/s)}$
I_e	Moment of inertia coefficient	$0.271\ \mathrm{Kgm}^2$
B_e	Viscous friction coefficient	$0.271\,\mathrm{Nms}$

The car robot is driven from an initial state $x(t_0)$ to a target state x_T. To avoid the obstacle and use minimal energy, the following optimal control problem can be formulated,

$$\min\ J(u) \ =\ \int_0^{20} (u_r^2 + u_l^2)dt \tag{33}$$

$$\text{s.t.}\quad \dot{x}(t) \ =\ f(x(t), u(t)) \tag{34}$$

$$1 \ \leq\ (x_1(t) - 5)^2 + (x_2(t) - 5)^2 \tag{35}$$

$$x(0) \ =\ [0, 0, 0, 0, 0]^T \tag{36}$$

$$x(20) \ =\ [10, 10, 0, 0, 0]^T \tag{37}$$

$$-1 \leq u_i(t) \leq 1, i = r, l \tag{38}$$

where Eq. (34) represents the dynamic model from Eqs. (28)–(32).

5.2   Simulation Results

The original optimal control problem was discretized by CVP method, and the time nodes of controls and constraints are both chosen as 50. The converted NLP problem has 100 decision variables and 50 inequality constraints. The initial controls are $u_r{}^0(t) = u_l^0(t) = 0, t \in [0, 20]$. To evaluate the efficiency of gradient calculation, the gradients of objective and constraints are calculated by 100 times. The time cost for three method are given in Table 2. It is shown that, to calculate the gradient of objective, adjoint equation (AE) and exact derivative (ED) method are more efficient. Because ED method calculates the Jacobian in state equation solving, it takes much time than AD. But for gradients of constraints, AE method need solve adjoint equation for each non-linear constraints, the time cost is directly proportional to number of constraints. But for ED method, by using the storage Jacobian it saves much time.

Table 2. Time cost(ms) for gradients calculation

Method	Objective gradient	Constraint gradient
Forward difference	256	11410
Adjoint equation	10	482
Exact derivative	18	93

To solve the NLP active-set SQP method was used, The trajectories of optimal control and optimal states are shown in Fig. 2.

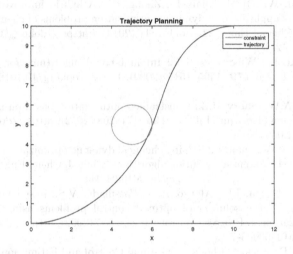

Fig. 2. Optimal trajectory.

6   Conclusion

When solving trajectory planning problem by optimal control method, the gradients of path constraints can be efficiently calculated with exact derivative method. The method is an application of automatic differentiation in dynamic optimization, but the implementation method given in this article doesn't need any automatic differentiation software package. From the numerical example, the exact derivative method shows its high accuracy and computational efficiency. It is very suitable to solve trajectory planning with obstacle avoidance.

Acknowledgement. This research was supported by the National Natural Science Foundation of China (Grant No. 51604296 and 61573378) and the Fundamental Research Funds for the Central University (Grant No. 19CX02066A).

References

1. Kameswaran, S., Biegler, L.T.: Simultaneous dynamic optimization strategies: recent advances and challenges. Comput. Chem. Eng. **30**, 1560–1575 (2006). https://doi.org/10.1016/j.compchemeng.2006.05.034
2. Liu, X., Chen, L., Hu, Y.: Solution of chemical dynamic optimization using the simultaneous strategies. Chin. J. Chem. Eng. **21**, 55–63 (2013). https://doi.org/10.1016/S1004-9541(13)60441-3
3. Benson, D.: A gauss pseudospectral transcription for optimal control (2005)
4. Goh, C.J., Teo, K.L.: Control parametrization: a unified approach to optimal control problems with general constraints. Automatica **24**, 3–18 (1988). https://doi.org/10.1016/0005-1098(88)90003-9
5. Sun, F., Du, W., Qi, R., Qian, F., Zhong, W.: A hybrid improved genetic algorithm and its application in dynamic optimization problems of chemical processes. Chin. J. Chem. Eng. **21**, 144–154 (2013). https://doi.org/10.1016/S1004-9541(13)60452-8
6. Trojanowski, K., Wierzchoń, S.T.: Immune-based algorithms for dynamic optimization. Inf. Sci. **179**, 1495–1515 (2009). https://doi.org/10.1016/j.ins.2008.11.014
7. Mohamed, A.W., Sabry, H.Z.: Constrained optimization based on modified differential evolution algorithm. Inf. Sci. **194**, 171–208 (2012). https://doi.org/10.1016/j.ins.2012.01.008
8. Chen, X., Du, W., Qian, F.: Solving chemical dynamic optimization problems with ranking-based differential evolution algorithms. Chin. J. Chem. Eng. **24**, 1600–1608 (2016). https://doi.org/10.1016/j.cjche.2016.04.044
9. Canto, E.B., Banga, J.R., Alonso, A.A., Vassiliadis, V.S.: Restricted second order information for the solution of optimal control problems using control vector parameterization. J. Process Control **12**, 243–255 (2002). https://doi.org/10.1016/S0959-1524(01)00008-7
10. Betts, J.T.: Practical Methods for Optimal Control and Estimation Using Nonlinear Programming. Society for Industrial and Applied Mathematics, Philadelphia (2010)
11. Sanz-Serna, J.M.: Symplectic runge-kutta schemes for adjoint equations, automatic differentiation, optimal control, and more. SIAM Rev. **58**, 3–33 (2016). https://doi.org/10.1137/151002769
12. Hu, Y., Liu, X., Xue, A.: An improved control vector iteration approach for nonlinear dynamic optimization (I) problems without path constraints. Chin. J. Chem. Eng. **20**, 1053–1058 (2012). https://doi.org/10.1016/S1004-9541(12)60586-2
13. Liu, X., Hu, Y., Feng, J., Liu, K.: A novel penalty approach for nonlinear dynamic optimization problems with inequality path constraints. IEEE Trans. Autom. Control **59**, 2863–2867 (2014). https://doi.org/10.1109/TAC.2014.2317293
14. Bloss, K.F., Biegler, L.T., Schiesser, W.E.: Dynamic process optimization through adjoint formulations and constraint aggregation. Ind. Eng. Chem. Res. **38**, 421–432 (1999). https://doi.org/10.1021/ie9804733
15. Poon, N.M.K., Martins, J.R.R.A.: An adaptive approach to constraint aggregation using adjoint sensitivity analysis. Struct. Multi. Optim. **34**, 61–73 (2007). https://doi.org/10.1007/s00158-006-0061-7
16. Zhang, Q., Li, S., Lei, Y., Zhang, X.: Newton-conjugate gradient (CG) augmented Lagrangian method for path constrained dynamic process optimization. J. Control Theory Appl. **10**, 223–228 (2012). https://doi.org/10.1007/s11768-012-0032-z

17. Griesse, R., Walther, A.: Evaluating gradients in optimal control: continuous adjoints versus automatic differentiation. J. Optim. Theory Appl. **122**, 63–86 (2004). https://doi.org/10.1023/B:JOTA.0000041731.71309.f1
18. Walther, A.: Automatic differentiation of explicit Runge-Kutta methods for optimal control. Comput. Optim. Applic. **36**, 83–108 (2007). https://doi.org/10.1007/s10589-006-0397-3
19. Birgina, E., Evtusenko, Y.: Automatic differentiation and spectral projected gradient methods for optimal control problems. Optim. Methods Softw. **10**(2), 125–146 (1998)
20. Birgina, E., Evtusenko, Y.: Automatic differentiation and spectral projected gradient methods for optimal control problems. Optim. Methods Softw. **10**, 125–146 (1998). https://doi.org/10.1080/10556789808805707
21. Zhang, X., Li, S., Lu, S.: Exact derivative calculation for Solving optimal control problem numerically. J. Sys. Sci. Math. Scis. **35**(7), 812–822 (2015)
22. Nocedal, J.: Numerical Optimization. Springer, New York (2006)
23. Abdulwahhab, O.W., Abbas, N.H.: Design and stability analysis of a fractional order state feedback controller for trajectory tracking of a differential drive robot. Int. J. Control Autom. Syst. **16**, 2790–2800 (2018). https://doi.org/10.1007/s12555-017-0234-8
24. Zhang, Y., Hong, D., Chung, J.H., Velinsky, S.A.: Dynamic model based robust tracking control of a differentially steered wheeled mobile robot. In: Proceedings of the 1998 American Control Conference. ACC (IEEE Cat. No. 98CH36207), vol. 2, pp. 850–855 (1998). https://doi.org/10.1109/ACC.1998.703528

Automotive Systems

Co-simulation Based on ADAMS and Simulink for Direct Yaw Moment Control System of 4WD-EV

Wang Yaping[1,2], Zhang Liping[3], Cao Sen[2], and Zhang Zheng[2(✉)]

[1] Institute of Automotive Engineering,
Shaan Xi Communications Technical College, Xi'an 710018, China
[2] Institute of Robotics and Intelligent Systems,
School of Mechanical Engineering, Xi'an Jiaotong University,
Xi'an 710049, China
zhangzh@mail.xjtu.edu.cn, 2889221067@qq.com
[3] Key Laboratory of Road Construction and Equipment of MOE,
Chang'an University, Xi'an, China

Abstract. A direct yaw moment control system using fuzzy logic is developed for 4 wheel drive electric vehicle (4WD-EV). The upper layer of the controller is a fuzzy PI controller to calculate desired yaw moment, inputs are the errors between the actual value and reference of side slip angle and yaw rate; the under layer distribute the torque properly on each wheel applying fuzzy logic rules, the rules are made in consideration of the contribution of each wheel to the required yaw moment and the driving limit of the vehicle. A vehicle dynamics model is established using ADAMS/Car, and co-simulation is carried out with the control system established in MATLAB/Simulink. The results show that the control system can effectively improve vehicle's handling and stability in different situations.

Keywords: Independent drive · Electric vehicle · Direct yaw moment control · Co-simulation

1 Introduction

With the advantage of multi-energy resource, simple structure, convenient use and pollutant emissions less, electric vehicle is one of the important ways to improve the energy shortage and environmental pollution [1]. Traditional vehicle dynamics control system make the longitudinal force of each wheel not equal to adjust the motor status by joint control of braking and engine or braking and transmission system [2]. Independent drive electric vehicle can take full advantage of rapid response of motor and high degree accuracy of torque to independent drive each wheel by using hub motor or in-wheel motor. It can improve the dynamic performance of vehicle under complicated

The Project was Supported by the Key Laboratory of Expressway Construction Machinery of Shaanxi Province, 300102259513.

H. Yu et al. (Eds.): ICIRA 2019, LNAI 11745, pp. 595–606, 2019.
https://doi.org/10.1007/978-3-030-27529-7_50

and extreme working condition by actively regulating the torque of each wheel to obtain yaw moment. That is to say, compared with electronic stability program (ESP) of traditional vehicle, direct yaw moment control (DYC) is more flexible and efficient in implementation.

The crux of DYC is to calculate a perfect yaw torque by distinguishing the vehicle running state. The study group of Jalali [3] designs a three-dimensional fuzzy controller, the inputs of fuzzy logic rules are the errors ($\Delta\beta$) between the actual value (β) and reference (β_d) of side slip angle, the errors ($\Delta\gamma$) and differential ($d(\Delta\gamma)/dt$) between the actual value (γ) and reference (γ_d) of yaw rate. Two main control variable of vehicle running state are taken into account and differential link is used to depress the over-shoot. With larger scale and complex relationship between variables, rich expert experience is required in making fuzzy logic rules. In order to simplify the formulation of fuzzy logic rules, in this paper, two control variable were controlled by fuzzy PI controller. A perfect yaw moment is calculated by the allocation of two outputs on the basis of side slip angle size. The allocation is formulated according to β theory proposed by Shibahata [4].

Torque distribution is mainly by optimization method in most of the relevant literatures after obtain the demand torque of whole vehicle. The establishment of objective function concentrated on stability of tire adhesion utilization [5], economy of average working efficiency of motor [6] and so on. The two objective functions are established and optimal allocation strategy is formulated by using fuzzy weight function. However, the different effect to yaw moment by the output of each wheel is ignored [7]. In this paper, the fuzzy rule is fabricated on the basis of simulation result of optimal distribution and ultimate analysis of vehicle driving [8]. The input is the requirement for vehicle drive torque and yaw moment.

The distribution of outputs by four wheels can obtain yaw moment more effectively under the prerequisite of driving. A vehicle dynamics models of control object and control algorithm are established in ADAMS/Car and MATLAB/Simulink respectively. Co-simulation is carried out and the accuracy and reliability of the designed DYC control system are verified.

2 Direct Yaw Moment Control System

2.1 System Structure of DYC

The schematic diagram of direct yaw moment control is shown in Fig. 1. For example, oversteer with turn left, the clockwise compensation of yaw moment can be obtained by increasing the driving force of left wheel or decreasing the driving force of right wheel. Thus, the vehicle would be corrected to the desired trajectory.

The DYC system of four wheel independent drive electric vehicle is shown in Fig. 2. The torque of vehicle is distributed between front and rear axles by the inputs of driver pedal without yaw moment. Torque command of the four wheels is obtained by superposing the outputs of DYC system. The control variables of DYC system are yaw rate and side slip angle. The expectations reflect the desired state of vehicle running, which can be calculated by the reference model with two degree of freedom [9]. The calculation formula are as follows:

$$\gamma_d = \min\left\{\left|\frac{u}{L(1+Ku^2)}\delta\right|, \left|\frac{0.85\mu g}{u}\right|\right\} sign(\delta) \tag{1}$$

$$\beta_d = 0 \tag{2}$$

Where: δ is front wheel steering angle, u is longitudinal velocity of vehicle, L is wheel base, μ is road adhesion coefficient.

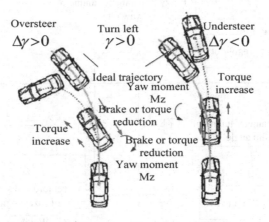

Fig. 1. The schematic diagram of DYC

According to the characteristics of the tire, driving force would decrease when slip rate is too large. Greater yaw moment cannot be produced by increasing of torque. Therefore, the output of slip rate controller is set as the saturation limit of DYC output. The final torque command is sent to the four motor controller by CAN bus to ensure the stable operation of vehicle under the requirements of driver.

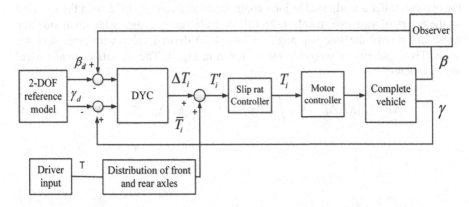

Fig. 2. The DYC system of four wheel independent drive electric vehicle

The block diagram of DYC algorithm with two layers is shown in Fig. 3. By choosing appropriate control variables in the upper layer, the differential torque can be calculated by PID controller using self-tuning parameter. Then, the differential torque is distributed to the four driving motor efficiently in the under layer. With 8 groups fuzzy rules (2 groups of output scaling parameters, 2 groups of output integral parameter, 4 groups of distribution coefficient of output torque), the whole algorithm can improve the sensitive parameters and nonlinear problem in the controller, which is easy to implement by gathering engineering experience efficiently.

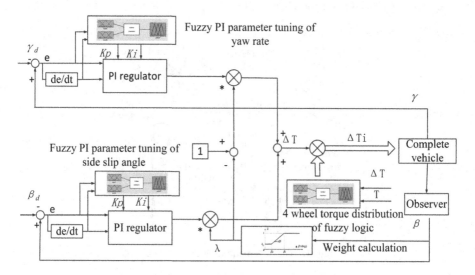

Fig. 3. The block diagram of DYC algorithm

2.2   The Calculation of Differential Torque

In this study, two fuzzy controller are designed individually. The parameters of yaw rate and side slip angle PI controller can be adjusted adaptively. The output weights of the two controller are adjusted in joint control, which are set by β-Method theory. That is, the errors of yaw rate mainly reflect the vehicle running state with small side slip angle and control the side slip angle to follow the desired value with large side slip angle. The regularity of weight value is shown in Fig. 4. The outputs of joint control are as follows:

$$\Delta T = \lambda(K_{p\beta}\Delta\beta + K_{i\beta}\int \Delta\beta dt) + (1-\lambda)(K_{p\gamma}\Delta\gamma + K_{i\gamma}\int \Delta\gamma dt) \qquad (3)$$

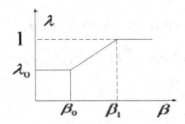

Fig. 4. The regularity of weight value

The fuzzy sets of input and output are{NB, NM, NS, ZO, PS, PM, PB}, the basic domain of yaw rate errors (e) and error variation (ec) are [–0.12, +0.12] and [–1, 1], the basic domain of side slip angle errors (e) and error variation (ec) are [–6°, +6°] and [–1, 1], the domain of Kp is [0, 500], the domain of Ki is [0, 100], the fuzzy rule is conditional statement of "if…then…". The fuzzy rule of PI fuzzy controller is shown in Table 1 [10], and the outputs are Kp and Ki individually.

Table 1. The fuzzy rule of PI fuzzy controller

e	ec						
	NB	NM	NS	ZO	PS	PM	PB
NB	PB/NB	PB/NB	PM/NM	PM/NM	PS/NS	ZO/ZO	ZO/ZO
NM	PB/NB	PB/NB	PM/NM	PS/NS	PS/NS	ZO/ZO	NS/ZO
NS	PM/NB	PM/NM	PM/NS	PS/NS	ZO/ZO	NS/PS	NS/PS
ZO	PM/NM	PM/NM	PS/NS	ZO/ZO	NS/PS	NM/PM	NM/PM
PS	PS/NM	PS/NS	ZO/ZO	NS/PS	NS/PS	NM/PM	NM/PB
PM	PS/ZO	ZO/ZO	NS/PS	NM/PS	NM/PM	NM/PB	NB/PB
PB	ZO/ZO	ZO/ZO	NM/PS	NM/PM	NM/PM	NB/PB	NB/PB

2.3 The Distribution Principle of the Four Wheel Torque

By total differential moment distributed to the four driving wheels, the constraints include the contribution of each wheel to yaw moment, the attachment limit of each wheel and the driving limit of motor. By the formula 4, as in the condition of left turn driving, when $F_{Xi} > 0$ and $F_{Yi} < 0$, $M_{Z2} > 0$ and $M_{Z3} < 0$ can be determined and the directions of M_{Z1} and M_{Z4} are uncertain. Based on this, when the driving moment of outer front wheel or inner rear wheel increases, the yaw moment in positive direction can be applied effectively. To control the yaw moment directions of inner front wheel or outer rear wheel is influenced by the value of imposed moment. In a word, the effect of outer front wheel and inner rear wheel to the output of yaw moment is more obvious than the other two wheels.

$$I_z\dot{\gamma} = (-\frac{B}{2}\cos\ \delta + a\ \sin\ \delta)F_{X1} + (a\ \cos\ \delta + \frac{B}{2}\sin\ \delta)F_{Y1} + (\frac{B}{2}\cos\ \delta + a\ \sin\ \delta)F_{X2}$$

$$+ (a\ \cos\ \delta - \frac{B}{2}\sin\ \delta)F_{Y2} - \frac{B}{2}F_{X3} - bF_{Y3} + \frac{B}{2}F_{X4} - bF_{Y4}$$

$$= M_{z1} + M_{z2} + M_{z3} + M_{z4}$$

$$(4)$$

Load transfer is existed in the driving condition, the load of inner wheel is smaller than the outer wheel and the load of front wheel is smaller than the rear wheel. According to the friction column theory, the wheel with small load will reach the limit of attachment first. Therefore, increasing the torque of rear wheel can use more surplus adhesion in the driving condition, and greater proportion of rear wheel would be distributed.

Let the driving torque is T_{lim}, when reaches the limit of attachment, the maximum output torque of motor is T_{max}, the torque distributed of front wheel is T_f, as rear wheel is T_r. When the adhesion limit is not reached, the torque increase on one side is equal to the decrease on the other side so as not to change the driving force of the vehicle. At this point, the driving torque of front axle also is the output of front axle T_f, and the maximum differential torque is $-2T_{max} + T_f$. When reaches the limit of attachment, the torque decreased on one side is larger than increased on the other side, and the maximum differential torque of front axle output is $-T_{max} - T_{lim}$. Then, the driving torque of front axle is $T_{max} - T_{lim}$, and the same as rear axle.

After comprehensively analyzing the three kinds of constraints, the maximum yaw moment is obtained by the most efficient way at the attachment limit of each wheel and the driving limit of motor. The effect to the yaw moment by each wheel is nonlinear. Considering this characteristics, the fuzzy rule of torque distribution coefficient of each wheel is set to summarize the above experiences. The basic principles are as follows: (1) With small T and ΔT, the equal and opposite differential torque are applied on the inside and outside wheel respectively. In order to make smaller weight setting of front wheel to reduce the burden of controller, the weight setting becomes larger with the increase of ΔT. (2) With medium T, larger ΔT, and the single wheel driving torque is increased to the limit value, the decreased torque value in single side of wheels is larger than the increased value in the other side, that to obtain larger differential torque. (3) With lager T and ΔT, the driving torques of vehicle are decreased in the inside and outside to ensure the steering stability of vehicle, and the torque value in one side is larger than the other side to ensure the requirement of ΔT.

The fuzzy rule is shown in Table 2 [11]. The input is the requirements of actual yaw moment and driving torque, and the output is torque distribution coefficient (s_i) of the four wheels. The requirements ΔT_i of each wheel are calculated by formula 5. Eventually, the control system is created in Simulink, as shown in Fig. 5.

$$\Delta T_i = \frac{s_i}{s_2 - s_1 + s_4 - s_3}\Delta T \qquad (5)$$

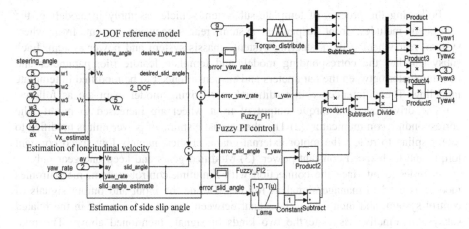

Fig. 5. The model of control system in Simulink

Table 2. The fuzzy rule for torque distribution coefficient of the four wheels

T	ΔT					
	NB	NM	NS	PS	PM	PB
PS	PM/NM/ PM/NM	PM/NM/ PB/NB	PS/NS/ PB/NB	NS/PS/ NB/PB	NM/PM/ NB/PB	NM/PM/ NM/PM
PM	PS/NM/ PS/NM	PM/NM/ PM/NM	PM/NM/ PB/NB	NM/PM/ NB/PB	NM/PM/ NM/PM	NM/PS/ NM/PS
PB	NB/NS/ NB/NS	PS/NM/ PS/NM	PM/NM/ PM/NM	NM/PM/ NM/PM	NM/PS/ NM/PS	NS/NB/ NS/NB

3 The Multi-body Dynamic Model of the Vehicle

ADAMS/Car modules is a mature analysis software package of vehicle multi-body dynamics, which includes lots of model library such as tire model, road model and so on. The common car model in ADAMS/Car is rear driving of rear-engine model. According to the characteristics of four wheel independent drive electric vehicle, new model is built, as shown in Fig. 6.

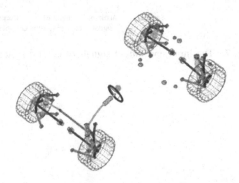

Fig. 6. The dynamic model of four wheel independent drive electric vehicle

Following the process of template-subsystem-vehicle assembly in modeling, the subsystem includes: front suspension system, rear suspension system, front wheel system, rear wheel system, steering system, chassis system and power system. Each subsystem has the corresponding model, and template feature file, parameter and communicator between the parameters and suspension need to be modified in template modeling. The differences with traditional rear driving model main are as follows: (1) The drive axle and torque output of front wheel are increased to modify the corresponding communicator. (2) The characteristic spline of power unit is modified to motor spline to reflect the motor external characteristics, namely low speed constant torque and high speed constant power. (3) Modified gears and keep one gear only.

In order to interface the connection with Simulink control system, mechatronics module is used to manage signal as follows: Define the input and output signals of control system, and then set up the signal between sensor and actuator in the related subsystem. Finally, associate the two kinds of signals mentioned above. The relationship of control system signals between input and output are shown in Fig. 7.

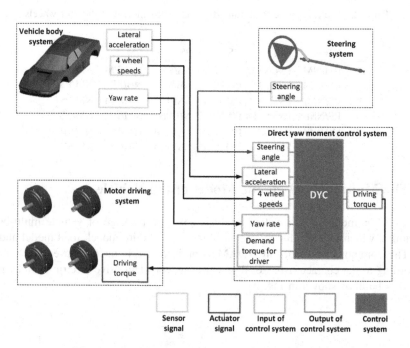

Fig. 7. The input and output signals of control system

4   Co-simulating

4.1   Simulation Structure

After building the model of control object and controller, the input and output of which are connected to carry out the co-simulating. The simulation model is shown in Fig. 8. The parameters of vehicle are as follows: the distance between front axle and centroid (a) is 1.233 m, the distance between rear axle and centroid (b) is 1.327 m, L is 2.56 m, the wheel track (B) is 1.52 m, the height from centroid to the ground (h_g) is 0.450 m, the radius of wheel (R) is 0.32 m, the vehicle weight (m) is 1316 kg, the moment of inertia (I_z) is 2046 kg·m^2, the cornering stiffness of front wheel (K_f) is 50000 kg·m/rad, the cornering stiffness of rear wheel (K_r) is 80000 kg·m/rad, the single motor power is 10 Kw and the maximum torque is 144 N·m.

The single lane change test of sinusoidal steering is selected to verify the effect of vehicle operational stability by control system. The initiative time of sinusoidal steering is 0.5, and replied to straight line at 2.5 s after one period. In order to compare the adaptability in different conditions, road adhesion coefficient is 0.9 and initial vehicle speed is 60 km/h for common condition, road adhesion coefficient is 0.3 and initial vehicle speed is 90 km/h for dangerous condition.

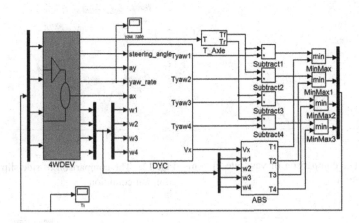

Fig. 8. The model of co-simulating

4.2   Simulation Result

In the working condition of sinusoidal steering, the desired trajectory of vehicle is replied to straight line. Controller can track the desired trajectory well under the controlling, as shown in Figs. 9 and 10. Especially under the condition of low road adhesion coefficient and high vehicle speed, the vehicle will lose stability completely without control, and combined control can further decrease the tracking errors.

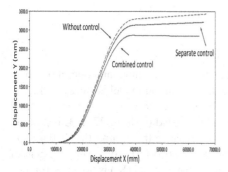

Fig. 9. The comparison of trajectory in common condition

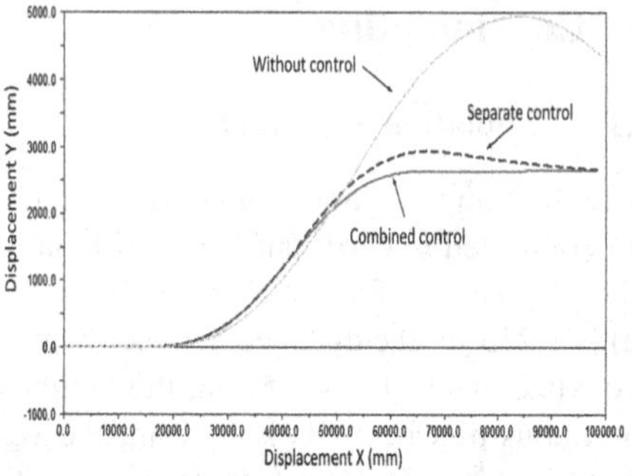

Fig. 10. The comparison of trajectory in dangerous condition

The yaw rate and side slip angle of vehicle in Figs. 11, 12, 13, 14, 15 and 16 illustrates that the two control variables could follow the reference value well under the control. In dangerous condition, the side slip angle is larger and the yaw rate is unable to converge to zero without the control.

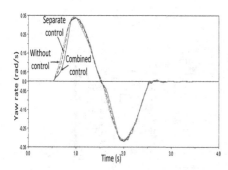

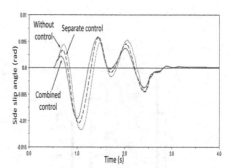

Fig. 11. The comparison of yaw rate in common condition

Fig. 12. The comparison of side slip angle in common condition

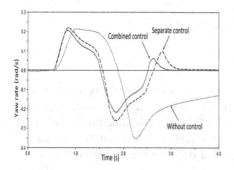

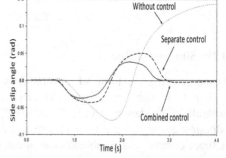

Fig. 13. The comparison of yaw rate in dangerous condition

Fig. 14. The comparison of side slip angle in dangerous condition

In the two conditions, outputs of the four wheel are shown in Figs. 15 and 16, and the torque is distributed between the front and rear axles. In common condition, the output torque of left and right wheels with front and rear axles is symmetric. In dangerous condition, the decreased torque of single side is larger than the other side to reduce the speed and make the vehicle return to steady state quickly. The simulation results show that the designed fuzzy controller in the study can keep the yaw stability of vehicle with sinusoidal steering, and have great adaptive to the working condition.

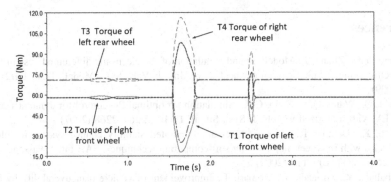

Fig. 15. The torque output under combined control in common condition

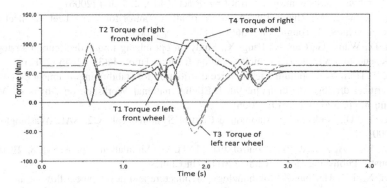

Fig. 16. The torque output under combined control in dangerous condition

5 Conclusions

(1) A more precise dynamics model of 4 wheel independent driving electric vehicle is established using ADAMS/Car, and co-simulation is carried out by combining DYC control model and multi-body dynamic model of the vehicle. The experiments of sinusoidal steering is carried out in different working conditions, which verifies the validity and applicability of DYC algorithm.

(2) In order to obtain the yaw torque value, the fuzzy PI controller is designed based on the errors between the actual value and reference of side slip angle and yaw

rate. Also, the effect of yaw moment to each wheel and driving limit are analyzed to distribute the torque. The co-simulation results show that the vehicle can track the desired trajectory of the driver better with the effect of controller. Especially in the high speed and low adhesion coefficient road, the increase of side slip angle can be controlled well, thus suppressed the shortage and oversteer of vehicle. Meanwhile, vehicle performance with combined control is better than the single control of yaw rate.

References

1. Zhao, Y.E., Zhang, J.: Modelling and simulation of the electronic differential system for an electric vehicle with two-motor-wheel drive. Int. J. Veh. Syst. Model. Test. 4(1/2), 117 (2009)
2. Jin, L.Q., Wang, Q.N., Song, C.X.: Simulation for optimal PD control for dynamics control of EV with motorized wheels. J. Syst. Simul. 19(10), 2264–2268 (2007)
3. Jalali, K., Uchida, T., Mcphee, J., et al.: Integrated stability control system for electric vehicles with in-wheel motors using soft computing techniques. SAE Int. J. Passeng. Cars-Electron. 2(1), 109–119 (2009)
4. Hibahata, Y., Shimada, K., Tomari, T.: Improvement of vehicle maneuverability by direct yaw moment control. Veh. Syst. Dyn. 22(1), 465–481 (1993)
5. Mokhiamar, O., Abe, M.: How the four wheels should share forces in an optimum cooperative chassis control. Control Eng. Pract. 14(3), 295–304 (2006)
6. Yu, Z., Jiang, W., Zhang, L.: Torque distribution control for four wheel in-wheel motor electric vehicle. J. Tongji Univ. 36(8), 1115–1119 (2008)
7. Xu, D., Wang, G., Cao, B., Feng, X.: Study on optimizing torque distribution strategy for independent 4WD electric vehicle. J. Xi'an Jiaotong Univ. 46(3), 42–46 (2012)
8. He, P., Hori, Y.: Optimum traction force distribution for stability improvement of 4WD EV in critical driving condition. In: 9th IEEE International Workshop on Advanced Motion Control, pp. 596–601. IEEE (2006)
9. Kieccke, U., Nielsen, L.: Automotive Control Systems, vol. 322. SAE, Washington DC (2000)
10. Liu, J.K.: Advanced PID Control the MATLAB Simulation, pp. 115–128. Electronic Industry Publishing House, China (2011). (In Chinese)
11. Wei, X., Dai, H., Sun, Z.: Methodology, architecture and development flow of automotive embedded systems. J. Tongji Univ. 40(7), 1064–1070 (2012)

Simulation Analysis of PID Closed-Loop
Control of Current of SBW

Zhanfeng Li[✉] and Shuang Du

Institute of Automotive Engineering,
Shaanxi College of Communication Technology, Xi'an 710018, China
369699861@qq.com

Abstract. SBW controls automobile steering by intelligent mechanical and electric transferring equipments. How to control the steering electricmotor, that determines steering track of the automobile. The dynamics model of the steering electromotor is established in the paper, and simulation analysis of PID closed-loop control of current of SBW is studied. The result of control is satisfied with the control requirement of SBW.

Keywords: Simulation · PID · Closed-loop · Current

1 Introduction

SBW refers to the elimination of the mechanical connection between the steering wheel and the steerable wheel, which is replaced by wires and controller. The core of control technology is intelligent mechanical and electric transferring equipments, which convert electric signals of the driver's turning the steering wheel into mechanical motion, and transfer dynamic informations feed back to the driver by electric signals. Thus Steering is controlled intelligently. Figure 1 means the structure of SBW.

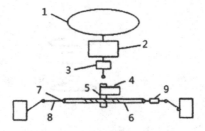

Fig. 1. Structure of SBW (1 - steering wheel; 2 - electromagnetic motor; 3 - angle sensor; 4 - steering electromotor; 5 - pinion; 6 - rack; 7 - steering knuckle; 8 - steering tie rod; 9 - steering tie rod displacement sensor)

2 Dynamic Model of SBW and Steering Electromotor Established

We use permanent magnet brush dc motor as power source of SBW, based on the motor features. SBW adopts switching mode to drive the steering electromotor by controlling the armature voltage of it. SBW should adopt reversible PWM voltage regulation control to drive the steering electromotor, because the vehicle needs to run left or right. Figure 2 means H-type reversible driving system by PWM controlled, which is satisfied with the requirement of SBW steering electromotor.

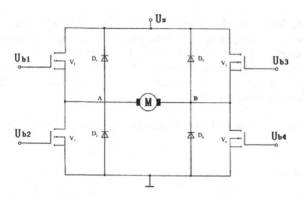

Fig. 2. H-type reversible driving system by PWM controlled

For study on the steering electromotor of SBW, we should know the dynamic relationship between SBW and the steering electromotor first, so the dynamic models of SBW and the steering electromotor need to be established.

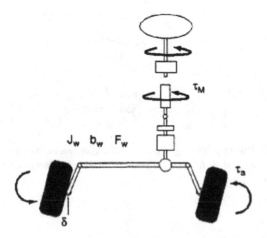

Fig. 3. Model of SBW

Figure 3 means model of SBW. Because of no mechanism connection between the steering wheel and the steerable wheels, Eq. (1) is the dynamic equation of the steerable wheel of SBW:

$$J_W \ddot{\delta} + b_W \dot{\delta} + T_f + T_a = r_s r_p T_M \tag{1}$$

Including:

J_W - Rotational Inertia of The Steering System;
b_W - Steering Damping of The Steering System;
T_f - Frictional Resistance Moment;
T_a - Steering Aligning Torque;
r_s - Transmission Ratio of The Steering System;
r_p - Moment Amplification Factor of The Power Steering System, it is a constant here.

T_M - The Steering Electromotor Torque, it is calculated as Eq. (2):

$$T_M = k_M i_M r_g \eta \tag{2}$$

Including: k_M - Electromotor Constant; i_M - Electromotor Current; r_g - Transmission Ratio of Reducing Mechanism; η - Electromotor Efficiency.

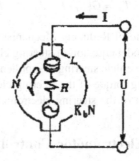

Fig. 4. Model of steering electromotor

Figure 4 means model of steering electromotor. The relationship between U, L, R, K_b, N, I, t is Eq. (3):

$$U = L\frac{dI}{dt} + RI + K_b N \tag{3}$$

Including: U - Terminal Voltage; L - Inductance; R - Armature Resistance; K_b - Back Electromotor Force Constant; N - Rotate Speed; I - Current; t - Time.

Equation (4) is the dynamic equation of the steering electromotor:

$$T_m - T_o - T_f = J_m \frac{d\omega}{dt} \qquad (4)$$

Including:

T_m - Electromagnetic Torque of Electromotor, $T_m = K_t \cdot I$, K_t - Torque Coefficient of Electromotor;

T_o - Output Torque of Electromotor;

T_f - Consumed Torque of Motor Rotor Overcoming Friction, $T_f = B_m\omega$;

ω - Angular Velocity of Motor Rotor, $\omega = 2\pi N = \dot{\delta}_m$, δ_m - Rotating Angle of Armature;

J_m - Rotational Inertia of Motor Rotor.

T_o, Output Torque of Electromotor, is calculated as Eq. (5):

$$T_o = K_t \cdot I - J_m \ddot{\delta}_m - B_m \dot{\delta}_m \qquad (5)$$

T_z, Steering Torque by Steering Electromotor, which is the torque that output torque of electromotor is amplified by reduxing mechanism. It is calculated as Eq. (6):

$$T_z = G \cdot T_o = G(K_t \cdot I - J_m \ddot{\delta}_m - B_m \dot{\delta}_m) \qquad (6)$$

Including: G - Reduction Ratio of Reducing Mechanism.

Equation (6) is the dynamic model equation of steering electromotor. As we know, the torque that is necessary for the vehicle steering is supplied by the steering electromotor, then we can control the steering torque of the steering electromotor by controlling the armature voltage or the current of the steering electromotor.

3   Torque of Steering Electromotor Control Strategy

Figures 5 and 6 mean Voltage-controlled and Current-controlled for torque by steering electromotor.

Fig. 5. Voltage-controlled block diagram

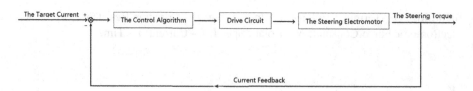

Fig. 6. Current-controlled block diagram

Voltage-controlled is open-loop control mode. It is easy to design control system and easily achieved. Theses are advantages of the mode. But control accuracy is not high. The steering torque of the steering electromotor (reflected by the armature current) is changed just only with the armature voltage, and the control system can not realize the influence of the electromotor torque according to changing of the load. While, current closed-loop control mode is based on the speciality that the electromotor torque is proportional with the electromotor current. When the signals of the steering wheel rotation angle (or torque) and the vehicle speed are inputed to the controller of SCM (Single Chip Micyoco), the controller determines the target current of the steering electromotor based on the speciality of power assisting, then the current sensor feeds back the actual current of the electromotor armature to the controller, which compares it with the target current. The current controller regulates and outputs PWM signals to the drive circuit, which drives the steering electromotor working for the steering task. The current controller makes the error between the actual electromotor armature current and the target current small enough, then the system gets smooth and steady as soon as possible.

Based on the dynamic model equations of SBW and the steering electromotor, we simulate the two control modes.

The target current is determined based on the speciality of SBW power assisting, then it and the actual electromotor current get a closed-loop, which achieves PWM chopping signals, that control the drive circuit by current computational algorithm. Thus, the key of the closed-loop control of the steering electromotor current is to formulate the control algorithm of the target current. We choose PID control algorithm, which is the most widely used in the industrial process. Its form is simple and fixed, thus it can keep in good robustness and reliability in widely operating conditions. It is easily realized with programmes, and it is permitted that regulating the system in simple and direct methods. PID controllers apply mature technology, its structure is easy and its parameters are easily regulated. Its 3 control parameters need PID optimal-tuning when it is in used. NCD, software tool box of Matlab/Simulink can be used to optimize design specially for nonlinear control system, in virtue of which, optimal design of system parameters can be realized.

After the PID control parameters are set, the electromotor torque of the different control strategies is simulated under the target current step input. The results are shown in Figs. 7 and 8. Since the electromotor torque is proportional to its armature current, the armature current and its response effect can reflect the control effect of the electromotor torque.

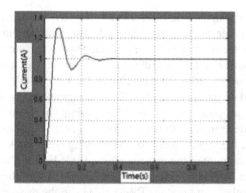

Fig. 7. Armature current response under voltage control

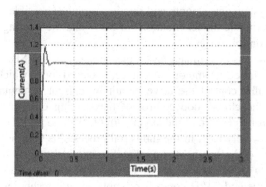

Fig. 8. Armature current response under current control

The results show that the current closed-loop control can make the output current of the steering electromotor, driven by PWM, quickly track the target current value, and the current PID closed-loop control can effectively reduce the overshoot and adjustment time of the system. It shows that the current PID closed-loop control strategy can ensure that the steering torque provided by the steering electromotor for the vehicle can accurately track the torque required by the vehicle to achieve the expected steering target, and the control effect meets the requirements.

4 Conclusion

SBW is a brand new steering system which grows up with the latest achievements of electronic technology development and is a significant innovation in the development history of automobile steering system. While, the key to complete power steering is whether the control strategy is reasonable and effective. In this paper, the dynamic model of steering electromotor and its two torque control models, namely voltage open-loop control and current PID closed-loop control, are established, and are simulated, compared. The results show that the current PID closed-loop control can realize the accurate tracking control of the target current and the tracking control of the steering torque provided by the steering electromotor for vehicle steering, and the control results meet the control requirements of SBW steering electromotor.

References

1. Pei, F.: In the era of automatic driving, the wire control technology completely eliminating mechanical connection. Automob. Parts **29**, 36–37 (2018)
2. Zhang, B., Zhang, J., et al.: Research on current control of permanent magnet synchronous motor for road feeling simulation. J. Jilin Univ. (Eng. Technol. Ed.), 1–9 (2019). https://doi.org/10.13229/j.cnki.jdxbgxb20180616
3. Zhao, L., Chen, W., et al.: Research on control strategy of SBW based on extension sliding mode. J. Mech. Eng. **55**(02), 126–134 (2019)
4. Li, C., Xiong, L., et al.: Review on research progress of automobile steer-by-wire system. Automob. Technol. (04), 23–34 (2018)
5. Wu, M., Zhang, F., et al.: The control strategy research of unnamed vehicles steering-by-wire system. Comput. Simul. **33**(12), 163–168 (2016)
6. Huang, C., Naghdy, F., et al.: Shared control of highly automated vehicles using steer-by-wire systems. IEEE/CAA J. Autom. Sin. **6**(02), 410–423 (2019)
7. Zhao, L., Cong, G., et al.: Research on torque characteristics of steering wheel of wire-controlled steering vehicle. J. Mech. Eng. **54**(24), 138–146 (2018)
8. Cong, G., Liu, Y., et al.: Simulation of road feel and hardware-in-the-loop test for steer-by-wire system. J. Hefei Univ. Technol. (Nat. Sci.) **41**(11), 1479–1483 (2018)

Mechatronics in Energy Systems

Characteristic Analysis and Disturbance Control of Hydraulic Transmission System for Driving Torque Extraction Electric Power Generation in Coal Sampling Robot

Haibo Xu[1(✉)], Li Liu[1], Jun Wang[2], Rui Wang[1], and Xiaodong Liu[1]

[1] Xi'an Jiaotong University, Xi'an 710049, Shanxi, China
hbxu@mail.xjtu.edu.cn, liuli521@stu.xjtu.edu.cn
[2] Xi'an Hongyu Mining Special Mobile Equipment Co.,
Xi'an 710075, Shanxi, China

Abstract. Coal sampling robot needs to work in the field for a long time. The energy supply of car-borne electrical appliances determines the duration of the coal sampling robot. Driving torque extraction generation satisfies not only the demand of electricity consumption but also the regenerative braking. Because of complicated road conditions and uncertain load, the speed of engine will fluctuate. In order to solve the problem of motor speed fluctuation caused by unstable input speed and load change of hydraulic transmission system, the structure and operation parameters of the system are analyzed in this paper, and measures are obtained to optimize system characteristics. A fuzzy PID control algorithm of compensating the instability of input speed and the change of load is proposed to reduce the fluctuation of output speed of the system.

Keywords: Coal sampling robot ·
Driving torque extraction power generation · Hydraulic system ·
Fuzzy PID control

1 Introduction

In order to generate electricity from automobile engine, the generator is driven by the torque extraction device. Vehicle engine speed is fluctuating, while the generator requires constant speed, which requires the design of a speed control system between them. Therefore, a pump-motor volume speed regulation system with rated power of 30 kW is designed, the mathematical model based on transfer function is established, and time-domain and frequency-domain analysis are carried out in this paper. The response characteristics of the system under different input speed and load changes are analyzed, and the measures to improve the system characteristics are put forward. PID control and fuzzy PID control algorithms are used to simulate the system, which meets the technical requirements of Class III power stations in *General Technical Conditions for Mobile Power Stations*. In the case of input speed fluctuation, the optimal control effect is also obtained (Fig. 1).

H. Yu et al. (Eds.): ICIRA 2019, LNAI 11745, pp. 617–626, 2019.
https://doi.org/10.1007/978-3-030-27529-7_52

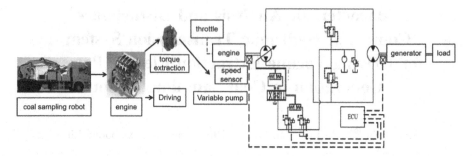

Fig. 1. The torque extraction and pump-motor volume speed regulation system.

2   Design and Mathematical Model Establishment of Hydraulic Drive System for Driving Power Generation

2.1   Design of Hydraulic Drive System for Driving Power Generation

Main Technical Indicators of Coal Sampling Robot Power Generation System.
Input rotational Speed: 800–3000 r/min; Maximum output power: 35 kW; Rated power: 30 kW; Output rotational Speed: 1500 r/min; Allowed steady input speed deviation: ±0.5%; The volume speed regulation method that variable displacement pump controls the constant displacement motor is chosen, which can avoid throttling loss. This system uses closed hydraulic circuit. Slippage pump supplements the flow of the overflow which returns the tank and meanwhile provides power for variable displacement adjusting mechanism for variable displacement pump [1].

Selection of Main Hydraulic Devices. The main hydraulic components include: variable displacement pump, constant displacement motor, slippage pump, hydraulic pipe fittings, etc. To ensure that the system meets the predetermined requirements, it is necessary to select and calculate the hydraulic components, determine the system working pressure, pump and motor displacement and other parameters. In this paper the hydraulic speed control system adopts Linde HPV105-02E1 electro-hydraulic proportional control variable pump and HMF50-02 constant displacement motor.

2.2   Establishment of Mathematical Model of Hydraulic Drive System

Mathematical Model of Electro-Hydraulic Proportional Variable Pump. Electrohydraulic proportional variable displacement pump can be expressed by first-order inertia link:

$$\frac{D_p}{u} = \frac{k_p}{t_d s + 1} \tag{1}$$

In equation:D_p—Gradient displacement of variable displacement pump; u—Input voltage; k_p—flow gain; t_d—time constant. $k_p = 1.2 \times 10^{-6}$, $t_d = 0.035$.

Mathematical Model of Pump-Motor System. The Laplace transformation of the pump flow equation is obtained:

$$Q_p(s) = D_p(s) - C_{tp}P_p(s) \tag{2}$$

The Laplace transformation of system flow continuity equation of high pressure cavity is obtained:

$$Q_p(s) = C_{tm}p_p(s) + D_m s\theta_m(s) + \frac{V_0}{\beta_e}sp_p(s) \tag{3}$$

The Laplace transformation of balance equation between motor and load torque is obtained:

$$D_m p_p(s) = (J_m s^2 + B_m s + G)\theta_m(s) + T_L(s) \tag{4}$$

According to above Eqs. (2), (3) and (4), the transfer function of pump-motor is obtained.

$$\theta_m = \frac{\frac{D_p n_p}{D_m} - \frac{C_t}{D_m^2}\left(1 + \frac{V_0}{\beta_e C_t}s\right)T_L}{\frac{V_0 J_t}{\beta_e D_m^2}s^3 + \left(\frac{C_t J_t}{D_m^2} + \frac{B_m V_0}{\beta_e D_m^2}\right)s^2 + \left(1 + \frac{C_t B_m}{D_m^2} + \frac{GV_0}{\beta_e D_m^2}\right)s + \frac{GC_t}{D_m^2}} \tag{5}$$

According to actual situations, simplify the formula by ignoring some minor factors:

$$\theta(s) = \frac{\frac{D_p n_p}{D_m} - \frac{C_t}{D_m^2}\left(1 + \frac{V_0}{\beta_e C_t}s\right)T_L}{s\left(\frac{s^2}{\omega_h^2} + \frac{2\xi}{\omega_h}s + 1\right)} \tag{6}$$

In equation: ω_h——natural frequency, $\omega_h = \sqrt{\frac{\beta_e D_m^2}{V_0 J_t}}$

ξ_h——damping ratio, $\xi_h = \frac{C_t}{2D_m}\sqrt{\frac{\beta_e J_t}{V_0}} + \frac{B_m}{2D_m}\sqrt{\frac{V_0}{\beta_e J_t}}$

Because of $\dot{\theta}(s) = s\theta(s)$, The transfer functions of pump-controlled motor system with variable pump displacement as input and load moment as input are respectively displayed as below [2] (Table 1):

$$\frac{\dot{\theta}(s)}{D_p(s)} = \frac{\frac{n_p}{D_m}}{\frac{s^2}{\omega_h^2} + \frac{2\xi}{\omega_h}s + 1} \tag{7}$$

$$\frac{\dot{\theta}(s)}{T_L(s)} = \frac{-\frac{C_t}{D_m^2}\left(1 + \frac{V_0}{\beta_e C_t}s\right)}{\frac{s^2}{\omega_h^2} + \frac{2\xi}{\omega_h}s + 1} \tag{8}$$

Table 1. Parameters table of hydraulic transmission system for driving power extraction generation.

Name	Symbol	Value	Unit
Rated displacement of variable displacement pump	D_{max}	105	ml/r
Maximum continuous rotational speed of variable pump	n	2800	r/min
Rated pressure of variable pump	p_p	420	bar
Maximum input torque of pump	T_{max}	670	Nm
Maximum output power of pump	P_{max}	204	kW
Rotating inertia value of pump	J_p	0.0149	kg m^2
Displacement gradient of variable displacement pump	k_p	1.67e-5	m^3/rad
Viscous damping coefficient of motor	B_m	0.35	N s/m
Moment of inertia converted to motor	J_t	0.065	kg m^2
Total leakage coefficient of pump-controlled motor system	C_t	3.25e-12	m^3/Pa s
Total volume of pump-controlled motor	V_0	5.5e-4	m^3
Efficiency of constant displacement hydraulic motor system	η_m	0.93	
Displacement of motor	D_m	51.3	ml/r
Elastic modulus of hydraulic oil	β_e	699.9	MPa
Output rotational speed of hydraulic motor	n_m	1500	r/min
Pipeline pressure drop	ΔP	0.012	MPa
Displacement of slippage pump	D_1	22.5	ml/r
Pressure of slippage pump	P_1	1.9	MPa

The parameters in the transfer function are calculated from the data in the table. Calculate natural frequency of pump-motor system and damping ratio of pump-motor system:

$$\omega_h = \sqrt{\frac{\beta_e D_m^2}{V_0 J_t}} = 48.19 \tag{9}$$

$$\xi_h = \frac{C_t}{2D_m}\sqrt{\frac{\beta_e J_t}{V_0}} + \frac{B_m}{2D_m}\sqrt{\frac{V_0}{\beta_e J_t}} = 0.19 \tag{10}$$

Mathematical Model of Velocity Sensor. Speed sensor is used for the feedback control of the drive system. And its dynamic response can be regarded as a first-order proportional link, whose transfer function is:

$$\frac{U(s)}{\dot{\theta}(s)} = k_f \qquad k_f = 0.019 \text{V} \cdot s/rad \tag{11}$$

The block diagram of transfer function of hydraulic transmission system for driving power generation is shown in Fig. 2.

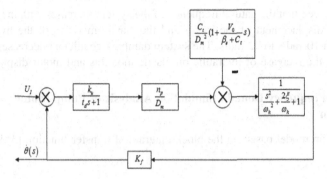

Fig. 2. The block diagram of transfer function of hydraulic transmission system for driving power generation

3 Characteristic Analysis of Driving Torque Extraction Power Generation System

3.1 Analysis of Damping Ratio and Natural Frequency of System

The open-loop transfer function of the system is:

$$G_k(s) = \frac{u_I(s)}{\dot{\theta}(s)} = \frac{k_u n_p (1 - \frac{C_t}{D_m^2}(1 + \frac{V_0}{\beta_e C_t}s)T_L)}{D_m(t_d s + 1)(\frac{s^2}{\omega_h^2} + \frac{2\xi}{\omega_h}s + 1)} \tag{12}$$

For second-order systems, natural frequencies and damping coefficients are the main performance indicators affecting system characteristics, and the elastic modulus of hydraulic oil β_e and motor displacement D_m play a decisive role in natural frequency and damping coefficient. Therefore, the correlative analysis of motor displacement and elastic modulus of hydraulic oil is made in this paper. The influences of gradient displacement of motor and elastic modulus of hydraulic oil are shown in Fig. 3

Natural Frequency and Damping coefficient Curve of Pump Motor System

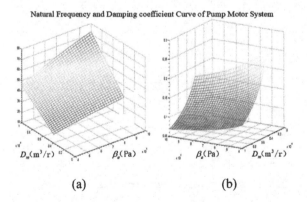

(a)   (b)

Fig. 3. The influences of gradient displacement of motor and elastic modulus of hydraulic oil: (a) displays the relationship between ω_h and D_m, β_e. (b) displays the relationship between ξ_h and D_m, β_e.

It can be seen that the natural frequency of the system increases with the increase of the gradient displacement of the motor and the elastic modulus of the hydraulic oil, ranging from 10 rad/s to 72 rad/s. The system damping coefficient decreases from 0.07 to 0.24 with the increase of hydraulic oil elastic modulus and motor displacement.

3.2   Time-Frequency Domain Simulation Analysis of Pump-Motor System

The simulation model based on the block diagram of transfer function [3] is shown in Fig. 4.

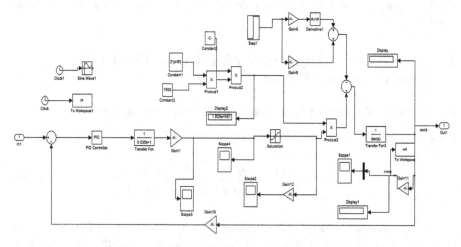

Fig. 4. Model of pump-motor volume speed regulation system.

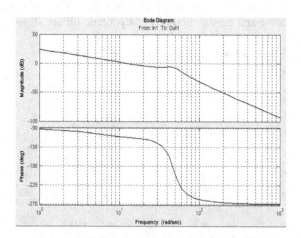

Fig. 5. The open-loop Bode diagram of the system.

The open-loop Bode diagram of the system is obtained, as shown in Fig. 5. It is known that the phase margin of the system is 60° and amplitude margin is 10 db. Therefore, this system is considerably stable.

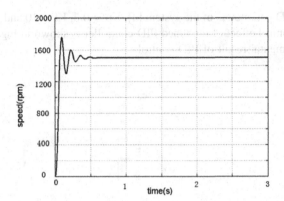

Fig. 6. Open-loop step response of system.

The system is simulated in time domain. The open loop step simulation result is shown in Fig. 6. The control voltage is 10.2 V and the pump input rotational speed is 1000 r/min. Without control algorithm, the system has a large overshoot, and the stabilization time is 0.4 s (Fig. 7).

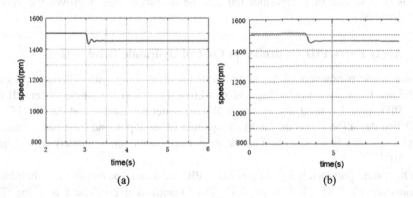

Fig. 7. 9.6 kW load is added suddenly: (a) is the result of simulation. (b) is the result of experiment.

4   Control of Hydraulic Drive System for Driving Torque Extraction Power Generation

4.1   Apply PID Controller to Control Hydraulic Drive System

By tuning the PID parameters of the system [4], Kp = 0.6, Ki = 10 and Kd = 0.027 are obtained. The control effect of the tuned PID controller is shown in Fig. 8(a). Figure 8 (b) is the experimental result of PID control.

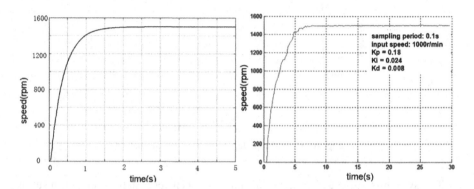

Fig. 8. (a) is the simulated result of PID control. (b) is the result of experiment of PID control.

According to the tuned PID control curve, the overshoot is zero and the response time is 0.75 s. The PID controller reduces the overshoot and improves the system characteristics.

4.2   Apply Fuzzy PID Controller to Control Hydraulic Drive System

Because some parameters of the system will fluctuate along with different operating conditions, there are time-varying and non-linear factors in the whole system. If the fuzzy PID control is used, the system will have better robustness and stability [5].

Define deviation E and deviation change rate EC as input, and their basic domains are [−3, 3] and [−3, 3]. The Quantization coefficients are separately $k_e = 1$ and $k_{ec} = 10^{-15}$.

The control parameters Kp, Ki and Kd of PID are defined as outputs, and their basic domains are [0, 0.8], [8, 12], [0, 0.4]. The Quantization coefficient is 1 [6]. The linguistic variables are NB-negative large, NM-negative medium, NS-negative small, ZE-zero, PS-positive small PM-positive medium and PB-positive large. Select triangular membership function. Fuzzy resolution method is gravity method [7].

In Fig. 9, it can be seen that the fuzzy PID control eliminates the steady-state error, improves the response speed of the system almost without overshoot and oscillation, and has the advantages of good dynamic effect of fuzzy control and high steady-state precision of PID control.

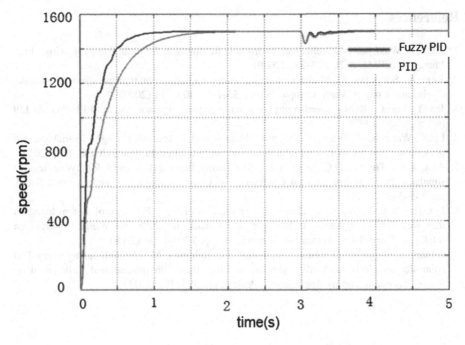

Fig. 9. Step response curve of fuzzy PID control.

5   Conclusion

According to the requirement of driving power generation system of coal sampling robot, The transmission scheme of the closed circuit of volume speed regulation of pump-controlled motor is designed.

According to the power requirement, the critical hydraulic components such as variable displacement pump, hydraulic motor and slippage pump are calculated and selected. The mathematical model is established using transfer function and the parameters in this model are calculated. According to the frequency domain analysis based on simulation model, it is proved that the system is considerably stable. The PID controller and the fuzzy PID controller are designed respectively, and the step signal simulation is carried out. The results show that the two controllers can eliminate the overshoot well, and the response time is less than 1 s.

Acknowledgment. Thanks to the support of Xi'an Hongyu Mining Special Mobile Equipment Co.

References

1. Tittla, I.: Wind power systems with hydrostatic transmission for clean energy. Environ. Eng. Manag. J. (EEMJ) **8**(2), 327–334 (2009)
2. Kugi, A., Schlacher, K.: Modeling and simulation of a hydrostatic transmission with variable-displacement pump. Math. Comput. Simul. **53**(4–6), 409–414 (2000)
3. Jen, Y., Lee, C.: Robust speed control of a pump-controlled motor system. IEEE-Proc.-D **139** (6), 503–509 (1992)
4. Li, X., Wang, X.-Z., Wang, Y.: Adaptive dynamic surface controller design of variable-speed pump controlled motor system with parametric uncertainties. In: IEEE CCDC, (12) (2014)
5. Ahn, K.K., Truong, D.Q., Soo, Y.H.: Self tuning fuzzy PID control for hydraulic load simulator. In: 2007 International Conference on Control, Automation and Systems, Seoul, pp. 345–349 (2007)
6. Liu, H., Zhou, J., Wang, S., Zhang, Z.: Application of fuzzy PID control system based on improved GA in hydraulic turbine generating units. In: 2008 7th World Congress on Intelligent Control and Automation, Chongqing, pp. 7790–7794 (2008)
7. Adnan, R., Tajjudin, M., Ishak, N., Ismail, H., Rahiman, M.H.F.: Self-tuning fuzzy PID controller for electro-hydraulic cylinder. In: 2011 IEEE 7th International Colloquium on Signal Processing and its Applications, Penang, pp. 395–398 (2011)

Human-Robot Interaction

Appearance-Based Gaze Tracking: A Brief Review

Jiaqi Jiang[1], Xiaolong Zhou[1,2(✉)], Sixian Chan[1], and Shengyong Chen[1,3]

[1] College of Computer Science and Technology,
Zhejiang University of Technology, Hangzhou, China
zxl@zjut.edu.cn
[2] College of Electrical and Information Engineering, Quzhou University,
Quzhou, China
[3] School of Computer Communication and Engineering,
Tianjin University of Technology, Tianjin, China

Abstract. Human gaze tracking plays an important role in the field of Human-Computer Interaction. This paper presents a brief review on appearance-based gaze tracking. Based on the appearance of human eyes, input features can be classified into three categories according to the different ways of extracting human eyes features, namely, complete human eye image, pixel-based feature and 3D reconstruction image. The estimation process from human eye feature to fixation point mainly uses different mapping functions. In this paper, common mapping functions and related algorithms are described in detail: k-nearest neighbor (KNN), random forest (RF) regression, gaussian process (GP) regression, support vector machines (SVM) and artificial neural networks (ANN). This paper evaluates the performance of these gaze tracking algorithms using different mapping functions. Based on the results of the evaluation, potential challenges are summarized and the future directions of gaze estimation are prospected.

Keywords: Gaze tracking · HCI · Appearance-based · Mapping

1 Introduction

The eyes are one of the most important sensory organs in the human body, which is the inevitable result of the long evolution of life to the advanced form. More than 90% of external information is obtained through the eyes. Eye gazing plays an important role in nonverbal communication as well as Human-Computer Interaction (HCI) [1–3]. Gaze tracking can be used as an analytical tool in HCI to make the interaction between human and computer more simple, natural and efficient. Gaze tracking plays an important role in many applications, including marketing and consumer research [4], immersive VR research [5], education research [6], et al.

There have been an increasing number of recent methods proposed for gaze tracking, which can be roughly classified into two major categories: model-based and appearance-based methods. The former calculates the specific geometric eye model to

H. Yu et al. (Eds.): ICIRA 2019, LNAI 11745, pp. 629–640, 2019.
https://doi.org/10.1007/978-3-030-27529-7_53

estimate gaze direction relying on invariant facial features such as pupil center [7], eye corners [8] and corneal infrared reflection [9]. The latter extracts input features from the human eye appearance images and establishes a mapping relation to realize gaze estimation. Common input eye features can be roughly divided into three categories: complete human eye images [10, 11], pixel-based features [12–14], and 3D reconstructed images [15]. The model-based gaze tracking methods require sophisticated hardware which may be composed by infrared light and high-definition cameras. Such methods are more suitable for controlled environments, e.g., in the laboratory, rather than in daily entertainment scenes. In contrast, the appearance-based methods usually only need a single camera to capture the user eye images. Certain eye features are generated from the complete eye images, and then a gaze mapping function is learned that maps the eye image to the gaze direction. Common eye features include a complete human eye image and the pixel-related information extracted from it, including color, gradient, light histogram, etc. Such a mapping function can be learned using various regression techniques, including k-Nearest Neighbor (KNN) [15–17], Random Forest (RF) regression [18–21], Gaussian Process (GP) regression [23–26], Support Vector Machines (SVM) [15, 27–29] and Artificial Neural Networks (ANN) [31–38].

The rest of this paper is organized as follows. Section 2 presents the common mapping functions and their related gaze tracking methods in detail: KNN, RF, GP, SVM and ANN. The advantages and disadvantages of these functions are briefly described. In Sect. 3, the performance of different mapping functions on appearance-based gaze tracking are evaluated. The potential challenges are summarized and the research directions of gaze estimation are prospected.

2   Appearance-Based Gaze Tracking

The estimation process from human eye feature to fixation point (gaze direction) mainly adopts different mapping functions, including establishing regression function and different clustering methods. The commonly used mapping functions mainly includes KNN, RF regression, GP regression, SVM, ANN and the convolutional neural network expanded on it.

2.1   *K*-Nearest-Neighbor

KNN is to calculate the distance between different eigenvalues to realize classification. Given the training set and the label, KNN first compares the characteristics of the input test data with the corresponding characteristics in the training set, and then calculates the distance between the training data and the test data, and finally gets the k points with the minimum distance (that is, the most similar) according to the distance ordering. Most of the categories of k points are the categories of this point.

The KNN algorithm needs to calculate the Euclidean distance between training data, so it will lead to excessive computational complexity in the case of large sample set calculation, and this algorithm is suitable for the case of small sample.

Zhang et al. [16] first extracted three low-dimensional features, including the color opponency, gray scale intensities and direction information. Secondly, the feature vector was gotten by normalized averaging the three features information, and minimum redundancy maximum relevance (MRMR) feature selection was used to reduce high dimensional image data to low dimensional feature vector. Finally, a KNN classifier with $k = 13$ was used to learn the mapping from image features to gaze direction. The reason why this method could use KNN algorithm was that it directly divided the gaze direction into 13 categories, and the value of k was not large, so the regression problem was changed to the classification problem.

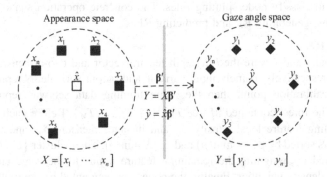

Fig. 1. The overall framework of neighbor regression [17]

As shown in Fig. 1, Wang et al. [17] proposed a gaze estimation method by combining with neighbor selection and neighbor regression. To find the closest set of samples, neighbor selection used features to achieve this goal, including head pose information, pupil center feature and eye appearance feature. This operation took up a large part of the total execution time, however, k-neural network adopted k-d tree structure in each feature space, it could achieve faster query speed. The neighbor regression improved the previous gaze estimation based on k-nearest neighbors that considered the correlation between samples and gaze angles to build models between the appearance space and gaze angle space. To save time, Weighted Least Squares Regression (WLSR) is selected as the regression method. Wood et al. [15] reconstructed the human eye image by scanning the 3D face with high resolution, used the KNN algorithm to obtain the gaze vector by matching the rendered human eye images to the images from MPIIGaze dataset.

From the existing KNN-based gaze tracking methods, it is worth considering how to balance the value of k and the time consumption. In contrast, KNN algorithm is more suitable for the case of fewer samples.

2.2 Random Forest Regression

RF is a classifier that contains multiple decision trees. It uses random samples to generate decision trees, called random decision tree. RF extracts some samples from the original data that need to be put back to generate the sample set and repeats the above steps to generate multiple sets. A decision tree is generated for each sample set, however, there is no correlation between decision trees. After obtaining the forest, a new test data is input into each decision tree, and the corresponding output value is generated. The output of the test data is the average output of each tree in the forest. RF is widely used in head pose estimation, feature selection and recommendation system. In recent years, RF has been employed in gaze tracking.

Obviously, RF can process high-dimensional data without feature selection, and the training speed is fast because it can operate in parallel. In order to solve the problem of head posture under deep illumination, Wang et al. [18] added the depth feature to the traditional line-of-sight estimation based on appearance, and applied the RF regression with cluster-to-classify node splitting rules. The concrete operation steps are divided into two steps: generating RF and predicting RF.

Generating RF

Assuming that x and y were the i-th depth feature vector and two-dimensional line of sight vector respectively, namely input variable and output variable, N represented the number of calibration point, then the entire training data set was represented by $\{x_i, y_i\}_{i=1}^N$. The forest contained M tree $T = \{T_1, T_2, \ldots, T_M\}$. Before each node splitting, computing feature local density ρ_m and distance measure δ_m, and recognizing cluster centers sorted by $\rho_m > \min(\rho)$ and $\delta_m > \min(\delta)$. Then, cluster $\{C_1, C_2, \ldots, C_k\}$ was completed by assigning the remaining feature points to the same cluster as its nearest high-density neighbor. Finally, the node was segmented by computing

$$f = \min_{w_k} \|w_k\|_2 + Z \sum_{i=1}^m (\max(0, 1 - d_i^k w_k^T x_i))^2 \qquad (1)$$

where w_k was the k-th cluster weight vector, Z was the penalty parameter. If $x_i \in C_k$, $d_i^k = 1$, otherwise, $d_i^k = -1$. Repeating the above steps until all nodes were partitioned to produce each random tree, then getting the regression value y_{pre}^i of current tree T_i.

Predicting RF

Entering the test sample x_{test} into each random tree, selecting the optimal splitting variables w_k and splitting points K, the gaze vector of the test set was the average of the regression values for each tree.

RF processed high-dimensional data without feature selection, and there was a large number of missing data, it had a strong anti-interference ability. The experimental results were the best when the number of features equaled to 160. Therefore, in the feature extraction stage, functions should be extracted as many as possible, however, with the increase of the number of features, the experimental results would also become worse. Excessive features may lead to redundancy (feature correlation is too high, part of consumption performance), noise (part of features have a negative impact on the predicted results), overfitting and other problems.

Sugano et al. [19] proposed a gaze estimation method using RF regression. Because this method collected the largest and fully calibrated multi-view gaze dataset and performed a 3D reconstruction eye images to build the input vector, RF regression could handle large-scale regression problems at a lower computational cost. Kacete et al. [20] used RF regression to estimate the gaze vector from the depth information with the face information. This method could handle real data scenarios presenting strong head pose changes. In general, the RF method was suitable for processing high-dimensional data. It could do parallel processing as well as the training speed was relatively fast. However, there would be overfitting in some regression problems with high noise. Huang et al. [21] studied gaze tracking on tablets. The various practical factors were performed extensive evaluation by the baseline algorithm which was based on multi-level HOG feature and RF regressor.

2.3 Gaussian Processers

GP [22] is a collection of random variables indexed by time or space, and the distributions of various derived quantities can be obtained explicitly. GP is different from the general regression algorithm in that the general regression algorithm is given the input x to get the corresponding output y, while the GP is to get the distribution of the function $f(x)$. The advantage of the GP is that it can get not only the estimate of the output, but also the confidence interval of the estimate.

For the training set D: (X, Y), let $f(X) = Y$, then the vector $f = [f(x_1), f(x_2), \ldots, f(x_n)]$ can be obtained. The test set of prediction x_i is defined as X^*, and the corresponding predicted value is f^*. According to the Bayes formula:

$$p(f^*|f) = \frac{p(f|f^*)p(f^*)}{p(f)} = \frac{p(f,f^*)}{p(f)} \tag{2}$$

the joint probability distribution between samples in the training set f is calculated first, and then the posterior probability distribution of f^* is calculated according to the prior probability distribution of the prediction set f^*. However, GP is not suitable for large data sets. For data sets with sample size N, the complexity of the traditional GP regression can reach $O(N^3)$.

Wojke et al. [23] generated a lower dimensional gaze manifold using GP latent variable model with the eye patches and the corresponding gaze points. In this particular application, only two potential dimensions are used to capture relevant information. Standard GP regression was used to establish the mapping relationship between the screen coordinates and the two-dimensional feature space, and the mapping relationship was used to generate eye-patches for each gaze point in the screen coordinates. Finally, the gaze point was estimated by non-linear optimization. Williams et al. [24] introduced a semi-supervised GP regression model to learn a mapping with only partially labelled training data. This model combined probability filters and the ability to learn from semi-supervised data simplified the process of collecting training data. In order to reduce the data set, Ferhat et al. [25] used an average eye image of the subjects for each calibration target as input to train GP estimator. Sugano et al. [26] also used the average human eye image as input. The gaze probability maps were formed by clustering with the saliency maps instead of gaze points, and the mapping from the average human eye image to the gaze probability graph was constructed by the GP.

In summary, the predicted value is probability of GP. The confidence interval is calculated and then a prediction of a specific field of interest is obtained based on the relevant information. However, this method does not support large data sets, also is not sparse, so before using such methods often have to deal with these two problems.

2.4   Support Vector Machines

SVM solves linear separable problems first, however, in some cases it cannot find linearly separable partition planes. Therefore, SVM needs to use the well-known "nuclear mechanism" to map these data into high-dimensional space, and transforms the original low-dimensional nonlinear regression problem into a high-dimensional linear regression problem. The performance of SVM depends on the construction of kernel function and the selection of corresponding parameters. However, for data sets with sample size N, the time complexity of SVM regression is $O(N^3)$, which greatly limits the scalability of large data sets.

For the general regression problem, $f(x)$ is learned from the training sample to make it as close as possible to y and the loss is zero only when $f(x)$ is completely the same as the real value. However, SVM regression can tolerate the deviation of $f(x)$ and y with the maximum of ξ, and only when the deviation value is greater than e, the loss will be calculated. If the training sample is between the interval bands with a width of 2ξ, the prediction could be considered correct.

Huang et al. [27] used iris center as input features of the SVM regression to build up mapping function. Unlike the former, Zhu et al. [28] built up an approximate generalized gaze mapping function from the pupil-glint vector and 3D eye position to the screen coordinate. Wu et al. [29] located the eye region by modifying the characteristics of active appearance model, and used SVM to classify the five gaze directions. Chuang et al. [30] defined a feature descriptor by the locations and scales of face parts. Then the feature descriptor was supplied to an SVM gaze classifier to get the gaze direction. In general, SVM is robust, and a small number of support vectors can determine the final result, such as the iris center as input. In the actual gaze tracking, it is obviously not affected by different users. However, with the increase of training samples, this method cannot be implemented and it is difficult to solve the problem of multi-classification.

2.5   Artificial Neural Network

ANN is an operational model, which abstracts the neural network of human brain from the perspective of information processing and forms different networks by connecting a large number of neurons in different ways. Each neuron represents a specific activation function, and the connection between two neurons has a weight of w_i. The output of the network varies according to the connection mode, weight value and excitation function of the network. The network itself can form an approximation to an algorithm or function.

Baluja and Pomerleau [31] developed an ANN-based gaze tracking system that was tested extensively on three architectures epochs. This system could achieve an accuracy of $1.5°$ that only used images of the eyeball and cornea as input. However, in order to get more information about the head pose, it took three minutes to extract the high pixel images. Yu et al. [32] proposed a method of gaze tracking based on BP neural network, and used particle swarm optimization algorithm to optimize the regression model of connection weight and threshold values. This method could accurately extract the eye-gaze features when the image pickup requirements were low. However, this method still could not achieve the full range of gaze tracking.

Convolutional Neural Network (CNN) is a special deep artificial neural network. On the one hand, the connections between neurons are local connections. For example, each layer node of BP network is a one-dimensional ordering state, and the network nodes between layers are completely connected. It's a simple one-dimensional convolutional network from a fully connected to a locally connected, and if it extends to two dimensions, it's a CNN. On the other hand, the weights between neurons on the same feature graph are the same. At present, with the development of neural network, the gaze-tracking method based on convolution network is more popular. Sewell and Komogortsev [33] used a multimodal CNN model to learn the mapping from the input features to gaze angles in the normalized space, the input features including both eye image and head pose information. As shown in the Fig. 2, which was the architecture of the proposed multimodal CNN. This model used LeNet network architecture, including two convolution layers, two max pooling layers and a fully connected layer, in which the head pose vectors were added to the output of the fully connected layer.

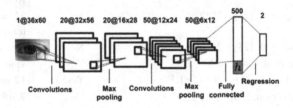

Fig. 2. Architecture of multimodal CNN [33]

Zhang et al. [34] used CNN to encode face images and imposed spatial weights on feature maps to flexibly suppress or enhance the information of different face regions. Cheng et al. [35] used the eye images and head pose information as input to complete judgement of the notion of two eye asymmetry. Zhang et al. [36] focused on the effect of variable head pose and proposed a novel branched CNN architecture that improved the robustness of gaze classifiers without increasing the computational cost. Palmero et al. [37] used face, eye region and face landmarks as separate information flows in CNN to estimate gaze in static images. It was the first time that the gaze dynamic characteristics were considered in the method. The learning features of all frames were input into a many-to-one recurrent module sequentially, and the 3D gaze vector of the last frame were predicted. Fischer et al. [38] recorded a new dataset of different head postures in order to improve the robustness of gaze estimation, and applied semantic image inpainting to the area covered by glasses to eliminate the obtrusiveness of the glasses and built a birdge between training and test images. Yu et al. [39] introduced a constrained landmark-Gaze model to get the relation of eye landmark locations and gaze directions.

In general, the training process of CNN model is long, but its accuracy and robustness are better than most standard machine learning algorithms.

Table 1. Summary of the appearance-based methods which are simply classified by means of mapping for facilitating user's access. Head pose shows whether the method has head-free movement or not, symbol $\approx$ means that the method allows a range of head movement, symbol ✓ means the method with fixed head pose, symbol—xmeans the method with free head movement.

Mapping	Reference	Year	Accuracy	Head pose	Calibration	Training dataset
KNN	Zhang et al. [16]	2011	/	✓	No	17 subjects
	Wang et al. [17]	2017	7.5° on SynthesEyes, 4.8° under UnityEyes	–	No	SynthesEyes, UnityEyes
	Wood et al. [15]	2016	9.95°	–	No	UnityEyes
RF regression	Wang et al. [18]	2016	1.53°	–	Yes	6 subjects with 25 training points
	Sugnao et al. [19]	2014	Average 6.5°	–	No	50 subjects with 10 grids
	Kacete et al. [20]	2016	Average 3.8°	–	No	200 k synthetic RGB-D samples
	Huang et al. [21]	2017	/	–	No	51 subjects with 35 training points
GP	Wojke et al. [23]	2016	/	$\approx$	No	400 samples
	Blake et al. [24]	2006	0.83°	–	Yes	videos
	Ferhat et al. [25]	2014	<1.5°	✓	Yes	12 subjects
	Sugano et al. [26]	2013	3.5°	✓	No	7 subjects with 80 short clips
SVM	Huang et al. [27]	2011	0.4°	✓	Yes	/
	Zhu et al. [28]	2006	1.5°	$\approx$	No	2757 samples
	Wu et al. [29]	2014	/	✓	No	15 subjects with 800 images
	Chuang et al. [30]	2014	/	✓	No	videos
ANN	Baluja et al. [31]	1993	Average 1.7°	$\approx$	Yes	2000 images
	Yu et al. [32]	2016	/	✓	Yes	50 subjects with the 15 training points
	Sewell et al. [33]	2010	<3.68°	$\approx$	Yes	5 subjects with the 50 training points
CNN (special ANN)	Zhang et al. [34]	2016	4.8° on MPIIGaze, 6.0° on EyeDiap	–	No	MPIIGaze, EyeDiap
	Cheng et al. [35]	2018	Average 5.0°	–	No	Modified MPIIGaze, UT Multiview, EyeDiap

(*continued*)

Table 1. (*continued*)

Mapping	Reference	Year	Accuracy	Head pose	Calibration	Training dataset
	Zhang et al. [36]		7.74°	–	No	MPIIGaze
	Palmero et al. [37]	2018	Average 6.2°	–	No	EyeDaip
	Fischer et al. [38]	2018	4.3° on MPIIGaze, 5.1° on UT Multiview	–	No	MPIIGaze, UT Multiview
	Yu et al. [39]	2018	5.4° on Eyediap, 5.7° on UT Multiview	–	No	UTMultiview, Eyediap

3 Discussions and Conclusion

3.1 Discussions

As shown in Table 1, each type of method has its advantages and limitations. It is difficult to compare the accuracy accurately because of the different evaluation criteria, but it is obvious that all the methods can achieve a good performance with a high estimation accuracy. However, most of them only can handle small head movements and achieve high accuracy in the special cases. With the development of commercial application, it is an inevitable trend to propose gaze tracking method with free head movement. Apart from the head pose, most methods require calibration procedure. The complex calibration process is inconvenient for the commercial application. To reduce the calibration points or without calibration is the direction of future development. Methods in recent years have tended to study gaze tracking without calibration, but the price is the reduction of tracking accuracy. Therefore, how to maintain a high tracking accuracy without personal calibration is one of the future research directions.

Obviously, appearance-based gaze tracking methods have showed great potential in various applications and achieved a high tracking accuracy, but some challenges still exist and need to be further researched.

(a) Free head movements

Most of the appearance-based gaze tracking methods require the user under a fixed head pose or a limited head moving range, which limit the user's moving space and result in a bad user experience in HCI applications. Therefore, it is necessary to develop an effective gaze tracking method that can handle free head movement. The latest methods take this problem into account, and most of the algorithms add the head pose vector to the feature extraction process. However, experiments show that this method is far from enough to offset the errors caused by head posture.

(b) Non-calibration or auto-calibration

Since the difference of personal eye parameters in different individuals, most gaze tracking methods require personal calibration process. On the one hand, calibration process requires user's involvement, which leads to a low degree of automation. On the other hand, calibration accuracy greatly affects the gaze tracking accuracy. Therefore, it is urgent to propose a robust gaze tracking method with auto-calibration or without calibration to achieve automation and stability. Although the latest algorithms almost reduce the calibration process, some experiments show that individual calibration in the testing process still has an optimization effect on the accuracy of the algorithm. Therefore, to solve this problem, the calibration process should be avoided in the training process and achieve robustness and automation, while the testing process can use the calibration appropriately, as long as the calibration process is not complicated.

(c) Reduction of training samples

Appearance-based gaze tracking methods normally require large training samples to obtain high accuracy. However, this will bring large computational cost. KNN, SVM and GP algorithms do not support large data sets, and neural network method also takes a long time. Therefore, how to reduce the training samples by discovering some more effective feature descriptors to improve the tracking efficiency while maintaining the accuracy remains a challenging task.

(d) Incorporating the merits of multiple methods

In recent years, all kinds of methods have their advantages and disadvantages. Taking the advantages of good methods and avoiding the disadvantages can greatly improve the calculation cost and accuracy of methods. For example, Wang et al. [18] uses the advantages of convolutional neural network to extract depth features, and uses the advantages of parallel computation of random forests to accelerate the mapping speed.

3.2   Conclusion

In this paper, a review on appearance-based gaze tracking methods has been presented. The mainstream feature input extraction methods based on human-eye appearance image have been introduced. Five classified appearance-based gaze tracking methods according to the mapping manner have been presented in detail. Finally, four challenging issues have been summarized and discussed for future research.

Acknowledgement. This work was supported by National Natural Science Foundation of China (61876168, U1509207), National Key R&D Program of China (2018YFB1305200), and Zhejiang Provincial Natural Science Foundation of China (LY18F030020).

References

1. Stiefelhagen, R., Yang, J.: Gaze tracking for multimodal human-computer interaction. In: 1997 IEEE International Conference on Acoustics, Speech, and Signal Processing. IEEE, Munich (1997)
2. Morimoto, C.H., Mimica, M.R.M.: Eye gaze tracking techniques for interactive applications. Comput. Vis. Image Underst. **98**(1), 4–24 (2015)
3. Sawahata, Y., Khosla, R., Komine, K.: Determining comprehension and quality of TV programs using eye-gaze tracking. Pattern Recogn. **41**(5), 1610–1626 (2008)
4. Guan, Q., Tang, F., Zhou, X., Min, H.: A survey of 3D eye model based gaze tracking. J. Comput.-Aided Des. Comput. Graph. **29**(9), 1579–1589 (2017)

5. Pham, C., Thiele, S., Parkinson, J., Li, S.: Alcohol warning label awareness and attention: a multi-method study. Alcohol Alcohol. **53**(1), 1–7 (2017)
6. Pfeiffer, T.: Towards gaze interaction in immersive virtual reality : evaluation of a monocular eye tracking set-up. In: Schumann, M., Kuhlen, T. (eds.) Virtuelle und Erweiterte RealitatFunfter Workshop der GIFachgruppe VRAR, pp. 81–92. Shaker Verlag (2008)
7. Valenti, R., Gevers, T.: Accurate eye center location and tracking using isophote curvature. In: IEEE Conference on Computer Vision & Pattern Recognition, vol. 1, pp. 1–8. IEEE, Alaska (2008)
8. Valenti, R., Staiano, J., Sebe, N., Gevers, T.: Webcam-based visual gaze estimation. In: Foggia, P., Sansone, C., Vento, M. (eds.) ICIAP 2009. LNCS, vol. 5716, pp. 662–671. Springer, Heidelberg (2009). https://doi.org/10.1007/978-3-642-04146-4_71
9. Guestrin, E.D., Eizenman, M.: General theory of remote gaze estimation using the pupil center and corneal reflections. IEEE Trans. Biomed. Eng. **53**(6), 1124–1133 (2006)
10. Zhang, Y., Bulling, A., Gellersen, H.: Discrimination of gaze directions using low-level eye image features. In: Proceedings of the 1st International Workshop on Pervasive Eye Tracking & Mobile Eye-Based Interaction, pp. 9–14. ACM, Beijing (2011)
11. Wang, Y.: Appearance-based gaze estimation using deep features and random forest regression. Knowl.-Based Syst. **110**, 293–301 (2016)
12. Tan, K., Kriegman, D.J., Ahuja, N.: Appearance-based eye gaze estimation. In: 6th IEEE Workshop on Applications of Computer Vision, p. 191. IEEE Computer Society, Orlando (2002)
13. Martinez, F., Carbone, A., Pissaloux, E.: Gaze estimation using local features and non-linear regression. In: 19th IEEE International Conference on Image Processing, pp. 1961–1964. IEEE, Orlando (2013)
14. Guo, Z., Zhou, Z., Liu, Z.: Appearance-based gaze estimation under slight head motion. Multimed. Tools Appl. **76**(2), 2203–2222 (2016)
15. Wood, E.,Tadas, B., Louis, M., Peter, R., Andreas, B.: Learning an appearance-based gaze estimator from one million synthesised images. In: Proceedings of the Ninth Biennial ACM Symposium on Eye Tracking Research and Applications, pp. 131–138. ACM, New York (2016)
16. Zhang,Y., Bulling, A., Gellersen, H.: Discrimination of gaze directions using low-level eye image features. In: Proceedings of the 1st International Workshop on Pervasive Eye Tracking & Mobile Eye-based Interaction, pp. 9–14. ACM, New York (2011)
17. Wang, Y., Zhao, T., Ding, X.: Learning a gaze estimator with neighbor selection from large-scale synthetic eye images. Knowl.-Based Syst. **139**, 41–49 (2017)
18. Wang, Y.: Appearance-based gaze estimation using deep features and random forest regression. Knowl. Based Syst. **110**, 293–301 (2016)
19. Sugano, Y., Matsushita, Y., Sato, Y.: Learning-by-Synthesis for Appearance-Based 3D Gaze Estimation. In: 2014 IEEE Conference on Computer Vision and Pattern Recognition (CVPR), pp. 1821–1828. IEEE, Columbus (2014)
20. Kacete, A., Séguier, R., Collobert, M., Royan, J.: Unconstrained gaze estimation using random forest regression voting. In: Lai, S.-H., Lepetit, V., Nishino, K., Sato, Y. (eds.) ACCV 2016. LNCS, vol. 10113, pp. 419–432. Springer, Cham (2017). https://doi.org/10.1007/978-3-319-54187-7_28
21. Huang, Q., Veeraraghavan, A., Sabharwal, A.: Tabletgaze: dataset and analysis for unconstrained appearance-based gaze estimation in mobile tablets. Mach. Vis. Appl. **28**(5–6), 445–461 (2017)
22. Ounpraseuth, S.T.: Gaussian processes for machine learning. Int. J. Neural Syst. **14**(2), 69–106 (2004)

23. Wojke, N.: Gaze-estimation for consumer-grade cameras using a Gaussian process latent variable model. Pattern Recogn. Image Anal. **26**(1), 248–255 (2016)

24. Williams, O., Blake, A.: Sparse and semi-supervised visual mapping with the S^3 GP. In: 2016 IEEE Computer Society Conference on Computer Vision & Pattern Recognition, pp. 230–237. IEEE, New York (2006)

25. Ferhat, O., Vilarino, F., Sánchez, F.J.: A cheap portable eye-tracker solution for common setups. J. Eye Mov. Res. **7**(3), 1–10 (2014)

26. Sugano, Y., Matsushita, Y.: Appearance-based gaze estimation using visual saliency. IEEE Trans. Pattern Anal. Mach. Intell. **35**(2), 329–341 (2013)

27. Huang, Y., Dong, X., Hao, M.: Eye gaze calibration based on support vector regression machine. In: 9th World Congress on Intelligent Control and Automation, pp. 454–456. IEEE, Taipei (2011)

28. Zhu, Z., Ji, Q., Bennett, K.P.: Nonlinear eye gaze mapping function estimation via support vector regression. In: 18th International Conference on Pattern Recognition, pp. 1132–1135. IEEE, Hong Kong (2006)

29. Wu, Y.L., Yeh, C.T., Wei, H.: Gaze direction estimation using support vector machine with active appearance model. Multimed. Tools Appl. **70**(3), 2037–2062 (2014)

30. Chuang, M.-C., Bala, R., Bernal, E.A., Paul, P., Burry, A.: Estimating gaze direction of vehicle drivers using a smartphone camera. In: Proceedings of the IEEE Conference on Computer Vision and Pattern Recognition Workshops, pp. 165–170. IEEE, Columbus (2014)

31. Baluja, S., Pomerleau, D.: Non-intrusive gaze tracking using artificial neural networks. Adv. Neural. Inf. Process. Syst. **98**(1), 753–760 (1993)

32. Yu, L., Xu, J., Huang, S.: Eye-gaze tracking system based on particle swarm optimization and BP neural network. In: 12th World Congress on Intelligent Control and Automation, pp. 1269–1273. IEEE, Guilin (2016)

33. Sewell, W., Komogortsev, O.: Real-time eye gaze tracking with an unmodified commodity webcam employing a neural network. In: Mynatt, E.D., Schoner, D., Fitzpatrick, G., Hudson, S.E., Edwards, W.K., Rodden, T. (eds.) Proceedings of the Extended Abstracts on Human Factors in Computing Systems (CHI EA 2010), pp. 3739–3744. ACM, Atlanta (2010)

34. Zhang, X., Sugano, Y., Fritz, M.: It's written all over your face: full-face appearance-based gaze estimation. Comput. Vis. Pattern Recogn. **1**(5), 2299–2308 (2016)

35. Cheng, Y., Lu, F., Zhang, X.: Appearance-based gaze estimation via evaluation-guided asymmetric regression. In: Ferrari, V., Hebert, M., Sminchisescu, C., Weiss, Y. (eds.) Computer Vision – ECCV 2018. LNCS, vol. 11218, pp. 105–121. Springer, Cham (2018). https://doi.org/10.1007/978-3-030-01264-9_7

36. Zhang, C., Rui, Y., Cai, J.: Efficient eye typing with 9-direction gaze estimation. Multimed. Tools Appl. **77**(15), 1–18 (2017)

37. Palmero, C., Selva, J., Bagheri, M. A., Escalera, S.: Recurrent CNN for 3D gaze estimation using appearance and shape cues. Comput. Vis. Pattern Recogn. **1**(3), 1–13 (2018)

38. Fischer, T., Chang, H.J., Demiris, Y.: RT-GENE: real-time eye gaze estimation in natural environments. In: Ferrari, V., Hebert, M., Sminchisescu, C., Weiss, Y. (eds.) ECCV 2018. LNCS, vol. 11214, pp. 339–357. Springer, Cham (2018). https://doi.org/10.1007/978-3-030-01249-6_21

39. Yu, Y., Liu, G., Odobez, J.-M.: Deep multitask gaze estimation with a constrained landmark-gaze model. In: Leal-Taixé, L., Roth, S. (eds.) ECCV 2018. LNCS, vol. 11130, pp. 456–474. Springer, Cham (2019). https://doi.org/10.1007/978-3-030-11012-3_35

Language and Robotics: Complex Sentence Understanding

Seng-Beng Ho[1,2(✉)] and Zhaoxia Wang[1,3]

[1] Institute of High Performance Computing, A*STAR, Singapore, Singapore
hosengbeng@gmail.com, wangz.ihpc@gmail.com
[2] AI Programme, A*STAR, Singapore, Singapore
[3] Nanjing University of Information Science and Technology, Nanjing, China

Abstract. Existing robotic systems can take actions based on natural language commands but they tend to be only simple commands. On the other hand, in the domain of Natural Language Processing (NLP), complex sentences are processed, but this NLP domain does not make close contact with robotics. The beginning of computer processing of natural language, when traced back to a system such as Winograd's SHRUDLU, conceived in 1973, actually aimed to address the issues of Natural Language Understanding (NLU) of relatively complex sentences by a robotic system which in turn takes actions accordingly based on the natural language input. NLU, in the robotic context, thus constitutes taking the correct actions from language instructions. This paper explores the use of cognitive linguistic constructs as well as other constructs such as spatial relationship constructs to configure an NLU system for translating complex natural language instructions into actions to be taken by a robot. This research work illustrates that two important steps are necessary: the first step is to translate a language-dependent surface sentential structure into a language independent deep-level predicate representation, and then the next step is to translate the predicate representation into grounded real-world references and constructs that enable a robot to carry out the language instructions accordingly.

Keywords: Natural language understanding · Robotics ·
Language and robotics · Predicate meaning representation · Grounding ·
Semantic grounding · Predicate to referent grounding ·
Complex sentence understanding

1 Introduction

This paper explores the relationship between language and robotics as well as the representational and computational devices needed for the understanding of complex natural language instructions. In the past decade or more, the research in Artificial Intelligence (AI) has splintered into many different "sub-areas" such as Natural Language Processing (NLP), Computer Vision (CV), robotics, machine learning, etc. In some cases, there are stronger connections, such as between machine learning and the other fields, because machine learning has to be applied to some problems (NLP, CV, etc.). There are also strong connections between CV and robotics. However, even though robotics is connected to NLP in the sense that some robotic systems do employ

© Springer Nature Switzerland AG 2019
H. Yu et al. (Eds.): ICIRA 2019, LNAI 11745, pp. 641–654, 2019.
https://doi.org/10.1007/978-3-030-27529-7_54

NLP when it is desired that robots respond to natural language commands, these commands tend to be relatively simple [1–3]. On the other hand, NLP people largely proceed with their research as though robotics does not exist [4–7]. But there is actually a very strong connection between the two aspects of intelligent systems. One of the very first NLU systems, Winograd's SHRUDLU, conceived in 1973, consists of a toy-world in which a robotic arm is made to carry out actions based on natural language commands [8]. This work illustrates the inseparability between language and robotics: through carrying out the respective actions correctly, the system demonstrate that it really "understands" the natural language input, and this distinguishes NLU from "merely" NLP. And from a robotic system's point of view, it would naturally benefit from being able to carry out actions based on natural language commands.

This paper first reviews some of the representative past work which demonstrates the close connections between language and robotics, and then proceeds to describe a method to enable robots to receive complex natural language commands and carry out the respective actions accordingly. This research will contribute to human-like next generation AI.

2   Review of Relevant Work

Recent work in NLP focuses more on the "processing" aspect of natural language rather than addresses the issue of "understanding" [4–7]. E.g., a machine translation could output a string of words given another string of words in another language, but it does not really "understand" what they mean, nor perhaps does it really matter as far as the task is concerned. However, there has also not been many attempts in trying to define what "understanding" really entails. Ho and Wang [9] attempts to clarify what "understanding" really entails and in the subsequent discussions we will demonstrate that the process discussed not only clarifies what "understanding" really entails, it also provides an NLU framework for robots to receive complex natural language commands and act on them accordingly.

One of the earliest works relevant to NLU is Winograd's SHRUDLU system, conceived in 1973 [8]. Figure 1 shows a "toy-world" used in the system. The system basically involves a user typing in a series of commands and the system would answer some questions, or through a robotic arm, would carry out a series of actions accordingly. Thus, from the outset, language and robotics are intertwined in this paradigm of NLU. It is almost like Winograd is declaring "understanding is under-standing how to act."

Issues of ambiguous reference are resolved through some built-in heuristics as well as clarifications requested by the system to the human user giving the commands. For example, as shown in the figure, it uses heuristics to determine what "it" refers to in one sentence and which block is being referred to in another sentence.

SHRUDLU suffered from the issue of scalability. At that time (the 70's) there was no machine learning or computer vision to assist in learning rules, say, for mapping between words and their referents in the real world, and hence the knowledge used had to be hand-coded. However, today there are systems that can achieve both the learning and word referents as well as the grammatical rules is possible concurrently [10].

>> Pick up a big grey block.
➤ Ok.

>> Find a block that is taller than the one you are holding and put it on the cylinder.
> BY "IT," I ASSUME YOU MEAN THE BLOCK WHICH IS TALLER THAN THE ONE I AM HOLDING.
Ok.

>> What is the block supported by?
➤ THE CYLINDER.
(If this question was asked earlier, it would have responded "I DON'T UNDERSTAND WHICH BOX
YOU MEAN")

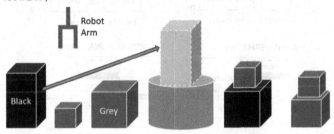

Fig. 1. Winograd's SHRUDLU system [8].

Another piece of natural language related research that came from the 1970's that is relevant to robotics and vision is Schank and Abelson's work on Scripts [11]. Scripts basically consist of Causal-Spatio-Temporal (CST) descriptions of an event, such as the happenings in a restaurant, that allow complex question-answering exchanges to take place. Suppose someone says something like "I went to the Restaurant yesterday. I didn't leave a tip," the Restaurant Script may allow questions such as this to be responded to by a system: "Was the service bad?" as this piece of knowledge is encoded in the script's processes describing what happen and why in a typical restaurant. If a Restaurant is simply defined as "an establishment where food can be purchase," as in a typical dictionary definition, "deep understanding" reflected by this sophisticated linguistic response cannot be achieved.

In the 70's these Scripts were hand-coded but recently it has been shown that CST graphs are learnable through observing the environment directly [12, 13].

There has been a number of linguistic paradigms [14] that attempt to formulate semantics – i.e., the meaning of meaning, or what meaning entails. Among all these paradigms, "cognitive linguistics" is most suited for providing useful representational constructs for AI and robotics [15].

Figure 2 shows some examples of representational constructs proposed in cognitive linguistics to describe spatial and temporal relationships. Figure 2(a) depicts the "above" and "below" relationships. It can be shown that as far as the objects involved are concerned (Object1 and Object2), the spatial arrangement between them remains the same in both descriptions. However, in a sentence such as "Object1 is *above* Object2," cognitive linguistics identifies Object1 as the Trajector (TR) and Object2 as the Landmark (LM). TR is like a "focus" of the sentence and LM is like a "reference." Therefore, should the positions of TR and LM be interchanged, then the language description becomes "Object2 is *below* Object1." Thus *above* and *below* are in a complementary relationship, depending on the TR and LM.

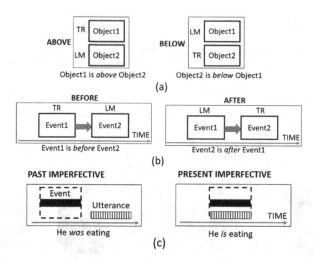

Fig. 2. Cognitive linguistics representations of (a) *above* and *below*; (b) *before* and *after*; (c) past and present imperfective [15].

Figure 2(b) depicts a similar situation, but in the temporal domain – the "before" and "after" relationships. The two events, Event1 and Event2, bear the same relative relationship in time in both situations, but there are two possible sentential descriptions arising from it, depending on which is the TR and LM.

Figure 2(c) depicts the meaning of the present imperfective and the past imperfective tenses in a temporal picture. The corresponding tense is used depending on the temporal relationship between the utterer of the sentence and the event itself.

In the following, we will leverage some of these cognitive linguistic representations for the use of robotic language understanding.

3   Language and Robotics: Complex Sentence Understanding

In this section, we elucidate the intimate connections between language and robotics, and show how some of the concepts reviewed above can be integrated to bear on the problems of complex sentence understanding. Due to the limitation of space, the discussions here are not meant to be exhaustive but merely illustrative.

3.1   Basic Instructions

We consider two kinds of instructions given to a robot:

AFFORDANCE:
Use OBJECT1 for TASK1 (AFFORDANCE)

TEMPORAL SEQUENCE:
Do TASK1 *then (begin to do)* TASK2
After you *have done* TASK1 *then* do TASK2
Do TASK1 *until* TASK2/EVENT1 *begins*
While you *are doing* TASK1, do TASK2

The first kind of instructions is to inform the robot what entity can be used to achieve a certain goal, i.e., what can *afford* what. (E.g., "use the screw driver to screw the screw" – a screw driver affords screwing of screws.) The second kind of instructions is to inform the robot what *temporal steps* it should take. Here we are assuming that words like "use," "for," "do," "you," etc. have built-in procedural meanings (i.e., procedures are used to implement them) and we do not explore how they may be represented explicitly such as in the cognitive linguistics examples for certain concepts in Fig. 2.

For the words in italics, such as *"then," "after," "while," "have done," "are doing," "until," "begin,"* they are grounded in the corresponding cognitive linguistic constructs such as shown in Fig. 2.

Note that of course when a certain instruction such as "use a screw driver to screw the screw" is given to a totally naïve "infant" robotic system, the system still needs to work out, through a problem solving process, *how* exactly to use the screw driver. But this instruction at least helps to cut down the search space tremendously, otherwise thousands of objects may have to be tried.

Of course, the system can recurse: it can ask further questions and receive further language instructions: "How do I use that screw driver?" The answer(s) may be:

(1) *"First,* you pick-up that screw driver, and *then* you position the screw driver such that its long axis is aligned with the long axis of the screw, and *then* you insert the tip of the screw driver into the grooves on the top part of the screw, and *then* you rotate the screw driver around its long axis in a clockwise direction..."

The system may further ask, "How do I pick up the screw driver?" And the answer may be:

(2) *"First,* you position your hand directly above the screw driver's handle area, *then* you rotate your hand until the main axis of the gap between your fingers is aligned with the long axis of the screw driver's handle, *then* you lower your hand until these two axes coincide, *then* you close your fingers onto the handle, ..."

If these complex language instructions can be "understood," the appropriate actions can be carried out. This will be explored in the subsequent sections. Figure 3 shows how the various sentences above can be represented in an explicit temporal representation through a syntactic transformation process.

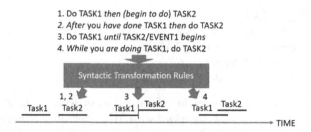

Fig. 3. Syntactic transformation converts the sentences 1, 2, 3, and 4 into the corresponding temporal structures.

There is ambiguity inherent in the co-temporal instruction *while* and the temporal instruction *after...then*. The two tasks in a *while* construct may begin at the same time or at slightly different times, though they must overlap temporally, and the two tasks in the *after...then* construct may be separated by any amount of time. The robotic system may (i) decide on the time interval based on some earlier learned typical values; (ii) decide on the time interval based on the knowledge about the tasks at hand; and (iii) ask for further instructions.

For (iii), further language processing is needed, and the instructions may be:

Do TASK2 *while* doing TASK1, *begin* TASK2 **1 minute** *after starting* TASK1
Do TASK2 *after* TASK1, *begin* TASK2 **1 minute** *after stopping* TASK1

The new words introduced here and their corresponding progressive versions are "*start*" and "*stop*". *Start* has the same meaning in this context as *begin*.

For the case of "Do TASK1 *until* TASK2/EVENT1 *begins*," it implies that TASK1 could have continued but its termination is effected by the beginning of TASKS2 or another EVENT1.

3.2   Complex Instructions

There are a number of basic constructs that are needed before the complex instructions (1) and (2) discussed above can be "understood" and they are described as follows.

Basic Constructs Needed

Objects and Parts

Figure 4 shows an arrow-shaped object. For a longish and asymmetrical object such as this, it is typical for humans to identify, say by pointing or through the use of words, a "front" and a "back" parts. These parts could also be identified by their shapes – the "rectangular" part and the "triangular" part. The center of gravity (CG) of an object could also be its dividing point, and a *back* and *front* parts of the object with respect to the CG can thus be identified, which will not coincide exactly with the identification based on the shapes. If the object is symmetrical (i.e., no "triangular" vs "rectangular" region), then these are more likely to be referred to as "left" and "right" parts.

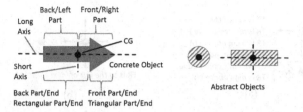

Fig. 4. An object and its parts. Definitions of Center of Gravity (CG), and long and short axes. Abstract objects are hatched and used in subsequent discussions.

Other than the CG, there are the "long axis" and "short axis" which could typically be identified for a longish object.

Predicate representations can be used to identify or refer to the various subparts of the object involved, such as *Long-Axis*(Object1), *Front-Part*(Object1), *CG*(Object1), etc.

A concrete object such as the arrow-shaped object have sub-structures that are identifiable as its parts. In the following discussion, we will also use "abstract" objects, which could represent "any" objects, and these are shown as hatched shapes in Fig. 4 – the circular one represents something that is more or less symmetrical with no clear distinction of a *long* and *short axes*, and in the rectangular one, *long* and *short axes* can be discerned.

Spatial Relationships

Spatial relationships are very fundamental to the positioning and placement of objects and entities for the purpose of subsequent goal-oriented actions. Figure 5 shows some very fundamental spatial relationships.

Figure 5(a) shows the "above" relationship. In the spirit of cognitive linguistics as discussed in Sect. 2.3, the focus of the relationship is the Trajector, TR, and the reference, the Landmark, LM. In a sentence like, "A is *above* B," A is the TR and B is the LM. And as shown in Fig. 5(a), when a relationship such as "TR is above LM" is specified, there could be a range of locations in which TR can be positioned with respect to LM, and this is shown as two arrows showing the tolerable relative positions of the CG in which the *above* relation still holds. However, if more specific relationships are specified, such as "TR is 5 cm above LM," then the location range is more constrained.

These tolerable relative positions may be derived from observational statistics of the relative positions of the real-world instances of objects in which the relationship of *above* holds. These probabilities can then be used to determine what is a most "typical" configuration for the *above* spatial relationship.

Specifications such as this in Fig. 5(a) and in the rest of the figures can be used for **recognition** as well as **generation**. For recognition, the specification is mapped onto two real world objects, and if they satisfy this specification, they are in the above spatial relation.

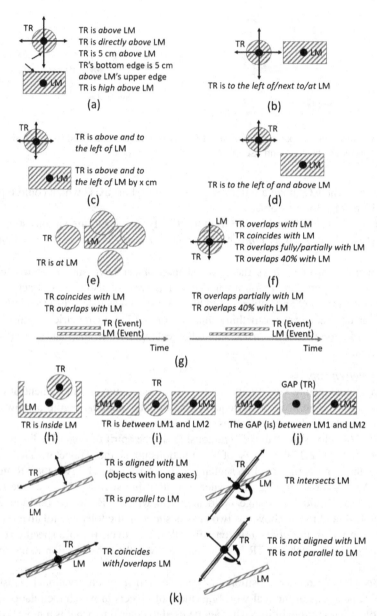

Fig. 5. Spatial relations. (a) *above*; (b) *to the left* or *right/next to/at*; (c) *above and to the left of*; (d) *to the left of and above*; (e) *at*; (f) *overlap/coincide with*, fully or partially; (g) temporal *overlap/coincide with*, fully or partially; (h) *inside*; (i) *between*; (j) a GAP as an object, *between*; (k) entities with longish spatial extent. The horizontal and vertical double arrows indicate the ranges of positions of the corresponding CGs.

For generation, the specification would direct the placement of the objects involved accordingly, using the concepts as well as probabilities learned earlier as a guide to produce the "typical" situation, taking consideration of other constraints (e.g., there may be other blockages so that the next most probable placement is selected).

Figure 5(b) shows the "to the left of" (and similarly "to the right of") relationships. If the objects are very close together, the description could be "next to" or "at."

Figure 5(c) shows a combination of *above* and *left of*. The situation is more of an *above* than a *left of*, so the word order is *above and to the left of*. If the situation is more *left of* than *above*, than it may be more likely to be described as *left of and above* such as shown in Fig. 5(d). Note that in both Figs. 5(c) and (d), the range of allowable positions of the TR is smaller than those in Fig. 5(a) and (b).

Figure 5(e) shows that other than the very nearby kind of *left of* or *right of*, even if there is some overlap between the TR and LM, the relationship could be "the TR is *at* the LM." Figure 5(f) shows the "overlap" situation. Sometime, "coincide" may be used to describe the same situation.

Figure 5(g) shows the concept of *overlap/coincide* applied to a temporal situation in which one *event* is a TR and another an LM. One can also say "Event1 (TR) is *next to* Event2 (LM)" but there is no corresponding situation of "Event1 is above Event 2."

Figure 5(h) shows a situation in which the LM is a container-like object and the TR is likely to be described as "inside" the LM rather than just *overlap* with the LM. All the other relationships of *above, to the left, to the right, next to*, etc. can also be characterized as "outside," if LM is container-like.

Figure 5(i) shows the "between" relationship. Figure 5(j) shows how a "gap" could be characterized as an "object" and the relationship of *between* could be applied here.

Figure 5(k) shows entities with spatial extents in which the relative orientation between the entities is important. In the case of entities with a longish spatial extent (i.e., a long axis can be defined), they can be *in parallel* to each other or *aligned* with each other, or *not in parallel* or *not aligned* with each other. The entities can also *intersect* each other or *coincide/overlap with* each other as shown in the same figure. Even though *intersect* is a little like *overlap*, for longish objects in which the "overlapping" area is small, *intersect* is used to describe the relationship instead.

Sentence to Action Predicates Transformation

Sentences are "surface" structures and different languages may represent the same "deep" structure (i.e., "meaning") using different surface structures (e.g., in some languages such as English, the word order is SUBJECT—VERB—OBJECT, while in some other languages, e.g., Japanese, it could be SUBJECT—OBJECT—VERB). Even within the same language, a passive voice and an active voice surface structure map onto the same deep structure (e.g., Mary *kicks* John has the same "meaning" as John is *kicked* by Mary). Whatever the surface structure, we should have transformation rules that map them into the same deep structure if they are indeed the same in meaning. In the following, we show an example of a Spatial Predicate and an example of an Action Predicate created from the surface structure sentences.

TR is *above* LM
→ **Above**(TR, LM) – **Spatial** Predicate

Mary *kicks* John **or** John is kicked by Mary
→ **Kick**(John, Mary) – **Action** Predicate

Next, we show an example of the use of the concept of **Until**. (Fig. 3)

John *moves* his hand *until* it is next to the Wall
→ **Move**(John, *Hand*(John), **Until**(*Next-To*(*Hand*(John), Wall))

Usually what follows **Until** is a condition to be met to terminate the earlier action. And usually, the concept of "positioning" is used to describe a similar situation more succinctly as follows:

John *positions* himself at the door
→ **Move**(John, John, **Until**(*At*(John, Door))

Note that the **Move** Action Predicate could be a simple movement or the more complex sequence of steps generated through a problem solving process – i.e., the **Until** predicate specifies a Goal State, and a problem solving process is called to generate the sequence of move actions to reach that state from the current state.

Predicate to Referent Conversion: Representation and Action

Having derived the predicate descriptions from sentences as described above, the next step of processing is to convert the predicates to their referents. One kind of predicate we discussed above is a predicate that specifies a subpart of an object. Figure 6 depicts an example of referencing the *Long-Axis* of an object.

Figure 6 shows that in the process of referencing the *Long-Axis* of an object, the equation of the *Long-Axis* is returned (some other forms of representation, such as an analogical representation, for the long-axis may be used instead of an equation). Similarly, something like **Top-Surface**(ObjectA) will return the equation or some other representational form for the top surface. If the predicate is **Front-Part**(ObjectA), then a volumetric representation of that front part is returned.

Figure 7 shows how a spatial predicate is converted into a referent. Suppose the spatial predicate *Above* is used to describe the spatial relationship between two specific objects, ObjectA and ObjectB. The process begins with the recall of the grounded representation of *Above*, shown on the left side of the figure (see Fig. 5(a)). Then the specific concrete instances ObjectA and ObjectB are bounded to the respective abstract objects in the grounded representation, and a *grounded and specific* concrete representation of *Above*(ObjectA, ObjectB) is output. This specific concrete representation of *Above*(ObjectA, ObjectB) contains a range of possible positions for ObjectA, relative to ObjectB.

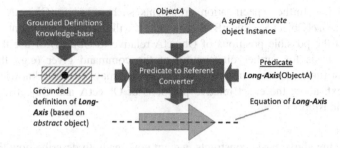

Fig. 6. Predicate to Referent Converter: An **Aspect-of-Object** Predicate, *Long-axis*, references the long axis of an ObjectA, and the Predicate to Reference Converter outputs the equation or other forms of representation of the long axis.

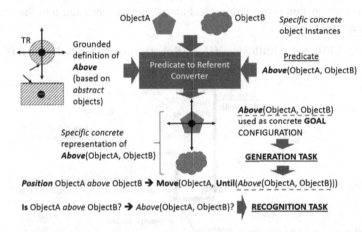

Fig. 7. Predicate to Referent Converter: A **Spatial Predicate** *above* is converted into the corresponding referent. Note the distinction between a RECOGNITION TASK and a GENERATION TASK, and the corresponding predicate representations are shown.

The use of this specific representation can be for answering a query such as "Is ObjectA above ObjectB?", i.e., "*Above*(ObjectA, ObjectB)?" For this task, this concrete representation can be used to match to the current specific ObjectA and ObjectB in their corresponding specific locations to see if the *Above* relationship really holds. This is a RECOGNITION TASK.

This specific representation can also be used for a GENERATION TASK. I.e., suppose currently ObjectA and ObjectB are not in an *Above* relationship. The specific concrete representation of *Above*(ObjectA, ObjectB) is then used to specify a desired GOAL CONFIGURATION for a problem solving process to take actions to achieve that goal.

Because there is still a range of possible positions of ObjectA relative to ObjectB, before the problem solving process can use the goal, it may take the most typical relation positions (such as ObjectA is **directly** above ObjectB), or if the *Above* relationship has further specification arguments such as *Above*(ObjectA, ObjectB, **Directly**), *Above*(ObjectA, ObjectB, **5 cm**), etc., it will use those arguments to restrict the range of the possible positions of ObjectA relative to ObjectB or use those arguments as a basis for further questioning of the command giver (e.g., the human involved) for further specific instructions. The system may also have knowledge, for a given context, about the exact relative positions of ObjectA and ObjectB, given the *Above* relationship.

Integration

Armed with the above basic constructs, we are now ready to describe how the system may process the complex instructions (2) from Sect. 3.1.

Figure 8 depicts a robotic hand with fingers and a screw driver with two subparts, the *Handle* and the *Shank*. The operation instructed by the first sentence "position your hand directly above the screw driver's handle" is shown. Through the Sentence to Predicate transformation process described above, this is translated into the following predicate representation:

$$\textbf{Move}(Hand(\text{Robot}), \textbf{Until}(Above(Hand(\text{Robot}), Handle(\text{Screw-Driver}), \textbf{Directly})$$

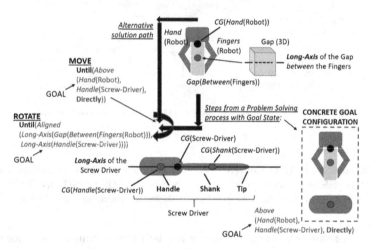

Fig. 8. A situation with a robot hand and a screw driver, and the robot is instructed to position its hand directly above the screw driver's handle.

To carry out this action, first the Predicate to Referent process discussed above and depicted in Fig. 7 is engaged to derive the CONCRETE GOAL CONFIGURATION of *Above*(*Hand*(Robot), *Handle*(Screw-Driver), **Directly**) as shown. Then, a problem solving process, employing either forward or backward chaining, is used to derive the action steps to bring the hand to the designated position. There could be more than one solution derived from the problem solving process.

Figure 9 illustrates the rest of the Sentence to Predicate conversion process and further Predicate to Referent conversion process will derive the corresponding actions.

Figure 8 also illustrates the goal of the **Rotate** action involved. **Rotate…Until** is also an action like the earlier **Move…Until** that will launch a problem solving process if needed. Note that in Fig. 9 a variant of the **Move** Action Predicate is introduced in which the direction of movement is specified in an argument.

A similar process can be used to process and understand the other complex sentence example (1) used in Sect. 3.1.

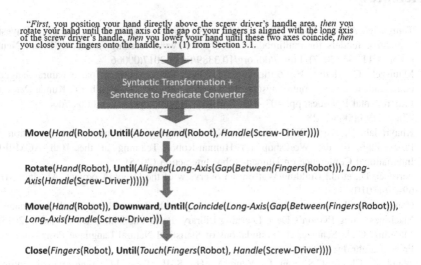

"First, you position your hand directly above the screw driver's handle area, then you rotate your hand until the main axis of the gap of your fingers is aligned with the long axis of the screw driver's handle, then you lower your hand until these two axes coincide, then you close your fingers onto the handle, …" (1) from Section 3.1.

Syntactic Transformation +
Sentence to Predicate Converter

Move(*Hand*(Robot), **Until**(*Above*(*Hand*(Robot), *Handle*(Screw-Driver))))

Rotate(*Hand*(Robot), **Until**(*Aligned*(*Long-Axis*(*Gap*(*Between*(*Fingers*(Robot))), *Long-Axis*(*Handle*(Screw-Driver))))))

Move(*Hand*(Robot)), **Downward**, **Until**(*Coincide*(*Long-Axis*(*Gap*(*Between*(*Fingers*(Robot))), *Long-Axis*(*Handle*(Screw-Driver)))))

Close(*Fingers*(Robot), **Until**(*Touch*(*Fingers*(Robot), *Handle*(Screw-Driver))))

Fig. 9. The complete Predicate representation of the complex sentence under consideration.

4 Conclusion and Summary

This paper analyzed the connection between language and robotics and successfully demonstrated how complex natural language instructions can be processed by a robotic system that will then carry out the actions accordingly. Two goals have been achieved at once for two seemingly disparate domains – it elucidates the meaning of meaning for the domain of linguistics and NLU, and it also elucidates the representational and computational processes for a robot to convert natural language instructions to actions.

This paper first reviewed and analyzed the previous works in linguistics, AI NLP and NLU, and robotics that point to a direction of how NLU can be applied to robotics. The paper then elucidates the steps of converting the temporal order embedded in certain natural language instructions to an explicit temporal representation for tasks to be carried out accordingly. Following that, a Sentence to Predicate conversion process is elucidated, followed by a Predicate to Referent process that grounds the meaning of the sentence in real-world constructs of spatial relations, spatial arrangements, and action sequences. This enables the robot to carry out the instructions accordingly.

Further work includes bringing in more of the cognitive linguistic constructs, such as those illustrated in Fig. 2, to represent the meaning of even more complex sentences, finessing the representational constructs for spatial relationship and spatial arrangements so that they can participate in the recognition and generation processes as discussed, and upgrade the 3 major blocks of processing, the Syntactic Transformation Rules, the Sentence to Predicate Converter, and the Predicate to Referent Converter, to handle more general and complex sentences. This will bring about the development of truly intelligent robots which can perform human-like understanding in the future.

References

1. Taniguchi, A., Taniguchi, T., Cangelosi, A.: Cross-situational learning with Bayesian generative models for multimodal category and word learning in robots. Front. Neuro-robotics **11**, 66 (2017). https://doi.org/10.3389/fnbot.2017.00066
2. Matuszek, C., Herbst, E., Zettlemoyer, L., Fox, D.: Learning to parse natural language commands to a robot control system. In: Desai, J., Dudek, G., Khatib, O., Kumar, V. (eds.) Experimental Robotics, pp. 403–415. Springer, Heidelberg (2013). https://doi.org/10.1007/978-3-319-00065-7_28
3. Khayrallah, H., Trott, S., Feldman, J.: Natural language for human robot interaction. In: Proceedings of the Workshop on Human-Robot Teaming at the 10th ACM/IEEE International Conference on Human-Robot Interaction (2015)
4. Ferrucci, D., et al.: Building Watson: an overview of the DeepQA project. AI Mag. **31**(3), 59–79 (2010)
5. Ganegedara, T.: Natural Language Processing with TensorFlow: Teach Language to Machines Using Python's Deep Learning Library. Packt Publishing, Birmingham (2018)
6. Manning, C.D., Schutze, H.: Foundations of Statistical Natural Language Processing. MIT Press, Cambridge (1999)
7. Wang, Z., Chong, C.S., Lan, L., Yang, Y., Ho, S.-B., Tong, J.C.: Fine-grained sentiment analysis of social media with emotion sensing. In: IEEE Future Technologies Conference 2016 (FTC 2016), San Francisco, United States, 6–7 December 2016
8. Winograd, T.: A procedural model of language understanding. In: Schank, R., Colby, K.M. (eds.) Computer Models of Thought and Language. W. H. Freeman & Company, San Francisco (1973)
9. Ho, S.-B., Wang, Z.: On true language understanding. In: 5th International Conference on AI and Security, New York, 26–28 July 2019
10. Alomari, M., Duckworth, P., Hogg, D.C., Cohn, A.G.: Natural language acquisition and grounding for embodied robotic systems. In: Proceedings of the 31st AAAI Conference on Artificial Intelligence (2017)
11. Schank, R., Abelson, R.: Scripts, Plans, Goals, and Understanding. Lawrence Erlbaum Associates, Hillsdale (1977)
12. Pei, M., Jia, Y., Zhu, S.-C.: Parsing video events with goal inference and intent prediction. In: International Conference on Computer Vision. IEEE, New Jersey (2011)
13. Si, Z., Pei, M., Yao, B., Zhu, S.-C.: Unsupervised learning of AND-OR grammar and semantics from video. In: International Conference on Computer Vision. IEEE, New Jersey (2011)
14. Cruse, A.: Meaning in Language. Oxford University Press, Oxford (2011)
15. Langacker, R.W.: Foundation of Cognitive Grammar, vols. I and II. Stanford University Press, Stanford (1987)

Dynamic Motion Planning Algorithm in Human-Robot Collision Avoidance

Lei Zhu, Zijing Chi, Fan Zhou, and Chungang Zhuang$^{(\boxtimes)}$

State Key Laboratory of Mechanical System and Vibration,
School of Mechanical Engineering, Shanghai Jiao Tong University,
Shanghai 200240, China
cgzhuang@sjtu.edu.cn

Abstract. The collision-free robotic motion planning algorithm in a dynamic environment is an effective method for the prevention of collision in a human-robot interaction scenario. In this paper, an improvement of the Rapidly-exploring Random Tree (RRT) algorithm is proposed to avoid the potential collision between robot and human by taking the costmap of robot workspace into consideration. The depth camera and Kalman filter are applied to estimate the positions and velocities of dynamic obstacles. The main contribution of this paper is that the spatiotemporal information of moving obstacles is integrated into the robotic motion planning algorithm with the costmap of workspace. Besides, a new costmap generation method is designed based on the velocities of moving obstacles. Finally, a local replanning method is used to accelerate the robotic motion planning algorithm. Experimental results show that the proposed method can efficiently protect human workers from colliding with the robot and the robot can dynamically generate a collision-free path in the human-robot coexisting environment.

Keywords: Motion planning · Rapidly-exploring Random Tree ·
Dynamic environment · Human-Robot Interaction

1 Introduction

In the past two decades, cooperation with industrial robots becomes a trend in manufacturing industry. The research on Human-Robot Interaction (HRI) for robot manipulator programming in industrial applications is envisioned to combining human's flexibility and robot's productivity [1]. It is important to ensure the safety of human workers in the human-robot coexistence scenarios. The injury from the robot can be reduced or eliminated by the application of collaborative robots, but collaborative robots cannot perform the heavy load task. The contact between robots and humans will also result in the emergency stop of the robots [2]. Indeed, the robot collision avoidance method is an effective approach to handle this problem, the goal of which is to guide the robot to avoid the moving obstacles and complete the original tasks.

The typical robot collision avoidance method can be roughly divided into two steps: (1) modeling the dynamic environment with human workers; (2) algorithms for avoiding the potential collision. The development of the stereo vision system has had a significant impact on the research of environment construction. It provides a low-cost

© Springer Nature Switzerland AG 2019
H. Yu et al. (Eds.): ICIRA 2019, LNAI 11745, pp. 655–666, 2019.
https://doi.org/10.1007/978-3-030-27529-7_55

and stable vision sensor system. Various algorithms have been proposed to provide an obstacle-avoidance and collision-free path for the robot in a dynamic environment. However, few of them has been applied in the production line to improve the human-robot collaboration. There are some reasons: (a) the robotic motion planning algorithm is usually in a high dimensional configuration space. Moving obstacles in Cartesian space are hardly mapped to configuration space; (b) the environment of basic motion planning is stationary. Thus, the generated path is only related to space relationship, which ignored the influence of obstacles' movement; (c) the calculating time of algorithms may not meet the real-time requirements as the sampling and collision checking processes are time-consuming.

In this paper, while several methods have been proposed to prevent the collision in a human-robot interaction scenario, we here mainly focus on adapting improved RRT algorithm for collision-free robotic motion planning. In detail, the moving object detection and tracking algorithms are used to calculate the spatiotemporal relations (including relative position and velocity) between the robot and human by the depth camera. Then, the relative velocity is taken into consideration to generate an environment costmap with artificial potential field method. The costmap is defined as the criterion of risk level and it is used to determine which part of the path is interfered with the movement trend of the moving obstacles. Finally, a Costmap Based Rapidly-exploring Random Tree (CB-RRT) algorithm is proposed. The expanding direction of CB-RRT is guided by the costmap in local motion planning. Our main contribution is using velocity based costmap method to process the original path for local motion planning and applying the CB-RRT method in the collision-free motion planning.

The paper is organized as follows. Section 2 reviews some related work on human-robot interaction and motion planning algorithms. Our method of generating velocity based artificial potential field costmap and the CB-RRT in local motion planning are introduced in Sect. 3. Section 4 demonstrates the experimental results. The conclusion and future work are summarized in Sect. 5.

2   Related Work

An extensive overview of the robot collision avoidance method in human-robot interaction is provided. In addition, the motion planning algorithms in dynamic environment are introduced in this section.

The problem of human-robot interaction has been studied from various perspectives. There is a number of works aiming at the perception of human and robot in a co-existence environment. A method for quickly determining the minimum distance between the robot and unknown obstacles with a 2D camera is presented in [3]. However, the distance evaluated by RGB image is not accuracy. A concept of depth space is proposed to estimate the robot-obstacles distance based on depth image acquired by a stereo vision system [4]. The parallel computation method is used to accelerate collision check algorithms [5]. These works emphasize the distance between the robot and human while the velocity is taken into consideration in this paper. The preprocessed point cloud of the environment is used to calculate the minimum distance and to evaluate the velocity with the Kalman filter [6]. More recently, [7] Proposes to generate an attractive and repulsive potential field for the robot end effector. The robot can preserve the original task in the workspace and avoid the collision. However, the posture of the robot end effector is changed and only the control points on the robot could avoid the obstacles by the potential field algorithm. A trajectory manager algorithm based on the neural network model is proposed in [8], while it is based upon the assumption that the workspace is discretized in 3D-Matrices with a resolution of $5 \times 5 \times 3$. The workspace is divided into three different zones based on the minimum distance [9, 10]. The behavior of the robot is changed by the obstacles' locations. The human arm occupancy is predicted to generate a robot collision-free path [11, 12]. Instead of the human arm motion, these papers consider the nearest part between the human and robot. [1] Proposes to divide the obstacles avoiding path-planning process into two steps: convex feasible set algorithm (CFS) for the long term planning and the safe set algorithm (SSA) for the short term planning. In this paper, the related potential dangerous path is changed install of the entire remaining path. All the aforementioned works do not emphasize the effect of relative velocity on human-robot interaction. It helps the robot react in the right direction responding to the moving obstacles.

Rapidly-exploring random tree (RRT) is a major class of sampling methods. The RRT algorithm and its variants had been widely used in kinematic problems because of its simplicity and efficiency [13]. The extensions of RRT methods mainly focus on finding the optimal path and improving planning speed. In [14], the Transition based RRT (T-RRT) takes the configuration space costmap into consideration and the transition test is used to accept or reject potential states. The exploratory strength of RRTs and minimal work path are the advantages of T-RRT, but their work was based on the existence of the costmap. In [15], each random sampling node is biased toward the vector field direction in Vector Field Rapidly-exploring Random Tree (VF-RRT). As it does not reject potential states by costmaps, it is more efficient than T-RRT. [16] Proposed RRT* method to obtain a provably asymptotically optimal path after the initial path planned quickly with the basic RRT. These extensions of RRT methods above are based on the assumption of the stationary environment. In [17], DRRTs is proposed to dealing with the dynamic environment. This work focuses on removing the newly-invalid part of the path and growing the newly-generated tree. [18] Uses the velocity vectors of moving obstacles as the reference. However, only the optimal path is examined in the selection of the goal. The replanning process cannot meet the real-time requirements. [19] Focuses on the reconnecting and regrowing algorithms to repair the selected branches and the valid paths by RRT*FND. But the scenery is considered to be stationary in the process of reconnecting and regrowing. The newly planned path is not optimal. All the aforementioned works do not emphasize on the influence of obstacles' velocities, which play a key role in the robot collision avoidance behavior. In this work, we explore the new states in the search tree of CB-RRT by combining the velocities and local replanning methods under a dynamic environment. The planned path is more optimal and efficient.

3 Proposed Method

The main contribution in this paper is the construction of a HRI system of human workers co-existing with industrial manipulators. This paper focuses on the costmap generation based on the positions and velocities of moving obstacles and the costmap guided replanning with CB-RRT. Comparing with common HRI system, our work pays more attention to the part of the robot original path affected by moving obstacles. Besides, the newly generated local path is related to the moving trend of dynamic obstacles. This section introduces our HRI system in detail.

3.1 The Perception of Environment

In a common HRI system, dynamic obstacles (including humans) interfere with the workspace of the robot. The movements of obstacles are uncertain and unsustainable. The depth camera is used to calculate the positions and velocities of the moving obstacles. The vision algorithm includes the following four steps: (a) generating the static background; (b) removing robot in the image; (c) locating the moving obstacles; (d) estimating the velocities of the obstacles.

Generating the Static Background. The stationary obstacles in the workspace can be regarded as the background. At the beginning of the system, the static background is generated to remove the stationary obstacles. Since the depth information has been obtained, the furthest distances of the pixels are regarded as the background region:

$$I_{bg}(i,j) = \max_{t < t_{times}} I_t(i,j)) \tag{1}$$

where the $I_{bg}(i,j)$ and $I_t(i,j)$ are the static background and depth image captured by camera and t_{times} is the total number of images to calculate the background.

Removing Robot in the Image. The robot is in the camera field of view. The movement of robot interferes with the detection of moving obstacles. Since the robot position and joints angle can be available from the robot controller, it is reasonable to use robot URDF model to represent the projection of the robot on the background depth image [20]. The workflow of the removing method is shown in Fig. 1.

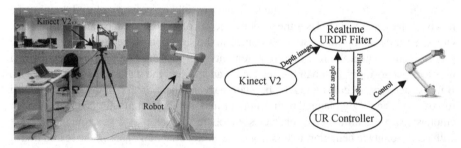

Fig. 1. The layout of robot and camera (left) and the workflow of the removing method (right).

Locating the Moving Obstacles. The background depth image without the robot and stationary obstacles is obtained in the previous part of the paper. The robust way to identify the moving obstacles and locate them in the Cartesian coordinate system is the background subtraction method:

$$I_{obs}(i,j) = f(\mathbf{x}) = \begin{cases} I_t(i,j), |I_t(i,j) - I_{bg}(i,j)| < 0 \\ 0, |I_t(i,j) - I_{bg}(i,j)| > 0 \end{cases} \tag{2}$$

where the $I_{obs}(i,j)$ is the depth image segmented by obstacles. The positions of obstacles in the workspace are determined by camera internal and external parameters.

Estimating the Velocities of the Obstacles. The velocities of obstacles are estimated and updated by Kalman filter, which provides a more robust result. In the 3-D workspace, the state of the moving obstacle is $S_k = (x_k, y_k, z_k, \dot{x}_k, \dot{y}_k, \dot{z}_k)^T$, where k refers to the time-step. As the depth camera acquisition frequency is up to 30 Hz, the movement of the obstacle is regarded as uniform motion. The state vector $\hat{S}_k$ is updated from the output of the Kalman filter. The updated positions and velocities of the obstacles are calculated by camera internal and external parameters.

3.2 The Generation of Costmap

The dynamic obstacles' positions and velocities have an impact on the robot original planned path. A costmap generation algorithm related to the velocity is proposed in this section. In Sect. 3.1, the spatiotemporal information of moving obstacles is evaluated by the depth camera. Consider a generic Cartesian point as $P_{obs} = (x_{obs}, y_{obs})^T$. The velocity of the point is $V_{obs} = (\dot{x}_{obs}, \dot{y}_{obs})^T$. The costmap of dynamic obstacles' positions and velocities are generated individually. The cost function of the position is:

$$U_p(X) = \begin{cases} \frac{1}{2}\eta(\frac{1}{\rho(P_{obs},X)} - \frac{1}{\rho_0})^2, \rho(P_{obs}, X) \le \rho_0 \\ 0, \rho(P_{obs}, X) > \rho_0 \end{cases} \tag{3}$$

where X is the position $(x, y)^T$ in the robot workspace. ρ_0 is the effective influence distance of obstacles and $\eta > 0$ is a scaling factor.

The velocities of moving obstacles also have an influence on the robot original path. If the obstacles move toward the robot, the value of cost function in the moving direction should be higher and this value decreases with the time passed. So the cost function of velocity can be defined by the equation of a plane. This paper chooses three non-collinear points $P_1 = (x_{obs}, y_{obs}, z_{obs})$, $P_2 = (x_{obs} + \dot{x}_{obs} \times t, y_{obs} + \dot{y}_{obs} \times t, 0)$ and $P_3 = (x_3, y_3, 0)$, where t is a constant value of time and $\overrightarrow{P_1P_2} \cdot \overrightarrow{P_2P_3} = 0$. The cost function of velocity is the plane which passes through P_1, P_2, P_3. The corresponding cost function of velocity is:

$$U_v(X) = \begin{cases} ax + by + c, 0 < U_v(X) < Z_{obs} \text{ and } \rho\left(\overrightarrow{P1P2}, X\right) \le \rho_2 \\ 0, others \end{cases} \tag{4}$$

where $\rho\left(\overrightarrow{P1P2}, X\right)$ is the Euclidean distance between X and $\overrightarrow{P1P2}$, ρ_2 is a parameter that limits the effect of the obstacles at the vertical direction in the movement direction. The constant values a, b, c meet the following requirement:

$$\begin{cases} Z_{obs} = a \times x_{obs} + b \times y_{obs} + c \\ 0 = a \times x_3 + b \times y_3 + c \\ 0 = a \times (x_{obs} + \dot{x}_{obs} \times t) \\ \quad + b \times (y_{obs} + \dot{y}_{obs} \times t) + c \end{cases} \tag{5}$$

The costmap of the dynamic environment integrates the position and velocity cost function, it can be calculated by:

$$U_{obs}(X) = \begin{cases} U_p(X) + \beta \times U_v(X), \, U_{obs}(X) < U_{max} \\ U_{max}, \, U_{obs}(X) \geq U_{max} \end{cases} \tag{6}$$

where the β is a scaling factor to adjust the weight between position and velocity. U_{max} is an upper limit value to prevent the interference of noise.

The corresponding gradient $F_{obs}(X)$ is:

$$F_{obs}(X) = -\frac{\partial U}{\partial X} \tag{7}$$

The costmap of moving obstacles in the workspace is generated above. The elevation in the costmap corresponds to the probability of collision. Since the velocities of moving obstacles are taken into consideration, the positions and movement trends of the obstacles affect the robotic motion planning together. Then, the costmap is used to determine whether the robot original planned path has the potential risk of collision with obstacles.

The original path of the robot is composed of a set of ordered points. In this work, the original path is discretized into a series of grid points in the same resolution as the costmap. The discretized line method is the same as Bresenham's line algorithm [21]. A new energy function U_{grid} is defined to estimate the level of grid points impacted from moving obstacles:

$$U_{grid} = \sum_{i=1}^{n} U_{obs}(P_i) \tag{8}$$

where $\{P_i | i = 1, 2, \ldots, n\}$ is a set of ordered grid points discretized from the robot original path.

The algorithm for determining the potential collision between the grid points and moving obstacles is based on the value of U_{grid}. In this algorithm, the value of U_{grid} is a sum of the costmap values. If it is higher than a certain standard system value, it means that the completely original path is affected by obstacles and the collision is going to occur.

In this situation, the system raises an interruption to handle the potential collision. Since the costmap value of each grid points can be obtained, the affected part in the original path is found with these grid points. Typically, the original path is divided into two shorter paths by removing the affected part. The initial and final grid points of the removed path are saved as the root and goal positions for the CB-RRT algorithm in the next section. Only the affected part of the path needs to be replanned instead of the whole path. The basic algorithm for the affected path estimation and the local path preparation are shown in Algorithm 1.

Algorithm 1. PreparePath(*costmap, original path*)

Input: the generated *costmap*, robot original path: *original path*

Output: *localpath1, localpath2, P_{start}, P_{goal}*

  1: PATH ← BresenhamLine(*original path*)
  2: **for** each path point p in PATH **do**
  3:    CostmapValue ← sum(costmap(p))
  4:    **if** CostmapValue > Safety Threshold **then**
  5:      affected path ← costmap(p)≠0
  6:      P_{start} ← the beginning of affected path
  7:      P_{goal} ← the end of affected path
  8:      *localpath1, localpath2* ← remove the affected path from the original path
  9:    **end if**
10: **end for**

3.3 Replanning with CB-RRT

The basic RRT method in robotic motion planning [22] is divided into three steps: 1. the sampling method; 2. distance measure; 3. local planner. As the sampling method is a random sampling strategy, the path has no relationship with the positions and velocities of dynamic obstacles. Traditionally, the original path is replanned from the root to goal once it was occupied by obstacles, which results in an inefficient and time-consuming process. These two aspects can be improved to achieve a new path in high quality. In fact, only the path around the moving obstacles needs to be replanned. As an improved RRT algorithm, the CB-RRT is proposed based on the following assumptions: (a). the robot workspace is a two-dimensional Cartesian coordinate system. (b). the dynamic obstacles are moving at a constant speed.

The costmap of the moving obstacles is generated in the previous section. The root and goal positions of the local motion planning are obtained in Sect. 3.2. The information is used as a precondition of CB-RRT. Different from other improved RRT method, the gradient value of the costmap is taken into consideration to offset the new state. The biased point is added to the search tree then. A probability of this offset is set to prevent the path from being stuck in local minimal of the costmap.

First, the root of the local motion planning task is used as an initial state X_{start} of the search tree T. A random point X_{samp} in the workspace is chosen by the sampler. The closest node $X_{nearest}$ in the search tree T is found by calculating the Euclidean distances between the X_{samp} and each node in the search tree T. The new state X_{new} is chosen in the direction of $\overrightarrow{X_{nearest}X_{samp}}$ with the fix stepsize w. In basic RRT method, the system will often use a straight line to connect $X_{nearest}$ to X_{new}. If this line has no intersection with obstacles, the new state X_{new} is added to the search tree T. while the newly added node is random and has no relationship with the moving obstacles. In this article, once the new state X_{new} is found, the gradient vector X_{map} generated from the costmap is used to bias the state. A kind of vector addition method is adopted to generate the new state X_{pf}:

$$X_{pf} = X_{new} + mX_{map} \tag{9}$$

An upper limit of the X_{map} is set to prevent the effect of the local maximum in costmap. Besides, it is known that the local minimal value of costmap results in a failure motion planning in potential filed planning algorithm. As the newly added node of the search tree T is guided by the costmap, the local minimal value of costmap will cause the failure of path generation either. In line 8 at Algorithm 2, a probability value p_{bias} is used to remove the bias of X_{map}. The new state X_{pf} is connected to the $X_{nearest}$ and added to the search tree T if the line is collision-free.

Once the local path is generated, this part of the path is integrated with the original path. Comparing with the original path, the new generated local path is shorter and takes less computation time.

Algorithm 2. CB-RRT(map, $costmap$, P_{start}, P_{goal})

Input: map, the generated $costmap$, $localpath1$, $localpath2$, P_{start}, P_{goal}

Output: replanned path: $repath$

1: initialize search tree T with P_{start}
2: **while** T is less than the maximum tree size **do**
3:    $X_{samp} \leftarrow$ sample from map
4:    $X_{nearest} \leftarrow$ nearest node in T to X_{samp}
5:    employ a local planner to find a motion from $X_{nearest}$ to X_{new} in the
       direction of X_{samp}
6:    $X_{map} \leftarrow$ the gradient vector at X_{new}
7:    $X_{pf} \leftarrow$ vector sum of X_{map} and mX_{new}
8:    **if** random(1) $< p_{bias}$ **then**
9:       employ a local planner to find a motion form $X_{nearest}$ to X_{pf}
10:   **else then**
11:      employ a local planner to find a motion form $X_{nearest}$ to X_{new}
12:   **if** the motion is collision-free **then**
13:      add X_{new} or X_{pf} to T with an edge from $X_{nearest}$ to X_{new} or X_{pf}
14:      **if** X_{new} or X_{pf} is in P_{goal} **then**
15:         $repath \leftarrow T$
16:         **Return SUCCESS**
17:      **end if**
18:   **end if**
19: **end while**
20: **Return FAILURE**

---

4 Experimental Results

In this section, the scenario is designed to verify the performance of human-robot interaction system. The experiments include three parts corresponding to Sect. 3. Experiment 1 estimates the performance of the perception of the environment with the real environment. Experiment 2 and experiment 3 test and verify the generation of costmap and path planned by CB-RRT in a simulation environment. The background of the scenario is that the robot end effector moves from place A to B to finish a pick-and-place task. A human worker approached and occupied its original path.

Experiment 1 has been performed on the Universal Robot UR5 robot arm. The depth camera Kinect V2 form Microsoft is used to calculate the location and velocity of the dynamic obstacle. The system is running on Ubuntu 16.04 and ROS Kinetic. The intrinsic and extrinsic matrix of the camera has been calibrated well before the experiment. The distance between the moving obstacle and the robot is shown in Fig. 2. The error measured by the depth camera meets the requirement of human-robot interaction operation.

Fig. 2. Real-time distance and velocity estimation between the robot and moving obstacle.

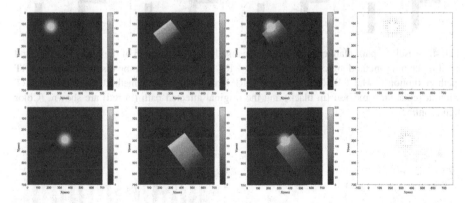

Fig. 3. The costmap of moving obstacles when the velocity is 5 mm/s (top) and 10 mm/s (bottom). The graph from left to right is the costmap corresponding to position, velocity, position and velocity, and the gradient of the costmap respectively.

Experiment 2 and experiment 3 are simulated in Matlab R2017b. The obstacles and free workspace are represented by a binary map (0 represents obstacles). The workspace of the manipulator is defined as a 700 × 700 mm grid. The different shapes of static obstacles are placed in the workspace. The position and the velocity of moving obstacle are represented by the circle with a radius of 30 mm. Figure 3 shows the costmap of different positions and velocities of dynamic obstacles separately. From the simulation results above, the position and velocity directly affect the costmap. The closer position and faster speed will lead to an increase in the costmap value.

Experiment 3 illustrates that the robot path is replanned with CB-RRT while the original path was occupied. The basic RRT algorithm is introduced as a comparison. The search times of the tree are recorded as the criterion of the path quality. Figure 4 shows that the newly generated path (in green) is biased to the direction of moving obstacle's velocity. Which is good for the movement of the robot to avoid obstacles. The original path affected by the moving obstacles is detected and is used for local motion planning.

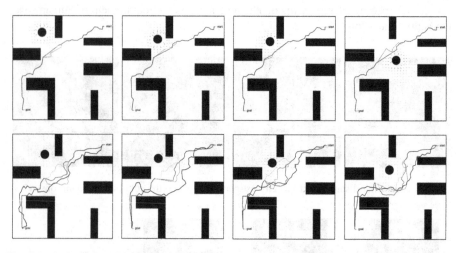

Fig. 4. Result of path planned with RRT series method. The costmap of dynamic obstacles and local replanning method are considered by CB-RRT (upon) and the comparison with basic RRT method (bottom). The CB-RRT (in green), RRT with replanning method (in yellow), RRT without replanning method (in black) and the original affected path (in red) are shown. (Color figure online)

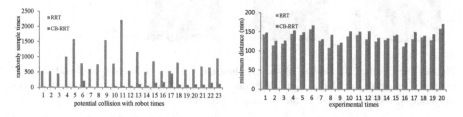

Fig. 5. The randomly sample times between basic RRT and CB-RRT (left) and the average of the minimum distance among the new generated path and moving obstacles (right).

The comparison with basic RRT method is shown in the Fig. 5. The sample times in RRT series method has been reduced by the local motion planning method applied in CB-RRT. The fewer sample times improve the real-time performance of the human-robot interaction system. Also, the average distance between the newly generated path and moving obstacles by CB-RRT is greater than basic RRT. The greater distance provides a more safety range between robot and moving obstacles.

5 Conclusion

In this paper, we revisit the research on robot collision avoidance to dynamic obstacles and propose an improved RRT method (CB-RRT) by taking the position and velocity into consideration during the exploration of new states in the search trees. A robust algorithm for detecting the moving obstacles and estimating spatiotemporal information was applied to the HRI system. A costmap generation method in the dynamic environment was designed. The basic RRT method was improved by biasing to the gradient of the costmap. Besides, the local replanning method was introduced to accelerate the motion planning speed and to improve real-time performance. Simulations and experimental results confirmed the good performance of the method. Further work will focus on extending the collision avoidance method to the whole robot instead of end-effector. The performance in a complex environment will be optimized either.

Acknowledgments. This work is partially supported by National Natural Science Foundation of China (51775344).

References

1. Liu, C., Tomizuka, M.: Robot Safe Interaction System for Intelligent Industrial Co-Robots. arXiv preprint arXiv:1808.03983 (2018)
2. Flacco, F., Kröger, T., De Luca, A., Khatib, O.: A depth space approach to human-robot collision avoidance. In: 2012 IEEE International Conference on Robotics and Automation (ICRA), pp. 338–345. IEEE, St. Paul (2012)
3. Kuhn, S., Henrich, D.: Fast vision-based minimum distance determination between known and unkown objects. In: 2007 IEEE/RSJ International Conference on Intelligent Robots and Systems, pp. 2186–2191. IEEE, San Diego (2007)
4. De Luca, A., Flacco, F.: Integrated control for pHRI: collision avoidance, detection, reaction and collaboration. In: 2012 4th IEEE RAS & EMBS International Conference on Biomedical Robotics and Biomechatronics (BioRob), pp. 288–295. IEEE, Rome (2012)
5. Cefalo, M., Magrini, E., Oriolo, G.: Parallel collision check for sensor based real-time motion planning. In: 2017 IEEE International Conference on Robotics and Automation (ICRA), pp. 1936–1943. IEEE, Singapore (2017)
6. Meguenani, A., Padois, V., Da Silva, J., Hoarau, A., Bidaud, P.: Energy based control for safe human-robot physical interaction. In: Kulić, D., Nakamura, Y., Khatib, O., Venture, G. (eds.) ISER 2016. SPAR, vol. 1, pp. 809–818. Springer, Cham (2017). https://doi.org/10.1007/978-3-319-50115-4_70

7. Chen, J.H., Song, K.T.: Collision-free motion planning for human-robot collaborative safety under cartesian constraint. In: 2018 IEEE International Conference on Robotics and Automation (ICRA), pp. 1–7. IEEE, Brisbane (2018)
8. Meziane, R., Otis, M.J.D., Ezzaidi, H.: Human-robot collaboration while sharing production activities in dynamic environment: SPADER system. Robot. Comput.-Integr. Manuf. **48**, 243–253 (2017)
9. Nikolakis, N., Maratos, V., Makris, S.: A cyber physical system (CPS) approach for safe human-robot collaboration in a shared workplace. Robot. Comput.-Integr. Manuf. **56**, 233–243 (2019)
10. Bdiwi, M., Pfeifer, M., Sterzing, A.: A new strategy for ensuring human safety during various levels of interaction with industrial robots. CIRP Ann. **66**(1), 453–456 (2017)
11. Pereira, A., Althoff, M.: Overapproximative human arm occupancy prediction for collision avoidance. IEEE Trans. Autom. Sci. Eng. **15**(2), 818–831 (2018)
12. Wang, Y., Ye, X., Yang, Y., Zhang, W.: Collision-free trajectory planning in human-robot interaction through hand movement prediction from vision. In: 2017 IEEE-RAS 17th International Conference on Humanoid Robotics (Humanoids), pp. 305–310. IEEE, Birmingham (2017)
13. Lynch, K.M., Park, F.C.: Modern Robotics: Mechanics, Planning, and Control, 1st edn. Cambridge University Press, Cambridge (2017)
14. Jaillet, L., Cortés, J., Siméon, T.: Sampling-based path planning on configuration-space costmaps. IEEE Trans. Rob. **26**(4), 635–646 (2010)
15. Ko, I., Kim, B., Park, F.C.: VF-RRT: introducing optimization into randomized motion planning. In: 2013 9th Asian Control Conference (ASCC), pp. 1–5. IEEE, Istanbul (2013)
16. Karaman, S., Walter, M.R., Perez, A., Frazzoli, E., Teller, S.: Anytime motion planning using the RRT. In: 2011 IEEE International Conference on Robotics and Automation (ICRA), pp. 1478–1483. IEEE, Shanghai (2011)
17. Ferguson, D., Kalra, N., Stentz, A.: Replanning with RRTs. In: Proceedings 2006 IEEE International Conference on Robotics and Automation (ICRA), pp. 1243–1248. IEEE, Orlando (2006)
18. Connell, D., La, H.M.: Dynamic path planning and replanning for mobile robots using RRT. In: 2017 IEEE International Conference on Systems, Man, and Cybernetics (SMC), pp. 1429–1434. IEEE, Banff (2017)
19. Adiyatov, O., Varol, H.A.: A novel RRT*-based algorithm for motion planning in dynamic environments. In: 2017 IEEE International Conference on Mechatronics and Automation (ICMA), pp. 1416–1421. IEEE, Takamatsu (2017)
20. Real-time URDF filter. https://github.com/blodow/realtime_urdf_filter. Accessed 26 Apr 2019
21. Wright, W.E.: Parallelization of Bresenham's line and circle algorithms. IEEE Comput. Graphics Appl. **10**(5), 60–67 (1990)
22. LaValle, S.M.: Planning Algorithms, 1st edn. Cambridge University Press, Cambridge (2006)

Dynamics Modeling of a 2-DOFs Mechanism with Rigid Joint and Flexible Joint

Yanlin Chen, Baizhe Song, Xianmin Zhang, and Yanjiang Huang[✉]

South China University of Technology, Guangzhou 510640, China
mehuangyj@scut.edu.cn

Abstract. The integration of robot and human will become the essential feature of the new generation of robot. Therefore, higher requirements are required for the safety, positioning accuracy and real-time performance of the robot. The rigid-flexible coupling can be realized by adding suitable flexible joints or components on the basis of traditional rigid manipulator to improve the safety of robot. The positioning accuracy and real time performance of the robot can be improved by accurate dynamic modeling and complete consideration of its motion state and motion characteristics.

In this paper, the flexible body dynamics modeling method is used for theoretical analysis, and the dynamics modeling method of rigid body robot is combined with the flexible joint to complete the dynamic modeling of 2 DoF rigid-flexible coupling mechanism. Then verify the dynamic model, through Adams own dynamic model solution simulation and Adams and Matlab united simulation means, proved that the established dynamic model is accurate. Then the rigid-flexible coupling mechanism with 2 DoF was designed to complete the construction of the experimental prototype and the verification and analysis of the actual data.

Keywords: Dynamic modeling · Rigid-flexible coupling mechanism · 2 DoF series robot

1 Introduction

With the development of the times, robots are more and more be emphasized on man-machine collaboration, which has higher requirements for the safety, positioning accuracy and real-time performance for robots. Robot design based on Human Robot Interaction (HRI) and physical human-robot Interaction (pHRI) [1] has gradually attracted researchers' attention. In the development of human-machine integration and human-machine interaction, a kind of mechanical arm joint is improved, which is series elastic drive joints (SEA) [2]. In SEA, flexible parts are introduced into the joint to transfer the energy and power generated in the process of robot collision, so as to eliminate or reduce the human body injury in the collision.

As a complex multi-input and multi-output system, the robot make it difficult to control and built a certain mathematical [3, 4]. Since the mechanical structure of industrial robots is mostly in the form of series manipulator [5], the 2 DoF series manipulator with relatively simple structure is often taken as the research object in the

© Springer Nature Switzerland AG 2019
H. Yu et al. (Eds.): ICIRA 2019, LNAI 11745, pp. 667–678, 2019.
https://doi.org/10.1007/978-3-030-27529-7_56

process of studying the dynamic characteristics of industrial robots. The control results can be extended to n degrees of freedom due to the structural characteristics of the series manipulator. Such a simplified research method can not only reduce the difficulty of establishing mathematical models, but also significantly improve the accuracy of the research [6]. 2 DoF planar mechanisms are also common in dynamic modeling, and lagrangian method is often used to study the dynamic characteristics of mechanisms [7].

The 2 DoF rigid-flexible coupling mechanism is basically composed by adding the flexible mechanism [8–10] into the forearm driving joint, so as to realize the rigid-flexible coupling of the 2 DoF manipulator. The SEA joints added in this paper replace the original rigid mechanical arm actuator which is directly rigidly connected with the motor and the reducer with flexible joint parts. The joints transfer torque and displacement through their own deformation and have good low impedance and good compliance [11].

In order to ensure the stability and accuracy of the robot's dynamic performance, dynamic modeling and verification is an important task in the process of improving the safety of robot. Dynamics on the basis of Newton's laws of motion, the main research work and the relationship of force and operation of the macro object [12]. Robot dynamics modeling [13] is mainly through the position descriptions, homogeneous coordinate transformation method to establish on the basis of the robot kinematics equation. By means of Lagrange method, Newton-Euler method or Kane methods, the connection between the robot motion characteristics and the forces on the relevant joints is established through the robot joint angular acceleration, gravitational potential energy, kinetic energy and other parameters, so as to solve the problem of robot dynamics.

After the flexible joint is added into the traditional two-degree-of-freedom tandem manipulator, the dynamic modeling method is changed [14]. Modeling method for the dynamics of flexible body [16, 17], the real question is how to reveal the mechanism of the coupled, from the basic principle of mechanics to describe the coupled dynamics and establish more accurate dynamics model, need specific experiment verifies the correctness of the model at the same time, so as to realize the accurate control of two degrees of freedom coupled mechanism motion [15].

The purpose of this study is to establish a reasonable dynamic model for the rigid-flexible coupling mechanism with 2 DoF, which can better reflect the dynamic characteristics of the 2 DoF series manipulator after adding the flexible joint, and lay a foundation for the follow-up vibration research, trajectory tracking and other work.

2 Dynamics Modeling of 2 DoF Rigid Flexible Coupling Mechanism

The dynamic methods for solving the robot mechanism are mainly divided into Lagrange method and Newton-Euler method. This paper is mainly solved by Lagrange method, which is described as:

$$\frac{d\partial L}{\partial t \partial \dot{\Theta}} - \frac{\partial L}{\partial \Theta} = \tau \tag{1}$$

$$L = K - U \tag{2}$$

When L it is a Lagrangian, Θ is scalar function of joint position, $\dot{\Theta}$ is scalar function of joint velocity, K is kinetic energy of robot mechanism, U is potential energy of robot mechanism.

The rigid flexible coupling mechanism model diagram is shown in Fig. 1. Motor 1 and link 1 are rigidly connected. Motor 2 and link 1 are rigidly connected. Motor 2 and link 2 are connected through spring.

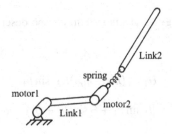

Fig. 1. The rigid flexible coupling mechanism model diagram

2.1 Establishment of Ideal Undamped Dynamic Model

According to formula 1, the ideal undamped dynamic model is established firstly. We simplified the model to some extent, including setting the link and motor as the concentrated mass, and the mass was concentrated at the end of the link. The total kinetic energy K of the system can be described as:

$$K = K_1 + K_2 + K_{motor1} + K_{motor2} \tag{3}$$

$$K_1 = \frac{1}{2} m_1 l_1^2 \dot{\theta}_1^2 + \frac{1}{2} I_{ZZ_1} \dot{\theta}_1^2 \tag{4}$$

$$K_2 = \frac{1}{2} m_2 \cdot \begin{bmatrix} -l_1 s_1 \dot{\theta}_1 - l_2 s_{12}(\dot{\theta}_1 + \dot{q}_2) \\ l_1 c_2 \dot{\theta}_1 + l_2 c_2(\dot{\theta}_1 + \dot{q}_2) \\ 0 \end{bmatrix}^2 + \frac{1}{2} I_{ZZ_2}(\dot{\theta}_1^2 + 2\dot{\theta}_1 \dot{q}_2 + \dot{q}_2^2) \tag{5}$$

$$K_{motor1} = \frac{1}{2} I_{r_1 zz} n_1^2 \dot{\theta}_1^2 \tag{6}$$

$$K_{motor2} = \frac{1}{2} m_{r2} l_1^2 \dot{\theta}_1^2 + \frac{1}{2} I_{r_2 zz}(\dot{\theta}_1 + n_2 \dot{\theta}_2)^2 \tag{7}$$

When $c_{12} = c_1c_2 - s_1s_2$, $s_{12} = c_1s_2 - s_1c_2$, $c_1 = \cos\theta_1$, $c_2 = \cos q_2$, $s_1 = \sin\theta_1$, $s_2 = \sin q_2$. K_1, K_2 is the kinetic energy of Link1, Link2. K_{motor1}, K_{motor2} is the rotary inertia kinetic energy of the motor1's rotor and the motor2's rotor .m1 is the concentrated mass of Link1 and motor1, m2 is the concentrated mass of Link2 and motor2. m_{r2} is the quality of motor2's rotor. l1, l2 is the length of the Link1 and Link2. n1, n2 is the reduction ratio of motor1 and motor2. $(\theta_1, \dot\theta_1, \ddot\theta_1)$ is the motor as a function of position, velocity, and acceleration after reduce the speed, which is also the Link1's position, velocity, and acceleration. $(\theta_2, \dot\theta_2, \ddot\theta_2)$ is the motor2 as a function of position, velocity, and acceleration after reduce the speed. $(q_2, \dot q_2, \ddot q_2)$ is the Link2 as a function of position, velocity, and acceleration. The kinematic parameters are different because there is a spring connection between link 2 and the motor2. I_{zz1}, I_{zz2} is the moment of inertia of the Link1 and Link2. I_{r_1zz}, I_{r_2zz} is the moment of inertia of the motor1's rotor and the motor2's rotor.

The total potential energy U of the system can be described as:

$$U = U_1 + U_2 + U_{elas} \tag{8}$$

$$U_1 = (m_1 + m_{r2})l_1g\,\sin\theta_1 \tag{9}$$

$$U_2 = [l_1\sin\theta_1 + l_2\sin(\theta_1 + q_2)] \cdot m_2g \tag{10}$$

$$U_{elas} = \frac{1}{2}k(q_2 - \theta_2)^2 \tag{11}$$

When U_1, U_2 is the gravitational potential energy of two concentrated mass points. g is acceleration of gravity. U_{elas} is the elastic potential energy of a spring, k is spring stiffness.

According to formula (1), (2):

$$\frac{d\partial K}{\partial t\partial\dot\Theta} - \frac{\partial K}{\partial\Theta} + \frac{\partial U}{\partial\Theta} = \tau \tag{12}$$

$$\Theta = (\theta_1, \theta_2, q_2)^{\mathrm{T}} \tag{13}$$

$$\tau = (\tau_1, \tau_2, 0)^{\mathrm{T}} \tag{14}$$

When τ_1, τ_2 is driving moment of motor1 and motor2 after reduce the speed.

Combining with the formula (3)–(14) and ignoring the moment of inertia I_{zz}. Three unknowns τ_1, τ_2, q_2 are given by input θ_1, θ_2. The relationship between input Angle and output torque, angular displacement, angular velocity and angular acceleration is established.

In order to verify that the dynamic equation can be solved, we used matlab to solve it and called Adams algorithm to solve the ordinary differential equation. The function called is ode113. In the parameters of matlab, we set m1 = 2.65 kg, m2 = 1.52 kg, $\theta_1 = \theta_2 = \sin(0.5\pi t)$, l1 = l2 = 300 mm, K = 197 N·m/rad (This is the real value in the later experiment, so the simulation value is also set to the same), g = 9.8 m/s^2.

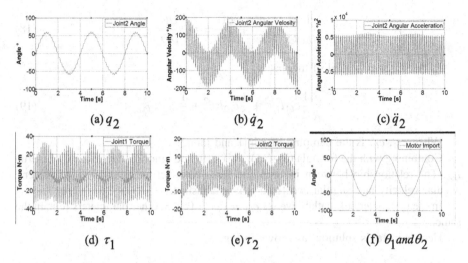

(a) q_2 (b) $\dot{q}_2$ (c) $\ddot{q}_2$

(d) τ_1 (e) τ_2 (f) θ_1 and θ_2

Fig. 2. The resulting waveform by matlab without damping.

Here is matab's solution, as shown in Fig. 2:

2.2 Establishment of a Damped Real Dynamic Model

According to the ideal dynamic model in 3.3, the influence of damping is introduced. The damping exists at two revolute joints. Formula (1), (13) is now described as [18]:

$$\frac{d\partial L}{\partial t\partial\Theta} - \frac{\partial L}{\partial\Theta} = Q_K \tag{15}$$

$$\frac{d\partial K}{\partial t\partial\Theta} - \frac{\partial K}{\partial\Theta} + \frac{\partial U}{\partial\Theta} = \tau - Q_z \tag{16}$$

When Q_K is a generalized force, which includes various influences such as external active force, force, and viscous resistance. In this article, dynamic modeling is simplified and only external active force and viscous resistance are considered. In the complete particle system described by generalized coordinate q_1, q_2, ..., q_{3n-x}, there is viscous resistance, which is proportional to the first power of velocity [19, 20] ($c_{Li}\dot{x}_i, c_{Li}\dot{y}_i, c_{Li}\dot{z}_i$). According to the generalized resistance generated by viscous resistance on generalized coordinate q_k [21]:

$$-\sum_{i=1}^{N}\left(c_{Lxi}\dot{x}_i\frac{\partial x_i}{\partial q_k} + c_{Lyi}\dot{y}_i\frac{\partial y_i}{\partial q_k} + c_{Lzi}\dot{z}_i\frac{\partial z_i}{\partial q_k}\right) = -\frac{\partial}{\partial q_k}\left[\frac{1}{2}\sum_{i=1}^{N}\left(c_{Lxi}\dot{x}_i + c_{Lyi}\dot{y}_i + c_{Lzi}\dot{z}_i\right)\right] \tag{17}$$

Set $\frac{1}{2}\sum_{i=1}^{N}\left(c_{Lxi}\dot{x}_i + c_{Lyi}\dot{y}_i + c_{Lzi}\dot{z}_i\right) = F$, so the formula (19) is now described as:

$$\frac{d\partial K}{\partial t\partial \Theta} - \frac{\partial K}{\partial \Theta} + \frac{\partial U}{\partial \Theta} = \tau - \frac{\partial F}{\partial \Theta} \qquad (18)$$

In the dynamic model of this paper,

$$F = \frac{1}{2}c_{L1}l_1^2\theta_1^2 + \frac{1}{2}c_{L2}l_2^2\theta_2^2 + \frac{1}{2}c_{L2}l_2^2\dot{q}_2^2 \qquad (19)$$

When c_{L1}, c_{L2} is the damping of joint1 and joint2.

Combining with the formula (3)–(11), (15)–(19) and ignoring the moment of inertia I_{ZZ}. The relationship between input Angle and output torque, angular displacement, angular velocity and angular acceleration is established.

In the parameters of matlab, we set $c_{L1} = c_{L2} = 0.015$, other parameters remain the same.

Here is matab's solution, as shown in Fig. 3:

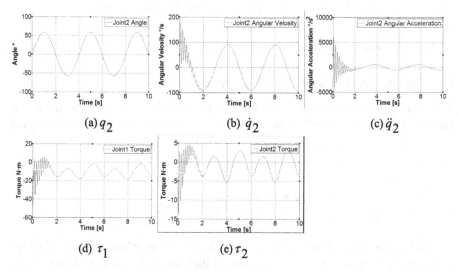

Fig. 3. The resulting waveform by matlab with damping

3 Simulation Verification of Dynamic Model

This chapter through the software Adams simulation, and Adams and Matlab united simulation, to solve the dynamics model. By means of software simulation, the relationship between angular displacement, angular velocity, angular acceleration and driving torque of 2 DoF coupling mechanism is obtained, and the relationship is compared with the results of dynamic model analysis in Chap. 2 to verify the rationality and integrity of dynamic modeling. The model established in Adams is shown in the Fig. 4 (The Settings of each parameter are the same as those in Chap. 2):

Fig. 4. ADAMS physical model

3.1 Dynamic Model Calculation Based on Adams

According to the undamped and damped condition in the above dynamic modeling, a corresponding simplified model was established in the Adams virtual prototype to measure the rotation Angle of the flexible joint, the rotation Angle velocity of the flexible joint, the rotation Angle acceleration of the flexible joint, the torque at joint 1 and the torque at joint 2, as shown in Figs. 5 and 6.

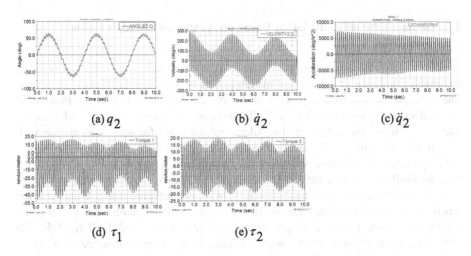

Fig. 5. The resulting waveform by Adams without damping

Comparing Fig. 2 with Fig. 5 and comparing Fig. 3 with Fig. 6, it can find that the theory and simulation of joint 2 angle are in good agreement. Both of them have oscillatory wavelet in the trend of macroscopic sine wave sin(0.5 πt). About 2 joints angle velocity, acceleration, two joint driving moment in the theory and simulation waveform is approaching, but the simulation value is bigger, the existing reason is that the theoretical value on numerical calculation time ignores the influence of the rotational inertia, at the same time, the simulation values tend towards convergence trend, analyze its reasons may be Adams in solving ordinary differential equations using numerical differential algorithm in the process of each iteration to ignore the mantissa.

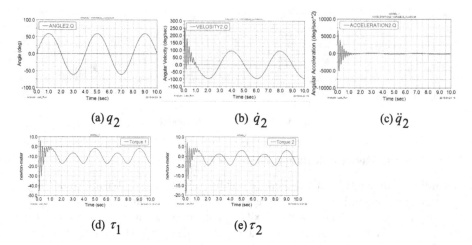

(a) q_2 (b) $\dot{q}_2$ (c) $\ddot{q}_2$

(d) τ_1 (e) τ_2

Fig. 6. The resulting waveform by Adams with damping

3.2 Dynamic Model Calculation Based on Adams and Matlab United Simulation

In order to solve the convergence problem in adams simulation, we use the method of the united simulation of Adams and matlab to obtain more accurate simulation results. The united simulation design process of Adams and matlab is as follows. Firstly, the physical model is established in the Adams virtual prototype module, and then the interface of input and output of this Adams model is set for data transmission with matlab software. The transfer function of the dynamic model is provided by the Adams virtual prototype model module set for data transmission. The joint position parameters in Adams software provide the rotation angle input 1 and the rotation angle input 2, that is, the input interface of this transfer function. In Adams software, variable and function functions are used to obtain the flexible rotation angle, rotation velocity, rotation acceleration, joint 1 joint 2 torque during the motion of the 2 DoF rigid-flexible coupling mechanism, namely the output interface of this transfer function. See Fig. 7:

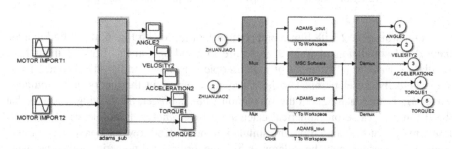

Fig. 7. System block diagram of joint simulation

Matlab/Simulink module was used to construct the system block diagram. The virtual prototype system model module established in the ADAMS/View environment was imported into Simulink. The parameters of each module and the required measurement quantity were set. After setting the simulation parameters, the virtual prototype model is simulated jointly and the simulation curve is shown in Figs. 9 and 10.

Comparing Figs. 2 and 5 with Fig. 8, and comparing Figs. 3 and 6 with Fig. 9, it can find that the theory and simulation of joint 2 angle are in good agreement. About 2 joints angle velocity, acceleration, two joint driving moment in the theory and united simulation waveform is approaching, and the value of united simulation value is similar to Adams simulation. The reason is that the physical model is built in Adams, so there is a moment of inertia. At the same time, there is no convergence trend in united simulation because matlab is adopted to solve the problem.

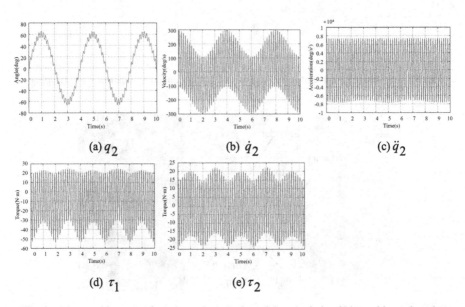

Fig. 8. The resulting waveform by Adams and matlab united simulation without damping

4 Experiment

The experimental device is shown in the Fig. 10. Link 1 and Link 2 is driven by the belt drive of the motor1 and motor2. The actual position of link 2 is measured by the encoder, which is q_2.

676   Y. Chen et al.

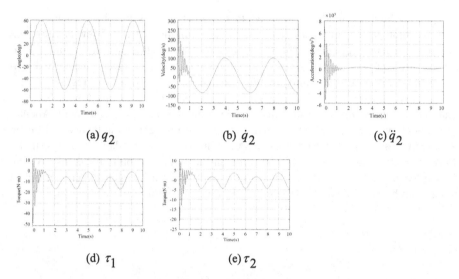

(a) q_2 (b) $\dot{q}_2$ (c) $\ddot{q}_2$

(d) τ_1 (e) τ_2

Fig. 9. The resulting waveform by Adams and matlab united simulation with damping

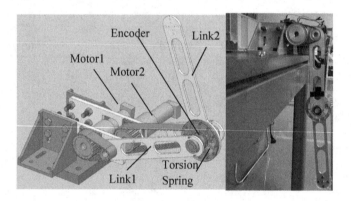

Fig. 10. Experimental models and real objects

The experimental parameters are the same as the proposed parameters above, and the position, angular velocity and angular acceleration of the q_2 can be obtained, as shown in Fig. 11.

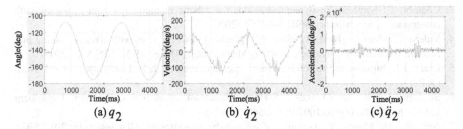

Fig. 11. The resulting waveform in experiment

The flexible Angle encoder can obtain the sine wave state which has a small range of oscillation at the start-up moment and a short time, but tends to be stable due to the existence of damping. On the experiment of flexible rotation discrete points difference operation, approximate angle acceleration of the flexible joint is obtained, we can see, in the starting moment and short time has a relatively large angular velocity oscillations, then quickly stable oscillation, the overall trend and speed of numerical within the scope of the theory and simulation is reliable. The acceleration is solved by differentiating the velocity result again. Therefore, the waveform error of the flexible angular acceleration obtained by the two differential treatments is large, and the cumulative effect caused by the cumulative error is difficult to avoid making the angular acceleration of the flexible joint. In the subsequent experiments, acceleration sensor and torque sensor will be added for measurement.

5 Conclusion

In this paper, the flexible body dynamics modeling method is used for theoretical analysis, and the dynamics modeling method of rigid body robot is combined with the flexible joint to complete the dynamic modeling of 2 DoF rigid-flexible coupling mechanism. Then verify the dynamic model, through Adams and Matlab united simulation and Adams own dynamic model solution simulation means, proved that the established dynamic model is accurate. Then the rigid-flexible coupling mechanism with 2 DoF was designed to complete the construction of the experimental prototype and the verification and analysis of the actual data.

Acknowledgements. Research supported by National Nature foundation of China under Grant 91748111, Fundamental Research Funds for the Central Universities under Grant 2018ZD27.

References

1. Santis, A.D., Siciliano, B., Luca, A.D., et al.: An atlas of physical human–robot interaction. J. Mech. Mach. Theor. **43**(3), 253–270 (2008)
2. Pratt, G.A., Williamson, M.M.: Series elastic actuators. In: International Conference on Intelligent Robots and Systems, p. 399 (1995)

3. Chettibi, T.: Synthesis of dynamic motions for robotic manipulators with geometric path constraints. J. Mechatron. **16**(9), 547–563 (2006)
4. Valero, F., Mata, V., Besa, A.: Trajectory planning in workspaces with obstacles taking into account the dynamic robot behaviour. J. Mech. Mach. Theor. **41**(5), 525–536 (2005)
5. Craig, J.J.: Introduction to robotics mechanics and control. J. Pediatr. Gastroenterol. Nutr. (1990)
6. Siciliano, B., Khatib, O. (eds.): Springer Handbook of Robotics. Springer, Heidelberg (2016). https://doi.org/10.1007/978-3-540-30301-5
7. Ishibashi, N., Maeda, Y.: Learning of inverse-dynamics for SCARA robot. In: 2011 SICE Annual Conference (SICE), Proceedings of IEEE, pp. 1300–1303 (2011)
8. Howell, L.L.: Compliant Mechanisms. Wiley, New York (2001)
9. Her, I.: Methodology for Compliant Mechanism Design. Purdue University, Indiana (1986)
10. Burns, R.H., Crossley, F.: Kinetostatic synthesis of flexible link mechanisms. In: Mechanical Engineering, vol. 90, p. 67 (1968)
11. Megahed, S.F.M.: Principles of Robot Modelling and Simulation, pp. 186–191. Wiley, Hoboken (1993)
12. Qu, J., Zhang, F., Fu, Y., et al.: Adaptive neural network visual servoing of dual-arm robot for cyclic motion. Ind. Rob.: Int. J. **44**(2), 210–221 (2017)
13. Yang, Y., Pan, S., Zhou, Z.: Dynamics control and simulation of two DOF robot computer engineering. J. Ind. Control Comput. **30**(08), 102–104 (2017)
14. Dwivedy, S.K., Eberhard, P.: Dynamic analysis of flexible manipulators, a literature review. J. Mech. Mach. Theor. **41**, 749–777 (2006)
15. Benosman, M., Le, V.G.: Control of flexible manipulator: a survey. J. Robotica **22**, 533–545 (2004)
16. García-Vallejo, D., Mayo, J., Escalona, J.L., Domínguez, J.: Three-dimensional formulation of rigid-flexible multibody systems with flexible beam elements. J. Multibody Syst. Dyn. **20**(1), 1–28 (2008)
17. Liu, J.Y., Lu, H.: Rigid-flexible coupling dynamics of three-dimensional hub-beams system. Multibody Syst. Dyn. **18**(4), 487–510 (2007)
18. Hongliang, T., Dalin, Z.: Second kind lagrange equation of nonlinear nonautonomous nonconservative damping system. J. China Three Gorges Univ. (Nat. Sci.) **05**, 435–439 (2006)
19. Ou, J.P., Guan, X.: Magnetorheological fluid and smart damper for structure vibration control. Earthquake Engineering and Engineering Vibration (1998)
20. Xu, H.: The kinematical equation for the dual- arm damped robot. Appl. Energy Technol. **09**, 42–44 (2008)
21. Fu, W., Wang, Y., Wang, H., Zhang, Y.: Simulation analysis of semi-active control of structures with magnetorheological variable damper. Earthq. Eng. Eng. Vibr. (2003)

Haptic Joystick Impedance Control
with Gravity Compensation

Yong-Jin Ock[1], Zhan-Ming Gu[1], Jong-Woo An[1],
and Jang-Myung Lee[2(✉)]

[1] Department of Electrical, Electronic and Computer Engineering,
Pusan National University, Busan 609-735, Korea
{yongjin7379,guzhanming7379,jongwoo7379}@pusan.ac.kr
[2] Department of Electronic Engineering, Pusan National University,
Busan 609-735, Korea
jmlee@pusan.ac.kr

Abstract. Due to the gravity of the joystick during the remote control using the joystick, If you use it for a long time, the driver's muscles may become tired. In order to achieve the impedance control of the joystick gravity environment, this paper proposed an impedance control method based on gravity compensation in the gravity environment. The control of the end force of the joystick is implemented in a joint space- based position impedance control algorithm. This paper proposed a gravity compensation algorithm that can calculate the compensation force required for the current position according to each joint angle, and generate corresponding force to compensate the end gravity in real time. The experimental results showed that the method can compensate the influence of gravity on the measured value of the F/T sensor at the end of the joystick in real time, so that the joystick can achieve impedance control at any end position without any external equipment in the gravity environment.

Keywords: Haptic joystick · Gravity compensation · Kinematics ·
Impedance control

1 Introduction

This paper proposed a new type of parallel structure joystick. It can be seen as three parallel manipulators. The space manipulator running on the geosynchronous orbit works in a micro gravity environment, and the impedance control is not interfered by additional forces such as gravity, which can be easily realized. However, the impedance control problem in the gravity environment has not been solved very well. The most important reason is that real-time gravity compensation is not well per-formed. Now the manipulator gravity compensation generally adopts the passive compensation method by means of external mechanical devices. The spring mechanism can be used to design gravity compensation devices [1]. These passive compensation devices are not only economically expensive, but also the motion of the manipulator has effect and limitation. Another compensation method is using adaptive control and dynamic equation analysis. Adapt control is energy-based concepts can compensate gravity

© Springer Nature Switzerland AG 2019
H. Yu et al. (Eds.): ICIRA 2019, LNAI 11745, pp. 679–687, 2019.
https://doi.org/10.1007/978-3-030-27529-7_57

based on gravity compensation method [2] and the theory of Lipunov control [3]. Dynamic Equation Analysis [4–7] is accurate but computational intensive and is not suitable for use as a real-time calibration algorithm. This paper proposed a new gravity compensation algorithm based on spatial position. We obtained the cur-rent position through kinematics equation and analyzed the influence of the directional and rotation transformation on gravity to estimate the gravity of the current position.

2   Kinematics of the Haptic Joystick

This paper presents a parallel structure with three serial manipulators shown in Fig. 1. The serial manipulator consists of one passive joint and two active joints. In Fig. 1, the grey joints are active joints, while the white joints are passive joints. Three series manipulators with 3DOF are connected to the upper plate through passive spherical joints. The movement of the upper plate relative to the lower plate is generated by the movement of the serial manipulator.

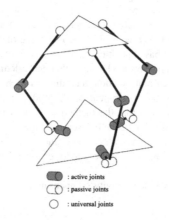

: active joints
: passive joints
: universal joints

Fig. 1. Structure of joystick

From the structural point of view, the joystick proposed by this paper is composed of three parallel series mechanisms. The position of the end effector of the serial manipulator is the same as that of each connecting point on the upper board. Therefore, the position and movement direction of the upper plate can be obtained by geometric relationship. Equations 1–3 is the kinematics equation of the position of the end effector obtained by Jacobian matrix. Figure 2 illustrates the angle selected in the equation [10], [11] (Table 1).

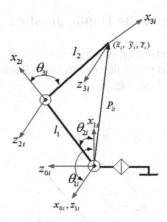

Fig. 2. 3 Motion generation principle of joystick

Table 1. Denavit–Hartenberg parameter of Manipulator.

Link	a	d	α	θ
1	0	0	90	θ_1
2	l_1	0	0	θ_2
3	l_2	0	0	θ_3

The kinematics solution of the series link is represented by the product of the homogeneous matrix defined by the following Eq. 1, and it is expressed by Eq. 2.

$$H = R(\theta_i, Z)T(d_i, Z)T(\alpha_i, X)R(\alpha_i, X) \tag{1}$$

$$^n_0H = {}^n_0H^2_{i1}H \cdots {}^n_{n-1}H_i = \begin{bmatrix} {}^n_0R & {}^0P_n \\ 0 & 1 \end{bmatrix} \tag{2}$$

Here ^n_0R is the rotation matrix between the {0} coordinate and the {n} coordinate, and ^0P_n is the position vector between the {0} coordinate and the {n} coordinate. If we hope to obtain the kinematics of this serial link, the equation is as follows.

$$^n_0H = {}^n_0H^2_{i1}H \cdots {}^n_{n-1}H_i = \begin{bmatrix} {}^n_0R & {}^0P_n \\ 0 & 1 \end{bmatrix} \tag{3}$$

$$
\begin{aligned}
X_i &= l_1 \cos(\theta_{2i}) + l_2 \cos(\theta_{2i} + \theta_{3i}) \\
Y_i &= \sin(\theta_{1i})(l_1 \sin(\theta_{2i}) + l_2 \sin(\theta_{2i} + \theta_{3i})) \\
Z_i &= l_1 \cos(\theta_{1i}) \sin(\theta_{2i}) + l_2 \cos(\theta_{1i}) \sin(\theta_{2i} + \theta_{3i})
\end{aligned} \tag{4}
$$

3   Inverse Kinematics of the Haptic Joystick

The inverse kinematic analysis of θ_{1i} is shown in Fig. 3. In the actual physical system, the region where the solution exists due to mechanical deformation is from 0 to π, so that Eq. 5 can be expressed from Fig. 3.

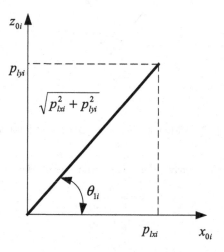

Fig. 3. θ_{1i} Inverse kinematics analysis

$$\theta_{1i} = a \cos\left(\frac{p_{lxi}}{\sqrt{p_{lxi}^2 + p_{lyi}^2}}\right) \tag{5}$$

Figure 4 shows the inverse kinematic analysis of θ_{2i} and θ_{3i} in the serial link.

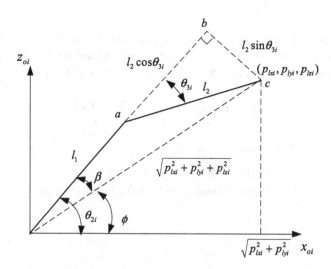

Fig. 4. θ_{2i}, θ_{3i} Inverse kinematics analysis

In Fig. 4, we can obtain Eq. 6 by applying the cosine law to the $\triangle abc$

$$p_{lxi}^2 + p_{lyi}^2 + p_{lyi}^2 = l_1^2 + l_2^2 - 2l_1 l_2 \cos(180° - \theta_{3i}) \tag{6}$$

Equation 7 can be obtained by summing the Eq. 6.

$$\cos\theta_{3i} = \frac{p_{lxi}^2 + p_{lyi}^2 + p_{lyi}^2 - l_1^2 - l_2^2}{2l_1 l_2} \tag{7}$$

$$\theta_{3i} = -a\,\cos\left(\frac{p_{lxi}^2 + p_{lyi}^2 + p_{lyi}^2 - l_1^2 - l_2^2}{2l_1 l_2}\right)$$

θ_{2i} is a passive joint and it cannot be directly controlled, but can be obtained from Eq. 8 as shown in Fig. 4

$$\theta_{2i} = \varphi + \beta = a\,\tan 2(p_{lxi}, \sqrt{p_{lxi}^2 + p_{lyi}^2}) \pm a\,\tan 2(l_2 s_{3i}, l_1 + l_2 c_{3i}) \tag{8}$$

Here, β has a positive value when θ_{3i} has this negative value, and a negative value when θ_{3i} has a positive value. Since in this system θ_{3i} always has a negative value, θ_{2i} can be uniformly given as Eq. 9

$$\theta_{2i} = a\,\tan 2(p_{lxi}, \sqrt{p_{lxi}^2 + p_{lyi}^2}) - a\,\tan 2(l_2 s_{3i}, l_1 + l_2 c_{3i}) \tag{9}$$

4   Impedance Control Based in Gravity Compensation

The gravity compensation algorithm we proposed is to calculate the torque of each joint to generate a corresponding force to counteract the influence of gravity on the joystick. The compensated force we need is shown in Eq. 10.

$$G(q) = g(q)\gamma \tag{10}$$

$$g(q) = \begin{bmatrix} g_{11}(q) & g_{12}(q) & \cdots & g_{1(n-1)}(q) & g_{1n}(q) \\ 0 & g_{22}(q) & \cdots & g_{2(n-1)}(q) & g_{2n}(q) \\ \cdots & \cdots & \cdots & \cdots & \cdots \\ 0 & 0 & \cdots & g_{(n-1)(n-1)}(q) & g_{(n-1)n}(q) \\ 0 & 0 & \cdots & 0 & g_{nn}(q) \end{bmatrix}$$

$$g_{ij}(q) = g^T(\partial R_0^j / \partial q_i)p_i$$

$$\gamma = \begin{bmatrix} \gamma_1 \\ \gamma_2 \\ \gamma_3 \\ \dots \\ \gamma_{n-1} \\ \gamma_n \end{bmatrix} = \begin{bmatrix} m_1 l_1^c + l_1 \sum_{k=2}^{n} m_k \\ m_2 l_2^c + l_2 \sum_{k=3}^{n} m_k \\ m_3 l_3^c + l_3 \sum_{k=4}^{n} m_k \\ \dots \\ m_{n-1} l_{n-1}^c + l_{n-1} m_n \\ m_n l_n^c \end{bmatrix}$$

Here, $G(q)$ is the gravity to be compensated, $g(q)$ is the gravity constant of each joint under the influence of rotation, q is the current angle of each joint, R_0^j is the rotation component of the matrix, γ is the product of the link mass and the gravity direction distance, p_i is the directional vector that frame i pointing to the center of mass of link i, l_i^c is the distance between the origin of frame i and the mass center of link i, l_i is the distance between the origin of frame i and that of frame $i+1$.

Apply the gravity compensation algorithm to the impedance control of the joystick [12] as shown in Fig. 5. Figure 5 is a block diagram of the principle of impedance control with gravity compensation algorithm proposed in this paper. The impedance control method is implemented by the position-based impedance control strategy of the joint space. The impedance model of the joystick is shown in Eq. 11.

$$(M_d s^2 + B_d s + K_d)(x - x_e) = F_h \tag{11}$$

$M_d s^2 + B_d s + K_d$ is the expected impedance modeling of the system, and M_d is the ideal inertia parameter of the joystick. It has a great influence on the high-speed motion with large acceleration or the motion that generates the impulse. B_d is the ideal damping parameter of the joystick, which has a great influence on the medium speed motion or large disturbance. K_d is the ideal stiffness parameter of the joystick, which has a great influence on the low speed motion near the equilibrium state. M_d, B_d, and K_d are all 3 by 3 diagonal matrices, and each element of the diagonal represents the desired impedance characteristic of the X, Y, and Z axis translation and rotation, respectively.

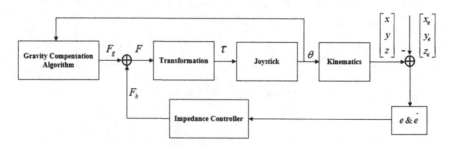

Fig. 5. Impedance control block

Here, x_e, y_e, z_e is the coordinates of the previous position, because any motion can be divided into infinitesimal differential elements and all elements are uniform motion. Therefore, the motion state of the next second can be inferred from the last second differential element.

5 Experiment

The haptic joystick used in the experiment is shown in Fig. 6. The motors and encoders of joint controllers designed for each serial manipulator was Maxon Motor's DCX22L GB KL 12V and ENX16 EASY Absolute SSI, and the motor and encoder are combined into one system. Two joint controllers control the two active joints respectively. In the structure of the joystick we designed, the length of each link is 10 cm, the radius of the upper plate is 9.6 cm, and the radius of the bottom plate is 19.2 cm.

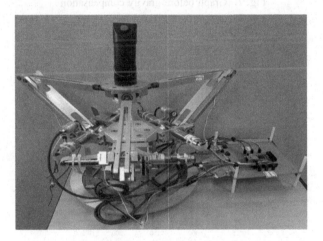

Fig. 6. Haptic joystick used in experiments

We move the joystick separately without gravity compensation and with gravity compensation. The force in the x, y, z axis directions measured by the FT sensor is shown in the Figs. 7 and 8.

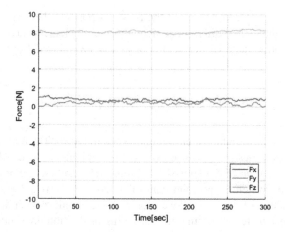

Fig. 7. Graph before gravity compensation

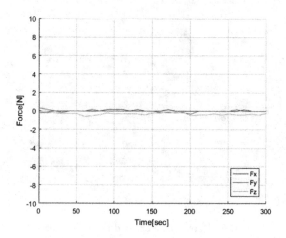

Fig. 8. Graph after gravity compensation

If gravity compensation is not performed as shown in Fig. 6 above, A force of 8 [N] in the Z-axis direction is generated at the contact point between the user and the haptic joystick. At this time, fatigue can accumulate because the user continues to use force to maintain position. Even in the case of the X axis and the Y axis, a slight weight change due to gravity occurs. In Fig. 7, the force applied to the X, Y and Z axes is compensated by gravity compensation using the motor, so that the force generated at the contact point is kept close to 0 [N]. This allows the user to conveniently and precisely control the haptic joystick with less effort.

6 Conclusion

This paper proposed a new method of impedance control based on gravity compensation. The gravity compensation algorithm proposed in this paper can calculate the compensation force required for the current position according to each joint angle, and generate corresponding force to compensate the gravity in real time. In the experiment, the torque sensor was used to measure the interaction between the operator and the joystick to prove its effectiveness.

Acknowledgment. This research was financially supported by the Ministry of trade, Industry and Energy (MOTIE), Korea Institute for Advancement of Technology (KIAT) through the Robot Business Belt Development Project (A012000009).

This research was funded and conducted under 「the Competency Development Program for Industry Specialists」 of the Korean Ministry of Trade, Industry and Energy (MOTIE), operated by Korea Institute for Advancement of Technology (KIAT). (No. P0008473, The development of high skilled and innovative manpower to lead the Innovation based on Robot).

References

1. Stienen, A.H.A., et al.: Freebal: dedicated gravity compensation for the upper extremities. In: Proceedings of the 2007 IEEE 10th International Conference on Rehabilitation Robotics, Noordwijk, Netherlands (2007)
2. De Luca, A., Siciliano, B.: An asymptotically stable joint PD controller for robot arms with flexible links under gravity. In: 1992 Proceedings of the 31st IEEE Conference on Decision and Control, Tucson, AZ, USA (1992)
3. Kelly, R.: PD control with desired gravity compensation of robotic manipulators: a review. Int. J. Robot. Res. **16**(5), 660–672 (1997)
4. Ott, C., Albu-Schaffer, A., Kugi, A., Stamigioli, S., Hirzinger, G.: A passivity based Cartesian impedance controller for flexible joint robots - part I: torque feedback and gravity compensation. In: IEEE International Conference on Robotics and Automation, New Orleans, LA (2004)
5. Kim, M.G., Park, I.G.: Initial investigation of gravity and friction compensation of 2-DOF robot manipulator for programming by demonstration. In: 2015 12th International Conference on Ubiquitous Robots and Ambient Intelligence (URAI), Goyang, South Korea (2015)
6. Víctores, J.G., Martinez, S., Balaguer, C.: Sensorless friction and gravity compensation. In: 2014 IEEE-RAS International Conference on Humanoid Robots, Madrid, Spain (2014)
7. Shioi, Y., Sakai, S.: Casimir based gravity compensations for hydraulic arms. In: 2017 56th Annual Conference of the Society of Instrument and Control Engineers of Japan (SICE), Kanazawa, Japan (2017)
8. Lee, S.S., Lee, J.M.: Design of a general purpose 6-DOF haptic interface. Mechatronics **13**(7), 697–722 (2003)
9. Kim, S.W., Kim, T.E., Lee, J.M.: Impedance feedback control system for dynamic control of haptic interface and operators arm. J. Inst. Control Robot. Syst. **24**(4), 361–368 (2018)
10. Park, H., Lee, S.C., Lee, S.S., Lee, J.M.: A robust adaptive impedance control algorithm for haptic interfaces. J. Control Autom. Syst. Eng. **8**(5), 393–400 (2002)

Landmark-Based Virtual Path Estimation for Assisted UAV FPV Tele-Operation with Augmented Reality

Santiago Grijalva[1] and Wilbert G. Aguilar[1,2,3(✉)]

[1] CICTE, Universidad de las Fuerzas Armadas ESPE, Sangolquí, Ecuador
wgaguilar@espe.edu.ec
[2] FIS, Escuela Politécnica Nacional, Quito, Ecuador
[3] GREC, Universitat Politècnica de Catalunya, Barcelona, Spain

Abstract. In this paper we proposed an Assisted UAV Tele-Operation System, specifically for FPV navigation based on Artificial Landmarks in obstacle free environments. The system estimates the optimal path through landmarks and traces an artificial route to be followed. Path recognition uses color space and morphological transformation such as eroding and dilating to reduce noise due to different lighting environments. Once path is recognized ORB detector is used for getting a set of the most representative pixels coordinates, this is done for each ROI (Region of Interest) in the camera image. Later, the median of each pixel coordinate in the specific ROI is considered for interpolation needed to trace the route. Parrot's drone Bebop 2 was used for the purpose of this study as it has a fisheye lens camera that allows us to face downwards to detect the landmarks.

Keywords: UAV · Tele-Operation · Augmented reality · Landmark

1 Introduction

Unmanned Aerial Vehicles (UAVs) [1, 2] are widely used in recent applications such as 3D mapping [3, 4], topographic survey [5], precision farming [6], surveillance systems [7–10], rescue, military reconnaissance [11, 12], disaster area identification, etc. [13–16]. Most of this applications show advance in fully autonomous UAVs [17–19], but human-machine interfacing will always be present for specific applications, therefore development of efficient assistance systems during flights it is critical and shall be capable to give enough information to the tele-operator for a prompt response.

Vehicle teleoperation first appeared in the early 1900s but it was not until the 1970s that systems became widely used [20]. Since then tele-operation has been dependent on operator's expertise and requires training, especially when First Person View (FPV) mode limits the operator's field of view, decreasing awareness of the environment.

Nowadays augmented and virtual reality applications are used mostly for general entertainment. DronePrix AR by EdgyBees is an Augmented Reality application for DJI's Drone Mavic Pro that allows the user to interact with a virtual racing track. Furthermore, there are other types of application [21–23] such as Augmented Reality

© Springer Nature Switzerland AG 2019
H. Yu et al. (Eds.): ICIRA 2019, LNAI 11745, pp. 688–700, 2019.
https://doi.org/10.1007/978-3-030-27529-7_58

Maps or Augmented Reality (AR) for drone navigation. The present document resides in the last study case; we propose a system that allows the tele operator to be aware of that path that must be followed making use of an estimated landmark-based virtual path [13, 24, 25] traced in arrow shape in an AR application.

This paper is organized as follows: Sect. 2 presents a quick review of the literature about Vehicles Teleoperation and the different approaches to offer full guidance, security and comfort to the tele-operator. Section 3 presents our first approach to give the tele operator assistance during a UAV flight, despite of being addressed to artificial landmarks at first, it can be easily used on natural landmarks or paths; experimental results and test conditions, in addition, a comparison with hand-traced optimal path are presented in Sect. 4. conclusions and future work are presented in the last section.

2   Related Works

Bilateral systems for UAV teleoperation [26] are very common [27–29] as they may involve time delay due to signal loss, Lam et al. presented a study for obstacle avoidance in a tele operation system for a UAV that had a response delay to tele operator commands.

Military applications for UAVs are the most common due to their ability to navigate in complex environments. Chen in 2010 [30] presented a simulation of a military reconnaissance environment where the UAV showed exocentric vision of the whole space while the Unmanned Ground Station (UGV) showed egocentric perspective of the environment [31]. This study case is very different from others as the tele operation resides on the UGV while the UAV assists giving an overview visual feedback.

Haptic and visual feedback started to lead in assisted teleoperation systems, in [27, 32–34] presented bilateral haptic teleoperation of under actuated UAV, in [32] tele operator receives haptic feedback from the environment as a function of the distance to an obstacle or the approach rate.

Lee et al. [28, 35] presented a novel haptic teleoperation control framework for multiple UAVs, this framework consists of three layers, UAV control layer, Virtual Point Control Layer and the teleoperation layer in which the tele operator is capable to drive one or all the UAVs present in the framework.

Studies for natural path recognition are important to provide the tele-operator trust information. Approaches based on monocular camera such as [36, 37] achieved very accurate results. [38] Detected paths based on monocular images from a ground robot named ExaBot, this study includes horizon detection based on morphological transformation and path detection based on color transformations. Even though this is not guided for assisted teleoperation is similar to our study.

Obstacle detection [39] and object tracking [21, 40] is as well important for guidance in UAV as it provides valuable information about the environment, feature point detection approaches had been used to detect obstacles or track objects and landmarks [38, 39, 41].

Aleotti et al. implemented an Augmented Reality Interface that allows a tele-operator to be aware of the environment while the UAV equipped with a gamma-ray detector alert of possible nuclear radiation sources in the display [42].

3 Our Approach

Our system consists of three main factors: Tele-operator, Parrot Bebop 2.0 and a ground station (GS). Image processing is done off-board in the GS. UAV connects to the GS through a Wi-Fi signal emitted by itself. Then a *nodelet* is raised in the ground station letting the drone publish ROS Messages, specifically it publishes the video capture in *image_raw* topic as a *sensor_msgs/Image* message. To convert ROS Images we use *cv_bridge* that let us interface directly with the video capture on OpenCV. After image processing, estimated virtual path is presented to the tele-operator in GS's screen to send control commands depending on the UAV positioning in relation to the artificial route (Fig. 1).

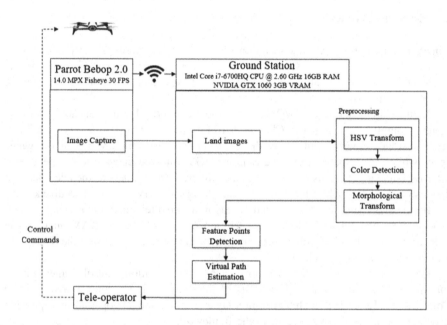

Fig. 1. Proposed system overview

The proposed system makes use of an input image (856 × 480 pixels) from a monocular camera facing downwards to obtain a processed image with the artificial path to be followed by the tele-operator. For this, the following steps must take place in image processing:

3.1 Color Space Transformation and Color Detection

The input image obtained from the UAV's camera needs to be transformed from the BGR color space to HSV color space. This is widely used in applications that detect a specific color with different brightness and saturation levels, thus HSV help us achieving acceptable results in different lighting conditions. Figures 2, 3 and 4 show raw image and masked input image for three different lighting levels.

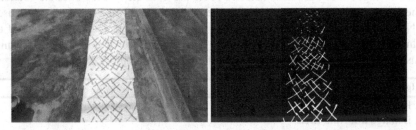

Fig. 2. Raw image from UAV's camera (Left) and masked input image (Right) for ∼ 10000 lx (Color figure online)

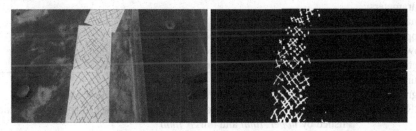

Fig. 3. Raw image from UAV's camera (Left) and masked input image (Right) for ∼ 2000 lx (Color figure online)

Fig. 4. Raw image from UAV's camera (Left) and masked input image (Right) for ∼ 300 lx (Color figure online)

3.2 Morphological Transformation

Once color was successfully detected, erode transformation takes place first to reduce noise that might have been miss-detected in the previous step, as it erodes the boundary of the foreground object by the size of the kernel, in this study a 2×2 kernel was used.

Next, a dilation transform is applied to the eroded one, to increase the size of the landmarks that have been almost eroded. This method is also known as Opening Transformation. Algorithm 1 summarizes the proposed preprocessing method.

Algorithm 1: Input image preprocessing
1: Read *image* from Bebop 2
2: **if** *image* **not** *Nule* **then**
3:    *hsv_image* = **brg8_to_hsv**(*image*)
4:    *mask* = **inRange**(*hsv_image, upper_limit, lower_limit*)
5:    *erosion* = **erode**(*mask, kernel*)
6:    *dilation* = **dilate**(*erosion, kernel*)

Parameters	
image:	Raw input image
upper_limit:	HSV upper color limit for color detection
lower_limit:	HSV lower color limit for color detection
kernel:	2x2 ones matrix for erode and dilate functions

Functions	
bgr8_to_hsv:	Converts input image from BGT color space to HSV color space
inRange:	Filters all pixels which pixel's intensities are not in the range established by *upper_limit* and *lower_limit*
erode:	Erodes the input image
dilate:	Dilates the input image

3.3 Feature Points Detection

To reduce the number of pixels obtained in the previous step, ORB OpenCV's algorithm was used to detect feature points. We divided the image obtained in the previous step in different regions of interest. Then detection takes place for each ROI (Fig. 5), drastically reducing the number of points to be processed. Once a max number of 100 points is detected for each ROI, median point of the set for each ROI is considered for the route interpolation, as it is not biased by noise that might have not been filtered in the previous steps.

Fig. 5. ORB feature points (Blue) and median point for each ROI (Red) (Color figure online)

Algorithm 2: Feature point detection and median calculation for each ROI

1: Divide *image* in *n* ROIs
2: **for each** *ROI* :
3:   *feature_points* = **orb_detect**(*image*)
4:     **if length**(*feature_points*) > *threshold* **then**
5:       *x_median* = **median**(*feature_points_x*)
6:       *y_median* = **median**(*feature_points_y*)
7:       *std_x* = **std**(*feature_points_x*)
8:       *std_y* = **std**(*feature_points_y*)
9:       **append** *x_median* to *new_x_points*
10:       **append** *y_median* to *new_y_points*
11:   **end if**
12: **end for**

Parameters	
image:	Preprocessed image
n:	Number of ROIs
threshold:	Minimum number of features to calculate median and standard deviation for ROI

Functions	
ord_detect:	Detects feature points using ORB detector
length:	Calculates size of vector
median:	Calculates median for the input vector
std:	Calculates standard deviation for the input vector
append:	Appends a value to a vector

3.4 Route Tracing

From points detected for each ROI in the previous step, a polynomial regression is done in real-time. To avoid excessive refreshing of the traced route that might end up in misunderstanding to the tele-operator, the following algorithm is applied:

Algorithm 3: Route tracing and refreshing
1: Store previous points as *old_points*
2: Calculate *new_points* using **Algorithm 2**
3: **if length**(*new_x_points*) > **length**(*old_x_points*) **then**
4:   *old_points* = *new_points*
5: **else if length**(*new_x_points*) < **length**(*old_x_points*) **then**
6:   *old_points* = *new_points*
8: **else**
9:   **for each** *point* in *new_points*
10:    **if** *new_point_x* > *old_point_x* + 2*std_x **then**
11:       *old_point_x* = *new_point_x*
12:    **else** *new_point_x* < *old_point_x* − 2*std_y **then**
13:       *old_point_x* = *new_point_x*
14:    **end if**
15: **end for**
16: **end if**
17: Repeat 3 to 16 for *new_y_points*
18: Polynomial regression with *old_x_points* and *old_y_points*
19: Evaluate *x_points* with obtained polynomial
20: Trace estimated virtual path

Parameters	
std_x:	Standard deviation for x pixel coordinate
std_y:	Standard deviation for y pixel coordinate
Functions	
length:	Calculates size of vector

4   Results and Discussion

The proposed system was tested experimentally in several scenarios, we defined them as follows (Figs. 6, 7 and 8):

Fig. 6. Smooth curve like artificial landmark path (Color figure online)

Fig. 7. Sharp bend like artificial landmark path (Color figure online)

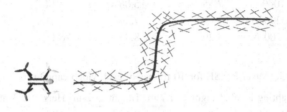

Fig. 8. Left and right turn like artificial landmark path (Color figure online)

a. Route design: It refers to the path formed by the artificial landmarks. Three possible routes were considered: (a) Smooth curve, (b) Sharp bend, (c) Left and right turn.
b. Height: The distance between the UAV and the ground: (a) 1.7 m, (b) 2 m, (c) 2.3 m.
c. Lighting level: The average illuminance depending of the environment: (a) Outdoor Full Daylight $\sim$10000 lx, (b) Outdoor Midday Light $\sim$2000 lx, (c) Outdoor Night Light $\sim$300 lx.

Merging all different conditions, we get 27 possible scenarios. For each one a video capture is recorded for later offline processing. We sample each video capture in 10 different most representative frames, an optimal route is hand traced in OpenCV then the algorithm runs for the same frames and takes the Root Mean Squared Error (RMSE) described by Eq. (1).

$$RMSE = \sqrt{\frac{1}{n}\sum\nolimits_{i=1}^{n}\left(\widehat{Y}_l - Y_i\right)^2} \tag{1}$$

where

    RMSE: Root mean squared error
    n: Number of frames
    $\widehat{Y}_l$: Estimated path i-th point
    Y_i: Optimal path i-th point

    Tables 1, 2 and 3, present the mean of RMSE in pixels for each video capture.

Table 1. Mean RMSE for 10 frames of each video capture for Route 1

Lighting level	Height 1: 1.7 m	Height 2: 2 m	Height: 2.3 m
∼ 10000 lx	7.44	8.08	6.49
∼ 2000 lx	7.62	6.59	5.36
∼ 300 lx	8.59	5.65	4.71

Table 2. Mean RMSE for 10 frames of each video capture for Route 2

Lighting level	Height 1: 1.7 m	Height 2: 2 m	Height: 2.3 m
∼ 10000 lx	7.55	5.06	5.14
∼ 2000 lx	9.64	7.29	5.61
∼ 300 lx	8.29	8.05	6.13

Table 3. Mean RMSE for 10 frames of each video capture for Route 3

Lighting level	Height 1: 1.7 m	Height 2: 2 m	Height: 2.3 m
∼ 10000 lx	9.61	8.3	7.39
∼ 2000 lx	13.72	12.86	8.76
∼ 300 lx	12.85	6.94	6.15

Tables 4, 5 and 6 present absolute error for total length of the estimated virtual path, relative to the length of the diagonal obtained from the image resolution (856 × 480) calculated as follows:

$$d = \sqrt{h^2 + w^2} \tag{2}$$

where

d: Diagonal length in pixels
h: Height of raw image in pixels
w: Width of raw image in pixels

Table 4. Absolute relative error for path length in Route 1

Lighting level	Height 1: 1.7 m	Height 2: 2 m	Height: 2.3 m
∼ 10000 lx	1.72	1.79	1.29
∼ 2000 lx	2.32	2.13	0.83
∼ 300 lx	2.67	2.25	0.91

Table 5. Absolute relative error for path length in Route 2

Lighting level	Height 1: 1.7 m	Height 2: 2 m	Height: 2.3 m
∼ 10000 lx	2.50	1.32	1.24
∼ 2000 lx	4.17	2.78	1.65
∼ 300 lx	2.82	2.81	1.41

Table 6. Absolute relative error for path length in Route 3

Lighting level	Height 1: 1.7 m	Height 2: 2 m	Height: 2.3 m
~ 10000 lx	1.70	1.71	2.05
~ 2000 lx	4.88	3.2	2.09
~ 300 lx	3.86	2.12	1.24

Figure 9 show a comparison between estimated virtual path and optimal path, blue arrows represent the estimations and red ones represent the hand-traced path, this is the presentation to graphical display to the tele-operator.

Fig. 9. Arrowed line showing the estimated virtual (blue) and optimal (red) path for Sharp Bend (Left) and Smooth Curve (Right) (Color figure online)

5   Conclusions and Future Work

Optimal path estimation through computer vision algorithm makes possible to trace the route according to landmarks positioning, providing assistance for the tele operator to control accurately an UAV during flights. According to Tables 1, 2 and 3 optimal path estimation reduces RMSE as it increases the maximum height, they also show that RMSE increases in lighting levels lower than 2000 lx, tele operator must choose a height over 2 m and environments where there are higher lighting levels than 2000 lx to get more accurate results. Tables 4, 5 and 6 present a minimum percentage error of 0.83% and a maximum of 4.88%, this means that the tele-operator is not going to be aware of the error due to human visual limitations, resulting in trust information to take prompt responses. Estimated virtual path is presented to the tele-operator through a computer display in augmented reality-like application, although there is no more information than the estimated route, this represents a first approach to a complex system where the tele operator gets full environment information. In future works we propose a system that can provide a visual feedback about possible obstacles and estimated route in natural landmarks, specifically in military application, as in this study is not possible to face downwards and forward due to hardware limitations.

References

1. Orbea, D., Moposita, J., Aguilar, W.G., Paredes, M., Reyes, R.P., Montoya, L.: Vertical take off and landing with fixed rotor. In: Chilean Conference on Electrical, Electronics Engineering, Information and Communication Technologies (CHILECON), Pucón, Chile (2017)
2. Orbea, D., Moposita, J., Aguilar, W.G., Paredes, M., León, G., Jara-Olmedo, A.: Math model of UAV multi rotor prototype with fixed wing aerodynamic structure for a flight simulator. In: De Paolis, L.T., Bourdot, P., Mongelli, A. (eds.) AVR 2017. LNCS, vol. 10324, pp. 199–211. Springer, Cham (2017). https://doi.org/10.1007/978-3-319-60922-5_15
3. Aguilar, W.G., Rodríguez, G.A., Álvarez, L., Sandoval, S., Quisaguano, F., Limaico, A.: Visual SLAM with a RGB-D camera on a quadrotor UAV using on-board processing. In: Rojas, I., Joya, G., Catala, A. (eds.) IWANN 2017. LNCS, vol. 10306, pp. 596–606. Springer, Cham (2017). https://doi.org/10.1007/978-3-319-59147-6_51
4. Aguilar, W.G., Rodríguez, G.A., Álvarez, L., Sandoval, S., Quisaguano, F., Limaico, A.: Real-time 3D modeling with a RGB-D camera and on-board processing. In: De Paolis, L.T., Bourdot, P., Mongelli, A. (eds.) AVR 2017. LNCS, vol. 10325, pp. 410–419. Springer, Cham (2017). https://doi.org/10.1007/978-3-319-60928-7_35
5. Basantes, J.: Capture and processing of geospatial data with laser scanner system for 3D modeling and virtual reality of Amazonian Caves. In: IEEE Ecuador Technical Chapters Meeting (ETCM), Samborondón, Ecuador (2018)
6. Pardo, J.A., Aguilar, W.G., Toulkeridis, T.: Wireless communication system for the transmission of thermal images from a UAV. In: Chilean Conference on Electrical, Electronics Engineering, Information and Communication Technologies (CHILECON), Pucón, Chile (2017)
7. Aguilar, W.G., Angulo, C.: Real-time model-based video stabilization for microaerial vehicles. Neural Proc. Lett. 43(2), 459–477 (2016)
8. Aguilar, W.G., Angulo, C.: Real-time video stabilization without phantom movements for micro aerial vehicles. EURASIP J. Image Video Process. 1, 1–13 (2014)
9. Aguilar, W.G., et al.: Real-time detection and simulation of abnormal crowd behavior. In: De Paolis, L.T., Bourdot, P., Mongelli, A. (eds.) AVR 2017. LNCS, vol. 10325, pp. 420–428. Springer, Cham (2017). https://doi.org/10.1007/978-3-319-60928-7_36
10. Aguilar, W.G., et al.: Statistical abnormal crowd behavior detection and simulation for real-time applications. In: Huang, Y., Wu, H., Liu, H., Yin, Z. (eds.) ICIRA 2017. LNCS (LNAI), vol. 10463, pp. 671–682. Springer, Cham (2017). https://doi.org/10.1007/978-3-319-65292-4_58
11. Jara-Olmedo, A., Medina-Pazmiño, W., Tozer, T., Aguilar, W.G., Pardo, J.A.: E-services from emergency communication network: aerial platform evaluation. In: International Conference on eDemocracy & eGovernment (ICEDEG) (2018)
12. Jara-Olmedo, A., Medina-Pazmiño, W., Mesías, R., Araujo-Villaroel, B., Aguilar, W.G., Pardo, J.A.: Interface of optimal electro-optical/infrared for unmanned aerial vehicles. In: Rocha, Á., Guarda, T. (eds.) MICRADS 2018. SIST, vol. 94, pp. 372–380. Springer, Cham (2018). https://doi.org/10.1007/978-3-319-78605-6_32
13. Aguilar, W., Morales, S.: 3D environment mapping using the kinect V2 and path planning based on RRT algorithms. Electronics 5, 70 (2016)
14. Zhang, J., Liu, W., Wu, Y.: Novel technique for vision-based UAV navigation. IEEE Trans. Aerosp. Electron. Syst. 47(4), 2731–2741 (2011)
15. Zhang, C., Kovacs, J.M.: The application of small unmanned aerial systems for precision agriculture: a review. Precis. Agriculture 13(6), 693–712 (2012)

16. Nex, F., Fabio, R.: UAV for 3D mapping applications: a review. Appl. Geomat. **6**(1), 1–15 (2013)
17. Aguilar, W.G., Angulo, C., Costa-Castello, R.: Autonomous navigation control for quadrotors in trajectories tracking. In: Huang, Y., Wu, H., Liu, H., Yin, Z. (eds.) ICIRA 2017. LNCS (LNAI), vol. 10464, pp. 287–297. Springer, Cham (2017). https://doi.org/10. 1007/978-3-319-65298-6_27
18. Aguilar, W.G., Salcedo, V.S., Sandoval, D.S., Cobeña, B.: Developing of a video-based model for UAV autonomous navigation. In: Barone, D.A.C., Teles, E.O., Brackmann, C. P. (eds.) LAWCN 2017. CCIS, vol. 720, pp. 94–105. Springer, Cham (2017). https://doi.org/ 10.1007/978-3-319-71011-2_8
19. Salcedo, V.S., Aguilar, W.G., Cobeña, B., Pardo, J.A., Proaño, Z.: On-board target virtualization using image features for UAV autonomous tracking. In: Boudriga, N., Alouini, M.-S., Rekhis, S., Sabir, E., Pollin, S. (eds.) UNet 2018. LNCS, vol. 11277, pp. 384–391. Springer, Cham (2018). https://doi.org/10.1007/978-3-030-02849-7_34
20. Fong, T., Thorpe, C.: Vehicle teleoperation interfaces. Auton. Robots **11**(1), 9–18 (2001)
21. Aguilar, W.G., Luna, M., Moya, J., Abad, V., Parra, H., Ruiz, H.: Pedestrian detection for UAVs using cascade classifiers with meanshift. In: IEEE 11th International Conference on Semantic Computing (ICSC), San Diego (2017)
22. Aguilar, W., Rodriguez, G., Álvarez, L.: On-board visual SLAM on a UGV using a RGB-D camera. Intell. Robot. Appl. **10464**, 298–308 (2017)
23. Amaguaña, F., Collaguazo, B., Tituaña, J.: Simulation system based on augmented reality for optimization of training tactics on military operations. Augment. Reality Virtual Reality Comput. Graph. **10850**, 298–308 (2017)
24. Aguilar, W.G., Manosalvas, J.F., Guillén, J.A., Collaguazo, B.: Robust motion estimation based on multiple monocular camera for indoor autonomous navigation of micro aerial vehicle. In: De Paolis, L.T., Bourdot, P. (eds.) AVR 2018. LNCS, vol. 10851, pp. 547–561. Springer, Cham (2018). https://doi.org/10.1007/978-3-319-95282-6_39
25. Aguilar, W.G., Abad, V., Ruiz, H., Aguilar, J., Aguilar-Castillo, F.: RRT-based path planning for virtual bronchoscopy simulator. In: De Paolis, L.T., Bourdot, P., Mongelli, A. (eds.) AVR 2017. LNCS, vol. 10325, pp. 155–165. Springer, Cham (2017). https://doi.org/ 10.1007/978-3-319-60928-7_13
26. Aguilar, W.G., Cobeña, B., Rodriguez, G., Salcedo, V.S., Collaguazo, B.: SVM and RGB-D sensor based gesture recognition for UAV control. In: De Paolis, L.T., Bourdot, P. (eds.) AVR 2018. LNCS, vol. 10851, pp. 713–719. Springer, Cham (2018). https://doi.org/10. 1007/978-3-319-95282-6_50
27. RifaïM, H., Hua, D., Hamel, T., Morin, P.: Haptic-based bilateral teleoperation of underactuated unmanned aerial vehicles. IFAC Proc. Volumes (IFAC-PapersOnline) **44**, 13782–13788 (2011)
28. Lee, D., Franchi, A., Son, H.I., Ha, C., Heinrich, H., Giordano, P.R.: Semi-autonomous haptic teleoperation control architecture of multiple unmanned aerial vehicles. IEEE/ASME Trans. Mechatron. **18**, 1334–1345 (2013)
29. Lam, T., D'Amelio, V., Mulder, M., Van Paassen, M.M: UAV tele-operation using haptics with a degraded visual interface. In: Conference Proceedings - IEEE International Conference on Systems, Man and Cybernetics, vol. 3, pp. 2440–2445 (2007)
30. Chen, J.: UAV-guided navigation for ground robot tele-operation in a military reconnaissance environment. Ergonomics **53**(8), 940–950 (2010)
31. Galarza, J., Pérez, E., Serrano, E., Tapia, A., Aguilar, Wilbert G.: Pose estimation based on monocular visual odometry and lane detection for intelligent vehicles. In: De Paolis, L.T., Bourdot, P. (eds.) AVR 2018. LNCS, vol. 10851, pp. 562–566. Springer, Cham (2018). https://doi.org/10.1007/978-3-319-95282-6_40

32. Omari, S., Hua, M., Dueard, G., Hamel, T.: Bilateral haptic teleoperation of VTOL UAVs. In: IEEE International Conference on Robotics and Automation (ICRA), pp. 2393–2399 (2013)
33. Smisek, J., Sunil, E., Van Paassen, M.M., Abbink, D.A., Mulder, M.: Neuromuscular-system-based tuning of a haptic shared control interface for UAV teleoperation. IEEE Trans. Hum.-Mach. Syst. **47**(4), 449–461 (2017)
34. Kanso, A., Elhajj, I.H., Shammas, E., Asmar, D.: Enhanced teleoperation of UAVs with haptic feedback. In: IEEE/ASME International Conference on Advanced Intelligent Mechatronics, AIM, pp. 305–310 (2015)
35. Lee, D., Franchi, A., Giordano, P., Son, H., Bülthoff, H.H.: Haptic teleoperation of multiple unmanned aerial vehicles over the internet. In: Proceedings - IEEE International Conference on Robotics and Automation, pp. 1341–1347 (2011)
36. Guoqin, G.: Navigating path recognition for greenhouse mobile robot based on K-means algorithm. Trans. Chin. Soc. Agric. Eng. **30**, 25–33 (2014)
37. Al-kaff, A., Meng, Q., Mart, D.: Monocular vision-based obstacle detection/avoidance for unamnned aerial vehicles. In: IEEE Intelligent Vehicles Symposium (2016)
38. De Cristóforis, P., Nitsche, M.A., Krajník, T., Mejail, M.: Real-time monocular image-based path detection: a GPU-based embedded solution for on-board execution on mobile robots. J. Real-Time Image Process. **11**(2), 335–348 (2016)
39. Aguilar, W., Casaliglla, V., Pólit, J.: Obstacle avoidance based-visual navigation for micro aerial vehicles. Electronics **6**, 10 (2017)
40. Aguilar, W.G., et al.: Pedestrian detection for UAVs using cascade classifiers and saliency maps. In: Rojas, I., Joya, G., Catala, A. (eds.) IWANN 2017. LNCS, vol. 10306, pp. 563–574. Springer, Cham (2017). https://doi.org/10.1007/978-3-319-59147-6_48
41. Odelga, M., Stegagno, P., Bulthoff, H.H.: Obstacle detection, tracking and avoidance for a teleoperated UAV. In: Proceedings - IEEE International Conference on Robotics and Automation, pp. 2984–2990 (2016)
42. Aleotti, J., et al.: Detection of nuclear sources by UAV teleoperation using a visuo-haptic augmented reality interface. Sensors **17**(10), 1–22 (2017)

Concurrent Probabilistic Motion Primitives for Obstacle Avoidance and Human-Robot Collaboration

Jian Fu[✉], ChaoQi Wang, JinYu Du, and Fan Luo

School of Automation, Wuhan University of Technology, Wuhan 430070, China
fujian@whut.edu.cn

Abstract. The paper proposed a new method to endow a robot with the ability of human-robot collaboration and online obstacle avoidance simultaneously. In other words, we construct a probabilistic model for human-robot collaboration primitives to learn the nonlinear correlation between human and robot joint space and Cartesian space both based on interaction trajectories from the demonstration. This multidimensional probabilistic model not only helps to infer robot collaboration motion depending on the human action by the correlation between human and robot in joint space but also convenient to conduct robot obstacle avoidance reverse kinetics from cartesian space via the correlation between them. Specifically, as for the latter, a modulation matrix is established from the obstacle form to automatically generate robot obstacle avoidance trajectory in Cartesian space. Obstacle avoidance in the human-robot collaboration experimental is investigated, and its simulation results verify the feasibility and efficiency of the algorithm.

Keywords: Human-robot collaboration ·
Concurrent probabilistic movement primitive · Imitation learning ·
Online obstacle avoidance

1 Introduction

An important aspect of collaborative robots is to be able to recognize human motions [1, 2] and quickly generate corresponding robot trajectories to match the predicted human motion. Probabilistic movement primitive (ProMP) [3] model has been used to solve the problem of motion recognition and trajectory generation, and training data needs to be neatly aligned so that they can well capture spatial correlation [4–6]. Specifically, collaborative ProMP [7] allows the robot and human movement trajectory generation together, the model correlates the trajectories parameters of human and robot in the execution of tasks and infer the robot trajectories according to the observed partial human actions based on conditional probabilities theory [8, 9]. The collaborative

---

The authors acknowledge the National Natural Science Foundation of China (61773299, 515754112), Excellent Dissertation Cultivation Funds of Wuhan University of Technology (2017-YS-067).

H. Yu et al. (Eds.): ICIRA 2019, LNAI 11745, pp. 701–714, 2019.
https://doi.org/10.1007/978-3-030-27529-7_59

ProMP can be carried out in joint space and Cartesian space respectively [10]. Let's consider the special scenarios, such as robot obstacles avoiding in collaborative tasks [11]. The location of obstacles detected by sensors in space is usually Cartesian coordinates, and obstacle avoidance tasks are usually carried out in Cartesian space [12]. In addition, the classical collaboration ProMP [7] only focuses on the task planning of joint space, so as to cannot meet the requirements of the task.

In order to get better interaction performance in the collaborative ProMP framework, we propose a Concurrent Probabilistic Movement Primitive(CProMP) framework, which can be used for concurrent planning in joint space and cartesian space. The framework provides many kinds of collaboration way for human-robot collaboration and has better generalization ability. Moreover, in order to solve the above problem, the collaboration framework combined with the online obstacle avoidance strategy [13] to extend the CProMP framework. The obstacle avoidance method ensures good coordination with the CProMP framework. Specifically, the online obstacle avoidance method establishes a dynamic system modulation matrix based on the size, position and shape information of obstacles, moreover, the dynamic system is used to describe the trajectory in real-time modulation and ensure the safety of the robot under uncertain environment to reach target position [14]. However, the obstacle avoidance trajectory which is obtained by combining the collaborative framework with the online obstacle avoidance method is in Cartesian space. In order to drive the robot, the common method is to obtain the joint angle through inverse kinematics, but many feasible solutions will be obtained in this way, which will consume a lot of time to get the optimal solution. But we can solve it by using the CProMP framework, because when we do a collaborative demonstration task, the obstacle avoidance trajectory will have the corresponding solution in the robot joint space. In other words, our proposed methods make it convenient to conduct robot obstacle avoidance reverse kinetics from Cartesian space via the correlation between them. At last, the CProMP framework and online obstacle avoidance can be used alternately to obtain joint data and drive the robot. Thus, we achieved the algorithm of human-robot collaboration and obstacle avoidance in two spaces.

2   Collaborative Probabilistic Movement Primitives

2.1   Probabilistic Movement Primitives

Probabilistic movement primitives represent the distribution of trajectories, a single motion can be modeled as $\tau = \{q_t\}_{t=0...T}$. A robotic joint is usually called a degree of freedom (DOF). In the probabilistic movement primitive, each DOF is represented as the position q_t at the time t, and the trajectory with $y_t = q_t$ and length T is represented as $y_{1:T}$. A smooth trajectory can be parameterized by linear regression of N Gaussian basis functions, so it can be represented as

$$y_t = \psi_{t_h}^T \omega + \varepsilon_y \tag{1}$$

In addition, the observation probability of the whole trajectory can be represented as

$$p(\mathbf{y}_{1:T}|\omega) = \prod_{1}^{T} \mathcal{N}(\mathbf{y}_t|\psi_t^T \omega, \Sigma_\mathbf{y}) \tag{2}$$

Where ψ_t is the Gaussian basis function of $N \times 1$ dimension, $\omega \in \mathbb{R}^{N \times 1}$ is the corresponding weight, ε_y is Gaussian noise with mean zero and covariance $\Sigma_\mathbf{y}$.

Assuming there are M demonstration trajectories, then M sets of weights can be obtained by linear fitting of the basis function, namely $\omega = \{\omega_1, \cdots, \omega_m, \cdots, \omega_M\}$

Define ω to be a probability distribution with parameter θ, namely $\theta = \{\mu_\omega, \Sigma_\omega\}$. The distribution of the whole trajectory is given by integrating ω

$$
\begin{aligned}
p(\mathbf{y}_{1:T}; \theta) &= \int p(\mathbf{y}_{1:T}|\omega)p(\omega; \theta)d\omega \\
&= \mathcal{N}(\mathbf{y}_t; \boldsymbol{\Psi}_t^T \boldsymbol{\mu}_\omega, \boldsymbol{\Psi}_t^T \Sigma_\omega \boldsymbol{\Psi}_t + \Sigma_\mathbf{y})
\end{aligned}
\tag{3}
$$

2.2 Correlating Human and Robot Movements with Probabilistic Movement Primitives

Collaborative probabilistic movement primitives can correlate the correlations of multiple DOFs. Suppose that the human has P DOFs and the robot has Q DOFs. Similarly, in ProMPs, the state vector of the motion at time t is represented as follows:

$$\mathbf{y}_t = \left[y_{1,t}^H, y_{2,t}^H, \cdots, y_{P,t}^H, y_{1,t}^R, y_{2,t}^R, \cdots, y_{Q,t}^R \right]^T \tag{4}$$

Where superscript $(.)^H$ and $(.)^R$ represent the DOFs of human and robot respectively. ProMPs is used to parameterize Eq. (4) as follows:

$$p(\mathbf{y}_t|\bar{\omega}) = N(\mathbf{y}_t|H_t^T \bar{\omega}, \Sigma_\mathbf{y})| \tag{5}$$

Where $H_t^T = \text{diag}\left((\psi_t^T)_1, \cdots, (\psi_t^T)_P, (\psi_t^T)_1, \cdots, (\psi_t^T)_Q \right)$ have P + Q diagonal entries, and P + Q training trajectory are provided for each collaborative demonstration task. The weight vector $\bar{\omega}_i$ represents the relationship between the human and robot weight parameters of the ith group and a multi-DOF weight vector is regressed as,

$$\bar{\omega}_i = \left[(\omega_1^H)^T, \cdots, (\omega_P^H)^T, (\omega_1^R)^T, \cdots, (\omega_Q^R)^T \right] \tag{6}$$

A large number of demonstration trajectories are required to find correlations between the various joints of human and robot. According to Eqs. (1) and (5), we can get M groups weight parameters of the demonstration trajectories for the same task, it can be represented as $\bar{\omega}_1, \cdots, \bar{\omega}_M$. Where, each group weight parameters can also be managed with θ, namely $\theta = N(\mu_\omega, \Sigma_\omega)$.

According to condition probability theory, in order to infer the trajectory of the robot, we need to calculate the posterior distribution of the robot trajectory parameters through the known joint distribution of human-robot trajectory parameters under the condition of partial motion of the observed human. That is,

$$
\begin{aligned}
\mu_\omega^+ &= \mu_\omega + K\left(y_{t:t'}^* - H_{t:t'}^T \mu_\omega\right) \\
\Sigma_\omega^+ &= \Sigma_\omega - K\left(H_{t:t'}^T \Sigma_\omega\right) \\
K &= \Sigma_\omega H_{t:t'}\left(\Sigma_y^* + H_{t:t'}^T \Sigma_\omega H_{t:t'}\right)^{-1}
\end{aligned}
\tag{7}
$$

Where superscript $(.)^+$ represents the posterior probability of the parameter, $y_{t:t'}^*$ represents the observed values in consecutive moments, and can also represent the observed values in discontinuous moments.

The trajectory distribution of human and robot motion can be predicted by the weight of integral posterior distribution.

$$
p\left(\mathbf{y}_{1:T}; \theta^+\right) = \int p(\mathbf{y}_{1:T}|\overline{\omega})p(\overline{\omega}; \theta)d\overline{\omega}
\tag{8}
$$

3 Two-Space Based Collaborative Probabilistic Movement Primitives

Though ProMP works well in the scenario of human-robot collaboration, it only concerns the correlation between human and robot in joint space. However, in most applications such as hand over, obstacle avoidance, etc., we usually more focus on the collaborative states in the Cartesian for both cooperators, and it is a challenge for ProMP. Therefore, we propose concurrent probabilistic movement primitives in two spaces to solve the above problem in the paper. The CProMP framework can plan the trajectory in two spaces simultaneously and the model also can plan the trajectory in a single space according to the task.

A reasonable extension is made to Eq. (4), assuming that there is also M group human-robot demonstration trajectories, then:

$$
y_t = \left[y_{1,t}^H, y_{2,t}^H, \cdots, y_{P,t}^H, X_t^H, Y_t^H, Z_t^H, y_{1,t}^R, y_{2,t}^R, \cdots, y_{Q,t}^R, X_t^R, Y_t^R, Z_t^R\right]^T
\tag{9}
$$

Where, $y_{i,t}^H$ represents the position of the i-th joint at time t, X_t^H, y_t^H, Z_t^H represents the position of the end of the upper limb in cartesian space at time t, $y_{i,t}^R$ represents the position of the i-th joint of the robot at time t, X_t^R, y_t^R, Z_t^R represents the position of the end of the robot at time t. The end position can be obtained from the forward kinematics.

Suppose we also have M sets of model trajectories $[y^1, \cdots, y^M]$. According to Eqs. (5) and (6), ProMP is used to parameterize the trajectory, then:

$$\Omega_i = \left[\omega_1^H, \cdots, \omega_P^H, \omega_x^H, \omega_y^H, \omega_z^H, \omega_1^R, \cdots, \omega_Q^R, \omega_x^R, \omega_y^R, \omega_z^R \right]^T \tag{10}$$

Where, $(.)_i$ represents the human-robot joint weight parameters of the model trajectory in i group, and the statistical law of the model trajectory can be obtained by extension according to Eq. (5), namely the joint probability distribution between human upper limbs and robot motion:

$$p(\Omega) \sim N(\mu_\Omega, \Sigma_\Omega)$$

$$= \left(\begin{bmatrix} \mu_P^H \\ \mu_E^H \\ \mu_Q^R \\ \mu_E^R \end{bmatrix}, \begin{bmatrix} \Sigma_{PP}^{HH} & \Sigma_{PE}^{HH} & \Sigma_{PQ}^{HR} & \Sigma_{PE}^{HR} \\ \Sigma_{EP}^{HH} & \Sigma_{EE}^{HH} & \Sigma_{EQ}^{HR} & \Sigma_{EE}^{HR} \\ \Sigma_{QP}^{HH} & \Sigma_{QE}^{HH} & \Sigma_{QO}^{HR} & \Sigma_{QE}^{HR} \\ \Sigma_{EP}^{HH} & \Sigma_{EE}^{HH} & \Sigma_{EQ}^{HR} & \Sigma_{EE}^{HR} \end{bmatrix} \right) \tag{11}$$

Where μ_Ω denotes the mean of the human-robot weight parameter, Σ_Ω denotes the covariance of the human-robot weight parameter, μ_P^H denotes the joint trajectory parameter of the human, μ_E^H denotes the end trajectory parameter of the human, and similarly, μ_Q^R denotes the joint trajectory parameter of the robot, μ_E^R denotes the end trajectory parameter of the robot. Each element in Eq. (11) can be obtained using the following equation.

$$\mu_\omega = \frac{1}{M} \sum_{i=1}^{M} \omega_i,$$
$$\Sigma_\omega = \frac{1}{M-1} \sum_{i=1}^{M} (\omega_i - \mu_\omega)(\omega_i - \mu_\omega)^T \tag{12}$$

There are many ways to infer the trajectory of the robot. The posterior distribution of weight $\Omega \sim N(\mu_\Omega^+, \Sigma_\Omega^+)$ can be calculated by taking the motion of human upper limbs as the condition. Since the motion of the robot was not observed, the observation vector can be represented as

$$y^O = \left[y_1^O, \cdots, y_P^O, X_H^O, Y_H^O, Z_H^O, 0, \cdots, 0 \right]^T \tag{13}$$

Where $(.)^O$ represents the observed human motion, and Eq. (7) can be used to obtain the posterior trajectory parameters of the robot.

The CProMP framework can use a variety of modes to infer the trajectory of the robot. For example, the joint data of the human upper limb can be used to infer the end position of the robot and the joint data of the robot. Similarly, the end position of the human upper limb can also infer the data of the robot in two space. When CProMP framework is not used for task planning, CProMP can be reduced to the ProMP framework, which is a very flexible framework.

4 Online Obstacle Avoidance Algorithm

The CProMP can effectively reproduce and generalize the human-robot collaborative demonstration task, but the framework cannot be completed autonomously for other tasks different from the demonstration movement, such as obstacle avoidance task.

Obstacle avoidance is a necessary strategy in the industrial and family environment, so we join the obstacle avoidance strategy to extend the CProMP framework to solve the above problems. In particular, the obstacle avoidance method can immediately change the trajectory of the robot to avoid collisions with the robot based on the global stability of the dynamic system and the surface form of the obstacles. Next, we reuse CProMP framework for secondary planning to get the joint space angle of robot, rather than use inverse kinematics to solve joint space angle of robot, because of there will get a lot of solutions, but there is no need to consider such a problem with the CProMP framework. As a result, the CProMP framework and the online obstacle avoidance method can be used alternately to accomplish our task.

Firstly, the robot motion predicted is represented by an independent ordinary differential equation of the SEDS model [15].

$$\dot{x} = f(x) \tag{14}$$

Where x represents the state of the system, the state usually represented as the position $\{x, y, z\}$ in Cartesian space, and $f(.)$ represents a nonlinear continuous function.

Suppose a d-dimensional spherical obstacle has a spherical center of x^o and a radius of r^o. According to the above information and the knowledge of fluid mechanics [12], the modulation equation of the spherical obstacle on the robot configuration space can be obtained as follows:

$$\phi^S(x; x^o, r^o) = \left(1 + \frac{(r^o)^2}{(x - x^O)^T (x - x^o)}\right)(x - x^O) \tag{15}$$

As can be seen from Eq. (14), the output of the dynamic system in this paper is the velocity. Therefore, Eq. (15) needs to be converted into the modulation of the velocity. In other words, the Jacobi equation can be obtained as follows:

$$\begin{aligned} M(x; x^o, r^o) &= \nabla \phi^s(x; x^o, r^o) \\ &= I + \left(\tfrac{r^o}{\tilde{x}^T \tilde{x}}\right)^2 (\tilde{x}^T \tilde{x} I - 2\tilde{x}\tilde{x}^T) \end{aligned} \tag{16}$$

Where $M(.)$ represents the dynamic modulation equation for the velocity, $\tilde{x}$ represents the reference coordinate system with the center of the obstacle, namely

$\tilde{x} = x - x^0$, and I represents the identity matrix. Therefore, the final model of real-time obstacle avoidance based on Eqs. (14) and (16) can be obtained as follows:

$$\dot{x} = M^s\left(x; x^0, r^0\right) f(x) \tag{17}$$

Then, the sphere is generalized as a convex obstacle:

$$\Gamma\left(x^b\right) = \sum_{i=1}^{d} \left(\frac{1}{c_i} \times \frac{x_i^b - x_i^o}{a_i}\right)^{b_i} = 1 \tag{18}$$

Where x^b represents the point on the boundary of the ellipsoid, d represents the dimension of the obstacle, a_i and b_i are the parameters of adjusting the obstacle shape and size. c_i represents the safe distance between modulated trajectory and obstacle.

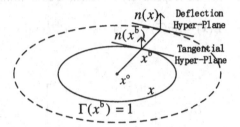

Fig. 1. Obstacle hyper-plane

Obstacle avoidance usually requires the robot's end position to move the outside of obstacle, namely $\{x|x \in R^a \cap \Gamma(x) > 1\}$. According to Eq. (17), $M(.)$ is used to adjust the speed of the robot. Therefore, it can be concluded that the speed direction of the robot's end on the obstacle along the normal direction of its boundary is required to be zero. That is,

$$n\left(x^b\right)^T \dot{x}^b = 0 \tag{19}$$

Where $\dot{x}^b$ represents the velocity at a point x^b on the obstacle surface and $n\left(x^b\right)$ represents the normal vector of the tangent plane of a point x^b on the obstacle surface, as shown in Fig. 1.

Next, it is necessary to verify whether the robot trajectory modulated by $M(x; x^o, r^o)$ satisfying Eq. (19). The normal vector of the point on the obstacle can be obtained by taking the partial derivative of $\Gamma(\tilde{x})$ with respect to each element in $x = \{x_1, \cdots, x_d\}$. That is,

$$n\left(\tilde{x}^b\right) = \left[\frac{\partial \Gamma\left(\tilde{x}^b\right)}{\partial x_1^b}, \cdots, \frac{\partial \Gamma\left(\tilde{x}^b\right)}{\partial x_d^b}\right]^T \tag{20}$$

Each point on the hyperplane of the obstacle can be represented as a linear combination of d-1 basis vectors, and a group of such vectors $e^1, \cdots, e^{d-1}$ can be obtained from Eq. (21), as shown below:

$$e^i_j(\tilde{x}) = \begin{cases} -\frac{\partial(\tilde{x})}{\partial x_i} & j = 1 \\ \frac{\partial \Gamma(\tilde{x})}{\partial x_1} & j = i \neq 1 \\ 0 & j \neq 1, j_n \neq i \end{cases} \quad i \in 1..d-1, j \in 1..d \tag{21}$$

Then the eigenvalue of the dynamic modulation matrix $M(x; x^o, r^o)$ is decomposed to obtain the following form

$$M(\tilde{x}) = E(\tilde{x})D(\tilde{x})E(\tilde{x})^{-1} \tag{22}$$

Where, $E(\tilde{x})$ and $D(\tilde{x})$ are respectively represented as follows

$$E(\tilde{x}) = [n(\tilde{x}) \quad e^l(\tilde{x}) \quad \cdots \quad e^{d-1}(\tilde{x})] \tag{23}$$

and,

$$D(\tilde{x}) = \begin{bmatrix} \lambda^1(\tilde{x}) & & \mathbf{0} \\ & \ddots & \\ \mathbf{0} & & \lambda^d(\tilde{x}) \end{bmatrix} \tag{24}$$

Where,

$$\begin{cases} \lambda'(x) = 1 - \frac{1}{|\Gamma(\tilde{x})|^{\frac{1}{p}}} \\ \lambda^i(\tilde{x}) = 1 + \frac{1}{|\Gamma(\tilde{x})|^{\frac{1}{p}}} \end{cases} \quad 2 \leq i \leq d \tag{25}$$

Where $\rho(\rho > 0)$ represents the reaction distance, and the default is 1. The larger the response distance, the earlier the dynamic modulation of the robot trajectory to the obstacle.

Next, it can be obtained from Eqs. (20), (21), (22), (23), (24), (25) that:

$$\begin{aligned} n(x^b)^T \dot{x}^b &= n(x^b)E(\tilde{x}^b, r^o)D(\tilde{x}^b, r^o)E(\tilde{x}^b)^{-1}f(x^b) \\ &= \begin{bmatrix} 1 \\ [\mathbf{0}]_{d-1} \end{bmatrix}^T D(\tilde{x}^b, r^o)E(\tilde{x}^b, r^o)^{-1}f(x^b) \\ &= [\mathbf{0}]^T_d E(\tilde{x}^b, r^o)^{-1}f(x^b) = 0 \end{aligned} \tag{26}$$

According to Eq. (26), when an obstacle is in the way of robot collaborative motion trajectory, the modulation matrix will produce extra velocity component which is perpendicular to the normal of the current position. In this way, the desired trajectory will not enter the obstacle, which can meet the requirement of obstacle avoidance.

The robot joint space data is obtained by using the CProMP for the secondary planning obstacle avoidance trajectory. According to Eq. (13), the observable motion at this time is

$$y^O = \left[y_1^O, \cdots, y_P^O, X_H^O, Y_H^O, Z_H^O, 0, \cdots, 0, X_R^O, Y_R^O, Z_R^O\right]^T \tag{27}$$

Due to the observation value is as known above, thus the robot joint data is obtained according to the CProMP by using Eqs. (7) and (10), thereby achieving the obstacle avoidance requirement of human-robot collaboration.

5 Experimental Results and Analysis

5.1 Two-Space Based Collaborative ProMP Experiment

We employ ur5 robot and Xsens sensor collects data and the base coordinate system of the robot as the global coordinate system, so the coordinate system of the human collaborator can be measured as [−148,0,53.5]. We set up a human-robot collaboration task that uses ur5 to transfer bottles to human collaborator, and repeatedly collect data of five joints of human upper limbs and five joints of UR5 robot, and set the data of the sixth joint of the robot is 0.

Figure 2 shows the human-robot demonstration trajectory in two space. Figure 2(a) show demonstration trajectory of human-robot in joint space, the upper row shows joint trajectory of human and the bottom row show the joint trajectory of the robot. Figure 2(b) shows demonstration trajectory of human-robot in Cartesian space, the upper row shows the trajectory of human and the bottom row show the trajectory of the robot. The red curve in Fig. 2 represents the mean trajectory of multiple groups of demonstration. The Cartesian trajectory of human and robot is obtained by forward kinematics and coordinate transformation.

After collecting actions of multiple demonstrations for the same task, Eq. (11) is used to calculate the joint probability density between human and robot trajectories, and the robot's motion is estimated according to the observed partial human motion, as shown in Fig. 3, which similar to Fig. 2. The black circle on Fig. 3(a) upper row represents the observed human movement and trajectory distribution of other joint is calculated, all the red curves represent the posterior predicted trajectory, and Fig. 3(b) represents the predicted trajectory in Cartesian space, the green area represents the demonstration trajectory distribution.

The collected human-robot demonstration trajectories are used to calculate the correlation between trajectory parameters, among which 90% are used to train the correlation and 10% is used to test its correlation. As can be seen from Fig. 4, the predicted trajectories are basically within the range of variance, and the test result is relatively ideal. In addition, we compared the Euclidean distance between the predicted trajectory of the robot in the test data set and the end position of the sample trajectory, as shown in Fig. 4. The calculated posterior trajectory of the robot has a little deviation from the test trajectory and with good experimental results.

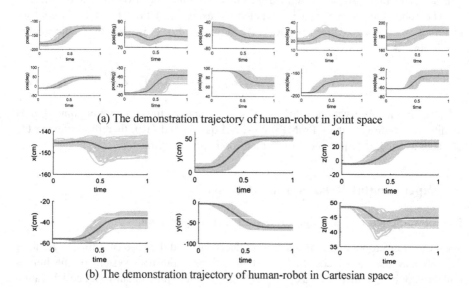

(a) The demonstration trajectory of human-robot in joint space

(b) The demonstration trajectory of human-robot in Cartesian space

Fig. 2. The demonstration trajectory of human-robot in two space (Color figure online)

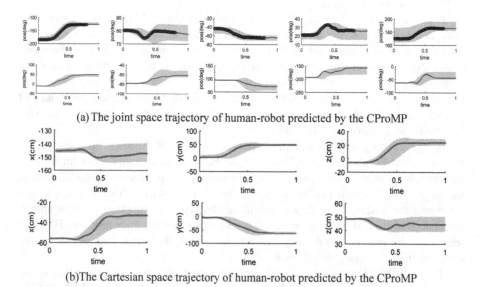

(a) The joint space trajectory of human-robot predicted by the CProMP

(b)The Cartesian space trajectory of human-robot predicted by the CProMP

Fig. 3. The human-robot trajectory predicted by the CProMP (Color figure online)

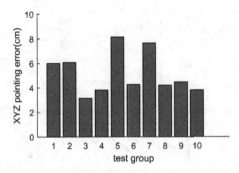

Fig. 4. Robot error in reaching at each of the test end positions

5.2 Two-Space Based Human-Robot Collaborative Obstacle Avoidance Experiment

The CProMP framework extends its strategy with online obstacle avoidance to achieve better interactive effects. This experiment is aimed at the end of the robot to avoid obstacles, without considering other parts of the robot. The trajectory of the robot predicted by the CProMP method is planned using the online obstacle avoidance method, so as to obtain the trajectory of obstacle avoidance, as shown in Fig. 5. The trajectory in the joint space of the robot is obtained by continuing the secondary planning with the CProMP framework.

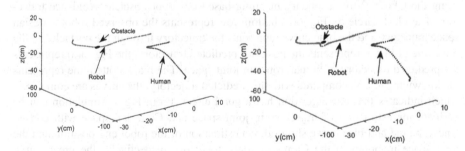

Fig. 5. The human-robot trajectory of obstacle avoidance in the target coordinate system

We can see from the previous section, the posterior robot Cartesian space data are obtained by using the spatial data of human upper limb joints as the condition. And global stability of the dynamic system constructs a model of imitation learning in the target coordinate system, namely all predicted the end of the robot trajectory coordinates as (0, 0, 0), as shown in Fig. 5. Specifically, a spherical obstacle with a radius of 2 cm and a safety distance of 1.2 cm is supposed to established at (−17.8, 22.8, −3.75), the left figure shows the trajectory of human-robot under obstacles and the right figure shows the obstacle avoidance trajectory of human-robot based on the online obstacle avoidance algorithm.

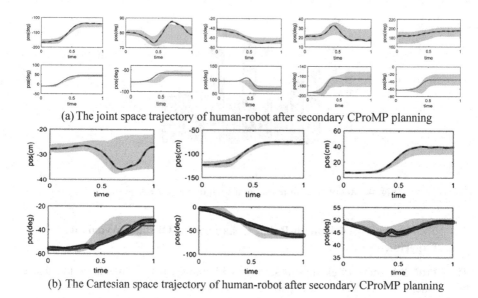

(a) The joint space trajectory of human-robot after secondary CProMP planning

(b) The Cartesian space trajectory of human-robot after secondary CProMP planning

Fig. 6. The human-robot trajectory after secondary CProMP planning (Color figure online)

The obstacle avoidance algorithm is real-time, which can modulate the trajectory of the robot in real time for obstacles which is in the way of the robot's forward trajectory. Then, Fig. 6 shows the trajectory of the robot joint space can be directly driven by using the CProMP for secondary planning based on robot obstacle avoidance trajectory. The black circle on Fig. 6(b) bottom row represents the observed robot cartesian space trajectory and the blue curve represents the trajectory through the obstacle, all the red curve of Fig. 6 represents the posterior predicted trajectory, the Fig. 6(a) represents the predicted trajectory of human-robot in joint space. The black dotted line represents the known trajectory, compared with the predicted trajectory, the curves are coincident, which indicates that our algorithm has a good effect. From Fig. 7 simulation can be verified, the estimation of trajectory in joint space and Cartesian space with consistency, the red and blue curve shows direct estimation of the robot end position and the joint space mapping to the Cartesian space trajectory respectively, the green curve shows the obstacle avoidance trajectory based on the online obstacle avoidance algorithm. From the results of this section, it can be seen that the human-robot collaborative obstacle avoidance algorithm in two space is effective. By using the obstacle avoidance algorithm to expand the CProMP framework, the human-robot collaboration effect is greatly increased.

In summary, in the experiment in Sect. 5.1, the robot Cartesian space trajectory is obtained by CProMP on the condition of the observed upper limb joint data. In the experiment of Sect. 5.2, the online obstacle avoidance algorithm is used to modulate the Cartesian space trajectory of the robot to avoid the obstacles, thus obtaining the obstacle avoidance trajectory. Then, the CProMP is used again to predict the joint space data of the robot based on the obstacle avoidance trajectory.

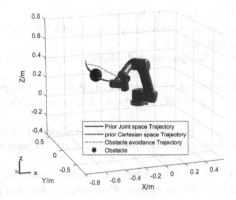

Fig. 7. UR5 robot simulation

6 Conclusions

The paper proposed a method of CProMP that can be used for joint space and Cartesian space planning or concurrent planning for human-robot collaboration, which solves the problem of human-robot collaboration in a single space. The framework has a stronger generalization ability than ProMP. To expand our framework, we continue to design human-robot collaboration tasks, the online obstacle avoidance method is further combined to extend the CProMP framework, the secondary planning is carried out for Cartesian space on the basis of human-robot collaboration to drive the robot conveniently. So as to achieve the skill acquisition of human-robot collaborative obstacle avoidance and obtain a better human-robot interaction experience.

References

1. Akkaladevi, S., Heindl, C., Angerer, A., Minichberger, J.: Action recognition for human robot interaction in industrial applications. In: IEEE International Conference on Computer Graphics (2016)
2. Wang, Z., et al.: Probabilistic movement modeling for intention inference in human–robot interaction. Int. J. Robot. Res. **32**(7), 841–858 (2013)
3. Paraschos, A., Daniel, C., Peters, J., Neumann, G.: Probabilistic movement primitives. In: Advances in Neural Information Processing Systems, pp. 2616–2624 (2014)
4. Sylvain, C., Florent, G., Aude, B.: On learning, representing, and generalizing a task in a humanoid robot. IEEE Trans. Syst. Man Cybern. Part B **37**(2), 286–298 (2007)
5. Gu, Y., Alterovitz, R.: Demonstration-Guided Motion Planning (2017)
6. Perez-D'Arpino, C., Shah, J.A.: Fast target prediction of human reaching motion for cooperative human-robot manipulation tasks using time series classification. In: IEEE International Conference on Robotics & Automation (2015)
7. Maeda, G.J., Neumann, G., Ewerton, M., Lioutikov, R., Kroemer, O., Peters, J.: Probabilistic movement primitives for coordination of multiple human-robot collaborative tasks. Auton. Robot **41**(3), 593–612 (2017)

8. Ewerton, M., Maeda, G., Peters, J., Neumann, G.: Learning motor skills from partially observed movements executed at different speeds. In: IEEE/RSJ International Conference on Intelligent Robots & Systems (2015)
9. Bishop, C.M.: Pattern Recognition and Machine Learning (Information Science and Statistics) (2006)
10. Gomez-Gonzalez, S., Neumann, G., Scholkopf, B., Peters, J.: Using probabilistic movement primitives for striking movements. In: IEEE-RAS International Conference on Humanoid Robots (2017)
11. Amor, H.B., Neumann, G., Kamthe, S., Kroemer, O., Peters, J.: Interaction primitives for human-robot cooperation tasks. In: IEEE International Conference on Robotics & Automation (2014)
12. Saveriano, M., Lee, D.: Distance based dynamical system modulation for reactive avoidance of moving obstacles. In: IEEE International Conference on Robotics & Automation (2014)
13. Khansari-Zadeh, S.M., Billard, A.: A dynamical system approach to realtime obstacle avoidance. Auton. Robot $32(4)$, 433–454 (2012)
14. Feder, H.J.S., Slotine, J.J.E.: Real-time path planning using harmonic potentials in dynamic environments. In: IEEE International Conference on Robotics & Automation (1997)
15. Khansari-Zadeh, S.M., Billard, A.: Learning stable nonlinear dynamical systems with gaussian mixture models. IEEE Trans. Robot. $27(5)$, 943–957 (2011). https://doi.org/10.1109/TRO.2011.2159412

Author Index

Printed in the United States
By Bookmasters